A COMMERCIAL LAW OF PRIVACY AND SECURITY FOR THE INTERNET OF THINGS

In the Internet of Things (IoT) era, online activities are no longer limited to desktop or laptop computers, smartphones, and tablets. Instead, these activities now include ordinary tasks, such as using an internet-connected refrigerator or washing machine. At the same time, the IoT provides unlimited opportunities for household objects to serve as surveillance devices that continually monitor, collect, and process vast quantities of our data. In this work, Stacy-Ann Elvy critically examines the consumer implications of the IoT through the lens of commercial law and privacy and security law. The book provides concrete legal solutions to remedy inadequacies in the law that will help usher in a more robust commercial law of privacy and security that protects consumer interests.

Stacy-Ann Elvy is a professor of law and Martin Luther King, Jr. Hall Research Scholar at the University of California, Davis School of Law. She is an expert on commercial law and its relationship to emerging technology, and she teaches courses on commercial law, privacy law, and information security law. Her scholarship has been published in leading legal journals and books, including the *Columbia Law Review, Boston College Law Review, Washington & Lee Law Review, Research Handbook on the Law of Artificial Intelligence*, and the *University of Michigan Journal of Gender and Law*. In 2019 Professor Elvy received both the Otto L. Walter Distinguished Writing Award and the UC Davis CAMPSSAH Faculty Scholar Award. She is also an adviser to the American Law Institute's *Principles for a Data Economy* project and received the Rising Legal Star Award from the *New York Law Journal* in 2016.

A Commercial Law of Privacy and Security for the Internet of Things

STACY-ANN ELVY

University of California, Davis

CAMBRIDGE
UNIVERSITY PRESS

University Printing House, Cambridge CB2 8BS, United Kingdom

One Liberty Plaza, 20th Floor, New York, NY 10006, USA

477 Williamstown Road, Port Melbourne, VIC 3207, Australia

314–321, 3rd Floor, Plot 3, Splendor Forum, Jasola District Centre,
New Delhi – 110025, India

103 Penang Road, #05–06/07, Visioncrest Commercial, Singapore 238467

Cambridge University Press is part of the University of Cambridge.

It furthers the University's mission by disseminating knowledge in the pursuit of
education, learning, and research at the highest international levels of excellence.

www.cambridge.org
Information on this title: www.cambridge.org/9781108482035
DOI: 10.1017/9781108699235

© Stacy-Ann Elvy 2021

First published 2021

A catalogue record for this publication is available from the British Library.

Library of Congress Cataloging-in-Publication Data
NAMES: Elvy, Stacy-Ann, 1980– author.
TITLE: A commercial law of privacy and security for the internet of things / Stacy-Ann Elvy,
University of California, Davis.
DESCRIPTION: Cambridge, United Kingdom ; New York, NY : Cambridge University Press,
2021. | Includes index.
IDENTIFIERS: LCCN 2021000582 (print) | LCCN 2021000583 (ebook) | ISBN 9781108482035
(hardback) | ISBN 9781108741781 (paperback) | ISBN 9781108699235 (ebook)
SUBJECTS: LCSH: Internet of things – Law and legislation – United States. | Data protection –
Law and legislation – United States. | Computer security – Law and legislation – United
States.
CLASSIFICATION: LCC KF390.5.C6 E48 2021 (print) | LCC KF390.5.C6 (ebook) | DDC 343.7309/944–
dc23
LC record available at https://lccn.loc.gov/2021000582
LC ebook record available at https://lccn.loc.gov/2021000583

ISBN 978-1-108-48203-5 Hardback
ISBN 978-1-108-74178-1 Paperback

Cambridge University Press has no responsibility for the persistence or accuracy of
URLs for external or third-party internet websites referred to in this publication
and does not guarantee that any content on such websites is, or will remain,
accurate or appropriate.

For Hannah

Contents

Acknowledgments

While writing this book over the last four years, I received many productive and helpful comments from scholars in the commercial law and privacy and security law fields. For valuable feedback and insights, I am particularly grateful to the following individuals: Afra Afsharipour, Ryan Calo, Nordia Elvy, Joshua A. T. Fairfield, Pamela Foohey, Jim Hawkins, Courtney G. Joslin, Emily Kadens, Sonya Katyal, Nancy Kim, Mark Lemley, Michael Madison, Andrea M. Matwyshyn, Stephen McJohn, David Owen, Frank Pasquale, Menesh Patel, Aaron Perzanowski, Jennifer E. Rothman, Margaret Ryznar, Amy J. Schmitz, Lauren Scholz, Paul Schwartz, Stephen Sepinuck, Peter Swire, Olivier Sylvain, Charlotte Tschider, Andrew Keane Woods, Erick Zacks, and Jonathan Zittrain.

This book also benefited from feedback at various conferences, including the 2019 Privacy Law Scholars Conference and the 15th Annual International Conference on Contract. For their research, cite checking, and Bluebooking efforts and general help in preparing the manuscript, I am indebted to my research assistants Jessica Gillotte, Rachel Rubens, Dillon Jackson, Stephanie Dong, Niharika Sachdeva, Kayla Lindgren, Ryan Isola, Lavneet Dhillon, and Justin Schwartz. This book would not have been possible without the support of UC Davis School of Law and its distinguished faculty.

Some sections of this book were adapted from parts of my previously published articles. However, the ideas that I present represent important developments and growth in my thoughts on the commercial law of privacy and security. These articles include: *Commodifying Consumer Data in the Era of the Internet of Things*, 59 BOSTON COLLEGE L. REV. 423 (2018), *Paying for Privacy and the Personal Data Economy*, 117 COLUMBIA L. REV. 1369 (2017), *Hybrid Transactions and the Internet of Things: Goods, Services or Software?* 74 WASH. & LEE L. REV. 75 (2017), and *Contracting in the Age of the Internet of Things: Article 2 of the UCC and Beyond*, 44 HOFSTRA L. REV. 839 (2016).

Introduction

We now live in a world where we can obtain current information about a global pandemic from our smartphones and Internet of Things (IoT) devices.[1] The recent novel coronavirus (COVID-19) outbreak is not just a public health emergency. The pandemic has forced us to further evaluate the extent to which privacy should give way to public health threats and resulting technological innovations.[2] It directly raises questions about whether legal frameworks governing our privacy should be relaxed to address public health concerns, and if any such relaxation will continue post pandemic to permanently undermine our privacy.[3]

The outbreak also highlights privacy concerns about corporate and government actors' use of data collected from smartphones, mobile applications (mobile app(s)), facial recognition and geo-location technologies, and IoT devices, such as

---

[1] *See, e.g.,* Rebecca Heilweil, *Here's What Alexa and Other Smart Speakers Say About the Coronavirus,* Vox (Mar. 13, 2020, 3:40 PM), www.vox.com/recode/2020/3/13/21178361/alexa-google-assistant-coronavirus; Neil Selwyn & Mark Andrejevic, *The New Transparency: Smartphones, Data Tracking, and COVID-19,* Lens, Monash U. (Mar. 9, 2020), https://lens.monash.edu/@education/2020/03/09/1379796/the-new-transparency-smartphones-data-tracking-and-covid-19?amp=1&__twitter_impres sion=true; *see also* Dep't of Health & Human Servs., Ctr. for Disease Control, What You Should Know About COVID-19 to Protect Yourself and Others (2020), www.cdc.gov/coronavirus/2019-ncov/downloads/2019-ncov-factsheet.pdf ("The virus that causes COVID-19 is a new coronavirus").

[2] *See* Vincent Manancourt, *Coronavirus Tests Europe's Resolve on Privacy,* Politico, www.politico.eu /article/coronavirus-tests-europe-resolve-on-privacy-tracking-apps-germany-italy/ (last updated Mar. 11, 2020, 12:28 AM); *see also* Carrie Cordero & Richard Fontaine, *Health Surveillance Is Here to Stay,* Wall St. J. (Mar. 27, 2020, 4:04 PM), www.wsj.com/articles/health-surveillance-is-here-to-stay–11585339451.

[3] *See* Simon Chandler, *Coronavirus Could Infect Privacy and Civil Liberties Forever,* Forbes (Mar. 23, 2020, 11:59 AM), www.forbes.com/sites/simonchandler/2020/03/23/coronavirus-could-infect-privacy-and-civil-liberties-forever/#5583c1ba365d; Allison Grande, *COVID-19 Fuels Heated Fight over CCPA Enforcement Timing,* Law360 (Mar. 27, 2020, 8:39 PM), www.law360.com/articles/1257124/covid-19-fuels-heated-fight-over-ccpa-enforcement-timing; Ryan Grim, *Coronavirus Spending Bill Could Be Used to Cement Spying Powers, Surveillance Critics in Congress Warned,* Intercept (Feb. 27, 2020, 12:33 PM), https://theintercept .com/2020/02/27/coronavirus-spending-bill-surveillance-patriot-act/; Manancourt, *supra* note 2; *Statement of the European Data Protection Board on the Processing of Personal Data in the Context of the COVID Outbreak* (Mar. 19, 2020), https://edpb.europa.eu/sites/edpb/files/files/news/edpb_statement_2020_proces singpersonaldataandcovid-19_en.pdf.

internet-connected thermometers and fever detection cameras.[4] The IoT is a network of internet-connected physical objects, systems, and software.[5] IoT devices and other technologies can be used to unmask our identities and monitor our health status, movements, location, and physical and behavioral responses to the pandemic, including assessing our compliance with social distancing guidelines and shelter in place orders.[6] To detect pandemic patterns, 2,000 health workers in San Francisco agreed to wear IoT rings manufactured by a startup firm.[7] The rings can monitor wearers' temperatures, heart rates, daily steps, and sleep patterns.[8] The city of St. Augustine, Florida plans to distribute hundreds of IoT thermometers to its citizens as part of a pandemic pilot study in partnership with an IoT thermometer

---

[4] *See, e.g.,* Dylan Byers, *The U.S. Wants Smartphone Location Data to Fight Coronavirus. Privacy Advocates Are Worried,* NBC NEWS (Mar. 18, 2020, 11:01 AM), www.nbcnews.com/news/amp/ncna1162821?__twitter_impression=true; Joseph Cox, *Surveillance Company Says It's Deploying "Coronavirus-Detecting" Cameras in US,* VICE (Mar. 17, 2020, 12:43 PM), www.vice.com/en_us/article/epg8xe/surveillance-company-deploying-coronavirus-detecting-cameras; April Glaser, "Fever Detection" Cameras to Fight Coronavirus? Experts Say They Don't Work, NBC NEWS (Mar. 27, 2020, 4:01 pm), www.nbcnews.com /tech/security/fever-detection-cameras-fight-coronavirus-experts-say-they-don-t-n1170791, Donald G. McNeil Jr., *Can Smart Thermometers Track the Spread of the Coronavirus,* N.Y. TIMES (Mar. 18, 2020), www.nytimes.com/2020/03/18/health/coronavirus-fever-thermometers.html#click=https://t.co/hzE6K2Fmtn; Jason Murdock, *Mobile App Could Help Stop Coronavirus Without Resorting to China-Like Surveillance,* NEWSWEEK (Mar. 17, 2020, 1:09 PM), www.newsweek.com/coronavius-covid19-mobile-app-alerts-trace-infections-oxford-university-research-1492754?amp=1&__twitter_impression=true.

[5] ARUBA, IoT AND THE SMART DIGITAL WORKPLACE: OPPORTUNITIES AND CHALLENGES 3 (2018), www .arubanetworks.com/assets/wp/WP_SmartDigitalWorkplaceIoT.pdf (The IoT "can be defined as a universe of devices, software, and systems that interact directly with the physical environment while communicating with each other and the IT infrastructure"); *see also* CISCO, AN INTRODUCTION TO THE INTERNET OF THINGS (IoT): PART 1. OF "THE IoT SERIES" 2 (2013), www.cisco.com/c/dam/en_us/solutions/trends/iot/introduction_to_IoT_november.pdf (describing the IoT and noting that the term was coined by Kevin Ashton); INTEL, MAKING THE CONNECTION: HOW THE INTERNET OF THINGS ENGAGES CONSUMERS AND BENEFITS BUSINESS 3 (2016), www.intel.com/content/dam/www/public/us/en/documents/white-papers/how-iot-engages-consumers-benefits-business-paper.pdf (The IoT "uses the founding protocols of the internet to allow any electronic machine, device, object or sensor to send data to anywhere else on the network. This could be to another machine, database, application or device (e.g., smartphone).").

[6] *See, e.g.,* Kirsten Grind, Robert McMillan & Anna Wilde Mathews, *To Track Virus, Governments Weigh Surveillance Tools That Push Privacy Limits,* WALL ST. J. (Mar. 17, 2020, 7:55 PM), www.wsj.com /amp/articles/to-track-virus-governments-weigh-surveillance-tools-that-push-privacy-limits -11584479841; Tim Hornyak, *What America Can Learn from China's Use of Robot and Telemedicine to Combat the Virus,* CNBC, www.cnbc.com/2020/03/18/how-china-is-using-robots-and-telemedicine-to -combat-the-coronavirus.html (last updated Mar. 18, 2020, 9:06 AM); Issie Lapowsky, *Facebook Data Can Help Measure Social Distancing in California,* PROTOCOL (Mar. 17, 2020), www.protocol.com /facebook-data-help-california-coronavirus-2645513228.amp.html?__twitter_impression=true.

[7] Lisa Eadicicco, *Emergency Medical Workers in San Francisco Are Wearing Smart Rings that Can Monitor Body Temperature in an Effort to Detect COVID-19 Symptoms Early,* BUS. INSIDER (Mar. 24, 2020, 10:38 AM), www.businessinsider.com/coronavirus-smart-ring-san-francisco-hospitals-covid19-symptoms-study-oura-2020-3?amp.

[8] *Id.*

maker.[9] Amazon is already using IoT thermal cameras in some of its warehouses to identify and screen its workers who may be infected with the virus.[10] Government actors are reportedly already collecting the anonymized smartphone location data of millions of US citizens to track both the virus and individuals' movements.[11] The data are reportedly provided by mobile advertisers.[12]

As of the date of writing, it is unclear how much pandemic-related data will be collected, used, and disclosed and whether any corresponding limitations will be imposed. Depending on how these disease-related data are used and disclosed, there could be unintended consequences for COVID-19 victims, such as stigmatization. In South Korea, the government sends public safety text messages to citizens containing the location history, age range, and gender of those infected with the virus.[13] Although these disclosures may contribute to decreasing the spread of the virus, they have in some cases reportedly led to social shaming as well as embarrassing inferences of marital affairs, insurance fraud, and involvement with prostitutes.[14]

Containing the pandemic and ensuring public health and safety are without a doubt important societal and governmental goals. Many lives depend on these efforts. However, it is currently unclear whether a delicate and appropriate balance will be struck between public health protection and privacy, both of which have individual, collective, and societal value.[15] Privacy and public health goals can bolster and inform each other. They are not mutually exclusive. As legal scholars have noted, privacy can enable the development of civil society, "democratic deliberation," and individual autonomy.[16]

Technology giants' involvement in global pandemic responses also raises concerns about how much access, if any, these companies should have to our health-related and other pandemic-related data, and whether these companies can be

---

[9] Sheldon Gardner, *Coronavirus: St. Augustine to Use Smart Thermometers Against COVID-19*, St. Augustine (Mar. 31, 2020, 10:51 AM), www.staugustine.com/news/20200331/coronavirus-st-augustine-to-use-smart-thermometers-against-covid-19.

[10] Jeffrey Dastin & Krystal Hu, *Exclusive: Amazon Deploys Thermal Cameras at Warehouses to Scan for Fevers Faster*, Reuters (Apr. 18, 2020, 4:07 AM), www.reuters.com/article/us-health-coronavirus-amazon-com-cameras/exclusive-amazon-deploys-thermal-cameras-at-warehouses-to-scan-for-fevers-faster-idUSKBN2200HT.

[11] Byron Tau, *Government Tracking How People Move Around in Coronavirus Pandemic*, Wall. St. J. (Mar. 28, 2020), www.wsj.com/articles/government-tracking-how-people-move-around-in-coronavirus-pandemic-11585393202.

[12] *Id.*

[13] Nemo Kim, *"More Scary than Coronavirus": South Korea's Health Alerts Expose Private Lives*, Guardian (Mar. 5, 2020, 11:46 PM), www.theguardian.com/world/2020/mar/06/more-scary-than-coronavirus-south-koreas-health-alerts-expose-private-lives.

[14] *Id.*

[15] *See generally* Priscilla M. Regan , Legislating Privacy: Technology, Social Values and Public Policy (1995) (noting that privacy has individual, collective, and societal value); James P. Nehf, *Recognizing the Societal Value in Information Privacy*, 78 Wash. L. Rev. 1 (2003) (noting the same).

[16] Julie E. Cohen, *Examined Lives: Informational Privacy and the Subject as Object*, 52 Stan. L. Rev. 1373, 1423–28 (2000); Paul M. Schwartz, *Privacy and Democracy in Cyberspace*, 52 Vand. L. Rev. 1609, 1647–58 (1999).

trusted to place societal interests above corporate goals. For example, Verily, Google's "sister company," is reportedly participating in pandemic relief efforts.[17] Apple and Google are working on a joint effort to enable pandemic contact tracing through users' devices.[18] Technology companies could use COVID-19 surveillance data about us to aid pandemic responses as well as to simultaneously or subsequently monetize and exploit these data to advance their own corporate objectives.[19] These companies' history of corporate data monetization and exploitation leaves some room for doubt. Only time can provide definitive answers to these questions. There is also the related question of whether changed circumstances resulting from the pandemic, such as the large number of individuals working from home, will contribute to data security vulnerabilities. Technology firms' participation in pandemic response efforts, and their resulting access to sensitive COVID-19 data, also raises concerns about whether effective measures will be taken to secure such data from unauthorized access. Data breaches are common, and many IoT devices are insecure.

The global pandemic is indeed the most recent development to generate privacy and security concerns. These issues are also germane and similar to pre-existing privacy and information security debates, including those involving IoT products. These questions include how to balance technological innovations against privacy, which is an important societal value, and how to regulate corporate and government actors' collection and processing of our data and surveillance of our activities.[20] The volume and types of data about us that are now easily available to companies have increased exponentially because of the IoT. The use of IoT devices, services, and systems in pandemic response efforts illustrates the established and ubiquitous nature of the IoT. What does the IoT's proliferation mean for us as consumers? This book seeks to shed light on this question by exploring the consumer ramifications of the IoT primarily through the lens of commercial law and privacy and security law, with a central focus on corporate conduct.

The IoT and various other technological developments allow companies to extend their digital dominance over our lives and activities and provide multiple opportunities for once-ordinary household objects to serve as surveillance equipment capable of continuously monitoring and collecting vast quantities of our data.

---

[17] *See* Mason Marks, *You Shouldn't Have to Give Google Your Data to Access a COVID-19 Test*, SLATE (Mar. 17, 2020, 3:05 PM), https://slate.com/technology/2020/03/covid19-coronavirus-testing-google-walmart-target-privacy.amp?__twitter_impression=true.

[18] *Apple and Google Partner on COVID-19 Contact Tracing Technology*, APPLE (Apr. 10, 2020), www.apple.com/newsroom/2020/04/apple-and-google-partner-on-covid-19-contact-tracing-technology/; Russell Brandom, *Apple and Google Pledge to Shut Down Coronavirus Tracker When Pandemic Ends*, VERGE (Apr. 24, 2020, 12:15 PM), www.theverge.com/2020/4/24/21234457/apple-google-coronavirus-contact-tracing-tracker-exposure-notification-shut-down; Jack Nicas & Daisuke Wakabayashi, *Apple and Google Team Up to "Contact Trace" the Coronavirus*, N.Y. TIMES (Apr. 10, 2020), www.nytimes.com/2020/04/10/technology/apple-google-coronavirus-contact-tracing.html.

[19] Marks, *supra* note 17.

[20] REGAN, *supra* note 15, at 212–31.

Various IoT companies use privacy-invasive user default settings on IoT devices. Many smart televisions capture our viewing data by default.[21] To avoid data collection we must change default settings and, in some cases, must muddle through complicated privacy controls in order to do so.[22] In 2019, the average home had eleven connected products.[23] This number is expected to increase steadily as the IoT and mobile telecommunication systems expand.[24] If most IoT devices, mobile apps, and websites are collecting our data by default, how many mobile apps, websites, and device settings can each of us realistically review and revise to protect our privacy?

Consider that in 2019, Google and Amazon requested that IoT device makers who offer compatible devices design their products and services to ensure that they provide continuous streams of data to the technology giants.[25] For instance, an Alexa-enabled IoT device manufactured by a third-party IoT device maker must provide data to Amazon whenever the device is operational and also whenever it is turned off even if the consumer did not direct Alexa to turn the device on or off.[26] Similarly, IoT televisions can send continuous data streams about the channel they are tuned to, and IoT locks can send data about whether or not door bolts are engaged.[27] Prior to the change, these types of information were primarily provided to Amazon when a consumer issued a voice command to Alexa to operate third-party IoT devices.[28] These changes were reportedly made to increase IoT devices' performance and functionality.[29] From these continuous streams of data technology giants can glean unprecedentedly detailed information about us and our in-home behaviors, including our sleep and wake habits, the amount of time we spend at home, how frequently we use IoT products, and much more. Amazon dominates the

---

[21] Eli Blumenthal, *Just Got a New TV or Streamer? You Need to Change These Privacy Settings*, CNET (Dec. 30, 2019, 3:30 AM), www.cnet.com/google-amp/news/just-got-a-new-tv-or-streamer-you-need-to-change-these-privacy-settings/.

[22] *Id.*

[23] Todd Spangler, *U.S. Households Have an Average of 11 Connected Devices – and 5G Should Push That Even Higher*, VARIETY (Dec. 10, 2019, 8:48 AM), https://variety.com/2019/digital/news/u-s-households-have-an-average-of-11-connected-devices-and-5g-should-push-that-even-higher-1203431225/.

[24] *See* KEVIN WESTCOTT ET AL., DELOITTE CTR. FOR TECH., MEDIA & TELECOMM., BUILD IT AND THEY WILL EMBRACE IT 2(2019), www2.deloitte.com/content/dam/insights/us/articles/6457_Mobile-trends-survey/DI_Build-it-and-they-will-embrace-it.pdf.

[25] Matt Day, *Your Smart Light Can Tell Amazon and Google When You Go to Bed*, BLOOMBERG (Feb. 12, 2019, 2:00 AM), www.bloomberg.com/news/articles/2019-02-12/your-smart-light-can-tell-amazon-and-google-when-you-go-to-bed; *see also* David Priest, *Smart Home Developers Raise Concerns About Alexa and Google Assistant Security*, CNET (Mar. 15, 2020, 5:00 AM), www.cnet.com/news/smart-home-developers-raise-concerns-about-alexa-and-google-assistant-security/.

[26] Day, *supra* note 25.

[27] *See id.*

[28] *Id.*

[29] *See id.*; Terell Wilkins, *What You Need to Know About Amazon, Google, Smart Homes and Privacy*, SPECTRUM (Feb. 23, 2019, 8:59 AM), www.thespectrum.com/story/news/2019/02/23/p-c-periodicals-what-you-need-know-smart-home-privacy/2955184002/.

IoT smart speaker market.[30] Even if smaller IoT device manufacturers oppose technology giants' privacy-invasive practices, these smaller firms may be required to implement such practices or lose access to big technology firms' platforms, which could decrease consumers' willingness to purchase their products.[31]

Also, consider that Amazon's workers can listen to smart speaker users' Alexa conversations conducted in their homes.[32] Apple's external contractors can also reportedly review Siri conversations from users' Apple Watch and other Apple devices.[33] Technology giants' employees' and contractors' access to our IoT data is concerning in light of growing insider security threats.[34] Additionally, employees, contractors, and third parties with knowledge of the strength and weaknesses of related security infrastructure can pose a threat as well. It was, for example, a former Amazon employee who exploited a firewall weakness to carry out the 2019 Capital One data breach, which exposed the data of 106 million consumers that were stored in Amazon's cloud service.[35]

Design problems in IoT devices can also cause inadvertent data collection. Apple's Siri can mistakenly capture conversations when an individual wearing an Apple Watch lifts their wrist.[36] Similarly, smart speakers, including Amazon's Echo, can be accidentally activated and record in-home conversations.[37] One study of smart speakers found that these IoT devices could be erroneously activated nineteen times per day.[38]

---

[30]   Kim Lyons, *Amazon Is Still Crushing Google and Apple in the Smart Speaker Market*, VERGE (Feb. 10, 2020, 4:57 PM), www.theverge.com/2020/2/10/21131988/amazon-alexa-echo-google-apple-smart-home-speaker.

[31]   Priest, *supra* note 25.

[32]   Kate O'Flaherty, *Amazon Staff Are Listening to Alexa Conversations – Here's What to Do*, FORBES (Apr. 12, 2019, 11:54 AM), www.forbes.com/sites/kateoflahertyuk/2019/04/12/amazon-staff-are-listening-to-alexa-conversations-heres-what-to-do/#756908e771a2.

[33]   Kate O'Flaherty, *Apple Siri Eavesdropping Puts Millions of Users at Risk*, FORBES (July 28, 2019, 8:26 AM), www.forbes.com/sites/kateoflahertyuk/2019/07/28/apple-siri-eavesdropping-puts-millions-of-users-at-risk/#1d7d969ea530.

[34]   *Insider Threats: How Co-Workers Became a Bigger Security Headache*, DICE (Feb. 27, 2020), https://insights.dice.com/2020/02/27/insider-threats-co-workers-bigger-security-headache/. *See generally* OBSERVE IT, 2020 COST OF INSIDER THREATS GLOBAL REPORT (2020), www.observeit.com/cost-of-insider-threats/.

[35]   Robert McMillan, *Capital One Breach Casts Shadow over Cloud Security*, WALL ST. J. (July 30, 2019, 6:57 PM), www.wsj.com/articles/capital-one-breach-casts-shadow-over-cloud-security-11564516541; James Rundle & Catherine Stupp, *Capital One Breach Highlights Dangers of Insider Threats*, WALL ST. J. (July 31, 2019, 5:30 AM), www.wsj.com/articles/capital-one-breach-highlights-dangers-of-insider-threats-11564565402.

[36]   O'Flaherty, *supra* note 33.

[37]   Sara Morrison, *Alexa Records You More Often than You Think*, VOX (Feb. 21, 2020, 7:10 AM), www.vox.com/recode/2020/2/21/21032140/alexa-amazon-google-home-siri-apple-microsoft-cortana-recording; *see also* Kate O'Flaherty, *Amazon, Apple, Google Eavesdropping: Should You Ditch Your Smart Speaker?*, FORBES (Feb. 26, 2020, 10:12 AM), www.forbes.com/sites/kateoflahertyuk/2020/02/26/new-amazon-apple-google-eavesdropping-threat-should-you-quit-your-smart-speaker/#2f5cd710428d.

[38]   *See* DANIEL J. DUBOIS ET AL., MON(IOT)R RESEARCH GRP., WHEN SPEAKERS ARE ALL EARS: UNDERSTANDING WHEN SMART SPEAKERS MISTAKENLY RECORD CONVERSATIONS, https://moniotrlab.ccis.neu.edu/smart-speakers-study/ (last updated Feb. 14, 2020).

The mobile fitness apps we download to our smartphones and use in conjunction with our IoT devices, such as smart watches, also raise privacy concerns. In 2020, an individual using the Runkeeper fitness app to track workouts became a suspect in a burglary after police obtained a geofence warrant to access data from all devices close to the crime scene.[39] The individual was subsequently cleared, but by using the mobile app he provided location data.[40] State actors' use of geofence warrants has increased steadily in the last few years.[41] IoT devices and associated mobile apps that collect our location data provide additional venues for data disclosures and geofence warrant requests. Solving crimes is an important government objective, but so too is privacy protection. The number of IoT devices that will needlessly collect our location data is only growing. In 2020, Asics announced plans to reveal a prototype of a smart running sneaker with embedded sensors that could work in conjunction with the company's Runkeeper app.[42] As more IoT devices flood the market, there are more potential methods for others to obtain access to information about us.

An increasing number of IoT devices are insecure. In 2019, the Food and Drug Administration announced that an implantable IoT cardiac device was susceptible to hacking.[43] IoT insulin pumps have also been found to have security flaws that allow hackers to remotely control the devices and revise dosage settings.[44] Some IoT companies and industries also have limited data security expertise.[45] A growing

---

[39] Kim Lyons, *Google Location Data Turned a Random Biker into a Burglary Suspect*, VERGE (Mar. 7, 2020, 5:23 PM), www.theverge.com/platform/amp/2020/3/7/21169533/florida-google-runkeeper-geofence-police-privacy.

[40] *Id.*

[41] Jennifer Valentino-DeVries, *Tracking Phones, Google Is a Dragnet for the Police*, N.Y. TIMES (Apr. 13, 2019), www.nytimes.com/interactive/2019/04/13/us/google-location-tracking-police.html?mtrref=www.drudgereport.com&mtrref=www.nytimes.com.

[42] Vinciane Ngomsi, *ASICS to Launch an Entire Collection of Smart Shoes That Make You a Faster and Stronger Runner*, YAHOO SPORTS (Jan. 11, 2020, 10:21 AM), sports.yahoo.com/asics-to-launch-an-entire-collection-of-smart-running-shoes-heres-where-to-snag-your-own-pair-182150380.html; *see also ASICS Opens Doors to Innovation Labs at CES 2020*, PR NEWSWIRE (Jan. 7, 2020, 4:24 PM), www.prnewswire.com/news-releases/asics-opens-doors-to-innovation-labs-at-ces-2020-300983086.html.

[43] U.S. FOOD & DRUG ADMIN., CYBERSECURITY VULNERABILITIES AFFECTING MEDTRONIC IMPLANTABLE CARDIAC DEVICES, PROGRAMMERS, AND HOME MONITORS: FDA SAFETY COMMUNICATION (Mar. 21, 2019), www.fda.gov/medical-devices/safety-communications/cybersecurity-vulnerabilities-affecting-medtronic-implantable-cardiac-devices-programmers-and-home; *see also* Dave Johnson, *Can Pacemakers (and Other Medical Devices) Really Be Hacked?*, HOW-TO GEEK (July 18, 2019, 6:40 AM), www.howtogeek.com/427904/can-pacemakers-and-other-medical-devices-really-be-hacked/;
Liam Tung, *FDA Warning: Scores of Heart Implants Can Be Hacked from 20ft Away*, ZDNET (Mar. 22, 2019, 11:49 AM), www.zdnet.com/google-amp/article/fda-warning-scores-of-heart-implants-can-be-hacked-from-20ft-away/.

[44] Aimee Picchi, *Medtronic Recalls Insulin Pumps Because Hackers Could Hijack Device*, CBS NEWS (June 28, 2019, 9:16 AM), www.cbsnews.com/news/medtronic-insulin-pump-recall-fda-says-hackers-could-hijack-device/.

[45] Alison DeNisco Rayome, *Your Sex Tech Devices May Be Spying on You*, CNET (Jan. 18, 2020, 8:01 AM), www.cnet.com/google-amp/news/your-sex-tech-devices-may-be-spying-on-you/; *see also* Rose Minutaglio, *Is Your Sex Toy Spying on You?*, ELLE (Oct. 14, 2019), www.elle.com/culture/tech/

number of sex toys are now connected to the Internet and are controlled through mobile apps.[46] Many of these devices pose serious privacy risks and are insecure. They collect intimate data, including the exact date and time of use, frequency of orgasms, and vibration settings.[47] Consider that a Standard Innovation IoT sex toy and mobile app, which both users and their partners could remotely control, collected users' email addresses as well as information about their sexual habits without their consent.[48] These data could be used to identify users. The class action lawsuit that followed was subsequently settled.[49] IoT sex toys that are accompanied by cameras pose an even greater risk as they can capture users engaging in sexual acts.[50] For instance, researchers were able to easily hack the video feed of a Svakom IoT sex toy.[51] The data collected by these devices and the associated mobile apps could be used to stigmatize, blackmail, and harass victims.[52]

The IoT also allows companies to extend their digital control over us post transaction. In the subprime auto lending industry, lenders require subprime borrowers to accept installation of monitoring devices in their vehicles. These devices allow lenders to observe users' location and remotely disable their vehicles. Also, consider that in 2020, Tesla allegedly remotely disabled the autopilot feature in a consumer's vehicle after the car was sold without providing notice and obtaining prior consent.[53] IoT companies can also remotely disable our devices when we provide negative online reviews of their products.[54] IoT firms can "brick" our devices after we purchase them

---

a28846210/smart-sex-toy-dildo-butt-plug-hacking/; Danny Palmer, *Cybersecurity: These Are the Internet of Things Devices That Are Most Targeted by Hackers*, ZDNET (June 12, 2019, 9:00 AM), www .zdnet.com/google-amp/article/cybersecurity-these-are-the-internet-of-things-devices-that-are-most -targeted-by-hackers/.

[46] DeNisco Rayome, *supra* note 45; *see also* Press Release, Access Now, Access Now Asks U.S. FTC to Investigate Vulnerabilities in Internet-Enabled Sex Toy (Apr. 26, 2017, 9:04 AM), www.accessnow.org /access-now-asks-u-s-ftc-investigate-vulnerabilities-internet-enabled-sex-toy/.

[47] DeNisco Rayome, *supra* note 45; *see also* Shayna Possess, *Vibrator Gets Too Intimate by Tracking Usage Info, Suit Says*, LAW360 (Sept. 15, 2016, 3:57 PM), www.law360.com/articles/840299/vibrator-gets -too-intimate-by-tracking-usage-info-suit-says.

[48] Possess, *supra* note 47.

[49] *See* Judgment, N.P. v. Standard Innovation, No. 1:16-cv-8655, 2017 WL 10544062 (N.D. Ill. Aug. 15, 2017); Report and Recommendation, N.P. v. Standard Innovation, No. 16-cv-8655, 2017 WL 10544061 (N.D. Ill. July 25, 2017); *see also* Ry Crist, *Screwed by Sex Toy Spying? You May Get $10k*, CNET (Mar. 14, 2017, 8:30 AM), www.cnet.com/news/app-enabled-sex-toy-users-get-10000-each -after-privacy-breach/#ftag=CAD-00-10aag7d; Diana Novak Jones, *Web-Enabled Vibrator Class Action Ends with $3.75M Deal*, LAW360 (Aug. 15, 2017, 4:39 pm), www.law360.com/articles/954375.

[50] Complaint and Request for Investigation, Injunction and Other Relief, *In re* Svakom Design USA Ltd. (Apr. 26, 2017), www.accessnow.org/cms/assets/uploads/2017/04/AccessNow-FTCComp-Svakom.pdf.

[51] *Id.* at 3–4.

[52] Access Now, *supra* note 46.

[53] Jason Torchinsky, *Tesla Remotely Removes Autopilot Features from Customer's Used Tesla Without Any Notice*, JALOPNICK (Feb. 6, 2020, 4:10 PM), https://jalopnik.com/tesla-remotely-removes-autopilot- features-from-customer-1841472617.

[54] Rob Price, *The Maker of an Internet-Connected Garage Door Disabled a Customer's Device over a Bad Review*, BUS. INSIDER (Apr. 5, 2017, 3:51 AM), www.businessinsider.com/iot-garage-door-opener- garadget-kills-customers-device-bad-amazon-review-2017-4.

by failing to provide the necessary software updates and by also terminating the online services that are necessary for our devices to function. The Revolv smart hub is one such example. Thus, in the IoT setting we may purchase devices, but we now have significantly less control over how these devices function. Instead, it is the company that manufactures the device and provides the services required for device functionality that has true control over us and our devices.

The IoT may provide some benefits to individuals, including increased efficiency, convenience, and enhanced seamless and responsive user experiences.[55] It could also be beneficial to specific groups of consumers, such as those that are disabled, by increasing their access to services and goods and ability to participate in daily activities.[56] However, these groups of consumers are not immune to the privacy and security concerns the IoT raises. Moreover, while the IoT increasingly invades our lives and technology firms obtain more detailed access to information about us and our families, these companies are also able to simultaneously obfuscate their data mining and manipulation activities by using non-disclosure agreements, trade secrecy, and various other tactics.[57] Companies use these data analytics practices to determine how to treat us and what opportunities we will receive. Various legal frameworks strongly protect the secrecy of corporate entities in the commerce context, but the law fails to sufficiently do the same with respect to our privacy.[58] As a result, the various IoT concerns I have discussed so far are likely just the tip of the iceberg. If left unchecked, the harms the IoT generates will outweigh its possible benefits, if they do not already.

Many of the IoT examples discussed earlier raise several legal questions that implicate both privacy and security law and commercial law. For instance, companies often disclose their data collection and use practices in their privacy policies. Companies' online terms and conditions, which often contain mandatory arbitration provisions, can also incorporate privacy policies. Companies obtain rights in our data and permission to collect and use our data through these documents. Further, many IoT devices lack the traditional screens found on smartphones and computers that are typically used to display privacy policies and terms of service as well as any amended provisions. If an IoT company suffers a cybersecurity incident or if an IoT product causes physical or what are often seen as intangible privacy harms, are existing contract law principles addressing consent and products liability law adequate in today's IoT age? I argue in this book that they are not. Contract law is

---

[55] *See* Steve Ranger, *What Is the IoT? Everything You Need to Know About the Internet of Things Right Now*, ZDNET (Feb. 3, 2020, 2:45 PM), www.zdnet.com/article/what-is-the-internet-of-things-everything-you-need-to-know-about-the-iot-right-now/.

[56] LAUREN SMITH ET AL., FUTURE OF PRIVACY FORUM, THE INTERNET OF THINGS (IoT) AND PEOPLE WITH DISABILITIES: EXPLORING THE BENEFITS, CHALLENGES, AND PRIVACY TENSIONS (2019), https://fpf.org/wp-content/uploads/2019/01/2019_01_29-The_Internet_of_Things_and_Persons_with_Disabilities_For_Print_FINAL.pdf.

[57] FRANK PASQUALE, BLACK BOX SOCIETY 2–3 (2015).

[58] *Id.*

a core source of technology giants' "economic power."[59] Contract law and products liability law must evolve to acknowledge the realities of the circumstances surrounding consent in the IoT era as well as the new types of harms that the IoT raises. Another complicating factor is the role of large technology companies, such as Amazon, that both manufacture IoT devices and provide a platform for third-party sellers to sell IoT devices and other items. Courts' interpretation of federal law and state products liability laws can limit platform companies' exposure to liability for privacy-invasive and insecure IoT devices sold by third parties on their platforms. Consider that a *Wall Street Journal* investigation determined that 4,152 items for sale on Amazon's website were "declared unsafe by federal agencies."[60] Many of these products were potentially deceptively labeled, including 2,000 toy and medication listings.[61]

In the IoT setting, not only must we concern ourselves with the prospect of insecure and privacy-invasive IoT devices that we purchase directly from companies, we must also consider largely overlooked risks that the IoT raises and which are enabled by multiple sources of commercial law and corporate law. Companies use corporate and commercial law frameworks to facilitate data transfers among themselves. Companies' privacy policies and terms of service often contain provisions that enable our data to be disclosed and transferred in corporate transactions. The data that IoT devices and connected mobile apps collect about us can be transferred and sold to others in bankruptcy proceedings. For instance, if the maker of an IoT sex toy goes bankrupt, one if its most valuable assets is likely to be the email addresses and masturbatory habits of individuals using its products. There is also the possibility that companies could use their rights in our data to secure loans by granting lenders a lien on those rights.

Technology giants, such as Amazon and Google, continue to solidify their data market dominance and power by acquiring smaller IoT companies. Google's acquisition of Nest and Amazon's acquisition of Ring are but a few of these examples. Through these acquisitions, technology companies not only acquire a steady stream of talent and the rights to products acquired companies offer, but they also obtain the data we provided to acquired companies. These data acquisitions allow technology

---

[59] Julie E. Cohen, Between Truth and Power: The Legal Constructions of Informational Capitalism 63 (2019); Amy Kapczynski, *The Law of Information Capitalism*, 129 Yale L. J. 1460, 1482, 1489–90 (2020); Margaret Jane Radin , Boilerplate: The Fine Print, Vanishing Rights, and the Rule of Law 7–9, 12–15 (2013).

[60] Alexandra Berzon, Shane Shifflett & Justin Scheck, *Amazon Has Ceded Control of Its Site. The Result: Thousands of Banned, Unsafe or Mislabeled Products*, Wall St. J. (Aug. 23, 2019, 8:56 am), www.wsj.com/articles/amazon-has-ceded-control-of-its-site-the-result-thousands-of-banned-unsafe-or -mislabeled-products-11566564990 [hereinafter *Amazon Has Ceded Control*]; *see also* Alexandra Berzon, Shane Shifflett & Justin Scheck, *Senators Want Answers About Listings for Unsafe Merchandise on Amazon.com*, Wall St. J. (Aug. 29, 2019, 6:39 pm), www.wsj.com/articles/ democratic-senators-want-answers-about-listings-for-unsafe-merchandise-on-amazon-com -11567101615.

[61] Berzon et al., *Amazon Has Ceded Control, supra* note 60.

giants to know us more intimately than we even know ourselves. For example, Amazon collects and documents every motion its Ring doorbells detect "down to the millisecond" as well as data on users' interactions with the Ring mobile app, including mobile network and model information.[62] These data have also been reportedly disclosed to third-party advertising firms.[63] Inferences and patterns from these data could reveal detailed information about our lives, including how frequently we socialize with others and for how long.[64] Even more alarming is the possibility that Ring doorbells could one day be designed with vehicle license plate image collection and facial recognition tools.[65]

This book's arguments can be broken down into four main points. First, despite the IoT's possible benefits, it disrupts our privacy across a large range of contexts, raises significant data security concerns, and further enables corporate digital domination. Many existing privacy and security law frameworks, including federal and state statutes, do not fully remedy these concerns. Second, I contend that various commercial law frameworks can exacerbate and further enable the privacy, information security, and digital domination concerns the IoT raises, and provide various vehicles for the collection, transfer, and disclosure of our data, while in some cases allowing companies to shield themselves from liability. Third, I offer a comprehensive set of solutions to address deficiencies in covered sources of privacy and security law and commercial law. Fourth, the book offers three non-exhaustive reasons that in combination could explain the seeming disconnect between commercial law and privacy law and the consumer concerns of today's connected world. Stated differently, I attempt to shed light on why these legal frameworks are inadequate.

All of these reasons likely coalesce and contribute to a setting that allows corporate actors to use commercial law frameworks to undermine and assault our privacy and security. Privacy has long had a definitional problem.[66] There are various definitions and views of privacy.[67] Privacy harms are often perceived as ambiguous, intangible, and abstract. Yet, privacy may be no more difficult to define than other abstract concepts and values that we have ensured that our legal system adequately protects. It is likely that there are strong corporate interests that are deeply invested in

---

[62] Leo Kelion, *Amazon's Ring Logs Every Doorbell Press and App Action*, BBC News (Mar. 4, 2020), www.bbc.com/news/amp/technology-51709247; *see also* Brian X. Chen, *Your Doorbell Camera Spied on You. Now What?*, N.Y. Times (Feb. 19, 2020), www.nytimes.com/2020/02/19/technology/personaltech/ring-doorbell-camera-spying.html.

[63] Chen, *supra* note 62.

[64] Kelion, *supra* note 62.

[65] Kate Cox, *Leaked Pics from Amazon Ring Show Potential New Surveillance Features*, ARSTechnica (Apr. 22, 2020, 4:45 AM), https://arstechnica.com/tech-policy/2020/04/ring-cameras-may-someday-scan-license-plates-and-faces-leak-shows/.

[66] Daniel Solove , Understanding Privacy 2 (2008) ("Nobody can articulate what [privacy] means."); *see also* Helen Nissenbaum , Privacy in Context: Technology, Policy, and the integrity of Social Life 2 (2010) ("[A]ttempts to define [privacy] have been notoriously controversial.").

[67] Regan, *supra* note 15, at XIII.

and have contributed to privacy's perceived definitional problem.[68] If there is ambiguity in articulating the rights that should be protected and harms that should be guarded against under a specific source of law, it is likely more difficult for external sources of law to adequately account for these harms.

Another possible explanation is that despite the overlap of some concepts in both the commercial law and privacy law fields, such as autonomy and anonymity, privacy law and commercial law have historically focused primarily on addressing a distinct set of questions. Unlike privacy law discourse, which has predominantly explored questions and claims related to knowledge, access, and the use of information about us, commercial law has long had a heavy focus on issues relating to trade involving individuals, merchants, and entities. Privacy and commercial law are increasingly overlapping in the IoT world. This melding of the privacy and commercial law worlds predates the IoT.[69] However, the IoT exacerbates the consumer harms that arise from privacy and security law's and commercial law's inadequate recognition and resolution of issues caused by the growing overlap.

Another related reason is that despite distinct inquiries, both commercial law and privacy law historically reflect varying levels of deference to corporate practices. This deference has likely contributed to an environment that allows corporate actors to use both bodies of law to best serve their interests. In the privacy context, this deference has taken the form of a self-regulatory approach to data privacy and notice and choice. An industry self-regulatory regime primarily dependent on notice and choice has historically dominated the United States' approach to consumer data protection.[70] Powerful technology companies have played a significant role in blocking proposed consumer privacy and security laws while advocating for self-

---

[68] SHOSHANA ZUBOFF, THE AGE OF SURVEILLANCE CAPITALISM: THE FIGHT FOR A HUMAN FUTURE AT THE NEW FRONTIER OF POWER 47, 48, 85–87, 90, 96, 105 (2019).

[69] *Id.* at XI (noting that "[b]eginning in the 1960s, an array of technological and social changes precipitated challenges to individual privacy," including computers, wiretapping, miniature cameras and "parabolic microphones"); *see also* SOLOVE, *supra* note 66, at 4 ("[S]tarting in the 1960s, the topic of privacy received steadily increasing attention" because of the "profound proliferation of new information technologies," including the computer).

[70] Florencia Marotta-Wurgler, *Understanding Privacy Policies: Content, Self-Regulation, and Markets* 2 (NYU Law & Econ., Working Paper No. 435, 2016), https://pdfs.semanticscholar.org/281b/f65790a32e149cd7c1686dbb9a6eabb19e2d.pdf ("For the most part, consumer information has been protected by a self-regulatory regime articulated by the Federal Trade Commission (FTC) that has generally been referred to as 'Notice and Choice' and is predominantly based on disclosure."); *see also* CHRIS JAY HOOFNAGLE, FEDERAL TRADE COMMISSION PRIVACY LAW AND POLICY 146, 153 (2016) (noting that in the privacy context, "the FTC begins its regulatory process by first encouraging industries to self-regulate" and "[t]hroughout most of the FTC's history, it has endorsed self-regulatory approaches to promote the [fair information practices principles], while threatening the internet industry that it might endorse legislation"); FED. TRADE COMM'N, PRIVACY ONLINE: A REPORT TO CONGRESS i–ii (1998), www.ftc.gov/sites/default/files/documents/reports/privacy-online-report-congress/priv-23a.pdf (noting that the FTC's "goal has been to encourage and facilitate effective self-regulation as the preferred approach to protecting consumer privacy online . . . [and finding] that industry association guidelines generally encourage members to provide notice of their information practices and some choice with respect thereto").

regulation and the notice and choice model.[71] The privacy notice and choice regime has, to some extent, been duplicated in commercial law as well.

Outside of privacy law's influence, commercial law has for some time displayed a high regard for the development of commercial practices.[72] This respect for business custom appears to go beyond a mere recognition that commercial practices will evolve over time. Deference to commercial practices is evidenced by the Uniform Commercial Code's (UCC) provisions. The UCC is an important source of commercial law in the United States. Article 1 of the UCC states that one of the core purposes of the code is "to permit the continued expansion of commercial practices through custom, usage and agreement of the parties."[73] Given that one of the underlying purposes of the UCC is to facilitate the expansion of commercial practices, the development of modern commercial practices involving data trade arrangements and the potential applicability of the code to such transactions is in keeping with this goal. Indeed, the UCC was drafted to be flexible so that its provisions could "be applied by the courts in the light of unforeseen and new circumstances and practices."[74] This esteemed view of commercial practices combined with the role corporate advocates play in the UCC revision processes, the UCC's goal of uniformity, and the complicated mechanism for the approval of UCC amendments, may explain why the UCC has not yet been revised to more adequately reflect consumer perspectives. Although there are currently several UCC provisions directly addressing consumers, the UCC has on the whole been unwelcoming to consumer protection issues. Efforts to revise the code to more effectively address consumer concerns have failed.[75] The Bankruptcy Code, which regulates some aspects of commercial practices, also suffers from a similar problem.

---

[71] ZUBOFF, *supra* note 68, at 105–08; *see also* Frank Pasquale, *Privacy, Antitrust, and Power*, 20 GEO. MASON L. REV. 1009, 1009–24 (2013); Daniel J. Solove & Woodrow Hartzog, *The FTC and the New Common Law of Privacy*, 114 COLUM. L. REV. 583, 592–95 (2014).

[72] *See, e.g.*, U.C.C. § 8-113 cmt. (AM. LAW INST. & UNIF. LAW COMM'N 2020) ("For securities transactions, whatever benefits a statute of frauds may play in filtering out fraudulent claims are outweighed by the obstacles it places in the development of modern commercial practices in the securities business."); Henry D. Gabriel, *The Inapplicability of the United Nations Convention on the International Sale of Goods as a Model for the Revision of Article Two of the Uniform Commercial Code*, 72 TUL. L. REV. 1995, 1996 (1998) ("The Uniform Commercial Code ... attempts to reflect modern commercial practices."); Grant Gilmore, *The Commercial Doctrine of Good Faith Purchase*, 63 YALE L.J. 1057, 1065 n.22 (1954) ("The principal effect of the 'reasonable commercial standards' language may be to make evidence of business practice more easily admissible."); Ingrid Michelsen Hillinger, *The Article 2 Merchant Rules: Karl Llewellyn's Attempt to Achieve The Good, The True, The Beautiful in Commercial Law*, 73 GEO. L.J. 1141, 1150–51 (1985); Allen R. Kamp, *Legal Development: Between-the-Wars Social Thought: Karl Llewellyn, Legal Realism, and the Uniform Commercial Code in Context*, 59 ALB. L. REV. 325, 334 (1995) (citation omitted) ("The UCC was written largely to supplant the common law by clearing 'statute and case law debris from the field so that commercial law could follow the natural flow of commerce.'").

[73] U.C.C. § 1-103 (AM. LAW INST. & UNIF. LAW COMM'N 2001).

[74] *Id.* at cmt. 1.

[75] *See* Henry Gabriel, *Uniform Commercial Code Article Two Revisions: The View of the Trenches*, 23 BARRY L. REV. 129, 149–51 (2018). *See generally* Jean Braucher, *Foreword: Consumer Protection and the*

Many of the privacy and security harms the IoT raises lie at the unique intersection of the privacy and security law world and the commercial law world – the commercial law of privacy and security.[76] As such, a comprehensive approach that addresses inadequacies found in various sources of privacy and security law and commercial law at both the federal and state level is needed in order to sufficiently remedy these harms, and to better account for the increasing overlap between commercial law and privacy and security concerns in the IoT age.

Before we continue, a quick note about the term commercial law as used in this book. This term is used primarily to refer to legal frameworks governing commercial activities and practices. There are multiple sources of commercial law. The UCC and the Bankruptcy Code are the primary sources of law impacting commercial activity that this book covers. As Linda Rusch and Stephen Sepinuck note, "[c]ommercial law may be based upon contract law, but it also encompasses property-law concepts, tort rules, and agency principles."[77] Commercial transactions are often subject to multiple sources of law rather than being governed by a single legal regime.[78] Article 2 of the UCC contains important contract law rules as well as warranty rules. This book also covers sources of contract law and products liability law that are external to the UCC, but which are also important for an in-depth analysis and understanding of the IoT's consumer implications and the effect of the contract law and warranty provisions found in the UCC. Consumer protection legislation also significantly impacts commercial law and vice versa. The UCC contains provisions deferring to both federal and state consumer protection laws. As such, in some sections of this book, I also explore the role of consumer protection legislation, such as the Fair Debt Collection Practices Act. This book also considers the ramifications of corporate mergers and acquisitions, as these transactions present consumer concerns that are similar to those governed by traditional sources of commercial law. Privacy policies and conditions of use significantly determine companies' ability to transfer our data in corporate transactions, and contract law principles can impact the validity of such instruments.

As mentioned earlier, there is an ever-increasing blurring of the lines separating the privacy and security law world and the commercial law world. This blending began at least as early as the 1960s and perhaps even earlier.[79] The rise of the

---

Uniform Commercial Code, 75 WASH. U. L.Q. 1 (1997); Edward, L. Rubin, *The Code, the Consumer, and the Institutional Structure of the Common Law*, 75 WASH. U. L.Q. 11 (1997).

[76] To my knowledge, the term "commercial law of privacy" was coined by Michael Madison in his review of my previous scholarship in this area. *See* Michael Madison, *Money for Your Life: Understanding Modern Privacy*, JOTWELL (Jan. 8, 2018), https://cyber.jotwell.com/money-life-understanding-modern-privacy/ (reviewing Stacy-Ann Elvy, *Paying for Privacy and the Personal Data Economy*, 117 COLUM. L. REV. 1369 (2017)).

[77] LINDA J. RUSCH & STEPHEN L. SEPINUCK, COMMERCIAL LAW: PROBLEMS AND MATERIALS ON SALES AND PAYMENTS 15 (2nd ed. 2015).

[78] *Id.* at 14 ("Commercial transactions do not fall neatly under one legal regime.").

[79] *See, e.g.*, NISSENBAUM, *supra* note 66, at 1 (information technology discourse has been a "fixture in public discourse at least since the 1960s, when the dominant concern was massive databases of government and other large institutions housed in large stand-alone computers"); REGAN, *supra*

computer, modern databases, big data, and companies' free and freemium data business models and others, has created an ever-increasing overlap between privacy and security law and commercial law.[80] These business and technological developments have pushed us deeper into the realm of the commercial law of privacy and security. The IoT's rise and the corresponding exponential increase in data increases the meddling of the privacy and security and commercial law worlds, and exacerbates unaddressed harms. The result is that our concerns about privacy and security are intricately connected to the commercial law frameworks that allow companies to exploit our data and endanger our privacy and our sense of security. In today's connected world, our concerns about "who should know us and how"[81] are determined by the privacy law and commercial law frameworks that govern consent, and firms' data collection, monetization, transfer, and disclosure practices.

Commercial law and in some cases corporate law frameworks are directly implicated by the pressing privacy and data security questions the IoT raises. These questions include but are not limited to how the law and our society should respond to and evaluate: (1) the proliferation of the IoT and firms' related implementation of business models and product design and data practices that in combination work to invade our privacy, continuously surveil our activities and cause us harm; (2) the extent to which existing commercial law, privacy law, and security law frameworks should be adjusted to adequately remedy IoT privacy and security harms; (3) consumer consent to companies' data practices, including in transactions subject to Article 2 of the UCC, and the implications of such consent; (4) companies' use of asset collection technology and IoT devices to digitally dominate and restrain our activities in lending transactions, including those subject to Article 9 of the UCC; (5) technology firms' use of mergers and acquisitions to solidify their market dominance to collect and exploit more data about us; (6) companies' possible use of our data and the rights associated with such data in secured financing transactions under Article 9 of the UCC; and (7) businesses' disclosure and transfer of our data in bankruptcy proceedings. This book attempts to answers these questions and it provides several solutions to lead the way forward.

I propose a comprehensive set of recommendations to remedy the deficiencies I identify in various privacy and security law and commercial law frameworks. On the topic of privacy and information security, federal and state legislation must effectively constrain the transfer, disclosure, and use of consumer data in commercial transactions and must disincentivize business models and offerings

---

note 15, at XI; ROBERT ELLIS SMITH, BEN FRANKLIN'S WEB SITE: PRIVACY AND CURIOSITY FROM PLYMOUTH ROCK TO THE INTERNET 146 (2004) ("Each time when there was renewed interest in protecting privacy it was in reaction to new technology. First, in the years before 1890, came cameras, telephones, and high-speed publishing; second, around 1970, came the development of computers; and third, in the late 1990s, the coming of personal computers and the World Wide Web brought renewed interest in this subject.").

[80] *See generally* ZUBOFF, *supra* note 68.

[81] SARAH E. IGO, THE KNOWN CITIZEN: A HISTORY OF PRIVACY IN MODERN AMERICA 350 (2018).

that primarily rely on consumer data to the detriment of consumer interests. We should not have to accept terms and conditions and privacy policies that authorize nefarious and seemingly benign data collection and use practices that are unrelated to consumer products in order to access services and goods.

A comprehensive baseline privacy and information security federal statute that does more than mandate notice and choice and that establishes the contours of acceptable and unacceptable data practices is a key step in safeguarding consumers in the age of the IoT, and addressing current and possible future harms resulting from existing legal frameworks' inability to sufficiently account for the blending of the commercial law and privacy law worlds. The Federal Trade Commission (FTC), the U.S. Government Accountability Office, academics, consumer advocates, and others have long recommended that Congress enact various versions of a comprehensive federal privacy and security statute to better protect consumer interests.[82] The FTC has acknowledged that the privacy and security harms the IoT generates provide further evidence of the pressing need for Congress to adopt

---

[82] *See, e.g.*, U.S. Gov't Accountability Office, Internet Privacy: Additional Federal Authority Could Enhance Consumer Protection and Provide Flexibility 32–34, 38 (2019), www.gao.gov /assets/700/696437.pdf; Joseph Simons, Chairman, Fed. Trade Comm'n, Federal Trade Commission: Protecting Consumers and Fostering Competition in the 21st Century 7 (Sept. 25, 2019), www.ftc.gov /system/files/documents/public_statements/1545285/appropriations_committee_testimony_092519.pdf; Mark E. Budnitz, *Touching, Tapping, and Talking: The Formation of Contracts in Cyberspace*, 43 Nova L. Rev. 235, 272–79 (2019); Shaun G. Jamison, *Creating a National Data Privacy Law for the United States*, 10 Cybaris 1 (2019); Paul Ohm, *Broken Promises of Privacy: Responding to the Surprising Failure of Anonymization*, 57 UCLA L. Rev. 1701, 1762–64 (2010); W. Gregory Voss, *Obstacles to Transatlantic Harmonization of Data Privacy Law in Context*, 2019 U. Ill. J.L. Tech. & Pol'y 405, 458–61 (2019); Comments from the Future of Privacy Forum to U.S. Dept. of Comm. National Telecommunications and Information Administration (Nov. 9, 2018), www.ntia.doc.gov/files/ntia/publications/ntia_request_ for_comments_future_of_privacy_forum.pdf; Müge Fazlioglu, *White Paper – Consensus and Controversy in the Debate over US Federal Data Privacy Legislation*, Int'l Ass'n Privacy Professionals, https://iapp.org/resources/article/consensus-and-controversy-in-the-debate-over-us-federal-data-privacy-legislation/ (last updated Oct. 2019); Gennie Gebhart, *EFF's Recommendations for Consumer Data Privacy Laws*, Electronic Frontier Found. (Jun. 17, 2019), www.eff.org/deeplinks/ 2019/06/effs-recommendations-consumer-data-privacy-laws; *34 Organizations Unite to Release Principles for Privacy Legislation*, Media Alliance (Nov. 12, 2018), https://media-alliance.org/2018/11/34-organizations-unite-to-release-principles-for-privacy-legislation-2/. *See generally* Laura Moy, Associate Professor of Law, Georgetown Univ. Law Ctr., Statement Before the United States Senate Committee on Commerce, Science, and Transportation: Examining Legislative Proposals to Protect Consumer Data Privacy (Dec. 4, 2019), www.commerce.senate.gov/services/files/9BBAE979-05DE-46B0-AB8B-F352E54111F1; Maureen K. Ohlhausen, Co-Chair, 21st Century Privacy Coalition, Congress Needs to Enact a National, Comprehensive Consumer Privacy Framework, Testimony Before the Senate Committee on Commerce, Science, and Transportation (Dec. 4, 2019), www.commerce.senate.gov /services/files/30994150-8879-48B7-9BC0-625D8C81A7F2; Michelle Richardson, Dir. of Privacy & Data, Ctr. for Democracy & Tech., Statement Before the United States Senate Committee on Commerce, Science and Technology: Examining Legislative Proposals to Protect Consumer Data Privacy (Dec. 4, 2019), www.commerce.senate.gov/services/files/7F60A1BB-C8FD-420A-938C-D414BAC7FB71; Justin Brookman, Dir., Privacy & Tech. Policy, Small Business Perspectives on a Federal Data Privacy Framework, Statement Before the Senate Subcommittee on Manufacturing, Trade, and Consumer Protection (Mar. 26, 2019), www.commerce.senate.gov/services/files/18A4DA06-E09B-42CB-9FD3-01EE4DFC85C0; Stacey Gray, Senior Counsel, Future of Privacy Forum, Enlisting

a general privacy and data security statute.[83] However, an extensive approach is needed to fully reconcile provisions in commercial law and privacy law frameworks that enable consumer harms. Thus, in addition to joining earlier calls for the adoption of baseline privacy and security legislation, I also propose revisions to important sources of law governing commercial activity, such as the UCC, the Bankruptcy Code, debt collection laws, and products liability law as well as courts' interpretation of contract law principles. The goal of this extensive two-pronged approach – a baseline privacy and security statute and revisions to various sources of law impacting commercial practices – is to better remedy consumer harms resulting from the growing overlap between commercial law and privacy law in the IoT age.

BOOK OUTLINE

This book comprises three parts: (I) Privacy and Security in the Connected Era; (II) Commercial Law's Impact on Privacy, Security, and Liability, and (III) Concrete Legal Solutions for a Commercial Law of Privacy and Security. Part I evaluates the vast consumer privacy and security ramifications of the IoT and various applicable privacy and information security legal frameworks. Chapter 1 begins by exploring privacy's definitional problem and it exposes the significant privacy problems that the IoT raises, which are often facilitated by technology companies' various data business models and programs. These privacy harms include worsening unequal access to privacy and security, decreased anonymity, reduced ability to determine what happens to our data, decreased ability to shield our lives from corporate and government actors, digital colonization of our private spaces, and negative shaping of the opportunities we receive and our behaviors. I explore the various types of data that IoT devices, mobile apps, and services collect, and identify potential corporate beneficiaries of the digital colonization of our lives, including companies that make and sell IoT devices and provide IoT services, internet service providers, data brokers, and social media companies.

Chapter 2 uncovers the security failures of IoT devices, software, and associated systems and it also explores the limits of anonymization and aggregation. There are both internal and external sources of security vulnerabilities in the IoT setting. Companies also attempt to use their privacy policies and terms of service to limit their liability for security failings. Although useful, state data breach notification

Big Data in the Fight Against Coronavirus, Testimony and Statement Before the Senate Committee on Commerce, Science, and Transportation (Apr. 9, 2020), www.commerce.senate.gov/services/files/F24D0AF8-D939-4D14-A963-372B9357DD7E [hereinafter, Gray Testimony]. Other scholars have also proposed broad revisions to US privacy law to fill existing gaps through a model privacy regime. Daniel J. Solove & Chris Jay Hoofnagle, *A Model Regime of Privacy Protection*, 2006 U. Ill. L. Rev. 357 (2006).

[83] Fed. Trade Comm'n, Internet of Things: Privacy & Security in a Connected World 49–51 (2015), www.ftc.gov/system/files/documents/reports/federal-trade-commission-staff-report-november-2013-workshop-entitled-internet-things-privacy/150127iotrpt.pdf.

statutes and solely voluntary security frameworks by themselves are unlikely to fully remedy IoT security concerns. Courts' limited view of privacy and security harms and standing requirements are a significant hurdle to consumer remedy in security lawsuits.

Chapter 3 presents an overview and critique of several leading privacy and security legal frameworks applicable to the IoT. The frameworks covered in Chapter 3 include state statutes specifically adopted to address IoT harms, the 2018 California Consumer Privacy Act, data broker legislation, biometric and health-related data statutes, laws applicable to children's data and student data, and the FTC's efforts in this area. I argue that many of these frameworks are in need of improvement and are unlikely to comprehensively address the privacy and security harms discussed in Chapters 1 and 2 for several reasons. The United States' sectoral approach to privacy is prone to gaps. For instance, much of the health-related data that IoT devices collect are not subject to the federal Health Insurance Portability and Accountability Act. The absence of a federal statute that creates baseline privacy and security protections also enables unequal access to privacy and security between citizens of different states. There are significant drawbacks to the FTC's previous self-regulatory approach to consumer data protection. Privacy laws at both the federal and state level over-rely on notice and choice as the primary safeguard of our privacy and security, and in some cases statutory language constrains the possible impact and effectiveness of statutes in the IoT setting. Through their lobbying efforts, technology firms have successfully undermined efforts to adopt and revise privacy and security laws to protect consumers.

Part II offers a critical survey of the legal frameworks impacting commercial and corporate practices, which allow companies to transfer and disclose our data in corporate transactions, obtain our consent to collect and process our data, digitally dominate our lives and devices, and escape liability for defective IoT devices. In Chapter 4, I explore the issue of assent to contract terms and offer a brief account of the history of commercial law and its high regard for commercial practices. This historical exploration facilitates a clearer understanding of commercial law's current consent problem as well as the various other inadequacies in commercial law's handling of the privacy, security, and digital domination issues covered in Chapters 5, 6, and 7. In Chapter 4, I primarily discuss traditional contract law principles found in Article 2 of the UCC, and other important sources of contract law. I argue that the IoT complicates the already confusing world of online con-tracting. Courts frequently apply a reasonable notice and opportunity to review standard to determine consumer assent to online contracting terms, but the IoT disrupts the traditional assent analysis. The IoT worsens information asymmetry and the increasing distance between us as consumers and contract terms. In applying the notice and opportunity to review standard, consumers are often found to be bound to online contracting terms, such as mandatory arbitration provisions and class action waivers, despite empirical evidence showing limited consumer understanding of online contract terms.[84] Chapter 4 also discusses the possibility that in the future IoT devices may be transformed into objects that can act autonomously and contract on our behalf. I turn to agency law to highlight possible concerns with such transactions.

Chapter 5 uncovers inadequacies in products liability law and warranty principles in the IoT age. Previous attempts to amend Article 2 of the UCC to deal with consumer concerns have been unsuccessful for several possible reasons, including the UCC drafting processes' reliance on industry practices and approval of proposed UCC amendments. Historically, under products liability law, and under Article 2 of the UCC, there is a strong distinction between services and products. For instance, Article 2 of the UCC and its accompanying implied warranties apply to "transactions in goods." I argue that the connected nature of services, hardware, and software in the IoT setting, as well as the multiplicity of providers, renders the historical distinction between services and products obsolete. The IoT also makes it more difficult to assess liability for defects. Products liability law and warranty rules fail to capture some of the unique digital domination harms the IoT raises, including device bricking, the termination of integral services, and the denial of necessary software updates. Narrow definitions of the term seller under products liability law fail to sufficiently address technology giants' complicated role as sellers and platform providers. The federal Communications Decency Act also contributes to this problem. As it stands, warranty rules and products liability law's limited coverage of products and sellers can insulate companies from liability for wrongdoing in the IoT setting.

Chapter 6 then turns a critical eye toward the subprime auto lending and vehicle title lending industries to demonstrate the various harms that flow from IoT devices and technology that allow lenders to remotely track us and disable our vehicles. These harms include privacy intrusions, loss of device control, digital restraints, and significant lifestyle interruptions. All of these harms can occur post transaction and both before and after an individual is in default under a lending agreement. Historically marginalized consumers are particularly at risk. These technologies exacerbate unequal access to privacy and security and debt criminalization concerns, and relevant consumer protection legislation does not currently sufficiently address these harms. Chapter 6 also covers the role of the Bankruptcy Code and Article 9 of the UCC in facilitating these harms, and it also exposes inadequacies in state legislation regulating remote disablement devices. Like privacy law's failures, these remote disablement state statutes also rely significantly on notice and choice. This chapter also explores failed attempts to amend Article 9 of the UCC to

---

[84] *See, e.g.,* Yannis Bakos et al., *Does Anyone Read the Fine Print? Consumer Attention to Standard-Form Contracts,* 43 J. LEGAL STUD. 1 (2014); Jeff Sovern et al., *"Whimsy Little Contracts" with Unexpected Consequences: An Empirical Analysis of Consumer Understanding of Arbitration Agreements,* 75 MD. L. REV. 1 (2015).

comprehensively resolve pressing consumer issues, such as abusive deficiency claims in secured transactions.

In Chapter 7, I expose corporate use of privacy policies and conditions of use to authorize consumer data transfers in mergers and acquisition, bankruptcy proceedings, and secured financing transactions. Chapter 7 shows how corporate and commercial frameworks allow companies to transfer our data in ways that are opaque and potentially harmful to us as consumers. The 2005 amendments to the Bankruptcy Code also reflect privacy law's overreliance on notice and choice and do not adequately deal with data transfers in bankruptcy proceedings.

In Parts I and II of this book I argue that several sources of privacy law, security law, and commercial law have not been sufficiently revised and restructured to account for the rise of the commercial law of privacy and security. An extensive approach is necessary to correct this problem. Part III provides concrete legal solutions at every level to remedy inadequacies in existing commercial law and privacy and security law frameworks to better safeguard our interests as consumers and account for the increasing overlap between the privacy law and commercial law worlds. These inadequacies are found in various sources of privacy and security law, and commercial law at both the state and federal level. Chapter 8 offers federal- and state-level solutions primarily to correct state and federal privacy frameworks' overreliance on notice and choice and to better account for the privacy and security IoT harms that lie at the intersection of the privacy and security law and commercial law worlds. Chapter 9 provides several federal- and state-level proposals to facilitate a more effective commercial law of privacy and security by addressing shortcomings in various sources of law regulating commercial practices as well as including certain provisions in the federal baseline privacy and security legislation proposed in Chapter 8.

Chapter 8's proposed level reforms include movement away from an excessive reliance on the notice and choice model through the adoption of a baseline federal privacy and security statute inspired by several principles from the European General Data Protection Regulation and certain consumer-friendly provisions contained in the existing patchwork of domestic privacy law frameworks and previously proposed legislation. This section joins previous calls of privacy scholars and advocates in support of relying on some aspects of the European data protection approach in restructuring US privacy frameworks.[85] A federal baseline privacy and security statute need not preempt more protective state legislation. Such a statute could shed light on permissible and impermissible data practices; constrain the transfer,

---

[85] *See, e.g.,* Nehf, *supra* note 15; *see also* REGAN, *supra* note 15, at 234; David H. Flaherty, *The Need for an American Privacy Protection Commission,* 1 GOV. INFO. Q. 235 (1984); Karl Manheim & Lyric Kaplan, *Artificial Intelligence: Risks to Privacy and Democracy,* 21 YALE J.L. & TECH. 106, 181–82 (2019); Alexander Tsesis, *Data Subjects' Privacy Rights: Regulation of Personal Data Retention and Erasure,* 90 U. COLO. L. REV. 593, 627 (2019); Alexander Tsesis, *The Right to Erasure: Privacy, Data Brokers, and the Indefinite Retention of Data,* 49 WAKE FOREST L. REV. 433 (2014); Gray Testimony, *supra* note 82.

disclosure, and use of consumer data in commercial transactions; provide special protections for sensitive data, such as children's data, biometric, and health-related data; and disincentivize business models and offerings that primarily rely on consumer data to the detriment of consumer interests. Additionally, in the absence of a federal baseline privacy and security statute, this chapter calls for the adoption and revision of state privacy and security legislation to provide similar baseline privacy rights and granular security obligations recommended for federal legislation.

Chapter 9 builds on the proposals discussed in Chapter 8 and contends that a wide-ranging approach to addressing privacy and security deficiencies will also require significant changes to legal frameworks governing commercial practices that impact privacy and security, and that are found in state and federal law. The recommendations proposed in Chapter 9 include: (1) guidance on how to address the consent challenges the IoT raises via contract law principles applicable to assessing consumer assent to online contract terms. These recommendations include, but are not limited to, requiring courts to specifically consider the extent to which the consumer grasps the implications of the agreement's terms. I also use some aspects of Nancy Kim's recent consentability theory to offer a concrete framework to apply and expand on my earlier recommendations; (2) a prohibition on mandatory arbitration provisions in consumer transactions; (3) a new functional theory of warranty and products liability law that extends liability principles to the services and software associated with the functionality of IoT consumer devices; (4) amendments to the Communications Decency Act to prevent platforms from using the statute to obtain immunity from products liability claims; (5) amendments to the Fair Debt Collection Practices Act and state lending laws to deal with digital domination harms and debt collection abuses; (6) revisions to the Bankruptcy Code to more effectively address the transfer and disclosure of consumer data in bankruptcy proceedings and to correct the overreliance on notice and choice; and (7) amendments to Article 9 of the UCC to address the possible transfer and disclosure of consumer data in secured financing transactions. Antitrust law and its enforcers can also play a significant role in tackling consumer harms. I offer a few concluding words in Chapter 9.

PART I

Privacy and Security in the Connected Era

1

Privacy in the Internet of Things World

There are various definitions of privacy, and for some time now, privacy harms have been characterized as intractable and ambiguous. In this chapter, I argue that regardless of how one conceptualizes privacy the ubiquitous nature of IoT devices and the data they generate, together with corporate data business models and programs, create significant privacy concerns for all of us. The brisk expansion of the IoT has increased "the volume, velocity, variety and value of data."[1] The IoT has made new types of data that were never before widely available to organizations more easily accessible. IoT devices and connected mobile apps and services observe and collect many types of data about us, including health-related and biometric data.

The IoT allows corporate entities to colonize and obtain access to traditionally private areas and activities while simultaneously reducing our public and private anonymity. This unyielding corporate infiltration also has implications for other aspects of our privacy, including further limiting our ability to determine what happens to information about us and reducing our capacity to shield ourselves and our emotions, lifestyles, and children from the prying eyes of corporate and state actors alike. The pervasive data collection made permissible by IoT devices and companies' data business models also amplifies concerns about unequal access to privacy and security. A sharp distinction is further exploited between those who can afford privacy and security and those who cannot. IoT data combined with other sources of information can also be used to facilitate discrimination, negatively impact the opportunities that we receive, transform our behaviors, and modify our actions in real time for the benefit of organizations. Historically marginalized groups and members of other vulnerable groups, including children and low-income consumers, are particularly at risk.

---

[1] Terrell McSweeny, Comm'r, FED. TRADE COMM'N, Remarks at TecNation 2016, 8 (Sept. 20, 2016) (transcript available on the Federal Trade Commission's website).

DEFINING PRIVACY

As Daniel Solove observes, there are multiple "conceptions of privacy."[2] What follows is a brief description of some views of privacy. In 1890, Samuel Warren and Louis Brandeis attempted to identify a legal right to privacy, and defined privacy as the "right to be let alone" in a now famous law review article, written in response to the development of "instantaneous photographs" and the press's use of same.[3] Many legal scholars regard this article as the "foundation of privacy law in the United States."[4] Privacy has also been described as the ability or need to seclude oneself, including one's identity or certain aspects of oneself, from others.[5] Privacy is often defined as the ability to control others' access to data about us.[6] It has also been viewed as important to protecting "integrity of personality" and ensuring the intimacy needed to create and maintain relationships.[7] There is also a historical distinction between privacy protection for activities conducted in the private sphere versus those performed in the public sphere.

Recall that privacy is also conceptualized as a societal value and a public good.[8] Under this view, privacy is described as central to our democratic system, and our privacy can be better protected when we all have a "minimum level of privacy."[9] As Priscilla Regan has noted, viewing privacy only as an individual right ignores the social importance of privacy and allows policy discussions to be framed as a balancing act between individual privacy rights and other competing interests with social value.[10] The result is that privacy

---

[2]   Daniel Solove, Understanding Privacy 8 (2008); Daniel J. Solove, *Conceptualizing Privacy*, 90 Calif. L. Rev. 1087, 1092 (2002).

[3]   *Id.* at 15; Samuel Warren & Louis Brandeis, *The Right to Privacy*, 4 Harv. L. Rev. 193, 195 (1890).

[4]   Solove, *supra* note 2, at 15. *See also,* Jennifer E. Rothman, The Right of Publicity: Privacy Reimagined For A Public World 15–16 (2018).

[5]   Solove, *supra* note 2, at 1102 (describing privacy as "limited access to self" and noting that "this conception recognizes the individual's desire for concealment and for being apart from others"); *see also* Robert Ellis Smith, Ben Franklin's Web Site: Privacy and Curiosity from Plymouth Rock to the Internet 88 (2004)(privacy "is the desire by each of us for physical space where we can be free of interruption, intrusion, embarrassment or accountability").

[6]   *See, e.g.,* Helen Nissenbaum, Privacy in Context: Technology, Policy, and the Integrity of Social Life 2 (2010); Smith, *supra* note 5, at 88 ("Just what is privacy? . . . the attempt to control the time and manner of disclosures of personal information about ourselves.") Ari Ezra Waldman, Privacy as Trust: Information Privacy for an Information Age 6, 20 (2018); Alan F. Westin, Privacy and Freedom 7 (1967).

[7]   Solove, *supra* note 2, at 29–37.

[8]   *See generally,* Priscilla M. Regan, Legislating Privacy: Technology, Social Values and Public Policy (1995); James P. Nehf, *Recognizing the Societal Value in Information Privacy*, 78 Wash. L. Rev. 1 (2003); Paul M. Schwartz, *Property, Privacy, and Personal Data*, 117 Harv. L. Rev. 2055, 2084–85 (2004); Joshua A. T. Fairfield & Christoph Engel, *Privacy as a Public Good*, 65 Duke L.J. 385 (2015).

[9]   Regan, *supra* note 8, at xv, 225 ("[P]rivacy is a common value in that it is shared by individuals, a public value in that it has value to the democratic political system, and a collective value in that technology and market forces make it increasingly difficult for any one person to have privacy unless everyone has a similar minimum level of privacy.").

[10]   Regan, *supra* note 8, at 212–13.

advocates must then show that individual privacy harms outweigh the social benefits of any competing interests.[11]

Because there are so many different theories of privacy it has been difficult to cement a unified concept of privacy that adequately protects individuals and to clearly articulate privacy harms.[12] Instead, the privacy as control narrative, which largely benefits corporate interests, has dominated legal responses to privacy and security issues. Corporate entities are beneficiaries of the view of privacy as an abstract concept worthy of less protection, and as a solely individual value in direct competition with more important societal goals.

Despite privacy's definitional problem, claims of privacy, including some of those found in privacy law discourse, have primarily focused on the following inquiries: "who ha[s] the right to know, what ought to be publicly known and who and what should remain unknown."[13] These inquiries are common to several debates spanning multiple decades, including debates about the development of "instantaneous photography" and print journalism that alarmed Warren and Brandeis, "confessional memoirs," and state and corporate databases.[14] These questions are also germane to current debates about the global pandemic, corporate algorithms and big data.[15] Inquiries about who should be able to obtain information about us and what can happen when others possess information about us are core questions that are also relevant to privacy and security claims in the IoT setting.[16]

IOT DATA DELUGE

In the age of the IoT, ordinary objects are transformed into services with an unquenchable appetite for our data. Almost any physical object can now be connected to the Internet – watches, vacuums, vehicles, toasters, refrigerators, ovens,

---

[11] *Id.*

[12] SOLOVE, *supra* note 2, at 8–9 (observing that "the attempt to locate the 'essential' or 'core' characteristics of privacy has led to failure" and arguing "privacy should be conceptualized from the bottom up rather than the top down, from particular contexts rather than in the abstract").

[13] SARAH E. IGO, THE KNOWN CITIZEN: A HISTORY OF PRIVACY IN MODERN AMERICA 11–12, 350 (2018); *see also* DAVID H. FLAHERTY, PRIVACY IN COLONIAL NEW ENGLAND 1 (1967) ("In both the past and present American experience, concern for personal privacy has meant the desire of individuals to choose freely under what circumstances, and to what extent, they should expose themselves, their attitudes, and their behaviors to others."); REGAN, *supra* note 8, at 4, 43 (noting that "privacy is seen as an individual interest" and choice and privacy is often regarded "as a civil liberty, a right to be free of outside interference"); SMITH, *supra* note 5, at 135 (contending that "in the end the question of privacy throughout our history comes down to the relationships of the individual to large organizations and the method by which those large organizations foster and use new technology").

[14] IGO, *supra* note 13, at 11–12; *see also* SMITH, *supra* note 5, at 135 (noting that "in the first half of our history, Americans seemed to pursue, the first, physical privacy; in the second half – after the Civil War – Americans seemed in pursuit of the second, 'informational privacy,'" and discussing the rise of various technological developments).

[15] IGO, *supra* note 13, at 12.

[16] *Id.* at 350 (noting that the corollary to the question "[w]ho should know us and how" is "what might be altered by others' possession of that knowledge").

clothes, implantable devices, and much more.[17] All of these internet-enabled objects, along with the connected mobile apps and other online services, collect mountains of data. IoT objects obtain data about our consumption and usage rates and information about device functionality. Consider that Tommy Hilfiger's Xplore clothing line are manufactured with a smart chip to track how frequently individuals wear their clothes.[18] Frequent wearers of the brand's clothing will be given rewards.[19] Data from IoT devices and associated sensors allow companies to glean detailed information about our behaviors and interactions with IoT devices and could further transform us into corporate products and resources.[20]

IoT devices also have the capacity to collect location data. Companies have long used mobile apps to track our location. Even mundane apps, such as the Weather Channel app, collect our location data every few seconds.[21] The data can be used to reveal our identities and daily habits. Mobile location-based advertisement spending (much of which is possible because of the sale and disclosure of location data collected from our mobile apps) is expected to reach $32.4 billion by 2021.[22] IoT devices' reliance on mobile apps for functionality allows companies to further expand their mobile app data collection efforts. Technology companies that manufacture IoT products and provide various shopping platforms and services can also access our financial data and purchasing history.[23]

[17]   *See, e.g.*, Richard Baguley & Colin McDonald, *Appliance Science: The Internet of Toasters (and Other Things)*, CNET (Mar. 2, 2015, 11:26AM), www.cnet.com/news/appliance-science-the-internet-of-toasters-and-other-things/; Devin Pickell, *5 IoT Devices that Could Change Our Lives in the Very Near Future*, G2 (Sept. 21, 2018), https://learn.g2crowd.com/iot-devices; Darren Quick, *Neato's Robot Vacuum Cleaner Joins the Internet of Things*, NEW ATLAS (Sept. 7, 2015), https://newatlas.com/neatos-botvac-connected-robot-vacuum-ifa-2015/39286/; Hope Reese, *How Implanted Microchips Are Extending IoT from Objects to Human Beings*, TECHREPUBLIC (July 27, 2017, 4:05 AM), www.techre public.com/article/how-implanted-microchips-are-extending-iot-from-objects-to-human-beings/ #googDisableSync; Michael Sawh, *The Best Smart Clothing: From Biometric Shirts to Contactless Payment Jackets*, WAREABLE (Apr. 16, 2018), www.wareable.com/smart-clothing/best-smart-clothing.

[18]   Sam Wolfson, *Track Suits: Tommy Hilfiger's Creepy New Clothes Know How Much You Wear Them*, GUARDIAN (July 26, 2018, 12:47 PM), https://amp.theguardian.com/fashion/2018/jul/26/tommy-hilfiger-new-clothing-line-monitor-customers?__twitter_impression=true.

[19]   *Id.*

[20]   BRETT FRISCHMANN & EVAN SELINGER, RE-ENGINEERING HUMANITY 131 (2018); Kate Crawford & Vladan Joler, *Anatomy of an AI System*, AI NOW INST. & SHARE LAB (Sept. 7, 2018), https://anato myof.ai (contending that Amazon Echo users are "simultaneously a consumer, a resource, a worker, and a product . . . as their voice commands are collected, analyzed and retained for the purposes of building an ever-larger corpus of human voices and instructions").

[21]   Lauren Berg, *Weather Channel App Secretly Mines User Data, LA Says*, LAW360 (Jan. 4, 2019, 5:43 PM), www.law360.com/articles/1115318/weather-channel-app-secretly-mines-user-data-la-says; Jennifer Valentino-DeVries et al., *Your Apps Know Where You Were Last Night, and They're Not Keeping It Secret*, N.Y. TIMES (Dec. 10, 2018), www.nytimes.com/interactive/2018/12/10/business/location-data-privacy-apps.html.

[22]   *Location-Targeted Mobile Ad Spend to Reach over $32 Billion in 2021*, BIA ADVISORY SERVICES (Jan. 24, 2017), www.biakelsey.com/location-targeted-mobile-ad-spend-reach-32-billion-2021/; *see also* Valentino-DeVries et al., *supra* note 21.

[23]   *See* Drew Harwell, *Your Banking Data Was Once Off-Limits to Tech Companies. Now They're Racing to Get It.*, WASH. POST (Aug. 7, 2018, 12:31 PM), www.washingtonpost.com/technology/2018/08/07/your-

Immutable biometric data, such as a fingerprint scan, are also collected by IoT products. Our voice recordings and photographs can be used to generate voice and face prints that can be later used to identify us. IoT devices are notorious for their ability to generate biometric related data. Biometrics are increasingly becoming "the most widespread user interface for customers to interact with their various digital devices."[24] Real estate developers are currently building "smart apartments" and other structures that utilize IoT devices that can be operated by voice command.[25] Landlords are already using smart technology to control tenants' access to building areas.[26] More companies are using biometrics for authentication purposes, and biometric authentication will play an important role in the IoT context. Apple smartphones now use facial recognition technology.[27] Inadequately stored and communicated biometric identifiers may be at risk of disclosure and interception by third parties.

IoT objects have also created a boom in the collection of real-time health-related data, including COVID-19–related data, heart rates, sleep patterns, calories burned, body temperature, and oxygen levels.[28] Consider that UPRIGHT GO, a wearable IoT device, together with the associated mobile app, can generate continuous real-time data about users' postures.[29] Similarly, the Spire Stone device collects data on users' breathing patterns to assess and reduce stress levels.[30] The prototype of another wearable device can measure the cortisol levels in human sweat and expose our emotional state.[31] Wearable X's smart yoga pants and associated mobile app can monitor and collect information about a wearer's posture and alignment.[32]

banking-data-was-once-off-limits-tech-companies-now-theyre-racing-get-it/?outputType=amp&tid=ss_tw&utm_term=.8a15a8a1fa93&__twitter_impression=true.

[24] Paul Schaus, *Biometric Deployments Must Consider the "Internet of Things,"* PAYMENTSSOURCE (Aug. 9, 2016, 12:01 AM), www.paymentssource.com/news/paythink/biometric-deployments-must-consider-the-internet-of-things-3024711-1.html.

[25] C. J. Hughes, *The Latest in Apartment Technology: Fridge Cams and Robotic Valets,* N.Y. TIMES (Dec. 15, 2017), www.nytimes.com/2017/12/15/realestate/apartment-technology-fridge-cams-robotic-valets.html.

[26] Corina Knoll, *When a Phone App Opens Your Apartment Door, but You Just Want a Key,* N.Y. TIMES (Mar. 23, 2019), www.nytimes.com/2019/03/23/nyregion/keyless-apartment-entry-nyc.html#click=https://t.co/HTwCYg63YI.

[27] Arielle Pardes, *Facial Recognition Tech Is Ready for Its Post-Phone Future,* WIRED (Sept. 10, 2018, 7:00 AM), www.wired.com/story/future-of-facial-recognition-technology/.

[28] *See generally* Adam Thierer, *The Internet of Things and Wearable Technology: Addressing Privacy and Security Concerns Without Derailing Innovation,* 21 RICH. J.L. & TECH. 6 (2015); Andrea M. Matwyshyn, *The "Internet of Bodies" Is Here. Are Courts and Regulators Ready?* WALL ST. J. (Nov. 12, 2018, 11:19 AM) www.wsj.com/articles/the-internet-of-bodies-is-here-are-courts-and-regulators-ready-1542039566; Jonathan M. Peake, Graham Kerr & John P. Sullivan, *A Critical Review of Consumer Wearables, Mobile Applications, and Equipment for Providing Biofeedback, Monitoring Stress, and Sleep in Physically Active Populations,* 9 FRONTIERS PHYSIOLOGY 1 (Jun. 28, 2018).

[29] *See How UPRIGHT Works,* UPRIGHT, www.uprightpose.com/how-it-works/ (last visited Jan. 30, 2019).

[30] SPIRE HEALTH, https://spire.io/pages/stone (last visited Jan. 30, 2019).

[31] Taylor Kubota, *Wearable Device from Stanford Measures Cortisol in Sweat,* STAN. NEWS (July 20, 2018), https://news.stanford.edu/2018/07/20/wearable-device-measures-cortisol-sweat/.

[32] Ray A. Smith, *The Future of Everything Work Clothes, Reimagined for an Age of Wearable Tech,* WALL ST. J. (Jan. 2, 2020, 11:04 AM), www.wsj.com/articles/work-clothes-reimagined-for-an-age-of-wearable-tech-11577981068?redirect=amp#click=https://t.co/WGjLTJJKsz.

IoT products also frequently observe and collect consumer environmental data. I use the term environmental data to refer to our physical surroundings. This includes our neighborhoods, places of employment, and other places we frequent. For example, by bringing IoT objects into our homes, IoT device manufacturers and other third parties could potentially access home layout data.[33] Information about other household members (such as children) can also be observed and collected using IoT devices.[34] Employers are also increasingly using IoT objects and sensors to track employees.[35] Wearable devices and sensors embedded within employees' identification badges, and work equipment, monitor workers' location, activities, productivity levels, and emotional state.[36]

The rise of smart cities further enables the collection of environmental data directly related to individuals. Internet-enabled city infrastructure allows various entities to monitor neighborhoods and easily observe our activities and habits. Low-income neighborhoods and people of color are especially vulnerable to the misuse of environmental data. Even roads and highways can be connected to the Internet. Technology start-up Integrated Roadways has developed "smart pavement" technology that embeds internet connectivity into ordinary roads.[37] These smart roads can serve as a platform for IoT vehicles. In fact, electronic sensors are already embedded in local roads in Kansas City.[38] IoT city energy meters can provide data about the time at which energy is used as well as generate 2,880 readings per month, in contrast to predecessor analog meters that provide only one reading per month.[39]

DATA BUSINESS MODELS AND PROGRAMS

Companies' traditional data business models enable what author Shoshana Zuboff has aptly described as "surveillance capitalism," the goal of which is to "predict and

---

[33]   *See* Dan Price, *Smart Home Data Collection: Are Companies Going Too Far?*, MUO (Sept. 28, 2017), www.makeuseof.com/tag/smart-home-data-collection/.

[34]   *See* Natasha Lomas, *Call for Smart Home Devices to Bake in Privacy Safeguards for Kids*, TECHCRUNCH (Sept. 18, 2018, 4:01 PM), https://techcrunch.com/2018/09/18/call-for-smart-home-devices-to-bake-in-privacy-safeguards-for-kids/.

[35]   Scott R. Peppet, *Regulating the Internet of Things: First Steps Toward Managing Discrimination, Privacy, Security, and Consent*, 93 TEX. L. REV. 85, 112 (2014).

[36]   Stuart Frankel, *Employers Are Using Workplace Wearables to Find Out How Happy and Productive We Are*, QUARTZ (Aug. 11, 2016), https://qz.com/754989/employers-are-using-workplace-wearables-to-find-out-how-happy-and-productive-we-are/; Gene Marks, *These Office Sensors Can Track Employees Wherever They Go*, WASH. POST (Feb. 15, 2017, 10:38 AM), www.washingtonpost.com/news/on-small-business/wp/2017/02/15/these-office-sensors-can-track-employees-wherever-they-go/?noredirect=on&utm_term=.98653ef8ced3.

[37]   INTEGRATED ROADWAYS, http://integratedroadways.com/ (last visited Jan. 30, 2019).

[38]   Timothy Williams, *In High-Tech Cities, No More Potholes, but What About Privacy?*, N.Y. TIMES (Jan. 1, 2019), www.nytimes.com/2019/01/01/us/kansas-city-smart-technology.html.

[39]   Allison Grande, *Smart Meter Data Needs Privacy Protection, 7th Circ. Told*, LAW360 (Mar. 2, 2017, 8:34 PM), www.law360.com/articles/897628/smart-meter-data-needs-privacy-protection-7th-circ-told.

modify human behavior as a means to produce revenue and market control."[40] Companies have long collected, monetized, and disclosed our data with impunity. Given the variety and quality of IoT data that are now available, continuous streams of these data allow companies to expand surveillance capitalism. The drastic increase in data, in conjunction with traditional and nascent business models, lays the foundation for continued data abuse and monetization, which have even more far-reaching consequences in the IoT context.

Technology companies have historically used traditional free and freemium (a combination of the terms "free" and "premium") business models. The free business model, operating through the concept of "data as payment," provides users with access to the company's offerings without charging a monetary fee. For instance, the now-shuttered Shiru Cafe in Rhode Island provided free beverages to college students in exchange for their data, including their names, telephone numbers, and majors.[41] Technology companies, such as Facebook and Twitter, also use the free business model.[42] Once an individual uses a free mobile app or other free service, the user engages in an unequal bargain in which their generated data are collected and monetized by the organization providing the free product.[43] In such transactions, our data could be viewed as the "things of value" that are transferred as consideration in exchange for the free service or product.[44] Even companies providing free antivirus programs have collected data about our online searches, clicks, and purchases.[45] These data can then be sold to and monetized by large technology companies, including Google and Microsoft.[46] Similarly, Facebook has reportedly given other technology companies, such as Netflix, detailed access to consumers'

---

[40] SHOSHANA ZUBOFF , THE AGE OF SURVEILLANCE CAPITALISM: THE FIGHT FOR A HUMAN FUTURE AT THE NEW FRONTIER OF POWER (2019) (discussing surveillance capitalism); Shoshana Zuboff, *Big Other: Surveillance Capitalism and the Prospects of an Information Civilization*, 30 J. INFO. TECH. 75, 75 (2015) (defining and discussing surveillance capitalism).

[41] Allie Reed, *Shiru Cafe Shutters All U.S. Locations*, BROWN DAILY HERALD (Sept. 18, 2019), www.browndailyherald.com/2019/09/18/shiru-cafe-shutters-u-s-locations/; Chaiel Schaffel, *No Cash Needed at This Cafe. Students Pay the Tab with Their Personal Data*, NPR (Sept. 29, 2018, 7:37 AM), www.npr.org/sections/thesalt/2018/09/29/643386327/no-cash-needed-at-this-cafe-stu dents-pay-the-tab-with-their-personal-data.

[42] *See* Sourobh Das, *How Does Twitter Make Money? Twitter Business Model*, FEEDOUGH.COM (Feb. 3, 2019), www.feedough.com/how-does-twitter-make-money/; Luis Perez-Breva, *Facebook Has to Change Its Business Model Because It's Using Us as Unpaid Laborers*, MARKETWATCH (Apr. 12, 2018, 11:42 AM), www.marketwatch.com/story/facebook-has-to-change-its-business-model-because-its-using-us-as-unpaid-laborers-2018-04-12.

[43] Chris Jay Hoofnagle & Jan Whittington, *Free: Accounting for the Costs of the Internet's Most Popular Price*, 61 UCLA L. REV. 606, 624–25 (2014); *see also* 16 C.F.R. § 251.1 (2017).

[44] *See generally*, Andrea M. Matwyshyn, *Privacy, the Hacker Way*, 87 S. CAL. L. REV. 1 (2013).

[45] Michael Kan, *The Cost of Avast's Free Antivirus: Companies Can Spy on Your Clicks*, PC MAG. (Jan. 27, 2020), www.pcmag.com/news/the-cost-of-avasts-free-antivirus-companies-can-spy-on-your-clicks.

[46] Joseph Cox, *Leaked Documents Expose the Secretive Market for Your Web Browsing Data*, VICE (Jan. 27, 2020, 6:00 AM), www.vice.com/en_us/article/qjdkq7/avast-antivirus-sells-user-browsing-data-investigation.

data (including private messages).[47] Thus, we voluntarily and involuntarily trade our data and attention away to acquire free products.[48]

In addition to the free business model, companies can also use the freemium data business model wherein the introductory aspects or portions of a product are provided to users without a monetary charge, but users must pay a fee to access the product's advanced features.[49] Yahoo and LinkedIn have used the freemium data business model.[50] Companies that use this model often generate revenue from advertisements and subscription fees paid by consumers for upgraded options. These companies also obtain data from users who access the free aspects of their products as well as data provided by consumers who pay a monetary price to access upgraded product features. For instance, Yahoo scans and scrapes data from the emails of consumers who use its free email service as well as users who pay for its advertisement-free email service.[51] Additionally, as Chris Hoofnagle and Jan Whittington have noted, companies using a freemium model "devote remarkable amounts of attention and investment to the collection of data from and about free-riding consumers of their products."[52]

Today, IoT companies are employing business strategies akin to traditional data business models. Much like the technology giants that use free and freemium business models to vacuum up our data, IoT companies are increasingly using data collected by IoT devices to compete with other companies and to subsidize the costs of the IoT products they sell us.[53] Soon, we will all become more accustomed to devices that collect extensive data about us in exchange for cheaper

---

[47] Gabriel J. X. Dance et al., *As Facebook Raised a Privacy Wall, It Carved an Opening for Tech Giants*, N.Y. TIMES (Dec. 18, 2018), www.nytimes.com/2018/12/18/technology/facebook-privacy.html.

[48] Stacy-Ann Elvy, *Paying for Privacy and the Personal Data Economy*, 117 COLUM. L. REV. 1369, 1385 (2017); Adam B. Thimmesch, *Transacting in Data: Tax, Privacy, and the New Economy*, 94 DENV. L. REV. 145, 147 (2016) (contending that the data-as-payment model is a "barter transaction" and that "the digital products of today's economy are not free even though they are provided without a cash charge" because "consumers buy access to those products with their data").

[49] Mariana Bravo & Katherine Ondeck, *When the Money Is Gone: The Legal Aftermath of Wire Fraud*, LAW360 (May 19, 2017, 11:54 AM), www.law360.com/articles/925861/when-the-money-is-gone-the-legal-aftermath-of-wire-fraud (describing Yahoo Mail as a freemium email account); Jason Kincaid, *Startup School: Wired Editor Chris Anderson on Freemium Business Models*, TECHCRUNCH (Oct. 24, 2009, 11:55 AM), https://techcrunch.com/2009/10/24/startup-school-wired-editor-chris-anderson-on-freemium-business-models/ (suggesting that Yahoo Mail is based on a freemium business model); Vineet Kumar, *Making "Freemium" Work*, HARV. BUS. REV. (May 2014), http://hbr.org/2014/05/making-freemium-work.

[50] Kumar, *supra* note 49.

[51] Matt Binder, *Yahoo and AOL Will Continue to Scan Your Emails for Precious Advertising Data*, MASHABLE (Aug. 28, 2018), https://mashable.com/article/yahoo-aol-email-scanning-ad-data/#LKSpO4ofVsqn; Shannon Liao, *How to Opt out of Yahoo Mail's Invasive Data Scanning*, VERGE (Aug. 28, 2018, 7:20 PM), www.theverge.com/2018/8/28/17793964/how-to-opt-out-yahoo-mail-email-data-scanning-advertising.

[52] Hoofnagle & Whittington, *supra* note 43, at 634.

[53] *See, e.g.*, Nilay Patel, *Taking the Smarts out of Smart TVs Would Make Them More Expensive*, VERGE, www.theverge.com/2019/1/7/18172397/airplay-2-homekit-vizio-tv-bill-baxter-interview-vergecast-ces-2019 (last updated Jan. 7, 2019, 7:46 PM).

products. Also consider that the data IoT vehicles collect may soon be more valuable to businesses and generate more profits than IoT vehicle sales.[54]

Companies often offer the accompanying mobile apps – which enable consumers to use the IoT devices – without requiring consumers to pay an additional monetary fee. For example, many of the IoT devices Samsung sells are accompanied by a free SmartThings mobile app that can be used to control Samsung and SmartThings-compatible IoT devices.[55] Our use of free services and products may complicate the application of those areas of consumer protection law that rely on individuals acting as buyers who exchange money for services or products.[56] Technology companies that have historically used the free business model can encourage consumers to trade access to their IoT data for more free services. Companies that sell IoT devices can also obtain data about us from businesses that use the traditional free business model. For instance, a consumer that purchases a Fitbit wearable device (which collects health-related data) can sync their account with various social media sites, such as Facebook.[57] Fitbit then obtains access to the user's social media information, including their friend lists.[58]

Somewhat similar to the traditional freemium model, IoT companies also offer upgraded IoT online services for additional prices on a subscription basis. After purchasing a Nest security camera accompanied by a free mobile app, a consumer receives a free trial of the company's video storage service.[59] At the end of the free trial period, the consumer must pay an additional subscription fee to store and review future videos.[60]

IoT devices can also serve as an envoy for the purchase of other products IoT companies offer. For example, Amazon gave its IoT dash button for free to its Amazon Prime subscription consumers.[61] The dash button was used to purchase subsequent products directly from Amazon with a push of a button.[62] Similarly, an

---

[54] Matt McFarland, *Your Car's Data May Soon Be More Valuable than the Car Itself*, CNN (Feb. 7, 2017, 9:05 AM), https://money.cnn.com/2017/02/07/technology/car-data-value/index.html.

[55] *SmartThings*, SAMSUNG, www.samsung.com/global/galaxy/apps/smartthings/ (last visited Jan. 31, 2019).

[56] Ellis v. Cartoon Network, Inc., 803 F.3d 1251, 1252–56 (11th Cir. 2015); *In re* Facebook Privacy Litig., 791 F. Supp. 2d 705, 715 (N.D. Cal. 2011); Elvy, *supra* note 48, at 1386; Hoofnagle & Whittington, *supra* note 43, at 657–62; Chris Jay Hoofnagle et al., *The Tethered Economy*, 87 GEO. WASH. L. REV. 783, 794 n.63 (2019) (citing Stacy-Ann Elvy, *Hybrid Transactions and the Internet of Things: Goods, Services, or Software?*, 74 WASH. & LEE L. REV. 77 (2017)).

[57] *See Fitbit Privacy Policy*, FITBIT, www.fitbit.com/legal/privacy-policy (last visited Feb. 1, 2019).

[58] *Id.*

[59] *See Google Nest Cam Indoor*, GOOGLE STORE, https://store.google.com/us/product/nest_cam?hl=en-US&GoogleNest (last visited Feb. 14, 2020); *FAQs About the Free Nest Aware Trial for Nest Cameras*, GOOGLE NEST HELP, https://support.google.com/googlenest/answer/9248198?hl=en&co=GENIE .Platform%3DiOS&oco=0 (last visited Feb. 14, 2020) [hereinafter *Nest Aware FAQs*].

[60] *See Nest Aware FAQs*, *supra* note 59.

[61] Amazon Prime consumers received a credit equal to the cost of the Dash button. *See* Sarah Silbert, *What Is the Amazon Dash Button?*, LIFEWIRE, www.lifewire.com/amazon-dash-buttons-4129293 (last updated Jan. 23, 2020). Amazon eventually discontinued the device.

[62] *Id.*

IoT product, such as a connected water pitcher, that is accompanied by Amazon's dash replenishment service and a free mobile app can reorder supplies directly from Amazon even though the IoT device is manufactured by a third party.[63] The result of course is that both the device manufacturer and Amazon can obtain data about users' purchasing habits, among other things. In both the freemium and free business models, and their IoT variations, many consumers may fail to fully understand the extent to which they have traded away their data and attention in exchange for a product. Consumers have historically had little control over their data and privacy under traditional data business models. These problems are heightened in the IoT context.

Technology companies also use other data business models or programs, such as the pay for privacy (PFP) and personal data economy (PDE) models. These models share some characteristics with older data business models. Companies using PFP business models or programs offer privacy or security-centered products at moderate or expensive prices, or via privacy-invasive discounts and rewards that require consumers to pay higher fees to protect their privacy. For instance, AT&T previously offered monthly discounts to consumers who allowed AT&T to use their web-browsing information "to tailor ads and offers."[64] Users who wanted to protect their privacy had to pay "as much as $66" more per month.[65] Similarly, the Verizon Up program gives consumers rewards, such as credits towards the purchase of new devices and other discounts, in exchange for obtaining access to consumers' browsing history, location, app usage, demographic data, and preferences.[66] Once collected, the data are shared with third parties, including Verizon related entities and other Verizon business partners.[67]

Organizations that offer virtual private network (VPN) products, which mask consumers' online identities, require users to pay subscription fees and are PFP products.[68] VPNs may not provide full online privacy protection to consumers and some VPN companies have even sold consumers' data, including browsing history,

---

[63] *See Amazon Dash Replenishment Program Continues to Grow, Adding New Device Manufacturers and Auto-Replenishment Products*, Bus. Wire (Jan. 10, 2018, 9:00 AM), www.businesswire.com/news/home/20180110005410/en/Amazon-Dash-Replenishment-Program-Continues-Grow-Adding.

[64] Dan Gillmor, *AT&T Wants to Know: How Much Would You Pay for a Little Online Privacy?*, Guardian (Dec. 13, 2013, 1:45 PM), www.theguardian.com/commentisfree/2013/dec/13/at-t-austin-uverse-experiment-user-data.

[65] Letter from Elizabeth Warren, Senator, U.S. Senate, to Tom Wheeler, Chairman, Fed. Commc'n Comm'n (June 21, 2016), https://perma.cc/9WWT-7362 [hereinafter Warren Letter] (explaining that AT&T's discount program may have required "consumers to pay as much as $66 in additional monthly costs for service that maintains their privacy").

[66] Chaim Gartenberg, *Verizon's New Rewards Program Lets It Track Your Browsing History*, Verge (Aug. 2, 2017, 2:50 PM), www.theverge.com/2017/8/2/16085062/verizon-up-rewards-program-track-browsing-history-data-select-oath.

[67] *Id.*

[68] Max Eddy, *The Best VPN Services for 2020*, PC Mag., www.pcmag.com/picks/the-best-vpn-services (last updated Feb. 13, 2020).

while others adopt lax cybersecurity practices.[69] The COVID-19 pandemic has increased interest in VPN services.[70] In the IoT space, F-Secure Sense, which retails for $199, is a connected router that connects to and secures users' in-home IoT devices from cyberattacks.[71] Consumers must pay a subscription fee to access premium cybersecurity features and services beyond the one-year initial free period.[72] A study discussing PFP models, and evaluating the impact of mobile apps found that approximately half of the studied paid apps shared the same types of consumer data as the free versions of the app, even though consumers tend to expect more privacy and cybersecurity protection when they have paid for an app rather than received it for free.[73]

Companies that adopt a PDE business model or program provide users with a platform to control, aggregate, analyze, and in some cases monetize their IoT data and other sources of information.[74] Datacoup buys data directly from consumers for a monetary price.[75] Inrupt aims to vest consumers with control of their data through personal data pods that consumers can use to grant and revoke companies' access to their data.[76] Nebula Genomics' platform allows users to obtain insights from their DNA, while also providing rewards to those consumers who elect to share their data with third parties.[77] Meeco and Digi.me provide platforms that allow consumers to curate and obtain insights from their data.[78] Other PDE-like companies, such as Killi, match consumers with data buyers and facilitate payments from businesses to users as compensation for completing surveys about their preferences.[79]

[69] Romain Dillet, *How I Made My Own WireGuard VPN Server*, TECHCRUNCH (July 28, 2018, 7:17 AM), https://techcrunch.com/2018/07/28/how-i-made-my-own-wireguard-vpn-server/; *see also* MUHAMMAD IKRAM ET AL., AN ANALYSIS OF THE PRIVACY AND SECURITY RISKS OF ANDROID VPN PERMISSION-ENABLED APPS, INTERNET MEASUREMENT CONFERENCE (2016), www.icir.org/vern/papers/vpn-apps-imc16.pdf (a study finding several privacy and cybersecurity failures by VPN providers).

[70] Adam Janofsky, *Coronavirus Fears Sparks a Rush of Interest in the Humble VPN*, PROTOCOL (Mar. 4, 2020), www.protocol.com/vpn-unexpected-coronavirus-winner.

[71] Max Eddy & Victoria Song, *F-Secure Sense Preview*, PC MAG. (Nov. 8, 2017), www.pcmag.com/review/357074/f-secure-sense.

[72] Dan Dziedzic, *F-Secure Sense Keeps Hackers out of Your Connected Devices*, CNET (Sept. 26, 2017, 8:24 AM), www.cnet.com/reviews/f-secure-sense-preview/.

[73] Kenneth A. Bamberger et al., *Can You Pay for Privacy? Consumer Expectations and the Behavior of Free and Paid Apps*, 35 BERKELEY TECH. L.J. 327, 327–36 (2020).

[74] PDE companies appear to be similar to the "infomediaries" of the dot com era. *But see* Elvy, *supra* note 48, at 1419 n.238 (distinguishing infomediaries from PDE companies).

[75] *See* DATACOUP, http://datacoup.com/ (last visited Feb. 4, 2019).

[76] K. G. Orphanides, *How Tim Berners-Lee's Inrupt Project Plans to Fix the Web*, WIRED (Feb. 15, 2019), www.wired.co.uk/article/inrupt-tim-berners-lee.

[77] *How It Works*, NEBULA GENOMICS, https://nebula.org (last visited Feb. 4, 2019); *see also* Jeff Bauter Engel, *Nebula Genomics Touts Free DNA Sequencing to Coax Health Data Sharing*, XCONOMY (Nov. 15, 2018), https://xconomy.com/boston/2018/11/15/nebula-genomics-touts-free-dna-sequencing-to-coax-health-data-sharing/.

[78] *See* Irina Bolychevsky & Simon Worthington, *Are Personal Data Stores About to Become the Next Big Thing?*, MEDIUM (Oct. 4, 2018), https://medium.com/@shevski/are-personal-data-stores-about-to-become-the-next-big-thing-b767295ed842; Elvy, *supra* note 48, at 1393–1400.

[79] KILLI, www.killi.io/killi-app/ (last visited Apr. 4, 2019).

In contrast to traditional data models like the free model, in which companies' offerings are seemingly unconnected to data transfers, organizations using PDE data business models could increase transparency surrounding data-trade arrangements. However, it is unclear whether this transparency and consumer understanding of data value and data-trade arrangements will extend to how companies use the consumer data obtained through PDE marketplaces. Additionally, creating more marketplaces for us to actively trade our data in exchange for money, rewards, or discounts may simply provide new platforms and mechanisms for companies to further commodify and profit from our data. Consider that Facebook recently announced plans to pay users for their voice recordings through its viewpoints app in order to refine the speech recognition systems associated with its IoT devices.[80]

CORPORATE INVASION OF THE PRIVATE SPHERE

Many IoT devices are Trojan horses. These devices further muddle the lines between the public and private spheres. Corporate data business models, combined with the proliferation of IoT devices, enable organizations to colonize intimate spaces under the pretense of providing us with convenience. Surveillance and data collection intensify once we begin to use IoT devices and associated mobile apps and services.

With the IoT's rise, conversations and activities that could once be performed at home without disclosure to multiple corporate institutions can now be easily observed, monitored, and shared by corporate entities and their associates. For instance, IoT televisions are accompanied by various software programs and inter-active services that allow technology companies and device makers to collect data about almost everything shown on our smart television sets, as well as data about other devices connected to these IoT televisions.[81] Also, consider that Samba TV, a company that tracks individuals' viewing habits in partnership with television manufacturers via software installed on IoT televisions, allows companies to target advertisements to consumers based on these data.[82] Unsurprisingly, the interface that prompts users to authorize the Samba TV data collection does not clearly inform individuals about the types and amount of data the company will collect.[83] Consumers must click on multiple subsequent screens to view the company's approximately 6,500-word terms of service and 4,000-word privacy policy.[84] Users

---

[80]   Tim Bradshaw, *Facebook Offers to Pay Users for Their Voice Recordings*, Ars Technica (Feb. 20, 2020, 10:33 AM), https://arstechnica.com/tech-policy/2020/02/facebook-offers-to-pay-users-for-their-voice-recordings/; Jay Peters, *Facebook Will Now Pay You for Voice Recordings*, Verge (Feb. 20, 2020, 3:00 PM), www.theverge.com/platform/amp/2020/2/20/21145584/facebook-pay-record-voice-speech-rec ognition-viewpoints-prounuciations-app.

[81]   Sapna Maheshwari, *How Smart TVs in Millions of U.S. Homes Track More Than What's on Tonight*, N.Y. Times (July 5, 2018), www.nytimes.com/2018/07/05/business/media/tv-viewer-tracking.html.

[82]   *Id.*

[83]   *Id.*

[84]   *Id.*

are lulled into believing that they are merely receiving convenient viewing recommendations while the company collects massive quantities of data. One study evaluating streaming devices associated with smart TVs, such as Amazon's firestick, found that these devices enable widespread data collection and transmissions.[85]

IoT devices give corporate entities a front row seat to view and obtain data about our in-home activities. As the Samba TV example discussed earlier illustrates, companies can obtain access to our data through the online terms of service and privacy policies that we agree to. These agreements are broadly written to protect companies' ability to collect, transfer, and disclose our data. Many IoT devices and digital assistants continuously listen to in-home conversations. These devices may eventually be able to determine the status of personal relationships and suggest methods to resolve disputes.[86] We can no longer assume that our homes will be a refuge free from prying eyes. Since the pandemic has forced us to spend more time at home, IoT companies will likely be able to collect even more data about us and how we use our in-home IoT devices. Confidential conversations, including those between attorneys working from home and their clients, could be recorded by in-home IoT devices during the pandemic.[87]

Those of us who are surveillance averse and proactive about protecting our privacy are not immune to this corporate invasion. For instance, a privacy-conscious person may elect not to use IoT devices in their home to limit corporate surveillance. Assume that this individual visits a family member's abode that is awash in various IoT devices, including a smart speaker, an IoT doorbell, and an IoT television. By entering their family member's IoT home, the surveillance-averse consumer's image, voice, and conversations could be recorded, stored, and possibly obtained by third parties. Many children have very little influence in determining whether their in-home activities will also be observed by the IoT devices their parents elect to bring home. Human error can also inadvertently lead to the disclosure of the private conversations and data IoT devices record. For example, a German consumer obtained access to 1,700 Alexa voice recordings of another user after links to the recordings were erroneously sent by an Amazon employee.[88] The recordings were used to identify the unsuspecting consumer.[89]

---

[85] HOOMAN MOHAJERI MOGHADDAM ET AL., WATCHING YOU WATCH: THE TRACKING ECOSYSTEM OF OVER-THE-TOP TV STREAMING DEVICES, ACM SIGSAC CONFERENCE 12 (2019), https://tv-watches-you.princeton.edu/tv-tracking-acm-ccs19.pdf.

[86] Daniel Jones, Alexa Will Be Able to Tell When Your Relationship Is Ending, Experts Predict, N.Y. POST (Nov. 29, 2018, 11:59 AM), https://nypost.com/2018/11/29/alexa-will-be-able-to-tell-when-your-relationship-is-ending-experts-predict/.

[87] Crystal Tse & Jonathan Browning, *Locked-Down Lawyers Warned Alexa Is Hearing Confidential Calls*, BLOOMBERG (Mar. 20, 2020, 9:59 AM), www.bloomberg.com/news/articles/2020-03-20/locked-down-lawyers-warned-alexa-is-hearing-confidential-calls.

[88] *Amazon Error Allowed Alexa User to Eavesdrop on Another Home*, REUTERS (Dec. 20, 2018, 2:32 AM), www.reuters.com/article/us-amazon-data-security/amazon-error-allowed-alexa-user-to-eavesdrop-on-another-home-idUSKCN1OJ15J.

[89] *Id.*

Not only are our homes being colonized by IoT devices, but our bodies are too. Wearable and implantable devices allow organizations to obtain deep insights and real-time data about our physical, mental, and emotional well-being. Where once a person could attempt to hide a racing heart rate, an individual wearing an IoT fitness device cannot always mask their rising heart rate from the device's manufacturer. Internet-connected devices implanted in an individual's body (the so-called Internet of Bodies) can be used to control bodily functions through a smartphone mobile app connected to the implanted device.[90] Additionally, even when IoT devices are not located in ordinary homes or implanted in our bodies they can capture vulnerable and significant life events. For example, a COVID-19 victim's vocal request to Alexa for pain relief was recorded and stored by an Amazon Echo smart speaker in a nursing home.[91]

Regardless of how one defines privacy, data business models that enable the corporate colonization of our private spaces through IoT devices and services limit our access to privacy in multiple ways. The IoT diminishes our ability to be "let alone" from surveillance.[92] It restricts our ability to conceal aspects of our personalities, events, emotions, facts and matters from others and our capacity to effectively share specific things with only a select group of people. It lowers societal and individual expectations of privacy by conditioning us to accept constant and unrelenting surveillance. It decreases our ability to control intimate aspects of our lives and our ability to limit others' access to our lives. Companies' exploitation of the IoT data deluge for multiple purposes (many of which are unrelated to the initial purpose of data collection and in some cases conducted without our consent) also diminishes our autonomy and our ability to control what happens to information about us. The ubiquitous nature of IoT devices also negatively impacts our ability to know, understand, and keep track of the volume, nature, and quality of data multiple entities collect about us. This reduction facilitates "exclusion" which reduces data collectors' accountability.[93] The disclosure of the intimate data the IoT generates could also negatively impact our ability to maintain relationships with others. The IoT also enables multiple actors to distort information about us for their benefit and appropriate our likeness, images, and identities with more ease.[94] The biometric data IoT devices collect combined with machine learning technology could be used to create believable deepfakes targeting individuals. Additionally, the IoT amplifies

---

[90]   *See* Andrea M. Matwyshyn, *The Internet of Bodies*, 61 WM. & MARY L. REV. 77, 81 (2019); *Internet of Bodies: What's Getting into You*, EMERGO (July 29, 2019), www.emergobyul.com/blog/2019/07/internet-bodies-whats-getting-you.

[91]   Janelle Griffith, *Nursing Home Patient Asked Amazon Alexa for Help as She Lay Dying of Coronavirus, Sister Says*, NBC NEWS, www.nbcnews.com/news/us-news/nursing-home-patient-asked-amazon-alexa-help-she-lay-dying-n1180131 (last updated Apr. 10, 2020, 9:29 AM).

[92]   *See* Warren & Brandeis, *supra* note 3, at 193.

[93]   *See* Daniel J. Solove, *A Taxonomy of Privacy*, 154 U. PA. L. REV. 477, 522–25 (2006) (describing exclusion as a privacy harm).

[94]   *See id.* at 545–52 (describing the privacy harms of appropriation and distortion).

our sense of cyber-insecurity and increases the ability of third parties to threaten us with data disclosure. The more data that companies hoard the more likely it is that a data breach will lead to the disclosure of our information. The data breach stakes are higher in the IoT context given the granular, more accurate, and often intimate nature of IoT data. For instance, an IoT breach could involve a live video feed of an individual in the nude.

One frequent critique of IoT privacy concerns is that we choose to purchase, install, and wear IoT devices and are complicit in allowing companies to invade our private spaces. However, IoT products are becoming the norm. The newer models of once basic objects are all now connected to the Internet. Today, if you are looking to buy a new television, you would be hard pressed to find one that lacks either a direct internet connection or the capacity to be connected to the Internet using a separate device. Approximately 75 percent of all televisions in use are connected to the Internet.[95] To use many of the features advertised by IoT companies as essential to device function-ality, we must generally use the internet-connected aspects of the IoT product and the free mobile apps companies provide. For example, a Nest security camera is only useful to the extent that the consumer enables internet connectivity and can view videos through the accompanying mobile app.[96] Similarly, the Ring doorbell is useless without the accompanying mobile app, and users must consent to having their video footage centrally stored on Amazon's servers.[97]

Various corporate entities are benefiting from the IoT's proliferation. Companies that manufacture and sell IoT devices and provide IoT-specific services and prod-ucts are direct beneficiaries. For instance, in order to improve the Alexa digital assistant software, Amazon's workers and external contractors are given access to the voice recordings Echo smart speakers capture in our homes.[98] Similarly, executives and employees of Ring IoT doorbell products were given unprecedented access to view unencrypted and continuous video feeds and files from users' cameras to compensate for gaps in facial recognition software linked to the company's Neighbors system (another service the company provides).[99] While annotating

[95] Alan Wolk, *Why ACR Data Is Poised to Become the Future of TV Measurement*, FORBES (Feb. 19, 2018, 3:27 PM), www.forbes.com/sites/alanwolk/2018/02/19/why-acr-data-is-poised-to-become-the-future-of-tv-measurement/#5a5274aa1821.

[96] *See FAQs About Outdoor Nest Cameras*, GOOGLE NEST HELP, https://support.google.com/googlenest/answer/9251085?hl=en#outdoor-faq-good-enough (last visited Feb. 17, 2020).

[97] Tristan Greene, *Why Amazon's Ring and Facial Recognition Technology Are a Clear and Present Danger to Society*, THENEXTWEB (Jan. 31, 2020, 2:37 PM), https://thenextweb.com/artificial-intelli gence/2020/01/31/why-amazons-ring-and-facial-recognition-technology-are-a-clear-and-present-dan ger-to-society/.

[98] Matt Day et al., *Amazon Workers Are Listening to What You Tell Alexa*, BLOOMBERG (Apr. 10, 2019, 3:34 PM), www.bloomberg.com/news/articles/2019-04-10/is-anyone-listening-to-you-on-alexa-a-global-team-reviews-audio.

[99] Sam Biddle, *For Owners of Amazon's Ring Security Cameras, Strangers May Have Been Watching Too*, INTERCEPT (Jan. 10, 2019, 9:34 AM), https://theintercept.com/2019/01/10/amazon-ring-security-camera/.

video files, employees observed users kissing and operating guns.[100] Ring products have also been subject to several consumer cybersecurity complaints, including hacking.[101] These examples illustrate that not only are IoT companies profiting from the direct sale of IoT devices and services, but they are also benefiting from using in unexpected ways the data gathered from our ongoing use of the IoT devices they sell to us.

IoT data are also ripe for acquisition by traditional data brokers. Acxiom, one of the largest data brokers, has "more than 23,000 computer servers" scrutinizing the data of millions of individuals.[102] Data brokers' possible access to IoT data would allow these entities to build even more detailed and accurate dossiers on all of us. Data brokers obtain information about us from public sources as well as from organizations with whom they enter into cooperative agreements. IoT companies could very easily enter into such data sharing agreements with data brokers and other business partners. Data brokers and other companies can also provide IoT businesses with information about us as well.

As Chris Hoofnagle notes, technology giants such as Facebook and Google compensate developers with access to our data and are "the modern data brokers" of our time.[103] These companies trade our data to external mobile developers who are obscurely described as "partners" and "service providers" in privacy policies.[104] Developers have long designed mobile apps to obtain more data about us "than is available through the web and to enhance lock-in."[105] Facebook has also entered the IoT market. The company sells various IoT smart display and video calling devices with Alexa capabilities.[106] These devices are accompanied by smart cameras and microphones that track users' in-home movements and listen to conversations.[107] Users' device-related data can be used for targeted advertisements.[108]

---

[100] *Id.*

[101] *See* Complaint, Orange v. Ring L.L.C., No. 2:19-cv-10899 (C.D. Cal. Dec. 26, 2019); Jonathan Stempel, *Amazon's Ring Cameras Are Vulnerable to Hackers, Lawsuit in U.S. Claims*, REUTERS (Dec. 27, 2019, 12:49 PM), www.reuters.com/article/us-amazon-com-ring-lawsuit-idUSKBN1YV1LQ; Daniel Wroclawski, *3,000 Ring Doorbell and Camera Accounts May Be Vulnerable to Hackers*, CONSUMER REPORTS (Dec. 19, 2019), www.consumerreports.org/hacking/ring-doorbell-accounts-may-be-vulnerable-to-hackers/.

[102] Natasha Singer, *Mapping, and Sharing, the Consumer Genome*, N.Y. TIMES (June 16, 2012), www.nytimes.com/2012/06/17/technology/acxiom-the-quiet-giant-of-consumer-database-marketing.html.

[103] CHRIS HOOFNAGLE, UNIV. OF CAL., BERKELEY, FACEBOOK AND GOOGLE ARE THE NEW DATA BROKERS 3, 5, 8 (2019), https://docs.wixstatic.com/ugd/36ef64_f2c9212728c0421597f297cc931c1181.pdf.

[104] *Id.* at 4.

[105] *Id.* at 2.

[106] *Smart Video Calling to Fit Every Family*, PORTAL https://portal.facebook.com/products/ (last visited Apr. 13, 2020).

[107] Ry Crist, *Facebook's New Portal Smart Displays: Who's Listening and What's Happening to Your Data*, CNET (Oct. 4, 2019, 12:24 PM), www.cnet.com/how-to/facebook-portal-smart-display-privacy-concerns/.

[108] *Id.*; *Data Policy*, FACEBOOK, www.facebook.com/policy/ (last visited Apr. 13, 2020).

IoT device manufacturers can also use external developers to generate the mobile apps that IoT devices rely on. As IoT devices proliferate, there will be a corresponding increase in the number of mobile apps, thereby creating more opportunities for IoT device manufacturers, developers, and other third parties to collect our data. Consider that marketing and analytics companies can obtain users' IoT device data through third-party trackers associated with IoT apps, regardless of whether the user pays for the IoT device, associated services, or mobile app. The third-party trackers in the Android Ring doorbell mobile app allow marketing companies to obtain paying users' "names, private IP addresses, mobile network carriers, persistent identifiers, and sensor data on" Ring devices.[109]

Internet Service Providers (ISPs) are another potential corporate beneficiary of the proliferation of IoT devices and the corresponding corporate colonization of our private spaces. IoT devices that are designed for use in our homes generally require internet access via a Wi-Fi network in order for us to operate and control these devices. ISPs provide us with access to the Internet. Although somewhat controversial, the Federal Communications Commission (FCC) has noted that ISPs can "see a tremendous amount of their customers' personal information that passes over that [i]nternet connection, including their browsing habits."[110] Verizon has used behavior-tracking tools to surreptitiously monitor customers' online activities.[111] ISPs have also sold our location data to third parties and opposed web browser providers' implementation of privacy and cybersecurity features to block data snoopers.[112] In some instances, they have continued to sell our location data even after promising not to do so.[113]

---

[109] Bill Budington, *Ring Doorbell App Packed with Third-Party Trackers*, Electronic Frontier Found. (Jan. 27, 2020), www.eff.org/deeplinks/2020/01/ring-doorbell-app-packed-third-party-trackers.

[110] Fed. Comm. Commission, Fact Sheet: The FCC Adopts Order to Give Broadband Consumers Increased Choice over Their Personal Information 1, http://apps.fcc.gov/edocs_public/attach match/DOC-341938A1.pdf.

[111] Karl Bode, *Verizon May Soon Get to Enjoy a Lawsuit over Its Sneaky Use of Perma-Cookies*, Techdirt (Nov. 7, 2014, 7:51 AM), www.techdirt.com/articles/20141105/11315029057/verizon-may-soon-get-to-enjoy-lawsuit-over-their-sneaky-use-perma-cookies.shtml.

[112] *See, e.g.*, Kelcee Griffis, *Big Telecoms Face $200M in Fines for Mobile Data Sales*, Law360 (Feb. 28, 2020, 1:56 PM), www.law360.com/technology/articles/1248664; Kelcee Griffis, *Verizon, AT&T Say They Will Cut Off Location Data Sellers*, Law360 (June 19, 2018, 9:28 PM), www.law360.com/articles/1055184/verizon-at-t-say-they-will-cut-off-location-data-sellers; Andrew Kragie, *Mozilla to Congress: Don't Trust ISPs on Data Tracking*, Law360 (Nov. 4, 2019, 6:28 PM), www.law360.com/cybersecurity-privacy/articles/1216616/mozilla-to-congress-don-t-trust-isps-on-data-tracking?nl_pk=8bca81a9-bf53-40e6-b4c6-; Will Oremus, *The Privacy Scandal that Should Be Bigger than Cambridge Analytica*, Slate (May 21, 2018, 12:51 PM), https://amp.slate.com/technology/2018/05/the-locationsmart-scandal-is-bigger-than-cambridge-analytica-heres-why-no-one-is-talking-about-it.html? wpsrc=sh_all_dt_tw_ru&__twitter_impression=true.;4d8c2eda4ebe&utm_source=newsletter& utm_medium=email&utm_campaign=cybersecurity-privacy.

[113] Jon Brodkin, *Ajit Pai: Carrier Sales of Phone-Location Data Is Illegal, FCC Plans Punishment*, Ars Technica (Jan. 31, 2020, 1:10 PM), https://arstechnica.com/tech-policy/2020/01/ajit-pai-carrier-sales-of-phone-location-data-is-illegal-fcc-plans-punishment/.

Increasingly, ISPs are supplementing their traditional business models by providing new services that collect more of our data. Verizon's Yahoo acquisition allows it to provide email services directly to consumers and obtain direct access to their consumers' email contents.[114] This expansion will continue in the IoT era. The recent T-Mobile and Sprint merger will decrease "the number of national wireless carriers from four to three" and could solidify these companies' market power.[115] ISPs are also increasingly entering the IoT space. ISPs are likely to monitor and collect data generated from our in-home use of IoT devices and services. Consider that Verizon sells several IoT devices, including the Nest thermostat.[116] Comcast intends to offer its own IoT home platform, which will allow consumers to control their IoT devices through its services.[117] Verizon also offers to its consumers a VPN service called Safe Wi-Fi.[118] The applicable terms of service for Safe Wi-Fi provides that the company does not collect data transmitted through its VPN service, but the terms of service also reference Verizon's privacy policy, which authorizes it to collect data, including browsing history.[119] VPN products will become even more useful in the IoT setting in which every activity leaves an online digital trial.

This invasion of our private spaces also enables non-corporate entities to monitor us. These entities include hackers and other individuals with malicious intentions. IoT products can be used to harass and control domestic abuse victims.[120] Women

[114] *See* Andrew Liptak, *Oath's New Privacy Policy Allows It to Scan Your Yahoo and AOL Mail for Targeted Advertising*, VERGE (Apr. 14, 2018, 12:27 PM), www.theverge.com/2018/4/14/17237864/oath-aol-yahoo-email-privacy-terms-scan-ads.

[115] Letter from Edward J. Markey, Amy Klobuchar, Tom Udall, Tammy Baldwin & Richard Blumenthal, Senators, U.S. Senate, to Roger Wicker, Chairman, Comm. on Commerce, Sci. & Transp., & Maria Cantwell, Ranking Member, Comm. on Commerce, Sci. & Transp. (Jan. 24, 2019), www.markey.senate.gov/imo/media/doc/TMobile-Sprint.pdf; Edmund Lee, *T-Mobile and Sprint Are Cleared to Merge as the Big Get Bigger*, N.Y. TIMES (Feb. 11, 2020), www.nytimes.com/2020/02/11/business/media/t-mobile-sprint-merger.html.

[116] *Smart Home*, VERIZON, www.verizonwireless.com/smart-home/ (last visited Feb. 5, 2019).

[117] Todd Spangler, *Comcast Wants to Turn Xfinity into an "Internet of Things" Smart-Home Platform*, VARIETY (Jan. 10, 2018, 9:00 AM), https://variety.com/2018/digital/news/comcast-xfinity-internet-of-things-home-automation-1202657823/.

[118] Karl Bode, *Verizon Didn't Bother to Write a Privacy Policy for Its "Privacy Protecting" VPN*, VICE: MOTHERBOARD (Aug. 6, 2018, 11:28 AM), https://motherboard.vice.com/en_us/article/a3q4gz/verizon-didnt-bother-to-write-a-privacy-policy-for-safe-wi-fi-privacy-protecting-vpn.

[119] *Terms of Service for the Verizon Safe Wi-Fi App*, VERIZON, www.verizonwireless.com/support/safe-wifi-legal/ (last visited Feb. 5, 2019) ("Neither Verizon nor its third party licensor(s) or vendors access or collect any information that you send or receive through your Safe Wi-Fi secure connection. . . . For more information . . . see the Verizon privacy policy."); *Full Privacy Policy*, VERIZON, www.verizon.com/about/privacy/full-privacy-policy (last visited Feb. 5, 2019) (describing the types of information Verizon collects as including "information about your browsing, searching and buying activities; IP address" and "call records containing phone numbers you call and receive calls from, websites you visit, text records, wireless location, application and feature usage, product and device-specific information and identifiers . . . and other similar information").

[120] Nellie Bowles, *Thermostats, Locks and Lights: Digital Tools of Domestic Abuse*, N.Y. TIMES (June 23, 2018), www.nytimes.com/2018/06/23/technology/smart-home-devices-domestic-abuse.html.

across the country have reported having their IoT light bulbs, locks, doorbells, and air conditioners switched on and off remotely by abusers who seek to observe and extend their dominance over their victims.[121] Data generated from IoT devices, including voice recordings from smart speakers, are also susceptible to use in criminal proceedings. Government agents can request access to the data collected by IoT in-home and wearable devices. This has significant societal implications. Consider that Ring provides law enforcement with access to videos recorded by users' Ring devices and has provided training to law enforcement on how best to entice Ring owners to disclose video footage without obtaining a warrant.[122] To increase a neighborhood's use of Ring products, the company has given discounts on Ring devices to law enforcement officials which are then provided to communities.[123] The increased and invasive government and corporate surveillance that the IoT enables infringes core democratic ideals. It could decrease our willingness to associate with and engage in unpopular political activities. IoT devices, and accompanying services and mobile apps, allow various corporate entities, hackers, and other third parties, including state actors, to surveil our activities with alarming consequences.

ERODING ANONYMITY

The very nature of the Internet has put our anonymity in peril. Whenever we access the Internet via a smartphone, computer, or tablet, our internet protocol (IP) address restricts our ability to be fully anonymous in online transactions.[124] Our online activities can be traced back to us using our IP addresses. Consider that the automatic content recognition process used in connection with IoT televisions allows providers to determine our IP addresses and the websites and apps we visit.[125] Some IoT devices have their own individual IP addresses.[126] Although it may be difficult to prove exactly which individual within a household used a certain online device at a specific time, at a minimum, IP addresses can reveal our

---

[121] *Id.*

[122] Rani Molla, *How Amazon's Ring Is Creating a Surveillance Network with Video Doorbells*, VOX: RECODE (Jan. 28, 2020, 12:08 PM), www.vox.com/platform/amp/2019/9/5/20849846/amazon-ring-explainer-video-doorbell-hacks.

[123] *Id.*

[124] WILLIAM MCGEVERAN, PRIVACY AND DATA PROTECTION LAW 328 (2016) (describing IP addresses as "the unique ID of an internet connection, which can reveal location, organizations like companies and schools that host the connection, and sometimes identity").

[125] Wolk, *supra* note 95.

[126] *See* Azmi Jafarey, *The Internet of Things & IP Address Needs*, NETWORK COMPUTING (Apr. 16, 2015), www.networkcomputing.com/networking/internet-things-ip-address-needs (suggesting IoT devices will need a traditional IP address); Charles Sun, Opinion, *No IoT Without IPv6*, COMPUTERWORLD (May 19, 2016, 4:00 AM), www.computerworld.com/article/3071625/internet-of-things/no-iot-without-ipv6.html ("[N]ot every IoT device will need an IP address, but IPv4 can accommodate less than 20% of [IoT] devices.").

location.[127] Combining an IP address with other data sources could reveal detailed information about each user and their preferences.[128]

As one commentator has observed, "the only way to stay truly anonymous online is to not go online at all."[129] By expanding our online activities to include the performance of tasks that we historically performed offline, the IoT further erodes our ability to be fully anonymous. Mundane offline activities, such as drinking water, turning on a light, vacuuming, ringing a doorbell, writing with a pen, wearing clothes, or closing a door, whether at home or at work, are transformed into online activities when performed through the use of IoT devices. These new online activities, which IoT devices and accompanying mobile apps observe and record, can be used to determine our identities.[130] Recall the Ring debacle mentioned earlier, wherein Ring employees watched users' videos and could thus identify them.[131] Also, recall that the inadvertently disclosed voice recordings of the Amazon consumer were used to reveal a consumer's identity.

More detailed data are now available for collection, interception, and identification than ever before. When once offline activity is converted into online activity, we must concern ourselves with the possibility of both corporate and government surveillance of these new online activities and communications, as well as the use of these data to reveal our identities. Indeed, data generated from our new online activities, even if anonymized, can be combined with other disparate sources of information to unmask our identities and behavioral patterns. As Chapter 2 will explore, companies' data anonymization techniques are not always effective. The transformation of offline activity to online activity may very well decrease our ability to be anonymous, while simultaneously further facilitating a privacy market for the sale of PFP products and services to fully or partially obscure our identities.

Anonymity reduction is not only limited to the offline–online conversion. The IoT also further reduces our ability to be anonymous in public. Not only can our identities be revealed, but we also lose our ability to keep our emotions, reactions, and characteristics to ourselves when in public. Biometric data, including those generated by IoT devices, fuel facial recognition technology. We can already control our IoT devices by using our voices. Google is moving closer to developing "gesture-controlled sensing technology" that would allow users to control their devices through hand gestures.[132] It is not too far of a stretch to imagine a scenario in

---

[127] Cale Guthrie Weissman, *What Is an IP Address and What Can It Reveal About You?*, Bus. Insider (May 18, 2015, 1:45 PM), www.businessinsider.com/ip-address-what-they-can-reveal-about-you-2015-5.

[128] *Id.*

[129] Eric Griffith, *How to Stay Anonymous Online*, PC Mag., www.pcmag.com/article2/0,2817,2363302,00 .asp (last updated Aug. 30, 2019).

[130] *See* Gilad Rosner & Erin Kenneally, Center for Long-Term Cybersecurity, Privacy and the Internet of Things: Emerging Frameworks for Policy and Design 15–16, https://cltc.berkeley.edu/wp-content/uploads/2018/06/CLTC_Privacy_of_the_IoT-1.pdf.

[131] Biddle, *supra* note 99.

[132] Peter Holley, *Google Moves Closer to Creating "Minority Report"-Style Sensors for Controlling Devices with Hand Gestures*, Wash. Post (Jan. 3, 2019, 1:00 PM), www.washingtonpost.com/technol

which facial recognition technology is directly connected to both device authentication and functionality, so that an individual could operate an IoT device with their facial features after the device scans the user's face and creates a face print.[133]

As Andrew Ferguson contends, existing surveillance technology and smart sensors within IoT devices could allow law enforcement officials to virtually track and monitor us.[134] Ferguson goes on to posit that the communications and data IoT devices emit can be intercepted and captured by third parties and government officials.[135] Law enforcement officials have used facial recognition technology in criminal investigations, and Amazon has reportedly made its facial recognition technology tools available to law enforcement officials.[136] Facial recognition technology continues to be prone to misidentifying racial minorities.[137]

Today, more companies are using facial recognition technology to track us and potentially unmask our identities. Facebook and Google have used facial recognition technology to identify individuals in photographs.[138] Even malls and stores can use facial detection technology and connected devices to identify shoppers and monitor their age, race, gender, and shopping habits.[139] Advancements in facial

ogy/2019/01/03/google-moves-closer-creating-minority-report-style-sensors-controlling-devices-with-hand-gestures/?utm_term=.c109bf35c48d.

[133] *Facial Recognition and Its Applications in the Internet of Things and Wearables*, ALTIUM (Sept. 21, 2017), https://resources.altium.com/pcb-design-blog/facial-recognition-and-its-applications-in-the-internet-of-things-and-wearables.

[134] *See* Andrew Guthrie Ferguson, *The Internet of Things and the Fourth Amendment of Effects*, 104 CALIF. L. REV. 805, 818–23 (2016) [hereinafter *Fourth Amendment of Effects*]. *See generally* ANDREW GUTHRIE FERGUSON, THE RISE OF BIG DATA POLICING: SURVEILLANCE, RACE AND THE FUTURE OF LAW ENFORCEMENT (2017) (e-book) ("If you add in 'smart devices' connected through the Internet of Things (Fitbits, smart bandages, smart cups) or sensors built into our transportation infrastructure, clothing, and bodies, you have a very revealing web of data about our activities.").

[135] *See* Ferguson, *Fourth Amendment of Effects*, *supra* note 134, at 820–21.

[136] Nick Wingfield, *Amazon Pushes Facial Recognition to Police. Critics See Surveillance Risk*, N.Y. TIMES (May 22, 2018), www.nytimes.com/2018/05/22/technology/amazon-facial-recognition.html.

[137] PATRICK GROTHER ET AL., NATIONAL INSTITUTE OF STANDARDS AND TECHNOLOGY, FACE RECOGNITION VENDOR TEST (FRVT), PART 3: DEMOGRAPHIC EFFECTS 2 (2019), https://nvlpubs.nist.gov/nistpubs/ir/2019/NIST.IR.8280.pdf; *Face Recognition*, ELECTRONIC FRONTIER FOUND., www.eff.org/pages/face-recognition (last updated Oct. 24, 2017); Jon Porter, *Federal Study of Top Facial Recognition Algorithms Finds 'Empirical Evidence' of Bias*, VERGE (Dec. 20, 2019), www.theverge.com/2019/12/20/21031255/facial-recognition-algorithm-bias-gender-race-age-federal-nest-investigation-analysis-amazon.

[138] Danny Thakkar, *Here Is How Google Makes Use of AI to Identify People and Objects on Images*, BAYOMETRIC, www.bayometric.com/google-uses-ai-to-identify-people-objects/; James Vincent, *Facebook's Facial Recognition Now Looks for You in Photos You're Not Tagged In*, VERGE (Dec. 19, 2017, 10:38 AM), www.theverge.com/2017/12/19/16794660/facebook-facial-recognition-tagging-photos.

[139] Eden Gillespie, *Are You Being Scanned? How Facial Recognition Technology Follows You, Even as You Shop*, GUARDIAN (Feb. 23, 2019, 9:11 PM), www.theguardian.com/technology/2019/feb/24/are-you-being-scanned-how-facial-recognition-technology-follows-you-even-as-you-shop; Sarah Rieger, *At Least Two Malls Are Using Facial Recognition Technology to Track Shoppers' Ages and Genders Without Telling*, CBC, www.cbc.ca/news/canada/calgary/calgary-malls-1.4760964 (last updated July 27, 2018); Ben Sobel, *Facial Recognition Technology Is Everywhere. It May Not Be Legal*, WASH. POST (June 11, 2015, 10:12 AM), www.washingtonpost.com/news/the-switch/wp/2015/06/11/facial-recognition-technology-is-everywhere-it-may-not-be-legal/?utm_term=.990800971bec.

detection technology can allow stores to provide individualized prices to specific returning consumers, and capture our moods and facial responses to advertisements and in-store products in real time.[140] Once malls and stores collect data about our facial responses and moods, the information can immediately be shared with advertisers, who then provide "tailored advertisements within seconds."[141] There is significant potential for discrimination with the unchecked use of this technology. Advocates of stores and shopping centers' use of facial detection technology (that lacks facial recognition capabilities) contend that they do not identify specific individuals but rather use the technology to assess the characteristics of a person.[142] However, even if our specific identities are not unmasked, our feelings and moods can be, and that still reduces our ability to be anonymous. Stated differently, what may be lost through the use of this technology is our ability to shield our emotions and reactions from corporate actors who seek to commodify our responses. These data could also be combined with other sources of information to eventually uncover our identities. Additionally, it is not entirely clear whether our facial expressions can accurately and consistently convey our emotions.[143] Companies could treat us differently based on the possibly unreliable and inaccurate emotions these technologies detect and assign to us.

The proliferation of smart cities and smart buildings that rely on IoT devices, such as internet-connected and networked surveillance cameras that collect biometric data, and which can be used in connection with facial recognition technology to identify persons in public, also decreases our public anonymity.[144] Many city cameras are connected to the Internet.[145] Even mundane connected city infrastructure that at first glance may transmit basic environmental data can also be used to decrease public anonymity. For instance, networked LED city lights and grids equipped with smart sensors can be used to capture street images.[146] San Diego has a reported 14,000 LED streetlights, and eventually sensor-enabled city lights could be used to record audio conversations.[147] Smart cities awash with connected and networked cameras and audio recorders enable remote tracking of our

---

[140]   Gillespie, *supra* note 139; Sobel, *supra* note 139.

[141]   Gillespie, *supra* note 139.

[142]   *Id.*

[143]   Douglas Heaven, *Why Faces Don't Always Tell the Truth About Feelings*, NATURE (Feb. 26, 2020), www.nature.com/articles/d41586-020-00507-5.

[144]   *See* Tammy Waitt, *New Trends in Smart Cities Include Wireless Broadband*, AM. SECURITY TODAY (Jan. 31, 2018), https://americansecuritytoday.com/new-trends-smart-cities-include-wireless-broadband-see-video/.

[145]   Niall Jenkins, *245 Million Video Surveillance Cameras Installed Globally in 2014*, INFORMA TECH (June 11, 2015), https://technology.ihs.com/532501/245-million-video-surveillance-cameras-installed-globally-in-2014; Jordan G. Teicher, *Gazing Back at the Surveillance Cameras that Watch Us*, N.Y. TIMES (Aug. 13, 2018), www.nytimes.com/2018/08/13/lens/surveillance-camera-photography.html.

[146]   Sarah Holder, *The Shadowy Side of LED Streetlights*, CITYLAB (Mar. 8, 2018), www.citylab.com/equity/2018/03/their-lights-were-watching-odd/554696/.

[147]   *Id.*

movements, affiliations, conversations, and location. Connected city devices can be used by the government to further track and observe "traditionally over-policed communities."[148] Law enforcement agents have already attempted to require suspects to unlock their devices using their biometric identifiers.[149] As Christopher Slobogin convincingly posits, "anonymity in public promotes freedom of action and an open society," and a "lack of public anonymity promotes conformity and an oppressive society."[150]

IoT devices increase the likelihood that activities performed in public will be captured and shared with corporate entities and others. This decreases our ability to be anonymous. Publicly shared images and videos captured by smartphones and IoT devices can be used to identify us. Consider that a Clearview AI mobile app customer can quickly identify an individual by uploading a picture of a person, including pictures publicly shared on social media websites.[151] IoT devices condition us to accept, and in some cases participate in, surveillance, thereby acting as tools of those corporations that seek to identify us. Amazon's Ring devices are accompanied by its Neighbors mobile app feature, which encourages Ring owners to post and share captured videos of others.[152] The cameras in Tesla vehicles have been used by vehicle owners to record and share online videos of the activities of others.[153] Some Tesla owners have shared captured videos of individuals online that are unrelated to vehicle accidents, safety, or security.[154] Some Ring owners have also publicly shared videos unrelated to home security of others who were unaware that they were being recorded.[155] Ring devices and Tesla vehicles' cameras may provide their owners with certain security and safety benefits, and perhaps even entertainment. However, we participate in corporate surveillance and also enable anonymity reduction when we publicly share images and videos captured by IoT devices of others engaging in mundane activities that are unrelated to safety or security without their permission.

[148] Chad Marlow, *How to Stop "Smart Cities" from Becoming "Surveillance Cities,"* ACLU (Sept. 17, 2018, 9:45 AM), www.aclu.org/blog/privacy-technology/surveillance-technologies/how-stop-smart-cities-becoming-surveillance-cities.

[149] Stewart Bishop, *Feds Can't Force Biometric Use to Unlock Phones: Judge*, LAW360 (Jan. 14, 2019, 8:55 PM), www.law360.com/articles/1118407/feds-can-t-force-biometric-use-to-unlock-phones-judge.

[150] CHRISTOPHER SLOBOGIN, PRIVACY AT RISK: THE NEW GOVERNMENT SURVEILLANCE AND THE FOURTH AMENDMENT 92 (2007).

[151] Kashmir Hill, *The Secretive Company That Might End Privacy as We Know It*, N.Y. TIMES, www.nytimes.com/2020/01/18/technology/clearview-privacy-facial-recognition.html (last updated Feb. 10, 2020).

[152] *Safer Neighborhoods, Together*, RING, https://store.ring.com/neighbors (last visited Apr. 25, 2020).

[153] Fred Lambert, *Tesla's Millions of Cameras Are Capturing Some Crazy Things – Videos*, ELECTREK (Jul. 24, 2019, 5:04 AM), https://electrek.co/2019/06/24/tesla-cameras-sentry-mode-crazy-videos/amp/.

[154] *Id.*

[155] John Herrman, *Who's Watching Your Porch?*, N.Y. TIMES, www.nytimes.com/2020/01/19/style/ring-video-doorbell-home-security.html (last updated Jan. 20, 2020).

UNEQUAL ACCESS TO PRIVACY AND SECURITY

Unequal access to privacy and security is a significant problem in the IoT era. Pervasive surveillance and the reduction in public and private anonymity together with companies' internet business models and programs allow organizations to further transform privacy and security into premium products. The gap between those that can afford privacy and cybersecurity and those that cannot is likely to increase. Those of us who can attempt to shield ourselves from increased government surveillance and the corporate penetration of intimate spaces will choose to do so. Those who cannot afford to do so will be at the mercy of corporate and government actors.

Consider that researchers and designers have developed various clothing and accessories, including masks, goggles, and other wearable products, to confuse facial recognition technology and prevent our identification (Privacy Wearables).[156] One such product retails for $164.[157] Another device, a wearable bracelet, is designed to stop smart speakers, security cameras, and other devices from listening to and recording the wearer's conversations.[158] Adversarial Fashion sells clothing designed to pollute and decrease the reliability of automated license plate reader database systems and devices that track us and our location.[159] In addition to Privacy Wearables, other products are now being sold to block IoT devices' surveillance features. For instance, Paranoid, a $49 device, can be used to automatically mute and un-mute the microphone in smart speakers.[160] Other anti-surveillance products that are available for purchase include Silent Pocket's faraday sleeves, which can

---

[156] Umberto Bacchi & Adela Suliman, *Face Masks to Decoy T-Shirts: The Rise of Anti-Surveillance Fashion*, REUTERS (Sept. 25, 2019, 10:00 PM), https://uk.reuters.com/article/brit ain-tech-fashion/feature-face-masks-to-decoy-t-shirts-the-rise-of-anti-surveillance-fashion-idUKL5N26A2K8; Melissa Hellmann, *Special Sunglasses, License-Plate Dresses: How to Be Anonymous in the Age of Surveillance*, SEATTLE TIMES, www.seattletimes.com/business/technol ogy/special-sunglasses-license-plate-dresses-juggalo-face-paint-how-to-be-anonymous-in-the-age-of-surveillance/ (last updated Jan. 13, 2020, 6:33 PM); Aaron Holmes, *These Clothes Use Outlandish Designs to Trick Facial Recognition Software into Thinking You're Not Human*, BUS. INSIDER (Mar. 10, 2020, 9:38 AM), www.businessinsider.com/clothes-accessories-that-out smart-facial-recognition-tech-2019-10; Jane C. Hu, *When Will TJ Maxx Sell Anti-Surveillance Fashion?* SLATE (Aug. 15, 2019, 10:52 AM), https://slate.com/technology/2019/08/facial-recogni tion-surveillance-fashion-hong-kong.html.

[157] Kashmir Hill, *Activate This "Bracelet of Silence," and Alexa Can't Eavesdrop*, N.Y. TIMES (Feb. 14, 2020), www.nytimes.com/2020/02/14/technology/alexa-jamming-bracelet-privacy-armor.html.

[158] *Id.*

[159] John Seabrook, *Dressing for the Surveillance Age*, NEW YORKER (Mar. 9, 2020), www.newyorker.com/ magazine/2020/03/16/dressing-for-the-surveillance-age; *Featured Collection*, ADVERSARIAL FASHION, https://adversarialfashion.com (last visited Apr. 14, 2020) ("The patterns on the goods in this shop are designed to trigger Automated License Plate Readers, injecting junk data in to the systems used by the State and its contractors to monitor and track civilians and their locations.").

[160] Dave Johnson, *Ensure Your Privacy Around Smart Speakers with a $39 Paranoid Auto-Mute Device*, CNET (Apr. 1, 2020, 4:33 PM), www.cnet.com/news/ensure-your-privacy-around-smart-speakers-with-a-39-paranoid-auto-mute-device/; *Paranoid Home Devices*, PARANOID, https://paranoid.com/products (last visited Apr. 13, 2020).

block GPS tracking, RFID chips and cellular and Wi-Fi connectivity on smart-phones, tablets, and other devices.[161]

These technological developments are admirable and, if widely adopted, could enable a robust anti-surveillance industry in the IoT age. However, the increasing number of anti-IoT surveillance products and Privacy Wearables may unintention-ally provide justifications for pervasive IoT surveillance and impede calls for adequate regulation. Advocates of corporate surveillance can contend that these products provide evidence that an underregulated data market can provide solutions to address privacy concerns. Stated differently, those of us who would like to avoid observation and monitoring can simply purchase Privacy Wearables and other types of anti-IoT surveillance products offered on the market. In such a setting, individuals will continue to bear the overwhelming burden of protecting their privacy (with the added expectation that we must pay for privacy by buying Privacy Wearables and other anti-surveillance products), while companies' intrusive monitoring of our lives remains unaddressed. IoT companies could also develop technologies to restrict the performance of Privacy Wearables and other types of anti-surveillance products.

Also recall that other types of PFP offerings, such as VPNs that mask our IP addresses and encrypt our data, are paid products. The cost of purchasing Privacy Wearables and other types of anti-surveillance devices and the monthly subscription fees associated with VPN accounts are expenses that we must incur to preserve some level of privacy. Offering these types of PFP products for free to consumers could also be problematic. Recall from our earlier discussion of the free business model that products that are offered for free to consumers are often data hoarders and surveillance facilitators. This is also likely to be the case with free Privacy Wearables and anti-IoT surveillance products. Additionally, many VPN companies limit the number of devices that can connect simultaneously to their services and charge higher fees for the connection of multiple devices.[162] Consumers with multiple in-home IoT devices could incur higher VPN costs to mask their online identity and protect their data while using these devices. The IoT is the future. Remember that eventually all basic consumer objects that lack an internet connection may be replaced by their IoT equivalents. Eventually, we may all have no choice but to purchase IoT products as replacements for older objects and incur higher expenses to protect our privacy.

As Chapter 2 will explore in detail, many of IoT objects lack basic security features. To fill this gap, IoT companies have begun offering security-centered products, such as F-Secure Sense, to accompany IoT in-home devices.[163] Similarly, in contrast to providers, such as Yahoo, that scan the free email accounts they provide to users, Helm offers a personal IoT email server and service that retails

---

[161] *Tech Is Threatening Your Privacy, Security and Health: Regain Control*, SILENT POCKET, https://silent-pocket.com/ (last visited Apr. 14, 2020).

[162] Eddy & Song, *supra* note 71.

[163] *See supra* text accompanying note 72.

for $299 in addition to an annual subscription fee.[164] These privacy and cybersecurity products are an additional cost that we must incur to protect our privacy and devices. It is likely that low-income consumers will be unable to afford the additional monetary expenses associated with PFP products. These consumers will be more susceptible to security failures, surveillance, and privacy invasions.

Organizations that offer IoT devices with consumer-friendly privacy and security features can charge higher prices for their products. Cash-strapped consumers that cannot afford to pay for privacy and cybersecurity-oriented IoT products could elect to purchase cheaper (or use free) IoT equivalents that lack sufficient privacy and security features. Recently adopted state laws may not sufficiently eradicate these concerns, as Chapter 3 will explore in detail.[165] A version of this is already occurring in the smartphone context. Research on smartphone usage indicates that iPhone users tend to have higher incomes than Android users.[166] As of the date of writing, prices for Apple's latest iPhones range from $749 to as much as $1,449, while some Android operating smartphones with weak privacy and security protections can be bought for as little as $49.99.[167] Technology experts have long critiqued Google's

---

[164]   Jeff John Roberts, *Would You Trade Gmail for This Personal Email Server? I Tried*, FORTUNE (Mar. 9, 2019, 12:48 PM), http://fortune.com/2019/03/09/helm-server-gmail-privacy/ (noting that the Helm server can "connect to the internet" through a user's "home or office Wi-Fi network").

[165]   *See* CAL. CIV. CODE §§ 1798.91.04–.91.06, .100–.199 (2018).

[166]   *See* Marianne Bertrand & Emir Kamenica, *Coming Apart? Cultural Distances in the United States over Time* (Nat'l Bureau of Econ. Research, Working Paper No. 24771, 2018) (a study of US cultural divides finding that "[a]cross all years in our data, no individual brand is as predictive of being high-income [top quartile for household] as owning an Apple iPhone in 2016"); Jim Edwards, *These Maps Show that Android Is for Poor People*, BUS. INSIDER (Apr. 3, 2014, 5:02 PM), www.businessinsider.com/android-is-for-poor-people-maps-2014-4 ("The rich, it seems, use iPhones while the poor tweet from Androids.... Android users are less lucrative than iPhone users.... It's a socio-economic split on class lines, in favor of iPhone over Android."); Aaron Smith, *Smartphone Ownership* 2013, PEW RES. CTR. (June 5, 2013), www.pewresearch.org/internet/2013/06/05/smartphone-ownership-2013/ ("[Cell phone owners] from the upper end of the income and education spectrum are much more likely than those with lower income and educational levels to say they own an iPhone."); Robert Williams, *Survey: iPhone Owners Spend More, Have Higher Incomes than Android Users*, MOBILE MARKETER (Oct. 31, 2018), www.mobilemarketer.com/news/survey-iphone-owners-spend-more-have-higher-incomes-than-android-users/541008/; *see also* PEW RESEARCH CTR., U.S. SMARTPHONE USE IN 2015, 3–4 (2015), www.pewresearch.org/wp-content/uploads/sites/9/2015/03/PI_Smartphones_0401151.pdf (describing the "smartphone-dependent" population); Monica Anderson & Madhumitha Kumar, *Digital Divide Persists Even as Lower-Income Americans Make Gains in Tech Adoption*, PEW RES. CTR. (May 7, 2019), www.pewresearch.org/fact-tank/2017/03/22/digital-divide-persists-even-as-lower-income-americans-make-gains-in-tech-adoption/ ("As of early 2019, 26% of adults living in households earning less than $30,000 a year are 'smartphone-dependent' internet users – meaning they own a smartphone but do not have broadband internet at home.").

[167]   *See* Dan Cohen, *It's Not Only Rich Teens that Have Smartphones*, ATLANTIC (Apr. 15, 2016), www.theatlantic.com/technology/archive/2016/04/not-only-rich-teens-have-cell-phones-digital-divide/478278/; Jessica Dolcourt, *iPhone XS, XR, XS Max: Apple's Three New iPhones Replace the iPhone X*, CNET (Sept. 13, 2018, 10:44 AM), www.cnet.com/news/iphone-xs-iphone-xr-iphone-xs-max-apple-three-new-iphones-replace-iphone-x/; Sascha Segan, *Get America's Cheapest Android Nougat Phone via Amazon*, PC MAG. (Mar. 24, 2017), www.pcmag.com/news/352602/get-americas-cheapest-android-nougat-phone-via-amazon (discussing Android phones ranging in price from $49.99 to $99.99).

lackluster efforts to encrypt Android operating devices, which have lagged significantly behind Apple devices.[168] A 2018 study found that Google collects significantly more user data through Android phones than Apple does through iPhones.[169] A 2019 case study of a low-cost Android operating smartphone found that "data exploitation and poor security is often built into the devices that people rely on as their only means of communication."[170] In a 2019 Human Data Commons Foundation study of eighteen device manufacturers, Apple received the highest score for its privacy and cybersecurity practices.[171]

Admittedly, both iPhone and Android smartphone users are victims of surveillance capitalism. Apple has allowed companies with traditional data business models to use its app store platform and devices to collect consumer data and, just as Google does, it profits from this invasion.[172] In fact, there are a plethora of data hoarding IoT apps used to operate IoT devices available in Apple's app store. While Apple devices are also not completely free from cybersecurity flaws and privacy concerns, iPhone users benefit from using products made by a corporation that is seemingly more proactive in taking steps to preserve a higher level of user privacy

[168] *See* Conner Forrest, *The State of Mobile Device Security: Android vs. iOS*, ZDNET (July 11, 2016, 11:02 AM), www.zdnet.com/article/the-state-of-mobile-device-security-android-vs-ios/ (contending that IOS systems offer more security than Android systems); Jack Nicas, *Google Faces Challenges in Encrypting Android Phones*, WALL ST. J. (Mar. 14, 2016, 7:58 PM), www.wsj.com/articles/google-faces-challenges-in-encrypting-android-phones-1457999906 ("Experts estimate fewer than 10% of the world's 1.4 billion Android phones are encrypted, compared with 95% of Apple Inc.'s iPhones."); Christopher Soghoian, *Your Smartphone Is a Civil Rights Issue*, TED (June 2016), www.ted.com/talks/christopher_soghoian_your_smartphone_is_a_civil_rights_issue (describing the encryption differences between Android and Apple); Liam Tung, *iPhone Encryption Is Six Years Ahead of Android: Cryptographer*, CSO (Nov. 25, 2016, 12:04 AM), www.cso.com.au/article/610671/iphone-encryption-six-years-ahead-android-cryptographer (describing Google's allegedly ineffective full-disk encryption system and comparing it to Apple's); Kaveh Waddell, *Encryption Is a Luxury*, ATLANTIC (Mar. 28, 2016), www.theatlantic.com/technology/archive/2016/03/the-digital-security-div ide/475590/ ("Most Android phones don't encrypt the data that's stored on the device.").

[169] DOUGLAS C. SCHMIDT , GOOGLE DATA COLLECTION 14 (2018), www.ftc.gov/system/files/documents/public_comments/2018/08/ftc-2018-0074-d-0018-155525.pdf (a study finding that iPhones' data "communication with Apple's servers were 10x less frequent than the Android device's communications with Google [and] [l]ocation data made up a very small fraction (~1%) of the net data sent to Apple servers from the iPhone . . . [and] Android phones communicated 4.4 MB of data per day (~130MB per month) with Google servers, which is 6x more than what Google servers communicated through the iPhone device").

[170] *Buying a Smart Phone on the Cheap? Privacy Might Be the Price You Have to Pay*, PRIVACY INT'L (Sept. 20, 2019), http://privacyinternational.org/long-read/3226/buying-smart-phone-cheap-privacy-might-be-price-you-have-pay; *see also* JULIEN GAMBA ET AL., AN ANALYSIS OF PRE-INSTALLED ANDROID SOFTWARE (2019), https://arxiv.org/abs/1905.02713 (a study of multiple Android operating devices finding that the "supply chain around Android's open source model lacks transparency and has facilitated potentially harmful behaviors and backdoored access to sensitive data and services without user consent or awareness").

[171] GREG MCMULLEN & ROCHELLE FAIRFIELD, HUMAN DATA COMMONS FOUND., 2019 QUANTIFIED SELF REPORT CARD, https://humandatacommons.org/wp-content/uploads/2019/11/HDC-Quantified-Self-Report-Card-2019.pdf.

[172] Ian Bogost, *Apple's Empty Grandstanding About Privacy*, ATLANTIC (Jan. 31, 2019), www.theatlantic.com/technology/archive/2019/01/apples-hypocritical-defense-data-privacy/581680/.

and cybersecurity. Similarly, even if individual PFP products (such as Privacy Wearables) cannot guarantee absolute freedom from all forms of corporate and government surveillance, those of us who can afford to purchase these products achieve a higher (although not complete) level of privacy and security protection. Thus, consumers who are aware of and who can financially afford expenses associated with PFP and security-centered products "obtain at least some level of data protection when compared to those who cannot afford to pay for such products and services."[173] Also, consider that in early 2019 Apple banned a Facebook research mobile app.[174] Once installed, that mobile app had given Facebook unlimited access to users' smartphones and allowed the company to collect users' smartphone data transmissions and decrypt encrypted data traffic.[175] Facebook eventually shuttered the app to placate Apple, but the app continued to be available for a longer period on Android phones.[176]

As the IoT expands, it will become increasingly difficult to unplug from the Internet. Unplugging from the Internet will come at a high cost.[177] According to the chief technology officer of Vizio, it could be more expensive to offer a television without an internet connection and data collection capabilities.[178] Vizio would reportedly "have to charge higher prices for hardware if they didn't run content, advertising, and data businesses."[179] The wealthy will be able to more easily afford devices that are either not connected to the Internet (assuming that some companies continue to provide such products) or that provide privacy and security features, such as limited data collection.

Privacy-invasive discounts, such as the one AT&T previously adopted, can also force low-income consumers to choose between basic necessities and protecting their privacy through a more expensive phone plan.[180] A further complicating problem is that low-income and racial minority consumers continue to have "fewer options for online access."[181] These consumers could be subject to increased data surveillance when they eventually obtain online access to the extent that they cannot afford PFP IoT products, thereby compounding the existing socioeconomic digital divide.[182]

[173] Elvy, *supra* note 48, at 1402.
[174] Josh Constine, *Facebook Pays Teens to Install VPN that Spies on Them*, TECHCRUNCH (Jan. 29, 2019, 3:36 PM), https://techcrunch.com/2019/01/29/facebook-project-atlas/.
[175] Josh Constine, *Apple Bans Facebook's Research App that Paid Users for Data*, TECHCRUNCH (Jan. 30, 2019, 7:44 PM), https://techcrunch.com/2019/01/30/apple-bans-facebook-vpn/.
[176] *Id.*
[177] Olivier Sylvain, *Network Equality*, 67 HASTINGS L.J. 443, 447 (2016) ("The Internet has become the platform through which people learn about and seek jobs, health care, housing, and education.").
[178] Patel, *supra* note 53.
[179] *Id.*
[180] *See* Warren Letter, *supra* note 65, at 2; Sandra Fulton, *Pay-for-Privacy Schemes Put the Most Vulnerable Americans at Risk*, TRUTHOUT (May 13, 2016), https://truthout.org/articles/pay-for-priv acy-schemes-put-the-most-vulnerable-americans-at-risk/.
[181] Anderson & Kumar, *supra* note 166.
[182] *See generally* NAT'L TELECOMM. & INFO. ADMIN., FALLING THROUGH THE NET: DEFINING THE DIGITAL DIVIDE (1999) (discussing the existing digital divide).

Additionally, more technology companies may begin adopting PFP data business models. In response to user concerns about data privacy and recent data disclosure scandals, Facebook's Chief Operating Officer suggested that users should pay to protect their data and privacy.[183] However, companies' adoption of PFP data business models does not guarantee that our privacy and data will be absolutely protected. Paying for a non-PFP product also does not guarantee privacy. Indeed, we frequently pay for products even when companies monetize our data. Recall that Yahoo still scans the email messages of consumers that elect to pay for their ad-free email product.[184]

Personal data economy data business models also present unequal access to privacy concerns. Economically advantaged consumers may avoid transferring or disclosing their data in PDE marketplaces while their less well-off counterparts may sell their IoT data and other types of information at the first opportunity if compensation is provided. Low-income and other vulnerable groups of consumers could dominate the data selling market. Google has already used questionable and misleading data collection practices to target and induce racial minorities and the homeless to consent to selling their facial data to the company for a mere $5.[185] Additionally, data generated by the rich may be viewed as more valuable to data buyers, so, if the rich do participate in PDE marketplaces, they could be more handsomely compensated for their data than the poor.

Next, consider the case of children and the data they generate. Parents could intentionally engage in PDE marketplaces using child data. They may also unintentionally do so, such as when child-related IoT data is combined with household data or when parents and children share devices. Parents already provide companies with access to their children's data. Every post on social media about children, including pictures, leaves a digital trail. Like adults, children will also increasingly generate more data about themselves in the IoT setting. Recall the Facebook research mobile app mentioned earlier that was banned by Apple. Facebook paid children over thirteen years old $20 per month for their smartphone data, including browsing habits, shopping history, messages, and emails.[186] Some parents already receive significant compensation for monetizing their children's data. The plethora of YouTube family vlogs documenting children's daily lives and activities is one such example. It is entirely possible that child data may be traded in PDE marketplaces. The result of course is that children whose parents elect to avoid data trading

---

[183]   David Z. Morris, *Sheryl Sandberg Says Facebook Users Would Have to Pay for Total Privacy*, FORTUNE (Apr. 7, 2018, 9:58 AM), http://fortune.com/2018/04/07/sheryl-sandberg-says-facebook-users-would-have-to-pay-for-total-privacy/.

[184]   *See supra* note 51and accompanying text.

[185]   Ginger Adams Otis & Nancy Dillon, *Google Using Dubious Tactics to Target People with "Darker Skin" in Facial Recognition Project: Sources*, N.Y. DAILY NEWS (Oct. 2, 2019, 6:56 PM), www.nydailynews.com/news/national/ny-google-darker-skin-tones-facial-recognition-pixel-20191002-5vxpgowknffnvbmy5eg7epsf34-story.html.

[186]   Constine, *supra* note 174.

marketplaces or who can afford to purchase privacy- and cybersecurity-centered IoT products will receive more protection from surveillance. In an age in which more data about children are being collected than ever before, regulation that relies primarily on parental consent to protect children's privacy is doomed to fail.

Lastly, even COVID-19 pandemic response efforts could raise unequal access to privacy concerns. Government officials' decisions to distribute IoT products through partnerships with IoT device manufacturers to citizens in high-risk and racial minority neighborhoods to track the spread of the virus could mean that these groups of citizens will have more of their COVID-19–related data collected by companies than citizens in other neighborhoods. For example, in response to the pandemic, the City of St. Augustine announced plans to provide IoT thermometers to several groups of citizens, including residents of West Augustine, a predominately African American community with limited healthcare access.[187]

SHAPING OPPORTUNITIES AND BEHAVIORS

Privacy law scholars have long highlighted the dangers of big data. The IoT will make big data even bigger, with potentially significant consequences. Social media and website choice data can already be used to predict aspects of our personalities.[188] These types of inferences and more will only become increasingly accurate with the wealth of data that the IoT is expected to provide. All of the data the IoT generates will allow organizations to obtain deeper insights into our activities, behaviors, and tendencies. Companies can collect, analyze, and act upon IoT data at record speeds. Indeed, companies will be able to more precisely predict and influence our decisions and behaviors in real time. When organizations have the capacity to accurately observe, predict, influence, and shape our activities, preferences, and opportunities, consumer autonomy and choice are likely to decrease and there is more potential for discrimination.

Insights obtained from IoT data can be used to engender "new justifications [or methods] for exclusion."[189] IoT data could be used to deny opportunities to some of

[187]   Daniela Hernandez, *Coronavirus Trackers Try out AI Tools as Eyes Turn to Reopening*, WALL ST. J. (Apr. 19, 2020, 7:16 AM), www.wsj.com/amp/articles/coronavirus-trackers-try-out-ai-tools-as-eyes-turn-to-reopening-11587294000; *St. Augustine Distributing 900 Smart Thermometers to Help Monitor Community Health*, NEWS4JAX, www.news4jax.com/health/2020/04/19/st-augustine-to-distribute-900-smart-thermometers-to-help-monitor-community-health/?outputType=amp (last updated Apr. 26, 2020, 11:18 PM).

[188]   *See* Michal Kosinski et al., *Manifestations of User Personality in Website Choice and Behaviour on Online Social Networks*, 95 MACHINE LEARNING 357, 378 (2014).

[189]   *See generally* SAFIYA UMOJA NOBLE, ALGORITHMS OF OPPRESSION (2018); CATHY O'NEIL , WEAPONS OF MATH DESTRUCTION: HOW BIG DATA INCREASES INEQUALITY AND THREATENS DEMOCRACY (2016); FED. TRADE COMM'N, BIG DATA: A TOOL FOR INCLUSION OR EXCLUSION? 9–12 (2016), www.ftc.gov/system/files/documents/reports/big-data-tool-inclusion-or-exclusion-understanding-issues/160106big-data-rpt.pdf; Solon Barocas & Andrew D. Selbst, *Big Data's Disparate Impact*, 104 CALIF. L. REV. 671, 674 (2016); Stacy-Ann Elvy, *Commodifying Consumer Data in the Era of the Internet of Things*, 59 B.C. L.

us and more effectively influence the decisions we make. Consider that Facebook has allowed advertisers to "target users by their interests" and exclude users based on their race by, for instance, advertising housing options to only specific groups.[190] Analyzing data from users' pages, liked posts, and other activities allowed the company to assign users to an "Ethnic Affinity" category and enable exclusion.[191] The potential for exclusion is even greater in the IoT setting in light of the corporate colonization of intimate spaces and the mountains of real-time data IoT devices generate. Advancements in data analytics may lead to the development of new proxy traits that can enable discrimination. IoT data could be used to accurately deduce our race, gender, disability status, age, quality of life, income, and character traits.[192] Companies analyzing these data can then categorize us based on our personalities and tendencies and offer opportunities to those of us with traits companies deem preferable.[193]

Real-time product and service price fluctuations enabled by dynamic algorithmic pricing can also be problematic. For instance, Uber already uses algorithmic pricing to determine how much users are willing to pay for a ride and to adjust the price of rides each user sees.[194] The company can predict whether a user is likely to pay a higher price based on the battery power left on a user's cell phone.[195] A user with very low battery power is likely to pay a higher price to obtain a ride before their smartphone dies.[196] Dynamic pricing using algorithms that rely on IoT data will give companies additional insights into our "willingness to pay."[197] Armed with mountains of IoT data and other sources of information that reveal our individual attributes, companies can further exploit precarious situations and ordinary life moments alike. Based on these events and characteristics, they can charge each of us different prices for the same products, even when they are purchased at the same

---

REV. 423 (2018); Peppet, *supra* note 35, at 117–39; Olivier Sylvain, *Intermediary Design Duties*, 50 CONN. L. REV. 204 (2018).

[190] Julia Angwin & Terry Parris Jr., *Facebook Lets Advertisers Exclude Users by Race*, PROPUBLICA (Oct. 28, 2016, 1:00 PM), www.propublica.org/article/facebook-lets-advertisers-exclude-users-by-race; Matthew Guarnaccia, *HUD Accuses Facebook of Housing Discrimination in Ads*, LAW360 (Mar. 28, 2019, 10:52 AM), www.law360.com/articles/1143867/hud-accuses-facebook-of-housing-discrimin ation-in-ads.

[191] Angwin & Parris, *supra* note 190.

[192] Peppet, *supra* note 35, at 117–28.

[193] *Id.* at 125 (contending that existing anti-discrimination laws may not sufficiently guard against these concerns because these laws do "not prevent economic sorting based on our personalities, habits, and character traits").

[194] Nicole Martin, *Uber Charges More if They Think You're Willing to Pay More*, FORBES (Mar. 30, 2019, 12:58 PM), www.forbes.com/sites/nicolemartin1/2019/03/30/uber-charges-more-if-they-think-youre-willing-to-pay-more/#37abe8273654.

[195] *Id.*

[196] *Id.*

[197] *Id.* For a discussion of how form contracts can enable various forms of discrimination, see David Gilo & Ariel Porat, *The Hidden Role of Boilerplate and Standard-Form Contracts: Strategic Imposition of Transaction Costs, Segmentation of Consumers, and Anticompetitive Effects*, 104 MICH. L. REV. 983 (2006).

time. Members of historically marginalized groups who already pay higher prices for existing products are particularly vulnerable to dynamic price discrimination in the IoT setting.

Children are especially vulnerable to data exploitation in the IoT age. The ubiquitous nature of IoT devices, including toys, all but ensures that today's children begin leaving digital footprints much earlier than previous generations. The digital dossiers that companies compile about children from a young age will have long-term consequences once those children reach adulthood. Childhood and higher education institutions are also deploying IoT devices, mobile apps, and facial recognition technology to observe students' daily activities and collect and analyze data about students' behaviors.[198] There is already a robust and underregulated market for the sale of student data.[199] As schools increasingly continue to use IoT devices to monitor students, there will be a corresponding increase in the amount of student data available for trade.[200] Organizations could mine and analyze child and student data to predict or make "probabilistic inferences" about the adulthood and post-graduation preferences and behaviors of children and students. Eventually, data about children's experiences and behaviors could be analyzed to shape children's preferences and identities as well as determine the types of opportunities that children receive during childhood and negatively impact their lives and prospects during adulthood. Rising corporate and government surveillance of public and

---

[198]   James Vaznis, *Schools Are Collecting New Data in New Ways About Students with Cutting-Edge High-Tech*, Bos. Globe (Dec. 16, 2019, 8:20 PM), www.bostonglobe.com/metro/2019/12/16/schools-experiment-with-high-tech-student-monitoring/7sx3eMEqYTwO9zxzKjyEkK/story.html; *see also* Davey Alba, *Facial Recognition Moves into a New Front: Schools*, N.Y. Times (Feb. 6, 2020), www .nytimes.com/2020/02/06/business/facial-recognition-schools.html#click=https://t.co/ UA3iINywaZ (discussing facial recognition technology in New York schools); Meg Conlan, *The IoT Creates Opportunities and Challenges for K-12 Schools [#Infographic]*, EdTech (May 30, 2016), https://edtechmagazine.com/k12/article/2016/05/iot-creates-opportunities-and-challenges-k-12-schools-infographic (discussing IoT devices and services in schools); Drew Harwell, *Colleges Are Turning Students' Phones into Surveillance Machines, Tracking the Locations of Hundreds of Thousands*, Wash. Post (Dec. 24, 2019, 5:00 AM), www.washingtonpost.com/technology/2019/12/ 24/colleges-are-turning-students-phones-into-surveillance-machines-tracking-locations-hundreds-thousands/ (discussing colleges' use of mobile apps); Tom Simonite & Gregory Barber, *The Delicate Ethics of Using Facial Recognition in Schools*, Wired (Oct. 17, 2019, 6:00 AM), www .wired.com/story/delicate-ethics-facial-recognition-schools/ (discussing schools' use of facial recognition technology); *The Connected Classroom: How IoT Helps Schools with Education and Security*, IoT For All (Oct. 2, 2019), www.iotforall.com/smart-schools/ [hereinafter *The Connected Classroom*] (discussing IoT devices and services in schools); Atif Qazi, *How Will IoT Change the Education Sphere?*, Emerging EdTech (May 30, 2019), www.emergingedtech .com/2019/05/how-will-iot-change-impact-education/ (discussing IoT devices and services in schools).

[199]   N. Cameron Russell et al., *Transparency and the Marketplace for Student Data*, 22 Va. J.L. & Tech. 107, 114–18 (2019) (describing the student data broker marketplace and contending that "there is no federal privacy law in the United States that specifically targets the use, retention or resale of student data by private-sector data brokers.").

[200]   *See* Vaznis, *supra* note 198; *see also* Conlan, *supra* note 198; *The Connected Classroom*, *supra* note 198; Qazi, *supra* note 198.

private spheres increases children's digital footprints and will exacerbate privacy concerns for children.

Knowledge of pervasive surveillance could force us to change our behaviors and activities. Admittedly, it is also possible that IoT devices will become so ubiquitous that we will forget that IoT devices are monitoring our activities or that companies obtain detailed information about us from our use of these devices. To the extent that some of us do alter our behaviors in response to IoT surveillance, we may eventually revert back to our more authentic activities and natural tendencies over time. However, it is clear that technology companies have a voracious appetite for our data because of the insights our data can reveal about us and the possibility that these insights can be monetized and used to shape our behaviors. Insights from our data can be used to influence our willingness to consent to companies' data collection practices and our product selection choices. We may not even be aware of the extent to which companies are influencing our decisions or have the ability to monitor us. Consider, for example, Google's Nest Guard device (an IoT alarm key pad associated with the company's home security product line), which was manufactured and offered for sale in 2017 with a hidden microphone that the company only disclosed to device users in 2019.[201] Additionally, companies design and advertise IoT devices as products that will provide convenience to us while seamlessly operating in the background without constant human supervision or knowledge. For instance, the Roomba robotic vacuum cleans a consumer's home and also collects data on the location of walls, lamps, and thermostats.[202] It is likely that many of us are unaware of the extent of the data collected and the security risks posed by IoT devices.

Today, American businesses are already using our online activities to assign each of us scores based on our "overall trustworthiness."[203] Companies use these scores to reject user accounts and to determine those among us who will be subject to further screening in online transactions.[204] These "trust scores" are not accessible to us and our names are not required in order to analyze our online activities and generate a score.[205] Without sufficient federal oversight, companies' use of these scores could expand beyond fraud detection.

Consider China's burgeoning social rating system, which exemplifies the dangers of "trust scores" and data analytics in the IoT era. China's pilot social rating program also highlights the potential power of governments and companies to shape and

[201] Dave Lee, *Google Admits Error over Hidden Microphone*, BBC (Feb. 20, 2019), www.bbc.com/news/technology-47303077; Saqib Shah, *Google Put a Microphone in Nest Secure and Forgot to Tell Anyone*, ENGADGET (Feb. 20, 2019), www.engadget.com/2019/02/20/google-nest-secure-mic-forgot/.

[202] Maggie Astor, *Your Roomba May Be Mapping Your Home, Collecting Data that Could Be Shared*, N. Y. TIMES (July 25, 2017), www.nytimes.com/2017/07/25/technology/roomba-irobot-data-privacy.html.

[203] Christopher Mims, *The Secret Trust Scores Companies Use to Judge Us All*, WALL ST. J. (Apr. 6, 2019, 12:00 AM), www.wsj.com/articles/the-secret-trust-scores-companies-use-to-judge-us-all-11554523206.

[204] *Id.*

[205] *Id.*

control citizens' behaviors and opportunities. The system, which as of the date of writing is not yet fully unified, relies in part on facial recognition technology and on continuous surveillance of citizens' everyday activities and online habits.[206] Private companies work in conjunction with local governments to collect and share data.[207] Data from IoT devices and other sources of data are combined and analyzed to give individuals a dynamic reputational score or a social identity number linked to a reputational record.[208] The score can be used to determine the rewards and punishment that citizens receive.[209] A low social score or record can impact individuals' housing, career, travel, and lending options, among other things.[210] Individuals with a suboptimal rating could be unable to obtain acceptable school placements for their children, experience longer waiting times at hospitals, and be banned from traveling.[211] Pervasive surveillance and data collection in the IoT era is likely to give parties with access to IoT data the power to significantly influence and potentially shape our decisions, opportunities, and activities. As this chapter has shown, the IoT disrupts and endangers our privacy in various ways. However, as we will see in Chapter 2, the IoT also raises various security concerns as well.

---

[206] Nicole Kobie, *The Complicated Truth About China's Social Credit System*, WIRED (June 7, 2019), www.wired.co.uk/article/china-social-credit-system-explained ("There is no single, nationally coordinated system," but "pieces of the system are already in place, and the Chinese government appears to be targeting a 2020 goal to get the rest in place."); Alexandra Ma, *China Has Started Ranking Citizens with a Creepy "Social Credit" System – Here's What You Can Do Wrong, and the Embarrassing, Demeaning Ways They Can Punish You*, BUS. INSIDER (Oct. 29, 2018, 9:06 AM), www.businessinsider.com/china-social-credit-system-punishments-and-rewards-explained-2018-4.

[207] *See* Rebecca Fannin, *Social Credit Scoring in China Extends to Foreign Businesses, Creates New Risks*, FORBES (Oct. 8, 2019, 1:08 PM), www.forbes.com/sites/rebeccafannin/2019/10/08/social-credit-scoring-in-china-extends-to-foreign-businesses-creates-new-risks/#323457d55859; Daniel Sontag, *We, the Data: An Inside Look at China's Social Credit System*, MEDIUM (July 12, 2018), https://medium .com/connect-the-bots/we-the-data-an-inside-look-at-chinas-social-credit-system-b1a6152d4907.

[208] Kobie, *supra* note 206; Sontag, *supra* note 207.

[209] Fannin, *supra* note 207; Sontag, *supra* note 207.

[210] *See id.*

[211] *Id.*; *Chinese Social Credit System Bans Millions from Taking Trains, Flying*, AOL (Feb. 21, 2019, 8:32 AM), www.aol.co.uk/news/2019/02/21/chinese-social-credit-system-bans-millions-from-taking-trains-f/?guccounter=1&guce_referrer_us=aHR0cHM6Ly93d3cuZ29vZ2xlLmNvbS8&guce_referrer_cs=ZO6fH2BnZdqPz-qhgDFvSg ("Millions of Chinese citizens have now been banned from travelling by air or train as the government continues to expand its social credit system.").

2

Internet of Things Security Failures

Privacy and information security are distinct but related fields.[1] Security focuses on questions surrounding the extent to which related products, systems, and processes can effectively defend against "attacks on confidentiality, integrity and availability of code and information."[2] The field of information security often involves inquiries about the legal consequences of security failures.[3] In 2018, *The Economist* reported that "more than ninety percent of the world's data appeared in just the past two years."[4] In the last decade there have been multiple large-scale data breaches and inadvertent data exposures that have resulted in the disclosure of millions of our data. These include the data breaches and leaks at Google Plus, Equifax, Under Armour, Orbitz, Saks Fifth Avenue, Lord & Taylor, Panera Bread, Yahoo, and Facebook, among others. Data obtained from the 2018 Facebook hack have been offered for sale on the dark web.[5] In California alone, there were 657 data breaches impacting approximately 49 million records between 2012 and 2015.[6] In New York, organizations reported 1,583 data breaches in 2017 that revealed the data of 163 million individuals.[7] Nationwide, a Pew Research Center survey determined that 64 percent of American consumers have been victims of a data breach.[8] Since

---

[1]   JOANNA LYN GRAMA, LEGAL ISSUES IN INFORMATION SECURITY 37 (2011); Andrea M. Matwyshyn, Cyber!, 2017 BYU L. REV. 1109, 1137–42 (2017).

[2]   Matwyshn, *supra* note 1, at 1139–40.

[3]   *Id.* at 1140.

[4]   The Economist, *The Data Revolution: Privacy, Politics and Predictive Policing*, YOUTUBE (Oct. 3, 2018), www.youtube.com/watch?v=4ycCoDJqrpc&feature=em-uploademail.

[5]   Anthony Cuthbertson, *Facebook Hack: People's Accounts Appear for Sale on Dark Web*, INDEPENDENT (Oct. 2, 2018, 2:05 PM), www.independent.co.uk/life-style/gadgets-and-tech/news/facebook-hack-data-dark-web-login-details-cost-dream-market-a8564671.html; *see also* Dan Hall, *Hackers Selling Facebook Logins on the Dark Web for $2*, N.Y. POST (Oct. 1, 2018, 11:00 AM), https://nypost.com/2018/10/01/hackers-are-selling-facebook-logins-on-the-dark-web-for-2/.

[6]   KAMALA D. HARRIS , CAL. DEP'T OF JUSTICE, CALIFORNIA DATA BREACH REPORT 2012–2015, at iii (2016) https://oag.ca.gov/sites/all/files/agweb/pdfs/dbr/2016-data-breach-report.pdf.

[7]   N.Y. STATE ATTORNEY GEN., INFORMATION EXPOSED: 2017 DATA BREACHES IN NEW YORK STATE 3 (2017), https://ag.ny.gov/sites/default/files/data_breach_report_2017.pdf.

[8]   Aaron Smith, *Americans and Cybersecurity*, PEW RES. CTR. (Jan. 26, 2017), www.pewinternet.org/2017/01/26/americans-and-cybersecurity/.

we are already living in an era in which companies repeatedly fail to secure our data, the proliferation of the IoT is likely to exacerbate this problem.

IoT devices are notoriously insecure and give hackers multiple entry points into our homes and companies' networks, thereby increasing hackers' chances of obtaining highly sensitive data about us.[9] Many IoT devices pose security risks and enable "physical and financial threat[s]."[10] Even when data are not obtained or disclosed, hackers can take control of the operations of insecure IoT devices and use these devices to conduct wide-scale cyberattacks. In October 2016, a distributed denial-of-service (DDoS) attack weaponized IoT devices with weak security features to block access to multiple websites.[11] Recent research evaluating the consumer impact of DDoS attacks involving insecure IoT devices found that they "consume significantly more network bandwidth, creating a substantial direct consumer cost and increases in network latency leading to potentially degraded user experience[s]."[12] Manufacturers and software developers have inundated the consumer market with IoT devices that lack adequate security features. This continues to be the case despite the issuance of voluntary cybersecurity standards, such as the National Institute of Standards and Technology (NIST) cybersecurity framework.[13] NIST released core cybersecurity recommendations specifically for the IoT and a privacy framework toolkit for risk assessment.[14] In light of the voluntary and recent nature of NIST's IoT-specific recommendations, their impact on the cybersecurity issues discussed in this chapter remains to be seen.

---

[9]   *See e.g.*, Omer Shwartz et al., *Opening Pandora's Box: Effective Techniques for Reverse Engineering IoT Devices*, *in* Lecture Notes in Computer Science (2018), https://link.springer.com/chapter/10 .1007%2F978-3-319-75208-2_1. *But see* Robert Graham, *California's Bad IoT Law*, Errata Security (Sept. 10, 2018), https://blog.erratasec.com/2018/09/californias-bad-iot-law.html#.W6PwnZNKjX8 (contending that "[m]ost IoT devices exist behind firewalls, and are thus very difficult to hack").

[10] Woodrow Hartzog, Privacy's Blueprint: The Battle to Control the Design of New Technologies 268 (2018).

[11] Dave Lewis, *The DDoS Attack Against Dyn One Year Later*, Forbes (Oct. 23, 2017, 11:49 AM), www .forbes.com/sites/davelewis/2017/10/23/the-ddos-attack-against-dyn-one-year-later/#11d7ae251ae9.

[12] Kim Fong et al., Univ. of Cal., Berkeley, Sch. of Info. RIoT: Quantifying Consumer Costs of Insecure Internet of Things Devices 35, https://drive.google.com/file/d/ 1IivZwRbnQmEpIC6C3gYGPucxnxluIwuW/view.

[13] *See Cybersecurity Framework*, U.S. Dep't of Commerce, Nat'l Inst. of Standards & Tech., www .nist.gov/cyberframework (last visited Nov. 15, 2019); *see also* Rebecca Kelly Slaughter , Comm'r, Fed. Trade Comm'n, Raising the Standard: Bringing Security and Transparency to the Internet of Things?, Remarks at Open Technology Institute (July 26, 2018), www.ftc.gov/system/files/documents/pub lic_statements/1395854/slaughter_-_raising_the_standard_-_bringing_security_and_transparency_ to_the_internet_of_things_7-26.pdf (describing ongoing cybersecurity failures of IoT devices).

[14] *See* Michael Fagan et al., U.S. Dep't of Commerce, Nat'l Inst. of Standards & Tech., Foundational Cybersecurity Activities for IoT Device Manufacturers (May 2020), https:// nvlpubs.nist.gov/nistpubs/ir/2020/NIST.IR.8259.pdf. *See generally* Katie Boeckl et al., U.S. Dep't of Commerce, Nat'l Inst. of Standards & Tech., Considerations for Managing Internet of Things (IoT) Cybersecurity and Privacy Risks (2019), https://nvlpubs.nist.gov/nistpubs/ir/2019/NIST .IR.8228.pdf; U.S. Dep't of Commerce, Nat'l Inst. of Standards & Tech., NIST Privacy Framework: A Tool For Improving Privacy Through Enterprise Risk Management (2020), www .nist.gov/system/files/documents/2020/01/16/NIST%20Privacy%20Framework_V1.0.pdf.

This chapter begins by exploring the insecure nature of the IoT through concrete examples. It demonstrates that not only are many IoT devices insecure, but the networks, websites, and other devices connected to IoT devices and which transmit communications and store related data can also be insecure. Additionally, despite these pressing security concerns, some companies may attempt to use privacy policies and terms of use to negate liability for security failures. This chapter then highlights the limits of anonymization and aggregation as effective inoculation against security harms. Our data and privacy are increasingly at risk in the IoT setting even when our data are anonymized or aggregated. Lastly, when companies experience security failures, many courts have been unwilling to recognize the various consumer harms that result from data breaches. Standing requirements have been fatal to many consumer data breach lawsuits. I build on the work of other scholars by analyzing standing requirements in data breach lawsuits in federal courts. I argue that the IoT bolsters and underscores the need to heed calls to expand courts' perception of consumer harm in data breach lawsuits.

INTERNAL AND EXTERNAL INSECURITIES

Both internal and external vulnerabilities can impact the security of IoT data, devices, and associated systems. These security failures affect IoT devices designed for use by children, adults, and businesses. The connected nature of IoT devices, online services, cloud systems, and other related networks generate multiple sources of vulnerabilities that are ripe for exploitation. A U.S. Government Accountability Office (GAO) report on the IoT identified many ways in which insecure IoT devices and associated networks could be attacked.[15] These include malware, "[p]assive wiretapping," "[w]ar driving," "[s]tructured [q]uery [l]anguage injection," and "[z]ero-day exploit" attacks.[16]

IoT devices designed for use by children and the systems storing the data such devices generate are increasingly susceptible to cyberattacks. IoT toys are manufactured with various privacy-invasive features, such as speech recognition and GPS capabilities, cameras, and microphones.[17] In 2017, children's audio voice recordings and account information associated with CloudPets' IoT toys, which were reportedly held in "an insecure database," were accessed by hackers.[18] Despite the known

---

[15] *See generally* U.S. GOV'T ACCOUNTABILITY OFFICE, CTR. FOR SCI., TECH., & ENG'G, INTERNET OF THINGS: STATUS AND IMPLICATIONS OF AN INCREASINGLY CONNECTED WORLD (2017), www.gao.gov /assets/690/684590.pdf.

[16] *Id.* at 27.

[17] *See* FED. BUREAU OF INVESTIGATION, CONSUMER NOTICE: INTERNET-CONNECTED TOYS COULD PRESENT PRIVACY AND CONTACT CONCERNS FOR CHILDREN (2017), www.ic3.gov/media/2017/170717.aspx.

[18] Laura Hautala, *Smart Toy Flaws Make Hacking Kids' Info Child's Play*, CNET (Feb. 28, 2017, 2:49 PM), www.cnet.com/news/cloudpets-iot-smart-toy-flaws-hacking-kids-info-children-cybersecurity /#ftag=CAD-00-10aag7d; Selena Larson, *Stuffed Toys Leak Millions of Voice Recordings from Kids and Parents*, CNN (Feb. 27, 2017, 11:04 PM), https://money.cnn.com/2017/02/27/technology/cloudpets-data-leak-voices-photos/index.html.

security vulnerabilities, large retailers continued to permit listings for CloudPets' insecure toys to consumers for over a year before banning the products.[19] In 2015, VTech Electronics, an IoT toymaker and provider of various learning products, discovered a breach of its network that led to the disclosure of millions of children's data, including usernames, audio files, photographs, and physical addresses.[20] In 2017, a German agency described the IoT doll My Friend Cayla as "an illegal espionage apparatus."[21] There have been previous reports detailing hacks of the doll.[22] IoT baby monitors that are controlled through mobile applications have also been hacked and used to surreptitiously observe mothers and infants. In some instances, videos of children have been made public and hackers have communicated directly with children through insecure devices.[23] Given the extensive vulnerabilities of IoT toys, the FBI released a notice cautioning parents about the privacy and cybersecurity dangers of these products.[24] Likewise, the FTC issued a warning to parents about the privacy implications of IoT toys.[25] The vast quantities of sensitive data that are collected by IoT toys, including photographs, voice recordings, and frequently visited locations, could lead to child identity fraud and could also be used by dubious parties to engender trust in children and endanger their physical and emotional safety.[26]

Researchers evaluating IoT security risks have shown that by exploiting vulnerabilities in Alexa, Siri, and Google Assistant, undetectable commands can be sent to associated devices.[27] Once these devices receive the hidden command, researchers

[19] Ashley Carman, *Retailers Will Probably Keep Selling Kids Insecure Smart Toys Until They're Forced to Stop*, VERGE (June 10, 2018, 10:00 AM), www.theverge.com/circuitbreaker/2018/6/10/17442090/target-amazon-ebay-cloudpets-listing-removal-smart-toys.

[20] *See* Complaint at 7–12, United States v. VTech Electronics Ltd., No. 1:18-cv-114 (N.D. Ill. Jan. 8, 2018), www.ftc.gov/system/files/documents/cases/vtech_file_stamped_complaint_w_exs_1-8-18.pdf.

[21] Sheera Frenkel, *A Cute Toy Just Brought a Hacker into Your Home*, N.Y. TIMES (Dec. 21, 2017), www.nytimes.com/2017/12/21/technology/connected-toys-hacking.html; *see also* Philip Oltermann, *German Parents Told to Destroy Doll that Can Spy on Children*, GUARDIAN (Feb. 17, 2017, 11:53 AM), www.theguardian.com/world/2017/feb/17/german-parents-told-to-destroy-my-friend-cayla-doll-spy-on-children.

[22] *See German Parents Told to Destroy Cayla Dolls over Hacking Fears*, BBC NEWS (Feb. 17, 2017), www.bbc.com/news/world-europe-39002142.

[23] *See, e.g.*, Associated Press, *Russian Website Broadcasts Hacked Security Cameras, Baby Monitors Worldwide*, SYRACUSE, www.syracuse.com/news/index.ssf/2014/11/russian_website_broadcasts_hacked_security_cameras_baby_monitors_worldwide.html (last updated Mar. 22, 2019); *Baby Monitor Hacker Delivers Creepy Message to Child*, CBS NEWS (Apr. 23, 2015, 9:08 AM), www.cbsnews.com/news/baby-monitor-hacker-delivers-creepy-message-to-child/; Camila Domonoske, *S.C. Mom Says Baby Monitor was Hacked; Experts Say Many Devices Are Vulnerable*, NPR (June 5, 2018, 7:18 PM), www.npr.org/sections/thetwo-way/2018/06/05/617196788/s-c-mom-says-baby-monitor-was-hacked-experts-say-many-devices-are-vulnerable; *The Best Baby Monitor*, DON'T WASTE YOUR MONEY, www.wcpo.com/money/consumer/dont-waste-your-money/baby-monitor-hack (last updated July 18, 2019).

[24] *See* FED. BUREAU OF INVESTIGATION, *supra* note 17.

[25] *See* Cristina Miranda, *What to Ask Before Buying Internet-Connected Toys*, FED. TRADE COMM'N (Dec. 9, 2019), www.consumer.ftc.gov/blog/2019/12/what-ask-buying-internet-connected-toys.

[26] *See* FED. BUREAU OF INVESTIGATION, *supra* note 17.

[27] Craig S. Smith, *Alexa and Siri Can Hear This Hidden Command. You Can't.*, N.Y. TIMES (May 10, 2018), www.nytimes.com/2018/05/10/technology/alexa-siri-hidden-command-audio-attacks.html; *see also* Nicholas Carlini & David Wagner, *Audio Adversarial Examples: Targeted Attacks on Speech-to-*

have been able to direct the devices to dial telephone numbers and access websites.[28] Research in this area suggests that it may ultimately be possible for others to begin exploiting these vulnerabilities to surreptitiously observe and impact consumers' activities and purchase products without permission.[29] Security researchers have also hacked and remotely taken control of some of the physical operations of IoT vehicles.[30] According to Consumer Reports, vulnerabilities in several IoT televisions and streaming devices leave these devices susceptible to cyberattacks in which malicious actors can remotely control the devices' operations.[31] Hackers could cause televisions to display indecent content as well as increase the volume and switch channels. This lack of consumer control over IoT devices is a startling new development. Prior to the IoT, consumers could, with some degree of certainty, ensure that only parties in their household or guests could operate in-home objects and appliances. This is no longer the case. As the IoT colonizes more homes, consumers must concern themselves with external parties who have the capacity to control and operate their devices and access the data their devices collect. These parties could be hackers who seek to sell or use data for perverse purposes, or they could be established companies that seek to highjack IoT devices for advertisement purposes. For instance, in 2017, Burger King designed an advertisement to prompt certain Google devices in consumers' homes to search for and state the ingredients in its burgers.[32] Similarly, in 2017, Google sent an unprompted advertisement for a movie to consumers' in-home IoT speakers.[33]

In 2017, researchers exposed a significant security vulnerability that impacts almost every device connected to the Internet.[34] Hackers conducting a Key

---

Text, 2018 IEEE SECURITY AND PRIVACY WORKSHOPS (Mar. 30, 2018), https://arxiv.org/pdf/1801 .01944.pdf; Tavish Vaidya et al., *Cocaine Noodles: Exploiting the Gap Between Human and Machine Speech Recognition,* USENIX (2015), www.usenix.org/system/files/conference/woot15/ woot15-paper-vaidya.pdf.

[28] Smith, *supra* note 27.

[29] *See id.*

[30] *See generally* CHARLIE MILLER & CHRIS VALASEK , REMOTE EXPLOITATION OF AN UNALTERED PASSENGER VEHICLE (2015), http://illmatics.com/Remote%20Car%20Hacking.pdf; Steven Overly, *What We Know About Car Hacking, the CIA and Those WikiLeaks Claims,* WASH. POST (Mar. 8, 2017, 5:20 PM), www.washingtonpost.com/news/innovations/wp/2017/03/08/what-we-know-about-car-hacking- the-cia-and-those-wikileaks-claims/?utm_term=.5f693a239ede.

[31] *See Samsung and Roku Smart TVs Vulnerable to Hacking, Consumer Reports Finds,* CONSUMER REP. (Feb. 7, 2018), www.consumerreports.org/televisions/samsung-roku-smart-tvs-vulnerable-to-hacking- consumer-reports-finds/.

[32] *See* Sapna Maheshwari, *Burger King "O.K. Google" Ad Doesn't Seem O.K. with Google,* N.Y. TIMES (Apr. 12, 2017), www.nytimes.com/2017/04/12/business/burger-king-tv-ad-google-home.html?smid=pl- share.

[33] *See* Jack Nicas, *Google Tests Waters of Voice Ads on Speaker,* WALL. ST. J. (Mar. 16, 2017, 8:23 PM), www .wsj.com/articles/google-tests-waters-of-voice-ads-on-speaker-1489710193.

[34] *See* Mathy Vanhoef & Frank Piessens, *Key Reinstallation Attacks: Forcing Nonce Reuse in WPA2,* ASS'N FOR COMPUTING MACHINERY CONF. ON COMPUTER & COMM. SECURITY (2017), https://papers .mathyvanhoef.com/ccs2017.pdf; *see also* Katie Collins, *Wi-Fi Security Flaw KRACK Puts All Wireless Devices at Risk,* CNET (Oct. 16, 2017, 3:52 AM), www.cnet.com/news/krack-wi-fi-security-flaw-puts-all- wireless-devices-at-risk-of-hijack/.

Reinstallation Attack (KRACK) can "inject ransomware or viruses into websites," monitor consumers' online traffic, and collect sensitive data.[35] IoT devices are particularly vulnerable to KRACK attacks since unlike computers and smartphones that readily receive software updates, many IoT devices have not been designed to easily receive software updates to correct vulnerabilities.[36] Also, while larger manufacturers are able to quickly release software patches, smaller manufacturers struggle to do so. This leaves consumers of insecure IoT devices susceptible to cyberattacks until a patch is rolled out. According to one commentator, "IoT devices that never get the necessary updates are sitting ducks to KRACK attacks."[37] The Krook bug can also affect IoT devices. Hackers can also use various tools to identify vulnerable devices and systems, generate malware, and access cloud systems.[38] Additionally, there are other forms of hacking that involve the manipulation of machine learning systems.[39] For instance, a driverless IoT vehicle's "machine learning classifier" could be manipulated "into perceiving a stop sign as a speed limit."[40]

Even if a manufacturer provides an update to correct a vulnerability, if the update is not automatic, some consumers may not be aware that the software update is available, and others may elect not to install the update. Companies are already selling IoT devices that require software updates, including washing machines, refrigerators, stoves, microwaves, smart speakers, and vacuum cleaners. Consider that a Pew Research Center survey found that many consumers who use smartphones fail to adequately secure their devices. The survey results indicate that 28 percent of smartphone users do not use screen locks and approximately 40 percent of respondents only download and install software updates "when it's convenient."[41] Similarly, in the IoT setting, once multiple household appliances in our homes are connected to the Internet, many of us may neglect software updates for some or all of our IoT devices.

---

[35] Martin Coulter, *KRACK Attack: Researchers Reveal Major Security Flaw in ALL Wi-Fi Networks and Devices That Use Them*, Evening Standard (Oct. 16, 2017, 12:55 PM), www.standard.co.uk/news/techand gadgets/krack-attack-researchers-reveal-major-security-flaw-in-all-wifi-networks-a3659696.html. *See generally* Vanhoef & Piessens, *supra* note 34.

[36] Alfred Ng, *Why KRACK Could Hit Your Smart Home's Wi-Fi the Hardest*, CNET (Oct. 16, 2017, 12:38 PM), www.cnet.com/news/why-krack-wi-fi-attack-could-hit-your-smart-home-hardest/; *see also* Lily Hay Newman, *A New Way to Track Down Bugs Could Help Save IoT*, Wired (Jan. 18, 2018, 11:00 AM), www.wired.com/story/a-new-way-to-track-down-bugs-could-help-save-iot/.

[37] Ng, *supra* note 36.

[38] *See* McAfee, Economic Impact of Cybercrime — No Slowing Down 5 (2018), https://www .mcafee.com/enterprise/en-us/forms/gated-form.html?docID=5fee1c652573999d75e4388122bf72f5& tag=ec&eid=18TL_ECGLQ1_CT_WW&elqCampaignId=23163.

[39] Ivan Evtimov et al., *Is Tricking a Robot Hacking?*, 34 Berkeley Tech. L.J. 891, 893 (2019).

[40] *Id.*; Kevin Eykholt et al., *Robust Physical-World Attacks on Deep Learning Visual Classification*, IEEE/CVF Conf. on Computer Vision & Pattern Recognition 1625, 1626 (Apr. 10, 2018), https:// arxiv.org/pdf/1707.08945v5.pdf.

[41] Monica Anderson, *Many Smartphone Owners Don't Take Steps to Secure Their Devices*, Pew Res. Ctr. (Mar. 15, 2017), www.pewresearch.org/fact-tank/2017/03/15/many-smartphone-owners-dont-take-steps-to-secure-their-devices/; *see also* Smith, *supra* note 8.

Although there has been some movement toward standardization, there are various IoT standards and protocols which cause interoperability issues, among other things.[42] Companies adopt varying approaches to cybersecurity. The multiple IoT devices in our homes will likely be manufactured by different companies and software developers, which could be problematic from a security perspective because devices with different levels of security will be commingled in the same environment. For example, although the maker of a single device in a consumer's home may adopt effective security measures to limit or avoid intrusions and data exfiltration and disclosures, the manufacturer and software developer of another device in a consumer's home may not adopt such measures. Thus, as one commentator has noted, "the least secure device becomes the security level for all your devices."[43]

The possible use of the same common open source software in IoT devices and systems may make it much easier for security vulnerabilities to simultaneously impact multiple devices and networks that use the same technology platform.[44] Many IoT devices have lax, easily guessed manufacturer-set default passwords. Many of us also tend to reuse the same password across various accounts. In 2018, California enacted the first state statute to curb the insecurity that plagues IoT devices.[45] However, the statute has several limitations which will be explored in further detail in Chapter 3. Design malfunctions or errors can also inadvertently lead to the disclosure of consumer data. For instance, in 2018, Amazon's smart speaker recorded a private conversation in a consumer's home and mistakenly sent the recording to a third party.[46] Additionally, the rise of 5G may also enhance IoT cybersecurity vulnerabilities.[47]

---

[42] *Amazon, Apple, Google, and the Zigbee Alliance and Its Board Members Form Industry Working Group to Develop a New, Open Standard for Smart Home Device Connectivity*, ZIGBEE ALLIANCE (Dec. 18, 2019), https://zigbeealliance.org/news_and_articles/connectedhomeip/; Asokan Ashok, *Five Reasons Why IoT Is Not Ready for Prime Time*, FORBES (Sept. 20, 2018, 9:00 AM), www.forbes.com/sites/forbestechcouncil/2018/09/20/five-reasons-why-iot-is-not-ready-for-prime-time/#2d403a7278aa; EUR. UNION AGENCY FOR NETWORK & INFO. SEC., BASELINE SECURITY RECOMMENDATIONS FOR THE IoT IN THE CONTEXT OF CRITICAL INFORMATION INFRASTRUCTURES (2017), www.enisa.europa.eu/publications/baseline-security-recommendations-for-iot/at_download/fullReport; IEEE, IEEE DRAFT STANDARD FOR AN ARCHITECTURAL FRAMEWORK FOR THE INTERNET OF THINGS (Mar. 15, 2019), https://ieeexplore.ieee.org/document/8672168.

[43] Sarah Kellogg, *Every Breath You Take: Data Privacy and Your Wearable Fitness Device*, WASH. LAW. (Dec. 2015), www.dcbar.org/bar-resources/publications/washington-lawyer/articles/december-2015-data-privacy.cfm.

[44] *See* Marjorie Loeb et al., *Open-Source Software in Connected Vehicles: Pros and Cons*, LAW360 (Sept. 25, 2018, 2:21 PM), www.law360.com/articles/1085881/open-source-software-in-connected-vehicles-pros-and-cons.

[45] *See generally* CAL. CIV. CODE §§ 1798.91.04–.06 (West 2018).

[46] *See* Niraj Chokshi, *Is Alexa Listening? Amazon Echo Sent Out Recording of Couple's Conversation*, N. Y. TIMES (May 25, 2018), www.nytimes.com/2018/05/25/business/amazon-alexa-conversation-shared-echo.html.

[47] Tom Wheeler & David Simpson, *Why 5G Requires New Approaches to Cybersecurity*, BROOKINGS (Sept. 3, 2019), www.brookings.edu/research/why-5g-requires-new-approaches-to-cybersecurity/; Christopher Cole, *Trump Inks Pair Of Network Security, Broadband Bills*, LAW360 (Mar. 24, 2020,

Recall that many IoT devices can be controlled and operated through mobile applications and smartphones. These devices and a user's smartphone can communicate using "unencrypted" or "plain text" that can be viewed by parties that have the ability to observe consumers' online traffic.[48] Consider that despite advertising that its devices had an "unbreakable design," Tapplock, Inc., the maker of an IoT smart lock, failed to encrypt data flowing from its devices and mobile apps, which allowed researchers to create keys to unlock the devices.[49] Recent research evaluating the security of IoT devices found that even when IoT device communications are encrypted, "an eavesdropper can reliably learn a user's interactions with a device across a wide range of categories, opening the potential for profiling and other privacy invasive techniques."[50] According to a white paper released by Symantec, approximately "19% of all tested mobile apps that are used to control IoT devices did not use Secure Socket Layer (SSL) connections to the cloud."[51] A 2019 study of IoT devices determined that even when IoT devices communicate over Transport Layer Security (TLS), IoT companies often use "outdated or non-standard TLS librar-[ies]," and insecure settings can be used to configure the libraries.[52]

Consider that the privacy policy of SMA, a company that sells watches designed to protect minors by providing real-time GPS information, states that it will do its best to ensure the security of information entered online and notes that the company encrypts data to ensure security.[53] However, the company's weak authentication systems and unencrypted communications have made its devices and related systems susceptible to hacking.[54] The researchers who unmasked the SMA watch

---

3:23 PM), www.law360.com/articles/1256421/trump-inks-pair-of-network-security-broadband-bills (noting that "the Secure 5G and Beyond Act of 2020 ... requires the president to develop a strategy to 'ensure the security of next generation mobile telecommunications systems and infrastructure'"); *Statements & Releases: Bill Announcement*, WHITEHOUSE (Mar. 23, 2020), www.whitehouse.gov/briefings-statements/bill-announcement-90/ (noting that the Secure 5G and Beyond Act of 2020 was "signed into law").

[48] Ng, *supra* note 36; *see also* MARIO BALLANO BARCENA & CANDID WUEEST, SYMANTEC, SECURITY RESPONSE: INSECURITY IN THE INTERNET OF THINGS 12 (2015) https://docs.broadcom.com/doc/insecurity-in-the-internet-of-things-en.

[49] Lisa Weintraub Schifferle, *Tapplock Settlement: Smart Devices Need Smart Security*, FED. TRADE COMM'N (Apr. 6, 2020, 12:15 PM), www.ftc.gov/news-events/blogs/business-blog/2020/04/tapplock-settlement-smart-devices-need-smart-security.

[50] Jingjing Ren et al., *Information Exposure from Consumer IoT Devices: A Multidimensional, Network-Informed Measurement Approach*, ASS'N FOR COMPUTING MACHINERY INTERNET MEASUREMENT CONF. (2019), https://moniotrlab.ccis.neu.edu/wp-content/uploads/2019/09/ren-imc19.pdf.

[51] BARCENA & WUEEST, *supra* note 48, at 5.

[52] Danny Yuxing Huang et al., *IoT Inspector: Crowdsourcing Labeled Network Traffic from Smart Home Devices at Scale*, ARXIV, 1, 9 (Sept. 21, 2019), https://arxiv.org/pdf/1909.09848.pdf.

[53] *SMA Applicable Privacy Policy*, SMA WATCH, www.smawatch.com/page262 (last updated May 25, 2018).

[54] *See* John E. Dunn, *Kids' Smartwatch Security Tracker Can Be Hacked by Anyone*, NAKED SECURITY (Nov. 28, 2019), https://nakedsecurity.sophos.com/2019/11/28/kids-smartwatch-security-tracker-can-be-hacked-by-anyone/.

vulnerabilities could discover a child's identity, location, address, and age, among other things.[55] Research has also revealed authentication vulnerabilities associated with Google's IoT home speaker and Chromecast devices that can lead to the disclosure of consumers' location data.[56]

The devices reviewed in the Symantec study mentioned earlier also did not use mutual authentication between the server and client, and "many of the IoT cloud platforms included common web application vulnerabilities."[57] The third-party vendors that companies use to process, aggregate, and store data collected from IoT devices and associated mobile applications and services are also not immune to data breaches and accidental data disclosures. Businesses' use of established cloud service providers, such as Amazon's Web Services (AWS), may provide a false sense of data security, foster confusion about which parties are responsible for securing data, and compound the problem of determining liability for cybersecurity failures.[58] Companies can store user data in third-party cloud services and fail to establish sufficient security controls to prevent unauthorized access.[59] For example, Capital One allegedly used vulnerable security methods to store consumer data in AWS, which led to a data breach in 2019.[60] The data breach revealed the data of 106 million consumers and was conducted by a former AWS employee.[61] It is notable that AWS's shared responsibility model suggests that it is obligated to maintain cloud infrastructure but has no responsibility for data.[62] Instead, companies using AWS cloud services are "responsible for managing their data (including encryption options), classifying their assets, and using IAM tools to apply the appropriate permissions."[63] It is unclear whether cloud service providers should face liability (if any) under a theory of deceptive and unfair trade practices for data

[55] Maik Morgenstern, *Product Warning! Chinese Children's Watch Reveals Thousands of Children's Data*, INTERNET OF THINGS BLOG (Nov. 25, 2019), www.iot-tests.org/2019/11/product-warning-chinese-childrens-watch-reveals-thousands-of-childrens-data/.

[56] *See* Craig Young, *Google's Newest Feature: Find My Home*, TRIPWIRE (June 18, 2018), www.tripwire.com/state-of-security/vert/googles-newest-feature-find-my-home/; *see also* Matt Burgess, *Google Home's Data Leak Proves the IoT Is Still Deeply Flawed*, WIRED (June 20, 2018), www.wired.co.uk/article/google-home-chromecast-location-security-data-privacy-leak.

[57] BARCENA & WUEEST, *supra* note 48, at 5.

[58] *See* Eric Trexler, *To Protect Data, Organizations Must Stop Being "Cloud Dumb,"* NEXTGOV (Feb. 18, 2020), www.nextgov.com/ideas/2020/02/protect-data-organizations-must-stop-being-cloud-dumb/163157/.

[59] *See* Catherine Stupp & James Rundle, *Capital One Breach Highlights Shortfalls of Encryption*, WALL ST. J. (Aug. 2, 2019, 11:37 AM), www.wsj.com/articles/capital-one-breach-highlights-shortfalls-of-encryption-11564738200.

[60] *Id.*; *see also* Robert McMillan, *Capital One Breach Casts Shadow over Cloud Security*, WALL ST. J. (July 30, 2019, 6:57 PM), www.wsj.com/articles/capital-one-breach-casts-shadow-over-cloud-security-11564516541.

[61] Stupp & Rundle, *supra* note 59.

[62] *Shared Responsibility Model*, AWS AMAZON, https://aws.amazon.com/compliance/shared-responsibility-model/ (last visited Feb. 2, 2020).

[63] *Id.*

breaches involving data stored in their cloud infrastructure.[64] As more IoT device manufacturers rely on cloud service providers, such as AWS, questions about which entities' failures caused a data breach may become more pressing. There can also be internal confusion at an organizational level regarding who is responsibility for IoT device security and maintenance. Cisco's 2018 cybersecurity report indicates that ambiguities regarding which parties are responsible for securing IoT networks have led hackers to exploit "the fact that security teams are having difficulty defending both IoT and cloud environments."[65] According to the report, 83 percent of studied IoT devices had "critical vulnerabilities."[66]

The vast troves of data held by large data brokers, aggregators, and marketing firms are also concerning. It is only a matter of time before marketing firms and data brokers obtain widespread access to IoT data. Once IoT data are obtained, processed, and analyzed, the individual data profiles of consumers held by these companies could become more intimate and extensive, and any resulting disclosure of these data can cause even more harm. These companies have already proven that their primary business goal is to vacuum up and analyze as much data about consumers as possible, while failing to keep consumer data secure. The Equifax data breach exposed the data of millions of individuals. In 2018, lax security practices at Exactis, a data broker, caused the disclosure of 340 million consumer records that included names, telephone numbers, physical and email addresses, the "age, and gender of [consumers'] children," religion, smoking preferences, pets, apparel size, and other "interests" and "habits."[67] In 2018, Apollo, a data aggregator, accidentally made "212 million contact listings as well as nine billion data points" publicly accessible online.[68]

Insecure IoT devices are also problematic when used by companies in their daily operations. Vulnerabilities associated with IoT devices provide an entry point for hackers to access broader systems that are connected to these devices. An insecure IoT thermometer located in an aquarium in a casino was reportedly used to hack the casino's network and steal data.[69] A 2018 cybersecurity survey of approximately 1,100

---

[64] *See* Letter from Ron Wyden & Elizabeth Warren, Senators, U.S. Senate, to Joseph J. Simons, Chairman, Fed. Trade Comm'n (Oct. 24, 2019), www.wyden.senate.gov/imo/media/doc/102419%20Wyden%20Warren%20Letter%20to%20FTC%20RE%20Amazon%20Capital%20One%20Hack.pdf (discussing the Capital One data breach and Amazon's possible role in failing to adopt appropriate cybersecurity measures for its cloud infrastructure).

[65] Cisco, Annual Cybersecurity Report 4, 24 (2018), www.cisco.com/c/dam/m/digital/elq-cmcglobal/witb/acr2018/acr2018final.pdf?dtid=odicdc000016&ccid=cc000160&oid=anrsc005679&ecid=8196&elqTrackId=686210143d34494fa27ff73da9690a5b&elqaid=9452&elqat=2.

[66] *Id.* at 42.

[67] Andy Greenberg, *Marketing Firm Exactis Leaked a Personal Info Database with 340 Million Records*, Wired (June 27, 2018, 1:34 PM), www.wired.com/story/exactis-database-leak-340-million-records/.

[68] Lily Hay Newman, *A Recent Startup Breach Exposed Billions of Data Points*, Wired (Oct. 5, 2018, 12:40 PM), www.wired.com/story/apollo-breach-linkedin-salesforce-data/.

[69] *See* Oscar Williams-Grut, *Hackers Once Stole a Casino's High-Roller Database Through a Thermometer in the Lobby Fish Tank*, Bus. Insider (Apr. 15, 2018, 12:08 AM), www

information technology specialists found that "82% of respondents predict insecure IoT devices will likely cause a data breach in their organizations."[70]

LIMITING LIABILITY FOR DATA BREACHES, DISCLOSURES, AND LOSS

Despite the various insecurities that plague IoT devices and systems, some companies have attempted to limit their liability for inadvertent data disclosures, data loss, and third-party hacking. This is done through the use of limitation of liability provisions and disclaimers in companies' privacy policies and terms of use. Some companies also include language on their websites indicating that it is impossible to fully secure their website, services, and products. Whether such provisions can effectively limit companies' exposure to liability depends on contract law principles as well as whether any applicable federal or state statutes negate the effect of such provisions.

To return to a previous example, VTech's 2017 terms and conditions provide that the company does not guarantee the security of its Kid Connect software and services, and, further, it "disclaims any liability" related to the same.[71] The company's other 2015 terms and conditions also contained similar provisions.[72] Nest's terms and conditions also provide that it does not warrant that the services (which include its website, mobile applications, and subscription services) used in conjunction with its IoT devices "will be available on an uninterrupted, timely, secure or error-free basis."[73] Fitbit's privacy policy provides that "[n]o method of transmitting or storing data is completely secure."[74] The privacy policy of Owlet, a manufacturer of a wearable IoT sock that monitors and collects data about infants' heart rate, oxygen levels, and sleep patterns, states, "we cannot and do not guarantee the security of your information."[75] The terms of service of FiLIP, an IoT company that was in bankruptcy and previously sold IoT devices used by children, but now primarily provides a platform and mobile app for wearable devices, provides:

> We do not warrant that the functions contained in the FiLIP service or any materials or content contained therein will be completely secure, uninterrupted

.businessinsider.com/hackers-stole-a-casinos-database-through-a-thermometer-in-the-lobby-fish-tank-2018-4?r=UK&IR=T; *see also* Alex Schiffer, *How a Fish Tank Helped Hack a Casino*, WASH. POST (July 21, 2017, 6:26 AM), www.washingtonpost.com/news/innovations/wp/2017/07/21/how-a-fish-tank-helped-hack-a-casino/?noredirect=on&utm_term=.8e230b5d35c9.

70 PONEMON INST., 2018 STUDY ON GLOBAL MEGATRENDS IN CYBERSECURITY 1 (2018), www.raytheon.com/sites/default/files/2018-02/2018_Global_Cyber_Megatrends.pdf.

71 *Terms and Conditions of VTech Kid Connect and Kidiconnect*, VTECH, www.vtechda.com/legal/version/view.aspx?country=US&lang=eng&x=1&y=1 (last updated July 25, 2017).

72 *Terms and Conditions*, VTECH, http://contentcdn.vtechda.com/data/console/GB/1668/SystemUpgrade/FirmwareUpdateTnC_GBeng_V2_20160120-170000.txt (last updated Dec. 24, 2015).

73 *Terms of Service*, NEST, https://nest.com/legal/terms-of-service/ (last updated March 5, 2020).

74 *Fitbit Privacy Policy*, FITBIT, www.fitbit.com/legal/privacy-policy#info-security (last updated Dec. 18, 2019).

75 *Privacy Policy*, OWLET, https://owletcare.com/pages/privacy (last updated Jan. 2, 2020).

or error free, that defects will be corrected, or that the server that makes it available is free of viruses or other harmful components. . . . In no event will we be liable under any theory of tort, contract, strict liability or other legal or equitable theory for any direct, indirect, special, incidental, or other consequential damages, lost profits, lost data.[76]

In the class action lawsuit that followed the Yahoo data breach mentioned earlier, the district court found that the plaintiffs had sufficiently pled unconscionability with respect to the limitation of liability provision contained in Yahoo's conditions of use.[77] The provision prohibited damages that were not direct damages for losses related to "unauthorized access to or alteration of [users'] transmissions or data . . . or any other matter relating to the Yahoo! Service."[78] The court noted that the provision appeared close to the end of Yahoo's twelve-page-long conditions of use.[79] Yahoo's terms and conditions also noted that "no data transmission over the Internet or information storage technology can be guaranteed to be 100% secure."[80] In a previous decision in the case, the court noted that despite various disclaimers and security warnings, Yahoo had also promised to restrict access to consumers' personal information.[81] The court's decision seemingly calls into question the effectiveness of cybersecurity warnings, disclaimers, and limitation of liability provisions.

ANONYMIZATION AND AGGREGATION LIMITS

One critique of consumer concerns related to data breaches and disclosures is that even if data are intentionally or accidentally disclosed to third parties, or if a data breach results in data disclosure, consumers are adequately protected if the data are anonymized and aggregated. There is mounting evidence that such alleged protections are significantly ineffective. Anonymized data can be reidentified. At least two *New York Times* reports on anonymized cell phone location data found that consumers could be identified based on these data.[82] The anonymized data revealed how long individuals spent at sensitive locations, such as Planned Parenthood.[83]

---

[76] *Terms of Service*, FILIP, www.myfilip.com/terms-of-service/ (last visited Nov. 16, 2019); *The Open Platform for Family Connected Devices*, FILIP, www.myfilip.com (last visited Nov. 16, 2019).

[77] *In re* Yahoo! Inc. Customer Data Sec. Breach Litig., 313 F. Supp. 3d 1113, 1136–38 (N.D. Cal. 2018).

[78] *Id.* at 1136.

[79] *Id.* at 1137.

[80] *In re* Yahoo! Inc. Customer Data Sec. Breach Litig., No. 16-MD-02752-LHK, 2017 U.S. Dist. LEXIS 140212, at *158 (N.D. Cal. Aug. 30, 2017).

[81] *Id.* at *159.

[82] *See* Jennifer Valentino-DeVries et al., *Your Apps Know Where You Were Last Night, and They're Not Keeping It Secret*, N.Y. TIMES (Dec. 10, 2018), www.nytimes.com/interactive/2018/12/10/business/location-data-privacy-apps.html; *see also* Stuart A. Thompson & Charlie Warzel, *Twelve Million Phones, One Dataset, Zero Privacy*, N.Y. TIMES (Dec. 19, 2019), www.nytimes.com/interactive/2019/12/19/opinion/location-tracking-cell-phone.html.

[83] Valentino-DeVries et al., *supra* note 82.

Reidentification could be possible by identifying a smartphone that frequently visited a specific home address or by combining public records with where the device stayed during the night.[84]

Paul Ohm convincingly notes that organizations have disclosed "information [that can be used to reidentify consumers and which is] connected to sensitive data in supposedly anonymized databases, with absolute impunity."[85] Researchers have determined that an individual's zip code, gender, and date of birth are unique identifiers that can be combined to reidentify anonymized data.[86] Researchers conducting a study on anonymization and metadata were able to reidentify 90 percent of consumers from anonymized "credit card transactions for 1.1 million users."[87] The study found that "even data sets that provide coarse information . . . provide little anonymity and that women are more reidentifiable than men."[88] Other researchers were able to de-anonymize the anonymous movie rating data of some Netflix users and were able to determine the political preferences and other personal information of these Netflix subscribers.[89]

Even anonymized electronic health records and data can be reidentified.[90] In some cases, "simple code[s] could unlock . . . patients'" identifying information.[91] Sharona Hoffman notes that publicly available information, such as voter records, can be combined with anonymized health data to identify individuals.[92] Researchers have developed algorithms that can "reidentify individuals based on the uniqueness of [data] trails across unidentified and identified datasets."[93] Companies may also be able to make "probabilistic inferences" about consumers from anonymized data.[94] Also, recall that it is possible to combine anonymized and aggregated data with

---

[84] *See id.*

[85] Paul Ohm, *Broken Promises of Privacy: Responding to the Surprising Failure of Anonymization*, 57 UCLA L. Rev. 1701, 1703–05 (2010); *see also* Frederik Zuiderveen Borgesius et al., *Open Data, Privacy, and Fair Information Principles: Towards a Balancing Framework*, 30 Berkeley Tech. L.J. 2073, 2121 (2015) ("Irreversible anonymization is difficult – perhaps impossible.").

[86] Ohm, *supra* note 85, at 1719; *see also* Latanya Sweeney, *Simple Demographics Often Identify People Uniquel* 2–5 (Carnegie Mellon Univ., Working Paper No. 3, 2000).

[87] Yves-Alexandre de Montjoye et al., *Unique in the Shopping Mall: On the Reidentifiability of Credit Card Metadata*, 347 Sci. 536, 537 (2015).

[88] *Id.* at 536; *see also* Charlotte Jee, *You're Very Easy to Track Down, Even When Your Data Has Been Anonymized*, Tech. Rev. (Jul. 23, 2019), www.technologyreview.com/s/613996/youre-very-easy-to-track-down-even-when-your-data-has-been-anonymized/.

[89] *See* Arvind Narayanan & Vitaly Shmatikov, *Robust De-Anonymization of Large Sparse Datasets*, Inst. Electrical & Electronics Engineers (2008), www.cs.utexas.edu/~shmat/shmat_oako8netflix.pdf.

[90] *See* Sharona Hoffman, Electronic Health Records and Medical Big Data: Law and Policy 136–37 (2016).

[91] Adam Tanner, *The Hidden Global Trade in Patient Medical Data*, YaleGlobal Online (Jan. 24, 2017), http://yaleglobal.yale.edu/content/hidden-global-trade-patient-medical-data.

[92] Hoffman, *supra* note 90, at 136, 182.

[93] Bradley Malin et al., *Trail Re-Identification: Learning Who You Are from Where You Have Been*, Carnegie Mellon Univ., Lab. for Int'l Data Privacy 1, 1 (2003).

[94] Solon Barocas & Helen Nissenbaum, *Computing Ethics: Big Data's End Run Around Procedural Privacy Protections*, 57 Comm. Ass'n for Computing Machinery 31, 32 (2014).

information obtained from other sources to identify individuals. In short, research suggests that there are significant limits to the effectiveness of anonymization techniques.

THE STANDING HURDLE

Although a plethora of companies have experienced data breaches that have resulted in the disclosure of consumer data, courts have used standing requirements to restrict the ability of consumers to bring successful lawsuits against companies to remedy harms associated with data breaches. Standing can be a contested issue in both federal and state court. However, standing has proven to be a contentious issue in federal class action data breach cases in particular, and many of these cases have been dismissed for lack of standing. Even if the evidence suggests that a company did not implement adequate security measures to prevent a data breach, standing issues must first be addressed before the company's liability is evaluated.[95] As Daniel Solove and Danielle Citron have observed, "[n]o matter how derelict defendants might be with regard to security, no matter how much warning defendants have about prior hacks and breaches, if plaintiffs cannot show harm, they cannot succeed in their lawsuits."[96] Thus, in order for a data breach claim to proceed in federal court, a plaintiff must satisfy standing requirements.

In *Spokeo, Inc. v. Robins*, a recent Supreme Court case addressing the question of standing, the court stated: "[a] plaintiff invoking federal jurisdiction bears the burden of establishing the 'irreducible constitutional minimum' of standing by demonstrating (1) an injury in fact, (2) fairly traceable to the challenged conduct of the defendant, and (3) likely to be redressed by a favorable judicial decision."[97]

In *Clapper v. Amnesty International USA*, an important decision prior to *Spokeo*, the Court held that plaintiffs' "speculative fear" that their communications might be intercepted or observed was not sufficient to show a "threatened injury" for standing purposes.[98] As Solove and Citron have persuasively written, with some notable exceptions, most courts have used *Clapper* to dismiss data breach lawsuits for lack of standing.[99] In *Spokeo*, the court went on to state that in order to satisfy the "injury in fact" requirement, plaintiffs must show "'an invasion of a legally protected interest' that is 'concrete and particularized' and 'actual or imminent, not conjectural or hypothetical.'"[100] However, the court also indicated that both intangible harms closely connected to traditional harms historically recognized by English or American courts and "risk[s] of real harm" could, under certain circumstances, be

---

[95] Daniel J. Solove & Danielle Keats Citron, *Risk and Anxiety: A Theory of Data-Breach Harms*, 96 TEX. L. REV. 737, 739 (2018).

[96] *Id. See also,* Lauren Henry Scholz, *Privacy Remedies*, 94 IND. L.J. 653 (2019).

[97] Spokeo, Inc. v. Robins, 136 S. Ct. 1540, 1543 (2016).

[98] Clapper v. Amnesty Int'l USA, 568 U.S. 398, 410 (2013).

[99] *See* Solove & Citron, *supra* note 95, at 741.

[100] *Spokeo,* 136 S. Ct. at 1543.

viewed as concrete and therefore sufficient to satisfy the "injury in fact" requirement.[101] In the data breach or disclosure context, the pressing question after the *Spokeo* decision is: What types of intangible injuries and risks of harm are sufficient to satisfy standing requirements? Federal courts have reached different conclusions on this issue.[102]

Recent cases applying *Spokeo* and *Clapper* are potentially instructive on this point. In *In re VTech Data Breach Litigation*, the consumer class action filed after the VTech data breach, although there may have been standing based on overpayment, the court determined that the plaintiffs did not have standing with respect to their allegations of a "substantial risk of harm."[103] The court stated that unlike the data breach cases in which other courts found standing, "the data stolen [in the VTech case] did not include credit-card or debit-card information, or any other information that could easily be used in fraudulent transactions."[104] In *Antman v. Uber Techs., Inc.*, an ongoing data breach case involving Uber drivers, the district court concluded that the disclosure of bank account numbers and routing information, names, and driver's license numbers was not sufficient to establish "a credible threat of identity theft that risked real, immediate injury."[105] The court distinguished the few data breach cases in which judges have found standing by noting that in those cases the social security numbers, passwords, credit card numbers, and

[101]   *Id.* at 1549.

[102]   *See* Allison Grande, *The Biggest Privacy & Cybersecurity Developments of 2019*, LAW360 (Dec. 20, 2019, 1:25 PM), www.law360.com/consumerprotection/articles/1228763/the-biggest-privacy-cybersecurity-developments-of-2019?nl_pk=06d06a2b-64f8-4c4c-b81d-6950221f7573&utm_source=newsletter&utm_medium=email&utm_campaign=consumerprotection (discussing the circuit split on this issue); *see also* Allison Grande, *DC Circ. Piles onto Standing Split with Data Breach Ruling*, LAW360 (June 28, 2019, 5:32 PM), www.law360.com/articles/1173454/dc-circ-piles-onto-standing-split-with-data-breach-ruling (noting that "[w]hile the Sixth, Seventh and Ninth circuits have allowed data breach litigants to proceed based on the alleged heightened risk of future misuse, several appellate courts — the Second, Third, Fourth and Eighth — have imposed a heightened standard that requires some actual harm to have already manifested").

[103]   *In re* VTech Data Breach Litig., No. 15-CV-10889, 2017 U.S. Dist. LEXIS 103298, at *16 (N.D. Ill. July 5, 2017).

[104]   *Id.*

[105]   Antman v. Uber Techs., Inc., No. 15-cv-01175-LB, 2018 U.S. Dist. LEXIS 79371, at *24–26 (N.D. Cal. May 10, 2018) ("Mr. Antman specifies disclosure only of his name, driver's license information, and his bank account and routing number."); *see also* Antman v. Uber Techs., Inc., No. 3:15-cv-01175-LB, 2015 U.S. Dist. LEXIS 141945, at *14–15 (N.D. Cal. Oct. 19, 2015) (discussing personal information under California law); CAL. CIV. CODE § 1798.81.5 (West 2019) (defining personal information). The plaintiffs appealed the district court's dismissal. *See* Appellant's Opening Brief, Antman v. Uber Techs., Inc., No. 18-16100 (9th Cir. Oct. 17, 2018), https://dlbjbjzgnk95t.cloudfront.net/1093000/1093901/https-ecf-ca9-uscourts-gov-n-beam-servlet-transportroom-servlet-showdoc-009030424427.pdf; *United States Court of Appeals for the Ninth Circuit: Calendar for James R. Browning U.S. Courthouse, San Francisco*, U.S. COURTS, NINTH CIRCUIT, www.ca9.uscourts.gov/calendar/view.php?caseno=18-16100 (last visited Jan. 14, 2020); *see also* Linda Chiem, *Ex-Uber Drivers Ask 9th Circ. to Revive 2014 Data Hack Suit*, LAW360 (Oct. 19, 2018, 7:04 PM), www.law360.com/articles/1093901/ex-uber-drivers-ask-9th-circ-to-revive-2014-data-hack-suit.

addresses were disclosed, unlike the case before the court.[106] The court seemed to narrowly define the types of data disclosures that can generate a real risk of injury and identity theft.

The *Antman* court is not alone in using this rationale post *Spokeo* and *Clapper*. In *Alleruzzo v. SuperValu, Inc.*, another data breach lawsuit, the Eighth Circuit determined that some of the plaintiffs in a data breach lawsuit did not satisfy standing requirements by reasoning in part that the information related to debt and credit cards that was disclosed during the hack did not include "personally identifying information, such as social security numbers, birth dates, or driver's license number" and as such there was "little to no risk" that third parties would be able to use the data "to open unauthorized accounts in the plaintiffs' names."[107] The court also concluded that there was very little risk of "unauthorized charges" from the data disclosure.[108] Similarly, in *Whalen v. Michaels Stores, Inc.*, the Second Circuit found that the plaintiff could not show a credible "risk of future identity fraud" in the data breach lawsuit since the stolen credit card was canceled and "no other personally identifying information – such as her birth date or Social Security number – [was] alleged to have been stolen."[109]

Even courts that have found standing in data breach cases have done so by evaluating, in part, the nature and types of data that were disclosed. In *Attias v. CareFirst, Inc.*, the court held that there is "a substantial risk of identity theft" when "social security and credit card numbers" are obtained by unauthorized parties and such risk is sufficient for standing purposes.[110] The court also noted that the plaintiffs had spent funds to protect themselves from identity theft and suggested that the disclosure of subscriber identification numbers could also meet standing requirements "even if [plaintiffs'] social security numbers were never exposed to the data thief."[111] In *In re Office of Personnel Management Data Security Breach Litigation*, the D.C. Circuit determined that a high risk of identity theft was sufficient to meet standing requirements.[112] In contrast, other courts addressing data breach claims do not view an increased risk of identity theft as a harm that is sufficient for standing purposes, particularly when plaintiffs cannot prove or do not allege that their data have been misused.[113]

---

[106] *Antman*, 2018 U.S. Dist. LEXIS 79371, at *27–28 ("By contrast, fraud and identity theft are plausible risks with the account numbers and passwords disclosed in *Zappos*, the credit-card numbers and Social Security numbers in *Attias*, or the names, addresses, and Social Security numbers in *Krottner*.").

[107] Alleruzzo v. SuperValu, Inc. (*In re* SuperValu, Inc., Customer Data Sec. Breach Litig.), 870 F.3d 763, 770–74 (8th Cir. 2017) ("[W]e reverse the district court's dismissal of plaintiff Holmes for lack of Article III standing, [and] affirm the dismissal as to the remaining plaintiffs.").

[108] *Id.* at 770–71.

[109] Whalen v. Michaels Stores, Inc., 689 Fed. Appx. 89, 90 (2d Cir. 2017).

[110] Attias v. CareFirst, Inc., 865 F.3d 620, 627–28 (D.C. Cir. 2017), *cert. denied*, 138 S. Ct. 981 (2018).

[111] *Id.* at 628–29.

[112] Am. Fed'n of Gov't Emps. v. Office of Pers. Mgmt. (*In re* U.S. OPM Data Sec. Breach Litig.), 928 F.3d 42, 42 (D.C. Cir. 2019).

[113] Solove & Citron, *supra* note 95, at 750; *see also* Beck v. McDonald, 848 F.3d 262, 274 (4th Cir. 2017) (dismissing plaintiffs' claims for lack of standing and reasoning that "plaintiffs have uncovered no evidence that the information contained on the stolen laptop has been accessed or misused or that

So far in our standing discussion, we have seen cases in which a data breach has occurred, and data of some kind has been disclosed. In some instances, no data breach has occurred, but a company has manufactured an IoT product with significant security flaws. Standing is even more of a challenging issue in these cases. In these lawsuits consumers may allege that (1) they overpaid for the insecure IoT product, (2) the market value of the device has decreased significantly because of the security flaws, and (3) the device exposes them to an increased risk of hacking, which may lead to "injury or death," and they experience "fear and anxiety" as a result.[114] So far, these cases have primarily involved IoT vehicles. At least one court has found that there could be standing on the grounds of diminished value and overpayment of insecure IoT devices that have not been widely hacked.[115] But post *Clapper*, most courts are unwilling to find that an increased risk of hacking is sufficient for standing purposes.[116]

These cases suggest that post *Spokeo*, standing continues to be a significant hurdle for consumers. The holdings in these cases are problematic for several reasons. First, by narrowly defining the types of personal information that can lead to a substantial risk of harm and identity theft, courts may not adequately consider the types of data disclosures that may be prevalent in the IoT setting. Recall from Chapter 1 that IoT devices will collect highly sensitive data, such as immutable

---

they have suffered identity theft, nor, for that matter, that the thief stole the laptop with the intent to steal their private information"); Moore v. HighPoint Sols. LLC, No. 17-6266, 2018 U.S. Dist. LEXIS 94213, at *15 (D.N.J. June 5, 2018) (granting defendant's motion to dismiss for lack of standing and reasoning that "allegation[s] of an increased risk of identity theft [are] speculative and conclusory . . . but more importantly, Plaintiff has failed to allege actual misuse of her personal identifying information").

[114] Flynn v. FCA US LLC, No. 15-cv-0855-MJR-DGW, 2016 U.S. Dist. LEXIS 130614, at *22–24 (S.D. Ill. Sept. 23, 2016); *see also Search Results*, SUPREME COURT OF THE U.S., www.supremecourt.gov/search .aspx?filename=/docket/docketfiles/html/public/18-398.html (last visited Jan. 14, 2020) (Supreme Court denied petition for writ of certiorari on January 7, 2019).

[115] *See Flynn*, 2016 U.S. Dist. LEXIS 130614, at *10, *34 (stating that "overpayment or a drop in value suffices as an injury for standing purposes" but finding that plaintiffs "lack standing to pursue damages for a risk of harm or a fear of that risk" for "non-economic damages"). *But see* Birdsong v. Apple, Inc., 590 F.3d 955, 961 (9th Cir. 2009) (holding that plaintiffs' overpayment claim "does not constitute a distinct and palpable injury that is actual or imminent because it rests on a hypothetical risk of . . . loss to other consumers who may or may not choose to use [the product] in a risky manner").

[116] *See, e.g.,* Cahen v. Toyota Motor Corp., 717 Fed. Appx. 720, 723 (9th Cir. 2017) (finding that claims that "vehicles are vulnerable to being hacked because [the] vehicles' computer systems lack security" are speculative since no vehicles were hacked); Madstad Eng'g, Inc. v. U.S. Patent & Trademark Office, 756 F.3d 1366, 1374 (Fed. Cir. 2014) (affirming district court's dismissal for lack of standing and stating "[t]he mere fact that [plaintiff], like all other people and companies, faces cyber threats does not create standing"); CS Wang & Assoc. v. Wells Fargo Bank, N.A., 305 F. Supp. 3d 864, 881 (N.D. Ill. 2018) (finding standing on the basis of an "alleged violation of privacy" but noting that this finding does not extend "to the Plaintiffs' alternate theory that the Defendants' practice of storing the recordings in cloud-based computer systems accessible by the internet created a risk of data breach [,] [because the] Supreme Court [in *Clapper*] has explicitly denied that plaintiffs have standing based on such risks"); Oneal v. First Tenn. Bank, No. 4:17-CV-3-TAV-SKL, 2018 U.S. Dist. LEXIS 42383, at *36 (E.D. Tenn. Mar. 15, 2018) ("[P]laintiff has failed to plead a concrete risk of harm from a hypothetical future data breach.").

biometric data, health-related data, home-layout data (including the location of physical items in consumers' homes), and much more. If a court does not view the disclosure of bank account data as sensitive enough to create a concrete risk of harm for standing purposes, it is unlikely that such a court would find that data disclosures of other types of highly sensitive IoT data are sufficient. This is particularly true if IoT data are disclosed without being accompanied by the disclosure of passwords, social security numbers, or credit card information. The Exactis data breach discussed earlier did not appear to include social security numbers, passwords, or credit card information, and to date it is unclear whether malefic third parties have used the data.[117] However, the detailed and personal nature of the data could potentially make it easier for hackers and other malicious parties to conduct secondary hacks and facilitate other types of harms discussed later.[118] Under the parameters established in the case law discussed earlier, the Exactis data disclosure may not be viewed as creating a credible threat of future substantial harm despite the highly sensitive nature of the data.

Second, as Solove and Citron have persuasively argued, once consumers become aware that a data breach has disclosed their information, they may (1) become emotionally distressed, (2) refrain from exploring new financial and job options, and (3) have a higher "chance of being preyed upon by blackmailers, extortionists, and fraudsters promising quick fixes in exchange for data or money."[119] These concerns are magnified in the IoT context in light of the massive volume and new types of data that are being collected by IoT devices. These data are much more than simply unique combinations of numbers and letters assigned to us by governmental agencies. IoT data include information about our personal habits, behaviors, and daily activities and can go to the essence of who we are as individuals. Solove and Citron further argue that there are various areas of the law that already recognize risk and anxiety as valid harms and so too should courts in data breach cases.[120] In the IoT era, risk and anxiety are not just limited to emotional distress related to financial or economic injury.

A U.S. GAO report on cybersecurity found that most data breaches do not lead to reported identity theft.[121] Assuming this continues to be true, limiting the assessment of consumer harm to analyzing the possibility of identity theft, financial fraud, and other traditional economic injuries fails to encompass other types of harms. A University of California, Berkeley, Center for Long-Term Cybersecurity report describes a potential cybersecurity scenario in which "real-time emotional state"

---

[117]   Greenberg, *supra* note 67.
[118]   *See id.*
[119]   Solove & Citron, *supra* note 95, at 745–47.
[120]   *See id.* at 745.
[121]   U.S. Gov't Accountability Office, Personal Information: Data Breaches Are Frequent, but Evidence of Resulting Identity Theft Is Limited; However, the Full Extent Is Unknown 5 (2007), www.gao.gov/products/GAO-07-737.

data generated from IoT wearable devices are used to manipulate consumers.[122] IoT devices can collect information about consumers' mental and emotional state, and security vulnerabilities could enable the disclosure of such data. Research firm Gartner, Inc., projects that "by 2022, personal devices will know more about an individual's emotional state than his or her own family."[123] Facebook has reportedly requested patents for facial recognition technology that would permit it "to tailor ads based on users' facial expressions."[124]

Once highly sensitive IoT data are disclosed, the data could be used to manipulate consumers and increase the effectiveness and prevalence of "social engineering" attacks.[125] These types of disclosures could also impact consumers' future behaviors, activities, and opportunities, and enable profiling.[126] Malicious actors could use sensitive data to determine which individuals are more susceptible to specific types of manipulation or social engineering attacks, such as a phishing email with malware-infested attachments and links. Further, the data could be used to determine how best to psychologically control and impact our behaviors. Much like emotional marketing, emotional hacking could use IoT data about consumers' mental, physical, and emotional well-being to influence conduct and identify cognitive deficiencies and prejudices that are ripe for exploitation. Actors that seek to misuse these data to control and influence individuals could be motivated by financial, political, social, or personal concerns. Disclosures of immutable biometric data, such as voice and face prints that can be used to identify individuals, can facilitate impersonation in light of the frequency with which companies are now incorporating biometrics into IoT devices. Marketing and advertising firms are already incredibly effective at manipulating consumer perceptions and spending habits with the existing data that they have. Technology used by established companies to enable this process could become accessible to and deployed by hackers. Combining traditional sources of data with IoT data enhances threats of manipulation, targeting, profiling, and impersonation, as well as increasing the risk and anxiety associated with these potential threats. The impact of the disclosure of IoT data may have more long-lasting effects for vulnerable groups, such as children, who have longer digital footprints and data trails.

"Unwanted observation[s]" by third parties can be viewed as a significant privacy and cybersecurity harm.[127] Recall that the U.S. GAO IoT report discussed earlier

---

[122] UNIV. OF CAL., BERKELEY CTR. FOR LONG-TERM CYBERSECURITY, CYBERSECURITY FUTURES 2020, 7 (2016), https://cltc.berkeley.edu/wp-content/uploads/2016/04/cltcReport_04-27-04a_pages.pdf.

[123] Press Release, Gartner, Gartner Says Artificial Intelligence is a Game Changer for Personal Devices (Jan. 8, 2018), www.gartner.com/en/newsroom/press-releases/2018-01-08-gartner-says-artificial-intelligence-is-a-game-changer-for-personal-devices.

[124] *Facebook Inc: Biometric Data Class Action Ongoing in Illinois*, 19 CLASS ACTION REP. (2017).

[125] *See* Greenberg, *supra* note 67.

[126] *See id.*

[127] *See generally* M. Ryan Calo, *The Boundaries of Privacy Harm*, 86 IND. L.J. 1131 (2011).

highlighted "passive wiretapping" – observing and collecting IoT data – as a cybersecurity concern. The threat of unwanted observations and the anxiety associated with same is ever present in the IoT context. The stakes are higher for consumers whose IoT data are disclosed in a data breach. Imagine a scenario in which an in-home Nest security camera is hacked, and a malicious actor can not only turn the camera off and on, but can also observe live videos of all of the consumer's unclothed and clothed activities. The potential for extortion is high.[128] This type of surreptitious surveillance and the embarrassment and reputational injury that could follow should be viewed as a significant harm. If a data breach exposes these types of IoT data, courts should view this disclosure as being sufficient to establish a concrete and imminent risk of future harm for standing purposes, even if the data have not yet been misused and even if the data are not associated with traditional types of data that could cause identity theft. As Solove and Citron observe, it could take years before the party that obtains the data chooses to disclose or use it.[129] We should not have to adopt a wait-and-see approach or bear this risk of future harm and embarrassment.

The earlier sections of this chapter highlighted various insecurities plaguing IoT devices. The failure to acknowledge the risk of hacking and anxiety associated with insecure IoT devices ignores the very real and widespread security vulnerabilities plaguing IoT devices, services, and associated systems. Companies continue to introduce devices and services that are insecure, while simultaneously using standing requirements to avoid consumer claims about these devices. A hack of an insecure device that leads to data theft or unwanted observations could occur without consumers' knowledge. The Supreme Court indicated in *Clapper* that it is possible to find "standing based on a 'substantial risk' that [a] harm will occur, which may prompt plaintiffs to reasonably incur costs to mitigate or avoid that harm."[130] A known security vulnerability that has not been definitively and timely remedied, such that a significant risk of hacking remains, and which may generate "fear and anxiety" about the same, should count as a concrete injury for standing purposes. Additionally, with respect to DDoS attacks, consumer harms may also include a lack of device functionality or a "degraded user experience" even when data are not disclosed. These should also be viewed as concrete harms.

Every state has adopted a data breach notification statute (each of which has varying requirements), but these statutes cannot sufficiently remedy the harms

---

[128] Solove & Citron, *supra* note 95, at 774.

[129] *Id.* at 756.

[130] Clapper v. Amnesty Int'l USA, 568 U.S. 398, 414 n.5 (2013); *see also* Susan B. Anthony List v. Driehaus, 573 U.S. 149, 158 (2014) ("An allegation of future injury may suffice if the threatened injury is 'certainly impending,' or there is a 'substantial risk' that the harm will occur."); Solove & Citron, *supra* note 95, at 743 (noting that the Supreme Court did not elaborate on how to determine when a "substantial risk of harm" will occur).

discussed earlier.[131] Not all sensitive IoT data involved in data breaches will necessarily qualify as "personal information" under these varying statutes or meet the required risk of harm thresholds. As a result, associated data leaks or breaches may not trigger statutory reporting and notice requirements. Further, some of these statutes do not provide consumers with a private right of action.[132]

Additionally, state data security laws can also shield companies from liability. Consider that Ohio's data security statute provides an affirmative defense, which immunizes companies that adopt security practices in conformity with associated industry standards from data breach liability.[133] The California Consumer Privacy Act of 2018 (CCPA), which will be discussed in more detail in Chapter 3, gives consumers the right to sue for a data breach involving certain types of personal information.[134] Even when state law requires notification of a data breach, companies do not always immediately discover the breach or comply with their disclosure obligations. For instance, Verizon's 2018 data breach report found that "68% of breaches took months or longer to discover."[135] Yahoo took two years to disclose the hack that involved approximately 500 million accounts.[136] Equifax delayed disclosing its 2017 hack that impacted approximately 145 million individuals for four months.[137] The hack occurred because of the company's failure to timely address a known security weakness.[138] Calls to expand courts' understanding and perception of consumer harms in data breach cases are well warranted in the IoT era. As we will see in Chapter 3, despite the plethora of privacy and data security harms that the IoT generates, several notable privacy and security legal frameworks fail to adequately deal with these harms.

---

[131]   *See generally Security Breach Notification Laws*, NAT'L CONF. STATE LEGISLATURES (2019), www.ncsl.org /research/telecommunications-and-information-technology/security-breach-notification-laws.aspx.

[132]   Carol M. Hayes, *Comparative Analysis of Data Breach Laws: Comprehension, Interpretation, and External Sources of Legislative Text*, 23 LEWIS & CLARK L. REV. 1221, 1267 (2020).

[133]   *See* OHIO REV. CODE ANN. § 1354.02 (West 2019–20); *see also* Allison Grande, *Ohio's Data Security Law to Test Incentive-Driven Strategy*, LAW360 (Nov. 21, 2018, 8:42 PM), www.law360.com/cybersecur ity-privacy/articles/1104066/ohio-s-data-security-law-to-test-incentive-driven-strategy?nl_pk=d62df110-ded9-4a8a-aae8-6ca5f529ae34&utm_source=newsletter&utm_medium=email&utm_campaign=cy bersecurity-privacy.

[134]   *See* CAL. CIV. CODE § 1798.150 (West 2018); DANIEL J. SOLOVE & PAUL SCHWARTZ , INFORMATION PRIVACY LAW SUPPLEMENT 2 (6th ed. 2018) ("Although the CCPA lacks a private right of action for most violations, it creates a private right of action in the event of 'unauthorized access and exfiltration, theft, or disclosure' of a consumer's nonencrypted or nonredacted personal information.").

[135]   VERIZON, 2018 DATA BREACH INVESTIGATIONS REPORT 5 (11th ed. 2018), https://enterprise.verizon.com /resources/reports/2018/DBIR_2018_Report.pdf.

[136]   Andrea Peterson, *Yahoo Discovered Hack Leading to Major Data Breach Two Years Before It Was Disclosed*, WASH. POST (Nov. 10, 2016, 12:28 PM), www.washingtonpost.com/news/the-switch/wp/2016/ 11/10/yahoo-discovered-hack-leading-to-major-data-breach-two-years-before-it-was-disclosed/?noredir ect=on&utm_term=.45bf97547300.

[137]   Zack Whittaker, *Equifax Says More Private Data Was Stolen in 2017 Breach than First Revealed*, ZERO DAY (Feb. 12, 2018, 1:10 PM), www.zdnet.com/article/hackers-stole-more-equifax-data-than-first-thought/.

[138]   *See* Lily Hay Newman, *Equifax Officially Has No Excuse*, WIRED (Sept. 14, 2017, 1:27 PM), www .wired.com/story/equifax-breach-no-excuse/.

3

The Current Privacy and Data Security Legal Landscape

Most of the existing privacy and security legal frameworks at both the federal and state level provide incomplete safeguards against many of the privacy and information security harms highlighted in earlier chapters. Many of these frameworks have long been critiqued by privacy law experts for their lack of effectiveness. The IoT amplifies these inadequacies as it compounds existing privacy and security challenges.

At the state level, the patchwork of privacy and security legislation creates varying obligations for businesses without consistently ensuring that individuals receive adequate privacy and cybersecurity protection. State legislation also suffers from several shortcomings and is often replete with gaping privacy and security holes. Even the CCPA, the first privacy statute of its kind in the United States, has several limitations. Further, varying state privacy and security legislation also enables unequal access to privacy and security between citizens of different states. Unless state laws that provide more consumer protection have a constitutional extraterritorial impact in other states, those of us who are lucky enough to reside in states with more consumer-friendly privacy and security legislation will receive more shelter from privacy invasions and security failures than those who do not.

While some states have long taken a more protective approach to consumer issues, the magnitude of the privacy invasions and security failures the IoT creates stands in contrast to other aspects of consumer protection.[1] Now that companies have introduced the Internet, which already has no borders, to billions of once-ordinary objects, these objects (and the harms associated with them) are no longer subject to traditional geographical and jurisdictional boundaries.

At the federal level, the power of existing federal agencies to sufficiently address IoT-related problems is constrained in some instances by statutory authority and regulatory restrictions, some of which are self-imposed. These limits, combined with the American sectoral approach to privacy, which is characterized by legislation that

---

[1] *See generally* Nat'l Consumer Law Ctr., Consumer Protection in the States: A 50-State Evaluation of Unfair and Deceptive Practices Laws (2018), www.nclc.org/images/pdf/udap/udap-report.pdf (evaluating key differences in states' consumer protection legislation).

covers certain industries and specific types of data, significantly restrict privacy and security protections.[2] Lastly, privacy and security frameworks at both the state and federal level also continue to overrely on the notice and choice model as the primary means of safeguarding our privacy. To be clear, this book does not contend that companies should no longer provide consumers with any form of notice or that consumers should never be given a choice. Rather, it highlights the limits of depending excessively on the notice and choice model to safeguard our interests as consumers, and ultimately argues for the implementation of solutions to correct this overreliance.

PRIVACY LAW DISCOURSE

The 1973 Fair Information Practice (FIP) principles, which provide recommendations for the collection and use of data, have served as the foundation for several US privacy frameworks.[3] As we saw in Chapter 1, privacy law has long had a definitional problem. Despite this, the dominant view of privacy that is memorialized in many privacy frameworks today is that of privacy as control, which has been reduced to notice and choice.[4] The version of notice and choice that permeates US privacy laws

[2] In this chapter, I explore several (but not all) federal and state legal frameworks applicable to privacy and security issues. I do not cover state laws applicable to wiretapping and eavesdropping. It is unclear how helpful such laws will be to consumers who allege that IoT companies inappropriately listened to their in-home conversations, particularly if the conversations are not confidential or occurred in person. *See e.g., In re* Google Assistant Privacy Litigation, No. 19-cv-04286-BLF, 23–29 (N.D. Cal. May 6, 2020). I also do not discuss several federal statutes, such as the Electronic Communications Privacy Act (ECPA) and the Computer Fraud and Abuse Act (CFAA), primarily because efforts to use these statutes to address corporate online data collection have often failed. Daniel J. Solove & Paul M. Schwartz , Information Privacy Law 907 (6th ed. 2018) (discussing the impact of the CFAA's $5,000 threshold requirement); Daniel J. Solove & Woodrow Hartzog, *The FTC and the New Common Law of Privacy*, 114 Colum. L. Rev. 583, 591 (2014) [hereinafter Solove & Hartzog, *New Common Law*] (discussing the ECPA's limits and noting that the ECPA "was designed to regulate wiretapping and electronic snooping rather than commercial data gathering. The records maintained by internet retailers and websites were often held not to be 'communications' under the ECPA"); Cong. Research Serv., Data Protection Law: An Overview 25–30 (2019), https://fas.org/sgp/crs/misc/R45631.pdf (discussing the limits of the ECPA and the CFAA in addressing corporate data gathering and contending that "[a]s with [the] ECPA, internet users have attempted to use [the CFAA's] private right of action to sue companies tracking their online activity, arguing that companies' use of tracking devices constitutes an unauthorized access of their computers. . . . In practice, however such claims have typically been dismissed due to plaintiffs' failure to meet CFAA's damages threshold."); Bill Donahue, *LinkedIn Will Go to Supreme Court over Data Scraping*, Law360 (Jan. 27, 2020, 3:28 PM), www.law360.com/articles/1237505/linkedin-will-go-to-supreme-court-over-data-scraping (discussing the CFAA and data scraping lawsuits).

[3] U.S. Dep't of Health, Educ. & Welfare, Records, Computers, and the Rights of Citizens: Report of the Secretary's Advisory Committee on Automated Personal Data Systems 41–42 (1973), www.justice.gov/opcl/docs/rec-com-rights.pdf; Marc Rotenberg, *Fair Information Practices and the Architecture of Privacy (What Larry Doesn't Get)*, 2001 Stan. Tech. L. Rev. 1 (2001) (stating that the "Fair Information Practices played a significant role in framing privacy laws in the United States").

[4] Ari Ezra Waldman, Privacy as Trust: Information Privacy for an Information Age 30 (2018) ("This notion of privacy as control has arguably had a more profound impact on privacy law than any other

and regulation today does not fully embody the breadth of the FIP principles, such as the right to prohibit data that is obtained for a specific "purpose from being used for other purposes."[5] Corporations have also been heavily invested in advocating for self-regulation through a limited version of notice and choice and have repeatedly blocked legislation that would protect consumer privacy.

Notice implies that companies through their privacy policies and other statements provide us with information about the data they collect and how they use, disclose, and transfer our data.[6] Choice implies that as autonomous persons we have the option to consent to or reject companies' data practices, products, and services.[7] This view of privacy is also reflected in the FTC's approach to protecting consumer privacy and security.[8] More on this point later. Companies are the primary arbiters of how much of our data is collected and what happens to that information. Privacy legislation often reflects a compromise between the corporate beneficiaries of technologies and consumer advocates, with corporate beneficiaries exercising "more influence over the final legislation."[9] Overreliance on notice and choice has led to inadequate consumer data protection. This excessive reliance on a limited version of notice and choice and privacy law's definitional problem have likely also contributed to courts' inability to sufficiently account for harms in consumer data lawsuits, including when such cases involve claims grounded in commercial law, such as breach of implied warranties.

THE FTC AND CONSUMER PROTECTION

The FTC is the primary federal agency responsible for protecting consumer privacy and security. The FTC's core authority is based on the Federal Trade Commission Act (FTCA). Section 5 of the FTCA prohibits "unfair or deceptive acts or practices" impacting commerce.[10] The FTC uses this prohibition (whether intentionally or unintentionally) to attempt to fill regulatory gaps left open by the US sectoral privacy approach.[11] This prohibition on unfair and deceptive activities serves as the basis for

---

theory. It is first and foremost, at the core of the notice and choice approach to data privacy in the United States and Europe.").

[5]   Memorandum from Paul M. Schwartz, Professor, Univ. of Cal., Berkeley Sch. of Law & Daniel Solove, Professor, George Wash. Univ. Law Sch., on Notice and Choice: Implications for Digital Marketing to the Second NPLAN/BMSG Meeting on Digital Media and Marketing to Children 1 (2009), http://digitalads.org/documents/Schwartz_Solove_Notice_Choice_NPLAN_BMSG_memo .pdf [hereinafter Memorandum from Schwartz & Solove].

[6]   Daniel J. Solove & Woodrow Hartzog, *The FTC and the New Common Law of Privacy*, 114 COLUM. L. REV. 583, 592 (2014).

[7]   *Id.*; WALDMAN, *supra* note 4, at 31.

[8]   *Id.*

[9]   PRISCILLA M. REGAN, LEGISLATING PRIVACY: TECHNOLOGY, SOCIAL VALUES AND PUBLIC POLICY, XII (1995).

[10]   15 U.S.C. § 45(a)(1) (2020).

[11]   Solove & Hartzog, *New Common Law*, *supra* note 2, at 587–88 ("Because so many companies fall outside of specific sectoral privacy laws, the FTC is in many cases the primary source of regulation.").

many of the FTC's privacy and security enforcement activities. The agency's efforts in this area are constrained by the FTCA. For example, in "most privacy matters, the FTC cannot levy civil penalties."[12] The FTC has limited rulemaking authority.[13] In addition, common carriers are excluded from the FTC's coverage to the extent that such entities engage in common carrier activities.[14]

Historically, the FTC supported a self-regulatory approach to privacy because of a concern that regulation would hinder innovation.[15] In the privacy context, industry self-regulation includes corporate actors' adoption of practices and guidelines to regulate data collection and use as well as mechanisms for applying these guidelines to other corporate actors.[16] Examples of industry self-regulation include privacy certifications and seals programs, such as TRUSTe.[17] Self-regulation also took the form of notice and choice, with privacy policies playing a pivotal role in companies' purported provision of notice and choice to consumers.[18]

The FTC ultimately acknowledged the limits of overreliance on a self-regulatory approach to privacy, which failed to sufficiently incorporate FIPs principles and to

[12] CHRIS JAY HOOFNAGLE, FEDERAL TRADE COMMISSION PRIVACY LAW AND POLICY 113 (2016) [hereinafter FTC PRIVACY LAW AND POLICY]; *see also* Joseph Simons, Chairman, Fed. Trade Comm'n, Federal Trade Commission: Protecting Consumers and Fostering Competition in the 21st Century, Statement Before the Committee on Appropriations, Subcommittee on Financial Services and General Government, United States House of Representatives, at 7 (Sept. 25, 2019), www.ftc.gov /system/files/documents/public_statements/1545285/appropriations_committee_testimony_092519 .pdf [hereinafter Protecting Consumers and Fostering Competition] (noting that "[f]or example, Section 5 [of the FTCA] does not allow the Commission to seek civil penalties for the first offense").

[13] DANIEL J. SOLOVE & PAUL M. SCHWARTZ , CONSUMER PRIVACY AND DATA PROTECTION 161 (2015) ("The FTC lacks practical rulemaking authority."); *see also* HOOFNAGLE, FTC PRIVACY LAW AND POLICY, *supra* note 12, at 334 ("The Magnuson-Moss Warranty Act stripped the FTC of ordinary rule-making procedures, putting in its place a system for promulgating rules that is unwieldy and time consuming.").

[14] FTC v. AT&T Mobility LLC, 883 F.3d 848, 850 (9th Cir. 2018) (finding that common carriers are excluded "from FTC regulation only to the extent that a common carrier is engaging in common-carrier services").

[15] Solove & Hartzog, *New Common Law*, *supra* note 2, at 598.

[16] *Id.* at 589–99, 604; HOOFNAGLE, FTC PRIVACY LAW AND POLICY, *supra* note 12, at 175 ("Self-regulation is a form of governance where businesses themselves define the rules and their scope, and are entrusted with their enforcement."); *see also* Ira S. Rubinstein, *Privacy and Regulatory Innovation: Moving Beyond Voluntary Codes*, 6 I/S: J.L. & POL'Y 355, 356 (2011), www.ftc.gov/sites/default/files/documents/public_ comments/privacy-roundtables-comment-project-no.p095416-544506-00103/544506-00103.pdf ("Privacy self-regulation generally involves a trade association or group of firms establishing substantive rules concerning the collection, use and transfer of personal information and procedures for applying these rules to member firms.").

[17] Florencia Marotta-Wurgler, *Self-Regulation and Competition in Privacy Policies*, 45 J. LEGAL STUD. S13, S13 (2016) (a study of privacy policies finding that "[o]verall privacy policy content appears to be shaped at least as much by market forces as by a self-regulatory regime based on external guidelines"); *see also* HOOFNAGLE, FTC PRIVACY LAW AND POLICY, *supra* note 12 at 177–80 (discussing various self-regulatory guidelines, including privacy seal programs and FTC enforcement actions against privacy seal companies).

[18] Solove & Hartzog, *New Common Law*, *supra* note 2, at 592.

adequately safeguard consumer interests.[19] Recognizing these limitations as well as statutory inadequacies, the FTC has urged Congress to adopt comprehensive privacy and security legislation that would grant the FTC enforcement authority and the capacity to immediately issue civil penalties.[20] The FTC has encouraged "security by design," and pursued several companies in the IoT space for security and privacy violations, including Tapplock, Trendet, Vtech, Vizio, D-Link, and ASUS.[21] The FTC has also pursued privacy certifications and privacy seal programs through its deception enforcement authority.[22] However, the FTC's approach to protecting consumer privacy and security also relies heavily on notice and choice.[23]

Many of the cases that the FTC has brought against companies under its deception authority focus on reneged security and privacy pledges, illusory practices that entice consumers into disclosing their data, and insufficient notice of privacy practices.[24] In deception cases the FTC also considers companies' dealings with consumers, including whether any provided representations and statements (including qualifying communications) are clear and unambiguous, and whether consumers' interpretations or reactions to companies' practices are reasonable.[25]

In evaluating whether companies' privacy and cybersecurity practices are unfair, the FTC considers the extent to which a company's actions are unethical, whether consumers will suffer substantial injury in comparison to any potential benefits, and whether any related injuries could have been avoided.[26] The FTC has used its

---

[19]   *See generally*, Fed. Trade Comm'n, PRIVACY ONLINE: A REPORT TO CONGRESS (1998), www.ftc.gov/sites/ default/files/documents/reports/privacy-online-report-congress/priv-23a.pdf; FED. TRADE COMM'N, PRIVACY ONLINE: FAIR INFORMATION PRACTICES IN THE ELECTRONIC MARKETPLACE: A REPORT TO CONGRESS, at i–ii (2000), www.ftc.gov/sites/default/files/documents/reports/privacy-online-fair-information-practices-electronic-marketplace-federal-trade-commission-report/privacy2000text.pdf.

[20]   *See id.*; Simons, Protecting Consumers and Fostering Competition, *supra* note 12.

[21]   *See* Fed. Trade Comm'n, Bureau of Consumer Protection, Comments Before the Consumer Product Safety Comm'n (June 15, 2018), www.ftc.gov/system/files/documents/advocacy_documents/comment-staff-federal-trade-commissions-bureau-consumer-protection-consumer-product-safety /p185404_ftc_staff_comment_to_the_consumer_product_safety_commission.pdf [hereinafter FTC Comments Before the CPSC]; Press Release, Fed. Trade Comm'n, D-Link Agrees to Make Security Enhancements to Settle FTC Litigation (July 2, 2019), www.ftc.gov/news-events/press-releases/2019/07/ d-link-agrees-make-security-enhancements-settle-ftc-litigation; Press Release, Fed. Trade Comm'n, Tapplock Settlement: Smart Devices Need Smart Security (Apr. 6, 2020), www.ftc.gov/news-events /blogs/business-blog/2020/04/tapplock-settlement-smart-devices-need-smart-security.

[22]   HOOFNAGLE, FTC PRIVACY LAW AND POLICY, *supra* note 12at 177–80.

[23]   Memorandum from Schwartz & Solove, *supra* note 5.

[24]   *See* Woodrow Hartzog & Daniel J. Solove, *The Scope and Potential of FTC Data Protection*, 83 GEO. WASH. L. REV. 2230, 2233–47 (2015) [hereinafter *FTC Data Protection*].

[25]   *See* Stacy-Ann Elvy, *Paying for Privacy and the Personal Data Economy*, 117 COLUM. L. REV. 1369, 1432 (2017); *see also* HOOFNAGLE, FTC PRIVACY LAW AND POLICY, *supra* note 12, at 125; Letter from James C. Miller III, Chairman, Fed. Trade Comm'n, to John D. Dingell, Chairman, Comm. on Energy & Commerce U.S. House of Representatives (Oct. 14, 1983), www.ftc.gov/system/files/documents/pub lic_statements/410531/831014deceptionstmt.pdf [hereinafter FTC Policy Statement on Deception].

[26]   Letter from Michael Pertschuk, Chairman, Comm'rs, Fed. Trade Comm'n., to Wendell H. Ford, Chairman, Senate Consumer Subcomm. on Commerce, Sci. & Transp., & John C. Danforth, Ranking Minority Member, Senate Consumer Subcomm. on Commerce, Sci. & Transp. (Dec. 17,

unfairness authority to tackle several types of cases, including retroactive amendments to companies' privacy policies, dishonest consumer data collection and use, "unfair design," and unfair cybersecurity practices.[27] In connection with several of its cybersecurity enforcement actions against companies, the FTC has noted that consumer data would have been more adequately protected if the organization had adopted the NIST voluntary cybersecurity framework.[28]

The FTC's exercise of its deception and unfairness power is hampered by its overreliance on the notice and choice model, the deficiencies of which privacy law scholars have emphasized for some time.[29] Companies have significant control over how our dealings with them are structured and have sole control of the representations, disclosures, and statements that they make to us. Overreliance on the purported sufficiency of the notice and representations that companies make in their entire dealings and statements with us allows companies to continue to be the primary arbiters of what happens to our data. Even the FTC's enforcement actions against IoT companies have relied in part on the express and implicit promises that companies make to us.[30]

The FTC's 2015 IoT guidelines also reflect the FTC's recommendation that companies continue to primarily rely on notice and choice.[31] Recent indications by the FTC suggest that outdated notions of notice and choice will continue to be instrumental in the FTC's recommendations and enforcement actions. For instance, in response to a request for comments by the Consumer Product Safety

---

1980), www.ftc.gov/public-statements/1980/12/ftc-policy-statement-unfairness [hereinafter FTC Policy Statement on Unfairness] (describing "three factors" to evaluate the unfairness of a practice: "(1) whether the practice injures consumers; (2) whether it violates established public policy; and (3) whether [the conduct] is unethical or unscrupulous").

27 Solove & Hartzog, *New Common Law, supra* note 2, at 640.

28 *See* Andrea Arias, *The NIST Cybersecurity Framework and the FTC*, FED. TRADE COMM'N (Aug. 31, 2016, 2:34 PM), www.ftc.gov/news-events/blogs/business-blog/2016/08/nist-cybersecurity-framework-ftc.

29 *See, e.g.,* Fred H. Cate, *The Failure of Fair Information Practice Principles, in* CONSUMER PROTECTION IN THE AGE OF THE "INFORMATION ECONOMY" 341, 341 (Jane K. Winn ed., 2006); Kirsten E. Martin, *Privacy Notices as Tabula Rasa: An Empirical Investigation into How Complying with a Privacy Notice Is Related to Meeting Privacy Expectations Online*, 34 J. PUB. POL'Y & MARKETING 210, 211 (2015); Helen Nissenbaum, *A Contextual Approach to Privacy Online*, 140 DÆDALUS J. AM. ACAD. ARTS & SCI. 32, 34–35 (2011).

30 *See, e.g.,* Complaint, U.S. v. VTech Elecs. Ltd., No. 1:18-cv-114 (N.D. Ill. 2018), www.ftc.gov/enforcement/cases-proceedings/162-3032/vtech-electronics-limited; Complaint, Fed. Trade Comm'n v. D-Link Corp., No. 3:17-cv-00039 (N.D. Cal. 2017), www.ftc.gov/system/files/documents/cases/170105_d-link_complaint_and_exhibits.pdf; Complaint, *In re* TRENDnet, Inc., No. C-4426 (F.T.C. Jan. 16, 2014), www.ftc.gov/enforcement/cases-proceedings/122-3090/trendnet-inc-matter.

31 FED. TRADE COMM'N, INTERNET OF THINGS: PRIVACY & SECURITY IN A CONNECTED WORLD, v (2015) [hereinafter FTC IoT REPORT], www.ftc.gov/system/files/documents/reports/federal-trade-commission-staff-report-november-2013-workshop-entitled-internet-things-privacy/150127iotrpt.pdf (stating that the "staff believes that providing notice and choice remains important" in the IoT setting); *see also* FED. TRADE COMM'N, CAREFUL CONNECTIONS: BUILDING SECURITY IN THE INTERNET OF THINGS 6, 9 (2015), www.ftc.gov/system/files/documents/plain-language/pdf0199-carefulconnections-buildingsecurityinternetofthings.pdf (recommending that IoT device manufacturers provide notice to consumers about security features).

Commission (CPSC) about IoT safety issues, the FTC recommended that the CPSC consider obligating IoT manufacturers to publicly disclose their adherence to any standards adopted by the CPSC.[32] According to the FTC's comment, the goal of mandating such a disclosure would be to enable consumers to more effectively evaluate the privacy and cybersecurity features of IoT products, while allowing the FTC to take action against companies that misrepresent their adherence to the CPSC's standard.

Companies use their privacy policies to attempt to immunize themselves from liability, force us to consent to their data practices, and grant themselves the power to transfer, disclose, and manipulate our data. Overreliance on notice and choice also ignores the plethora of research about our lack of understanding about companies' data practices and privacy and cybersecurity disclosures.[33] A 2019 report by the Pew Research Center found that only 9 percent of respondents consistently read privacy policies before consenting to them and 63 percent of respondents had very little understanding of existing privacy laws and regulations.[34] Despite the prevalence of privacy policies, the Pew survey also found that 59 percent of respondents had very little understanding about how companies use their data.[35] Daniel Solove and Woodrow Hartzog have observed that the FTC "has not followed the empirical evidence [regarding consumers' failure to review or comprehend privacy policies] to the fullest extent."[36] In its 2015 IoT guidelines, the FTC not only recommended notice and choice in the IoT context, but it also indicated that data uses that are consistent with consumers' reasonable expectations do not require notice and choice.[37] These recommendations appear to have been provided without effectively considering and addressing the empirical evidence mentioned earlier about consumers' understanding of privacy policies and related issues. Also, recall the recent empirical study of companies' use of paid mobile apps discussed in Chapter 1. Not only did the study find that respondents erroneously believed that they could receive more privacy and cybersecurity protection if they purchased mobile apps rather than using the free versions of apps, but it also found that "there was no obvious way for

---

[32]   *See* FTC Comments Before the CPSC, *supra* note 21.

[33]   *See* Aleecia M. McDonald & Lorrie Faith Cranor, *The Cost of Reading Privacy Policies*, 4 J.L. & Pol'y for Info. Soc'y 543, 544, 566 (2008) (critiquing the effectiveness of the notice and choice model and discussing lack of consumer understanding of privacy policies); *see also* Martin, *supra* note 29, at 210 (contending that consumers "perceive[] the privacy notice as offering greater protections than the actual privacy notice").

[34]   Brooke Auxier et al., *Americans and Privacy: Concerned, Confused and Feeling Lack of Control over Their Personal Information*, Pew Res. Ctr. (Nov. 15, 2019), www.pewresearch.org/internet/2019/11/15/americans-and-privacy-concerned-confused-and-feeling-lack-of-control-over-their-personal-information/.

[35]   *Id.*

[36]   Solove & Hartzog, *New Common Law*, *supra* note 2, at 667–68 (contending that the FTC's deception authority should evolve to evaluate "the effect of particular practices on consumers with flawed assumptions and cognitive biases").

[37]   *See* FTC IoT Report, *supra* note 31.

a consumer to understand when paying for an app was likely to lead to better privacy and when it was not."[38]

In exercising its deception jurisdiction, the FTC has stated that an alleged deceptive "representation, omission or practice must be likely to mislead reasonable consumers under the circumstances."[39] The FTC's interpretation of its deception authority "is a self-imposed and voluntary restriction on the FTC's powers."[40] As Chris Hoofnagle notes, the FTCA is not restricted by a "reasonable person standard" and historically "lower standards were applied."[41] This focus on the reasonable expectations, interpretations, and reactions of consumers to a practice is inadequate in the IoT setting. Technology companies have tremendous power to impact reasonable interpretations of their practices by controlling and influencing our expectations, interpretations, and reactions. As Nancy Kim and Jeremy Telman have observed, technology companies already use "shaming and blaming" techniques to influence our decisions and to impact our privacy expectations.[42] By invading and colonizing traditionally private spaces, companies will have ever-increasing access to intimate information about us, including biometric, psychological, and other types of health-related data. The vast mountains of data the IoT generates will allow companies to expand their influence over us. Companies can easily analyze IoT data to generate new methods to groom us and to lower our expectations about privacy and cybersecurity, as well as control our interpretations and reactions to their representations and practices. If left unchecked, companies will wield significant power over how we respond and react to their practices.

Our privacy and security choices and expectations can also be influenced by the perceived trustworthiness of companies' services and products.[43] Increasingly, the IoT space is becoming dominated by large household names, such as Amazon and Google, and even ISPs are entering the IoT arena. For some consumers, these well-known and reputable companies may be more likely to elicit trust and thus consent to their data practices – in comparison to smaller and less well-known IoT brands. Even if some groups of consumers elect to use IoT devices manufactured by smaller companies, these smaller organizations may also utilize the IoT cloud and support services offered by larger companies, such as AWS. A single IoT device can contact and share data with multiple parties other than the manufacturer.[44] At least one

---

[38] Kenneth A. Bamberger et al., *Can You Pay for Privacy? Consumer Expectations and the Behavior of Free and Paid Apps*, 35 BERKELEY TECH. L.J. 327, 354 (2020).

[39] FTC Policy Statement on Deception, *supra* note 25.

[40] *See* Elvy, *supra* note 25, at 1432 n.288 (citing HOOFNAGLE, FTC PRIVACY LAW AND POLICY, *supra* note 12, at 122–23).

[41] HOOFNAGLE, FTC PRIVACY LAW AND POLICY, *supra* note 12, at 125.

[42] Nancy S. Kim & D. A. Jeremy Telman, *Internet Giants as Quasi-Governmental Actors and the Limits of Contractual Consent*, 80 MO. L. REV. 723, 736 (2015).

[43] Bamberger et al., *supra* note 38 at 358.

[44] Jingjing Ren et al., *Information Exposure from Consumer IoT Devices: A Multidimensional, Network-Informed Measurement Approach*, MON(IOT)R RES. GROUP (2019), https://moniotrlab.ccis.neu.edu /wp-content/uploads/2019/09/ren-imc19.pdf.

study of IoT devices found that companies that provide third-party services to support IoT devices can obtain detailed information about the devices in our homes and how we use them.[45] These data can be used to influence our privacy and cybersecurity expectations. Large IoT companies, such as Amazon, that provide IoT support and compatible platforms could also obtain IoT data even when consumers purchase IoT products manufactured by smaller companies. Additionally, as we will discuss in Chapter 7, technology giants can obtain our IoT data by acquiring smaller IoT companies. All of this works to extend the influence and power of large technology companies over us and our privacy and cybersecurity decisions, thereby undermining our autonomy. It is unclear whether the FTC will adequately take into account these concerns in exercising its deception and unfairness authority in the IoT setting. The FTC must more effectively consider companies' ability to groom our privacy and cybersecurity expectations.

Narrow views of consumer injury could also hamper the FTC's ability to sufficiently address privacy and cybersecurity harms. Although the FTC has in some cases focused on reputational and unwanted intrusion injuries, the FTC has also suggested that it is primarily concerned with remedying traditional injuries, such as financial, health, or safety harms.[46] Recall from our standing discussion in Chapter 2 that a narrow focus on traditional harms cannot adequately account for intangible harms in the IoT space.

Unequal access to privacy also does not fit squarely within existing FTC theories of unfair and deceptive trade practices.[47] For example, claims associated with insufficient cybersecurity standards, unfulfilled privacy policy promises, and

---

[45] *See id.*

[46] *See, e.g.,* Allison Grande, *Biz Groups Push FTC to Avoid "Theoretical" Privacy Harms,* LAW360 (Nov. 1, 2017, 9:06 PM), www.law360.com/articles/980724/biz-groups-push-ftc-to-avoid-theoretical-privacy-harms (noting that the former Acting Chair of the FTC has "repeatedly stress[ed] in recent remarks that her focus would be on concrete financial injury, health and safety injury, and broken privacy and data security promises"); Maureen K. Ohlhausen, Acting Chair, Fed. Trade Comm'n, Painting the Privacy Landscape: Informational Injury in FTC Privacy and Data Security Cases (Sept. 19, 2017), www.ftc.gov /system/files/documents/public_statements/1255113/privacy_speech_mkohlhausen.pdf (suggesting that other types of consumer injuries may be relevant under the FTC's authority, including "unwarranted intrusion injury" and "reputational injury," but noting that the FTC has "never brought an unfairness case based solely on reputational injury ... [however] in some of [the FTC's] deception cases, the effect on reputation is part of why a deceptive claim is material to consumers."); Fed. Trade Comm'n v. Eli Lilly and Co., No. 012-3214 (Fed. Trade Comm'n May 8, 2002), www.ftc.gov/enforcement/cases-proceedings /012-3214/eli-lilly-company-matter; Fed. Trade Comm'n v. Ruby Corp., No. 1:16-cv-02438 (D.D.C. 2016), www.ftc.gov/system/files/documents/cases/161214ashleymadisoncmplt1.pdf; TRENDnet, Inc., No. C-4426 (Fed. Trade Comm'n Jan. 16, 2014) (complaint), www.ftc.gov/enforcement/cases-proceedings/122-3090/ trendnet-inc-matter; *FTC Hearing 1: Session 3 The Regulation of Consumer Data,* FED. TRADE COMM'N (Sept. 14, 2018), www.ftc.gov/news-events/audio-video/video/ftc-hearing-1-competition-consumer-protection-21st-century-session-3; Press Release, Fed. Trade Comm'n, Aaron's Rent-To-Own Chain Settles FTC Charges that It Enabled Computer Spying by Franchisees (Oct. 22, 2013), www.ftc.gov/news-events/press-releases/2013/10/aarons-rent-own-chain-settles-ftc-charges-it-enabled-computer.

[47] *See* Solove & Hartzog, *New Common Law, supra* note 2, at 640 (discussing FTC unfair and deceptive trade practice theories).

retroactive amendments to privacy policies or settings that were made without sufficient notice and consent do not squarely address a central concern related to unequal access to privacy: that, because of social and economic circumstances and companies' use of data business models that enable widespread data collection, some of us will receive less privacy and cybersecurity protection than others. Notice and choice cannot remedy this concern. Although unequal access to privacy presents a significant societal harm, it may be beyond the current objective of the FTC.

In addition to the FTCA, the FTC is also responsible for enforcing several other statutes, including the Children's Online Privacy Protection Act (COPPA). COPPA is the primary federal statute that protects children's privacy. IoT companies that offer children products and services online are frequently subject to COPPA's requirements. Under COPPA's framework covered operators "cannot condition a child's participation in a game or prize offering on the child's disclosing more information than is reasonably necessary to participate in those activities."[48] Additionally, the FTC has indicated that under COPPA's framework, covered entities must retain children's covered data only for the duration of time necessary to complete the initial purpose for collection and companies should use reasonable practices to delete children's data.[49]

The FTC has taken action when companies inaccurately communicate their participation in COPPA self-regulatory programs to the public. In 2020, the FTC took action against Miniclip S.A. for misrepresenting its participation in a COPPA Safe Harbor program operated by the Children's Advertising Review Unit, "an investigative division of the advertising industry's system of self-regulation."[50] The FTC also approves COPPA Safe Harbor Programs.[51]

The COPPA framework is beset by several limitations, which severely restrict the FTC's ability to remedy the privacy concerns children will face in the IoT setting. COPPA applies only to children under the age of thirteen.[52] Children above the statutory age limit do not receive COPPA's limited protections. The statute also does not apply to data about children submitted by adults. This means that COPPA's protections are not applicable when a parent provides data about their child by using

[48] *Complying with COPPA: Frequently Asked Questions*, FTC, www.ftc.gov/tips-advice/business-center /guidance/complying-coppa-frequently-asked-questions (last visited Mar. 5, 2020).

[49] *Id.*

[50] U.S. Fed. Trade Comm'n, Statement of Commissioner Rohit Chopra Regarding Miniclip and the COPPA Safe Harbors Commission File No. 1923129 (May 18, 2020) www.ftc.gov/system/files/docu ments/public_statements/1575579/192_3129_miniclip_-_statement_of_cmr_chopra.pdf; *The Children's Advertising Review Unit (CARU)*, Better Bus. Bureau Nat'l Programs, https://bbbprograms.org /programs/all-programs/caru/CARU-COPPA-safe-harbor (last visited May 19, 2020).

[51] Statement of Commissioner Rohit Chopra, *supra* note 50.

[52] 15 U.S.C. § 6501(1) (2019); *see also* Paul M. Schwartz & Daniel J. Solove, *The PII Problem: Privacy and a New Concept of Personally Identifiable Information*, 86 N.Y.U. L. Rev. 1814, 1891–92 (2011) [hereinafter *The PII Problem*] (noting limitations of the COPPA framework, and that it applies only to children under the age of thirteen).

an IoT device, or when a parent submits child-related data for the purpose of participating in a PDE monetization program as discussed in Chapter 1.

Like other US privacy laws, COPPA is also hampered by a flawed overreliance on the notice and choice model.[53] Companies are required to provide direct notices to parents and post policies on their websites describing the types of information that the business collects and how the company will use and disclose the information.[54] Companies should obtain "verifiable parental consent" to collect, use, or disclose the data of children.[55] As we have discussed, consumers frequently do not read or understand privacy policies, and this practice may continue even though parental consent is received.[56] The COPPA third-party privacy self-regulatory programs can also obscure companies' actions on privacy-related issues, such as COPPA Safe Harbor performance.[57] These programs are given "lifetime approval," but instead should be subject to detailed frequent FTC review and Commission votes for continued accreditation.[58]

REGULATING ISPs

The American sectoral approach to privacy facilitates jurisdictional gaps. Under this sectoral approach, various laws and regulatory authorities govern distinct industries.[59] If the power of one regulatory body is restricted or if an agency fails to effectively govern an industry, regulatory holes can appear. The Congressional dismantling of the FCC's broadband privacy rules and the reversal of the classification of "broadband as a common carrier" service are perfect examples of these regulatory deficiencies.[60]

---

[53] *See* HOOFNAGLE, FTC PRIVACY LAW AND POLICY, *supra* note 12, at 202–08 (discussing COPPA's notice-and-choice framework). The FTC's enforcement of COPPA has also been criticized. *See generally* Angela J. Campbell, *Rethinking Children's Advertising Policies for the Digital Age*, 29 LOY. CONSUMER L. REV. 1, 21–35 (2016).

[54] *See* 15 U.S.C. § 6502(b)(1)(A)(i) (1998); 16 C.F.R. §§ 312.4(b)–(c) (2013); 16 C.F.R. § 312.4(d) (2013); HOOFNAGLE, FTC PRIVACY LAW AND POLICY, *supra* note 12, at 203 ("COPPA's notice requirements include a duty to provide a general privacy notice as well as special, direct notices to parents before the service collects information from children."); Elvy, *supra* note 25, at 1432–33.

[55] 15 U.S.C. § 6502(b)(1)(A)(ii) (1998); 16 C.F.R. § 312.5 (2013) (discussing parental consent and exceptions); *see also* Children's Online Privacy Protection Rule, 16 C.F.R. § 312.8 (2013) (noting that operators "must establish and maintain reasonable procedures to protect the confidentiality, security, and integrity of personal information collected from children").

[56] Under the COPPA framework, the mechanism used to obtain parental consent should be "reasonably calculated, in light of available technology, to ensure that the person providing consent is the child's parent." 16 C.F.R. § 312.5(b) (2013); see also HOOFNAGLE, FTC PRIVACY LAW AND POLICY, *supra* note 12, at 203–04 (discussing various ways to obtain parental consent).

[57] STATEMENT OF COMMISSIONER ROHIT CHOPRA, *supra* note 50.

[58] *Id.*; Allison Grande, *FTC Dem Says Kids' Privacy Programs Need More Scrutiny*, LAW360 (May 19, 2020, 9:29 PM) www.law360.com/articles/1275121/ftc-dem-says-kids-privacy-programs-need-more-scrutiny.

[59] Elvy, *supra* note 25, at 1429; *see also* Hartzog & Solove, *FTC Data Protection*, *supra* note 24, at 2267.

[60] Elvy, *supra* note 25, at 1373–74; 1430.

Recall from Chapter 1 that ISPs will also be beneficiaries of the widespread proliferation of IoT devices and the corporate infiltration of our private spaces. The FCC unsuccessfully attempted to regulate ISPs' ability to collect and share our geo-location, browsing history, "app usage history," and other types of data through the adoption of a specific set of privacy rules (FCC Privacy Rules).[61] These Obama-era privacy and cybersecurity rules would have imposed various restrictions on ISPs' use of PFP discount plans.[62] The rules also prohibited broadband internet access service providers from denying service to consumers who refused to waive their privacy rights.[63] Congress repealed the FCC Privacy Rules, which curtailed the FCC's ability to unilaterally adopt similar rules.[64] Although the rules would not have been a panacea for all ISP-related privacy issues, the rules were a step in the right direction. The rules were also intended to "give consumers the tools they need to choose how their [ISPs] use and share their personal data."[65] Forrester, a research and consulting firm, predicts that the repeal of the FCC's Privacy Rules will spell an eventual return of PFP ISP offerings.[66]

To date, it is unclear whether state laws in this area can effectively fill the gaps left open by the Congressional repeal of the FCC's Privacy Rules. A Maine statute adopted in 2019 restricts ISPs' use of PFP discount programs and prohibits ISPs from refusing to serve consumers who do not consent to the sale or disclosure of their data, among other things.[67] Several ISP trade groups have filed a lawsuit attacking the validity of the Maine statute.[68] These entities allege that several of the Maine statute's prohibitions and requirements violate the First Amendment and other

---

[61] *See Fact Sheet: The FCC Adopts Order to Give Broadband Consumers Increased Choice over Their Personal Information*, FED. COMM. COMMISSION, http://apps.fcc.gov/edocs_public/attachmatch/DOC-341938A1.pdf [hereinafter *FCC Fact Sheet*].

[62] *See* Protecting the Privacy of Customers of Broadband and Other Telecommunications Services, 81 Fed. Reg. 87,274 (Dec. 2, 2016) (to be codified at 47 C.F.R. pt. 64), *repealed by* Act of Apr. 3, 2017, Pub. L. No. 115-22, 131 Stat. 88 [hereinafter Customers of Broadband and Telecommunications Services].

[63] *Id.*

[64] *See id.* (providing for congressional disapproval of the FCC's "Protecting the Privacy of Customers of Broadband and Other Telecommunications Services" privacy rule); *see also* 5 U.S.C. § 801(b)(2) (1996) (noting that a rule that is "substantially the same" as an agency rule disapproved under the Congressional Review Act "may not be [re]issued" unless "specifically authorized by a law"); 163 CONG. REC. S1941 (daily ed. Mar. 23, 2017) (statement of Sen. McConnell regarding the Congressional Review Act resolution to disapprove of the FCC privacy rules); Jenna Ebersole, *Trump Signs Bill Nixing FCC's Broadband Privacy Rules*, LAW360 (Apr. 3, 2017, 8:14 PM), www.law360.com/articles/908812/trump-signs-bill-nixing-fcc-s-broadband-privacy-rules.

[65] *FCC Fact Sheet*, *supra* note 61, at 1.

[66] Jeff Dunn, *Trump Just Killed Obama's Internet-Privacy Rules – Here's What That Means for You*, BUS. INSIDER (Apr. 4, 2017, 7:55 AM), www.businessinsider.com/trump-fcc-privacy-rules-repeal-explained-2017-4/#-27.

[67] ME. REV. STAT. ANN. tit. 35, § 9301 (2019).

[68] Christopher Cole, *Internet Providers Sue Maine over Data Privacy Restrictions*, LAW360 (Feb. 18, 2020, 5:51 PM), www.law360.com/articles/1244916/internet-providers-sue-maine-over-data-privacy-restrictions.

constitutional provisions.[69] The lawsuit suggests that ISPs incorrectly believe that they have a First Amendment right to obtain and profit from our data without effective statutory restrictions.

ISPs' potential access to IoT-generated data and their expanded offerings, combined with the repeal of the FCC's Privacy Rules, are even more alarming in light of the FCC's reversal of its net neutrality rules.[70] These rules required equal treatment for all internet traffic.[71] The rules prevented ISPs from engaging in paid prioritization – that is, discriminating against specific types of internet traffic "in exchange for consideration" or to benefit affiliated entities.[72] Subject to a "reasonable network management exception," the rules also prohibited ISPs from throttling or blocking internet traffic.[73] Net neutrality rules hindered companies' ability to impose additional road blocks to access online content. This is significant given that, as the Pew Research Center reports, low-income and minority consumers continue to have "few[er] options for online access."[74] Without net neutrality, even when these groups of consumers obtain access to the Internet, they may face additional obstacles to access online content.[75] Net neutrality is thus a core "civil rights issue of our time."[76]

The FCC justified its net neutrality reversal order by arguing that its order restored the FTC's authority to effectively regulate ISPs.[77] In 2019, the FTC chairman noted that several of the activities that would have been restricted under the repealed net neutrality rules, such as "blocking, throttling, or paid prioritization" would "not be *per se* antitrust violations."[78] The chairman suggested that ISPs could

---

[69] *See* Complaint for Declaratory Judgment and Injunctive Relief, ACA Connects v. Aaron Frey, No. 1:20-cv-00055 (D. Me. Feb. 14, 2020), www.law360.com/articles/1244916/attachments/0 (last visited Feb. 19, 2020).

[70] *See* Restoring Internet Freedom, 83 Fed. Reg. 7,852, 7,852 (Feb. 22, 2018) (codified at 47 C.F.R. pts. 1, 8 & 20); Restoring Internet Freedom, 33 FCC Rcd. 311, 345 (2018).

[71] *See* Protecting and Promoting the Open Internet, 80 Fed. Reg. 19,738, 19,738 (Apr. 13, 2015) (codified at 47 C.F.R. pts. 1, 8 & 20); Protecting and Promoting the Open Internet, 30 FCC Rcd. 5601, 5603 (2015).

[72] Protecting and Promoting the Open Internet, 30 FCC Rcd. at 5608.

[73] *Id.* at 5610, 5651 ("[T]his Order contains an exception for reasonable network management, which applies to all but the paid prioritization rule.").

[74] *See* Aaron Smith, Pew Research Ctr., U.S. Smartphone Use in 2015 (2015), www.pewresearch.org /internet/2015/04/01/us-smartphone-use-in-2015/.

[75] *See* Adam Rhodes, *Activists See Net Neutrality as Civil Rights Battleground*, Law360 (Nov. 16, 2018, 5:45 PM), www.law360.com/articles/1093308/activists-see-net-neutrality-as-civil-rights-battleground; *see also* Olivier Sylvain, *Network Equality*, 67 Hastings L.J. 443, 447 (2016); Michael Copps, *Net Neutrality Is a Civil Rights Issue*, Common Cause (Dec. 5, 2013), www.commoncause.org/democracy-wire/net-neutrality-is-a-civil-rights-issue/.

[76] Rhodes, *supra* note 75; *see also What Is Net Neutrality?*, Am. Civ. Liberties Union, www.aclu.org /issues/free-speech/internet-speech/what-net-neutrality (last updated Dec. 2017).

[77] *See* Restoring Internet Freedom, 33 FCC Rcd. 311, 312 (2018) ("Our balanced approach also restores the authority of the nation's most experienced cop on the privacy beat – the Federal Trade Commission – to police the privacy practices of Internet Service Providers (ISPs).").

[78] Joseph J. Simons, Chairman, Fed. Trade Comm'n, Remarks at Eleventh Annual Telecom Policy Conference (Mar. 26, 2019), www.ftc.gov/system/files/documents/public_statements/1508991/free_sta te_foundation_speech_march_26.pdf.

engage in this behavior as long as they provided notice.[79] However, the FTC's ability and willingness to effectively protect consumers from the privacy-invasive tactics of ISPs is questionable. Former FTC commissioners have criticized the FCC's net neutrality reversal efforts and have argued that the reversal "create[s] an environment where neither the FCC nor FTC [can] protect the privacy of the customers of some of our largest broadband companies."[80] A 2019 study on the impact of net neutrality also challenges the accuracy of one of the FCC's central justifications for the net neutrality rollback – that net neutrality decreased ISPs' infrastructure investments.[81] The study concluded that the adoption of net neutrality rules in 2015 did not impact network investments.[82]

In 2019, the United States Court of Appeals for the District of Columbia Circuit upheld the FCC's reversal of its net neutrality rules, but vacated the portion of the FCC's net neutrality reversal order that prohibited states from adopting their own stringent net neutrality rules.[83] The court's decision has two potential implications. First, with the court's approval of the repeal of the FCC's net neutrality rules, ISPs are more free to engage in blocking and throttling and other types of anti-net neutrality behaviors, although some ISPs may adopt a more cautious approach in light of state statutes addressing net neutrality.[84] Second, even though the court struck down the FCC's efforts to blanketly preempt state net neutrality legislation, the court's decision does not uphold state net neutrality laws. Instead, the validity of state net neutrality laws will have to be litigated on a "case-by-case" basis.[85] This result continues the uncertainty around net neutrality principles and ISPs' privacy and cybersecurity obligations.

Several states, including California and Vermont, have adopted net neutrality rules and at least twenty-nine states have introduced net neutrality bills in previous legislative sessions.[86] California's net neutrality law both incorporates and goes

---

79 *Id.* ("[W]e could take action against ISPs if they block applications without adequately disclosing those practices or mislead consumers about what applications they block or how.").

80 Press Release, Joint Statement of FCC Commissioner Mignon Clyburn and FTC Commissioner Terrell McSweeny on Leaving Broadband Consumers and Competition Unprotected (Apr. 27, 2017), http://apps.fcc.gov/edocs_public/attachmatch/DOC-344627A1.pdf [hereinafter Clyburn & McSweeny Joint Statement].

81 *See* Christopher Alex Hooton, *Testing the Economics of the Net Neutrality Debate*, TELECOMM. POL'Y 3, 17 (2019), https://assets.documentcloud.org/documents/6430695/Net-Neutrality.pdf.

82 *Id.* at 17.

83 Mozilla Corp. v. Fed. Commc'ns Comm'n, 940 F.3d 1, 14 (D.C. Cir. 2019); Hailey Konnath, *DC Circ. Won't Rethink Ruling on Net Neutrality Rollback*, LAW360 (Feb. 6, 2020, 11:40 PM), www.law360.com /articles/1241825/dc-circ-won-t-rethink-ruling-on-net-neutrality-rollback.

84 *See, e.g., Mozilla Corp.*, 940 F.3d at 14 (and consolidated cases).

85 Kelcee Griffis, *Net Neutrality Ruling Leaves States' Roles Unsettled*, LAW360 (Oct. 1, 2019, 10:01 PM), www.law360.com/consumerprotection/articles/1204897/net-neutrality-ruling-leaves-states-roles-unset tled?nl_pk=06d06a2b-64f8-4c4c-b81d-6950221f7573&utm_source=newsletter&utm_medium= email&utm_campaign=consumerprotection.

86 Heather Morton, *Net Neutrality 2019 Legislation*, NAT'L CONF. STATE LEGS. (Oct. 1, 2019), www.ncsl.org /research/telecommunications-and-information-technology/net-neutrality-2019-legislation.aspx.

beyond several of the FCC's net neutrality principles.[87] For example, not only does the statute prohibit blocking and paid prioritization and mandate specific disclosures, but it also contains clear restrictions on zero-rating.[88] Other states have addressed the issue of net neutrality by adopting rules that ban throttling, blocking, and paid prioritizations; prohibiting ISPs that do not adhere to net neutrality principles from receiving state funds and contracts; or establishing a preference for ISPs that do.[89] California and Vermont agreed to suspend enforcement of their net neutrality statutes pending the DC Circuit's decision on the FCC's net neutrality repeal.[90] In light of the court's decision, it is likely that California and Vermont will begin enforcing their net neutrality statutes. California's statute was previously challenged by several ISP trade associations on the grounds that it violated the FCC's net neutrality reversal order and the dormant Commerce Clause of the Constitution, which invalidates laws that disproportionately burden interstate commerce.[91] Despite the robustness of some state net neutrality statutes, these laws may not withstand constitutional challenges and judicial scrutiny. If the patchwork of state net neutrality rules are upheld, unequal access to privacy may become an issue, unless such laws have a permissible extraterritorial reach. Individuals that are residents of states with robust net neutrality rules could receive more protection from ISPs' abusive data practices than those who live in other states that lack such protections.

If net neutrality principles at the state level are insufficient or are challenged and invalidated, ISPs will have the power to determine "the winners and losers" in the IoT world even if they are subject to some level of regulatory and legislative scrutiny.[92] ISPs could become the ultimate beneficiaries of the corporate penetration of our private spaces. ISPs could slow and block IoT traffic at will, while simultaneously collecting reams of IoT data. Consider that Verizon throttled the internet traffic of a California fire department during

---

[87] *See* S.B. 822, 2017-2018 Leg., Reg. Sess. (Cal. 2018).

[88] *See id.; see also* Cal. Civ. Code § 3101 (Deering 2019); Thomas B. Nachbar, *The Peculiar Case of State Network Neutrality Regulation*, 37 Cardozo Arts & Ent. L.J. 659, 667 (2019).

[89] Nachbar, *supra* note 88; Colo. Rev. Stat. Ann. § 40-15-209 (West 2019); Wash. Rev. Code Ann. § 19.385.020 (West 2019).

[90] *See* Complaint, U.S. v. California, No. 2:18-at-01539 (E.D. Cal. 2018); Kelcee Griffis, *California Will Stay Net Neutrality Law Pending DC Circ. Ruling*, Law360 (Oct. 26, 2018, 8:49 PM), www.law360.com /articles/1096271.

[91] *See* Dorothy Atkins, *Broadband Groups Sue to Block Calif. Net Neutrality Law*, Law360 (Oct. 3, 2018, 8:47 PM), www.law360.com/articles/1089130/broadband-groups-sue-to-block-calif-net-neutrality-law; *see also* Complaint, Am. Cable Ass'n v. Becerra, No. 2:18-at-01552 (E.D. Cal. Oct. 3, 2018); Nachbar, *supra* note 88, at 663 (contending that "state network neutrality laws are inherently violative of dormant Commerce Clause restrictions because the markets they actually seek to regulate – content markets – are primarily located outside the relevant states").

[92] Clyburn & McSweeny Joint Statement, *supra* note 80; Klint Finley, *The End of Net Neutrality Could Shackle the Internet of Things*, Wired (June 6, 2017, 7:00 AM), www.wired.com/2017/06/end-net-neutrality-shackle-internet-things/.

wildfires in 2018.[93] Assuming that there are no legal impediments, ISPs could favor the IoT traffic of their paying business partners and of those devices that they directly sell to consumers. Recall from Chapter 1 that ISPs are increasingly participating in the IoT space. Additionally, the mobile apps that consumers use to control and receive alerts from their IoT devices transmit data across the Internet. Internet traffic (including real-time mobile alerts) generated by competing IoT products and services not provided by ISPs as well as companies who are unwilling to pay to use "fast lanes" could be slowed significantly. IoT products and services affiliated with ISPs would be more attractive to consumers. The result is that consumers could be almost required to choose IoT products and services offered by or affiliated with ISPs.

THE CCPA

The CCPA provides California consumers with multiple rights, some of which are akin to those found under the European Union's General Data Protection Regulation (GDPR).[94] The CCPA grants California residents data deletion and data portability rights and the right to obtain certain information about the data covered companies collect about them.[95] The CCPA also provides California residents with the right to opt out of data sales (or opt in in the case of minors and their parents) and the right to obtain non-discriminatory service and pricing when exercising CCPA-granted rights.[96] The statute's definition of personal information includes data that can be reasonably associated with an individual or their household and biometric information.[97] Biometric information is broadly defined to include voice recordings, and health and exercise data that "contain[s] identifying information."[98] The CCPA's definition of personal information suggests that it will also govern certain types of data IoT devices collect.

The CCPA's influence and reach appears to be expanding. As of the date of writing, several state legislatures are considering adopting CCPA-like statutes.[99] In 2019, Nevada adopted an amendment to its privacy statute to provide

---

[93] Jon Brodkin, *Verizon Throttled Fire Department's "Unlimited" Data During Calif. Wildfire*, Ars Technica (Aug. 21, 2018, 12:49 PM), https://arstechnica.com/tech-policy/2018/08/verizon-throttled-fire-departments-unlimited-data-during-calif-wildfire/.

[94] *See* Cal. Civ. Code § 1798.198 (West 2020).

[95] *See id.* §§ 1798.100, 1798.105, 1798.110; Eur. Parl. & Council Regulation 2016/679 of Apr. 27, 2016, Protection of Natural Persons with Regard to the Processing of Personal Data and on the Free Movement of Such Data, and Repealing Directive 95/46/EC, 2016 OJ (L 119) 1, arts. 5, 12–15, 17, 20, 21 [hereinafter GDPR].

[96] Cal. Civ. Code §§ 1798.120, 1798.125, 1798.135.

[97] *Id.* § 1798.140.

[98] *Id.*

[99] Joseph J. Lazzarotti & Jason C. Gavejian, *State Law Developments in Consumer Privacy*, Nat'l L. Rev. (Mar. 15, 2019), www.natlawreview.com/article/state-law-developments-consumer-privacy.

consumers with the ability to opt out of certain data sales by institutions subject to the statute.[100] Although the Nevada statute's definition of a sale appears to be narrower than the California statute and therefore likely covers fewer transactions, the CCPA's influence is clear.[101] Also, consider that after California's adoption of its Online Privacy Protection Act, which required companies to post privacy policies, companies across the nation began to more prominently and frequently display their privacy policies.[102] The CCPA is likely to have a similar nationwide effect. Microsoft has announced plans to comply with the CCPA on a nationwide basis.[103] Additionally, in light of the multiple individual rights established by the CCPA, it has the potential to restrict companies' ability to freely transfer and disclose consumer data. The statute could have a significant and constitutionally permissible impact on technology companies' business models across the United States.[104]

Technology companies' lobbying efforts could successfully curtail the spread of CCPA-like statutes. These firms and the industry trade groups that represent their interests attempted to revise the CCPA to better protect themselves.[105] Technology companies are also proposing their own versions of privacy legislation in other states in order to maintain their business models and the existing overreliance on notice

---

[100] *See* S.B. 220, 2019 Leg., 80th Sess. (Nev. 2019).

[101] *See* CAL. CIV. CODE § 1798.140 (defining a sale as "selling, renting, releasing, disclosing, disseminating, making available, transferring, or otherwise communicating orally, in writing, or by electronic or other means, a consumer's personal information by the business to another business or a third party for monetary or other valuable consideration"); Nev. S.B. 220 (defining a sale as "the exchange of covered information for monetary consideration by the operator to a person for the person to license or sell the covered information to additional persons").

[102] *See* CAL. BUS. & PROF. CODE § 22575(a) (West 2019); *see also* Charlotte A. Tschider, *Regulating the Internet of Things: Discrimination, Privacy, and Cybersecurity in the Artificial Intelligence Age*, 96 DENV. U. L. REV. 87, 114 (2018) ("California's Online Privacy Protection Act of 2003 (CalOPPA) established privacy notice requirements most U.S.-based organizations follow as the most restrictive and prescriptive standard today."); Rich Ehisen, *Golden State Wields 'Stick' with Tough New Regulations. Ohio Takes 'Carrot' Approach.*, NAT'L CONF. STATE LEGS. (Nov. 20, 2018), www.ncsl.org/research/telecommu nications-and-information-technology/data-privacy-california-consumer-regulation.aspx.

[103] Julie Brill, *Microsoft Will Honor California's New Privacy Rights Throughout the United States*, MICROSOFT (Nov. 11, 2019), https://blogs.microsoft.com/on-the-issues/2019/11/11/microsoft-california-privacy-rights/.

[104] *See, e.g.*, Russell Spivak, *Too Big a Fish in the Digital Pond? The California Consumer Privacy Act and the Dormant Commerce Clause*, 88 U. CIN. L. REV. 475 (2020) (discussing the CCPA's impact and explaining why the statute "should survive any Commerce Clause challenge"); Anupam Chander, et al, *Catalyzing Privacy*, MINN. L. REV. (forthcoming), https://papers.ssrn.com/sol3/papers .cfm?abstract_id=3433922 (discussing preemption, dormant commerce clause and First Amendment challenges to the CCPA).

[105] Issie Lapowksy, *Tech Lobbyists Push to Defang California's Landmark Privacy Law*, WIRED (Apr. 4, 2019, 3:09 PM), www.wired.com/story/california-privacy-law-tech-lobby-bills-weaken/; Kartikay Mehrotra et. al, *Google and Other Tech Firms Seek to Weaken Landmark California Data-Privacy Law*, L.A. TIMES (Sept. 4, 2019, 2:32 PM), www.latimes.com/business/story/2019-09-04/google-and-other-tech-companies-attempt-to-water-down-privacy-law.

and choice.[106] In 2020, Washington state unsuccessfully attempted to move in the CCPA's direction. The state's proposed privacy statute was supported by several consumer advocacy groups and appears to have been inspired in part by the CCPA.[107] Technology companies successfully lobbied to block the proposed statute, which could have given consumers a private right of action.[108]

Despite the possible extraterritorial reach of the CCPA, the statute also highlights the uneven nature of privacy protections in the United States. Consider that a 2019 Comparitech ranking of state privacy laws found that California provided the most online privacy protection while Wyoming provided the least.[109] Unless technology companies begin extending CCPA rights to consumers in other states, California's residents will have significantly more privacy protection and rights with respect to their data in comparison to citizens of other states. This raises a significant unequal access to privacy problem. The level of privacy protection consumers receive depends on where they happen to reside. This result is even more problematic when one considers children, who oftentimes have little to no choice over where they reside. The CCPA contains several provisions that are aimed at safeguarding minors' data.[110]

Although the CCPA grants California residents extensive rights and allows them to obtain more control over their data in comparison to residents of other states, the statute's ability to fully remedy all of the IoT-related concerns noted in earlier chapters is questionable. The statute has several shortcomings. Like other privacy statutes, the CCPA's definition of personal information carves out deidentified and aggregated consumer data.[111] As discussed in Chapter 2, there are significant limits to companies' anonymization techniques, and aggregated and anonymized data can be de-anonymized.

As is the case with other privacy laws, the CCPA places the onus on individuals to protect their privacy. For instance, recall that the CCPA requires most consumers to proactively opt out of a data sale. Facebook is currently exploiting perceived

---

[106] Bennett Cyphers et. al, *Tech Lobbyists Are Pushing Bad Privacy Bills*, ELECTRONIC FRONTIER FOUND. (Mar. 6, 2020), www.eff.org/deeplinks/2020/03/tech-lobbyists-are-pushing-bad-privacy-bills-washington-state-can-and-must-do.

[107] Julie Brill, *The New Washington Privacy Act Raises the Bar for Privacy in the United States*, MICROSOFT BLOG (Jan. 24, 2020), https://blogs.microsoft.com/on-the-issues/2020/01/24/washington-privacy-act-protection/. *See generally* COMMONWEALTH OF WASH., PSSB 6281 EFFECT STATEMENT (to be codified at 19 WASH. REV. CODE §§ 1–19, https://app.leg.wa.gov/committeeschedules/Home/Document/209620#toolbar=0&navpanes=0.

[108] *Tech Companies Block Washington State Privacy Bill*, ELECTRONIC PRIVACY INFO. CTR. (Mar. 13, 2020), https://epic.org/2020/03/tech-companies-block-washingto.html; 2019 Legis. Bill Hist. WA S.B. 6281.

[109] *See* Paul Bischoff, *Internet Privacy Laws by State: Which US States Best Protect Privacy Online?*, COMPARITECH, www.comparitech.com/blog/vpn-privacy/which-us-states-best-protect-online-privacy/ (last updated Oct. 23, 2019).

[110] *See e.g.*, CAL. CIV. CODE § 1798.120 (West 2020).

[111] *See* A.B. 874, 2019-2020 Leg., Reg. Sess. (Cal. 2019).

ambiguities in the statute's definition of a sale to avoid compliance.[112] The company erroneously contends that its behavioral advertising practices do not qualify as a sale within the meaning of the statute and that it qualifies for a service provider exception.[113]

The CCPA's definition of a sale also excludes data asset sales in corporate transactions, such as mergers, and bankruptcy proceedings as long as certain notice and disclosure requirements are met.[114] The statute's safeguards for data sales in corporate transactions are inadequate. Prior notice sufficient to allow individuals to exercise their opt-out rights is required, if a third party who obtains consumer data subsequently materially alters the ways in which the data are used in a manner that is inconsistent with "promises made at the time of collection."[115] The efficacy of this qualification is dependent on the terms of a company's privacy policy at the time of the initial data collection. Additionally, the statute's qualification for retroactive unfair and deceptive privacy policy amendments may have little impact. As we will discuss in Chapter 7, companies routinely use their privacy policies to authorize corporate transactions. Privacy policies can be broadly drafted to authorize various anti-consumer data practices. As these terms are quite common in privacy policies, it is unlikely that a company will need to amend its privacy policy to authorize a data transfer as part of a corporate transaction immediately before a deal. With respect to data sales in corporate transactions, it is the language contained in the company's privacy policy that primarily determines the extent of the consumer's rights under the CCPA. Like many statutes before it, the CCPA vests covered companies with significant authority to determine how data is used once it is collected. The CCPA does not prohibit data collection or tracking.

Although the CCPA's protections for minors extend beyond COPPA's limited age range and other provisions, the CCPA authorizes the sale of child data as long as a parent, guardian, or the minor affirmatively consents.[116] As noted earlier, parents and minors under the age of sixteen are also likely to fail to read and understand companies' privacy notices and associated disclosures. These groups of consumers

---

[112] Ben Kochman, *California's New Privacy Law Faces Its First Big Challenge*, LAW360 (Jan. 30, 2020, 12:03 PM), www.law360.com/articles/1238022/california-s-new-privacy-law-faces-its-first-big-challenge; *see also* Patience Haggin, *Facebook Won't Change Web Tracking in Response to California Privacy Law*, WALL ST. J. (Dec. 12, 2019, 1:29 PM), www.wsj.com/articles/facebook-wont-change-web-tracking-in-response-to-california-privacy-law-11576175345.

[113] Kochman, *supra* note 112.

[114] CAL. CIV. CODE § 1798.140 (West 2020).

[115] *Id.*

[116] *Id.* § 1798.120(c) (A "business shall not sell the personal information of consumers if the business has actual knowledge that the consumer is less than 16 years of age, unless the consumer, in the case of consumers at least 13 years of age and less than 16 years of age, or the consumer's parent or guardian, in the case of consumers who are less than 13 years of age, has affirmatively authorized the sale of the consumer's personal information.").

are also not immune to companies' tactics to entice them to trade away rights in their data.

The CCPA's anti-discrimination provisions are unlikely to sufficiently address unequal access to privacy concerns.[117] The statute allows covered companies to freely use financial incentives (such as direct payments) to entice consumers to authorize the collection and sale of their data as long as the financial incentive is not "unjust, unreasonable, coercive, or usurious."[118] Covered entities can also charge different prices and provide goods and services of varying quality as long as the associated price and quality differences are "directly related to the value provided to the [business] by the consumer's data."[119] As of the date of writing, the final text of the CCPA Regulations issued by the California Attorney General (CCPA Regulations) have not yet been approved by the California Office of Administrative Law.[120] However, the CCPA Regulations provide that in determining the value of a consumer's data, a business can consider several factors, including the marginal and average value of the data to the business, revenue from the possible sale of data, and costs related to the sale and retention of the data, among other things.[121] Companies have the power to determine how much our data is worth to them. Under the statute companies can then discriminate and offer different prices and different quality of goods and services based on this value. Data about low-income consumers could be viewed as less valuable than data about more economically successful consumers. Low-income consumers could be more inclined to accept discounts in exchange for their data. They could also receive less of a discount on services and goods, less funds for consenting to the sale of their data or lower-quality goods than other groups of consumers.

The CCPA's approach to financial incentives is far from novel. It is quite similar to and suffers from the same limitations as the FCC's former approach to ISP PFP discount programs. In the repealed FCC Privacy Rules mentioned earlier, the FCC indicated that it would assess the validity of ISPs' financial incentive programs on a "case-by-case basis" and adopted heightened disclosure and choice standards for

---

[117] *Id.* § 1798.125 ("(1) A business shall not discriminate against a consumer because the consumer exercised any of the consumer's rights under this title, including, but not limited to, by: (A) Denying goods or services to the consumer. (B) Charging different prices or rates for goods or services, including through the use of discounts or other benefits or imposing penalties. (C) Providing a different level or quality of goods or services to the consumer. (D) Suggesting that the consumer will receive a different price or rate for goods or services or a different level or quality of goods or services. (2) Nothing in this subdivision prohibits a business from charging a consumer a different price or rate, or from providing a different level or quality of goods or services to the consumer, if that difference is reasonably related to the value provided to the business by the consumer's data.").

[118] Cal. Civ. Code § 1798.125 (West 2020).

[119] *Id.*

[120] Office of the Attorney Gen., California Consumer Privacy Act Regulations: Final Text of Regulations 2, https://oag.ca.gov/sites/all/files/agweb/pdfs/privacy/oal-sub-final-text-of-regs.pdf (last visited Jun. 10, 2020); *Proposed Regulations Package Submitted to OAL*, available at https://oag.ca.gov/privacy/ccpa (last visited Jun. 10, 2020).

[121] Office of the Attorney Gen., *supra* note 120 at 28–29.

such programs.[122] Similarly, the CCPA requires covered institutions to provide additional notice about their financial incentive programs and, like the repealed FCC Privacy Rules, requires consumers to opt in to such programs.[123] Consumers also have the ability to revoke consent to such programs under the CCPA.[124] As consumers, we are inundated daily with a plethora of disclosures and agreements that we are required to review. In a single online transaction, companies can provide us with separate privacy policies, terms and conditions, end-user license agreements, and warranty information for their products and services.[125] Imposing additional or heightened disclosure requirements simply adds to the long list of often incomprehensible documents that we must attempt to review and understand before making an artificial choice. Not surprisingly, as I have mentioned elsewhere in this book, consumers do not often read or understand companies' notices and disclosures.

The lessons learned from one ISP's use of a PFP financial incentive program are telling. After the adoption of its program, the ISP reported that a large segment of its customers chose to participate in the program and relinquished rights in their data in exchange for a monthly discount.[126] Recall from Chapter 1 that those consumers who did not opt in to the PFP discount program had to pay additional monthly fees. These types of offerings can force vulnerable groups of consumers to make difficult choices between privacy and other necessities and they allow companies to transform privacy into a luxury product that can only be afforded by a select group.[127] As one critic of the ISP's PFP discount program observed, "[f]or a struggling family, [the decision to pay to opt out of data sharing] could mean choosing between paying for privacy and paying for groceries or the public transportation needed to get to work."[128] The CCPA's approach to financial incentives creates similar concerns. Consumers often have a difficult time conceptualizing the intangible harms that can result from consenting to companies' data collection practices. Most consumers

---

[122] Customers of Broadband and Telecommunications Services, *supra* note 62, at 87,275, 87,317, 87,346.

[123] *See id.* at 87,275; CIV. § 1798.125.

[124] CIV. § 1798.125.

[125] Stacy-Ann Elvy, *Hybrid Transactions and the INTERNET of Things: Goods, Services, or Software?*, 74 WASH. & LEE L. REV. 77, 95–96 (2017).

[126] Customers of Broadband and Telecommunications Services, *supra* note 62, at 87,316–17.

[127] *See* Letter from Elizabeth Warren, Senator, U.S. Senate, to Tom Wheeler, Chairman, Fed. Commc'n Comm'n (June 21, 2016), https://perma.cc/9WWT-7362; *see also* Marc Rotenberg et al., Elec. Privacy Info. Ctr., Comments Before the Fed. Commc'ns Comm'n on Proposed Rule on Protecting the Privacy of Customers of Broadband and Other Telecommunications Services 25 (May 27, 2016), http://ecfsapi.fcc.gov/file/60002079241.pdf (urging the FCC to prohibit PFP offerings as "[f]inancial pressures reduce the voluntariness of consumer consent").

[128] Sandra Fulton, *Pay-for-Privacy Schemes Put the Most Vulnerable Americans at Risk*, Free Press (May 10, 2016), www.freepress.net/blog/2016/05/10/pay-privacy-schemes-put-most-vulnerable-americans-risk; *see also* Customers of Broadband and Telecommunications Services, *supra* note 62, at 87,274 ("Thirty-eight public interest organizations expressed concern that financial incentives can result in consumers paying up to $ 800 per year – $62 per month – for plans that protect their privacy.").

are likely to opt in to a financial incentive program that provides a monthly discount. Even if data about low-income and indigent consumers may be worth less than data about wealthier consumers, cheaper products and services are still likely to have significantly more appeal to low-income and cash-strapped consumers. These groups of consumers may be more likely to trade in their privacy for a financial incentive program even if they receive less of a discount or a lower-quality product than their wealthier counterparts. The CCPA's authorization of financial incentive programs also does not sufficiently account for the ways in which companies can use data about us to influence our decisions to consent to their data practices.

DATA BROKER LEGISLATION

Recall from Chapter 1 that data brokers (both modern and traditional) could obtain access to the vast quantities of data that we generate from our use of IoT devices. These entities will also be beneficiaries of the corporate colonization of our private spaces in the IoT setting. The FTC has called on Congress to adopt legislation to specifically govern the activities of data brokers and "to give consumers greater control over the immense amounts of personal information about them collected and shared by data brokers."[129] While Congress has yet to act on the FTC's recommendation, Vermont and California have passed legislation that specifically regulates data brokers' activities.[130]

The CCPA's text indicates that the data opt-out provisions are applicable to data brokers (companies that do not have a direct relationship with us, but that obtain our data from other businesses rather than directly from us).[131] The CCPA Regulations also indicate that the statutory data opt-out right applies to data brokers.[132] In 2019,

---

[129] Press Release, Fed. Trade Comm'n, FTC Recommends Congress Require the Data Broker Industry to be More Transparent and Give Consumers Greater Control over Their Personal Information (May 27, 2014), www.ftc.gov/news-events/press-releases/2014/05/ftc-recommends-congress-require-data-broker-industry-be-more; *see also* Fed. Trade Comm'n, Protecting Consumer Privacy in an Era of Rapid Change 11–12 (2012), www.ftc.gov/sites/default/files/documents/reports/federal-trade-commission-report-protecting-consumer-privacy-era-rapid-change-recommendations/120326priva cyreport.pdf (discussing data brokers and noting that "self-regulation has not gone far enough").

[130] *See* 9 Vt. Stat. Ann. §§ 2430, 2433, 2446, 2447 (West 2020); A.B. 1202, 2019 Leg., Reg. Sess. (Cal. 2019). A federal bill to address data brokers has been introduced but has not yet been adopted. *See* Data Broker List Act of 2019, S. 2342, 116th Cong. (2019), www.congress.gov/bill/116th-congress/senate-bill /2342?s=1&r=5.

[131] Cal. Civ. Code § 1798.115 (West 2020) ("A third party shall not sell personal information about a consumer that has been sold to the third party by a business unless the consumer has received explicit notice and is provided an opportunity to exercise the right to opt-out pursuant to Section 1798.120.")

[132] Office of the Attorney Gen., *supra* note 120, at 6 ("A data broker registered with the Attorney General pursuant to Civil Code section 1798.99.80 *et seq.* does not need to provide a notice at collection to the consumer if it has included in its registration submission a link to its online privacy policy that includes instructions on how a consumer can submit a request to opt-out.").

California also enacted additional provisions directly applicable to data brokers.[133] Covered institutions are required to register annually with the state and provide their contact information and any other types of information they choose to disclose.[134] The Vermont statute contains more detailed registration requirements. The Vermont statute requires data brokers that are subject to the Act to register with the Secretary of State yearly and provide the data broker's contact information as well as other types of information, including the types of data collection practices that consumers can and cannot opt out of and methods for exercising any such opt-out rights.[135] The statute also requires data brokers to adopt comprehensive cybersecurity standards to protect consumer data and provide information on the number of cybersecurity breaches.[136]

The Vermont statute has several shortcomings. The statute does not clearly require data brokers to provide consumers with the option to opt out of data sales, collection, or disclosures. Consumers are also not given the ability to request access to the information that data brokers collect about them or discover the identities of entities buying their data. Despite the statute's reference to "unique biometric data" and data that could lead to the reasonable identification of a person, it is not entirely clear whether the definition of "brokered personal information" also covers the various types of data IoT devices collect, such as sleep patterns and other types of health-related data.[137] Further, the statute imposes only negligible civil penalties for data broker registration violations.

Lastly, although the Vermont statute prohibits persons from acquiring covered data for purposes of fraud or harassment, it does not require data brokers to implement procedures to ensure that Vermont citizens' data are not disclosed to scammers or other third parties with dubious intentions.[138] Instead, the statute simply requires that data brokers disclose whether they have adopted such procedures. In practice, the Vermont statute's effectiveness may be questionable. Not all data brokers have complied with the statute's registration requirements. Many data brokers have failed to provide the detailed information required about their data collection practices.[139]

---

[133]   *See* Civ. §§ 1798.99.80–88; Allison Grande, *Modest Calif. Privacy Law Changes Leave Cos. Eyeing 2020*, Law360 (Oct. 3, 2019, 8:51 PM), www.law360.com/articles/1204190/modest-calif-privacy-law-changes-leave-cos-eyeing-2020; Shalin R. Sood et al., *CCPA and California's New Registration Requirement*, Nat'l L. Rev. (Sept. 16, 2019), www.natlawreview.com/article/ccpa-and-california-s-new-registration-requirement.

[134]   Civ. §§ 1798.99.80–88.

[135]   9 Vt. Stat. Ann. § 2446 (West 2019); *see also* Vt. Office of the Attorney Gen., Guidance on Vermont's Act 171 of 2018: Data Broker Regulation 6 (2018), https://ago.vermont.gov/wp-content/uploads/2018/12/2018-12-11-VT-Data-Broker-Regulation-Guidance.pdf.

[136]   Vt. § 2447.

[137]   *See id.* § 2430(1)(A) (West 2020).

[138]   *See id.* §§ 2431, 2446 (West 2019); *see also* Vt. Office of the Attorney Gen., *supra* note 135, at 8.

[139]   Douglas MacMillan, *Data Brokers Are Selling Your Secrets. How States Are Trying to Stop Them*, Wash. Post (June 24, 2019, 2:54 PM), www.washingtonpost.com/business/2019/06/24/data-brokers-are-getting-rich-by-selling-your-secrets-how-states-are-trying-stop-them/.

HEALTH-RELATED DATA

Recall from Chapter 1 the various types of health-related data that IoT devices can collect about us. These data can be disclosed and analyzed by companies to form a more accurate picture of our health, daily lifestyles, and preferences. The Food and Drug Administration (FDA) regulates medical devices, including those that are connected to the Internet.[140] The FDA has provided guidance and recommendations for entities manufacturing covered IoT devices and associated mobile medical applications and has issued cybersecurity warnings for related medical devices.[141] The FDA has also launched a pilot program for digital health-related products, including mobile applications, created by a select group of large technology companies.[142] There are sparse details on the program's appraisal process and this lack of transparency has been rightfully criticized by elected officials.[143] Not all IoT devices are subject to FDA regulation.[144] Minor-risk IoT devices that provide a "healthy lifestyle," such as smart watches and fitness trackers, may not be governed

[140] *See* David W. Opderbeck, *Artificial Intelligence in Pharmaceuticals, Biologics, and Medical Devices: Present and Future Regulatory Models*, 88 FORDHAM L. REV. 553, 554, 559–60 (2019).

[141] *See, e.g.*, *Cybersecurity*, U.S. FOOD & DRUG ADMIN., www.fda.gov/medical-devices/digital-health /cybersecurity (last updated Mar. 3, 2020); *Cybersecurity Vulnerabilities in a Widely-Used Third-Party Software Component May Introduce Risks During Use of Certain Medical Devices*, U.S. FOOD & DRUG ADMIN. (Oct. 1, 2019), www.fda.gov/medical-devices/safety-communications /urgent11-cybersecurity-vulnerabilities-widely-used-third-party-software-component-may-introduce; U.S. FOOD & DRUG ADMIN., POLICY FOR DEVICE SOFTWARE FUNCTIONS AND MOBILE MEDICAL APPLICATIONS: GUIDANCE FOR INDUSTRY AND FOOD AND DRUG ADMINISTRATION STAFF 14 (Sept. 26, 2019), www.fda.gov/regulatory-information/search-fda-guidance-documents/policy-device-software-functions-and-mobile-medical-applications; U.S. FOOD & DRUG ADMIN., POSTMARKET MANAGEMENT OF CYBERSECURITY IN MEDICAL DEVICES: GUIDANCE FOR INDUSTRY AND FOOD AND DRUG ADMINISTRATION STAFF 25 (DEC. 28, 2016), www.fda.gov/regulatory-information/search-fda-guidance-documents/postmarket-management-cybersecurity-medical-devices; U.S. FOOD & DRUG ADMIN., CONTENT OF PREMARKET SUBMISSIONS FOR MANAGEMENT OF CYBERSECURITY IN MEDICAL DEVICES: GUIDANCE FOR INDUSTRY AND FOOD AND DRUG ADMINISTRATION STAFF 17 (Oct. 2, 2014), www.fda.gov/media/86174/download.

[142] Letter from Elizabeth Warren, Patty Murray, Tina Smith, Senators, U.S. Senate, to Scott Gottlieb, Comm'r, U.S. Food & Drug Admin., & Jeffrey Shuren, Dir., Ctr. for Devices & Radiological Health, U.S. Food & Drug Admin. (Oct. 10, 2018), www.warren.senate.gov/imo/media/doc/2018.10.10%20Letter% 20to%20FDA%20on%20regulation%20of%20software%20as%20medical%20device.pdf; Kevin Stawicki, *FDA's Special Treatment of Big Tech Faces Mounting Scrutiny*, LAW360 (Nov. 12, 2019, 6:01 PM), www .law360.com/productliability/articles/1218770/fda-s-special-treatment-of-big-tech-faces-mounting-scrutiny? nl_pk=8ffa7ab4-c305-4fc6-b741-1815f1897c9e&utm_source=newsletter&utm_medium= email&utm_campaign=productliability.

[143] Stawicki, *supra* note 142.

[144] *See* Scott J. Shackelford et al., *Securing the Internet of Healthcare*, 19 MINN. J.L. SCI. & TECH. 405, 430 (2018) (contending that the statutory definition of a medical device "limits the scope the FDA is permitted to take by focusing only on devices that help heal or otherwise affect a patient's body as opposed to the constellation of devices that support a health provider's practice"); Tschider, *supra* note 102, at 123 (discussing IoT devices that are not subject to FDA regulation); *see also How to Determine If Your Product Is a Medical Device*, FOOD & DRUG ADMIN. (Dec. 16, 2018), www.fda.gov /medical-devices/classify-your-medical-device/product-medical-device (noting that devices that qualify as medical devices are subject to FDA requirements); *Overview of Device Regulation*, U.S. FOOD & DRUG ADMIN. (Aug. 31, 2018), www.fda.gov/medical-devices/device-advice-comprehensive-

by the FDA.[145] It is uncertain whether newer connected and hypothetical objects, such as ingestible smart pills that can track food consumption and digestion, will also fall in the "healthy lifestyle" category.[146] Thus, it is not entirely clear which IoT devices will be viewed as medical devices.[147] Devices that are not subject to the FDA will likely be regulated primarily by the FTC.[148]

The Health Insurance Portability and Accountability Act (HIPAA) is the primary federal statute that governs the use and disclosure of health-related data. HIPAA governs healthcare information when the data is collected by a healthcare provider, health plan, or healthcare clearinghouse, or the business associates of these entities.[149] The HIPAA framework restricts the ability of covered entities to freely disclose, transfer, and sell protected health-related data. Entities that are subject to HIPAA must comply with its associated privacy and cybersecurity rules for covered health data.[150]

The FTC and the U.S. Department of Health and Human Services Office for Civil Rights have both played a critical role in protecting consumer health-related data.[151] However, HIPAA's protection of healthcare information is not absolute. The HIPAA framework overrelies on the notice and consent model. It allows subject entities to use and share certain health-related data after receiving patient authorization and to disclose deidentified health-related data to third parties.[152] HIPAA's narrow set of protections do not apply to the majority of health-related data, including COVID-19 data, collected by IoT devices. This is because the vast majority of

regulatory-assistance/overview-device-regulation ("The FDA's Center for Devices and Radiological Health (CDRH) is responsible for regulating firms who manufacture, repackage, relabel, and/or import medical devices sold in the United States. In addition, CDRH regulates radiation-emitting electronic products (medical and non-medical) such as lasers, x-ray systems, ultrasound equipment, microwave ovens and color televisions."); Stawicki, *supra* note 142(noting that some "low-risk digital health" devices are not subject to FDA regulation).

[145] Andrea M. Matwyshyn, *The Internet of Bodies*, 61 Wm. & Mary L. Rev. 77, 95–96, 108 (2019).

[146] *Id.* at 108.

[147] *Id.*

[148] *Id.* at 133; Andrea M. Matwyshyn, *The "Internet of Bodies" Is Here. Are Courts and Regulators Ready?*, The Wall Street J. (Nov. 12, 2018, 11:19 AM), www.wsj.com/articles/the-internet-of-bodies-is-here-are-courts-and-regulators-ready-1542039566.

[149] 42 U.S.C. §§ 1320d–d-8 (2010) (statutory authority); 45 C.F.R. § 160.103(3) (2014) (defining a "covered entity" as a "health plan," "health care clearinghouse," "health care provider who transmits any health information in electronic form in connection with a transaction covered by this subchapter," or "business associate of another covered entity").

[150] *See* 45 C.F.R. §§ 160.101–160.105 (privacy rule); *id.* §§ 164.302–164.318 (security rule).

[151] *See HIPAA Enforcement*, U.S. Dep't of Health & Human Services, www.hhs.gov/hipaa/for-professionals/compliance-enforcement/index.html (last visited Nov. 24, 2019); *see also Mobile Health App Developers: FTC Best Practices*, Fed. Trade Comm'n (Apr. 2016); www.ftc.gov/tips-advice/business-center/guidance/mobile-health-app-developers-ftc-best-practices; *Sharing Consumer Health Information? Look to HIPAA and the FTC Act*, U.S. Dep't of Health & Human Serv. (Oct. 2016), www.hhs.gov/hipaa/for-professionals/special-topics/hipaa-ftc-act/index.html.

[152] *See* Sharona Hoffman , Electronic Health Records and Medical Big Data: Law and Policy 132 (2016); *see also* Stacy-Ann Elvy, *Commodifying Consumer Data in the Era of the Internet of Things*, 59 B.C. L. Rev. 423, 496–500 (2018).

IoT companies (manufacturers and service providers) are not subject to HIPAA's framework. Most IoT companies that sell or manufacture IoT devices that collect health-related data are unlikely to provide "medical or health services," health insurance plans, or process healthcare information, or qualify as business associates under HIPAA's framework.[153] As a result, the health-related data IoT devices collect will primarily be governed by a company's privacy policy, the FTC framework discussed earlier, and possibly state health laws.

Existing state laws in this area are also unlikely to sufficiently protect IoT health-related data. Sharona Hoffman has convincingly argued that state laws that regulate health-related data are "varied and inconsistent" and oftentimes provide only feeble protections for certain types of data.[154] Similarly, Daniel Solove and Paul Schwartz have observed that like HIPAA, most state health laws are not comprehensive and instead regulate only certain types of entities.[155]

Even when HIPAA's framework applies, its effectiveness is challenged by technological developments. Technology companies that provide cloud-computing and data analytic services to HIPAA-regulated companies are likely business associates under HIPAA. Despite HIPAA's applicability, these transactions provide opportunities for business associates to access, analyze (through machine learning), and potentially monetize patients' health records. Google's recent deal with health-system Ascension and reports about Google's access to patient data exemplify these concerns.[156] Patients were reportedly not aware of Google's involvement with their data and did not have the ability to opt out.[157] The data included names, prescription information, hospital records, and laboratory results, among other things.[158] Google is allegedly using

---

[153] *See* 42 U.S.C. § 17935(d)(2016) ("[p]rohibition on sale of electronic health records or protected health information" in the absence of individual consent subject to some exceptions); 45 C.F.R. § 160.103; *id.* § 164.502 (providing rules for use and disclosure of data by covered entities); *id.* § 164.508(a) (imposing consent requirements for the sale of protected health information and providing rules for the use and disclosure of health information for marketing purposes); *see also* Elvy, *supra* note 152at 496–500.

[154] HOFFMAN, *supra* note 152, at 135.

[155] SOLOVE & SCHWARTZ, *supra* note 2, at 508.

[156] *See* Tariq Shaukat, *Our Partnership with Ascension*, GOOGLE CLOUD (Nov. 11, 2019), https://cloud .google.com/blog/topics/inside-google-cloud/our-partnership-with-ascension; *see also* Jon Brodkin, *Google: You Can Trust Us with the Medical Data You Didn't Know We Already Had*, ARS TECHNICA (Nov. 13, 2019, 9:50 AM), https://arstechnica.com/tech-policy/2019/11/google-you-can-trust-us-with-the-medical-data-you-didnt-know-we-already-had/?amp=1; Jillian D'Onfro & Leah Rosenbaum, *Google Secretly Tests Medical Records Search Tool on Nation's Largest Nonprofit Health System, Documents Show*, FORBES (Nov. 11, 2019, 2:54 PM), www.forbes.com/sites/jilliandonfro/2019/11/11/google-ascension-project-nightingale-electronic-medical-records/#4ab43d5f7a0a (critiquing the Google–Ascension transaction and raising concerns about Google's access to patient records).

[157] *I'm the Google Whistleblower. The Medical Data of Millions of Americans Is at Risk*, GUARDIAN (Nov. 14, 2019), https://amp.theguardian.com/commentisfree/2019/nov/14/im-the-google-whistleblower-the -medical-data-of-millions-of-americans-is-at-risk.

[158] *See* Sidney Fussell, *Google's Totally Creepy, Totally Legal Health-Data Harvesting*, ATLANTIC (Nov. 14, 2019), www.theatlantic.com/technology/archive/2019/11/google-project-nightingale-all-your-health-data/601999/; Beth Mole, *Google Has Access to Detailed Health Records on Tens of Millions*

patients' health data to improve software powered by artificial intelligence, which makes recommendations for patient care.[159] Once fully developed, Google could further profit from the Ascension transaction by selling or licensing the software to other healthcare providers.[160] Patients whose data were transferred to Google are left to place their faith in Google's privacy policy and cybersecurity practices, while Google continues to vacuum up data for a profit and solidify its market power.

BIOMETRIC DATA

Several states are currently considering adopting biometric data statutes.[161] Some jurisdictions have also restricted the use of facial recognition technology by state actors.[162] To date, only a minority of states have adopted statutes or have amended existing privacy legislation to specifically address companies' collection of biometric data for commercial purposes.[163] The Illinois Biometric Information Privacy Act (BIPA) is the most stringent of these statutes and has been the subject of significant litigation. BIPA also contains more consumer-friendly provisions in comparison to the Texas and Washington biometric data statutes. Facebook's recent $550 million settlement of a class action lawsuit by Illinois residents alleging BIPA violations illustrates the strength and impact of BIPA.[164] BIPA also provides another example of unequal access to privacy between citizens of different states, as biometric data protection legislation in other states either does not exist or is significantly weaker.

Consumer advocates' attempts to adopt biometric data legislation in other states and to expand existing statutes in favor of consumers have been successfully hindered by large technology companies' lobbying tactics.[165] For instance, Facebook,

---

of Americans, Ars Technica (Nov. 11, 2019, 3:09 PM), https://arstechnica.com/science/2019/11/would-you-trust-google-with-your-medical-records-it-might-already-have-them/.

[159] Brodkin, *supra* note 156.

[160] *Id.*

[161] *2019 Consumer Data Privacy Legislation*, Nat'l Conf. State Legislatures (Jan. 3, 2020), www.ncsl.org/research/telecommunications-and-information-technology/consumer-data-privacy.aspx.

[162] *See, e.g.*, A.B. 1215, 2019 Leg. (Cal. 2019); Kate Conger, Richard Fausset & Serge F. Kovaleski, *San Francisco Bans Facial Recognition Technology*, N.Y. Times (May 14, 2019), www.nytimes.com/2019/05/14/us/facial-recognition-ban-san-francisco.html; Christine Fisher, *Oakland Bans City Use of Facial Recognition Software*, Engadget (July 17, 2019), www.engadget.com/2019/07/17/oakland-california-facial-recognition-ban/; Caroline Haskins, *A Second U.S. City Has Banned Facial Recognition*, Vice (June 27, 2019, 6:15 PM), www.vice.com/en_us/article/paj4ek/somerville-becomes-the-second-us-city-to-ban-facial-recognition.

[163] *See, e.g.*, Ark. Code Ann. § 4-110-103(7) (West 2019); Ill. Comp. Stat. Ann. 14/15 (West 2008); Tex. Bus. & Com. Code Ann. § 503.001 (West 2017); Wash. Rev. Code Ann. § 19.375.010 (West 2017).

[164] Natasha Singer & Mike Isaac, *Facebook to Pay $550 Million to Settle Facial Recognition Suit*, N.Y. Times (Jan. 29, 2020), www.nytimes.com/2020/01/29/technology/facebook-privacy-lawsuit-earnings.html.

[165] Facebook Inc: Biometric Data Class Action Ongoing in Illinois, Class Action Reporter (Beard Group, Inc., Washington, D.C.), Sept. 15, 2017, 7–8.

Google, and Verizon have successfully opposed biometric data legislation across the country by using several trade groups to represent their interests.[166] Washington's 2017 biometric data statute was passed only after being significantly weakened by technology companies' lobbying efforts.[167] In the last decade, large technology companies, such as Amazon and Facebook, have spent approximately "half a billion dollars" on lobbying.[168] These developments illustrate technology companies' vested interest in blocking privacy legislation and in keeping any existing legislation locked into overreliance on the notice and choice model.

Many of the existing biometric data state statutes suffer from several inadequacies that will limit their effectiveness in the IoT setting. These statutes also rely heavily on notice and choice, which, as discussed earlier, has its limitations. Washington's and Texas's biometric data statutes both impose general notice requirements for the collection of biometric identifiers.[169] BIPA requires that specific conditions be met to validate consumer consent to biometric data collection.[170] This includes requiring that institutions that collect biometric identifiers inform consumers of the purpose for which the data are being collected.[171] Both the Washington and Texas statutes permit institutions to sell and trade biometric data when notice and consent is met.[172] In contrast, BIPA prohibits such activities and also creates a right of action for statutory violations.[173] Although BIPA has stronger notice and consent requirements, the statute also relies on notice and consent to justify institutions collecting and storing biometric identifiers.

In *Rosenbach v. Six Flags Entertainment Corporation*, the Illinois Supreme Court held that individuals may bring suit as "aggrieved" parties under BIPA based on a statutory violation (such as a company's failure to satisfy notice and consent requirements) without having to prove "actual injury or adverse effect."[174] Standing limitations in federal courts can impact the reach and effectiveness of

---

[166] *Id.*

[167] *Id.*

[168] Tony Romm, *Tech Giants Led by Amazon, Facebook and Google Spent Nearly Half a Billion on Lobbying over the Past Decade, New Data Shows*, WASH. POST (Jan. 22, 2020, 6:32 AM), www .washingtonpost.com/technology/2020/01/22/amazon-facebook-google-lobbying-2019/.

[169] *See* TEX. BUS. & COM. § 503.001(b) (West 2017); WASH. REV. CODE ANN. § 19.375.020 (West 2017).

[170] *See* ILL. COMP. STAT. ANN. 14/15 (West 2008).

[171] *Id.*

[172] *See* TEX. BUS. & COM. § 503.001(c)(1); WASH. § 19.375.020(3).

[173] *See* ILL. 14/15(c), 14/20.

[174] Rosenbach v. Six Flags Entm't Corp., 129 N.E.3d 1197, 1200 (Ill. 2019); *see also* Patel v. Facebook, Inc., 932 F.3d 1264, 1275 (9th Cir. 2019) (finding that because "BIPA protects the plaintiffs' concrete privacy interests and violations of the procedures in BIPA actually harm or pose a material risk of harm to those privacy interests . . . the plaintiffs have alleged a concrete and particularized harm, sufficient to confer Article III standing"); Lauraann Wood, *Biggest Illinois Decisions So Far in 2019: Midyear Report*, LAW360 (July 8, 2019, 12:51 PM), www.law360.com/articles/1175051/biggest-illinois-decisions-so -far-in-2019-midyear-report.

BIPA. Individuals bringing suit under BIPA in federal court have had their cases dismissed for lack of standing.[175]

Statutory restrictions on the collection and disclosure of biometric data can also rely on the express terms of an institution's privacy policy as a means of protecting consumers. The Washington statute prohibits biometric identifier usage and disclosure practices that are "materially inconsistent with the terms under which" the data were collected in the absence of consumer consent.[176] Companies draft privacy policies to protect their interests. If the data collection terms initially provided in a privacy policy are drafted broadly to authorize various data practices, subsequent data uses (even for dubious purposes) could be permissible. Companies can also unilaterally amend their privacy policies. Even privacy policies that are narrowly drafted initially can be revised to authorize subsequent biometric data practices and uses as long as consumer consent is received.

Many of the state biometric data statutes also fail to sufficiently address the myriad ways in which companies can exercise significant influence over us to normalize invasive biometric data collection and transfer practices and to mislead us into consenting to these practices. Consider that in 2019, Google's contractors were able to obtain the facial images of consumers to advance its facial recognition technology by inaccurately describing the scan as a "selfie-game" or "survey" and a simple opportunity to test a new app.[177] Some of these representatives falsely told consumers that they were not being recorded.[178] Minority and homeless individuals were specifically targeted for facial data collection.[179]

Biometric data statutes can also exclude from their coverage the data that IoT devices collect. Washington's biometric data statute expressly carves out pictures, videos, and audio recordings from its definition of biometric identifiers.[180] Many of the statute's limited protections apply to biometric identifiers.[181] IoT devices will frequently collect, store, and disclose our facial images and audio recordings, which

---

[175] McGinnis v. U.S. Cold Storage, Inc., 382 F. Supp. 3d 813 (N.D. Ill. 2019); Rivera v. Google, Inc., 366 F. Supp. 3d 998 (N.D. Ill. 2018); Al Saikali et al., *Ill. Biometric Privacy Ruling Is Only the Beginning for BIPA*, LAW360 (Jan. 29, 2019, 5:00 PM), www.law360.com/articles/1123446/ill-biometric-privacy-ruling-is-only-the-beginning-for-bipa.

[176] WASH. REV. CODE ANN. § 19.375.020(5)(West 2017).

[177] Ginger Adams Otis & Nancy Dillon, *Google Using Dubious Tactics to Target People with "Darker Skin" in Facial Recognition Project: Sources*, N.Y. DAILY NEWS (Oct. 2, 2019, 6:56 PM), www.nydailynews.com/news/national/ny-google-darker-skin-tones-facial-recognition-pixel-20191002-5vxpgowknffnvbmy5eg7epsf34-story.html.

[178] *Id.; see also* Jack Nicas, *Atlanta Asks Google Whether It Targeted Black Homeless People*, N.Y. TIMES (Oct. 4, 2019), www.nytimes.com/2019/10/04/technology/google-facial-recognition-atlanta-homeless.html; Julia Carrie Wong, *Google Reportedly Targeted People with "Dark Skin" to Improve Facial Recognition*, GUARDIAN (Oct. 3, 2019, 5:11 PM), www.theguardian.com/technology/2019/oct/03/google-data-harvesting-facial-recognition-people-of-color.

[179] Nicas, *supra* note 178.

[180] WASH. § 19.375.010.

[181] *See id.* § 19.375.020.

can be easily transformed into biometric identifiers, such as voice and face prints. Yet, the statute seems to exclude much of these data from its coverage.

Whether the data that IoT devices collect are subject to a biometric data statute can be a critical issue in lawsuits relating to an institution's alleged violation of statutory requirements. For example, in *Nyltza Morales et al. v. Google.com, Inc.*, a lawsuit involving BIPA, Google argued that the voice recordings collected by Google Assistant (which is associated with multiple IoT devices) were not voice prints or biometric identifiers and were therefore not covered by BIPA.[182] The plaintiffs argued that Google had violated BIPA by failing to provide a written policy regarding its biometric data collection practices.[183] The case highlights the contradictory nature of companies' biometric data collection practices. Google has used third-party contractors to target vulnerable consumers and induce them to consent to the collection of video and audio recordings for the purpose of enhancing its facial recognition technology, but the company simultaneously argues in unrelated litigation that images and audio recordings are not biometric identifiers.

STUDENT DATA

Recall from Chapter 1 that some schools are deploying IoT devices to collect data about students. IoT slippers and glasses can track students' classroom movements and attentiveness to classroom materials.[184] The Family Educational Rights and Privacy Act (FERPA) is another federal statute that impacts children's data. FERPA regulates data in the educational setting.[185] FERPA's loopholes are significant.[186] The statute applies primarily to a narrow set of student data (those that qualify as educational records) and its applicability to commercial student data broker companies is questionable.[187] Valuable data generated from students' use of school-offered IoT

---

[182] Lauraann Wood, *Google Assistant Doesn't Collect Biometric Data, Court Told*, LAW360 (Oct. 3, 2019, 7:59 PM), www.law360.com/cybersecurity-privacy/articles/1205847/google-assistant-doesn-t-collect-biometric-data-court-told?nl_pk=8bca81a9-bf53-40e6-b4c6-4d8c2eda4ebe&utm_source=newsletter&utm_medium=email&utm_campaign=cybersecurity-privacy.

[183] Sarah Martinson, *Google Assistant Violates Biometric Law, Illinois Consumers Say*, LAW360 (July 17, 2019, 5:20 PM), www.law360.com/articles/1179260.

[184] *See* James Vaznis, *Schools Are Collecting New Data in New Ways About Students with Cutting-Edge High-Tech*, BOS. GLOBE (Dec. 16, 2019, 8:20 PM), www.bostonglobe.com/metro/2019/12/16/schools-experiment-with-high-tech-student-monitoring/7sx3eMEqYTwO9zxzKjyEkK/story.html.

[185] *See* 20 U.S.C. § 1232g (2013); 34 C.F.R. § 99 (2011).

[186] N. Russel Cameronl et al., *Transparency and the Marketplace for Student Data*, 22 VA. J.L. & TECH. 107, 114–18 (2019).

[187] *See* SOLOVE & SCHWARTZ, *supra* note 2, at 1008 ("FERPA covers only records and information from education records, not information per se."); Russell, *supra* note 186, at 117–18; *FERPA and Virtual Learning Related Resources*, U.S. DEP'T EDUC STUDENT PRIVACY POL'Y OFFICE (Mar. 2020), https://studentprivacy.ed.gov/sites/default/files/resource_document/file/FERPA%20%20Virtual%20Learning%20032020_FINAL.pdf [hereinafter, STUDENT PRIVACY POL'Y OFFICE] ("FERPA is the federal law that protects the privacy of personally identifiable information (PII) in students' education records."); Anisha Reddy, *Social (Media) Distancing: Online Learning During a Pandemic,*

devices and related mobile applications may not consistently fall under FERPA's scope.[188]

The coronavirus pandemic and resulting school closures have increased online distance learning for students of all ages.[189] The pandemic has highlighted the digital divide, with some groups of students (particularly those from low-income families) having limited access to high-speed Internet and online devices. Some educators have also turned to social media platforms to host virtual classes.[190] The pandemic creates additional opportunities for both technology companies that have not traditionally played a role in providing educational services and schools' education technology contractors to collect students' data. Traditional education technology companies are likely more versed in aiding schools to comply with FERPA's requirements than other types of technology companies.[191]

Information from the U.S. Department of Education on the pandemic's impact on online learning suggests that it is permissible to record students in their homes during virtual classes and share these recordings with certain parties as long as personally identifiable data from students' education records are not disclosed or consent is received.[192] Video recordings from online classroom sessions constitute

FERPASHERPA (Mar. 31, 2020), https://ferpasherpa.org/social-media-distancing-covid19/ ("schools, not companies, are subject to FERPA").

[188] Russell, *supra* note 186, at 117–18 ("Often, this student information outside of FERPA protection may be highly valuable to data brokers, such as metadata collected when students interact with a third-party app or service or detailed information about students' eating habits."); *see also* 20 U.S.C. § 1232g (a)(4) (West 2013) (defining educational records generally as records which "(i) contain information directly related to a student; and (ii) are maintained by an educational agency or institution or by a person acting for such agency or institution"); *id.* § 1232g(a)(5)(a) (defining "directory information"); *id.* § 1232g(a)(3) (defining "educational agency or institution" as "any public or private agency or institution which is the recipient of funds under any applicable program"); *Protecting Student Privacy While Using Online Educational Services: Requirements and Best Practices*, U.S. DEP'T EDUC. PRIVACY TECHNICAL ASSISTANCE CTR. (Feb. 2014), https://tech.ed.gov/wp-content/uploads/2014/09/Student-Privacy-and-Online-Educational-Services-February-2014.pdf (noting that "metadata that have been stripped of all direct and indirect identifiers are not considered protected information under FERPA because they are not PII").

[189] Madeline St. Amour, *Privacy and the Online Pivot*, INSIDE HIGHER ED (Mar. 25, 2020), www.insidehighered.com/news/2020/03/25/pivot-online-raises-concerns-ferpa-surveillance; Valerie Strauss, *As Schooling Rapidly Moves Online Across the Country, Concerns Rise About Student Data Privacy*, WASH. POST (Mar. 20, 2020, 6:00 AM), www.washingtonpost.com/education/2020/03/20/schooling-rapidly-moves-online-across-country-concerns-rise-about-student-data-privacy/.

[190] Reddy, *supra* note 187.

[191] *Id.*

[192] Kala Shah Suprenant, *FERPA & Virtual Learning During COVID-19*, U.S. DEP'T EDUC. STUDENT PRIVACY POL'Y OFFICE (Mar. 30, 2020), https://studentprivacy.ed.gov/sites/default/files/resource_document/file/FERPAandVirtualLearning.pdf; STUDENT PRIVACY POL'Y OFFICE, *supra* note 187; Dep't. of Educ. Family Educational Rights and Privacy Rule, 34 C.F.R § 99.3 (2012) ("The term [personally identifiable information] includes, but is not limited to – (a) The student's name; (b) The name of the student's parent or other family members; (c) The address of the student or student's family; (d) A personal identifier, such as the student's social security number, student number, or biometric record; (e) Other indirect identifiers, such as the student's date of birth, place of birth, and mother's maiden name; (f) Other information that, alone or in combination, is linked or linkable to a specific

education records under FERPA "if they directly relate to a student and are maintained by an educational agency or institution or by a party acting on their behalf."[193] This suggests that not all video recordings of students' online learning classrooms may qualify as educational records.

In addition to FERPA, states have also adopted or proposed legislation regulating student privacy, and privacy violations involving students' data can also be actionable under state unfair and deceptive trade practices statutes.[194] Consider that Google was sued in 2020 by New Mexico for allegedly improperly collecting and processing students' data through its education platform in violation of COPPA and the state's unfair and deceptive trade practices statute.[195] The complaint alleges in part that Google failed to live up to privacy promises about student data.[196] The lawsuit provides another example of privacy enforcement actions that are based on companies' privacy statements. Recall the limits of relying on a broken or reneged privacy promise theory as a central vehicle for protecting users. Companies continue to have significant power over the fate of our data as they primarily determine what promises they will make to us despite possible consumer outrage and objections. As of the date of writing, the lawsuit is unresolved. Google's possible use of student data to make predictions about students' academic performance and intelligence is problematic and goes beyond concerns about the use of student data for advertising purposes. Additionally, schools' use of Google's education platform and products gives the company early access to children's data and permits the company to condition students at a young age to use its products and services, including Gmail, Google Drive, and Google Docs.[197]

California's Student Online Personal Information Protection Act (SOPIPA) is one of the most notable state statutes regulating student data.[198] SOPIPA imposes restrictions on covered entities' ability to sell and disclose students' data.[199]

---

student that would allow a reasonable person in the school community, who does not have personal knowledge of the relevant circumstances, to identify the student with reasonable certainty; or (g) Information requested by a person who the educational agency or institution reasonably believes knows the identity of the student to whom the education record relates.").

[193] Suprenant, *supra* note 192.

[194] *State Student Privacy Laws*, FERPASHERPA, https://ferpasherpa.org/state-laws/ (last updated Aug. 8, 2019) (discussing state student privacy laws); *Student Data Privacy*, NAT'L CONF. STATE LEGS. (Oct. 26, 2018), www.ncsl.org/research/education/student-data-privacy.aspx.

[195] Yoree Koh, *New Mexico Sues Google over Children's Data Privacy*, WALL ST. J. (Feb. 20, 2020, 6:14 PM), www.wsj.com/articles/new-mexico-sues-google-over-childrens-data-privacy-11582240443?ns=prod/accounts-wsj; Nick Statt, *Google Sued by New Mexico Attorney General for Collecting Student Data Through Chromebooks*, VERGE (Feb. 20, 2020, 12:54 PM), www.theverge.com/2020/2/20/21145698/google-student-privacy-lawsuit-education-schools-chromebooks-new-mexico-balderas.

[196] Complaint, New Mexico v. Google LLC, No. 1:20-cv-00143-NF-KHR (D.N.M. Feb. 20, 2020), www.courthousenews.com/wp-content/uploads/2020/02/nm-google.pdf.

[197] *Id.* at 14.

[198] *See* CAL. BUS. & PROF. CODE §§ 22584–87 (Deering 2019).

[199] SOPIPA is applicable to "operators" of "an Internet Web site, online service, online application, or mobile application with actual knowledge that the site, service, or application is used primarily for K–12 school purposes and was designed and marketed for K–12 school purposes." BUS. & PROF.

Additionally, as Joel Reidenberg and others have argued, "data brokers already in possession of student data or who obtain such information from sources outside of SOPIPA's scope possess student data with few constraints."[200] It is not entirely clear whether SOPIPA and other similar state statutes can successfully mitigate the possible privacy- and security-related harms that students may face in the IoT setting.

IOT-SPECIFIC STATUTES

A minority of states have enacted IoT-specific legislation. Remember from Chapter 2 that multiple states have adopted data breach notification legislation, but these statutes are unlikely to effectively remedy the cybersecurity concerns that are associated with the IoT. There have been previous failed attempts at the federal level to enact security IoT legislation.[201] California and Oregon have adopted legislation that directly addresses IoT cybersecurity failures.

The California statute requires IoT device manufacturers to equip their devices with reasonable security measures that are suitable for the "nature and function of the device" and the types of data that the device may collect or transmit.[202] The statute also requires IoT devices to be designed to prevent unauthorized access.[203] IoT devices that are manufactured with unique default passwords or that require consumers to change default passwords prior to being used are deemed to have a "reasonable security feature."[204] The Oregon statute also requires covered institutions to adopt reasonable security measures and addresses the hard-coded password

---

§ 22584(a); *see also* Lothar Determann, California Privacy Law 410 (3rd. ed. 2018) ("SOPIPA was expanded upon by the Early Learning Personal Information Protection Act (ELPIPA), which requires operators of websites, online services, or applications used or marketed primarily to preschool or prekindergarten pupils to refrain from a variety of practices, including targeted advertising, profiling of students for other purposes, selling a pupil's information, or disclosing covered information unless certain other disclosures are made."); Russell, *supra* note 186, at 120 (noting that SOPIPA "valuably fills a gap between FERPA-covered educational institutions and private-sector vendors and websites servicing schools and K-12 students"); *State Student Privacy Policy*, Electronic Privacy Info. Ctr., https://epic.org/state-policy/student-privacy/ (last visited Jan. 31, 2020) (discussing SOPIPA).

[200] Russell, *supra* note 186, at 120; *Legal Overview: Key Laws Relevant to the Protection of Student Data*, Electronic Frontier Found., www.eff.org/issues/student-privacy/legalanalysis (last visited Jan. 31, 2020) (discussing SOPIPA loopholes).

[201] *See* S. 1691, 115th Cong. (2017) (proposing the "Internet of Things (IoT) Cybersecurity Improvement Act of 2017" to impose "security requirements" on IoT companies for IoT devices provided to the U.S. government); *see also* Allison Grande, *Senate Bill Would Up Internet of Things Device Security*, Law360 (Aug. 2, 2017, 8:57 PM), www.law360.com/articles/950047/senate-bill-would-up-internet-of-things-device-security; Adi Robertson, *California Just Became the First State with an Internet of Things Cybersecurity Law*, Verge (Sept. 28, 2018, 6:07 PM), www.theverge.com/2018/9/28/17874768/california-iot-smart-device-cybersecurity-bill-sb-327-signed-law.

[202] Cal. Civ. Code § 1798.91.04 (West 2020).

[203] *Id.*

[204] *Id.*

problem that plagues IoT devices.[205] Additionally, Oregon's statute provides that IoT device compliance with federal legislation or regulation may constitute a reasonable security measure.[206] The California statute contains a broader definition of the term "manufacturer" than the Oregon statute.[207] This suggests that the Oregon statute applies to a smaller set of entities. The Oregon statute's definition of connected devices is also expressly limited to consumer IoT devices.[208]

With the exception of passwords, the California statute does not provide significant guidance on what constitutes a reasonable security feature. One likely result of this ambiguity and lack of statutory guidance is that IoT device manufacturers will make the primary determination (at least initially) of what qualifies as a reasonable security feature. Thus, to some extent the statute appears to default to self-regulation, unless subsequent detailed IoT specific guidance is provided. A company may adopt what it believes are reasonable cybersecurity practices, but those measures may fail to adequately protect our data.

California's and Oregon's IoT statutes are not the only state data security laws that adopt a basic reasonable cybersecurity standard.[209] The National Conference of State Legislatures reports that in addition to data breach notification laws, at least twenty-five states have adopted general frameworks governing the data security activities of private entities.[210] As William McGeveran notes, most state data security frameworks impose a basic reasonable cybersecurity standard although some of these frameworks also provide additional guidance on data security obligations within a statute, by, for instance, referencing existing federal security frameworks, or in some cases through formal regulation and narrative reports.[211]

---

[205] *See* H.B. 2395, 80th Leg. Assemb., Reg. Sess. (Or. 2019); *see also Oregon Latest State to Require Reasonable Security for IoT Devices*, CROWELL MORING (June 7, 2019), www.crowell.com/NewsEvents/AlertsNewsletters/all/Oregon-Latest-State-to-Require-Reasonable-Security-for-IoT-Devices.

[206] Or. H.B. 2395; ORS § 646A.813.

[207] *Compare* CAL. CIV. CODE § 1798.91.05 (West 2020) (defining a "manufacturer" as "the person who manufactures, or contracts with another person to manufacture on the person's behalf, connected devices that are sold or offered for sale in California"), *with* ORS § 646A.813 (defining manufacturer as "a person that makes a connected device and sells or offers to sell the connected device").

[208] *See* ORS § 646A.813 (partially defining connected devices as those that are "used primarily for personal, family or household purposes"); *see also* Duane Pozza & Kathleen Scott, *States Continue to Move Forward on Their Own Privacy and Security Laws: Nevada, Maine, and Oregon Are the Latest*, WILEY CONNECT (July 22, 2019), www.wileyconnect.com/home/2019/7/22/states-continue-to-move-forward-on-their-own-privacy-and-security-laws-nevada-maine-and-oregon-are-the-latest (discussing the differences between the California and Oregon statutes).

[209] *See e.g.*, Cal Civ Code § 1798.81.5 (West 2020); Ark. Code § 4-110-104(b) (2005).

[210] *Data Security Laws: Private Sector*, NAT'L CONF. STATE LEGISLATURES (May 29, 2019), www.ncsl.org/research/telecommunications-and-information-technology/data-security-laws.aspx (but also noting that other state laws "address the security of health care data, financial or credit information, social security numbers or other specific types of data collected or maintained by businesses."); *Security Breach Notification Laws*, NAT'L CONF. STATE LEGISLATURES (Mar. 8, 2020), www.ncsl.org/research/telecommunications-and-information-technology/security-breach-notification-laws.aspx (noting that all fifty states have adopted data breach notification laws).

[211] William McGeveran *The Duty of Data Security*, 103 MINN. L. REV. 1135, 1153–58 (2019).

Returning to the California IoT statute, the law also does not sufficiently address cybersecurity incidents that result from consumers' tendency to use the same passwords across different accounts.[212] This tendency of some groups of consumers raises questions about personal responsibility, particularly in light of technological developments that make it easier for consumers to adopt unique passwords. However, as consumers, many of us are overwhelmed with the plethora of online accounts we are required to manage, and the multiple steps we must take to secure our privacy and security in order to engage in ordinary daily activities.

The statutory focus on single hard-coded passwords also fails to consider the interconnected nature of IoT devices, services, and systems. The mobile applications and websites consumers use to operate their devices normally require consumers to create usernames and passwords. IoT devices often rely on access to consumers' Wi-Fi passwords to obtain internet access. There are also distinct authentication systems for some services that are associated with IoT devices, such as Telnet.[213] Weaknesses in these passwords and related systems can also enable cyberattacks.[214] In 2019, researchers found that Telnet service-related vulnerabilities could impact more than "a million IoT radio devices."[215] Since many IoT devices require access to a Wi-Fi network in order to function, ISPs will also play a crucial role in network security and insecurity. Lax measures for the approval of third-party mobile applications and subsequent updates can also allow platform IoT services and products, such as Alexa and Google Home, to be weaponized by third parties to listen to and record in-home conversations and even obtain passwords for other services.[216]

---

[212] *See, e.g.*, Neil Vigdor, *Somebody's Watching: Hackers Breach Ring Home Security Cameras*, N.Y. TIMES (Dec. 15, 2019), www.nytimes.com/2019/12/15/us/Hacked-ring-home-security-cameras.html.

[213] *See California's Bad IoT Law*, ERRATA SECURITY (Sept. 10, 2018), https://blog.erratasec.com/2018/09/californias-bad-iot-law.html.

[214] *See id.*; *see also* Jeff Kosseff, *California's IoT Security Law Is Well-Intentioned, but a Comprehensive Federal Law is Needed*, TECH. & MARKETING L. BLOG (Oct. 5, 2018), https://blog.ericgoldman.org/archives/2018/10/californias-iot-security-law-is-well-intentioned-but-a-comprehensive-federal-law-is-needed-guest-blog-post.htm; Deepak Kumar et al., *All Things Considered: An Analysis of IoT Devices on Home Networks*, in PROCEEDINGS OF THE 28TH USENIX SECURITY SYMPOSIUM 1, 1 (2019), https://press.avast.com/hubfs/stanford_avast_state_of_iot.pdf ("A surprising number of [IoT] devices still support FTP and Telnet with weak credentials.").

[215] Charlie Osborne, *Telnet Backdoor Vulnerabilities Impact over a Million IoT Radio Devices*, ZDNET (Sept. 9, 2019), www.zdnet.com/google-amp/article/critical-vulnerabilities-impact-over-a-million-iot-radio-devices/.

[216] Dan Goodin, *Alexa and Google Home Abused to Eavesdrop and Phish Passwords*, ARS TECHNICA (Oct. 20, 2019, 4:05 PM), https://arstechnica.com/information-technology/2019/10/alexa-and-google-home-abused-to-eavesdrop-and-phish-passwords/; Catalin Cimpanu, *Alexa and Google Home Devices Leveraged to Phish and Evaesdrop on Users, Again*, ZDNet (Oct. 20, 2019), www.zdnet.com/article/alexa-and-google-home-devices-leveraged-to-phish-and-eavesdrop-on-users-again/. The problem of weak enforcement of platform policies and approval processes applicable to third-party apps also occurs in other contexts as well. *See* Shehroze Farooqi, et al., *Understanding Incentivized Mobile App Installs on Google Play Store*, ACM IMC (2020), https://dl.acm.org/doi/10.1145/3419394.3423662 (a study finding "a likely lack of enforcement from Google Play Store to detect the potential violations of their policies by incentivized installs.").

The Pew Research Center reports that "54% of internet users use public Wi-Fi networks, and many of these users are performing sensitive activities, such as online shopping (21%) or online banking (20%)."[217] Consumers may also use unsecured public or free Wi-Fi networks on their smartphones to access and control their in-home IoT devices. This is more likely to occur when a user has an unreliable cellular connection. The consistency of cellular data connectivity can depend on the carrier and the geographic region. Unsecured public networks pose a higher risk of data disclosure and interception.[218]

Both the Oregon and California statutes contain a narrow definition of connected devices that fails to consider the extent to which IoT devices rely on mobile applications and other types of online services. The statutes generally define connected devices as "devices" or "physical objects" that can be connected to the Internet.[219] As we will see in Chapter 5, statutory definitions of IoT devices can impact the availability of consumer-related remedies under products liability law and Article 2 of the UCC. With respect to enforcement, the California statute does not create a private cause of action but is instead enforced by state actors.[220]

California has also adopted legislation to address IoT televisions in particular.[221] This statute requires covered entities to clearly and concisely inform users of the voice recognition features of IoT televisions "during the initial setup or installation" of the device.[222] The statute also prohibits manufacturers and third-party contractors from selling or using certain voice recordings collected from covered devices for advertisement purposes.[223] The scope of the statute is quite narrow, which means that its impact is limited. The statute applies only to connected televisions and does not address other IoT devices with voice recognition and collection features, such as smart speakers. Amendments to the statute have been proposed to address this limitation, but have not yet been adopted as of the date of writing.[224]

This chapter has highlighted various gaps in existing privacy and security frameworks that call into question the ability of these frameworks to effectively deal with

---

[217] Monica Anderson, *Many Smartphone Owners Don't Take Steps to Secure Their Devices*, PEW RES. CTR. (Mar. 15, 2017), www.pewresearch.org/fact-tank/2017/03/15/many-smartphone-owners-dont-take-steps-to-secure-their-devices/.

[218] *See How to Avoid Public WiFi Security Risks*, KASPERSKY, https://usa.kaspersky.com/resource-center/preemptive-safety/public-wifi-risks (last visited Apr. 2, 2020).

[219] *See* CAL. CIV. CODE § 1798.91.05 (West 2020) ("'Connected device' means any device, or other physical object that is capable of connecting to the Internet, directly or indirectly, and that is assigned an Internet Protocol address or Bluetooth address."); H.B. 2395, 80th Leg. Assemb., Reg. Sess. (Or. 2019) (defining connected device as "a device or other physical object that: (A) Connects, directly or indirectly, to the Internet and is used primarily for personal, family or household purposes; and (B) Is assigned an Internet Protocol address or another address or number that identifies the connected device for the purpose of making a short-range wireless connection to another device").

[220] CAL. CIV. CODE § 1798.91.06(e) (West 2020).

[221] *See* CAL. BUS. & PROF. CODE § 22948.20 (West 2020).

[222] *Id.*

[223] *See id.*

[224] *See* A.B. 1395, 2019-2020 Leg., Reg. Sess. (Cal. 2019).

the IoT concerns discussed in Chapters 1 and 2. These concerns are not just confined to the world of privacy. Privacy and data security harms lie at the intersection of privacy law and commercial law. For example, commercial law's contract principles also determine the validity of the "choice" aspect of the notice and choice privacy regime. Commercial law's warranty rules and products liability law can also impact consumers' remedies for harmful and defective IoT devices. Commercial law's lending and debt collection rules can also facilitate privacy and corporate digital domination harms as well as allow companies to expand their market power and use various corporate transactions to consolidate, transfer, monetize, and disclose our data. Part II of this book primarily evaluates commercial law's role in enabling IoT harms.

Commercial Law's Impact on Privacy, Security, and Liability

4

Commercial Law's Consent Problem

Unlike privacy law discourse, which has primarily explored questions related to others' knowledge, access, and use of information about us, commercial law's central focus has been on issues related to trade involving persons, merchants, and entities. In the commercial law context, questions about knowledge and information are primarily connected to the exchange and disclosure of information needed to facilitate transactions between parties.[1] This distinct historical focus has likely contributed to commercial law's failure to adequately account for and address privacy, security, and digital domination harms. In some cases, commercial law also defers to corporate commercial practices as well.

As we discussed in Chapter 3, privacy scholars have long highlighted the many limits of the notice and choice framework.[2] Choice is about consent.[3] Commercial law is partly based upon contract law rules and principles that govern consent. Privacy policies give us the illusion of choice and control. Several legal scholars have critiqued the application of contract law principles that bind consumers to one-sided contract terms.[4] Consent to online contract terms can be a hotly contested

---

[1] *See, e.g.*, U.C.C. § 2-510 cmt. 2 (AM. LAW INST. & UNIF. LAW COMM'M 2020) ("However, if the goods have been destroyed prior to the cure or the buyer is unaware of their destruction at the time he waives the defect in the documents, the risk of the loss must still be borne by the seller, for the risk shifts only at the time of cure, waiver of documentary defects or acceptance of the goods.").

[2] *See, e.g.*, ARI EZRA WALDMAN, PRIVACY AS TRUST: INFORMATION PRIVACY FOR AN INFORMATION AGE 83 (2018) ("[N]otice-and-choice doesn't work."); Helen Nissenbaum, *A Contextual Approach to Privacy Online*, Fall, DÆDALUS J. AM. ACAD. ARTS & SCI., 32, 34 (2011) ("[T]here is considerable agreement that transparency-and-choice has failed.").

[3] WALDMAN, *supra* note 2, at 30.

[4] *See generally, e.g.*, Ian Ayres & Alan Schwartz, *The No-Reading Problem in Consumer Contract Law*, 66 STAN. L. REV. 545, 562 (2014); Stacy-Ann Elvy, *Contracting in the Age of the Internet of Things: Article 2 of the UCC and Beyond*, 44 HOFSTRA L. REV. 839 (2016); Nancy S. Kim, *Clicking and Cringing*, 86 OR. L. REV. 797 (2007) [hereinafter Kim, *Clicking*]; Juliet M. Moringiello, *Signals, Assent and Internet Contracting*, 57 RUTGERS L. REV. 1307 (2005); Todd D. Rakoff, *Contracts of Adhesion: An Essay in Reconstruction*, 96 HARV. L. REV. 1173, 1173 (1983). *But see* Randy E. Barnett, *Consenting to Form Contracts*, 71 FORDHAM L. REV. 627, 635–36 (2002); Jason Scott Johnston, *The Return of Bargain: An Economic Theory of How Standard-Form Contracts Enable Cooperative Negotiation between Businesses and Consumers*, 104 MICH. L. REV. 857 (2006).

issue in consumer lawsuits. The stakes are high: whether a consumer has assented to a company's terms and conditions has significant implications for the consumer's rights in the event of a dispute. These include whether the consumer is required to arbitrate her claims, whether the contract is subject to a limitation of liability clause, whether the consumer can bring a claim for breach of implied warranties, and possibly whether a consumer has consented to a company's data practices, including the collection and disclosure of the consumer's COVID-19–related data. Contract law principles play an essential role in the analysis of assent, but the IoT brings about unique challenges to established contract law rules. The IoT complicates the application of traditional assent doctrine in consumer transactions for several reasons.

Case law addressing the online contracting landscape is befuddling. Courts use several classifications for the different online formats companies use to display their terms and privacy policies. Courts do not always consistently and clearly apply these classifications. Courts' approval of online wrap contracts has contributed to technology giants' ongoing power over us.[5] Further, IoT devices lack the traditional screens that are used by consumers to view and agree to companies' terms and conditions and privacy policies and to configure privacy settings. This facilitates Contract Distancing and makes meaningful assent and notice much harder to achieve. I use the term "Contract Distancing" to refer to the growing distance in the IoT context between consumers, contract terms, and the traditional contract formation process.[6] By entering into a single IoT transaction, consumers are frequently required to assent to multiple different documents, including different terms of use, privacy policies, warranty agreements, end user licensing agreements (EULAs) and possibly service agreements, even when they contract with a single provider. Recall that various studies have shown that we frequently fail to read companies' conditions of use and privacy policies. With its multiplicity of providers and connected services, the IoT will only worsen this problem. The effect, of course, is that companies are free to continue to include anti-consumer contract provisions with impunity.

Rising levels of information asymmetry in contracting will give companies even more opportunities to shape and influence our contracting behaviors. Additionally, possible future developments in artificial intelligence and autonomous devices raise questions about the role of agency law in determining our contractual rights and obligations. Lastly, as several scholars have noted, privacy policies and even privacy settings do not adequately describe or depict companies' extensive data collection,

---

[5] Julie E. Cohen, Between Truth and Power: The Legal Constructions of Informational Capitalism 44, 63 (2019); Brett Frischmann & Evan Selinger, Re-Engineering Humanity 62–67 (2018); Margaret Radin, Boilerplate: The Fine Print, Vanishing Rights, and the Rule of Law 7–9, 12–15 (2013); Amy Kapczynski, *The Law of Information Capitalism*, 129 Yale L.J. 1460, 1501, 1503 (2020); Julie E. Cohen, *Law for the Platform Economy*, 51 U.C. Davis L. Rev. 133, 154–57 (2017).

[6] Elvy, *supra* note 4, at 843.

analytics, and sharing practices. In an IoT age where vast quantities of data are available to companies and Contract Distancing is the norm, privacy policy and privacy setting failures are even more glaring and potentially harmful.

COMMERCIAL LAW DISCOURSE

Before we discuss the role of privacy policies and the current contracting landscape, let us first turn to the origins of commercial law. This brief historical discussion will help us to better understand commercial law's current consent problem as well as the various other shortcomings in commercial law's handling of the privacy, data security, and digital domination issues explored in Chapters 5, 6, and 7. As with other areas of US law, historically some aspects of commercial law and practice were based on the earlier British experience.[7] As James Steven Rogers observes, "throughout the late eighteenth and early nineteenth centuries each system [US and British] freely drew upon authorities from the others."[8] Rogers' account of "early commercial practices" in Europe documents merchants' sale and transport of goods to foreign markets and the development of trade organizations in which merchants entrusted goods to agents or employees who acted on their behalf.[9]

Today, the UCC is a core aspect of US commercial law. Commercial laws adopted in the United States before the UCC came into being also reflect a focus on trade and commerce and rights in assets.[10] Much of commercial law continues to focus heavily on issues involving the transfer of rights and interests in various forms of collateral, while sometimes explicitly or implicitly allocating risks between contracting parties. Article 1 of the UCC notes that one of the underlying purposes of the code is to "simplify, clarify, and modernize the law governing

---

[7] JAMES Steven ROGERS, THE EARLY HISTORY OF THE LAW OF BILLS AND NOTES, xii (1995); *see also* Amelia H. Boss, *The Evolution of Commercial Law Norms: Lessons to Be Learned from Electronic Commerce,* 34 BROOK. J. INT'L L. 673, 673–81(2009)(noting the "common law influences of our mother country" on US commercial law).

[8] ROGERS, *supra* note 7, at xiv.

[9] *Id.* at 32–33.

[10] *See generally* Karl N. Llewellyn, *Why We Need the Uniform Commercial Code,* 10 U. FLA. L. REV. 367 (1957), https://chicagounbound.uchicago.edu/cgi/viewcontent.cgi?article=13353&context=journa l_articles (discussing various sources of early commercial law, such as the Uniform Sales Act); Uniform Sales Act (1906); *see also* Zipporah Batshaw Wiseman, *The Limits of Vision: Karl Llewellyn and the Merchant Rules,* 100 HARV. L. REV. 465, 474 n.31 (1987)(discussing the Uniform Sales Act and contending that it "was based on the British Sale of Goods Act of 1893"); Henry D. Gabriel, *The Inapplicability of the United Nations Convention on the International Sale of Goods as a Model for the Revision of Article Two of the Uniform Commercial Code,* 72 TUL. L. REV. 1995, 1999 (1998) ("The present Article Two replaces the Uniform Sales Act of 1906, which itself was based on the British Sale of Goods Act of 1893. Both of these earlier statutes attempted to codify the common law of sales."); Norman D. Lattin, *The Law of Sales in the Uniform Commercial Code,* 15 OHIO ST. L.J. 12, 12 (1954), https://kb.osu.edu/bitstream/handle/1811/67778/1/OSLJ_V15N1_0012.pdf; *Uniform Commercial Code,* UNIFORM L. COMMISSION, www.uniformlaws.org/acts/ucc (last visited Mar. 29, 2020).

commercial transactions."[11] Article 2 of the UCC governs transactions involving the purchase and sale of goods. Article 9 of the UCC regulates the assignment of rights in personal property. The Bankruptcy Code focuses on the transfer and regulation of assets in bankruptcy proceedings. Consumer protection law has had to adapt and respond to the commercial law frameworks that facilitate the transfer of rights in assets. Consumer protection regulation, such as the Fair Debt Collection Practices Act, governs debt collector actions in enforcing rights created via lending frameworks. United States commercial law is also not free from international influence, such as the United Nations Convention on Contracts for the International Sale of Goods.[12]

The seemingly inaccurate story of the law merchant – that "medieval merchants created a perfect private legal system out of commercial customs" – has appeared in several segments of modern commercial law.[13] Although "contracting is private ordering," research on the law merchant narrative has challenged the accuracy of this story.[14] The persistence of this narrative to some extent illustrates commercial law's regard for commercial practices.[15] As Emily Kadens argues, some commercial law scholars and others have used the story of the medieval law merchant narrative "as unassailable proof that private ordering can work."[16] Yet, several scholars have dispelled the traditional story of the law merchant as an entirely "distinct and cohesive body of law."[17] Research by scholars in this area suggests that historically merchants did not create uniform customs, but instead used law when necessary to supplement common contractual terms and sometimes requested that state actors (courts and governments) adopt rules to mitigate "the instability of custom."[18] J. H. Baker has argued that "substantive mercantile law . . . had no existence as a coherent system of principles before the common law itself developed the means of giving it expression."[19]

---

[11]   U.C.C. § 1-103 (Am. Law Inst. & Unif. Law Comm'n 2020).

[12]   United Nations Convention on Contracts for the International Sale of Goods, Apr. 11, 1980, 1489 U.N. T.S. 59, https://treaties.un.org/pages/ViewDetails.aspx?src=TREATY&mtdsg_no=X-10&chapter=10.

[13]   Emily Kadens, *The Myth of the Customary Law Merchant*, 90 Tex. L. Rev. 1153, 1153 (2012).

[14]   *Id.* at 1160.

[15]   *Id.* at 1153; *see also* J. H. Baker, *The Law Merchant and the Common Law Before 1700*, in The Legal Profession and the Common Law, Historical Essays 295, 320 (1986) (contending that "there was no incorporation of the law merchant into the common law before the eighteenth century").

[16]   Kadens, *supra* note 13, at 1153. *See generally* Emily Kadens, *The Medieval Law Merchant: The Tyranny of a Construct*, 7 J. Legal Analysis 251 (2015).

[17]   Benjamin Geva, *Forged Check Indorsement Losses Under the UCC: The Role of Policy in the Emergence of Law Merchant from Common Law*, 45 Wayne L. Rev. 1733, 1787 (2000); *see generally* Baker, *supra* note 15; Rogers, *supra* note 7, at xii; Kadens, *supra* note 15; Stephen E. Sachs, *From St. Ives to Cyberspace: The Modern Distortion of the Medieval "Law Merchant,"* 21 Am. U. Int'l L. Rev. 685 (2006); Hal S. Scott, *The Risk Fixers*, 91 Harv. L. Rev. 737, 738–39 (1978); Leon E. Trakman, *The Twenty-First Century Law Merchant*, 48 Am. Bus. L.J. (2011), www.austlii.edu.au/au/journals/UNSWLRS/2011/32.html.

[18]   Kadens, *supra* note 13, at 1205.

[19]   Baker, *supra* note 15 at 321.

Despite evidence that calls into question the validity of the law merchant narrative, the law merchant story continues to persist to some extent today. Some have suggested that courts could rely on a "law merchant of the Internet."[20] The law merchant narrative is also found in legal scholarship exploring cyberspace and privacy issues as well and has sometimes been used to justify calls for self-regulation in this area.[21] Several sources of commercial law continue to reference the law merchant narrative. The text and comments section of the UCC, the Bankruptcy Code, and other sources of commercial law make specific reference to "the law merchant."[22] The comments to Article 1 of the UCC note that "[a]pplication of the Code [under certain circumstances] may be justified . . . by the fact that it is in large part a reformulation and restatement of the law merchant and of the understanding of a business community which transcends state and even national boundaries."[23]

Although scholars debate the importance and impact of the UCC's reference to the false law merchant narrative, multiple cases applying commercial law principles reference the "law merchant."[24] Others contend that when courts refer to the "law merchant" they treat it as "synonymous with 'common law' or equity."[25] In an 1805 decision, a New York court stated "the law merchant is, however, the general law of commercial nations."[26] A federal district court observed in 2019 that "[t]he drafters of

[20] Am. B. Ass'n, *Achieving Legal and Business Order in Cyberspace: A Report on Global Jurisdiction Issues Created by the Internet*, 55 Bus. LAW. 1801, 1933 (2000); *see also* Sachs, *supra* note 17, at 687 ("In July 2000, the ABA panel suggested that courts should turn to 'a "law merchant" for the Internet' in enforcing mandatory, non-binding arbitration clauses, as well as in regulating the activities of automated software robots.").

[21] *See, e.g.*, Kadens, *supra* note 13, at 1160; Sachs, *supra* note 17, at 809–12 (describing legal scholarship in the cyberspace area reliance on the law merchant). *See generally* David R. Johnson & David Post, *Law and Borders – The Rise of Law in Cyberspace*, 48 STAN. L. REV. 1367 (1996); Joel R. Reidenberg, *Lex Informatica: The Formulation of Information Policy Rules Through Technology*, 76 TEX. L. REV. 553 (1998).

[22] *See, e.g.*, U.C.C. § 1-103; *id.* § 2-104 cmt. 2 ("The term 'merchant' as defined here roots in the 'law merchant' concept of a professional in business."); *id.* § 1-301 cmt. 3; Uniform Fraudulent Transfer Act § 12 (UNIF. LAW COMM'N 2014); 11 U.S.C. §§ 555, 556, 559, 561 (2020).

[23] U.C.C. § 1-301 cmt. 3.

[24] A search of the term "law merchant" in case law uncovered more than 4,000 cases ranging from 1784 through 2020. Results for "law merchant," LEXIS ADVANCE https://advance.lexis.com (search in search bar for "law merchant"); *see also, e.g.*, Ingrid Michelsen Hillinger, *The Article 2 Merchant Rules: Karl Llewellyn's Attempt to Achieve The Good, The True, The Beautiful in Commercial Law*, 73 GEO. L.J. 1141, 1148–50 (1985); Steve H. Nickles, *Problems of Sources of Law Relationships Under the Uniform Commercial Code – Part I: The Methodological Problem and the Civil Law Approach*, 31 ARK. L. REV. 1, 48 (1977); Peter Winship, *Contemporary Commercial Law Literature in the United States*, 43 OHIO ST. L.J. 643, 645 n.8 (1982).

[25] James Whitman, *Commercial Law and the American* Volk: *A Note on Llewellyn's German Sources for the Uniform Commercial Code*, 97 YALE L.J. 156, 174–75 (1987).

[26] Walden v. Le Roy, 2 Cai. R. 263, 265 (N.Y. Sup. Ct. 1805). *See generally The Evolution of the Court*, NYCOURTS.GOV, ww2.nycourts.gov/courts/1jd/supctmanh/A_Brief_history_of_the_Court.shtml ("The New York State Supreme Court was established in 1691, making it one of the oldest continuing courts of general jurisdiction in the United States. Pursuant to legislation adopted by the New York

the UCC set out to preserve and, where necessary, clarify and conform the law merchant with modern commercial practice."[27]

United States commercial law is not in fact an "embodiment[]of the law merchant," given evidence that calls into question the validity of the narrative.[28] Instead, commercial law has in some instances operated as a mechanism "for allocating risk among transactors."[29] Revisions to commercial law to meet technological challenges have sometimes transferred risks from firms to consumers.[30] The persistent law merchant narrative and the UCC's provisions indicate that commercial law's historic focus on the development of rules that enable the transfer of rights in assets also reflects its deep regard for corporate commercial practices.

Although the merchant juries proposed by Karl Llewellyn, the main drafter of Article 2 of the UCC, to determine the reasonableness of commercial practices was not adopted, the remaining framework associated with the merchant juries was retained in the UCC.[31] Research proving the inaccuracy of the law merchant narrative calls into question the references to the narrative currently found in various sources of commercial law and the assumption that courts should consistently turn to usage of trade, and defer to corporate commercial practices to resolve disputes.[32] Under the UCC, usage of trade can impact several topics, including but not limited to the interpretation of contract terms, the boundaries of the implied warranty of merchantability, and the creation and disclaimer of other implied warranties.[33] Some companies attempt to limit trade usages via their online terms

---

Assembly, the court, originally known as the Supreme Court of Judicature, was given jurisdiction over criminal and civil pleas.").

[27] Russell Barnett Ford of Tullahoma, Inc. v. H&S Bakery, Inc., 398 F. Supp. 3d 287, 300 (E.D. Tenn. 2019) (citing the Tennessee Court of Appeals).

[28] Scott, *supra* note 17, at 792.

[29] *Id.* at 737.

[30] Jean Braucher, *Rent-Seeking and Risk-Fixing in the New Statutory Law of Electronic Commerce: Difficulties in Moving Consumer Protection Online*, 2001 WIS. L. REV. 527, 529 (2001) ("The principal regulatory goal in E-Sign and UETA was elimination of legal risk for businesses as they switched from paper to electronic records for purposes of record retention, making disclosures and giving notices. But eliminating the risk for businesses in some instances meant shifting the risk to someone else. In the case of electronic consumer protection notices and disclosures, consumers are being assigned more risk that effective communication will not be achieved."); *see also* Scott, *supra* note 17, at 738–39.

[31] Allen R. Kamp, *Uptown Act: A History of the Uniform Commercial Code: 1940–49*, 51 SMU L. REV. 275, 290–93, 318 (1998); Whitman, *supra* note 25, at 174–75.

[32] *See* Kadens, *supra* note 13, at 1205; *see also* U.C.C. § 2-314(3) (AM. LAW INST. & UNIF. LAW COMM'N 2020) ("Unless excluded or modified (Section 2-316) other implied warranties may arise from course of dealing or usage of trade."); *id.* § 2-609(2) ("Between merchants the reasonableness of grounds for insecurity and the adequacy of any assurance offered shall be determined according to commercial standards."); Lisa Bernstein, *Merchant Law in a Merchant Court: Rethinking the Code's Search for Immanent Business Norms*, 144 U. PA. L. REV. 1765, 1768 (1996); Lisa Bernstein, *The Questionable Empirical Basis of Article 2's Incorporation Strategy: A Preliminary Study*, 66 U. CHI. L. REV. 710 (1999) [hereinafter Bernstein, *Article 2's Incorporation Strategy*].

[33] *See* U.C.C. § 2-314; *id.* § 2-202 cmt. 2; *id.* § 2-309 cmt. 1; *id.* § 2-316. *See generally* Lisa Bernstein, *Custom in the Courts*, 110 NW. U.L. REV. 63 (2015) [hereinafter Bernstein, *Custom in the Courts*];

of service.[34] The UCC's respect for commercial practices is found not only in its reference to usage of trade, but also by its inclusion of concepts related to commercial reasonableness and commercial standards.[35]

An official comment to section 1-303 states that "the very fact of commercial acceptance makes out a *prima facie* case that the usage is reasonable, and the burden is no longer on the usage to establish itself as being reasonable."[36] Consider that an empirical study of usage of trade in UCC case law found that trade usage is not generally proven "through the introduction of the types of 'objective evidence'" that advocates of the UCC's approach contend will decrease "the risk of interpretive error – such as expert witness testimony, industry trade codes, or statistical evidence that a particular practice is widely observed."[37] Instead, trade usage is frequently demonstrated through either the parties' testimony or those of their associates.[38] Thus, the original rationales for the UCC's incorporation approach to usage of trade may not be justified.[39]

It is currently the modern usage of trade to use electronic contracting formats that include anti-consumer terms and that negate meaningful consent in online consumer transactions. As David McGowan observes, courts can be more open to accepting usages of trade involving various online contracting formats in the e-commerce setting, such as "post-order shrink-wrap terms, as a method of forming an agreement as they either became more familiar with that method or c[o]me to accept economic arguments used to justify recognition of that method."[40] Over time courts began validating browsewrap and clickwrap and various other electronic contracting formats, which we will discuss in more detail later. These online formats are "usages currently observed by the great majority of decent dealers."[41] Today, modern commercial practices have evolved to include transactions involving our data that are facilitated through the use of these online contracting formats. Yet, courts have historically been reluctant to use the doctrine of unconscionability to aid consumers in the online setting. This problem is even more vexing in light of the various online contractual provisions that prevent consumers from accessing courts

---

Bernstein, *Article 2's Incorporation Strategy, supra* note 32; David McGowan, *Recognizing Usages of Trade: A Case Study from Electronic Commerce*, 8 WASH. U. J.L. & POL'Y 167 (2002).

[34] *See generally* Bernstein, *Custom in the Courts, supra* note 33.

[35] *See, e.g.,* U.C.C. § 1-201(20); *id.* cmt. 9; *id.* § 2-311 cmt. 2; *id.* § 2-609; *id.* § 2-612 cmt. 7; *id.* § 2-706 cmt. 1–5; *id.* § 4A-202; *id.* § 7-210 cmt. 1; *id.* § 9-607; Hillinger, *supra* note 24, at 1150–51.

[36] *See* U.C.C. § 1-303 cmt. 5.

[37] Bernstein, *Custom in the Courts, supra* note 33, at 63.

[38] *Id.*

[39] *Id.*

[40] McGowan, *supra* note 33, at 169, 177 ("a party might be found to have 'reason to know' of post-order or post-payment terms if the court finds that such terms amount to a usage of trade in a relevant market [and]a court can bind licensees, in either commercial or consumer markets, to post-order or post-payment terms if a court recognizes the use of such terms as a usage of trade."); Lisa Bernstein, *Merchant Law in a Modern Economy* 9–12 (Univ. of Chi. Law Sch. Coase-Sandor Inst. for Law & Econ. Research, Paper No. 639, 2013), http://ssrn.com/abstract=2242490.

[41] *See, e.g.,* U.C.C. § 1-303 cmt. 4.

and juries. This suggests that a new approach that establishes clearer rules to safeguard consumers from corporate overreach is needed to deal with the issue of consumer assent to online contractual terms.

Some proposed revisions to the UCC have been offered in part with the aim of updating the UCC in light of "modern commercial practices," such as electronic commerce.[42] However, the UCC's unresponsiveness to the consumer concerns these transactions raise continues (whether intentionally or unintentionally) the UCC's long-standing deference to the development of modern commercial practices. Historically, the UCC revision processes have not sufficiently accounted for consumer protection concerns.[43] These processes are not immune to corporate influence, and perhaps rightfully so, the UCC's drafters are "also continuously evaluat[ing] the anticipated political acceptability of their work."[44] Consumer protection issues are often viewed as controversial. From the UCC drafters' perspective, such issues could undermine uniformity efforts. Uniformity is a core goal of the UCC. Thus, even if many of the UCC's drafters do not oppose consumer protection regulation, they may oppose revising the code to address such issues in order to ensure that states adopt any proposed UCC amendments. Regardless of the reasons behind the UCC's meager consumer provisions, the result for consumers is the same – the UCC does not adequately deal with consumer protection issues. Although there are some specific provisions in the UCC dealing directly with consumer transactions, many consumer protection issues are left to other sources of law.[45] As Edward Rubin notes, "the [UCC] inherits the common law's blindness to consumer concerns, the very blindness which led directly to the law reform efforts of the consumer movement."[46]

There have been several missed opportunities to more adequately deal with consumer protection issues during proposed revisions to Articles 2 and 9 of the UCC.[47] For instance, the American Law Institute (ALI) and the National Conference of

---

[42]   Gabriel, *supra* note 10, at 141.

[43]   *See* Charles W. Mooney, Jr., *The Consumer Compromise in Revised UCC Article 9: Shame of It All*, 68 OHIO ST. L.J. 215, 216–17, 222–26 (2007). *See generally* Caroline Edwards, *Article 2 of the Uniform Commercial Code and Consumer Protection: The Refusal to Experiment*, 78 ST. JOHN'S L. REV. 663 (2004); Michael M. Greenfield, *The Role of Assent in Article 2 and Article 9*, 75 WASH. U. L.Q. 289 (1997); Gail Hillebrand, *The Uniform Commercial Code Drafting Process: Will Articles 2, 2B and 9 Be Fair to Consumers?*, 75 WASH. U. L.Q. 69 (1997); Gail Hillebrand, *What's Wrong with the Uniform Law Process?*, 52 HASTINGS L.J. 631, 631–32 (2001).

[44]   Jean Braucher, *Foreword: Consumer Protection and the Uniform Commercial Code*, 75 WASH. U. L.Q. 1, 8 (1997) [hereinafter Braucher, *Foreword*]; *see also* Frederick K. Beutel, *The Proposed Uniform [?] Commercial Code Should Not Be Adopted*, 61 YALE L.J. 334, 357–63 (1952). Robert Braucher, *The Legislative History of the Uniform Commercial Code*, 58 COLUM. L. REV. 798, 798–99 (1958); Gabriel, *supra* note 10, at 133–34.

[45]   *See, e.g.*, U.C.C. § 9-201(b) (AM. LAW INST. & UNIF. LAW COMM'N 2020); *id.* § 2-102; Braucher, *Foreword, supra* note 44, at 8; Jim Hawkins, *Protecting Consumers as Sellers*, 94 IND. L.J. 1407, 1408–09 (2019).

[46]   Edward, L. Rubin, *The Code, The Consumer, and the Institutional Structure of the Common Law*, 75 WASH. U. L.Q. 11, 14 (1997).

[47]   *See generally* Jean Braucher, *The Repo Code: A Study of Adjustment to Uncertainty in Commercial Law*, 75 WASH. U. L.Q. 549 (1997); Edwards, *supra* note 43; Edward J. Janger, *Predicting When the*

Commissioners on Uniform State Laws (ULC) attempted to revise the UCC to deal with the rise of computer information transactions through the inclusion of a proposed Article 2B, which would have been a new article in the UCC.[48] The proposed draft of Article 2B was not approved by the ALI.[49] Corporate actors in the software industry strongly influenced the drafting process, which resulted in a proposed statute that heavily favored the interests of industry.[50] Most of the proposed Article 2B drafting committee members allegedly routinely voted in support of provisions that protected software producers.[51] The failed Article 2B later became the Uniform Computer Information Transactions Act (UCITA) after the ALI withdrew from the project.[52] We will return to UCITA later on in this chapter.

In light of the UCC's failure to adequately deal with traditional consumer issues, it is not unexpected that the UCC has not to date sufficiently accounted for consumer privacy, security, and digital domination harms, which are even more abstract and intangible than traditional consumer harms. But the UCC is not the only source of commercial law that struggles to adequately address consumer protection issues, including privacy and data security concerns. The 2005 amendments to the Bankruptcy Code made it more difficult and expensive for consumers to file for and obtain adequate bankruptcy relief, with detrimental implications for low-income consumers.[53] The amendments were also a boon to automobile lenders who sought to limit consumers' ability to obtain adequate relief from vehicle loans

---

Uniform Law Process Will Fail: Article 9, Capture, and the Race to the Bottom, 83 Iowa L. Rev. 569 (1998); Jennifer S. Martin, *An Emerging Worldwide Standard for Protections of Consumers in the Sale of Goods: Did We Miss an Opportunity with Revised UCC Article 2?*, 41 Tex. Int'l L.J. 223 (2006); Mooney, Jr., *supra* note 43, at 216–17, 222–26.

[48] Juliet M. Moringiello & William L. Reynolds, *What's Software Got to Do With It? The ALI Principles of the Law of Software Contracts*, 84 Tul. L. Rev. 1541, 1542–43 (2010); Robert E. Scott, *The Rise and Fall of Article 2*, 62 La. L. Rev. 1009, 1048–50 (2002).

[49] Scott, *supra* note 48, at 1049.

[50] *Id.*

[51] Jean Braucher, *New Basics: Twelve Principles for Fair Commerce in Mass-Market Software and Other Digital Products*, in Consumer Protection in the Age of the "Information Economy" 166–67 (Jane K. Winn ed., 2006) [hereinafter Braucher, *New Basics*].

[52] *Id.*

[53] *See, e.g.*, A. Mechele Dickerson, *Race Matters in Bankruptcy Reform*, 71 Mo. L. Rev. 919, 920 (2006) (noting that the BAPCPA [Bankruptcy Abuse Prevention and Consumer Protection Act] made it harder for consumers to discharge their debts); Angela Littwin, *Adapting to BAPCPA*, 90 Am. Bankr. L.J. 183, 186–87 (2016) ("[T]he harm that remains a decade later [after the BAPCPA's adoption] boils down to the increased costs of filing and related ways that BAPCPA made consumer bankruptcy less accessible."); Angela Littwin, *The Affordability Paradox: How Consumer Bankruptcy's Greatest Weakness May Account for Its Surprising Success*, 52 Wm. & Mary L. Rev. 1933, 1935–36 (2011) (noting that the 2005 amendments to the bankruptcy code "increased the procedural burdens for everyone" and "made consumer bankruptcy more expensive for all debtors"); Andrew P. MacArthur, *Pay to Play: The Poor's Problems in the CAPCPA*, 25 Emory Bankr. Dev. J. 407, 407 (2009) ("The BAPCPA's additional fees and increased paperwork make bankruptcy access for the poor more difficult than for other classes, especially as fewer attorneys are likely to take their cases. Even if the poor are able to access the bankruptcy system, they are likely to be denied a fresh start.").

during bankruptcy.[54] As we will see in Chapter 6, subprime automobile lenders engage in several practices that enable privacy and digital domination harms. Additionally, as Chapter 7 notes, the 2005 bankruptcy amendments also failed to adequately address consumer privacy concerns in bankruptcy proceedings and overrely on the notice and choice regime.

THE ARTIFICE OF CHOICE AND CONTROL

Recall that companies primarily obtain rights in consumers' data through privacy policies and conditions of use. The contract law status of privacy policies has been the subject of significant debate.[55] Some case law suggests that privacy policies can qualify as contracts to the extent that contract formation requirements are satisfied.[56] Thus, the online contracting standards that we will explore in subsequent sections of this chapter that courts use to determine whether consumers are bound to companies' terms and conditions are also potentially applicable to privacy policies. Further, in some instances, IoT companies' terms and conditions also reference or incorporate their privacy policies. For instance, Owlet's terms of service states that "[b]y using the Products, you agree that we can use the personal data you provide in accordance with the terms of our Privacy Policy."[57] The company's terms and conditions also go on to provide that consumers assent to the terms "[b]y downloading, installing or otherwise accessing or using" the

[54] *See, e.g.*, 11 U.S.C. § 1325(a) (2019); Jean Braucher, *Rash and Ride-Through Redux: The Terms for Holding on to Cars, Homes and Other Collateral Under the 2005 Act*, 13 AM. BANKR. INST. L. REV. 457 (2005); Rajashri Chakrabarti & Nathaniel Pattison, *Auto Credit and the 2005 Bankruptcy Reform: The Impact of Eliminating Cramdowns*, 32 REV. FIN. STUD. 4734 (2019), https://academic.oup.com/rfs/article/32/12/4734/5425333 (noting that "[b]efore BAPCPA, a bankruptcy filer could reduce the amount owed on an undersecured auto loan to the market value of the car through a 'cramdown' but the 'anticramdown provision of BAPCPA prohibited cramdowns during the first 2.5 years of an auto loan'"); David Gray Carlson, *Cars and Homes in Chapter 13 after the 2005 Amendments to the Bankruptcy Code*, 14 AM. BANKR. INST. L. REV. 301 (2006); Pamela Foohey et al., *Driven To Bankruptcy*, 55 WAKE FOREST L. REV. (forthcoming 2020), https://papers.ssrn.com/sol3/papers.cfm?abstract_id=3451565 ("As part of BAPCPA, Congress enacted special protections for any purchase-money security interest in an automobile purchased within 910 days (i.e., two and a half years) before the bankruptcy filing" and if the provision applies "the chapter 13 plan must pay the full amount of the debt, not just the value of the collateral [and] the debtor's plan must use the interest rate in the contract even if the debtor could get a lower interest rate in a chapter 13 plan."); William C. Whitford, *A History of the Automobile Lender Provisions of BAPCPA*, 2007 U. ILL. L. REV. 143 (2007).

[55] *See, e.g., In re* Am. Airlines, Inc., Privacy Litig., 370 F. Supp. 2d 552, 561 (N.D. Tex. 2005); Warren E. Agin, *The New Regime for Treatment of Customer Data in Bankruptcy Cases*, 10 J. BANKR. L. & PRAC. 365, 369–70 (2001) (contending that privacy statements may be "executory" or non-executory" contracts depending on "whether it places continuing material obligations on each party" but a "privacy policy might not even qualify as an enforceable contract"); Daniel J. Solove & Woodrow Hartzog, *The FTC and the New Common Law of Privacy*, 114 COLUM. L. REV. 583, 595–96 (2014) (addressing whether privacy policies are contracts).

[56] *See, e.g., In re* JetBlue Airways Corp. Privacy Litig., 379 F. Supp. 2d 299, 316–17 (E.D.N.Y. 2005); *Am. Airlines*, 370 F. Supp. 2d at 561.

[57] *Terms and Conditions*, OWLET, https://owletcare.com/pages/terms (last updated May 8, 2019).

company's products.[58] Such incorporations and references of privacy policies in terms and conditions create a stronger argument for treating privacy policies as contracts.

If adopted, the ALI's proposed Restatement of the Law of Consumer Contracts (ALI Consumer Restatement) could provide some guidance on case law trends about whether privacy policies are indeed contracts or are simply statements of organizations' policies.[59] To date, it is unclear whether the ALI Consumer Restatement will sufficiently deal with this issue as well as other problems associated with the digitization of form contracts in a manner that adequately protects consumers' interests.[60] It also remains to be seen whether the proposed ALI Consumer Restatement will effectively address the Contract Distancing problem.

Even if privacy policies can qualify as contracts, companies attempt to limit their obligations to consumers through these policies. Recall the data security disclaimers discussed in Chapter 2. More importantly, companies' privacy policies have significant shortcomings that have long been problematic but that are particularly glaring in an IoT world plagued by Contract Distancing.

Privacy policies are notorious for their legalese and blundering inadequacies. Recall that consumers also misunderstand the very nature of privacy policies. Many consumers mistakenly believe that the existence of a privacy policy means that their data will not be disclosed or shared with third parties.[61] A GAO report on IoT

---

[58]   *Id.*

[59]   *See Restatement of the Law, Consumer Contracts*, AM. L. INST., www.ali.org/projects/show/consumer-contracts/ (last visited Nov. 15, 2018).

[60]   *See, e.g.*, Gregory Klass, *Empiricism and Privacy Policies in the Restatement of Consumer Contract Law*, 36 YALE J. ON REG. 45, 45 (2019) (a study finding "little support for the [proposed restatement's] claim that there is a clear trend recognizing privacy policies as contracts, and none for the claim that those decisions have been more influential than decisions coming out the other way"); Adam J. Levitin et al., *The Faulty Foundation of the Draft Restatement of Consumer Contracts*, 36 YALE J. ON REG. 447, 447 (2019) (critiquing the proposed restatement); Melvin Eisenberg, *The Proposed Restatement of Consumer Contracts, If Adopted, Would Drive a Dagger Through Consumers' Rights*, YALE J. ON REG. NOTICE & COMMENT BLOG (Mar. 20, 2019), http://yalejreg.com/nc/the-proposed-restatement-of-consumer-contracts-if-adopted-would-drive-a-dagger-through-consumers-rights-by-melvin-eisenberg/ (contending that the proposed restatement "seriously disfavors consumers"); Nancy Kim, *The Controversy over the Restatement of Consumer Contracts*, CONTRACTSPROF BLOG (May 7, 2019), https://lawprofessors.typepad.com/contractsprof_blog/2019/05/the-controversy-over-the -restatement-of-consumer-contracts.html (contending that the draft restatement "ignores the problems created by form and digitization and does nothing to address the problems created by ubiquitous digital contracts").

[61]   *See* PEW RESEARCH CTR., WHAT INTERNET USERS KNOW ABOUT TECHNOLOGY AND THE WEB 7 (2014), www.pewresearch.org/wp-content/uploads/sites/9/2014/11/PI_Web-IQ_112514_PDF.pdf (stating 52 percent of respondents believed that "when a company posts a privacy policy, it ensures that the company keeps confidential all the information it collects on users"); *see also* JOSEPH TUROW, LAUREN FELDMAN & KIMBERLY MELTZER, ANNENBERG PUB. POLICY CTR. OF THE UNIV. OF PA., OPEN TO EXPLOITATION: AMERICA'S SHOPPERS ONLINE AND OFFLINE 20 (2005), http://repository.upenn.edu/cgi/viewcontent.cgi?article=1035&context=asc_papers (determining that 59 percent of survey respondents said the statement "[w]hen a web site has a privacy policy, it means that the site will not share my information with other websites or companies" was true).

vehicles found that these devices collect significant amounts of data about consumers yet the manufacturers' privacy policies were not "written in plain language."[62] According to the report, the selected manufacturers insisted that they obtained consumer consent to their data collection practices, but many of the reviewed privacy policies did not accurately describe the purpose of the data collection, what types of data would be collected, or the manufacturers' data disclosure and use practices.[63] It is questionable whether one can provide a meaningful manifestation of assent to a privacy policy that obscurely describes a company's data collection and sharing practices. Consent to such a privacy policy is meaningless.

Admittedly, consumers' awareness and understanding of companies' data collection practices and privacy policies may be context dependent. For instance, a consumer that uses a health mobile application likely knows that that the application collects health-related data even if the consumer does not keenly grasp the implications of this type of data collection. However, a consumer that uses an IoT household device is most likely unaware of all of the types of, and extent to which, such data are collected, transferred, hoarded, and analyzed. Additionally, even when consumers decline to consent to data collection, organizations can "draw probabilistic inferences" about non-consenting individuals from the data supplied by consenting consumers, once a "representative sample" is reached.[64] This arguably renders a consumer's decision to decline to consent to data collection meaningless.[65]

IoT entities may also have multiple privacy policies that govern different aspects of their interactions with consumers. For example, Nest provides a separate privacy statement for its IoT devices and services and another for its websites.[66] Portions of consumers' data collected from IoT devices and associated services and websites may be governed by different privacy policies. This worsens the lack of reading problem.

Many companies also do not provide consumers with meaningful choices and control of their data through privacy policies. According to the GAO report mentioned earlier, consumers who were reluctant to share their data had "few options besides opting out of all" IoT services, such as "roadside assistance and automatic crash notification[s]."[67] Thus, in order to use all of the services that accompany these

---

[62]   U.S. Gov't Accountability Office, Vehicle Data Privacy: Industry and Federal Efforts Under Way, but NHTSA Needs to Define Its Role 17 (2017), www.gao.gov/assets/690/686284.pdf.

[63]   *See id.* at 18.

[64]   *See* Solon Barocas & Helen Nissenbaum, *Computing Ethics: Big Data's End Run Around Procedural Privacy Protections,* 57 Comm. Ass'n Computing Mach. 31, 32 (2014).

[65]   *See id.*

[66]   *Compare Privacy Policy for Nest Web Sites,* Nest, https://nest.com/legal/privacy-policy-for-nest-web-sites/ (last visited Jan. 4, 2020), *with Privacy Statement for Nest Products and Services,* Nest, https://nest.com/legal/privacy-statement-for-nest-products-and-services/ (last visited Jan. 4, 2020).

[67]   U.S. Gov't Accountability Office, *supra* note 62, at 7.

IoT vehicles, consumers are forced to manifest assent to privacy policies that do not adequately describe how the data will be used and which parties can have access to their data.

Similarly, makers of IoT devices that are Amazon dash replenishment service (DRS) enabled also collect data about the automatic orders placed by the device, among other things.[68] This occurs even though Amazon rather than the device manufacturer provides the replenishment service. Amazon's website provides that consumers may restrict the manufacturers' access to these data but doing so prevents the consumer from using DRS.[69] As we move further into an era in which all static objects become connected, companies will likely continue to provide consumers with no meaningful choice and little control over the data they generate unless required to do otherwise.

Privacy settings also lure consumers into believing that they can control their data trails. For instance, a 2018 Associated Press investigation into Google's data practices found that although privacy settings indicated that consumers could switch off location history data, Google's mobile applications continued to access consumers' location data without their knowledge.[70] In the lawsuits that followed, Google defended its actions by contending that users consented to the data collection via its privacy policy.[71]

As Nancy Kim and Jeremy Telman have observed, technology giants use the artifice of consent to undo the impact of rights granted or protected by legislation.[72] This problem extends to other types of organizations as well, even though such attempts are not always successful. For instance, according to a U.S. Department of Education letter, a charter school required parents to waive their rights under FERPA as a condition of student enrollment and educational services.[73] The relevant terms of use allowed the school's contractor, affiliates, and licensees to collect and disclose children's data, including messages, photographs, and personally identifiable information connected to school records.[74] These data could also be

---

[68] See *Amazon Dash Replenishment*, AMAZON, www.amazon.com/b/ref=s9_acss_bw_cg_dbpk5_md1_w?
node=15426532011&ref=cp_oft_db_drs_lm&pf_rd_m=ATVPDKIKX0DER&pf_rd_s=merchandised-
search-17&pf_rd_r=HNEJDFBW40898S96GTZ0&pf_rd_t=101&pf_rd_p=d722a022-7f6a-4d79-baf5-
27e10fd3a142&pf_rd_i=10667898011 (last visited Jan. 4, 2020).

[69] See id.

[70] Ryan Nakashima, *Google Tracks Your Movements, Like It or Not*, ASSOCIATED PRESS (Aug. 13, 2018),
www.apnews.com/828aefab64d4411bac257a07c1afoecb.

[71] See generally Defendant Google LLC's Motion to Dismiss, Patacsil v. Google, Inc., No. 5:18-cv-
05062-EJD, 2018 WL 9362364, at *4 (N.D. Cal. Oct. 22, 2018); Defendant Google LLC's Motion to
Dismiss, Lombardo v. Google, Inc., No. 5:18-cv-05288 (N.D. Cal. Oct. 22, 2018); Anne Cullen, *Google
Says IPhone, Android Users Agreed to Tracking*, LAW360 (Oct. 23, 2018, 8:06 PM), www.law360.com
/articles/1094780/google-says-iphone-android-users-agreed-to-tracking.

[72] See Nancy S. Kim & D. A. Jeremy Telman, *Internet Giants as Quasi-Governmental Actors and the
Limits of Contractual Consent*, 80 MO. L. REV. 723, 729, 738–39 (2015).

[73] See Letter from Dale King, Dir., Family Policy Compliance Office to U.S. Dep't of Educ. 6–7 (Nov.
2, 2017), https://studentprivacy.ed.gov/sites/default/files/resource_document/file/Agora%20Findings
%20letter%20FINAL%2011.2.17.pdf.

[74] Id.

disclosed to "future employers of [] student[s] without consent."[75] Remember from Chapters 1 and 3 that IoT devices are expected to play a central role in educational services, but that federal and state statutes do not always provide complete protections for students' data.[76]

The practice of using assent to contract terms to bind individuals to anti-consumer provisions while attempting to simultaneously limit the effect of consumer protection legislation will continue in the IoT age. Assent becomes less meaningful in contracting environments plagued by Contract Distancing, gross imbalances of information asymmetry, and privacy policies that fail to sufficiently describe data collection and sharing practices and provide us with meaningful choices all while purporting to grant organizations enforceable rights in our data.

THE CURRENT ONLINE CONTRACTING LANDSCAPE

The common law of contracts and Article 2 of the UCC provide primary contract law principles that govern assent issues associated with online contracts. The Restatement of the Law (Second) of Contracts (Contracts Restatement) serves as the primary "guide to the modern common law of contracts."[77] The Contracts Restatement provides that in order for a contract to be formed there must be "a manifestation of mutual assent."[78] The Contracts Restatement goes on to state that a "manifestation of assent may be made wholly or partly by written or spoken words or by other acts or by failure to act."[79] Article 2 of the UCC provides that a sale of goods contract can "be made in any manner sufficient to show agreement, including conduct by both parties which recognizes the existence of such a contract."[80] Various sources of commercial law give effect to electronic records and signatures and enable online contracting.[81] Other sources of relevant contract law that could apply to IoT transactions include UCITA and the ALI's Principles on the Law of Software Contracts (ALI Software Principles).

After the ALI withdrew from the Article 2B project discussed earlier, the ULC proceeded with the failed project by developing UCITA, a uniform law applicable to computer information transactions, including licenses of computer programs.[82] Although UCITA contains provisions applicable to mass-market license

---

[75] *Id.* at 6.

[76] Jeanette Cajide, *The Connected School: How IoT Could Impact Education*, HUFFINGTON POST, www .huffingtonpost.com/jeanette-cajide/the-connected-school-how-_b_8521612.html (last updated Dec. 6, 2017).

[77] *Restatement of the Law Second, Contracts*, AM. L. INST., www.ali.org/publications/show/contracts/ (last visited Nov. 16, 2018).

[78] RESTATEMENT (SECOND) OF CONTRACTS § 17 (AM. LAW INST. 1981).

[79] *Id.* § 19.

[80] U.C.C. § 2-204(1) (AM. LAW INST. & UNIF. LAW COMM'N 2002).

[81] UNIF. ELEC. TRANSACTIONS ACT § 1 (UNIF. LAW COMM'N 1999); 15 U.S.C. § 7001 (2018).

[82] Uniform Computer Information Transactions Act § 103(a) (UNIF. LAW COMM'N 2002); Braucher, *New Basics, supra* note 51, at 167.

transactions, such as a return right, it has faced significant opposition from consumer protection advocates and some industries.[83] Like proposed Article 2B, UCITA's provisions are primarily industry friendly and fail to protect consumer interests.[84] Consumers' use rights are primarily dependent on grants from the software producer, and UCITA generally approves of "broad contractual limitations on transfer."[85] UCITA's disclosure provisions were also criticized by state attorneys general and the FTC.[86] UCITA, like other sources of commercial law, also reflects deference to commercial practices.[87] One example of UCITA's deference to industry practices is found in its use of a "reason to know" standard in addressing the adoption of "subsequently presented" contract terms.[88] UCITA's comments indicate that reason to know may be inferred from "ordinary business practices or marketing approaches of which a party is or should be aware and from which a reasonable person would infer that terms will follow."[89] UCITA's impact on IoT transactions involving computer information is limited as only two states adopted it and some states enacted laws to prevent its application.[90] UCITA is a largely unsuccessful project. To the extent that UCITA is applicable, it appears to validate rolling contracts and approve of the delayed provision of contract terms in mass-market internet transactions.[91]

---

[83] UNIF. COMPUT. INFO. TRANSACTIONS ACT § 209(b); Braucher, *New Basics, supra* note 51, at 167; Robert Oakley, *Fairness in Electronic Contracting: Minimum Standards for Non-Negotiated Contracts*, 42 HOUS. L. REV. 1041, 1072–73 (2005); Michael L. Rustad & Maria Vittoria Onufrio, *The Exportability of the Principles of Software: Lost in Translation?*, 2 HASTINGS SCI. & TECH. L.J. 25, 37–38 (2010) [hereinafter, Rustad & Onufrio, *Exportability*].

[84] Braucher, *New Basics*, note 51, at 167–68; Michael L. Rustad & Elif Kavusturan, *A Commercial Law for Software Contracting*, 76 WASH & LEE L. REV. 775, 782–84, 808–09 (2019); Michael L. Rustad & Maria Vittoria Onufrio, *Reconceptualizing Consumer Terms of Use for a Globalized Knowledge Economy*, 14 U. PA. J. BUS. L. 1085, 1132–33 (2012) [hereinafter Rustad & Onufrio, *Reconceptualizing*]; Rustad & Onufrio, *Exportability, supra* note 83, at 37.

[85] Jean Braucher, *US Influence with a Twist: Lesson About Unfair Contract Terms from US Software Customers*, 15 AUSTL. COMPETITION & CONSUMER L.J. 5, 13 (2007) [hereinafter Braucher, *Twist*].

[86] Rustad & Onufrio, *Exportability, supra* note 83, at 39–40; Braucher, *Twist, supra* note 85, at 12.

[87] Richard A. Epstein, *Contract, Not Regulation: UCITA and High-Tech Consumers Meet Their Consumer Protection Critics*, in CONSUMER PROTECTION IN THE AGE OF THE "INFORMATION ECONOMY" 194 (Jane K. Winn ed., 2006) (noting that UCITA "puts express terms first, course of dealing second, and trade practice third").

[88] UNIF. COMPUT. INFO. TRANSACTIONS ACT § 208 (UNIF. LAW COMM'N 2002).

[89] *Id.* at cmt. 3(a).

[90] Rustad & Kavusturan, *supra* note 84, at 808; Braucher, *New Basics, supra* note 51, at 167.

[91] Braucher, *New Basics, supra* note 51, at 167–68; Scott, *supra* note 48, at 1049; Rustad & Onufrio, *Reconceptualizing, supra* note 84, at 1132; Rustad & Onufrio, *Exportability, supra* note 83, at 39–40, 39 n.60; Braucher, *Twist, supra* note 85, at 12; Va. Code Ann. § 59.1-502.8 (2020) ("A party adopts the terms of a record, including a standard form, as the terms of the contract if the party agrees to the record, such as by manifesting assent. (2) The terms of a record may be adopted pursuant to paragraph (1) after beginning performance or use if the parties had reason to know that their agreement would be represented in whole or part by a later record to be agreed on and there would not be an opportunity to review the record or a copy of it before performance or use begins."); Va. Code Ann. § 59.1-502.9 cmt. 5 (2020) ("Mass market licenses may be presented after initial general agreement from the licensee";

The ALI Software Principles represent the ALI's second effort to unify the law of software contracts after the failed Article 2B project discussed earlier.[92] The principles apply to software agreements, including licenses, and it provides that contract formation issues can be evaluated by using a reasonableness standard.[93] Although the principles contain a non-disclaimable implied warranty, the principles also reflect deference to commercial practices by largely deferring "to software industry practices when it comes to consumer protection."[94]

The ALI's Software Principles impact has so far been limited and courts have not relied on it to construe licensing contracts.[95] Additionally, the reporters of the ALI's Software Principles note that it does "not require a precontract disclosure of terms."[96] Instead, the principles establish a safe harbor that validates contracts of adhesion subject to some traditional limitations, such as unconscionability.[97] The safe harbor is dependent on software licensors making their forms accessible online, which is to some extent in keeping with privacy law's notice and choice regime. As Florencia Marotta-Wurgler observes, the principles' "drafters emphasize the regulation of disclosure rather than the regulation of terms. They anticipate that disclosure will promote the emergence of an informed minority, and it avoids the intrusive and controversial nature of direct regulation of term."[98]

In providing their online terms and conditions, organizations can select from a variety of contracting formats. In a clickwrap or clickthrough format, the consumer is required to select the "I agree" button or box, and the contract terms are frequently displayed on the screen.[99] There are also variations on clickthrough contracting formats such as scrollwrap agreements, which require the consumer to view the contract terms.[100] The ALI Software Principles appear to validate the use of

---

and UCITA "[a]llows such terms to be enforceable only if there is agreement, or if there is a manifestation of assent after a chance to review terms and only pursuant to the rule that a party that rejects terms for information must be given a cost free right to say no"); UNIF. COMPUT. INFO. TRANSACTIONS ACT §§ 208–09 cmt. 3, 5.

[92]   AM. L. INST., PRINCIPLES OF THE LAW OF SOFTWARE CONTRACTS (2010) [hereinafter SOFTWARE PRINCIPLES]; Rustad & Kavusturan, *supra* note 84, at 783.

[93]   SOFTWARE PRINCIPLES, *supra* note 92, at § 1.06.

[94]   Rustad & Kavusturan, *supra* note 84, at 783; SOFTWARE PRINCIPLES, *supra* note 92, at § 3.05(b).

[95]   Rustad & Kavusturan, *supra* note 84, at 783.

[96]   Robert A. Hillman & Maureen O'Rourke, *Defending Disclosure in Software Licensing*, 78 U. CHI. L. REV. 95, 104–05 (2011).

[97]   *Id.*

[98]   Florencia Marotta-Wurgler, *Will Increased Disclosure Help? Evaluating the Recommendations of the ALI's "Principles of the Law of Software Contracts,"* 78 U. CHI. L. REV. 165, 167 (2011).

[99]   LINDA J. RUSCH & STEPHEN L. SEPINUCK, COMMERCIAL LAW: PROBLEMS AND MATERIALS ON SALES AND PAYMENTS 60 (2012).

[100]   Meyer v. Uber Techs., Inc., 868 F.3d 66, 75–76 (2d Cir. 2017); *see also* Colin P. Marks, *Online and "As Is,"* 45 PEPP. L. REV. 1, 10–12 (2017) ("A further variation of the clickwrap agreement is the scrollwrap agreement. While clickwrap agreements require that users click a box, scrollwrap agreements force users to view the terms and conditions as part of the website's construction and design.").

clickwrap agreements through its safe harbor.[101] Consider that Marotta-Wurgler's study of the possible impact of the ALI Software Principles' disclosure regime on EULAs evaluated the "clickstreams of 47,399 households to 81 Internet software retailers."[102] The study found that requiring that contract terms be accessible to individuals did not cause an "economically significant increase" in individuals' review of contract terms.[103] More specifically, the study determined that requiring assent through clickwrap formats in close proximity to disclosed contractual terms "increases contract readership by at best on the order of 1 percent."[104] Thus, the study calls into question the effectiveness of the principles' notice safe harbor.

In another type of contracting format – browsewrap – the organization's terms and conditions are accessible through a website-displayed hyperlink.[105] When a sign-in wrap format is used, consumers are notified of the organization's terms of use and are informed that by registering for the service or product, or by completing the purchasing process, the consumer also agrees to the company's terms of use.[106]

In 2007, Nancy Kim observed that in examining consumer assent to online contract terms, if the consumer has "demonstrated assent" to an organization's terms of use, most "courts have focused on notice and an opportunity to read the relevant contractual terms."[107] Much of this observation remains true today and is applicable in the IoT context. A review of recent case law reveals that many courts continue to require that consumers be given an "opportunity to review" an organization's terms and conditions.[108] UCITA also incorporates the notice and

---

[101] SOFTWARE PRINCIPLES, *supra* note 92, § 2.02 cmt. c; Marotta-Wurgler, *supra* note 98, at 167; Hillman & O'Rourke, *supra* note 96, at 104 n.53.

[102] Marotta-Wurgler, *supra* note 98, at 165, 167.

[103] *Id.* at 168.

[104] *Id.* at 167–68.

[105] RUSCH & SEPINUCK, *supra* note 99, at 60.

[106] *Meyer*, 868 F.3d at 75–76; *see also* Marks, *supra* note 100, at 12 (contending that in sign-in wrap contracts "the website notifies users 'of the existence and applicability of the site's "terms of use" when proceeding through the website's sign-in or checkout process'").

[107] Kim, *Clicking*, *supra* note 4, at 818.

[108] Walsh v. Microsoft Corp., No. C14-424-MJP, 2014 WL 4168479, at *3 (W.D. Wash. Aug. 20, 2014) ("Online agreements are enforceable under Oregon law if a consumer has an opportunity to review the terms of the agreement and manifested assent to its terms."); *see also* Bernardino v. Barnes & Noble Booksellers, Inc., No. 17-CV-04570, 2017 WL 7309893, at *10 (S.D.N.Y. Nov. 20, 2017) (noting that plaintiff had "had ample opportunity to read" the disputed terms of use and finding that the disputed contract provision "met the key aspects of being reasonably conspicuous by virtue of the format and design of the 'Submit Order' page and the fact that customers could easily learn of the existence of and access and read the TOU before deciding to purchase a DVD"); Applebaum v. Lyft, Inc., 263 F. Supp. 3d 454, 465 (S.D.N.Y. 2017) ("[C]ourts have consistently found scrollwrap agreements enforceable because they present the consumer with a 'realistic opportunity' to review the terms of the contract *and* they require a physical manifestation of assent."); Kai Peng v. Uber Techs., Inc., 237 F. Supp. 3d 36, 47 (E.D.N.Y. 2017) ("A party may be bound to a 'click-wrap' agreement . . . by clicking a button declaring assent, so long as the party is given a 'sufficient opportunity to read the . . . agreement, and assents thereto after being provided with an unambiguous method of accepting or declining the offer.'").

opportunity to review standard as well.[109] In determining whether a consumer has assented to a company's terms and conditions, courts frequently assess whether reasonable notice of the terms was provided.[110] This involves evaluating "whether the user has actual or constructive knowledge" of the terms.[111] In *Metter v. Uber*, the district court stated "constructive notice occurs when the consumer has inquiry notice of the terms of service – like a hyperlinked alert – and takes an affirmative action to demonstrate assent to them."[112] Thus, in applying the reasonable notice standard, courts tend to evaluate whether a company's website places "a reasonably prudent user on inquiry notice" of the contested terms, particularly when it is unclear whether the consumer has actual knowledge of the terms and conditions.[113] In assessing the reasonableness of the notice provided, courts evaluate the screen or interface design, and the clarity of the terms at issue.[114]

The issue of actual or constructive knowledge of contract terms is a frequently contested question when a browsewrap agreement is used.[115] Notice can also be disputed when companies use other types of contracting formats, including

---

[109] Va. Code Ann. § 59.1-502.9 (2020); Va. Code Ann. § 59.1-501.13:1 (2020); UNIF. COMPUT. INFO. TRANSACTIONS ACT §§ 113, 208, 209.

[110] McKee v. Audible, Inc., No. CV-17-1941-GW(Ex), 2017 WL 4685039, at *5 (C.D. Cal. July 17, 2017) ("In the context of an electronic consumer transaction, the occurrence of mutual assent ordinarily turns on whether the consumer had reasonable notice of a merchant's terms of service agreement."); *see also* Mucciariello v. Viator, Inc., No. 18-14444, 2019 WL 4727896, at *4 (D.N.J. Sept. 27, 2019) (finding that plaintiff "was provided with reasonable notice of the hyperlinked Terms and Conditions").

[111] Nguyen v. Barnes & Noble Inc., 763 F.3d 1171, 1176 (9th Cir. 2014); *see also* Nicosia v. Amazon.com, Inc., 384 F. Supp. 3d 254, 266 (E.D.N.Y. 2019) ("A website user is deemed to be on inquiry notice of contract terms so long as the 'design and content' of the webpage renders 'existence' of those terms 'reasonably conspicuous.'"); Roller v. TV Guide Online Holdings, LLC, No. CV-12-306, 2013 WL 3322348, at *7 (Ark. June 27, 2013) ("[T]he dispositive issue in determining if an enforceable agreement existed is whether appellants had constructive or actual knowledge of the terms of the agreement and therefore agreed by their use of TV Guide's website to be bound by those terms."); NANCY S. KIM , WRAP CONTRACTS: FOUNDATIONS AND RAMIFICATIONS 41 (2013) ("[N]otice can be either actual or constructive.") [hereinafter KIM, WRAP CONTRACTS]. *See generally* Kurtis A. Kemper, Annotation, *Validity, Construction, and Application of Browsewrap Agreements*, 95 A.L.R.6TH 57 (listing several cases employing this standard).

[112] Metter v. Uber Techs., Inc., No. 16-cv-06652-RS, 2017 WL 1374579, at *2 (N.D. Cal. Apr. 17, 2017).

[113] *Applebaum*, 263 F. Supp. 3d at 465 ("[W]here . . . there is no evidence that the [mobile application] user had actual knowledge of the agreement, the validity of the . . . agreement turns on whether the [application] puts a reasonably prudent user on inquiry notice of the terms of the contract."); *see also McKee*, 2017 WL 4685039, at *5 ("Reasonable notice in this context requires that the consumer had either actual or constructive notice of the terms of service."); *In re* Zappos, Inc., 893 F. Supp. 2d 1058, 1064 (D. Nev. 2012) ("Because no affirmative action is required by the website user to agree to the terms of a contract other than his or her use of the website, the determination of the validity of a browsewrap contract depends on whether the user has actual or constructive knowledge of a website's terms and conditions.").

[114] KIM, WRAP CONTRACTS, *supra* note 111, at 127; *see also* Meyer v. Uber Techs., Inc., 868 F.3d 66, 78 (2d Cir. 2017) (evaluating the disputed screen design and language).

[115] *See, e.g.*, Lopez v. Terra's Kitchen, LLC, 331 F. Supp. 3d 1092, 1101 (S.D. Cal. 2018) (finding that the disputed terms and conditions provided via a browsewrap format did not provide inquiry notice).

clickthrough, scrollwrap, and sign-in wrap agreements.[116] Courts have acknowledged the potential validity of terms of use that are displayed using the scrollwrap
format.[117] The enforceability of sign-in wrap agreements also depends on whether
a company provides reasonable notice of its terms.[118] In traditional clickthrough
agreements, the combination of an adequate display of contract terms and the act of
selecting the "I agree" option is viewed as a demonstration of assent to contract
terms. As one district court noted, "[c]onstructive notice is generally clear where the
user is actually required to, and does click a button explicitly agreeing to the terms of
the contract."[119] Similarly, in *Meyer v. Uber Techs, Inc.*, the Second Circuit observed
that "'[c]ourts around the country recognize that [an] electronic "click" can suffice
to signify the acceptance of a contract,' and that '[t]here is nothing automatically
offensive about such agreements, as long as the layout and language of the site give
the user reasonable notice that a click will manifest assent to an agreement.'"[120]

Despite the cases mentioned earlier, courts' application of the notice and opportunity to- review principle and wrap classifications in the online contracting setting is
inconsistent and unclear. The "wrap" labels used to describe the different interface
formats companies use are ambiguous and confusing. In some instances, courts
merely provide descriptions of the various types of online contracting formats but do
not clearly label the agreement at issue as a particular type of "wrap" agreement.[121]
Some courts also fail to correctly label and differentiate between the multiple types
of "wrap" formats. For example, as the district court in *Applebaum v. Lyft, Inc.*
observed, "courts have not been consistent in distinguishing between scrollwrap and
clickwrap agreements."[122] In addition, courts continue to create new wrap labels. For
example, in *Bernardino v. Barnes & Noble Booksellers, Inc.*, the court simultaneously
acknowledged that the agreement at issue was likely a sign-in wrap agreement, but

---

[116] *See* Marks, *supra* note 100, at 11.
[117] *See, e.g.*, Dye v. Tamko Bldg. Prods., 908 F.3d 675, 678 (11th Cir. 2018) ("In this cyber age, you've also
almost certainly assented to the terms of a 'clickwrap' or 'scrollwrap' agreement – for instance, by
hitting 'I accept' when installing the latest operating system for your smartphone."); *Applebaum*, 263
F. Supp. 3d at 465 ("As relevant to this case, courts have consistently found scrollwrap agreements
enforceable because they present the consumer with a 'realistic opportunity' to review the terms of the
contract *and* they require a physical manifestation of assent."); Ranazzi v. Amazon.com, Inc., 46 N.
E.3d 213, 216 n.1, 217–18 (Ohio Ct. App. 2015) (describing the agreement at issue as a "scrollwrap
agreement" and finding that "appellant, by clicking 'I agree' on Intuit's license agreement or by
registering for an Amazon account and placing orders, accepted the terms of appellees' agreements,
including the arbitration provisions").
[118] *See McKee*, 2017 WL 4685039, at *6 (discussing several cases involving sign-in wrap contracts and
stating that "courts have also found constructive notice where sites contain a disclosure statement that
indicates that if a user signs up for a given service they accept the terms of service provided the design
of the website puts a reasonably prudent user on inquiry notice").
[119] *Id.*
[120] Meyer v. Uber Techs., Inc., 868 F.3d 66, 75 (2d Cir. 2017) (quoting *Sgouros v. TransUnion Corp.*, 817
F.3d 1029, 1033-34 (7th Cir. 2016).
[121] *Id.* at 75–76.
[122] *Applebaum*, 263 F. Supp. 3d at 465; *cf.* Berkson v. Gogo LLC, 97 F. Supp. 3d 359, 398 (E.D.N.Y.
2015).

also stated that it was more aptly described as a "checkout-wrap" agreement because the link to the company's conditions of use were provided during checkout.[123] In other cases, courts create a distinction between clickwrap agreements and hybrid clickwrap agreements and analogize the latter to browsewrap formats while noting that both are generally enforceable.[124]

Turning back to the notice standard, in *Meyer*, the Second Circuit had to evaluate whether, by clicking the register button, the lead plaintiff not only signed up for a mobile application, but also agreed to the terms of use at issue.[125] Central to this determination was whether notice of the disputed terms of service, which were provided only via a hyperlink below the register box, was reasonably conspicuous.[126] Like many online consumer contracting cases involving disputed terms and conditions, the court's finding on the notice and assent issue impacted whether the consumer plaintiffs would be forced to arbitrate their claims. The court found that the hyperlinked terms of service were conspicuous, reasoning that the average consumer "knows that text that is highlighted in blue and underlined is hyperlinked to another webpage where additional information will be found."[127] The court established a "reasonably prudent smartphone user" standard and found that the plaintiff unambiguously demonstrated assent to the contract terms because "[a] reasonable user would know that by clicking the registration button, he was agreeing to the terms and conditions accessible via the hyperlink, whether he clicked on the hyperlink or not."[128] In applying the "reasonable smartphone user" standard that it created, it appears that the court expressly assumed that smartphone users frequently enter into contracts using their smartphones and are aware of the contracting process.[129] The *Meyer* court seems to have relied on "judicial intuition" rather than empirical evidence to support its conclusions and findings about the "reasonably prudent smartphone user."[130] The ambiguity inherent in this intuitive approach could allow other courts to reach different

---

123 Bernardino v. Barnes & Noble Booksellers, Inc., No. 17-CV-04570, 2017 WL 7309893, at *3 (S.D.N.Y. Nov. 20, 2017) ("B&N's arbitration agreement falls under the 'sign-in-wrap' category of agreements; however, in this case, it is more appropriately labeled a 'checkout-wrap' agreement because the link to B&N's TOU was posted during the checkout process for purchasing a product.").

124 Zamber v. Am. Airlines, Inc., No. 16-23901-CV-MARTINEZ/GOODMAN, 2020 U.S. Dist. LEXIS 24851 (S.D. Fla. Feb. 10, 2020) (noting that "'clickwrap' agreements or hybrid-clickwrap browserwrap agreements are both routine and enforceable"); Hosseini v. Upstart Network, Inc., No. 19-cv-704, 2020 WL 573126 (E.D. Va. Feb. 5, 2020) (noting that both clickwrap and hybrid clickwrap agreements are enforceable).

125 *Meyer*, 868 F.3d at 70–73.

126 *See id.* at 77–79.

127 *Id.* at 77–78.

128 *Id.* at 79–80.

129 *See id.* at 77; *see also* Phillips v. Neutron Holdings, Inc., No. 3:18-CV-3382-S, 2019 WL 4861435, at *412 (N.D. Tex. Oct. 2, 2019) (citing *Meyer* and using the reasonable smartphone user standard).

130 Eric Goldman, *More Bad News for Uber's Contract Formation – Ramos v. Uber*, TECH. & MKTG. L. BLOG (June 4, 2018), https://blog.ericgoldman.org/archives/2018/06/more-bad-news-for-ubers-contract-formation-ramos-v-uber.htm.

holdings when applying this standard.[131] Continuing the theme of a reasonably prudent smartphone user, the district court in *Nicosia v. Amazon* suggested that there is no doubt

> that reasonably prudent internet users know that there are terms and conditions attached when they log onto Facebook, order merchandise on Amazon, or hail a ride on Uber? They know this, not because a loud, brightly-colored notice on the screen tells them so, but because it would be difficult to exist in our technological society without some generalized awareness of the fact.[132]

In contrast to the *Meyer* and *Nicosia* courts' assumptions regarding consumers' knowledge or awareness of online contracts, the Seventh Circuit in *Sgouros v. TransUnion Corp* suggested that courts should not presume that consumers who click a box or button in the online contracting setting have "notice of all contents not only of that page but of other content that requires further action (scrolling, following a link, etc.)."[133] The *Meyer* court attempted to distinguish the holding in *Sgouros* by reasoning that the interface at issue in *Meyer* was not misleading.[134] However, the *Sgouros* case suggests that a user's click of an "I agree" button should not automatically demonstrate meaningful assent, especially when the interface does not provide reasonable notice and suggests that the consumer is agreeing to "something else."[135] In *Meyer*, users who clicked the hyperlinked text had to click another button before being able to access the terms and conditions and had to scroll through multiple pages to view all of the applicable terms (including the arbitration provision).[136] It is questionable whether reasonable notice of Uber's terms was provided to users in *Meyer*, an issue that the court's opinion does not adequately address.

In *Cullinane v. Uber Techs*, the First Circuit determined that Uber's contract terms were not conspicuously displayed.[137] Applying Massachusetts law, the court relied in part on the UCC's definition of the term conspicuous.[138] The court reasoned that the hyperlinked terms and conditions did not look like a standard hyperlink and that the hyperlink, which was accompanied by other similarly depicted text, did not sufficiently "grab the user's attention."[139] Although the court briefly mentioned the *Meyer* decision, it did not address the "reasonably prudent smartphone user" standard.[140] The *Cullinane*

---

[131]   *See id.*

[132]   Nicosia v. Amazon.com, Inc., 384 F. Supp. 3d 254, 278 (E.D.N.Y. 2019).

[133]   Sgouros v. TransUnion Corp., 817 F.3d 1029, 1035 (7th Cir. 2016).

[134]   *Meyer*, 868 F.3d at 79.

[135]   *Sgouros*, 817 F.3d at 1035.

[136]   Meyer v. Kalanick, 200 F. Supp. 3d 408, 415 (S.D.N.Y. 2016).

[137]   Cullinane v. Uber Techs., Inc., 893 F.3d 53, 53 (1st Cir. 2018).

[138]   *See id.* at 62; U.C.C. § 1-201(b)(10) (AM. LAW INST. & UNIF. LAW COMM'N 2001) (defining "conspicuous").

[139]   *Cullinane*, 893 F.3d at 64; *see also* Geoffrey Wyatt, Jordan M. Schwartz & Zachary W. Martin, *1st Circ.'s Uber Ruling Imposes Burdens on App Design*, LAW360 (July 30, 2018, 1:45 PM), www .law360.com/articles/1067898/1st-circ-s-uber-ruling-imposes-burdens-on-app-design.

[140]   *See Cullinane*, 893 F.3d at 62–63.

court also suggested that Uber could have avoided questions related to contract formation by using a different contracting format that would require users to click the "I
agree" button to accept hyperlinked or displayed terms of use before proceeding to the
subsequent screen.[141]

The *Cullinane* decision appears to be in line with a minority of courts that are
hesitant to uphold form contracts absent clear satisfaction of contract formation
conditions.[142] Along similar lines, in *Berskon v. Gogo, LLC* the district court highlighted four factors to be considered when evaluating reasonable notice and assent.
These include whether (1) "[a]side from clicking the equivalent of sign-in (*e.g.*, log-
in, buy-now, purchase, etc.)," the consumer is aware that they are entering into
a contract; (2) the companies' terms and conditions are unambiguously available on
the company's website; (3) the importance of the contract terms were obscured by
the consumer's "physical manifestation of assent"; and (4) the company drew "the
consumer's attention to material terms," such as an arbitration provision.[143] This
four-part inquiry does much more than simply require formulaic applications of the
reasonable notice standard. It suggests that even if a consumer had general notice of
a company's terms and conditions, that notice does not automatically constitute
assent to or notice of specific contract terms, such as a class action waiver.[144]
Although only a minority of courts have expressly adopted the *Berkson* formulation,
the post-*Berkson* cases suggest that the law in this area remains unclear.[145]

In *Ramos v. Uber Tech*, a case involving another Uber mobile application, the
court also had to determine whether the plaintiff assented to Uber's terms and
conditions by completing the mobile application registration process.[146] The
New York court determined that the plaintiff did not unequivocally assent to
Uber's terms and conditions.[147] The court found that the interface and rectangular
box containing the phrase "Terms and Conditions and Privacy Policy" did not
provide reasonable notice.[148] The court reasoned that Uber's registration process

---

[141]   *Id.* at 62 ("We note at the outset that Uber chose not to use a common method of conspicuously
informing users of the existence and location of terms and conditions: requiring users to click a box
stating that they agree to a set of terms, often provided by hyperlink, before continuing to the next
screen. Instead, Uber chose to rely on simply displaying a notice of deemed acquiescence and a link
to the terms.")

[142]   *See* Martha Ertman, *Properly Restating the Law of Consumer Contracting*, JOTWELL (May 15, 2019),
https://contracts.jotwell.com/properly-restating-the-law-of-consumer-contracting/; *see also* Metter
v. Uber Techs., Inc., No. 16-cv-06652-RS, 2017 WL 1374579, at *4 (N.D. Cal. Apr. 17, 2017);
Kauders v. Uber Techs, Inc., No. SUCV20162180D, 2019 WL 510568, at *5 (Mass. Super. Ct. Jan.
3, 2019).

[143]   Berkson v. Gogo LLC, 97 F. Supp. 3d 359, 402 (E.D.N.Y. 2015).

[144]   *See* Nancy S. Kim, *Online Contracting: New Developments*, 72 BUS. LAW. 243, 243 (2017).

[145]   *See e.g.*, Starke v. Squaretrade, Inc., 913 F.3d 279 (2d Cir. 2019); Adwar Casting Co. v. Star Gems, Inc.,
342 F. Supp. 3d 297 (E.D.N.Y. 2018); Applebaum v. Lyft, Inc., 263 F. Supp. 3d 454 (S.D.N.Y. 2017);
McKee v. Audible, Inc., No. CV-17-1941-GW(Ex), 2017 WL 4685039 (C.D. Cal. July 17, 2017).

[146]   Ramos v Uber Techs., Inc., 77 N.Y.S.3d 296, 298–99 (N.Y. Sup. Ct. 2018).

[147]   *Id.* at 302.

[148]   *Id.* at 301.

did not compel users to view its terms and conditions and did not require users to clearly demonstrate acceptance of the disputed terms by, for instance, clicking the "I agree" button.[149]

One could attempt to reconcile the holdings in *Meyer*, *Cullinane*, and *Ramos* by contending that the interface layouts in each case were sufficiently different. However, all three interfaces at issue included the following language, a portion of which contained the hyperlinked terms: "By creating an Uber account, you agree to the ... 'Terms of Service & Privacy Policy.'"[150] Yet, the *Cullinane* and *Ramos* courts reached a different conclusion from the *Meyer* court. In *Cullinane* and *Ramos*, this language was depicted in white in a rectangular box against black payment and link card screens and in *Meyer* the hyperlinked language was in blue against a white screen.[151] The *Cullinane* court suggested a reasonable user may not have concluded that the phrase was hyperlinked because of its non-blue color, in contrast to the blue hyperlink used in *Meyer*.[152] In *Meyer*, the court noted that this language clearly prompted users to review the conditions of use and indicated that by completing the registration process they would be subject to the company's terms and conditions.[153] In *Ramos*, the court reasoned that this language was insufficient because a user could reasonably believe that the terms and conditions at issue were about access to social media accounts and the interface instructions did not include "any language or any indication" suggesting to the user that selecting the words "Terms & Conditions and Privacy Policy" would open a separate screen describing the company's conditions of use.[154]

In *Johnson v. Uber Technologies*, the district court also had to interpret similar language contained in Uber's mobile application.[155] The court stated that in applying the "reasonable notice" standard, it also assesses "whether a reasonable person would be misled, confused, misdirected, or distracted by the manner in which the terms and conditions are presented."[156] Citing *Meyer*, the court found that the statement "[b]y creating an Uber account, you agree to the Terms of Service & Privacy Policy" was unambiguous and conspicuous and reasonably notified users that they would be deemed to have agreed to the hyperlinked terms upon creating an account.[157] The payment screen in *Johnson* containing the disputed language and the hyperlink were in a non-blue color and was

---

[149] *Id.*
[150] *See* Cullinane v. Uber Techs., Inc., 893 F.3d 53, 62–63 (1st Cir. 2018); Meyer v. Uber Techs., Inc., 868 F.3d 66, 78 (2d. Cir. 2017); *Ramos*, 77 N.Y.S.3d at 300.
[151] *Cullinane*, 893 F.3d at 57–58; *Meyer*, 868 F.3d at 71; Exhibit A, *Ramos*, 77 N.Y.S.3d 296 (on file with author).
[152] *Cullinane*, 893 F.3d at 63.
[153] *Meyer*, 868 F.3d at 79.
[154] *Ramos*, 77 N.Y.S.3d at 301.
[155] *See* Johnson v. Uber Techs., Inc., No. 1:16-cv-05468, 2018 WL 4503938, at *4 (N.D. Ill. Sept. 20, 2018).
[156] *Id.*
[157] *Id.*

similar to the screens in *Ramos* and *Cullinane*.[158] Yet, the *Johnson* court found the notice reasonable. Although courts appear to be applying the same reasonable notice and opportunity to review standard, existing wrap terminology and courts' findings on the issue of assent are incredibly context dependent and unpredictable.

THE CONTRACT DISTANCING AND INFORMATION ASYMMETRY NORM

The answer to the question of whether a consumer can be said to assent to an IoT company's conditions of use has real-world implications for consumers' rights. Before the rise of online contracting, paper agreements imposed certain physical limits on organizations' contracting activities.[159] Courts' validation of various online contracting formats, such as browsewrap and clickthrough agreements, allowed organizations to expand "the reach of their contractual clauses."[160] Today, this expansion includes not only traditional warranty disclaimers and limitation of liability provisions, but also rights to use, process, and share consumer-generated data and content; disclaimers for cybersecurity failures and data loss; mandatory arbitration and class action waivers; and provisions that restrict consumers' property rights in the physical devices they purchase. The increase in data now available to companies because of the IoT's proliferation makes the inclusion of such provisions even more concerning. Increasingly, companies will have detailed, sensitive, and real-time access to data about us that they can use for more accurate and invasive targeted marketing and to discriminate against us. While targeted advertisements seem benign enough, if a consumer purchases a product or service after viewing an advertisement, that purchase and the consumer's associated rights are governed by a contract that the consumer has no ability to negotiate. Thus, targeted advertising is really targeted contracting. In the new interconnected world, the stakes are higher for all of us.

In the IoT context, the question of notice and opportunity to review becomes increasingly complex. Multiple individuals in a household, including minors, may use a single IoT device, but only one user may be required to review and consent to a company's terms and conditions.[161] Non-consenting members of the household (as well as guests) whose voices and images are recorded by IoT devices may never actually view a company's terms and conditions. Additionally, unlike computers, smartphones, and tablets, many (but not all) IoT devices lack the typical screens that

---

[158] *See id.* at *1; Defendant Uber's Statement of. Undisputed Material Facts in Support of Its Motion for Summary Judgment, *id.* (on file with author); Exhibit A, *Ramos*, 77 N.Y.S.3d 296 (on file with author).

[159] KIM, WRAP CONTRACTS, *supra* note 111, at 51.

[160] *Id.*

[161] *See, e.g.*, Report and Recommendation, Hall-O'Neil v. Amazon, No. 2:19-cv-00910-RAJ-MLP (W.D. Wash. Oct. 21, 2019); Venkat Balasubramani, *Amazon Can't Force Arbitration of Minors' Privacy Claims Based on Alexa Recordings – BF v. Amazon*, TECH. & MKTG. L. BLOG (Oct. 29, 2019), https://blog.ericgoldman.org/archives/2019/10/amazon-cant-force-arbitration-of-minors-privacy-claims-based-on-alexa-recordings-bf-v-amazon.htm.

companies use to display their privacy policies and terms of use.[162] Conditions of use and privacy policies cannot be displayed to consumers on many IoT devices prior to contracting. IoT devices provide easy incentives for consumers to fail to read and understand contract terms. Contract Distancing then becomes increasingly problematic. Consumers are likely to have less notice of contract terms and fewer opportunities to review contract terms and provide meaningful assent. The following examples illustrate this point.

Recall that Amazon's dash button was a small internet-connected device consumers used to access Amazon's reordering service to purchase products by pushing the button on the device.[163] The device lacked a physical screen, but with a simple click of the button a consumer could order new products. Consumers who used the dash button did not need to review or access the company's terms and conditions or click an online "I agree" button before clicking the physical button on the device to place subsequent orders. Similarly, consumers that use IoT smart speakers to "voice shop" (order goods and services using their voice) can enter into a contract to purchase products without viewing contract terms on the smart speakers, many of which lack screens. With the increased use of smart speakers, the problem of Contract Distancing will only worsen. It is estimated that by 2022, $40 billion "will be spent" in voice shopping.[164] Research conducted by Google and Peerless Insights on consumers' IoT smart speaker habits found that 62 percent of smart speaker owners who regularly use their devices intended to purchase goods and services via these devices.[165] While some commentators suggest that most consumers have been hesitant to use their smart speakers to voice shop, this will likely change as consumers become more comfortable with integrating smart speakers and other IoT devices into their daily routines, and as companies begin to address consumer concerns associated with voice shopping.[166] Also, the searches consumers conduct using IoT devices' voice features can provide

---

[162] *See, e.g., Samsung – Family Hub 27.7 Cu. Ft. 4-Door French Door Refrigerator – Stainless Steel*, BEST BUY, www.bestbuy.com/site/samsung-family-hub-27-7-cu-ft-4-door-french-door-refrigerator-stainless-steel/6196185.p?skuId=6196185&ref=212&loc=1&ds_rl=1260669&ds_rl=1266837&ref=30&loc=KW-4319&ds_rl=1266837&gclid=EAIaIQobChMI5s7tp4fS3gIVWMDICh1YnACQEAQYBSABEgKsnPD_BwE&gclsrc=aw.ds (last visited Jan. 4, 2020) (describing a smart refrigerator with a screen display).

[163] *See Amazon Dash*, AMAZON, www.amazon.com/Dash-Buttons/b?ie=UTF8&node=10667898011 (last visited Jan. 4, 2020).

[164] OC&C STRATEGY CONSULTANTS, THE TALKING SHOP: THE RISE OF VOICE COMMERCE 2 (2018), www.occstrategy.com/media/1285/the-talking-shop_uk.pdf.

[165] *How Voice Assistance Is Reshaping Consumer Behavior*, THINK WITH GOOGLE, www.thinkwithgoogle.com/data-collections/voice-assistance-emerging-technologies/ (last visited Jan. 4, 2020).

[166] *See* Laura Heller, *Consumers Are Passing on Voice Searches for Shopping, but Not for Long*, FORBES (Sept. 5, 2018, 12:45 PM), www.forbes.com/sites/lauraheller/2018/09/05/shoppers-pass-on-voice-but-not-for-long/#6db2841f2960; *see also* Priya Anand, *The Reality Behind Voice Shopping Hype*, INFO. (Aug. 6, 2018, 10:01 AM), www.theinformation.com/articles/the-reality-behind-voice-shopping-hype?jwt=eyJhbGciOiJIUzI1NiJ9.eyJzdWIiOiJsYXVyYS5oZWxsZXJAcGVyZm9ybWljys5jb2oiLCJleHAiOjE1NjUzMDUxNzcsIm4iOiJHdWVzdCIsInNjb3BlIjpbInNoYXJlIl19.5u-7WVeOeTd_XqPj8iempBXXSzy5fMMTlxY3G30yZgM&unlock=ab4ff5b29b88a818.

companies with insights into the products consumers would like to purchase, even if a voice shop purchase is not made. Amazon's "product search engine" capabilities already allows it to obtain data about products it does not offer for sale, but that its customers have searched for.[167] The COVID-19 pandemic and shelter in place orders that limit our ability to purchase goods and services in person may also increase our reliance on IoT devices and our willingness to use such devices to voice shop.

Other IoT offerings, such as Amazon's DRS, which allows compatible IoT devices to reorder goods automatically, also present a Contract Distancing problem.[168] A DRS-enabled device could also place subsequent consecutive orders for goods without the consumer reviewing Amazon's terms of service before the items are purchased. Also, consider that certain Tesla vehicles reportedly have the capacity to self-diagnose vehicle defects and order replacement parts.[169]

Since many IoT devices lack physical screens, companies provide notice of their privacy policies and conditions of use through their websites, the mobile applications that are frequently used to control IoT devices, or through email communications. If an IoT device has a physical screen, then terms of use could be displayed on the device. IoT companies can use the traditional "wrap" formats previously discussed to obtain valid consumer assent to anti-consumer contract terms. However, remember the concerns and ambiguities noted earlier regarding courts' "wrap" vocabulary. Courts will likely turn to the reasonable notice standard discussed earlier in this chapter to analyze consumer assent to contract terms in IoT transactions. The Contract Distancing problem remains although notice is given through an IoT mobile application or provided through the device when the consumer sets up and registers the device. Additionally, courts have found that there is blanket assent to all reasonable online contract provisions once there is a manifestation of assent and notice.[170] Thus, by simply selecting the "I agree" option displayed on a mobile application or the company's website, or ordering goods through IoT devices, an individual could be deemed to have assented to every term in

---

[167] *Williams-Sonoma Accuses Amazon of Copying Its Furniture*, AD AGE (Dec. 18, 2018), https://adage .com/article/tech/williams-sonoma-accuses-amazon-copying-furniture/316029.

[168] It is unclear what impact the Restore Online Shoppers' Confidence Act will have on the ability of consumers to end recurring fees in the IoT context. *See* 15 U.S.C. §§ 8401–8405 (2006); Duane C. Pozza, *New Issues Raised by Internet of Things Payments*, LAW360 (Jan. 4, 2019, 4:10 PM), www .law360.com/amp/articles/1115526.

[169] Mark Matousek, *Tesla Cars Can Now Figure Out Which Parts Need to Be Replaced and Order New Ones (TSLA)*, MARKETS INSIDER (May 7, 2019, 11:21 AM), https://markets.businessinsider.com/news/ stocks/tesla-cars-diagnose-parts-that-need-to-be-replaced-order-new-ones-2019-5-1028177759.

[170] Nicosia v. Amazon.com, Inc., 384 F. Supp. 3d 254, 279 (E.D.N.Y. 2019) (suggesting that even in the online setting, "Llewellyn had the answer: rather than scrutinizing hybridwrap agreements for contract formation issues, courts should recognize that such agreements, like other adhesive contracts, represent in substance a 'blanket assent' to any terms that are not objectively unreasonable"); Danielle Kie Hart, *Form & Substance in Nancy Kim's* Wrap Contracts, 44 SW. L. REV. 251, 253–54 (2014); Danielle Kie Hart, *In and Out – Contract Doctrines in Action*, 66 HASTINGS L.J. 1661, 1666 (2015).

a company's terms and conditions. Under the blanket assent theory, regardless of the wrap format used, the consent giver generally has the burden of finding, reviewing, and understanding a company's online terms, including data collection provisions.[171] The Contract Distancing problem the IoT raises suggests that it is time to limit the application of the blanket assent theory in the online context.

In the IoT context, even if a consumer can be said to be provided with an opportunity to review a company's terms and conditions, and clicks the "I agree" button after or while installing or registering for an IoT smartphone mobile application, the consumer may not be required to agree to the contract terms or view the terms prior to ordering products through the device. One might argue that by ordering products through an IoT device from a company, such as Amazon, the consumer consented to the company's terms of use upon registering for an account, or by continuing to use the company's website to order products. However, recall that there are multiple agreements, including EULAs, privacy policies, and different terms of service for a single IoT device that consumers are potentially subject to even when they contract with only one company. Additionally, the physical IoT device serves as a barrier to consumers' access to the terms displayed on the mobile device or the company's website. Thus, to review applicable terms and conditions the consumer that has ordered a product using their IoT device needs to reopen the mobile application or access the company's website, and search for the applicable terms and conditions or review any potential terms provided in email communications from the company. Being able to order goods through an IoT device, and having to take additional steps to review contract terms, further removes us as consumers from the contracting process and decreases our ability to access contract terms. Also, consider that companies send multiple emails to consumers, many of which are simply marketing emails rather than communications about a specific order or communications that are solely about a company's terms of service or privacy policy. The risk is that consumers who are inundated with both marketing and non-marketing emails from companies may simply delete any emails containing information about a company's terms of service or privacy policy without reviewing them. Additionally, the online contracting architecture all but ensures that consumers are generally not given the opportunity to revise a company's online contract terms or enter their own terms in the checkout process.[172]

As Juliet Moringiello and others have argued, when compared to physical paper contracts that typically require a physical signature, the ramifications of online contracting via browsewrap and clickthrough agreements seem less real to consumers.[173]

---

[171] KIM, WRAP CONTRACTS, *supra* note 111, at 127, 164, 175, 192.

[172] However, some PDE-like companies may provide opportunities to issue their own contract terms. Stacy-Ann Elvy, *Paying for Privacy and the Personal Data Economy*, 117 COLUM. L. REV. 1369, 1418 (2017).

[173] *See* KIM, WRAP CONTRACTS, *supra* note 111, at 58–62, 70–71 ("The proliferation of contracts on computer screens ... makes it difficult for consumers to discern their legal significance and easier

The *Sgouros* court similarly remarked that "a person using the Internet may not realize that she is agreeing to a contract at all, whereas a reasonable person signing a physical contract will rarely be unaware of that fact."[74] Research on the differences between companies' in-store and online contracts found that purchases made in person in a store often do not include the many anti-consumer provisions, such as implied warranty disclaimers, that are contained in companies' online contracts.[75] These issues are more troubling in the IoT setting. The IoT moves us deeper into the online contracting world. The ease with which we can order products using our IoT devices means that many of us will increasingly continue to underestimate the implications of online contracting. The potential consequences of assenting to a one-sided contract seem even further removed when one can simply rely on a device to order products. Stated differently, by further removing us from the potential consequences of assenting to a one-sided contract, IoT devices will lead us to even more drastically underestimate the ramifications of online contracting.

There is no meaningful assent when contract terms are not effectively displayed at the time of contracting and when we fail to understand the implications of those terms. Further, contract terms displayed through mobile applications and websites often do not consistently provide adequate or reasonable notice. Companies' terms of use are frequently long and contain legalese that is difficult for many of us to understand. As was the case in *Meyers*, consumers must scroll through multiple screens to review relevant documents in small font on smartphones, which typically have small screens. A court applying the "reasonably prudent smartphone user" standard to an IoT transaction could easily determine that constructive notice is provided and that consumers are on inquiry notice when IoT contract terms are displayed through the associated IoT mobile application.

The Contract Distancing problem will become more glaring if a large number of IoT devices are designed with the capacity to order products from websites that are not connected to the manufacturer of the device. In such a case, a consumer could also be subject to the online conditions of use or terms of service of the third-party retailers selling products purchased through the device in addition to the terms of use of the device manufacturer. A version of this scenario is already playing out with IoT devices that are manufactured by third parties, such as General Electric (GE), but which are enabled with Amazon's DRS. Consumers who purchase and enable these types of IoT devices are subject to multiple agreements, including Amazon's terms of service for its reorder services and GE's conditions of use and warranty agreement for its IoT products. Recall that even when consumers interact with only a single IoT company they are frequently required to enter into multiple agreements. For example, consumers that purchase and use the Amazon Key Home Kit

---

for them to ignore. Not surprisingly, consumers may manifest assent without being aware of what they are doing."); Moringiello, *supra* note 4, at 1316–17.

[74] Sgouros v. TransUnion Corp., 817 F.3d 1029, 1035 (7th Cir. 2016).

[75] *See* Marks, *supra* note 100, at 38–39.

(which includes an IoT lock, IoT camera, and accompanying services) are subject to six different terms of use and privacy policies.[176] These include Amazon's standard online privacy notice and terms of use as well as terms of use specific to each physical device and the Amazon key service.[177]

Remember that most consumers do not read online agreements and privacy policies.[178] This occurs even when consumers are purchasing products directly on their computers, tablets, or mobile phones. Indeed, scholars have observed that "the average person encounters so many privacy disclosures every year that it would take 76 days to read them."[179] The Second Circuit in *Meyer* acknowledged the lack of reading problem, but went on to state "that is the choice the user makes; the user is still on inquiry notice" for contracting purposes.[180] If consumers are forced to agree to and review multiple contracts to use ordinary household devices, consumers' unwillingness to read contract terms will only worsen in the IoT setting. As consumers become further removed from the contracting process through their use of IoT devices that can monitor their consumption rates and automatically order products on their behalf, Contract Distancing and a failure to read contract terms will become more prevalent. Moreover, more than 30 million American adults are unable to read.[181] Low literacy rates among vulnerable groups of consumers also worsen the lack of reading problem.

Additionally, not only are we distanced from contract terms, but the increasing levels of data information asymmetry in the IoT context allow companies to more accurately and precisely groom us for contracting and surveillance. We are unlikely to have equal access to the legion of data that will be generated from our use of IoT

---

[176] *See Terms and Conditions for Key by Amazon*, AMAZON, www.amazon.com/gp/help/customer/display .html?nodeId=202192590 (last visited Jan. 4, 2019).

[177] *See id.*

[178] *See, e.g.*, OMRI BEN-SHAHAR & CARL E. SCHNEIDER , MORE THAN YOU WANTED TO KNOW: THE FAILURE OF MANDATED DISCLOSURE (2014); Florencia Marotta-Wurgler, *Some Realities of Online Contracting*, 19 SUP. CT. ECON. REV. 11, 20 (2011); Aleecia M. McDonald & Lorrie Faith Cranor, *The Cost of Reading Privacy Policies*, 4 I/S J.L. & POL'Y INFO. SOC'Y 543, 568 (2008).

[179] Omri Ben-Shahar & Adam Chilton, *Simplification of Privacy Disclosures: An Experimental Test*, 45 J. LEGAL STUD. S41, S42 (2016).

[180] Meyer v. Uber Techs., Inc., 868 F.3d 66, 79 (2d Cir. 2017).

[181] *See U.S. Adult Literacy Facts*, PROLITERACY, https://proliteracy.org/Portals/0/pdf/PL_AdultLit Facts_US_flyer.pdf?ver=2016-05-06-145137-067 (last visited Jan. 4, 2020) ("More than 36 million adults in the United States cannot read, write or do basic math above a third grade level."); *see also* Willy E. Rice, *Unconscionable Judicial Disdain for Unsophisticated Consumers and Employees' Contractual Rights? Legal and Empirical Analyses of Courts' Mandatory Arbitration Rulings and the Systematic Erosion of Procedural and Substantive Unconscionability Defenses Under the Federal Arbitration Act, 1800–2015*, 25 B. U. PUB. INT. L.J. 143, 144–46 (2016) ("A fairly recent national study suggested that fourteen percent of the U.S. population is 'literally illiterate' . . . [and] among employed adults, 40% are functionally illiterate [and] 20% of employed adults are financially illiterate."); Valerie Strauss, *Hiding in Plain Sight: The Adult Literacy Crisis*, WASH. POST (Nov. 1, 2016, 4:00 AM), www.washingtonpost.com/news/answer-sheet/wp/ 2016/11/01/hiding-in-plain-sight-the-adult-literacy-crisis/ ("Approximately 32 million adults in the United States can't read, according to the U.S. Department of Education and the National Institute of Literacy.").

devices and services. While some companies are now providing US consumers with access to copies of the data they generate (the impetus for which is likely the GDPR and CCPA), this access may not always include the data analytics reports and consumer data that companies obtain from other entities. Thus, while we may have piecemeal access to the data that some companies collect about us, companies could potentially continue to horde the large data profiles and sets that they use to prey on many of us.

Recall from Chapter 3 that the CCPA will expand consumers' access to their data. The statute gives California consumers the right to request that certain organizations disclose "the categories" and "specific pieces of personal information" they collect about them.[182] The statute's definition of the term "collect" encompasses purchases of covered personal information.[183] Subject to some exceptions, this right could extend to consumer data a company collects from third parties as well as data obtained directly from consumers.[184] It is not entirely clear whether this right to access information extends to the data analytics report that companies generate about us and use to target us for contracting. The statute's broad definition of "personal information" excludes "publicly available information," but includes "inferences drawn from [other types of enumerated information] to create a profile about a consumer reflecting the consumer's preferences, characteristics, psychological trends, predispositions, behavior, attitudes, intelligence, abilities, and aptitudes."[185] To the extent that companies' data analytics reports qualify as personal information, it may be possible for California residents to access data analytics reports that are not deidentified or aggregated or subject to "trade secrets and intellectual property rights" protection.[186]

Companies' use of unilateral amendment provisions also presents Contract Distancing concerns. Online terms and conditions and privacy policies frequently note that companies may unilaterally amend these agreements. Companies could attempt to use unilateral amendment provisions to make mundane changes to their terms of use as well as to restrict consumers' abilities to bring suit in the event of a dispute. Warranty disclaimers, mandatory arbitration provisions, class action waivers, and limitation of liability provisions (and in some instances forum selection clauses) are but a few of the one-sided terms that companies can subsequently incorporate into their terms and conditions via unilateral amendment provisions,

---

[182] CAL. CIV. CODE § 1798.100 (West 2020); *see also id.* § 1798.110 (describing consumers' data disclosure rights); *id.* § 1798.140(c) (defining a "business" subject to the statute).

[183] *Id.* § 1798.140(e).

[184] *See id.* § 1798.145(d)–(f) (listing exceptions for the sale and disclosure of personal information under certain federal statutes).

[185] *Id.* § 1798.140(o).

[186] *See id.* Cal Civ Code § 1798.185 ("trade secrets should not be disclosed in response to a verifiable consumer request"); § 1798.110 ("This section does not require a business to do the following: ... Reidentify or otherwise link any data that, in the ordinary course of business, is not maintained in a manner that would be considered personal information."); A.B 874, 2019 Leg., Reg. Sess. (Cal. 2019) (noting that deidentified and aggregated data does not qualify as personal information).

assuming that such terms were not already included in the initial adhesion contract. A study of 500 sign-in wrap agreements "of the most popular websites in the U.S." determined that a large majority of these contracts allowed companies to covertly revise their terms and conditions after end-users accepted the terms of the original contract.[187] The study found that 81.6 percent of these contracts "facilitate non-transparent modifications by failing to require firms to inform consumers personally, publicly and in advance about the occurrence and contents of the change."[188]

Whether revised terms implemented through a unilateral amendment provision are enforceable against consumers can depend in part on whether appropriate notice of any revised terms was provided as well as whether consumers consented to the amended terms.[189] Consumers can be forced to consent to such revised terms or risk losing access to the company's service or products. As we will see in Chapter 5, IoT device functionality is often tethered to various ongoing online services and mobile applications that multiple companies provide. Thus, an individual who has previously purchased an IoT device is more likely to accept revised contract terms in order to ensure that the device that they have already paid for continues to function.

In *Rodman v. Safeway, Inc.*, the company's terms and conditions contained a unilateral amendment provision, which obligated users to review the company's terms and conditions for any subsequent revisions.[190] The court reasoned that users' assent to the amended terms could not "be inferred from their continued use" of the company's website "when they were never given notice that the [company's terms and conditions] had been altered."[191] In *Wainblat v. Comcast Cable Communications, LLC*, a 2019 decision, the district court validated an arbitration clause contained in a contract with a unilateral amendment provision.[192] Per the terms of the unilateral amendment provision, notice of any revised contract terms could be provided to consumers via a posting on the company's website, regular mail, email, or monthly bills.[193] The unilateral amendment clause also included the following provision: "[i]f you find any change to this Agreement to be unacceptable, you have the right to cancel your Service(s). Your continued receipt of the Service(s) for more than 30 days after we deliver notice of the change, however, will constitute your acceptance of the change."[194] The court rejected the plaintiff's argument that

---

[187]   Shmuel I. Becher & Uri Benoliel, *Sneak in Contracts: An Empirical Perspective*, 55 GA. L. REV. (forthcoming 2020), https://papers.ssrn.com/sol3/papers.cfm?abstract_id=3525212.

[188]   *See id.* at 5, 20.

[189]   *Id.* at 26–27, 41, 45; Andrea M. Matwyshyn, *Privacy, the Hacker Way*, 87 S. CAL. L. REV. 1, 59–62 (2013); *Online Contracts: We May Modify These Terms at Any Time, Right?*, AM. B. ASS'N (May 20, 2016), www.americanbar.org/groups/business_law/publications/blt/2016/05/07_moringiello/.

[190]   Rodman v. Safeway, Inc., No. 11-CV-03003-JST, 2015 WL 604985, at *11 (N.D. Cal. Feb. 12, 2015), *aff'd*, 694 F. App'x 612 (9th Cir. 2017).

[191]   *Id.* at 30–31.

[192]   Wainblat v. Comcast Cable Commc'ns, LLC, No. 19-10976-FDS, 2019 U.S. Dist. LEXIS 190650 (D. Mass. Nov. 4, 2019).

[193]   *Id.*

[194]   *Id.*

the arbitration clause was illusory and noted that the consumer had the ability to opt out of the contract within a thirty-day period.[195]

More recently, in *Vernita Miracle Pond et al. v. Shutterfly, Inc.*, a 2020 decision involving allegations of BIPA violations, the district court found that the plaintiff accepted Shutterfly's exercise of a preexisting unilateral amendment provision in its original terms of use to subsequently include an arbitration provision by continuing to use Shutterfly's website and order products from the company after the revised terms of use were posted on the website.[196] The court rejected the plaintiff's lack of notice arguments by reasoning that the plaintiff had consented to the initial click-wrap terms of use containing the unilateral amendment provision, which allowed Shutterfly to amend the terms of service without notice, with the exception of posting the revised terms to the website.[197] Thus, the plaintiff was bound by the arbitration provision.[198]

Without a traditional screen, most IoT devices cannot display any revised contract terms organizations implement via unilateral amendment provisions. An IoT device that is designed to automatically reorder products could place successive orders for goods without the consumer receiving sufficient notice of or reviewing the revised terms and conditions. In such an instance, a consumer is not provided with an adequate opportunity to review and understand amended terms prior to the IoT device's subsequent purchase of additional products. IoT companies' use of unilateral amendment provisions compounds the Contract Distancing problem. State law can require online companies to provide some description of the processes they use to inform users of amendments.[199] However, even when companies provide sufficient notice of their conditions of use, this notice fails to remedy one of the primary concerns associated with online consumer agreements: consumers' failure to review and understand conditions of use, privacy policies, and their implications.

In addition to providing disclosures and contract terms via mobile applications and websites, companies could also begin using home robots and IoT smart speakers to vocally provide consumers with contract terms prior to purchasing products.

---

[195] *Id.*

[196] Miracle-Pond v. Shutterfly, Inc., Case No. 19-cv-04722, 2020 WL 2513099, at *12–13 (N.D. Ill. May 15, 2020). *See also*, Lauraann Wood, *Shutterfly User Must Arbitrate Ill. Biometric Privacy Claim*, Law360 (May 15, 2020, 8:03 PM), www.law360.com/cybersecurity-privacy/articles/1274156/shutterfly-user-must-arbitrate-ill-biometric-privacy-claim?nl_pk=8bca81a9-bf53-40e6-b4c6-4d8c2eda4ebe&utm_source=newsletter&utm_medium=email&utm_campaign=cybersecurity-privacy.

[197] *Miracle-Pond*, 2020 WL 2513099, at 10–11, 14, 16.

[198] *Id.* at 16.

[199] *See, e.g.*, Cal. Bus. & Prof. Code §§ 22575–22579 (requiring certain companies to post a privacy policy that "[d]escribe[s] the process by which the operator notifies consumers" of "material changes" to a privacy policy); Del. Code Ann. tit. 6, § 1205C(b)(3) (2019–2020) (requiring certain companies to post privacy policies that "[d]escribe the process by which the operator notifies users of its commercial internet website, online or cloud computing service, online application, or mobile application of material changes to the operator's privacy policy for that internet website, online or cloud computing service, online application, or mobile application").

Thus, the IoT combined with other technological advancements could perhaps be used to provide new methods of notice and privacy protection to increase consumers' understanding of the privacy and other legal implications of online contracts. The effectiveness of any such potential notice is still questionable, particularly if the IoT device simply reads online terms of use and privacy policies to consumers rather than explaining the implications of these terms without legalese. Additionally, consumers could also ignore voice-provided contract terms or direct their smart speakers to stop reading the contract terms. Several studies and other scholarship in this area suggest that alternative means of notice, such as the use of shorter policies, tables, or icons to provide privacy notices, do not significantly avoid the pitfalls of traditional notice methods.[200] This may also be the case for new IoT methods of notice as well. Alternative notice through IoT devices may not increase consumers' understanding or readership of contract terms as it may be "that the cost of accessing the contract is not the issue; rather it is the expected benefit from reading it."[201]

Contract Distancing could also complicate contractual capacity issues. Consumers' use of IoT devices could make it difficult to determine whether a contracting party has knowledge of the other party's limited capacity.[202] This lack of knowledge could restrict vulnerable consumers' "power of avoidance" under existing contract law principles.[203] Moreover, it is unlikely that the traditional contract defense of unconscionability can sufficiently guard against the Contract Distancing problem and adequately protect consumer interests in the IoT era. Courts have significant discretion in applying the unconscionability doctrine. Several legal scholars have highlighted courts' continued reluctance to use the doctrine of unconscionability to protect consumer interests.[204] This is likely to

---

[200] Aleecia M. McDonald et al., *A Comparative Study of Online Privacy Policies and Formats*, in PRIVACY ENHANCING TECHNOLOGIES 37, 38 (Ian Goldberg & Mikhail Atallah eds., 2009); M. Ryan Calo, *Against Notice Skepticism in Privacy (and Elsewhere)*, 87 NOTRE DAME L. REV. 1027, 1033 (2012); Mike Hintze, *In Defense of the Long Privacy Statement*, 76 MD. L. REV. 1044, 1044 (2017); Lauren E. Willis, *Why Not Privacy by Default?*, 29 BERKELEY TECH. L.J. 61, 127 (2014); PEDRO GIOVANNI LEON ET AL., CARNEGIE MELLON U. CYLAB, WHAT DO ONLINE BEHAVIORAL ADVERTISING DISCLOSURES COMMUNICATE TO USERS? (2012), www.cylab.cmu.edu/files/pdfs/tech_reports/CMUCyLab12008.pdf; Joshua Gluck et al., *How Short Is Too Short? Implications of Length and Framing on the Effectives of Privacy Notices*, USENIX ASS'N 321, 321 (2016), www.usenix.org/system/files/conference/soups2016/soups2016-paper-gluck.pdf.

[201] Marotta-Wurgler, *supra* note 98, at 168.

[202] RESTATEMENT (SECOND) OF CONTRACTS § 12 (AM. LAW INST. 1981) ("A natural person who manifests assent to a transaction has full legal capacity to incur contractual duties thereby unless he is (a) under guardianship, or (b) an infant, or (c) mentally ill or defective, or (d) intoxicated.").

[203] *Id.* § 15 ("Where the contract is made on fair terms and the other party is without knowledge of the mental illness or defect, the power of avoidance under Subsection (1) terminates to the extent that the contract has been so performed in whole or in part or the circumstances have so changed that avoidance would be unjust.").

[204] *See, e.g.*, KIM, WRAP CONTRACTS, *supra* note 111, at 88; Brett M. Becker & John R. Sechrist II, *Claims of Unconscionability: An Empirical Study of the Prevailing Analysis in North Carolina*, 49 WAKE FOREST L. REV. 633, 634 (2014) (a study of unconscionability in one state finding that "unconscionability is a contract theory that rarely prevails"); Hazel Glenn Beh, *Curing the Infirmities of the Unconscionability Doctrine*, 66 HASTINGS L.J. 1011, 1014 (2015) (contending that courts are timid in

continue in the IoT setting. Additionally, as David Horton has observed, Supreme Court case law interpreting the Federal Arbitration Act (FAA) has been interpreted by some courts as limiting their ability to use the unconscionability doctrine to nullify anti-consumer arbitration provisions.[205]

THE MANDATORY ARBITRATION OBSTACLE

As we have seen, the issue of consumer consent has significant bearing on the application of arbitration and class action waiver clauses contained in a company's terms and conditions. The Supreme Court has supported companies' use of mandatory arbitration provisions in consumer transactions.[206] The FTC and Consumer Financial Protection Bureau (CFPB) have attempted to address companies' widespread use of mandatory arbitration provisions with limited success. The FTC has interpreted the Magnuson Moss Warranty Act (MMWA) to prohibit warrantors from forcing consumers into binding arbitration for breach of warranty claims under the statute, but some case law on this topic indicates that the FAA preempts the FTC's regulation on this issue.[207] The MMWA contains provisions applicable to certain warranties and limits companies' ability to disclaim implied warranties in certain consumer transactions, among other things.[208] The CFPB's mandatory arbitration rules in consumer financial transactions were repealed by Congress.[209]

Today, companies frequently include arbitration provisions in their agreements with consumers.[210] One study found that eighty-one businesses in the Fortune 100 use arbitration agreements in consumer transactions with seventy-eight of those companies also using class action waivers, and approximately two-thirds of US

---

utilizing the unconscionability doctrine and "[a]side from its use in recent arbitration cases, judges historically have not favored the doctrine, even in an era where consumer-targeted adhesionary standard form contracts abound"); Amy J. Schmitz, *Embracing Unconscionability's Safety Net Function*, 58 ALA. L. REV. 73, 76 (2006) (contending that courts should "ease rigid application of the two-prong unconscionability test in order to use the doctrine as a safety net to catch cases of contractual injustice that slip by formulaic contract defenses").

[205]   *See* David Horton, *Arbitration About Arbitration*, 70 STAN. L. REV. 363, 398–99 (2018).

[206]   *See, e.g.,* AT&T Mobility LLC v. Concepcion, 131 S. Ct. 1740 (2011).

[207]   16 C.F.R. § 703.5 (2015); 80 Fed. Reg. 42,710, 42,719 (July 20, 2015); Matteo Godi, *Administrative Regulation of Arbitration*, 36 YALE J. ON REG. 853, 864–65 (2019); Colin P. Marks, *Online Terms as In Terrorem Devices*, 78 MD. L. REV. 247, 281–82 (2019); Ryan Miller, *Next-Gen Arbitration: An Empirical Study of How Arbitration Agreements in Consumer Form Contracts Have Changed after Concepcion and American Express*, 32 GEO. J. LEGAL ETHICS 793, 802 n.75 (2019).

[208]   15 U.S.C. §§ 2301–2312 (2020); Marks, *supra* note 207, at 278.

[209]   Joint Resolution, Pub. L. No. 115-74, 131 Stat. 1243 (2017); 82 Fed. Reg. 33210 (July 19, 2017); Patricia A. McCoy, *Inside Job: The Assault on the Structure of the Consumer Financial Protection Bureau*, 103 MINN. L. REV. 2543, 2570–71 (2019); Eric Goldberg, *Correcting the Record on the CFPB's Arbitration Rules*, CONSUMER FIN. PROTECTION BUREAU (Oct. 16, 2017), www.consumerfinance.gov/about-us/blog/correcting-record-cfpbs-arbitration-rule/.

[210]   Scott Medintz, *Forced Arbitration: A Clause for Concern*, CONSUMER REP. (Jan. 30, 2020), www.consumerreports.org/mandatory-binding-arbitration/forced-arbitration-clause-for-concern/.

households are subject to "broad consumer arbitration agreements."[211] Forced arbitration provisions prohibit consumers from bringing various causes of action in courts and can allow corporations to shield themselves from liability despite possible wrongdoing. In the IoT context, these provisions can prohibit consumers from filing lawsuits resulting from defective IoT products and services and privacy and cybersecurity harms. Other critiques of mandatory arbitration provisions and processes include the cloaked nature of arbitration proceedings, arbitrator bias in favor of the companies that supply them with business, and the negative impact on consumers' and employees' willingness to bring individual arbitration claims.[212] A 2019 study of 40,775 filed arbitration cases between 2010 and 2016 found that arbitration tends to favor both repeat companies and repeat plaintiff attorneys.[213] The study determined that contrary to companies' claims, most arbitration cases are brought by attorneys rather than pro-se plaintiffs, but "the plaintiff win rate in arbitration is generally lower than its analogue in the judicial system" with pro-se plaintiffs having lower win rates.[214]

Companies can also abuse the arbitration process by requiring employees and consumers to arbitrate their disputes, but then attempt to renege on their contractual arbitration promises, for instance by failing to pay for filing fees.[215] Recently consumer advocates and FairShake, a startup company, have begun simultaneously filing a large number of individual arbitration claims against companies.[216] Consider that when faced with almost 6,000 individual arbitration claims by their workers, DoorDash attempted to obtain class action wide relief even though it contractually prohibited its workers from doing the same.[217] The company also attempted to persuade workers to agree to new arbitration terms that would change the structure of the arbitration.[218]

---

[211] Imre Stephen Szalai, *The Prevalence of Consumer Arbitration Agreements by America's Top Companies*, 52 U.C. Davis L. Rev. Online 233, 236 (2019).

[212] *See, e.g.*, Katherine Porter, Modern Consumer Law 556–58 (2016); *CFPB Finds Few Consumers File Arbitration Cases*, Consumer Fin. Protection Bureau (Dec. 12, 2013), www.consumerfinance.gov /about-us/newsroom/the-cfpb-finds-few-consumers-file-arbitration-cases/; Medintz, *supra* note 210; Katherine V. W. Stone & Alexander J. S. Colvin, *The Arbitration Epidemic*, Econ. Pol'y Inst. (Dec. 7, 2015), www.epi.org/publication/the-arbitration-epidemic/.

[213] Andrea Cann Chandrasekher & David Horton, *Arbitration Nation: Data from Four Providers*, 107 Calif. L. Rev. 1, 3–10 (2019).

[214] *Id.* at 54–61 (noting that the difference in win rates does not necessarily establish that "arbitration is less hospitable to plaintiffs than the court system" for several reasons).

[215] Abernathy v. Doordash, Inc., No. C-19-07545-WHA, 2020 U.S. Dist. LEXIS 23312 (N.D. Cal. Feb. 10, 2020); Hannah Albarazi, *Alsup Blasts DoorDash's "Hypocrisy," Orders 5K Arbitrations*, Law360 (Feb. 10, 2020, 11:11 PM), www.law360.com/articles/1242667/alsup-blasts-doordash-s-hypocrisy-orders-5k-arbitrations.

[216] Michael Corkery & Jessica Silver-Greenberg, *'Scared to Death' by Arbitration: Companies Drowning in Their Own System*, N.Y. Times (Apr. 6, 2020), www.nytimes.com/2020/04/06/business/arbitration-overload.html.

[217] *Abernathy*, 2020 U.S. Dist. LEXIS 23312.

[218] *Id.*; Albarazi, *supra* note 215.

Recall that in the IoT setting, consumers enter into multiple agreements with companies for a single product and service. These agreements can also include arbitration provisions as well. Rising levels of Contract Distancing likely ensure that we are less likely to review contract terms and understand the negative consequences discussed earlier of consenting to terms and conditions containing mandatory arbitration and class action waiver provisions. Consider that in *Hall-O'Neil v. Amazon, Inc.*, a 2019 putative class action lawsuit, plaintiff minors suing Amazon alleged that Alexa-enabled IoT devices collected and recorded their confidential conversations without their consent in violation of various laws.[219] Amazon moved to arbitrate the case, but the court rejected Amazon's equitable estoppel argument.[220] The court reasoned in part that the minor plaintiffs were not bound to the arbitration provision because they were "nonsignatories" to Amazon's terms and conditions containing the arbitration and class action waiver clauses and "did not knowingly exploit" Amazon's terms and conditions.[221] Despite the court's holding in favor of the plaintiff minors on the arbitration issue, the court also noted that Amazon could have inserted a provision in its terms and conditions that required the parents to consent to data collection and arbitration on behalf of their children.[222] The court's decision suggests that had such a provision been in place, the minors would have been bound by the arbitration clause. It is likely that Amazon and other technology companies will include such provisions in their terms and conditions going forward to avoid the issues in the *Hall* case, at least with respect to minors. Additionally, because the parents had consented to Amazon's various terms and conditions containing the arbitration provisions on several occasions, including while registering and creating accounts for their Alexa-enabled IoT devices and while making purchases from Amazon, the parents would be undisputedly subject to the arbitration clause if they sued on behalf of themselves.[223] Thus, despite renewed efforts by consumer advocates to hold companies accountable, there remains a strong need to prohibit the use of mandatory arbitration provisions in consumer contracts. Companies could attempt to change the arbitration structures, provisions, and processes to negate the future impact of courts' holdings in favor of plaintiffs and pro-consumer arbitration strategies, such as those adopted by FairShake. Additionally, an empirical study of approximately 5,000 consumer arbitration complaints filed between 2009 and 2013 found that

---

[219]   Complaint, Hall-O'Neil v. Amazon.com, Inc., No. 2:19-cv-00910-RAJ-MLP (W.D. Wash. June 11, 2019), www.courtlistener.com/docket/15760059/hall-oneil-v-amazoncom-inc/.

[220]   Order Adopting Report and Recommendation, B.F. by and through Fields v. Amazon.com, Inc., No. 2:19-cv-00910-RAJ-MLP, 2020 WL 1808908, at *2 (W.D. Wash. Apr. 9, 2020).

[221]   *Id.* (rejecting Amazon's equitable estoppel arguments in favor of the arbitration provision "[b]ecause Plaintiffs did not 'knowingly exploit' the agreements containing the arbitration clauses, they cannot be equitably estopped from avoiding them").

[222]   *Id.*; Lauren Berg, *Amazon Can't Arbitrate Kids' Alexa Privacy Battle*, LAW360 (Apr. 9, 2020, 10:42 PM), www.law360.com/articles/1262396.

[223]   Report and Recommendation, Hall-O'Neil. v. Amazon, No. 2:19-cv-00910-RAJ-MLP (W.D. Wash. Oct. 21, 2019), www.courtlistener.com/docket/15760059/hall-oneil-v-amazoncom-inc/.

when plaintiffs' attorneys filed "numerous free standing claims" against the same businesses they "inadvertently transformed some large corporations into 'extreme repeat players' . . . that win more and pay less in damages [in arbitration proceedings] than one shot entities."[224]

IOT DEVICES AS CONTRACTING AGENTS?

So far in our contracting discussion we have assumed that IoT devices are mere tools or "instrumentalities" consumers use in the same manner as computers and smartphones to enter into contracts, but this may not always be the case. Consider that Saudi Arabia granted citizenship to the robot Sophia, which has been described by commentators as the first "autonomous robot."[225] IoT objects enhanced by artificial intelligence may one day have the capacity to act autonomously. The current White House has expressed its intent to remove hurdles to artificial intelligence development, including what the administration describes as "[o]verly burdensome regulation."[226] The possible rise of artificially intelligent and autonomous IoT robots raises the question of what role, if any, agency law should play in evaluating consumers' rights and obligations in IoT contracts entered into by autonomous IoT robots. One could argue that the designer of the software and other forms of technology used to create the IoT robot will always maintain a significant degree of control over the robot, including the device's design and actions, and as such the robot can never truly be fully autonomous. Additionally, one might posit that a future in which IoT robots meet or exceed human intelligence levels is far off or may never come to fruition.

In the 1960s when the Jetsons cartoon was created, we could only dream of the possibilities of talking computers and cleaning robots. Obviously, we do not yet have flying cars, but consider that, in 2018, Google announced the Duplex, which it describes as a "fully autonomous" artificially intelligent system with the capacity to work with the Google Assistant to perform without "human involvement" certain limited tasks on behalf of consumers, such as phone calling and booking dining reservations and appointments for services.[227] Microsoft envisions a 2038 future in which its digital assistant Cortana places orders for products on behalf of consumers while they are

---

[224] David Horton & Andrea Cann Chandrasekher, *After the Revolution: An Empirical Study of Consumer Arbitration*, 104 GEO. L.J. 57 (2015).

[225] Roland Benedikter, *Citizen Robot*, CATO UNBOUND (Apr. 9, 2018), www.cato-unbound.org/2018/04/09/roland-benedikter/citizen-robot; *see also* Stephy Chung, *Meet Sophia: The Robot Who Laughs, Smiles and Frowns Just Like Us*, CNN (Nov. 2, 2018), www.cnn.com/style/article/sophia-robot-artificial-intelligence-smart-creativity/index.html.

[226] WHITE HOUSE OFFICE OF SCI. & TECH. POLICY, SUMMARY OF THE 2018 WHITE HOUSE SUMMIT ON ARTIFICIAL INTELLIGENCE FOR AMERICAN INDUSTRY 3 (May 10, 2018), www.whitehouse.gov/wp-content/uploads/2018/05/Summary-Report-of-White-House-AI-Summit.pdf.

[227] Yaniv Leviathan & Yossi Matias, *Google Duplex: An AI System for Accomplishing Real-World Tasks over the Phone*, GOOGLE AI BLOG (May 8, 2018), https://ai.googleblog.com/2018/05/duplex-ai-system-for-natural-conversation.html.

sleeping.[228] Today's IoT objects, including self-driving vehicles, Alexa- and Siri-enhanced devices, and smart vacuums that automate cleanings (such as the Roomba) bring us closer to realizing a Jetsonsian future.[229]

In 2018, US House of Representatives' Subcommittee on Information Technology Committee on Oversight and Government Reform chairman Will Hurd and member Robin Kelly released a white paper (SIT Report) which acknowledged that artificial intelligence "is an immature technology" but its reliance on volumes of personal data has the potential to "invade privacy" and facilitate bias.[230] The SIT Report also recommended consideration of possible consumer risks and concerns associated with the rise of artificial intelligence, as well as an evaluation of whether existing legal frameworks can sufficiently remedy those risks.[231] With that recommendation in mind consider the following question: under existing agency law, can or should IoT objects serve as contracting agents for humans, thereby creating legal obligations for consumers using such devices?

The Restatement of the Law (Third) of Agency (Agency Restatement) is a primary source of common law agency principles.[232] Section 1-103 of the UCC states that "[u]nless displaced by the specific provisions of the [UCC], the principles of law and equity, including ... principal and agent ... supplement its provisions."[233] This indicates that even if the UCC governs an IoT transaction, questions related to agency can be answered by consulting traditional agency principles. The Agency Restatement describes the concept of agency as a "fiduciary relationship that arises when one person (a 'principal') manifests assent to another person (an 'agent') that the agent shall act on the principal's behalf and subject to the principal's control, and the agent manifests assent or otherwise consents so to act."[234] When agency relationships are established and agents have the necessary authority, principals can be bound by their agents' actions.[235] Recall that anonymity protection is one aspect of privacy. Agency law also recognizes the value of anonymity.[236] The Agency Restatement permits the agent to act on the principal's behalf without disclosing the principal's identity.[237]

---

[228] Microsoft, The Future Computed: Artificial Intelligence and its Role in Society 5 (2018), https://blogs.microsoft.com/uploads/2018/02/The-Future-Computed_2.8.18.pdf.

[229] *See e.g.*, iRobot, www.irobot.com/ (last visited Jan. 4, 2020).

[230] U.S. House of Reps., Subcomm. on Info. Tech., White Paper (2018), https://oversight.house.gov/wp-content/uploads/2018/09/AI-White-Paper-.pdf.

[231] *Id.* at 1, 13.

[232] *See generally* Restatement (Third) of Agency (Am. Law Inst. 2006).

[233] U.C.C. § 1-103(b) (Am. Law Inst. & Unif. Law Comm'n 2001).

[234] Restatement (Third) of Agency § 1.01 (Am. Law Inst. 2006).

[235] *See id.* § 2.01–2.03.

[236] *Id.* § 6.11(4) cmt. d.

[237] *Id.* (discussing restrictions on the enforceability of contracts involving undisclosed principles); Jeffrey M. Skopek, *Anonymity, the Production of Goods and Institutional Design*, 82 Fordham L. Rev. 1751, 1754 n.19 (2014) (contending that "anonymous purchasing is facilitated by the law of agency, which generally allows an agent who enters into a contract on behalf of a principal to protect the anonymity of the principal – even by falsely representing that he is not acting on behalf of any principal," but

Imagine a consumer that requests that their autonomous IoT home robot search for and purchase household supplies and other household devices online. Assume further that the robot has the capacity to scan different websites and identify the best price for products and place orders for these products from different companies. Applying existing agency principles, one way to think about this example is that the autonomous robot should be seen as the agent of the consumer and could be said to manifest assent to the agency relationship by placing orders on the consumer's behalf. The consumer could be said to assent to the agency relationship by electing to use the device to purchase products on their behalf, thereby arguably creating an agency relationship between the IoT robot and the consumer. The IoT robot acting as the consumer's agent in our hypothetical has bound the consumer to the seller's online terms and conditions even though the consumer has not actively participated in the contracting process. Indeed, in this hypothetical the consumer never reads or actually sees the online terms and conditions, since the device and not the consumer searches for products, accesses various sellers' websites and places the online order. If the device is viewed as the agent of the consumer, the consumer is bound to the contract terms, despite the prevalence of Contract Distancing.

However, there are several potential challenges to using common law agency principles as the governing framework to evaluate the relationship between consumers and possibly autonomous IoT robots and consumers. The most obvious challenge to the application of traditional agency principles is that the Agency Restatement uses the term "person" to refer to agents and principals.[238] The Restatement's comments section goes on to provide that "an inanimate object" and a "computer program" cannot qualify as an agent.[239] This implies that agency principles are intended to apply only to parties with legal personhood. Some scholars have argued that robots should be considered "persons" under the law.[240] With the possible exception of the robot Sophia, robots and artificially intelligent entities or systems in general are not currently "persons." This presents a seemingly overwhelming challenge to applying traditional agency principles to assess transactions involving autonomous robots and consumers. Samir Chopra and Laurence White contend that despite the Agency Restatement's "person" requirement, the Restatement "cannot be understood as shutting the door on legal agency for artificial agents."[241] The Agency Restatement's comments section implies that the Restatement's position against computer programs and inanimate objects qualifying as agents relies on the presumption that "at present,

---

noting that "doing so will generally only affect the enforceability of the contract if the principal or agent had notice that the third party would not have dealt with the principal").

[238] *See, e.g.*, RESTATEMENT (THIRD) OF AGENCY § 1.01 cmts. a–c.

[239] *Id.* § 1.04 cmt. e.

[240] *See, e.g.*, SAMIR CHOPRA & LAURENCE F. WHITE , A LEGAL THEORY FOR AUTONOMOUS ARTIFICIAL AGENTS 87 (2011); *Open Letter to the European Commissions: Artificial Intelligence and Robotics*, ROBOTICS www.robotics-openletter.eu/ ("We believe that … [t]he creation of a Legal Status of an 'electronic person' for 'autonomous,' 'unpredictable' and 'self-learning' robots is justified.").

[241] CHOPRA & WHITE, *supra* note 240, at 157.

computer programs are instrumentalities of the persons who use them."[242] At some point in the future, IoT robots could meet or exceed human intelligence and possibly become autonomous. If this occurs, it is difficult to argue that an IoT device is a mere instrumentality or tool. If more states grant robots citizenship (as in the case with the robot Sophia) one might argue that such robots have the "capacity to be the holder of legal rights and the object of legal duties," and therefore qualify as "persons" for purposes of agency law.[243] In such an instance, the hypothetical posed earlier could become a reality. Moreover, traditional legal personhood for IoT robots may not need to be achieved in order for IoT robots to begin engaging in commercial transactions. Consider Shawn Bayern's observation that the existing structure of business organizations law could permit autonomous robots to mimic legal activities and rights, such as purchasing property, traditionally reserved for beings or entities with "legal personhood," by colonizing certain types of business entities with the aid of humans.[244]

Even if the Agency Restatement's "personhood" limitation can be overcome, there are still other challenges to applying traditional agency principles to bind consumers to contracts entered into on their behalf by IoT robots. First, agency is a fiduciary relationship and agents generally have certain responsibilities to their principals. These include the obligation to "act loyally in the principal's interest as well as on the principal's behalf."[245] Even if an IoT robot is truly autonomous, such devices would need to have sufficient intelligence to understand and perform the duty of loyalty.

Second, a potential conflict of interest may arise if IoT robots are viewed as consumers' agents but simultaneously collect and transfer data about consumers' activities and preferences to manufacturers and other IoT service and mobile application providers. The Agency Restatement provides that "[a]n agent has a duty ... not to use or communicate confidential information of the principal for the agent's own purposes or those of a third party."[246] Assuming that IoT robots qualify as consumers' agents, this duty of confidentiality is arguably breached when data about consumers is transferred to other parties, including the manufacturer. However, the Agency Restatement indicates that an agent may avoid allegations of breach of its duties "if the principal consents to the conduct."[247] In theory, one might contend that if the IoT robot manufacturer's conditions of use disclose that data will be collected and transferred to the manufacturer and the consumer manifests assent by, for instance, clicking an "I accept" option on their smartphone, then issues

---

[242]　Restatement (Third) of Agency § 1.04 cmt. e.

[243]　*Id.*

[244]　*See* Shawn Bayern, *The Implications of Modern Business-Entity Law for the Regulation of Autonomous Systems*, 19 Stan. Tech. L. Rev. 93, 94 (2015).

[245]　Restatement (Third) of Agency § 1.01 cmt. e; *see also id.* § 8.03 ("An agent has a duty not to deal with the principal as or on behalf of an adverse party in a transaction connected with the agency relationship.").

[246]　*Id.* § 8.05.

[247]　*Id.* § 8.06; *see also id.* § 8.03 cmt. c.

associated with a conflict of interest could be avoided, assuming all other agency law requirements are satisfied. As noted earlier, courts frequently hold that consumers are bound by clickwrap agreements.[248] Also, remember the limitations of the notice and opportunity to review paradigm and the Contract Distancing problem.

If the IoT robots of the future continue to collect and transfer reams of data about consumers to companies, it may be best to view such devices as agents of the companies that manufacture and design them or collect data about consumers rather than labeling these objects as consumers' agents for contracting purposes.[249] Moreover, through EULAs, companies retain control of and restrict consumers' rights in software associated with IoT devices. This is likely to continue even if IoT robots achieve human level intelligence and begin acting autonomously.

The unrestrained application of agency law principles to artificially intelligent and autonomous IoT robots combined with existing contract law assent standards could bind individuals to anti-consumer adhesions contracts despite the presence of overwhelming levels of Contract Distancing. If agency law becomes one of the legal frameworks that courts turn to in evaluating consumer assent to contracts facilitated by autonomous IoT robots, careful consideration must be given to the concerns noted in this chapter, including increased levels of Contract Distancing, data information asymmetry, and the data collection and surveillance role played by IoT robots. A one-to-one application of the reasonable notice and opportunity to review standard along with agency principles without an adequate evaluation of these risks could render the requirement of "mutual assent" meaningless in a Jetsonian future.

Contract law and agency law are not the only established sources of commercial law challenged by the IoT. There are also inadequacies plaguing Article 2's scope and warranty provisions, and products liability laws' ability to deal with IoT-specific harms, including digital domination harms and insecure and defective IoT devices. We turn to these issues next in Chapter 5.

---

[248] Mucciariello v. Viator, Inc., No. 18-14444, 2019 WL 4727896, at *3 (D.N.J. Sept. 27, 2019) ("While clickwrap agreements are routinely upheld . . . .").

[249] Elvy, *supra* note 4, at 861; Lauren Henry Scholz, *Algorithmic Contracts*, 20 STAN. TECH. L. REV. 128, 165 (2017).

5

Products Liability in the Internet of Things Age

The IoT raises several questions germane to traditional products liability law and the UCC's warranty provisions. These include how best to evaluate and remedy consumer harms related to insecure devices, malfunctioning devices, and the termination of services and software integral to a device's operations. Consider that the modern IoT vehicle with an infotainment system generates massive quantities of data about drivers, and that mobile applications can be used to impact the operations of these vehicles.[1] If the device or the databases storing these data are hacked and sensitive consumer data are disclosed to third parties, or consumers suffer economic injury as a result of the hack, should vehicle owners have a cause of action under products liability law or the UCC's warranty rules? And if so, against whom? This chapter begins to explore these questions and more.

Liability claims related to products often involve a mixture of tort law and contract law as well as common law and statutory law.[2] IoT companies may potentially be exposed to liability under several distinct theories of law for problematic devices, including strict liability, negligence, and warranty liability. At first glance the law of products liability and warranty principles would seem well suited to protect consumers in the IoT age. However, a review of the potential application of such rules to IoT consumer products reveals several shortcomings. The integrated nature of IoT devices that rely on services, software (both embedded and non-embedded), and hardware complicates assessments of liability under existing products liability law and warranty principles. The services and software that are needed for IoT devices to function may not qualify as "products" or "goods" for purposes of products liability law and Article 2 of the UCC. Stated differently, if the services and software are not "products" or "goods," then a cause of action under products liability law and Article 2 of the UCC cannot accrue for harms or damages associated with those aspects of IoT devices. Moreover, the termination of services and the denial of software

---

[1] Michael Wayland, *The Demise of the Car Key: Tesla, Lincoln Lead Auto Industry in Ditching Keys for Mobile Entry*, CNBC (Nov. 9, 2019, 10:15 AM), www.cnbc.com/2019/11/09/the-demise-of-the-car-key-tesla-lincoln-ditch-keys-for-mobile-entry.html.

[2] DAVID OWEN, OWEN'S PRODUCT LIABILITY LAW, 4 (3rd ed. 2015).

updates that are integral to device functionality may not be viewed as a defect for purposes of products liability law or a breach of warranty. The multiple parties involved in the manufacturing and post-distribution chain make it difficult to identify which entity is liable when consumers are harmed or incur damages. These parties include manufacturers, software developers, retailers, and service providers, to name a few. Further, the nature of online transactions in which IoT companies, such as Amazon, provide both a marketplace for third parties to sell products to consumers, while simultaneously selling products that they or other companies make directly to consumers highlights the limitations of narrowly defining "sellers" under products liability law. These restrictive definitions allow companies to insulate themselves from liability for defective products sold in their marketplaces. As interpreted by courts, the Communications Decency Act (CDA), a federal statute, also imposes limitations on companies' liability for defective products. Lastly, application of the economic loss doctrine may bar certain traditional liability claims, thereby limiting the types of suits that consumers may successfully bring.

WHAT IS A "PRODUCT" OR "GOOD?"

Article 2 of the UCC governs "transactions in goods."[3] Goods are generally defined as items that "are movable at the time of identification" to the sale contract.[4] Thus, Article 2 applies primarily to the sale of goods and it provides important warranty liability rules grounded in contract law. Article 2A of the UCC, which applies to the lease of goods, also contains a similar definition of "goods" and warranty principles.[5] Article 2 provides consumers with a cause of action for breach of warranties that have not been effectively disclaimed.[6] Article 2 provides various rules for disclaiming implied warranties, such as the implied warranty of merchantability and the implied warranty of fitness for a particular purpose.[7] Recall that the MMWA limits the effect of implied warranty disclaimers.[8] However, courts' interpretation of the provisions of the MMWA has restricted the Act's capacity to protect consumers.[9] Some state statutes restrict the effectiveness of warranty disclaimers in certain consumer transactions while other state statutes establish warranties similar to those found in the UCC.[10]

---

[3] U.C.C. § 2-102 (Am. Law Inst. & Unif. Law Comm'n 2002).

[4] *Id.* § 2-105(1).

[5] *See id.* §§ 2A-102, 2A-103(1)(h), 2A-212.

[6] *See id.* §§ 2-714(2), 2-316 (providing for warranty disclaimers).

[7] *See id.* § 2-316.

[8] 15 U.S.C. § 2308(a) (1975); *id.* § 2310(d).

[9] *See, e.g.*, Janet W. Steverson, *The Unfulfilled Promise of the Magnuson-Moss Warranty Act*, 18 Lewis & Clark L. Rev. 155, 176–77 (2014); Janet W. Steverson & Aaron Munter, *Then and Now: Reviving the Promise of the Magnuson-Moss Warranty Act*, 63 U. Kan. L. Rev. 227, 228 (2015).

[10] *See* Conn. Gen. Stat. Ann. § 42A-2-316 (West 2019); D.C. Code Ann. § 28:2-316.01 (West 2020); Kan. Stat. Ann. § 50-639(A) (2019–2020); Me. Rev. Stat. Ann. tit. 11, § 2-316(5) (2020); Md. Code Ann. Com. Law § 2-316.1 (LexisNexis 2020); Mass. Gen. Laws Ann. ch. 106, § 2-316A (LexisNexis 2020);

The effectiveness of a warranty disclaimer can be a hotly contested issue and can doom consumer claims in lawsuits involving privacy and security issues. For instance, in *In re Google Assistant Privacy Litigation*, a 2020 decision, the plaintiffs alleged that Google Assistant and various Google-enabled IoT devices collected their audio recordings, which the company uses to improve its voice recognition technology, among other things.[11] The plaintiffs brought several claims under state and federal law, including a breach of implied warranty claim under California's version of the UCC.[12] The district court granted the defendants' motion to dismiss the merchantability claim, reasoning in part that the plaintiffs had consented to Google's terms and conditions, which contained an effective warranty disclaimer.[13] The court granted plaintiffs leave to amend the complaint to further allege that the disclaimer was unconscionable.[14] However, recall that courts can be reluctant to grant consumer relief based on the unconscionability doctrine.

Previous attempts to amend Article 2 to effectively address consumer protection issues, such as warranty disclaimers, have failed.[15] In 1988, the UCC's Permanent Editorial Board began an evaluation of Article 2 to determine whether revisions were necessary.[16] As Henry Gabriel, the reporter for the Article 2 UCC revision process from 1999 through 2003, observes, "the proposed revisions of Article 2, from the time the process began until the time the revisions were withdrawn, took 24 years."[17] The initial drafting committee for the Article 2 revision process attempted to take a balanced approach to protecting buyers and sellers, in contrast to the Article 2B committee discussed in Chapter 4.[18] Revised Article 2's original reporters resigned and a new drafting committee was subsequently appointed.[19]

The 2003 proposed amendments to Article 2's warranty disclaimer provisions, which were ultimately withdrawn, would not have prohibited disclaimers in

---

MINN. STAT. § 325G.18 (2019); MISS. CODE ANN. § 11-7-18 (2019); VT. STAT. ANN. tit. 9A, § 2-316(5) (2019); W. VA. CODE § 46A-6-107 (2019).

[11] *In re* Google Assistant Privacy Litigation, No. 19-cv-04286-BLF, 2020 WL 2219022, at *1–3 (N.D. Cal. May 6, 2020).

[12] *Id.* at *3.

[13] *Id.* at *41–42.

[14] *Id.*

[15] Henry Gabriel, *Uniform Commercial Code Article Two Revisions: The View of the Trenches*, 23 BARRY L. REV. 129, 149–51 (2018); *PEB Study Group: Uniform Commercial Code, Article 2 Executive Summary*, 46 BUS. LAW. 1869 (1991).

[16] Am. Bar Assoc. Task Force, *An Appraisal of the March 1, 1990, Preliminary Report of the Uniform Commercial Code Article 2 Study Group*, 16 DEL. J. CORP. L. 981, 984 (1991); Donald F. Clifford, Jr., *Non-UCC Statutory Provisions Affecting Warranty Disclaimers and Remedies in Sales of Goods*, 71 N. C. L. REV. 1011 (1993).

[17] Gabriel, *supra* note 15, at 130.

[18] Jean Braucher, *New Basics: Twelve Principles for Fair Commerce in Mass-Market Software and Other Digital Products*, *in* CONSUMER PROTECTION IN THE AGE OF THE 'INFORMATION ECONOMY' 166 (Jane K. Winn ed., 2006); Linda J. Rusch, *A History and Perspective of Revised Article 2: The Never Ending Saga of a Search for Balance*, 52 SMU L. REV. 1683, 1689–90 (1999).

[19] Braucher, *supra* note 18, at 166.

consumer transactions.[20] Instead, the revisions would have imposed additional language requirements to effectively disclaim implied warranties.[21] The unsuccessful Article 2 revision process reflects a missed opportunity to have the UCC more adequately deal with existing ambiguities and consumer concerns, including companies' use of warranty disclaimers in consumer transactions. There are multiple reasons for the revisions' failures, including the fact that the circumstances surrounding Article 2's initial drafting indicate that the article was not "intended to be a consumer protection statute."[22] Structural hurdles in the UCC's drafting process have historically limited consumer advocates' perspectives and participation in the revision process.[23] These historical barriers include the complicated and lengthy duration of the revision process, costs that consumer advocates who are often short on resources must incur to participate in the process, drafting committees' limited consumer law practice backgrounds, which may limit their understanding of the consumer impact of corporate practices in consumer transactions, and the dominance of observers who represent corporate interests.[24] The UCC's drafters have long relied on corporate representatives during the drafting process to incorporate and reflect ongoing commercial practices.[25] Corporate support for the UCC and proposed amendments has for some time been critical to states' adoption of the UCC and related revisions, as corporate entities are well positioned to lobby against proposed legislation.[26] The reliance on industry practices and approval of proposed UCC amendments to some extent reflects the continuation of the UCC's history of deference to commercial practice and the goal of uniformity.

One of the most vexing issues under the UCC is when to apply Article 2 to agreements involving goods and non-goods. If a transaction involves the provision of both goods and non-goods, the majority of courts use a predominant purpose test to determine whether Article 2 should govern the transaction.[27] Article 2 and its accompanying warranty liability rules will only apply if the predominant purpose of the transaction is for the provision of goods. In applying this test courts use several factors, including "the nature and reasonableness of the purchaser's contractual expectations of acquiring a property interest in the goods"[28] and the "factual

---

[20]   *Revised Article 2*, U.C.C. § 2-316(2) (AM. LAW INST. & UNIF. LAW COMM'N, withdrawn 2011); Gabriel, *supra* note 15, at 149 n.94.

[21]   *Revised Article 2*, U.C.C. § 2-316(2) (AM. LAW INST. & UNIF. LAW COMM'N, withdrawn 2011).

[22]   Gabriel, *supra* note 15, at 133–39, 134 n.25.

[23]   Gail Hillebrand, *The Uniform Commercial Code Drafting Process: Will Articles 2, 2B and 9 Be Fair to Consumers?*, 75 WASH. U. L.Q. 69, 82–94 (1997).

[24]   *Id.*

[25]   Gabriel, *supra* note 15, at 133–39.

[26]   *Id.* at 133–34 ("[F]rom the beginning of the drafting of Article 2 in the 1940's, the philosophy behind the Code was to move away from the traditional legal formalism and instead focus on actual commercial practices.").

[27]   *See generally* Stacy-Ann Elvy, *Hybrid Transactions and the INTERNET of Things: Goods, Services, or Software?*, 74 WASH. & LEE L. REV. 77 (2017).

[28]   Colorado Carpet Installation, Inc. v. Palermo, 668 P.2d 1384, 1389 (Colo. 1983).

circumstances surrounding the negotiation, formation, and contemplated performance of the contract."[29] Different courts may use different factors in applying the test, making it difficult to determine pre contract whether a hybrid transaction is subject to Article 2.

The Restatement (Second) of Torts (Second Restatement) and the Restatement (Third) of Torts: Products Liability (Products Restatement) are central sources of products liability law. The majority of courts continue to rely on the strict liability principles set forth in the Second Restatement to evaluate defective products, but some courts use the Products Restatement.[30] Both restatements provide for liability for "defective" products in distinct ways.[31] The comments section of the Second Restatement contains a non-exhaustive list of items that are considered "products," including vehicles, stoves, and chairs.[32] The Products Restatement defines a product as "tangible personal property distributed commercially for use or consumption."[33] The Products Restatement goes on to provide that "other items" may be viewed as products to the extent that "their distribution and use" are similar to "tangible personal property."[34]

The Model Uniform Product Liability Act is another potential source of products liability law.[35] The model law's definition of the term "product" (or portions thereof) is used in at least three jurisdictions.[36] The model law defines the term product as "any object possessing intrinsic value, capable of delivery either as an assembled whole or as a component part or parts, and produced for introduction into trade or commerce."[37]

Under all of the aforementioned sources of law, the terms "product" or "goods" are limited to either tangible property, objects, or movable things. Recall that even California's ground-breaking IoT security statute discussed in Chapter 3 defines IoT products as "devices" or "physical objects."[38] These narrow definitions of the terms

---

[29] Glover Sch. & Office Equip. Co. v. Dave Hall, Inc., 372 A.2d 221, 223 (Del. Super. Ct. 1977).

[30] OWEN, *supra* note 2, at 245–46.

[31] *See* RESTATEMENT (THIRD) OF TORTS: PRODUCTS LIABILITY § 1 (AM. LAW INST.); RESTATEMENT (SECOND) OF TORTS § 402A (AM. LAW. INST.).

[32] RESTATEMENT (SECOND) OF TORTS § 402A cmt. d.

[33] RESTATEMENT (THIRD) OF TORTS: PRODUCTS LIABILITY § 19.

[34] *Id.*

[35] Model Uniform Product Liability Act, 44 Fed. Reg. 62,714, 62,733 (Oct. 31, 1979). As other commentators have noted, most jurisdictions have not adopted the model law. Hines v. JMJ Constr. Co., No. CV92-506329, 1993 Conn. Super. LEXIS 69, at *12 (Conn. Super. Ct. Jan. 7, 1993) (noting that Connecticut's product liability law is based on the Model Uniform Product Liability Act but Connecticut has not adopted the uniform law's definition of product); LOUIS FRUMER & MELVIN FRIEDMAN, PRODUCTS LIABILITY § 1:08 (rev. ed. 2018) (noting "a few states adopted several provisions of the UPLA, but no state adopted the Act in tot[al]"); OWEN, *supra* note 2, at 333–34.

[36] *See* ARIZ. REV. STAT. ANN. § 12-689 (LexisNexis 2020); IDAHO CODE § 6-1402 (2020); WASH. REV. CODE § 7.72.010 (2020).

[37] Model Uniform Product Liability Act, 44 Fed. Reg. at 62,719, 62,733.

[38] CAL. CIV. CODE § 1798.91.05 (Deering 2020) ("'Connected device' means any device, or other physical object that is capable of connecting to the Internet, directly or indirectly, and that is assigned an Internet Protocol address or Bluetooth address.").

"product" and "goods" pose significant challenges for consumers who seek to hold companies liable in the IoT era under multiple theories of liability. IoT devices rely on an intricate provision of ongoing services and external and internal software to function.[39] Indeed, IoT devices are "software-centric" products that are heavily dependent on firmware and sensors. Many IoT devices must receive software updates from manufacturers, and the mobile applications used in connection with these devices must also be periodically updated. The following examples of several IoT devices and services highlight these points.

Recall the Amazon dash button discussed in Chapters 1 and 4. Consumers using the dash button were able to register and configure their device, revise device settings, and receive order status notifications through Amazon's mobile application.[40] At least one manufacturer has also installed "virtual dash buttons" on their IoT home appliances.[41] Consumers who obtained the dash button acquired a physical object connected to a reordering service and an external software application– Amazon's mobile application.

Also, recall Amazon's DRS discussed in Chapters 1 and 4. DRS is integrated directly into various internet-connected products, including printers, home filters, washing machines, and coffee makers.[42] The service allows IoT devices to monitor the rate at which consumers use and consume products and automatically purchase additional products, among other things. Multiple companies have manufactured household appliances with DRS capabilities, including GE. A consumer that has purchased a GE IoT dishwasher that is accompanied by DRS obtains what could be viewed as a "movable," "tangible personal property," or "object," while simultaneously acquiring a right to use an ongoing reordering service and accompanying software – Amazon's reorder services, GE's appliance kitchen mobile application, and any software embedded within the dishwasher.[43] Through the GE mobile application consumers can remotely operate their IoT dishwashers. GE's various other IoT home appliances, such as refrigerators, washing machines, ovens, and microwaves, are also accompanied by mobile applications that allow consumers to remotely control device functions and receive alerts and warnings regarding device

---

[39] *See* Elvy, *supra* note 27; *see also* Rebecca Crootof, *The Internet of Torts: Expanding Civil Liability Standards to Address Corporate Remote Interference*, 69 DUKE L.J. 583, 587–88 n.14 (2019) (citing Elvy, *supra* note 27); Chris Jay Hoofnagle et al., *The Tethered Economy*, 87 GEO. WASH. L. REV. 783, 850–53 nn. 476–85 (2019) (citing Elvy, *supra* note 27).

[40] *See Help and Customer Service: Support for Dash Button Device*, AMAZON, www.amazon.com/gp/help/customer/display.html?nodeId=201730790 (last visited Jan. 4, 2020).

[41] Ry Crist, *Less Is More with Whirlpool's Clever Connected Fridge*, CNET (Jan. 10, 2018, 12:33 PM), www.cnet.com/news/less-is-more-with-whirlpools-clever-connected-fridge/.

[42] *Amazon Dash Replenishment*, AMAZON, www.amazon.com/b/ref=s9_acss_bw_cg_dbpk5_md1_w?node=15426532011&ref=cp_oft_db_drs_lm&pf_rd_m=ATVPDKIKX0DER&pf_rd_s=merchandised-search-17&pf_rd_r=HNEJDFBW40898S96GTZ0&pf_rd_t=101&pf_rd_p=d722a022-7f6a-4d79-baf5-27e10fd3a142&pf_rd_i=10667898011 (last visited Jan. 8, 2019).

[43] *See Smart Dishwashers*, GE APPLIANCES, www.geappliances.com/ge/connected-appliances/dishwashers.htm (last visited Feb. 4, 2019).

operations.[44] These devices can work seamlessly with various third-party IoT services and products, such as the Google Assistant and Amazon's Alexa.[45] Thus, consumers can also direct and operate their GE devices by using these third-party products and services.

Samsung's IoT refrigerators can be operated remotely through the company's mobile application. The refrigerators are accompanied by a built-in entertainment system that allows consumers to stream music and watch videos, and includes other features that allow device owners to send mobile messages and pictures to household members and purchase goods using the refrigerator.[46] Also, consider that various companies offer IoT products that can be integrated with and operated through Apple's home kit application and Apple devices. These products include light bulbs, locks, thermostats, and other items, all of which are manufactured by third-party companies, such as Phillips, August, Honeywell, and others.[47]

In addition to non-embedded software (such as mobile applications) and embedded software, many IoT devices also rely on cloud computing technology. For instance, an IoT company may offer data storage and subscription services to consumers that rely on cloud services and software. Consumers who purchase a Nest camera also obtain access to "Nest Aware," a subscription service that saves videos that the camera records in the cloud and provides "intelligent alerts" and "clips and time lapses."[48] Nest cameras' features can be managed through the company's mobile application. Cloud computing services play an integral role in providing software updates to IoT devices and in storing and processing the data these devices generate. Amazon provides (through AWS) an IoT service that permits IoT devices to "interact with cloud applications and other devices," allows companies to process and analyze IoT data, including building learning modules, and can be integrated with IoT edge-based software.[49] Fog or edge computing will also play an ever-increasing role in IoT device functionality and data processing.[50] The data

---

[44] See *Smart Microwave Ovens*, GE APPLIANCES, www.geappliances.com/ge/connected-appliances /microwave-ovens.htm (last visited Jan. 8, 2019); *Smart Ovens and Ranges*, GE APPLIANCES, www .geappliances.com/ge/connected-appliances/ranges-ovens-cooking.htm (last visited Jan. 8, 2019); *Connected Refrigerators*, GE APPLIANCES, www.geappliances.com/ge/connected-appliances/refriger ators.htm (last visited Jan. 8, 2019).

[45] *Voice Control*, GE APPLIANCES, www.geappliances.com/ge/connected-appliances/voice-activated-appliances.htm (last visited Jan. 8, 2019).

[46] *Family Hub*, SAMSUNG, www.samsung.com/us/explore/family-hub-refrigerator/connected-hub/ (last visited Jan. 8, 2019); *It's All on Your Fridge*, SAMSUNG, www.samsung.com/us/explore/family-hub-refrigerator/overview/ (last visited Jan. 8, 2019).

[47] *HomeKit*, APPLE, www.apple.com/shop/accessories/all-accessories/homekit (last visited Jan. 8, 2019).

[48] *Nest Aware*, GOOGLE, https://nest.com/cameras/nest-aware/ (last visited Jan. 8, 2019); *How Nest Cameras Store Your Recorded Video*, GOOGLE NEST HELP, https://nest.com/support/article/How-does-Nest-Cam-store-my-recorded-video (last visited Jan. 8, 2019).

[49] *AWS IoT Core*, AMAZON WEB SERV., https://aws.amazon.com/iot-core/?nc2=h_m1 (last visited Jan. 8, 2019).

[50] Alan Earls, *Fog Computing Brightens Prospects for Secure Edge Computing*, SCMAGAZINE (Jul. 25, 2019), www.scmagazine.com/home/security-news/cloud-security/despite-the-apparent-oxymoron-fog-

IoT devices generate can be processed through the cloud as well as through "fog nodes."[51] IoT devices that rely on fog technology are projected to be able to more quickly process and analyze data.[52] Cisco, IBM, and various other technology companies have supported use of fog or edge computing services in connection with the IoT.[53]

Software and services do not fall neatly within the definition of "goods" and "products" under the existing sources of law discussed earlier. Consumers who purchase IoT products rather than unconnected devices likely do so for the convenient services and software that allow them to remotely control and operate their devices and reorder products. As previously noted, the primary purpose for purchasing a device is relevant in assessing Article 2's (and its accompanying warranties) applicability to transactions that involve goods and non-goods. Embedded software and the physical device could be viewed as movable and a "good" for purposes of Article 2. The comments section to the proposed revisions to Article 2, which were ultimately abandoned, appears to have adopted this approach, but proposed Article 2 did not clearly deal with software issues.[54] As Jean Braucher notes, ambiguities in the proposed revisions to Article 2 had the potential to "throw in doubt the body of case law applying current Article 2 to software, without supplying an acceptable alternative and thus perhaps encouraging application of UCITA by analogy."[55]

Non-embedded software and IoT-associated services may not qualify as goods under Article 2. This software and these services are integral and essential to IoT products' functioning and could be described as the predominant purpose of the transaction, thereby removing an individual's purchase of an IoT device from Article 2's scope. Case law on Article 2's application to software is mixed, but courts have found that "mass-produced" software can qualify as a good.[56] Software could also be viewed as a service.

computing-brightens-prospects-for-secure-edge-computing/; David Linthicum, *Edge Computing vs. Fog Computing: Definitions and Enterprise Uses*, CISCO, www.cisco.com/c/en/us/solutions/enter prise-networks/edge-computing.html (last visited May 16, 2020); Marty Puranik, Opinion, *How Will the Cloud Be Able to Handle the Emergence of IoT*, NETWORK WORLD: BETWEEN TWO BYTES (Oct. 3, 2017, 4:00 AM), www.networkworld.com/article/3229667/cloud-computing/how-will-the-cloud-be-able-to-handle-the-emergence-of-iot.html.

51 CISCO, FOG COMPUTING AND THE INTERNET OF THINGS: EXTEND THE CLOUD TO WHERE THE THINGS ARE 1–4 (2015), www.cisco.com/c/dam/en_us/solutions/trends/iosppt/docs/computing-overview.pdf.

52 *See id.* at 2, 5.

53 Chris O'Connor, *IBM and Cisco: Understanding Critical Data on the Network Edge*, IBM: INTERNET OF THINGS BLOG (June 28, 2017), www.ibm.com/blogs/internet-of-things/ibm-and-cisco/.

54 *Revised Article 2*, U.C.C. § 2-103(k) cmt. 7 (AM. LAW INST. & UNIF. LAW COMM'N, withdrawn 2011); Braucher, *supra* note 18, at 166–67.

55 Braucher, *supra* note 18, at 166.

56 Simulados Software, LTD v. Photon Infotech Private, LTD, 40 F. Supp. 3d 1191, 1199–1200 (N.D. Cal. May 1, 2014) (discussing the holding of several relevant cases and stating "generally, courts have found that mass-produced, standardized, or generally available software, even with modifications and ancillary services included in the agreement, is a good that is covered by the UCC").

One could argue that mobile applications and other types of software external to, and relied upon by, IoT devices are mass-marketed software and should be treated as goods, but this argument is questionable. A further complicating factor is that software is often licensed rather than sold. When a consumer purchases an IoT device and uses a corresponding mobile application and embedded software, the consumer receives a license to use the software. Article 2 applies to sales, not licenses. However, as Nancy Kim has noted, "the sale of a software product does not exclude a license of the software."[57] Recognizing the unsettled nature of software's status under Article 2, a 2016 district court opinion stated:

> The applicability of the Uniform Commercial Code (UCC) to software is a question that has confounded courts in the digital age. For every court that finds that "the weight of authority favors application of common law and not the UCC with regard to software licenses," another finds that "courts nationally have consistently classified the sale of a software package as the sale of a good for UCC purposes."[58]

In *In re Sony Gaming Networks and Customer Data Security Breach Litigation*, a data breach class action, the district court concluded that Article 2 did not apply to transactions involving consumers and an online gaming network, and consequently dismissed the plaintiffs' Massachusetts implied warranty of merchantability claim.[59] The network (the defendant's "computer systems, servers and databases") allowed consumers to play online games using their video consoles as well as purchase other products and services, such as video games, provided by the online gaming network and other third-party companies.[60] The court reasoned that the predominant purpose of the transaction was for the provision of services (which are not movable) even though consumers needed to purchase a physical game console in order to access the online services the company provided.[61] This case is somewhat analogous to IoT companies' provision of physical devices along with ongoing services and software to consumers. In *Sony*, the court specifically noted that even if the transaction were viewed as a hybrid one, the sale of the video game console was incidental to the services provided by the online network.[62] The holding of the case suggests that some courts may view the predominant purpose of an IoT transaction as the provision of services, thereby removing the transaction from the scope of Article 2.

---

[57]　Nancy S. Kim, *The Software Licensing Dilemma*, 2008 BYU L. Rev. 1103, 1140 (2008).

[58]　SAS Inst., Inc. v. World Programming Ltd., No. 5:10-25-FL, 2016 U.S. Dist. LEXIS 79230, at *31 (E.D. N.C. June 17, 2016); *see also* Prairie River Home Care, Inc. v. Procura, LLC, No. 17-5121, 2018 U.S. Dist. LEXIS 126551, at *18–19 (D. Minn. July 30, 2018) (discussing software cases under Article 2).

[59]　*In re* Sony Gaming Networks, 996 F. Supp. 2d 942, 982–84 (S.D. Cal. 2014). *But see In re* VTech Data Breach Litig., Nos. 15 CV 10889, 15 CV 10891, 15 CV 11620, 15 CV 11885, 2018 U.S. Dist. LEXIS 65060, at *15 (N.D. Ill. Apr. 18, 2018).

[60]　*See Sony Gaming Networks*, 996 F. Supp. 2d at 954–55.

[61]　*See id.* at 983–84.

[62]　*Id.* at 983.

With respect to tort law, the services and external software connected to IoT devices are not "tangible" nor are they "objects" in the traditional sense. The Second Restatement's listing of products describes tangible items. While an automobile is included within this list, it is questionable whether the software and services associated with the modern-day "infotainment" IoT vehicle can be considered a "product" for purposes of the Second Restatement. Services are explicitly carved out of the Products Restatement's definition of "products."[63] The comments section of this Restatement goes on to provide that "it is irrelevant that the service provided relates directly to products commercially distributed."[64] With respect to hybrid transactions, the Products Restatement notes that when products and services are offered simultaneously, and in connection with "either the transaction taken as a whole, or the product component thereof," ownership of the product is transferred or the product is provided for consumption or use, the party offering such a combination will be deemed to sell or distribute a product.[65] Although ownership of an IoT device is arguably transferred to consumers, the external and internal software and services that are critical to the device's operations are not sold or transferred to consumers even if they can be said to be used or consumed.

As the Products Restatement notes, some legal scholars have argued that software could be categorized as a product for strict liability purposes.[66] The Products Restatement recognizes that whether software is a product for purposes of liability is up to the courts and it suggests that courts may rely on Article 2 case law addressing software.[67] But remember the limitations of Article 2 case law on this issue. The proliferation of the IoT highlights the urgent need to heed calls for tort reform. Although external IoT software and services can be said to be distributed and used in the same manner as "tangible personal property," the status of software under the Second Restatement and the Products Restatement remains unclear.[68] In *Winter*

[63] RESTATEMENT (THIRD) OF TORTS: PRODUCTS LIABILITY § 19(b) (AM. LAW INST.).

[64] *Id.* cmt. f.

[65] *Id.* § 20.

[66] *Id.* § 19 cmt. d. *See generally* Michael L. Rustad & Thomas H. Koenig, *The Tort of Negligent Enablement of Cybercrime*, 20 BERKELEY TECH. L.J. 1553, 1557 (2005); Michael Scott, *Tort Liability for Vendors of Insecure Software: Has the Time Finally Come?*, 67 MD. L. REV. 425 (2008).

[67] *See* RESTATEMENT (THIRD) OF TORTS: PRODUCTS LIABILITY § 19 cmt. d.

[68] OWEN, *supra* note 2, at 1045; *see also* James v. Meow Media, Inc., 300 F.3d 683, 688 (6th Cir. 2002) (finding that "video game cartridges, movie cassette, and internet transmissions are not sufficiently 'tangible' to constitute products in the sense of their communicative content"); Alan Butler, *Products Liability and the Internet of (Insecure) Things: Should Manufacturers Be Liable for Damages Caused by Hacked Devices?*, 50 U. MICH. J.L. REFORM 913, 915–16 (2017) (contending that academic scholars are "skeptical" of the application of products liability law to software defects and noting that "very few cases have" specifically addressed the issue); Mark A. Geistfeld, *A Roadmap for Autonomous Vehicles: State Tort Liability, Automobile Insurance, and Federal Safety Regulation*, 105 CALIF. L. REV. 1611, 1630 (2017) (discussing software's status under products liability law and stating "there is no established body of case law recognizing that a manufacturer incurs a tort duty for defective software"); James A. Henderson, Jr., *Tort vs. Technology: Accommodating Disruptive Innovation*, 47 ARIZ. ST. L.J. 1145, 1166 (2015) (contending that "even when alleged software defects cause physical harm, courts have denied recovery on the ground that the informational elements of IT are not products").

v. G.P. Putnam's Sons, the Ninth Circuit stated that "[p]roducts liability law is geared to the tangible world."[69] With the dawn of the IoT, services, data, and software reign supreme. If IoT software and services are not "products" or "goods" for purposes of products liability law or Article 2 of the UCC, then consumers cannot access related warranties and causes of action that rely on these definitions to remedy resulting harms.

The Uniform Computer Information Transactions Act and the ALI Software Principles are also possibly relevant sources of commercial law dealing with transactions involving goods and software. Although UCITA has only been adopted in a small number of states, its provisions could apply to a transaction involving software contained within goods if "the goods are a computer or a computer peripheral," or if giving the purchaser of the goods access to use the software is "ordinarily a material purpose of transactions in goods of the type sold or leased."[70] One could argue that IoT devices can be viewed as computer peripherals under UCITA because they are connected to a computer either directly or indirectly via a network.[71] However, UCITA's possible application to IoT transactions involving goods and software is far from certain. UCITA's comments section suggest that its coverage does not extend to software embedded within goods where "the embedded program is a mere part of the goods."[72] Software is routinely embedded within IoT devices. One could argue that the software embedded within an IoT device is an indistinguishable part of the device. Lastly, recall from Chapter 4 that there is significant consumer protection opposition to UCITA.

The ALI's Software Principles' application to IoT transactions is also questionable. As soft law, courts and parties can continue to ignore the principles.[73] The principles could be applied in certain transactions involving goods and non-

---

[69] Winter v. G.P. Putnam's Sons, 938 F.2d 1033, 1034 (9th Cir. 1991).

[70] UNIF. COMP. INFO. TRANSACTIONS ACT § 103(b), cmt. 4(b)(1), 4(b)(3) (2002); Va. Code Ann. § 59.1-501.3 (2020).

[71] PHILIP KOOPMAN & CEM KANER, THE PROBLEM OF EMBEDDED SOFTWARE IN UCITA AND DRAFTS OF REVISED ARTICLE 2 (2001), http://kaner.com/pdfs/embedd1.pdf; *see also Software Engineering and UCITA*, 18 J. MARSHALL J. COMPUTER & INFO. L. 435, 525 (stating that "if a copy of a program is contained in and sold or leased as part of a computer or computer peripheral (such as a printer or speakers or a scanner or a television that is connected to a computer) then the program is within the scope of UCITA under section 103(b)"). *But see* Linda J. Rusch, *Is the Saga of the Uniform Commercial Code Article 2 Revisions Over? A Brief Look at What NCCUSL Finally Approved*, 6 DEL. L. REV. 41, 45 (2003).

[72] UNIF. COMP. INFO. TRANSACTIONS ACT § 103 cmt. 4.b(3) (noting that "[UCITA] does not apply to a copy of a program on a computer chip embedded as part of an automobile engine and sold or leased as an indistinguishable part of the automobile containing the engine. On the other hand, [UCITA] does apply to a copy of a program contained on a computer chip in a computer and transferred along with the computer"); Va. Code Ann. § 59.1-501.3, cmt. 4(b)(3) (noting the same).

[73] Michael L. Rustad & Maria Vittoria Onufrio, *The Exportability of the Principles of Software: Lost in Translation?*, 2 HASTINGS SCI. & TECH. L.J. 25, 43–44 (2009).

embedded software.[74] With respect to embedded software, the principles exclude the transfer of embedded software in goods where the predominant purpose of the transaction is for the sale of goods rather than software.[75]

Recall that software is frequently included in IoT devices.[76] IoT devices are embedded systems. If a court concludes that the predominant purpose of the transaction involving software embedded within an IoT device is for the transfer of software rather than goods, the Software Principles may apply to the transaction.[77] However, the retention of the predominant purpose test to assess the principles' applicability to hybrid transactions involving the provision of goods and software is problematic given the deficiencies of the predominant purpose test discussed earlier in this chapter. The test can lead to ambiguous and inconsistent results. Additionally, the illustrations of transactions involving goods and embedded software described in the Software Principles suggests that a DVD player and a microwave with embedded software that are designed specifically for those products and are not provided "separately on the market" would not be subject to the principles.[78] Depending on whether an IoT device's software is designed specifically for the device and is available on the market separately, a court applying the principles to construe a license agreement involving the transfer of a consumer IoT device with embedded software could view the device in the same manner described in the illustrations.

DEFINING DEFECTS AND WARRANTY BREACHES

Even if IoT devices and all of their accompanying software, systems, and services were viewed as "products" or "goods," the unique harms that consumers suffer in the IoT context, which are associated with such software and services, may not qualify as a "defect" or rise to the level of a breach of implied warranty under existing products liability law and Article 2 of the UCC. These harms include malfunctions due to software and service-related problems, such as software update failures, cybersecurity flaws, and the termination of services and software critical to device operations. In the IoT setting, we must maintain an ongoing relationship with device makers, retailers, platform and service providers, and software developers in order to operate

---

[74] *See* Am. L. Inst., Principles of the Law of Software Contracts § 1.08(a), cmt. a, d illus.1 (2010) [hereinafter Software Principles]; Hannibal Travis, *The Principles of the Law of Software Contracts: At Odds with Copyright, Consumer, and European Law?*, 84 Tul. L. Rev. 1557, 1567 (2010).

[75] Am. L. Inst., Principles of the Law of Software Contracts §§ 1.06(b)–1.08, 2.02 (2010); *see also* Robert Hillman, *Contract Law in Context: The Case of Software Contracts*, 45 Wake Forest L. Rev. 669, 673 (2010) (noting that the Software Principles exclude "embedded software unless, measured objectively, the predominant purpose of the transferee is to obtain the software").

[76] *See generally* Aaron Perzanowski & Jason Schultz, The End of Ownership: Personal Property in the Digital Economy (2016); Terrell McSweeny, *Consumer Protection in the Age of Connected Everything*, 62 N.Y. L. Sch. L. Rev. 203, 212–13 (2018).

[77] *See* Software Principles, *supra* note 74, at § 1.07(a).

[78] *Id.* cmt. b.

our devices. Consumer products that may once have functioned for years without services or external software provided by a company now have a significantly shorter life span in the IoT context. Today, a company may exploit the connected nature of IoT devices, services, and software, and digitally dominate device owners by unilaterally deciding to remotely end device functionality. IoT companies may elect to terminate integral services and software because of expenses associated with fixing and maintaining device firmware, cybersecurity vulnerabilities, and costs associated with obtaining necessary software licenses. Companies may continue to advertise and sell IoT products that they eventually intend to "brick" and that are subject to temporary licenses that impact device functionality.

In 2016, the manufacturer of the Revolv smart home hub, elected to discontinue services and the mobile application used to control the device. As a result, the device could no longer function. In 2017, Logitech, the maker of an IoT product that allows users to control their in-home devices, announced that it would no longer provide cloud service for its harmony link product and that a software update would end device functionality in 2018.[79] The company reportedly chose not to renew an expensive "technology certificate license" associated with the device.[80] In 2018, Fitbit announced that it would terminate certain Pebble support services, including voice recognition, and end mobile application software updates.[81] In 2019, Mimobaby, a company that previously offered infant IoT onesies which collected audio, sleep, feeding, activity, and temperature data, announced that it would end support for all of its systems and products.[82] In 2020, Sonos, a maker of connected speakers, announced that it would no longer provide software updates for some of its products, several of which the company still sells directly to consumers.[83]

A lack of software updates can enable cybersecurity vulnerabilities not only in the device and the end-users' immediate network, but also in the broader online ecosystem. Recall from Chapter 2 that weaknesses in multiple IoT devices were exploited to facilitate the 2016 DDoS attack, which had widespread implications across the Internet. A device may lose functionality from malware deployed by third

---

[79] Swapna Krishna, *Logitech Will Brick All Harmony Link Devices in March*, ENGADGET (Nov. 9, 2017), www.engadget.com/2017/11/09/logitech-will-brick-harmony-link-in-march/; *see also* Liam Tung, *Logitech's Decision to Brick Harmony Link Leaves Owners Outraged*, ZDNET (Nov. 9, 2017, 1:13 PM), www.zdnet.com/article/logitechs-decision-to-brick-harmony-link-leaves-owners-outraged/.

[80] Tung, *supra* note 79.

[81] *See* Sam Rutherford, *Fitbit Is Killing Off Pebble in June, For Real This Time*, GIZMODO (Jan. 24, 2018, 7:15 PM), https://gizmodo.com/fitbit-is-killing-off-pebble-in-june-for-real-this-tim-1822394036; *Showing Pebblers Love with Longer Device Support*, FITBIT DEVELOPER, https://dev.fitbit.com/blog/2018-01-24-pebble-support/ (last visited Jan. 9, 2019).

[82] MIMOBABY, www.mimobaby.com/ (last visited Jan. 31, 2020) ("As of July 31, 2019, support for the Mimo system, products, and service has ended.").

[83] Alex Hern, *Sonos to Deny Software Updates to Owners of Older Equipment*, GUARDIAN (Jan. 23, 2020), www.theguardian.com/technology/2020/jan/23/sonos-to-deny-software-updates-to-owners-of-older-equipment; *see also A Letter from Our CEO: All Sonos Products Will Continue to Work Past May*, SONOS (Jan. 23, 2020), https://blog.sonos.com/en/a-letter-from-our-ceo/.

parties that enables "permanent denial of service" attacks.[84] The examples discussed earlier also highlight the ever-expanding ability of companies to control our devices and related activities post transaction. As the IoT proliferates, termination of consumer support services and software updates could become more widespread.

As we will discuss in more detail in Chapter 7, the acquisition of an IoT company by another firm increases the chances that a consumer device will be bricked. The functionality of the Revolv and Pebble devices were negatively impacted after the rights to the products were acquired by Nest and Fitbit, respectively. After Jibo's (the maker of an IoT home robot) assets were acquired by an investment firm, the company announced that devices would be bricked in 2019 once its servers went offline and its mobile app was shut down.[85] Patent disputes and resulting settlements between competitor IoT companies can also lead to bricking. For example, Flywheel's stationary in-home consumer IoT bikes, which retailed for about $1,999, lost functionality after related services were terminated because of a patent dispute between Flywheel and Peloton, the maker of another popular IoT bike.[86]

Recall that cloud services are an integral component of IoT device functionality as data processing and analytics are often provided through the cloud.[87] Once cloud services are terminated (whether because of a company's acquisition, bankruptcy, or a mere decision to increase profit by forcing consumers to buy new products), IoT devices may have little to no functionality.[88] Additionally, a company may elect to terminate only some service features while still allowing the device to have limited functionality, as evidenced by the Pebble debacle.[89]

---

[84] Lee Mathews, *A Malware Outbreak Is Bricking Insecure IoT Devices*, FORBES (Apr 10, 2017,12:30 PM),. www.forbes.com/sites/leemathews/2017/04/10/a-malware-outbreak-is-bricking-insecure-iot-devices /#7263a72529a3.

[85] A. J. Dellinger, *Social Robot Jibo Does One Last Dance Before Its Servers Shut Down*, ENGADGET (Mar. 4, 2019), www.engadget.com/amp/2019/03/04/social-robot-jibo-shutting-down-message/.

[86] Ashley Carman, *Flywheel Will Shut Down Its Virtual Classes After Admitting It Illegally Copied Peloton*, VERGE (Feb. 19, 2020, 3:49 PM), www.theverge.com/2020/2/19/21144268/flywheel-digital-classes-shut-down-peloton-exercise-trade-in; Natt Garun, *Flywheel Owners Found out That Their Bikes Were Bricked Through Peloton*, VERGE (Feb. 20, 2020, 11:52 AM), www.theverge.com/2020/2/20/ 21145349/flywheel-bike-shut-down-email-user-reactions-peloton-trade-in; Sara Randazzo, *Bike Maker Peloton Claims Flywheel Copied Its Technology*, WALL ST. J. (Sept. 13, 2018, 10:47 AM), www.wsj.com /articles/bike-maker-peloton-claims-flywheel-copied-its-technology-1536776620.

[87] *See* Jason Perlow, *All Your IoT Devices Are Doomed*, ZDNET (Sept. 4, 2019, 6:30 PM), www.zdnet.com /article/all-your-iot-devices-are-doomed/; *see also* Jason Perlow, *When Your IoT Goes Dark: Why Every Device Must Be Open Source and Multicloud*, ZDNET (Mar. 12, 2019, 6:22 PM), www.zdnet.com /article/when-your-iot-goes-dark-why-every-device-must-be-open-source-and-multicloud/.

[88] *See* Jason Perlow, *IoT Abandonware: When Your Cloud Service Leaves You Stranded*, ZDNET (Dec. 15, 2015, 3:06 PM), www.zdnet.com/article/iot-abandonware-when-your-cloud-service-leaves-you-stranded/.

[89] Rutherford, *supra* note 81(noting some features of the Pebble watch would still work); *see also* JONATHAN ZITTRAIN, THE FUTURE OF THE INTERNET AND HOW TO STOP IT 106 (2008) (discussing tethered appliances and contending that companies can "change them from afar, long after the devices have left warehouses and showrooms").

The increasing slate of companies that have either bricked or limited consumers' access to connected IoT services, systems, and software could also contribute to unequal access to privacy and security. Only those of us that can afford to continuously purchase updated versions of everyday devices will have consistent access to devices with software updates and patches and other security features. Those of us who cannot afford more secure products could be left with non-functioning products or with IoT devices that have partial functionality and lack security fixes. Recent evidence suggests that consumers are increasingly delaying their decision to upgrade and purchase new smartphones due to costs.[90] Some groups of consumers could make similar decisions with their IoT devices. However, companies could also use software updates to slow down IoT device performance, which could intentionally or unintentionally increase consumers' willingness to purchase new devices. Intentionally decreasing IoT device performance through software updates in order to force consumers to purchase the latest model of IoT devices is another form of digital domination.

It is questionable whether a company's decision to terminate consumers' access to support services and software that are required for device operations can be viewed as a defect under products liability law. The Products Restatement provides that a party that is in the "business of selling" or distributing defective products is liable for "harm to persons or property caused by the defect."[91] The Second Restatement provides for liability for defective products that are "unreasonably dangerous."[92] The origins or source of a defect in a consumer product could be found in the manufacturing process, the design process, or in a failure to provide adequate warnings.[93] Over the years courts have applied strict liability principles to manufacturing defect claims, while often evaluating design and warning claims under what appear to be negligence principles.[94] This is also reflected in some state products liability statutes.[95] Courts have used various tests to evaluate whether a product is

---

[90]   Abigail Ng, *Smartphone Users Are Waiting Longer Before Upgrading – Here's Why*, CNBC (May 17, 2019, 3:21 PM), www.cnbc.com/2019/05/17/smartphone-users-are-waiting-longer-before-upgrading-heres-why.html.

[91]   Restatement (Third) of Torts: Products Liability § 1 (Am. Law Inst.).

[92]   Restatement (Second) of Torts § 402A (Am. Law Inst.).

[93]   Dan Dobbs et al., Hornbook on Torts 805 (2nd ed. 2016).

[94]   *Id.* at 803, 805–06, 844 ("After the promulgation of the Second Restatement's § 402A ... Courts initially attempted to retain the language of strict liability for [manufacturing, defect and warning] claims, but they increasingly used negligence principles and approaches to decide design and warning defects claims, leaving strict liability to cases involving manufacturing."); Owen, *supra* note 2, at 35–38, 104, 556–57 ("Even while acknowledging that 'strict' liability in design and warning cases is really nothing more than negligence, most courts continue to pretend that it really is something more.").

[95]   Owen, *supra* note 2, at 106–07 ("Negligence principles also figure prominently in products liability reform legislation enacted in a number of states ... [and] in an increasing number of states, negligence principles are returning to the law of products liability as the dominant (and sometimes exclusive) tort law standard of liability in design and warning cases.").

defective for products liability purposes, including the "consumer expectations test" and the "risk utility test."[96]

A manufacturing defect typically occurs when there is an error in the production process that renders the product defective. These mistakes can occur, for instance, when there are problems with the parts or raw materials used to make the product or when errors occur in assembling the product's parts. A cessation of integral services or software does not occur during the manufacturing process. These events occur after the design and production process has ended. Although the comments to the Products Restatement indicate that a manufacturing "defect need not originate at [the] time of manufacture," terminating services and software arguably cannot be said to be a "physical departure from a product's intended design" if the manufacturer's specifications for the device provide a blueprint for the subsequent termination of support services and software.[97] Stated differently, a manufacturer's specifications could specifically contemplate producing a product that grants the company the ability to control and determine software and service functionality.

Similar problems also arise under the standards used by courts to evaluate design defects. Under the consumer expectations test, courts evaluate whether a "product is unreasonably dangerous to the consumer or user given the conditions and circumstances that foreseeably attend use of the product."[98] One could argue that designing a product that permits a company to terminate integral services does not comport with the expectations of the ordinary consumer. However, even if one agrees with this line of reasoning, a product is not necessarily "unreasonably dangerous" simply because the device maker retains post-transaction control of the product or because integral services are no longer provided. In fact, since the device may no longer function once services are terminated, any potential concerns related to the safety of the product become irrelevant. Further, in a setting in which companies routinely wield post-transaction control over devices, one might argue that the termination of integral services and software, as well as malfunctions associated with software update failures, are conditions "contemplated by the ultimate consumer."[99]

Under the risk utility test, a product is defective if it is designed without a safety feature or precaution and "the costs of a precaution are foreseeably less than the precaution's safety benefits."[100] This test focuses on the costs of implementing safety features in a product to avoid consumer harms. Courts consider various factors in applying the risk utility test, including "the manufacturer's ability to eliminate the unsafe character of the product without impairing its usefulness or making it too expensive to maintain its utility."[101] Exerting post-transaction control and ceasing the

---

[96]   Owen, *supra* note 2, at 289–306.
[97]   Restatement (Third) of Torts: Products Liability §§ 1 cmt. 1, 2 cmt. c, 8 cmt. 7(f) (Am. Law Inst.).
[98]   Branham v. Ford Motor Co., 701 S.E.2d 5, 13 (S.C. 2010).
[99]   Restatement (Second) of Torts § 402A cmt. g (Am. Law Inst.).
[100] Owen, *supra* note 2, at 493.
[101] *Id.* at 305, 491–93, 510–15. Dyvex Indus., Inc. v. Agilex Flavors & Fragrances, Inc., No. 12-CV-979, 2018 U.S. Dist. LEXIS 159241, at *8 (M.D. Penn. Sept. 18, 2018).

provision of integral services may not always be directly correlated to the safety of a product. The extent to which a product's safety is impacted depends on the type of IoT device at issue. There may be no "safety benefit" to designing a product that does not allow for remote termination of IoT services and software. Consumers may not suffer serious physical harm or injury as a result of the termination of connected software and service, malfunctioning software, or the temporary suspension of services. Indeed, much of the harm may be economic. However, when a software design defect has the potential to directly impact an IoT product's safety features, such as the brakes or ignition of a vehicle, a stronger argument exists for liability. If a company designs an IoT device to retain a default password and settings that can be easily guessed and accessed by hackers, this should be viewed as a design defect, but such a result is not guaranteed. Still, remember from Chapter 2 that even when companies manufacture and design devices that are insecure, courts have dismissed consumer lawsuits for lack of standing. In the data breach context, companies can allege that consumers' data, even if publicly disclosed, have not been misused by third parties.

With respect to a negligence claim, a company can attempt to avoid liability by contending that it exercised "due care" and complied with reasonable industry standards.[102] Industry standards for IoT devices are in flux and in the IoT setting companies are increasingly designing and manufacturing products that allow them to exert significant control over devices post transaction. These types of post-transaction control features are becoming the industry standard in consumer trans-actions. Recall from Chapter 3 that California's IoT security statute requires device manufacturers to adopt "reasonable security features."[103] Although the statute does not create a private right of action, it could influence products liability lawsuits involving IoT devices.[104] The statute specifically provides that it does not impose a duty on device manufacturers for third-party software that consumers choose to install on the device.[105] This provision could be read to absolve manufacturers of liability for third-party applications installed by consumers on their devices, even if the manufacturer advertises device compatibility with third-party applications that may impact device functionality. To return to a previous example, GE may have no liability with respect to third-party firms' applications under the California statute. Additionally, the use of the term "physical object" in the statute's definition of

---

[102]　OWEN, *supra* note 2, at 59–78 ("Negligence may occur at any stage of the design, manufacturing, or marketing process ... [and] a defendant's conformance to or violation of applicable customary standards of care is some evidence, though rarely conclusive, of whether a particular defendant in fact exercised due care in a particular situation.").

[103]　CAL. CIV. CODE § 1798.91.04 (Deering 2020).

[104]　LOTHAR DETERMANN, CALIFORNIA PRIVACY LAW: PRACTICAL GUIDE AND COMMENTARY U.S. FEDERAL AND CALIFORNIA LAW 68 (3rd ed. 2018) ("[P]rivate plaintiffs may nevertheless attempt to refer to the new law when they pursue other causes of action, for example, to show breach of a duty for purposes of asserting negligence.").

[105]　CAL. CIV. CODE § 1798.91.06.

"connected devices" could be used to exclude from liability third parties that provide only services and software associated with IoT devices.

It is also unclear whether a product is "unreasonably dangerous" and defective because a company fails to provide software updates after an IoT device is purchased or if the device does not receive the software update or if there are errors or glitches in the software update. This problem can be related to, but is oftentimes distinct from, a company's decision to "brick" a device by terminating support services and software. The Second Restatement suggests that the moment at which the product is distributed by the seller is a time frame that can be relevant in applying liability principles.[106] Software updates may be needed to continue device functionality as well as to correct software vulnerabilities and avoid security harms. These updates occur post transaction and after the IoT device has left "the seller's hands."[107] The Second Restatement's comments also indicate that a seller must take necessary precautions to allow a product "to remain safe for a normal length of time when handled in a normal manner."[108] In the IoT context, this comment suggests that even if one were to assume that a failure to provide software updates and services renders a product "unreasonably dangerous," the obligation to maintain software and services would not be continuous and could expire after a "normal length of time."

With respect to warning or marketing defects, if a company adequately notifies consumers at the time of purchase that it reserves the right to terminate supporting services and software, and may cease providing software updates, a failure to warn defect claim becomes dubious under products liability law. A company's "duty to warn" and "duty to instruct" are primarily correlated to informing consumers about dangerous aspects of the product when not safely used.[109] Thus, if a product is rendered dangerous because a company elects to terminate services and software support, a company could avoid warning defects claims by adequately notifying consumers of potential dangers. Recall that often consumers are already overburdened with the number of disclosures they must review and agree to in ordinary transactions. Some consumers may not review or take seriously a company's disclosures regarding potential termination of support services and software updates. Consumers may discover that a company has the ability to end the provision of necessary services and software only after the company announces its decision to do so.

---

[106] RESTATEMENT (SECOND) OF TORTS § 402A cmt. g (AM. LAW INST.) ("[I]t is expected to and does reach the user or consumer without substantial change in the condition in which it is sold.").

[107] *Id.*

[108] *Id.*

[109] *See* RESTATEMENT (THIRD) OF TORTS: PRODUCTS LIABILITY § 2(c) (AM. LAW INST.); DOBBS ET AL., *supra* note 93, at 288 ("Warnings must contain facts necessary to permit reasonable persons to understand the danger, and in some cases how to avoid it."); OWEN, *supra* note 2, at 557 ("to recover on a warning claim in negligence, the plaintiff must establish that the manufacturer failed to exercise reasonable care to provide adequate information in a reasonable manner to an appropriate person about a foreseeable risk that was significant enough to justify the costs of providing the information.").

Consider that Revolv hub ultimately offered to provide consumers with some monetary compensation after services were terminated. However, as one commentator noted, "[i]t's fair to assume that people who spent $300 on a centerpiece for their connected home setups also expected that it would be wrangling their gadgets for a lot longer than three years."[110] Logitech initially offered to provide new products to consumers whose devices were still subject to a warranty, and those whose warranties had expired would receive only a 35 percent discount on the purchase of another product.[111] Fitbit offered Pebble consumers a fifty dollar coupon code towards a new product.[112] Thus, it is the company that becomes the primary arbiter of whether consumers should be compensated for fully or partially "bricked" devices and the amount of such compensation. Additionally, although companies may in some instances be obligated to provide post-transaction warnings for dangers discovered after a product has been distributed, the law "in this area remains somewhat of a muddle."[113]

Turning now to the UCC, remember that Article 2 provides various implied warranties, including the implied warranty of merchantability and fitness for a particular purpose. Under Article 2, the implied warranty of merchantability arises in a contract for the sale of goods.[114] Article 2 contains a non-exhaustive list that attempts to define merchantability.[115] A good is merchantable to the extent that it is "fit for the ordinary purpose for which such goods are used," among other things.[116] Assuming that a court finds that an IoT consumer transaction involving the provision of a physical device, associated services, and software is subject to Article 2, only entities that qualify as "merchants with respect to goods of that kind" under Article 2 make the merchantability warranty. If a company elects to "brick" an IoT device, it is not entirely clear whether doing so would breach the implied warranty of merchantability. One might argue that a device is no longer fit for its ordinary purpose if it loses complete functionality after purchase. Another standard relevant in assessing merchantability is that the device should "pass without objection in the trade under the contract description."[117] Companies' ability to exert post-transaction control over

---

[110] Ry Crist, *Nest Pulls the Plug on the Revolv Smart Home Hub*, CNET (Apr. 6, 2016, 7:53 AM), www .cnet.com/news/nest-pulls-the-plug-on-the-revolv-smart-home-hub/.

[111] The company eventually elected to provide replacement products for all users. Krishna, *supra* note 79.

[112] Cosmin Vasile, *Fitbit to End Pebble Support in June, Offers $50 Discount to All Users*, PHONEARENA (Jan. 24, 2018) www.phonearena.com/news/Fitbit-to-end-Pebble-support-in-June-offers-50-discount-to-all-users_id101923; James Peckham, *Fitbit Ionic Review*, TECHRADER (Nov. 19, 2019), www .techradar.com/news/pebble-watch-owners-can-get-a-discounted-fitbit-ionic-but-theres-a-big-catch.

[113] *See* RESTATEMENT (THIRD) OF TORTS: PRODUCTS LIABILITY § 10; OWEN, *supra* note 2, at 701–05 (noting that "a number of states still refuse to adopt a post-sale duty to warn" but the majority of states recognize the post-sale duty to warn).

[114] U.C.C. § 2-314 (AM. LAW INST. & UNIF. LAW COMM'N 2002). Article 2A of the UCC also contains a merchantability warranty. *Id.* § 2A-212.

[115] *Id.* § 2-314 cmt. 6.

[116] *Id.* § 2-314(2)(c).

[117] *Id.* § 2-314(2)(a).

devices is becoming the standard in the consumer IoT industry. More importantly, Article 2's text and some case law suggests that "[t]he test for determining the breach of an implied warranty of merchantability, 'is to examine whether the goods were unmerchantable at the time of delivery.'"[118] Thus, a company that has provided a device that is not defective at the "time of delivery" may not have breached the implied warranty of merchantability. Arguably, if a product had full functionality at the time it was delivered or purchased by the consumer, a subsequent cessation of functionality (even if due to the direct actions of the seller in terminating supporting services and software) may not breach the implied warranty. Similarly, a seller's failure to provide software updates needed to remedy security vulnerabilities after the "time of delivery" may not breach the implied warranty. Since the merchantability warranty applies only in a "contract for sale," a company could posit that it should not be applicable to licensed software associated with IoT products and instead should be limited to only the physical device and possibly the embedded software. This would permit a company to cease providing critical external software and services, such as cloud systems and mobile applications, without breaching the warranty. Of course, all of this presumes that the company has not effectively disclaimed the implied warranty and that other state statutes or the MMWA do not prohibit such a disclaimer. If a warranty disclaimer is effective a consumer cannot bring a successful claim for breach of the implied warranty.

If a seller makes an express warranty that extends to the "future performance of the goods," then the consumer could potentially have a cause of action for breach of that warranty.[119] A company may offer express warranties for a short period of time. For instance, some of Logitech's harmony link devices were sold with a three-month warranty.[120]

With respect to warranty liability for security vulnerabilities, *Flynn v. FCA US LLC*, a case involving IoT vehicles with an insecure infotainment system that could be remotely controlled by hackers, may provide important precedent going forward.[121] In denying the defendant's motions for summary judgment on the plaintiff's breach of implied merchantability warranty claim, the court reasoned

---

[118]   Ada Cty. Highway Dist. v. Rhythm Eng'g, LLC, No. 1:15-cv-00584-CWD, 2016 U.S. Dist. LEXIS 119363, at *14 (D. Idaho Sept. 1, 2016); *see* U.C.C. § 2-725(2) ("A breach of warranty occurs when tender of delivery is made."); Oggi Trattoria & Caffe, Ltd. v. Isuzu Motors Am., Inc., 865 N.E.2d 334, 335 (Ill. Ct. App. 2007) ("An implied warranty of merchantability applies to the condition of the goods at the time of sale and is breached only if the defect in the goods existed when the goods left the seller's control."); *see also* Timothy Davis, *UCC Breach of Warranty and Contract Claims: Clarifying the Distinction*, 61 BAYLOR L. REV. 783, 787 n.13 (2009) (contending that "the [implied] warranty [of merchantability] does not extend to the future performance of the delivered goods").

[119]   U.C.C. § 2-725(2). Additionally, in some instances, state law can require manufacturers that make express warranties to provide "service and repair facilities" for consumer goods. CAL. CIV. CODE § 1793.2 (Deering 2020).

[120]   Krishna, *supra* note 79.

[121]   Flynn v. FCA US LLC, No. 15-cv-0855-MJR-DGW, 2018 U.S. Dist. LEXIS 111963 (S.D. Ill. July 5, 2018).

that the "plaintiffs provide[d] evidence that suggests that the . . . integration [system] in their vehicles is flawed such that the defect exists regardless of whether they, personally, have had their vehicles hacked."[122] The court's opinion indicates that the security defect in consumers' IoT vehicles may have been present at the time the vehicles "were produced and sold to the public."[123] This fact may have influenced the court's decision to keep the plaintiffs' breach of implied warranty claims under the MMWA alive. This suggests that to the extent that a cybersecurity defect arises after the "time of delivery," it may not constitute a breach of the implied warranty. This is an important point worth echoing. An IoT device or its software may be 'secure' at the time of distribution to consumers but may become insecure and vulnerable post production and distribution. If the implied warranty of merchantability is said to cover only defects that are present at the "time of delivery," then security vulnerabilities that arise subsequently may not be covered by the warranty. In contrast, one might also argue that even if a security defect arises after the device has been offered for sale to the public, the warranty is breached if the defect can be traced back to the time when the device was produced. The answer to this issue is not entirely clear.

Additionally, there is also the possible related question of whether resulting software updates issued by a company will sufficiently repair or cure all security and design defects, which may impact recoverable damages.[124] The UCC provides sellers with the ability to cure defects in certain instances, and preventing a seller from curing a defect can impact a buyer's breach of warranty claims in some cases.[125] Companies may also fail to timely release software updates and remedy defective systems. Consider that in *Banh v. Am. Honda Motor Co.*, the plaintiffs alleged that Honda failed to repair defects in the infotainment systems of their vehicles, and instead recommended that consumers wait for a corrective software update.[126] Authorized dealerships allegedly discouraged consumers from bringing their vehicles in to repair the defect as the dealerships could not fix the system issues which caused the safety risks.[127] The plaintiffs brought breach of implied merchantability warranty claims as well as several other claims, and contended that Honda failed to find an effective remedy for the infotainment defect.[128]

The lawsuit that followed the VTech data breach discussed in Chapter 2 also highlights two other potential problems in security lawsuits. In *In re VTech Data Breach Litigation*, the company "suspended its online services" after the data breach

---

[122]   *Id.* at *13.

[123]   *Id.*

[124]   *Id.* at *215–16; Flynn v. FCA US LLC, No. 3:15-cv-855-SMY-RJD, 2019 WL 4861015, *3–4 (S.D. Ill. Oct. 2, 2019).

[125]   U.C.C § 2-508 (AM. LAW INST. & UNIF. LAW COMM'N 2002); Wilson v. Scampoli, 228 A.2d 848 (1967).

[126]   Banh v. Am. Honda Motor Co., No. 2:19-CV-05984-RGK-AS, 2019 U.S. Dist. LEXIS 230700, *4 (C. D. Cal. Dec. 17, 2019).

[127]   *Id.*

[128]   *Id.* at *1–2; *4.

and the plaintiffs alleged that the company breached the implied warranty of merchantability.[129] Although the court concluded that Article 2 applied to the transaction involving the sale of the IoT toy and the associated online services, the court dismissed the warranty claim.[130] The court reasoned in part that the company did not promise on the toys' packaging that consumers' access to its services would be uninterrupted and that the plaintiffs' complaint did not sufficiently describe the ordinary purpose of the product.[131] Curiously, the court's opinion appears to focus on the merchantability of the physical toys rather than the online service. However, the existence of a data breach should suggest that there may, in fact, be something wrong with or unmerchantable about the services and networks provided by the company even if the physical toys appear to be fine. The case indicates that IoT service interruptions (particularly those that are temporary) may not be viewed by some courts as constituting a breach of the implied warranty of merchantability.

Lastly, privity requirements may limit the viability of implied warranty claims, unless an exception applies.[132] In the *VTech* case, the court also determined that the plaintiffs' claim for breach of the implied warranty of merchantability lacked privity.[133] The court's earlier opinion in 2017 noted that the plaintiffs did not allege that they purchased the toys "directly from VTech," but instead the plaintiffs argued that the "direct relationship exception to the privity requirement" applied.[134] In its 2018 decision the court reasoned that although other courts may have expanded this exception to apply to instances in which "manufacturers advertise directly to consumers," advertisements without more are not sufficient to defeat privity requirements under Illinois law.[135] As the *VTech* case illustrates, in some instances consumers do not purchase their IoT products directly from manufacturers and privity can then become a hurdle for plaintiffs seeking to bring a breach of implied warranty claim. Additionally, recall from Chapter 2 that third-party vendors hired by

---

[129] *In re* VTech Data Breach Litig., Nos. 15 CV 10889, 15 CV 10891, 15 CV 11620, 15 CV 11885, 2018 U.S. Dist. LEXIS 65060, at *4 (N.D. Ill. Apr. 18, 2018).

[130] *Id.*

[131] *See id.*

[132] *Id.* at *18 ("Illinois has recognized an exception to the privity requirement where there is a direct relationship between the manufacturer and the seller."); Mekertichian v. Mercedes-Benz U.S.A., LLC, 807 N.E.2d 1165, 1168 (Ill. Ct. App. 2004) ("In order for a plaintiff to file a claim for economic damages under the UCC for a breach of an implied warranty, he or she must be in vertical privity of contract with the seller . . . . This means that 'the UCC article II implied warranties give a buyer of goods a potential cause of action only against his immediate seller.'"); Owen, *supra* note 2, at 187 ("[M]any states which have abolished the requirement of vertical privity in *express* warranty cases have retained it in cases of implied warranties, such that the absence of privity may bar an implied warranty claim in the same case in which an express warranty claim is allowed.").

[133] *VTech Data Breach Litig.*, 2018 U.S. Dist. LEXIS 65060, at *19 (dismissing an implied warranty claim with prejudice); *In re* Vtech Data Breach Litig., Nos. 15 CV 10889, 15 CV 10891, 15 CV 11620, 15 CV 11885, 2017 U.S. Dist. LEXIS 103298, at *34 (N.D. Ill. July 5, 2017) (granting motion to dismiss merchantability claim).

[134] *VTech Data Breach Litig.*, 2017 U.S. Dist. LEXIS 103298, at *33.

[135] *VTech Data Breach Litig.*, 2018 U.S. Dist. LEXIS 65060, at *18.

manufacturers to process IoT data could adopt lax security practices leading to a data breach. Consumers are not in direct privity with such third-party vendors. Also, if the data disclosed concern individuals in a consumer's household, can those individuals also sue manufacturers, sellers, and third-party vendors in data breach cases? Of the three alternatives listed in Article 2 regarding third-party beneficiaries, most states have adopted the alternatives that require personal injury in order to waive privity requirements.[136] A data breach or disclosure may not necessarily lead to personal injuries.

WHO IS LIABLE?

Products liability rules apply primarily to manufacturers and certain other parties in the distribution chain. Many of Article 2's rules, including the implied warranty of merchantability, govern the actions of sellers of goods. Section 402(A) of the Second Restatement contains liability provisions applicable to "one who sells any product."[137] The Products Restatement authorizes liability for parties "engaged in the business of selling or otherwise distributing products" in certain instances.[138] Thus, whether a party is a manufacturer, distributor, or the seller of a product or good can determine liability. However, even if a company qualifies as a party that may face liability, the provisions of the CDA may limit the company's liability for defective products.[139]

When e-commerce platform companies sell products directly to consumers or manufacture IoT products, they qualify as sellers or manufacturers under products liability law and Article 2. However, when a defective or insecure product is manufactured and sold by third parties on e-commerce platforms, determining which party should be liable is more complicated. Remember from Chapter 4 that the IoT increases pre-existing levels of "Contract Distancing." The problem is further worsened when consumers use IoT devices, which do not have a visual screen to display contract terms and the identity of product manufacturers and sellers, to purchase defective and insecure products manufactured by third parties on e-commerce platforms.

---

[136]   U.C.C § 2-318 (Am. Law Inst. & Unif. Law Comm'n 2002); Owen, *supra* note 2, at 190 ("Most American jurisdictions, including half the states, adopted Alternative A, or something similar. Six and a half jurisdictions adopted Alternative B, or a close approximation, and fourteen and a half adopted Alternative C, or a close equivalent."); Juliet M. Moringiello, *Warranting Data Security*, 5 Brook. J. Corp. Fin. & Com. L. 63, 75 (2010) ("Although Article 2 of the UCC allows non-buyers affected by a product to sue for breach of warranty, most states, in their versions of Article 2, deny a cause of action to a third-party non-buyer in the absence of personal injury.").

[137]   Restatement (Second) of Torts § 402A (Am. Law Inst.).

[138]   Restatement (Third) of Torts: Products Liability § 1 (Am. Law Inst.).

[139]   *See* 47 U.S.C. § 230 (2019); *see also* Erie Ins. Co. v. Amazon.com Inc., No. 16-02679-RWT, 2018 WL 3046243, at *3 (D. Md. Jan. 22, 2018) ("[E]ven if I am incorrect with respect to my conclusion that Amazon is not a seller and therefore cannot be liable . . . I conclude that the CDA would preclude the claims in any event.").

State products liability statutes can expressly limit the parties who may face a products liability lawsuit. For instance, New Jersey's products liability statute provides that "[a] manufacturer or seller of a product shall be liable in a product liability action only if" certain requirements are met.[140] This suggests that only parties that are manufacturers or sellers of products may face products liability lawsuits in certain circumstances under this section of the New Jersey statute. The statute goes on to define a "product seller" as a party who "sells; distributes; leases; installs; ... packages; labels; markets; ... or otherwise is involved in placing a product in the line of commerce."[141] In *Allstate N.J. Insurance Company v. Amazon.com, Inc.*, a 2018 case interpreting the provisions of the New Jersey statute, the district court reasoned that notwithstanding the "broad language" contained in the statute's definition of product seller, a party is only a product seller if it had the power to exercise "control of the product itself" – that is, the ability to exercise dominance over, for example, the manner in which the product is sold."[142] The court reasoned that Amazon's storage and shipping of the product at issue (a defective battery) was not sufficient evidence of control and did not make Amazon a product seller under the New Jersey statute.[143]

Tennessee's products liability statute also appears to primarily limit liability to manufacturers and sellers of products.[144] The statute provides that product sellers ("other than the manufacturer") may face products liability action only if at least one of five enumerated requirements are met.[145] These requirements include that the "seller exercised substantial control over that aspect of the design, testing, manufacture, packaging or labeling of the product that caused the alleged harm for which recovery of damages is sought."[146] In *Fox v. Amazon*, the court found that Amazon was not a seller for purposes of the Tennessee statute because it

> did not hold title to the product sold . . ., did not set the price of the product, and did not create the text describing or making representations about the product . . . [and its] role in the transaction was to provide a mechanism to facilitate the interchange between the entity seeking to sell the product and the individual who sought to buy it.[147]

The court went on to state that even if Amazon had shipped the defective hoverboard directly to consumers, those services would be offered only to enable the

---

[140] N.J. Stat. Ann. § 2A:58C-2 (West 2019).

[141] *Id.* § 2A:58C-8.

[142] Allstate N.J. Ins. Co. v. Amazon.com, Inc., No. 17-2738, 2018 U.S. Dist. LEXIS 123081, at *20 (D.N.J. July 24, 2018).

[143] *Id.* at *23–24.

[144] *See* Tenn. Code Ann. § 29-28-102 (2019) (defining "manufacturer" and "seller").

[145] *Id.* § 29-28-106.

[146] *Id.*

[147] Fox v. Amazon.com, Inc., No. 3:16-cv-03013, 2018 U.S. Dist. LEXIS 90101, at *20–21 (M.D. Tenn. May 30, 2018).

transaction and would not make Amazon a seller.[148] On appeal, the Sixth Circuit Court of Appeals upheld the district court's determination that Amazon was not a seller within the meaning of the statute, but found that Amazon assumed a duty to warn, which arose from the company's emails to buyers about reports of possible defects in the devices.[149]

In *Oberdorf v. Amazon*, the district court noted that Pennsylvania adopted section 402A of the Second Restatement.[150] The district court likened Amazon to an auctioneer and found that Amazon was not a seller of the defective dog collar at issue because it had "no role in the selection of the goods to be sold."[151] Yet Amazon has significant control over the third-party sellers that are allowed to sell and select items for sale on its platform. On appeal, the Third Circuit correctly acknowledged Amazon's significant influence over third-party sellers, and through the use of a four-factor test the court found that Amazon was a seller under Pennsylvania Law.[152] As of the date of writing, the Third Circuit's findings are currently undergoing an en banc review.[153]

In *Eberhart v. Amazon*, the district court held that Amazon was not a seller for purposes of New York's products liability laws and therefore was not subject to strict liability.[154] The court reasoned that strict liability was reserved for manufacturers, and "certain sellers, such as retailers and distributors ... 'within the chain of distribution'" and Amazon was not within this chain since it did not own the defective coffeemaker.[155] The court stated that "Amazon is better characterized as

---

[148] *See id.* at *21–22.

[149] Fox v. Amazon.com, Inc., 930 F.3d 415, 425, 427 (6th Cir. 2019) ("[W]e are not convinced, on the record before us, that Defendant exercised sufficient control over Plaintiff Megan Fox's hoverboard to be deemed a 'seller' of the hoverboard under the TPLA. Thus, we hold that there is no genuine dispute of material fact regarding Plaintiffs' TPLA claim, and affirm the district court's dismissal and ... we hold that Defendant assumed a duty to warn Plaintiff Megan Fox of the dangers posed by the hoverboard when it sent her the December 12, 2015 email."). The court's opinion and its analysis and recital of the applicable Tennessee tort law provisions suggests that this duty to warn arose because Amazon "chose to send the December 12, 2015 email," which indicates that such a duty may not have arisen if the company had elected not to send the email. *Id.* at 426–27. The case was ultimately settled and the settlement terms "were not disclosed." Mike Curley, *Amazon Settles Suit over Hoverboard House Fire*, LAW360 (Apr. 10, 2020, 6:08 PM), www.law360.com/articles/1262643/amazon-settles-suit-over-hoverboard-house-fire.

[150] Oberdorf v. Amazon.com, Inc., 295 F. Supp. 3d 496, 499 (M.D. Penn. 2017).

[151] *Id.* at 501.

[152] Oberdorf v. Amazon.com, Inc., 930 F.3d 136, 144 (3d Cir. 2019) (relying on the following four factors to determine whether an entity is a seller: "(1) Whether the actor is the 'only member of the marketing chain available to the injured plaintiff for redress'; (2) Whether 'imposition of strict liability upon the actor serves as an incentive to safety'; (3) Whether the actor is 'in a better position than the consumer to prevent the circulation of defective products'; and (4) Whether 'the actor can distribute the cost of compensating for injuries resulting from defects by charging for it in his business, i.e., by adjustment of the rental terms.").

[153] *See* Oberdorf v. Amazon.com, Inc., 936 F.3d 182 (3d Cir. 2019).

[154] Eberhart v. Amazon.com, Inc., 325 F. Supp. 3d 393, 398 (S.D.N.Y. 2018).

[155] *Id.* at 397. In contrast, see State Farm Fire & Cas. Co. v. Amazon.com, Inc., 390 F. Supp. 3d 964 (W.D. Wisc. 2019) (finding that "Amazon otherwise serves all the traditional functions of both retail

a provider of services."[156] The *Eberhart* court went on to dismiss the plaintiff's negligence claim, reasoning that since Amazon was not the manufacturer, seller, or distributor of the defective product, it did not owe a duty to the plaintiff.[157] The court also granted Amazon's summary judgment motion on the plaintiff's warranty claim, finding that since Amazon had made no statements regarding the defective product it could not be subject to liability under a breach of express warranty claim.[158] Similarly, in *McDonald v. LG. Elecs, USA, Inc.*, the court dismissed a breach of implied warranty claim against Amazon, under Maryland's version of the UCC, involving a defective battery.[159] The court reasoned that because Amazon provided a "'platform' for the third-party sales" it was not a merchant or seller and therefore did not make the implied warranty of merchantability.[160] In addition, courts have also found that other companies, such as eBay, that similarly offer a marketplace to sell products are not subject to certain products liability claims.[161]

The *Allstate* case, discussed earlier, indicates that some courts may narrowly interpret the express language of state statutes and common law principles that suggest that e-commerce platform companies can be viewed as sellers. By providing a platform that offers products manufactured by third parties for sale, companies, such as Amazon, are arguably "involved in placing a product in the line of commerce" and are packaging and marketing goods and should qualify as product sellers under New Jersey's statute.[162] The New Jersey statute's definition of the term seller is based on common law principles and some courts continue to rely on common law cases that were decided prior to the statute's adoption.[163] The holdings of the cases discussed earlier become increasingly problematic for consumers in the IoT setting. When consumers are harmed by malfunctioning or insecure IoT devices the primary party that can be identified in a cause of action is the company on whose platform the product was sold. Yet the foregoing cases indicate that e-commerce platform providers are often not sellers or merchants, and therefore have no liability under those portions of products liability law and the UCC that depend on such definitions. Consumers who purchase IoT devices from third parties on online

seller and wholesale distributor. . . . Amazon is properly considered a seller for purposes of Wisconsin strict product liability law for products sold by third parties through Amazon.com.").

[156]   *Eberhart*, 325 F. Supp. 3d at 399.

[157]   *Id.* at 400.

[158]   *Id.*

[159]   McDonald v. LG Elecs. USA, Inc., 219 F. Supp. 3d 533, 542 (D. Md. 2016).

[160]   *Id.*

[161]   Inman v. Technicolor USA, Inc., No. 11-666, 2011 U.S. Dist. LEXIS 133220, at *19, *24 (W.D. Penn. Nov. 18, 2011).

[162]   N.J. Stat. Ann. § 2A:58C-8 (West 2019).

[163]   Papataros v. Amazon.com, Inc., No. 17-9836, 2019 U.S. Dist. LEXIS 144253, at *28, *29 (D.N.J. Aug. 26, 2019) (noting that the definition of seller in the New Jersey statute "draws on established common law: 'This definition encompasses entities within a product's chain of distribution and is consistent with most prior New Jersey case law . . . and the common law' and hence we look to pre-Act cases in construing the Act."); Agurto v. Guhr, 381 N.J. Super. 519 (2005) (noting the same).

platforms offered by companies, such as Amazon, may have little to no recourse under products liability laws or Article 2's warranty rules. The manufacturers and third-party sellers of defective or insecure products may be judgment-proof, leaving only the e-commerce platform as the viable defendant. In some instances, the consumer may be unable to uncover the identity of the manufacturer of the defective product purchased on an online platform.

Returning to the *Fox* case, the plaintiff purchased the defective hoverboard on Amazon's platform and the box containing the hoverboard did not indicate who manufactured or sold the item. The device manufacturer's identity was unknown and the sale receipt sent to the plaintiffs vaguely labeled the third-party seller as "DEAL."[164] As one commentator has observed, "[i]t has been well documented that American e-commerce platforms, such as Amazon and eBay, have become cesspools of counterfeits and other illegal and potentially dangerous goods."[165] Even counterfeit child products, such as car seats, have been reportedly sold on Amazon's marketplace by third-party vendors.[166] Amazon places the burden on device manufacturers to report counterfeit products sold by others on its platform.[167]

As the cost of sensors, hardware, and firmware decreases, manufacturers are routinely producing IoT devices that lack minimum security measures. A hacked or malfunctioning device can impact access to a consumer's home, in the case of IoT locks and garage door openers, and may have even more serious consequences for consumers when other types of IoT devices, such as child monitors and IoT diabetes monitors and other health-related products, are involved.[168] Consider that security researchers have identified vulnerabilities in an IoT pacemaker and its associated programmer that would allow hackers to remotely transmit unnecessary shocks to patients and withhold lifesaving shocks.[169] As of the date of writing, the manufacturer has reportedly failed to remedy the vulnerability.[170] An insecure IoT candle in a consumer's home could be used by a third party to commit remote arson

---

[164]   Fox v. Amazon.com, Inc., No. 3:16-cv-03013, 2018 U.S. Dist. LEXIS 90101, at *5–6 (M.D. Tenn. May 30, 2018).

[165]   Wade Shepard, *As Amazon and eBay Flood with Illegal Goods from China, Beijing Cracks Down on Foreign E-Commerce*, FORBES (Nov. 22, 2017, 11:48 PM), www.forbes.com/sites/wadeshepard/2017/11/22/as-amazon-and-ebay-flood-with-illegal-goods-from-china-beijing-cracks-down-on-foreign-e-commerce/#88fdc874dfd3.

[166]   Pamela Boykoff & Clare Sebastian, *Fake and Dangerous Kids Products Are Turning up for Sale on Amazon*, CNN (Dec. 23, 2019, 8:25 AM), https://amp.cnn.com/cnn/2019/12/20/tech/amazon-fake-kids-products/index.html.

[167]   *Id.*

[168]   *See* Crootof, *supra* note 39, at 588–90 (citing Elvy, *supra* note 27).

[169]   Lily Hay Newman, *A New Pacemaker Hack Puts Malware Directly on the Device*, WIRED (Aug. 9, 2018, 12:30 PM), www.wired.com/story/pacemaker-hack-malware-black-hat/; *see also Hack Attack Can Stop People's Hearts*, BBC (Aug. 9, 2018), www.bbc.com/news/av/technology-45118645/hack-attack-can-stop-people-s-hearts.

[170]   Newman, *supra* note 169; *Hack Attack Can Stop People's Hearts*, *supra* note 169.

that causes both property and bodily harms.[171] One such smart candle is compatible with Amazon's Alexa.[172] IoT candles are also sold by third-party sellers on Amazon's platform.[173] Additional consumer harms can also include a loss of sensitive data about children and other individuals in consumers' households.

Case law finding that e-commerce platforms are not sellers under products liability law incentivizes these companies to continue to offer a marketplace that enables the proliferation of insecure and malfunctioning devices that can be controlled post transaction by third-party sellers and manufacturers. An IoT garage door company remotely disabled a consumer's product after the consumer left a negative review. The IoT product was purchased on Amazon.[174] The defective product at issue in *Fox* was shipped from a seller in another country.[175] Commentators have suggested that many of the insecure IoT devices that were weaponized to conduct the 2016 DDOS attack that blocked access to some of the world's major websites were manufactured abroad by a foreign company.[176] Unlike the brick and mortar stores of old that could only connect third-party sellers of products to consumers within a small geographic region, and that oftentimes made discerning decisions about the products manufactured by others that they would offer for sale, today's internet platforms have no geographic boundaries. In 2018, Amazon opened a physical store, Amazon 4 Star, that sells both products manufactured by the company and third parties.[177] Excluding these e-commerce platforms from liability

---

[171] Andrew Liszewski, *The World's First Smart Candle Can Be Lit and Extinguished from Your Smartphone*, GIZMODO (Sept. 20, 2016, 8:00 AM), https://gizmodo.com/the-worlds-first-smart-candle-can-be-lit-and-extinguish-1786637893 (describing the LuDela IoT candle and noting that the candle can be "remotely ignited and extinguished" via a mobile app).

[172] *Better Light, Better Lives*, LUDELA, https://ludela.com/ (last visited Feb. 20, 2020) (noting that the IoT candle is "Alexa enabled").

[173] *PLAYBULB Candle Bluetooth Smart Flameless LED Candle for iPhone and Android*, AMAZON, www.amazon.com/PLAYBULB-Candle-Bluetooth-Flameless-Android/dp/B00O4LHNNS (last visited Feb. 20, 2020).

[174] Rob Price, *The Maker of an Internet-Connected Garage Door Disabled a Customer's Device over a Bad Review*, BUS. INSIDER (Apr. 5, 2017, 3:51 AM), www.businessinsider.com/iot-garage-door-opener-garadget-kills-customers-device-bad-amazon-review-2017-4.

[175] Fox v. Amazon.com, Inc., No. 3:16-cv-03013, 2018 U.S. Dist. LEXIS 90101, at *6 (M.D. Tenn. May 30, 2018) ("They appear to agree the hoverboard was shipped via Federal Express from China.").

[176] *See* Karl Bode, *Chinese Company Recalls Cameras, DVRs Used in Last Week's Massive DDoS Attack*, TECH DIRT (Oct. 24, 2016, 11:40 AM), www.techdirt.com/articles/20161024/08552535872/chinese-company-recalls-cameras-dvrs-used-last-weeks-massive-ddos-attack.shtml; *Hacked Cameras, DVRs Powered Today's Massive Internet Outage*, KREBS ON SECURITY (Oct. 21, 2016, 5:57 PM), https://krebsonsecurity.com/2016/10/hacked-cameras-dvrs-powered-todays-massive-internet-outage/; Michael Kan, *Chinese Firm Admits Its Hacked Products Were Behind Friday's DDOS Attack*, COMPUTER WORLD (Oct. 23, 2016, 1:45 PM), www.computerworld.com/article/3134097/security/chinese-firm-admits-its-hacked-products-were-behind-fridays-ddos-attack.html.

[177] Daniel Roberts, *Amazon's New 4-Star Store Is a Curated Mess*, YAHOO FINANCE (Sept. 30, 2018), https://finance.yahoo.com/news/amazons-new-4-star-store-curated-mess-114556311.html; Kaya Yurieff, *Inside Amazon's New Store That Only Sells Its Highest-Rated Stuff*, CNN (Sept. 27, 2018, 2:44 PM), https://money.cnn.com/2018/09/27/technology/amazon-4-star-store-opening/index.html.

under products liability law and Article 2 does not encourage such platform companies to make thoughtful decisions about which third-party sellers can offer products for sale on their platforms. Instead, it continues to enable platforms to inquire only retrospectively about the safety of products offered for sale on their platforms. Even more alarming is the possibility that international sellers and manufacturers of IoT products sold on domestic e-commerce platforms may have the capacity to monitor and collect data about us and our devices as well as control our activities post transaction, all while potentially escaping products liability claims by keeping their identities hidden when utilizing e-commerce platforms.

E-commerce platforms that qualify as providers of interactive computer services may also escape certain products liability claims associated with speech published by third parties under the CDA.[178] In *Oberdorf*, the district court found that Amazon was immune from negligence claims under Section 230 of the CDA, which provides in relevant part that "[no] provider or user of an interactive computer service shall be treated as the publisher or speaker of any information provided by another information content provider."[179] The *Oberdorf* district court reasoned that Amazon could not be held liable as the "publisher or speaker" of product statements and advertisements given to Amazon by the seller of the defective product.[180] In *McDonald*, the court stated that if a consumer proves that an e-commerce platform "played a *direct* role in tortious conduct – through its involvement in the sale or distribution of the defective product – Section 230" of the CDA will not immunize a defendant "from all products liability claims."[181] However, the court ultimately dismissed the plaintiff's failure to warn negligence claim based on CDA immunity.[182] Similarly, in *Erie Insurance Company v. Amazon.com, Inc.*, the district court found that Amazon was immune from a products liability lawsuit under the CDA.[183] Although on appeal the Fourth Circuit in *Erie* determined that the CDA did not shield Amazon from products liability claims because there was no claim "based on the content" of Amazon's published speech, the court concluded that Amazon was not a seller under Maryland's products liability law.[184]

---

[178] Hinton v. Amazon.com.DEDC, LLC, 72 F. Supp. 3d 685, 690 (S.D. Miss. 2014) (dismissing plaintiff's products liability claims against eBay based on CDA immunity).

[179] 47 U.S.C. § 230; Oberdorf v. Amazon.com, Inc., 295 F. Supp. 3d 496, 502–03 (M.D. Penn. 2017). For a discussion of CDA and products liability issues applicable to the sharing economy, see generally David Berke, *Products Liability in the Sharing Economy*, 33 YALE J. ON REG. 603 (2016).

[180] *Oberdorf*, 295 F. Supp. 3d at 502.

[181] McDonald v. LG Elecs. USA, Inc., 219 F. Supp. 3d 533, 537–40 (2016) (finding that "while plaintiff's negligence and breach of implied warranty claims (Counts VI and VII) are not barred under the [CDA], plaintiff's negligent failure to warn claim (Count V) falls within the scope of Section 230" of the CDA).

[182] *Id.* at 540.

[183] Erie Ins. Co. v. Amazon.com Inc., No. 16-02679, 2018 WL 3046243 (D. Md. Jan. 22, 2018). *But see* State Farm Fire & Cas. Co. v. Amazon.com, Inc., 390 F. Supp. 3d 964 (W.D. Wisc. 2019) (finding that "Amazon is not immune under the CDA for claims that it sold a defective product").

[184] Erie Ins. Co. v. Amazon.com Inc., 925 F. 3d 135, 139 (4th Cir. 2019).

In 2005, Michael Rustad and Thomas Koenig observed that "[c]ourts have stretched Congress' express language in 230 of the [CDA] from the narrow purpose of immunizing [ISPs] as publishers to the expanded purpose of shielding them from all tort liability."[185] More recent cases that have addressed this issue, including *Inman v. Technicolor USA* and *Hinton v. Amazon*, indicate that there remains some degree of confusion in the case law about how to handle products liability claims involving CDA immunity issues.[186] This becomes even more concerning for consumers in the IoT setting in light of the proliferation of insecure devices and the increased harms that consumers may suffer from defective products in their homes. Immunizing e-commerce platforms from products liability lawsuits allows them to continue to profit from the sale of malfunctioning and insecure devices as well as products that allow companies to control consumers' activities through their devices post transaction, while offering consumers no significant remedy when these products fail to function or cause harm. E-commerce platforms earn profits from charging selling and service fees to domestic and international sellers that choose to sell and fulfill product orders on their platforms.[187] E-commerce platform companies that routinely sell goods directly to consumers while also offering goods sold and manufactured by third parties should not be able to escape products liability actions based on CDA immunity. Additionally, platforms should not be able to avoid liability by drafting contracts that obligate third-party sellers to provide product descriptions to ensure CDA immunity.[188]

Consumers who purchase goods on online platforms may erroneously believe that the goods are being sold directly by the e-commerce platform rather than a third-party seller. This is likely to occur when the product is shipped and received by the consumer in packages displaying the platform's logo and when the platform recommends the product to the consumer. For instance, Amazon labels many products sold and manufactured by third-party sellers as "Amazon's Choice." An algorithm determines the products that will receive this label.[189] Such a designation is likely to suggest to consumers that the product is of good quality. A company's statements

---

[185] Michael L. Rustad & Thomas H. Koenig, *Rebooting Cybertort Law*, 80 WASH. L. REV. 335, 335 (2005); *see also* Michael L. Rustad & Thomas H. Koenig, *Cybertorts and Legal Lag: An Empirical Analysis*, 13 S. CAL. INTERDISCIPLINARY L.J. 77, 110–11 (2003). *See generally* JEFF KOSSEFF, THE TWENTY-SIX THAT CREATED THE INTERNET (2018) (discussing Section 230 and tort immunity). More recent legal scholarship has also critiqued companies' CDA immunity. *See, e.g.*, Danielle Keats Citron & Benjamin Wittes, *The Internet Will Not Break: Denying Bad Samaritans § 230 Immunity*, 86 FORDHAM L. REV. 401 (2017); Olivier Sylvain, *Recovering Tech's Humanity*, 119 COLUM. L. REV. F. 252 (2019).

[186] Inman v. Technicolor USA, Inc., No. 11-666, 2011 U.S. Dist. LEXIS 133220, at *19, *24 (W.D. Penn. Nov. 18, 2011); Hinton v. Amazon.com.DEDC, LLC, 72 F. Supp. 3d 685, 690 (S.D. Miss. 2014).

[187] *See e.g.*, *Pricing: Let's Talk Numbers*, AMAZON, https://sell.amazon.com/pricing.html (last visited May 16, 2020).

[188] Eberhart v. Amazon.com, Inc., 325 F. Supp. 3d 393 (S.D.N.Y. 2018) (describing Amazon's Service Business Solutions Agreement with third-party sellers).

[189] David Carnoy, *How Is "Amazon's Choice" Chosen? Amazon Won't Say*, CNET (Mar. 21, 2018, 4:00 AM), www.cnet.com/news/do-humans-choose-what-products-get-amazons-choice/.

regarding the quality of products are at the core of breach of express warranty claims. As consumers become further removed from the contracting process by using IoT devices that lack traditional screens to display contract terms, consumers may increasingly have no way of knowing at the time of contracting that a product is sold by a third-party seller rather than the e-commerce platform. For instance, a consumer could use an IoT smart speaker or personal assistant (with voice shopping capabilities) made by an e-commerce platform to purchase IoT devices and other items without knowing the identity of the seller. Companies that make IoT devices while simultaneously connecting these devices to their online platforms, which offer goods for sale by third parties, should be subject to some form of products liability for defective products purchased from third-party sellers on their websites. Case law unfortunately suggests that they may not be.

A further complicating factor in identifying potential defendants in products liability lawsuits in the IoT context is the plethora of parties that are involved in manufacturing, distributing, and servicing IoT products. Recall from the earlier portions of this chapter GE's various IoT products that are accompanied by a product reordering service, and GE's mobile application. If a device malfunctions, how does one go about identifying whether the malfunction is due to the physical device or its embedded software or, instead, a malfunction in the external systems and computer programs related to the device? Indeed, this is only the tip of the iceberg. Recall that the software, services, and sensor-centric nature of IoT devices means that these devices rely on a complicated combination of external and internal software, and services maintained by manufacturers, retailers, various software developers, and third-party data and cloud service providers. When a device malfunctions, is hacked, or causes harm, it may be particularly difficult to identify who should bear responsibility for the defect under products liability law.

As IoT devices become more widely used there may be a concomitant increase in the number of used or refurbished devices that are offered for sale. Existing and proposed right-to-repair statutes that require open product designs and disclosures to facilitate device repairs by consumers and independent companies can further enable the sale of refurbished and used products.[190] However, the IoT's proliferation combined with advanced telematics systems exposes loopholes in right-to-repair legislation.[191] For instance, IoT vehicle manufacturers have avoided compliance with Massachusetts' right-to-repair law by using wireless technology to limit

---

[190]   *See, e.g.,* Mass. Gen. Laws ch. 93K (LexisNexis 2019); Lothar Determann & Bruce Perens, *Open Cars*, 32 Berkeley Tech. L.J. 915, 959 (2017) (discussing right to repair statutes but noting that "such laws do not require car manufacturers to open ports to add-on accessories or software updates made by unaffiliated suppliers"); Nathan Proctor, *Right to Repair Wraps up a Big Year*, U.S. PIRG (Dec. 26, 2019), https://uspirg.org/blogs/blog/usp/right-repair-wraps-big-year (discussing proposed digital right to repair legislation).

[191]   Leah Chan Grinvald & Ofer Tur-Sinai, *Intellectual Property Law and the Right to Repair*, 88 Fordham L. Rev 63, 72 (2019).

independent repair companies' access to diagnostic and repair data needed to successfully repair IoT devices.[192] Additionally, as Joshua Fairfield has written, consumers do not generally have the ability to "sell or lend the digital version" of products that they have purchased.[193] Aaron Perzanowski and Jason Schultz have also observed the limits of consumer ownership of digital media.[194] Contractual restrictions imposed in terms of service agreements and EULAs combined with the integral nature of associated services and software may make it difficult for consumers to transfer functioning IoT products to other consumers. Thus, the market for the sale of used IoT products could be dominated by companies rather than consumers. Some IoT companies have recognized this problem and addressed it in their privacy policies or terms of service.[195]

While sellers of used products and goods can be exposed to liability under negligence and warranty theories, courts historically have been sharply divided about whether such sellers can be exposed to strict liability, with "a majority of courts" finding "that strict liability in tort ordinarily does *not* apply to the sale of used products unless the seller repaired or modified the product or otherwise caused the defect."[196] Some courts addressing this issue have considered several factors, including whether the used seller regularly deals in such products.[197] The Products Restatement specifically opines on this issue and provides for strict liability for

---

[192] Jonathan Ng, *Independent Auto Repair Shops Want Right-to-Repair Law Updated*, BOS. HERALD www .bostonherald.com/2019/06/18/independent-auto-repair-shops-want-right-to-repair-law-updated/ (last updated June 18, 2019, 10:49 PM), (discussing proposed amendments to Massachusetts' right-to-repair laws and noting that IoT vehicles "have built-in wireless technology providing diagnostic and repair information that independent repair shops can't access"); *see also* Press Release, The Massachusetts Right to Repair Coalition, Needed Update of MA Right to Repair Law Headed to Ballot (Dec. 5, 2019), www.prnewswire.com/news-releases/needed-update-of-ma-right-to-repair-law-headed-to-ballot-300969819.html (discussing proposed ballot initiative to supplement Massachusetts' right-to-repair law to address wireless technology).

[193] JOSHUA A. T. FAIRFIELD, OWNED: PROPERTY, PRIVACY, AND THE NEW DIGITAL SERFDOM 199–200 (2017).

[194] *See* Aaron Perzanowski & Jason Schultz, *Reconciling Intellectual and Personal Property*, 90 NOTRE DAME L. REV. 1211, 1214–17 (2015). *See generally* PERZANOWSKI & SCHULTZ, *supra* note 76.

[195] *Terms of Service*, NEST (May 23, 2018), https://nest.com/legal/terms-of-service/ ("If you transfer a Product to a new owner, your right to use the Services with respect to that Product automatically terminates and the new owner will have no right to use the Product or Services under your Account (as described below) and will need to register for a separate Account with Nest and accept these Terms.").

[196] OWEN, *supra* note 2, at 1027–28; *see also* FRUMER & FRIEDMAN, *supra* note 35, at § 5:06 ("[T]he controversy rages as to whether or not the doctrine of strict liability is applicable to a person or entity selling goods secondhand. Perhaps the prevailing view in American courts, by a small margin, is that a used product seller may not be held liable for strict liability, absent some affirmative activity with respect to the product such as remanufacture, reconditioning, repair, or modification."). *See generally* Tracy A. Bateman, *Products Liability: Application of Strict Liability Doctrine to Seller of Used Product*, 9 A.L.R.5th 1 (2017) (discussing the holdings of multiple cases involving the sale of used products and strict products liability).

[197] FRUMER & FRIEDMAN, *supra* note 35 ("[A]lthough a majority of states have opted for the better view excluding the used product seller from strict liability . . . the potential liability of used product sellers has also depended upon whether the seller repaired, reconditioned, remanufactured or modified the used product."); OWEN, *supra* note 2, at 1029.

commercial sellers and distributers of used products under certain circumstances, such as if the product is "remanufactured."[198] In some instances, state products liability statutes provide some clarity on used sellers' obligations, and some statutes exclude certain sellers of used products from the definition of "product seller."[199] Kansas's products liability statute explicitly provides that used product retail sellers are not subject to strict liability claims, and provides other instances in which such sellers may be excluded from products liability lawsuits.[200] Potential defects associated with IoT devices will become more problematic as IoT devices age and are resold to consumers after being used. Consumers may be unable to bring successful strict liability claims against sellers of used IoT devices in some jurisdictions. To the extent that a used retail seller's strict tort liability depends on whether the product has been modified or refurbished by the used seller, when a company modifies an IoT device to install asset collection devices the seller may arguably be subject to strict liability. But recall from our earlier discussions that the specific harms and defects that consumers may encounter with respect to IoT products do not always fit neatly within current theories of products liability.[201]

THE ECONOMIC LOSS DOCTRINE

Another complicating factor for consumers in products liability lawsuits is the potential application of the economic loss rule. Under the economic loss doctrine, negligence and strict liability claims are not available causes of action when a defective product causes only pure economic harm, unless an exception to the

[198] RESTATEMENT (THIRD) OF TORTS: PRODUCTS LIABILITY § 8 (AM. LAW INST.); *id.* § 8 cmt. b ("[W]hen a used product is remanufactured, strict liability under Subsection (c) is justified."); *see also* OWEN, *supra* note 2, at 1029 (contending that with respect to used sellers' and strict liability the Products Restatement "basically adopts the majority approach"); Richard C. Ausness, *Sailing Under False Colors: The Continuing Presence of Negligence Principles in "Strict" Products Liability Law*, 43 U. DAYTON L. REV. 265, 288 (2018) (stating used product sellers are subject to strict liability under the Products Restatement "only if a manufacturing defect is involved, if the product is remanufactured, or if the seller has failed to comply with an applicable product safety statute").

[199] CAL. CIV. CODE § 1795.5 (Deering 2020) (imposing obligations on sellers and distributors of used consumer goods that make express warranties); IDAHO CODE § 6-1402 (2020) (excluding commercial sellers of used products from the definition of "product seller" under certain circumstances); WASH. REV. CODE § 7.72.010 (2020) (same as Idaho).

[200] KAN. STAT. ANN. § 60-3306(b) (2019–2020) ("A product seller that is a retail seller of used products shall not be subject to liability in a product liability claim ... if ... (3) (A) Such seller resold the product after the product was used by a consumer or other product user; (B) the product was sold in substantially the same condition as it was when it was acquired for resale; (C) the manufacturer of the defective product or product component is subject to service of process either under the laws of the state of Kansas or the domicile of the person making the product liability claim; and (D) any judgment against the manufacturer obtained by the person making the product liability claim would be reasonably certain of being satisfied.").

[201] Additionally, with respect to vehicles, state statutes that apply to the sale of used vehicles may impose specific obligations on sellers of such products. MASS. GEN. LAWS ANN. ch. 90, § 7N 1/4 (LexisNexis 2020) ("No used motor vehicle shall be sold in the commonwealth by a dealer to a consumer unless accompanied by an express written warranty.").

economic loss doctrine applies.[202] Thus, if there is no personal injury or damage to property "other than the defective product itself," a consumer may not be able to recover under negligence or strict liability theories.[203] In 2018, the ALI approved a tentative draft of the "Restatement of the Law Third, Torts: Liability for Economic Harm."[204] The Restatement defines economic loss as "pecuniary damage not arising from injury to the plaintiff's person or from physical harm to the plaintiff's property."[205] The Restatement attempts to narrow the economic loss doctrine and provides that "[e]xcept as provided elsewhere in this Restatement, there is no liability in tort for economic loss caused by negligence in the performance or negotiation of a contract between the parties."[206] Many IoT consumers have a contractual relationship with the manufacturer or retailer of their IoT device, particularly when such parties provide terms of service agreements and EULAs that govern the device and associated services and software. Even for parties who do not have a direct

---

[202] *See, e.g.*, RESTATEMENT (THIRD) OF TORTS: PRODUCTS LIABILITY § 21 cmt. a (providing rules limiting the types of harms that are recoverable and stating "[s]ome categories of loss, including those often referred to as 'pure economic loss,' are more appropriately assigned to contract law."); *In re* Yahoo! Inc. Customer Data Sec. Breach Litig., 313 F. Supp. 3d 1113, 1133 (N.D. Cal. 2018) (finding that plaintiffs "pled a 'special relationship' with Defendants [and] so Plaintiffs' negligence and deceit by concealment claims are not barred by the economic-loss rule"); *In re* Sony Gaming Networks, 996 F. Supp. 2d 942, 967 (S.D. Cal. 2014) (stating that an exception to the economic loss rule "permits recovery for economic losses resulting from negligent misrepresentation" and noting that under California law "[i]n the absence of (1) personal injury, (2) physical damage to property, (3) a 'special relationship' existing between the parties, or (4) some other common law exception to the rule, recovery of purely economic loss is foreclosed"); Arco Prods. Co. v. May, 948 P.2d 263, 266 (Nev. 1997) ("[T]he economic loss doctrine applies to cases of strict products liability in exactly the same fashion as it applies to cases of negligence."); OWEN, *supra* note 2, at 266 ("[A] great majority of courts (and some legislatures, in products liability reform acts) have applied the 'economic loss rule' ... denying recovery in strict tort liability (or negligence) for pure economic loss – that is, for pecuniary losses a defective product causes other than those growing out of personal injuries or out of damage it causes to 'other property,' that is, apart from any damage a defective product may cause to itself."); Catherine M. Sharkey, *In Search of the Cheapest Cost Avoider: Another View of the Economic Loss Rule*, 85 U. CIN. L. REV. 1017, 1017 (2018) ("The economic loss rule is a judicially created doctrine invoked in strict liability or negligence (i.e., not intentional) tort cases to preclude tort liability in certain situations where a victim has suffered purely financial losses (i.e., no physical injury or damage to property.").

[203] RESTATEMENT (THIRD) OF TORTS: PRODUCTS LIABILITY § 21.

[204] *Restatement of the Law Third, Torts: Liability for Economic Harm – Now Available*, ALI ADVISER (Mar. 18, 2020), https://ali.org/news/articles/restatement-law-third-torts-liability-economic-harm-published/ ("This completes the fourth installment of the Restatement Third of Torts."); Pauline Toboulidis, *Restatement of the Law Third, Torts: Liability for Economic Harm Approved*, ALI ADVISER (May 21, 2018), www.thealiadviser.org/economic-harm-torts/the-american-law-institute-membership-approves-restatement-of-the-law-third-torts-liability-for-economic-harm/.

[205] RESTATEMENT OF THE LAW (THIRD) TORTS: LIAB. FOR ECON. HARM § 2 (AM. LAW INST. 2020).

[206] RESTATEMENT OF THE LAW (THIRD) TORTS: LIAB. FOR ECON. HARM § 3 cmt. a ("Courts have used the expression 'economic-loss rule' to refer to a variety of propositions.... [A] minority have used it to mean that there is, in general, no liability in tort for causing pure economic loss to another. This Restatement does not endorse that formulation because its breadth is potentially misleading. This Section instead states an economic-loss rule that is narrower and more robust, and that is followed by a majority of courts. It is limited to parties who have contracts.").

contractual relationship with an IoT provider, the economic loss rule may still serve as a bar to certain products liability claims.[207]

If the economic loss doctrine is applicable in the products liability context, a consumer is likely limited to causes of actions that arise under Article 2, such as a breach of warranty claim, or another source of law. In such instances, it is critical that Article 2 apply to a transaction in order for a consumer to have a viable products liability claim.[208] However, remember from our earlier discussion in this chapter that Article 2's application (including its accompanying warranties) to IoT products, services, and software is not guaranteed. Additionally, even if Article 2 were to apply to such a transaction, a company may successfully disclaim implied warranties except as prohibited by state or federal law.

Consumers do not always experience personal injury or property harms from defective IoT goods, services, and software. In such cases, consumers' products liability lawsuits are vulnerable to dismissal under the economic loss doctrine. Indeed, many of the harms that consumers may experience could be viewed as property harms directly related to the defective IoT product or pure economic or financial losses that are unrelated to personal and property injury harms. These include damages to the IoT product at issue, costs related to the termination of services and software support, and harms related to cybersecurity problems, such as data loss and disclosure to third parties and credit monitoring expenses associated with data breaches. With respect to damages to "other property," although consumer-related data may be viewed as intangible property from the perspective of companies that collect, analyze, and monetize such data, these data are not the "property" of consumers, and consumers cannot currently be said to have a "property or ownership" interest in such data. As it stands, one could not successfully avoid application of the economic loss rule by contending that data disclosure from a data breach is a "property harm" incurred by consumers. Even if this argument were viewed as valid, the data loss may be directly related to the "defective product itself" and thus still barred by the rule.

Several courts have dismissed data breach lawsuits, reasoning that the economic loss doctrine bars tort claims associated with such cases.[209] As Mark Geistfeld notes,

---

[207] See generally Catherine M. Sharkey, *Can Data Breach Claims Survive the Economic Loss Rule?*, 66 DEPAUL L. REV. 339 (2017) (discussing the "stranger economic loss rule").

[208] DOBBS ET AL., *supra* note 93, at 803–04.

[209] *In re* Target Corp. Customer Data Sec. Breach Litig., 66 F. Supp. 3d 1154, 1176 (D. Minn. 2014) (finding that "[t]he economic loss rule in Alaska, California, Illinois, Iowa, and Massachusetts appears to bar Plaintiffs' negligence claims under the laws of those states"); *In re* Sony Gaming Networks, 996 F. Supp. 2d 942, 973 (S.D. Cal. 2014) (granting a motion to dismiss "negligence claims based on the economic loss doctrine"); *In re* Michaels Stores Pin Pad Litig., 830 F. Supp. 2d 518, 531 (N.D. Ill. 2011) (dismissing plaintiffs' negligence claims under the economic loss doctrine and stating that "other courts dealing with data breach cases have also held that the economic loss doctrine bars the plaintiff's tort claim because the plaintiff has not suffered personal injury or property damage"); *see also* David W. Opderbeck, *Cybersecurity, Data Breaches, and the Economic Loss Doctrine in the Payment Card Industry*, 75 MD. L. REV. 935 (2016) (discussing several data breach cases and the economic loss rule); Sharkey, *supra* note 202(discussing the same).

when a data breach occurs, many identity theft victims "suffer economic loss caused by the failure of a business to protect their confidential information."[210] Consumers of IoT products are increasingly susceptible to data loss and data breaches. Application of the economic loss rule in the IoT setting could become even more problematic as insecure consumer IoT devices become ubiquitous and invasive data collection by insecure devices becomes the norm.

This chapter has exposed various gaps in products liability law and Article 2 of the UCC. Products liability law and Article 2 of the UCC will need to evolve to meet the products, privacy, security, and digital domination issues of the IoT age. Commercial law's lending frameworks and consumer protection legislation in the debt collection area must also evolve. The IoT and various technological developments allow corporate entities to extend their digital control over us post transaction. Chapter 6 discusses these points and more by turning to the subprime auto lending and vehicle title lending industries.

---

[210] Mark Geistfeld, *Protecting Confidential Information Entrusted to Others in Business Transactions: Data Breaches, Identity Theft, and Tort Liability*, 66 DePaul L. Rev. 385, 389 (2017).

6

Digital Domination in Consumer Lending Transactions

As we have seen so far in this book, the IoT comprises various connected devices, services, and systems. Connecting regular devices to the Internet has made it much easier for companies to protect their interests in consumer transactions. New technologies allow companies to continue to wield significant control over us and our devices beyond the point of sale, license, or lease. As Aaron Perzanowski and Jason Schultz have observed, the IoT "threatens our sense of control over the devices we purchase."[1] Of chief concern is companies' use of technology to control our devices and actions and digitally restrain our activities in lending transactions.

This chapter explores the rise of asset collection technology in consumer financing transactions in the IoT setting. I use the term asset collection technology to refer to the devices, networks, and services companies use in consumer financing transactions to enforce their rights in lending agreements and to access, control, and retrieve encumbered consumer collateral. This chapter primarily turns a critical eye toward the subprime auto lending and vehicle title lending industries to highlight two disturbing problems created by the proliferation of asset collection technology and IoT devices. First, when we participate in lending marketplaces with asset collection technology and IoT devices, we are vulnerable to privacy intrusions, loss of device control, the imposition of digital restraints, and notable lifestyle and daily interruptions post transaction. Existing laws can facilitate these harms. These concerns can also arise in other contexts as well.

Second, historically marginalized consumers – that is, low-income and racial minorities – have long experienced private "debt criminalization tactics," a term used by legal scholar Creola Johnson to describe, among other things, instances in which companies threaten to (and in many cases do) obtain warrants to arrest non-paying individuals.[2] Companies that engage in debt criminalization tactics

---

[1] AARON PERZANOWSKI & JASON SCHULTZ, THE END OF OWNERSHIP: PERSONAL PROPERTY IN THE DIGITAL ECONOMY 150 (2016).

[2] Creola Johnson, *Creditors' Use of Consumer Debt Criminalization Practices and Their Financial Abuse of Women*, 34 COLUM. J. GENDER & L. 5, 7 (2016).

frequently threaten to use the criminal justice system against debtors.[3] Consumer harms associated with asset collection technology and IoT devices and private debt criminalization tactics are likely to be disproportionately borne by low-income and racial minority consumers. This burden exacerbates unequal access to privacy and security concerns.

There are multiple consumer narratives in the CFPB complaint database describing privacy, digital domination, and debt criminalization harms. Despite the possible representative limits of the CFPB's complaint database, it contains the most extensive collection of consumers' experiences in lending transactions.[4] As lending and debt collection entities become increasingly empowered by technological developments in the IoT setting, there is more potential for discrimination, privacy intrusions, and the digital domination of all of us in the lending and debt collection processes.

BASIC STATE LAW LENDING FRAMEWORK

There are various federal and state laws that apply to consumer lending transactions.[5] Rather than focusing primarily on federal lending requirements, which have been well documented by various other legal scholars, this chapter primarily evaluates a specific set of state commercial laws applicable to consumer financial transactions. The connection between the IoT and asset collection technology in consumer lending transactions and relevant state laws has received minimal attention in legal scholarship.[6] As such, this chapter seeks to further discourse about consumer concerns associated with such technology in the IoT age.

---

[3] *See id.*

[4] *See* Pamela Foohey, *Calling on the CFPB for Help: Telling Stories and Consumer Protection*, 80 L. & CONTEMP. PROBS. 177, 184–86 (2017) (noting that low-income consumers may be less likely to submit complaints to the CFPB database as they have less access to the Internet and only a "particular subset" of racial minorities may submit complaints, but contending that "[d]espite these limitations, the [CFPB] [d]atabase remains the most comprehensive collection of people's stories about their experiences with consumer credit and banking products and services"); Angela K. Littwin, *Why Process Complaints? Then and Now*, 87 TEMP. L. REV. 895, 908–10 (2015)(discussing the representative limits of the CFPB's complaint database and noting that "Black consumers are slightly overrepresented in the CFPB data, and the percentage of Latino consumers . . . is nearly identical").

[5] There are several federal statutes and associated regulations that may apply to a consumer credit transaction, including but not limited to the Fair Debt Collection Practices Act and the Truth in Lending Act.

[6] Several articles have discussed starter-interrupt devices in various contexts, but few have focused exclusively on the IoT. *See generally* Kwesi D. Atta-Krah, Note, *Preventing a Boom from Turning Bust: Regulators Should Turn Their Attention to Starter Interrupt Devices Before the Subprime Auto Lending Bubble Bursts*, 101 IOWA L. REV. 1187 (2016); Laura Harper, Note, *Did the Repo Man Just Ghost Me? Technology's Contribution to Vehicle Repossession and How It Impacts the UCC*, 38 REV. LITIG. 373 (2019); Thomas B. Hudson & Daniel J. Laudicina, *The Emerging Law of Starter Interrupt Devices*, 61 BUS. LAW. 843 (2006); Elizabeth E. Joh, *Automated Seizures: Police Stops of Self-Driving Cars*, 94 N.Y.U. L. REV. ONLINE 292 (2019); Robbin Rahman, *Electronic Self-Help Repossession and You: A Computer Software Vendor's Guide to Staying Out of Jail*, 48 EMORY L.J. 1477, 1499 (1999);

Lending transactions involving the sale of goods between consumers and creditors are frequently subject to a state's version of Article 9 of the UCC. However, the provisions of Article 9 must defer to both state and federal consumer protection rules.[7] Article 9 generally applies to transactions that establish a "security interest in personal property."[8] There are several categories of personal property subject to Article 9.[9] IoT devices and the associated computer programs we use likely fall in the "consumer goods" or possibly the "general intangibles" categories of Article 9 property.[10]

Consider a consumer who has purchased an IoT device, such as an internet-connected vehicle, and has obtained a loan from a creditor to finance the transaction. In exchange for providing funding, the creditor takes a security interest (a lien) in the collateral (the IoT product). What happens if the consumer fails to pay back the loan? Article 9 does not define the term "default," and as a result, the parties' agreement is instructive on this point. Failure to make timely payments generally qualifies as a default under loan agreements. There are other events that may constitute a default. For instance, in a 2016 Georgia case, a consumer's vehicle was remotely disabled by the lender for failure to maintain car insurance, which, according to the lender, was an event of default under the loan agreement despite there being only a one-day gap in coverage.[11] Some laws also restrict the kinds of events that can permissibly constitute an event of default in consumer loan agreements.[12]

Once an event of default occurs, the creditor is given several rights in transactions governed by Article 9. A lender who has taken a security interest in a consumer's IoT device in exchange for providing funding (in many cases to acquire the device) may repossess the device if the consumer fails to pay back the loan, subject to certain requirements that I will explore in detail in later sections of this chapter.[13] Debtors may also have the ability to cure defaults and redeem collateral.[14] Once a secured

---

Andrew Schmidt, Note, *Pump the Brakes: What Financial Regulators Should Consider in Trying to Prevent a Subprime Auto Loan Bubble*, 107 CALIF. L. REV. 1345 (2019); Erica N. Sweeting, Comment, *Disabling Devices: Adopting Parameters for Addressing a Predatory Auto-Lending Technique on Subprime Borrowers*, 59 HOW. L.J. 817 (2016).

[7]   U.C.C. §§ 9-109(c)(1), 9-201(c) (AM. LAW INST. & UNIF. LAW COMM'N 2017); *see also* U.S. CONST. art. VI, cl. 2.

[8]   U.C.C. § 9-109(a)(1).

[9]   *See id.* § 9-102(a) (defining several categories of personal property).

[10] *See id.* § 9-102(a)(44) (defining goods to include various items as well as certain computer programs "embedded in goods"); *id.* § 9-102(a)(23) (defining consumer goods as "goods that are used or bought for use primarily for personal, family, or household purposes"); *id.* § 9-102(a)(42) (defining software as a general intangible).

[11] *See* Olympic Auto Sales, Inc. v. Geico Indem. Co., No. 15-1-01666-53, 2016 Ga. Super. LEXIS 4035, at *1 (Super. Ct. Ga. July 14, 2016).

[12] *See, e.g.*, UNIF. CONSUMER CREDIT CODE § 5.109 (UNIF. LAW COMM'N 1974) (describing permissible events of default).

[13] U.C.C. § 9-610(a).

[14] LINDA J. RUSCH & STEPHEN L. SEPINUCK, PROBLEMS AND MATERIALS ON SECURED TRANSACTIONS 160 (3rd ed. 2014); U.C.C. § 9-623.

party has repossessed collateral it can dispose of the collateral by selling it, among other things, to apply the collateral's value to the debt owed.[15] Article 9 requires the lender to ensure that the disposition is commercially reasonable.[16] This dependence on commercially reasonably practices in the disposition context also reflects the UCC's high regard for commercial practices, although the vagueness of this standard could in some cases be beneficial to debtors who have the resources to legally challenge the lender's actions.[17]

Article 9 has been amended several times since its initial adoption.[18] With a small number of exceptions, Article 9's rules generally apply similarly to corporate and consumer transactions.[19] The previous amendments to Article 9 reflect missed opportunities to comprehensively resolve pressing consumer issues in secured transactions in a manner that would be beneficial to consumer debtors.[20] Previous amendments failed to fully clarify the state of secured transactions law in consumer transactions, while simultaneously improving secured lenders rights in corporate transactions.[21] For instance, revisions to Article 9 could have adopted the transformation rule in purchase money security interest (PMSI) consumer transactions – meaning that the funds provided by the creditor were used by the consumer to acquire the product.[22] Under a transformation rule adopted by some courts, a refinancing or cross-collateralization destroys the PMSI status of a loan, thereby requiring the lender to perfect its interests.[23] Unperfected security interests and non-possessory non-PMSIs in certain household products can be avoided in bankruptcy proceedings.[24] In determining the issue of avoidance and applying relevant

---

[15] U.C.C. § 9-623.

[16] U.C.C. § 9-610.

[17] LYNN M. LoPUCKI ET AL., SECURED TRANSACTIONS A SYSTEMS APPROACH 83 (8th ed. 2016).

[18] RUSCH & SEPINUCK, *supra* note 14, at 49-50.

[19] *Making Repossessions Safer and Fairer: Model Consumer Amendments to Uniform Commercial Code Article 9*, NAT'L CONSUMER L. CTR. 1, 1 (2016), www.nclc.org/images/pdf/legislation/model_laws/model_consumer_amendments_uni_ccode.pdf.

[20] Jean Braucher, *Deadlock: Consumer Transactions Under Revised Article 9*, 73 AM. BANKR. L.J. 83 (1999); Charles W. Mooney, Jr., *The Consumer Compromise in Revised U.C.C. Article 9: The Shame of It All*, 68 OHIO ST. L.J. 215 (2007).

[21] Braucher, *supra* note 20, at 83.

[22] U.C.C. § 9-103 cmts. 7, 8; Braucher, *supra* note 20, at 96–97; PERMANENT EDITORIAL BD. STUDY GRP., PEB STUDY GROUP UNIFORM COMMERCIAL CODE ARTICLE 9, at 97–99 (1992), https://heinonline.org/HOL/P?h=hein.ali/alicco265&i=1 [hereinafter PEB REPORT].

[23] U.C.C. § 9-103 cmts. 7, 8; Braucher, *supra* note 20, at 96–97.
    U.C.C. § 9-103 cmts. 7, 8; Braucher, *supra* note 20, at 96–97; *See e.g.*, *In re* Keeton, 161 B.R. 410, 411 (Bankr. S.D. Ohio 1993); Hipps v. Landmark Financial Services of Georgia, Inc. (*In re* Hipps), 89 B.R. 264, 265 (Bankr. N.D. Ga. 1988); *see also* Nathan Goralnik, *The Over-Encumbered Trade-in in Chapter 13*, 29 EMORY BANKR. DEV. J. 15, 21 (2012) (noting that some jurisdictions adopt a transformation rule); Gail Hillebrand, *The Uniform Commercial Code Drafting Process: Will Articles 2, 2B and 9 Be Fair to Consumers?*, 75 WASH. U. L. Q. 69, 127–29 (1997) (discussing jurisdictions adopting the transformation rule); RUSCH & SEPINUCK, *supra* note 14, at 296-97 (same)

[24] *In re* Short, 170 B.R. 128, 132 (Bankr. S.D. Ill. 1994) ("Section §522(f)(2) [of the Bankruptcy Code] allows a debtor to avoid the fixing of a lien on property that would otherwise be exempt if such lien is a non-possessory, non-purchase money security interest"); Braucher, *supra* note 20, at 96–97.

bankruptcy rules, bankruptcy courts can turn to a state's version of Article 9 to define a PMSI.[25] The UCC drafters chose instead to adopt a dual status rule for corporate transactions, but failed to adequately resolve the issue in consumer transactions in a manner that would have been beneficial to consumers.[26]

Similarly, proposals to deal with the various approaches in consumer transactions for deficiency claims involving noncompliant secured lenders failed to be adopted.[27] We will explore the basics of deficiency claims later on in this chapter. During previous Article 9 amendment proceedings, secured lenders' representatives successfully opposed revisions to Article 9 that would favor consumers and in response consumer advocates agreed to a compromise that for the most part froze the status quo.[28] An "absolute bar rule" that prohibits a secured lender from recovering deficiencies in consumer transactions if the lender failed to comply with certain Article 9 provisions, such as the obligation to conduct a commercially reasonable disposition, failed to be adopted.[29] Instead Article 9's current provisions provide a rebuttable presumption rule for non-consumer transactions but fail to provide adequate guidance with respect to consumer transactions.[30] Ultimately, consumer advocates were left primarily to argue in courts for subsequent favorable decisions, which could be somewhat beneficial or certainly detrimental to consumer debtors, depending on the rule applied by courts and the evidenced introduced.[31] At least one

---

[25] U.C.C. § 9-103 cmt. 8; Braucher, *supra* note 20, at 96–97; *In re Short*, 170 B.R. at 132 ("The Bankruptcy Code does not define 'purchase money security interest' or specify how a lien's purchase money status is affected by refinancing or consolidation with other debt. Reference must be had, therefore, to the state law definition of 'purchase money security interest'.").

[26] U.C.C. § 9-103(f), cmt. 7(a), cmt. 8; Braucher, *supra* note 20, at 86.

[27] Mooney, *supra* note 20, at 223–24, 229; Braucher, *supra* note 20, at 86–88.

[28] Braucher, *supra* note 20, at 83, 86 (noting that secured lenders were also opposed to an approach that would "require that the debtor be credited for the wholesale value [of the collateral], based on collateral condition, minus expenses of repossession and sale (which could be reduced by eliminating the public foreclosure sale)"); Andrea Coles-Bjerre, *Trusting the Process and Mistrusting the Results: A Structural Perspective on Article 9's Low-Price Foreclosure Rule*, 9 AM. BANKR. INST. L. REV. 351, 372 (2001) (citing CONN. GEN. STAT. ANN. § 36a-785(g) (West 1996)); Hillebrand, *supra* note 23, at 134–40; Timothy G. Hayes, *Secured Creditors Holding Lien Creditors Hostage: Have a Little Faith in Revised Article 9*, 81 IND. L.J. 733, 747 (2006); Mooney, *supra* note 20, at 229. Currently § 9-626(a)(3) provides that when a sale fails to comply with Article 9's requirements "[i]n calculating the deficiency under it, the amount that would have been realized in a complying sale is treated as if it were the actual sale price"; LOPUCKI ET AL., *supra* note 17, at 8; U.C.C. § 9-626(a)(3).

[29] Braucher, *supra* note 20, at 86–88 (noting that "consumer advocates would have preferred codification of wholesale value approach or the 'absolute bar' approach for consumer transactions"); Mooney, *supra* note 20, at 223–24, 224 n.19 (describing the absolute bar rule and discussing proposed revisions to Article 9); Timothy R. Zinnecker, *The Default Provisions of Revised Article 9 of the Uniform Commercial Code: Part II*, 54 BUS. LAW. 1737, 1810–14 (1999) (discussing various approaches to the deficiency problem). *See also* PEB REPORT, *supra* note 22, at 201–05.

[30] U.C.C. § 9-626, cmts. 3–4 (noting that courts can "continue to apply established approaches" in consumer transactions); RUSCH & SEPINUCK, *supra* note 14, at 195–98; Braucher, *supra* note 20, at 86–87.

[31] Braucher, *supra* note 20, at 88; Mooney, *supra* note 20, at 222, 225; *see also* Coxall v. Clover Commercial Corp., 781 N.Y.S.2d 567 (N.Y. Civ. Ct. 2004).

state has adopted a non-uniform amendment to Article 9 to apply the rebuttable presumption rule to commercial and consumer transactions.[32]

In 1973, the Alaska Supreme Court observed "[u]sually, due to his poor financial position, the debtor has scant prospect of obtaining an attorney ... The possible [debtor] remedies [under Article 9] are thus illusory in most cases."[33] This remains true today to some extent. Challenging a secured lender's disposition of collateral as being commercially unreasonable typically obligates the debtor to place the secured lender's compliance in issue during litigation.[34] This often requires the debtor to be represented by a knowledgeable attorney, and the possible hiring of an expert on reasonable disposition prices.[35] Although the comments to Article 9 indicate that a few courts have applied the absolute bar approach, it also notes that some states adopted rules applicable to deficiencies, and other courts have applied various other rules to address the deficiency issue in consumer transactions, including a rebuttable presumption rule and an "offset rule" allowing a debtor to "offset against a claim to a deficiency all damages recoverable" due to the secured lender's noncompliance.[36]

In addition to Article 9, other sources of state law that apply specifically to consumer transactions, such as the Uniform Consumer Credit Code, also provide lenders with the ability to repossess collateral.[37] State statutes directly addressing automobile lending provide specific rules related to motor vehicle transactions, and these statutes can also authorize repossession of vehicles in the event of nonpayment.[38] Thus, existing state laws establish legal frameworks that give creditors the right of repossession. The introduction of asset collection technology and IoT devices in consumer financial transactions skews the debt collection process in favor of creditors to our detriment. The following discussions of these technology in the subprime auto lending industry highlights this point.

THE SUBPRIME AUTO LENDING INDUSTRY

The subprime auto lending industry provides loans to consumers at high interest rates to finance purchases of vehicles that are usually used or pre-owned. The

---

[32] WASH. REV. CODE ANN. § 62A.9A-626, Wash. cmt. (West 2020) ("Washington adopts the rebuttable presumption rule for all transactions."); RUSCH & SEPINUCK, *supra* note 14, at 197–98.

[33] *See* Moran v. Holman, 514 P. 2d 817, 820 (Alaska 1973); Braucher, *supra* note 20, at 103.

[34] U.C.C. § 9-626(a); Braucher, *supra* note 20, at 87.

[35] U.C.C. § 9-626(a); Braucher, *supra* note 20, at 87.

[36] U.C.C. § 9-626 cmt. 4.

[37] UNIF. CONSUMER CREDIT CODE § 5.112 (Unif. Law Comm'n) (permitting repossession without "the use of force or other breach of the peace"); 10A SARA JANE HUGHES & FRED H. MILLER, HAWKLAND'S UNIFORM COMMERCIAL CODE SERIES § 6:39, Westlaw (database updated Dec. 2018) ("The Uniform Consumer Credit Code (U3C), either the 1968, 1974 or a modified version, is the law in ten states.").

[38] CAROLYN L. CARTER ET AL., REPOSSESSIONS AND FORECLOSURES: CONSUMER CREDIT AND SALES LEGAL PRACTICES SERIES 96 (8th ed. 2013) (discussing various state statutes); NEV. REV. STAT. ANN. § 604A.5078 (West 2019) (authorizing repossession of vehicles and limiting creditors' right to deficiencies).

industry offers financing and vehicles to consumers with imperfect credit histories, often through indirect loans in which the dealer identifies the lender who provides financing to the consumer, and the lender subsequently purchases the loan from the dealer.[39] Instead of relying on third-party lenders, some subprime vehicle dealers also provide financing directly to consumers.[40] Many consumers who finance their vehicles enter into indirect lending transactions.[41]

Experian reports that in the third quarter of 2019, the average interest rates on vehicle loans for subprime and deep-subprime borrowers were 11.71% and 14.30% for new vehicles, respectively, and 16.89% and 19.72% for used vehicles, respectively.[42] At the end of 2018 there were "more subprime auto loan borrowers than ever, and thus a larger group of borrowers at high risk of delinquency."[43] More than 7 million consumers were "90 or more days delinquent" on their vehicle loans at the close of 2018, which is 1 million higher than the number of consumers who were delinquent on their vehicle loans in 2010, "when the overall delinquency rates were at their worst."[44] In the subprime auto lending context, some dealers have reportedly inflated the price of their vehicles, and in some cases have sold their vehicles to subprime borrowers for almost 35 percent more than the vehicles' market value.[45] Industry wide, approximately 300,000 vehicles of the total 24 million vehicle loans originated in 2018 "were repossessed within 12 months, up 17% from 2014."[46]

Large quantities of combined subprime auto loans are often sold to investors. Vehicle dealers receive compensation from indirect auto lenders for originating automobile loans.[47] The cost of this compensation is often borne by subprime consumers who then receive higher interest rates as car dealers are incentivized to

---

[39] CONSUMER FIN. PROT. BUREAU, EXAMINATION PROCEDURES: AUTO FINANCE (2015) [hereinafter EXAMINATION PROCEDURES]; CONSUMER FIN. PROT. BUREAU, INDIRECT AUTO LENDING AND COMPLIANCE WITH THE EQUAL CREDIT OPPORTUNITY ACT (2013) [hereinafter INDIRECT AUTO LENDING]; INDEP. DEM. CONF., ROAD TO CREDIT DANGER: PREDATORY SUBPRIME AUTO LENDING IN NEW YORK (2015); James A. Wilson, Jr. & Sandra L. DiChiara, *The Changing Landscape of Indirect Automobile Lending*, SUPERVISORY INSIGHTS, Summer 2005, at 29, 34 (noting that indirect vehicle loans involve subprime borrowers); Letter from Thomas H. Armstrong, Gen. Counsel, U.S. Gov't Accountability Office, to Patrick J. Toomey, Senator, U.S. Senate (Dec. 5, 2017), www .toomey.senate.gov/files/documents/GAO%20Lending.pdf (discussing indirect lending).

[40] EXAMINATION PROCEDURES, *supra* note 39, at 2–3; INDEP. DEM. CONF., *supra* note 39, at 4.

[41] *See* EXAMINATION PROCEDURES, *supra* note 39, at 3.

[42] Melinda Zabritski, *State of the Automotive Finance Market Q3 2019*, EXPERIAN 25 (2020), www .experian.com/content/dam/marketing/na/automotive/quarterly-webinars/credit-trends/q3-2019- experian-safm-revised.pdf.

[43] Andrew F. Haughwout et al., *Just Released: Auto Loans in High Gear*, LIBERTY ST. ECON. (Feb. 12, 2019), https://libertystreeteconomics.newyorkfed.org/2019/02/just-released-auto-loans-in-high- gear.html.

[44] *Id.*

[45] Anjali Kamat, *The Big Business of Subprime Auto Loans*, NPR (Dec. 12, 2019, 5:00 AM), www.npr.org /2019/12/12/787337997/the-big-business-of-subprime-auto-loans.

[46] AnnaMaria Andriotis & Ben Eisen, *Dealerships Give Car Buyers Some Advice: Just Stop Paying Your Loan*, WALL ST. J. (Feb. 15, 2020, 5:30 AM), www.wsj.com/articles/dealerships-give-car-buyers-some- advice-just-stop-paying-your-loan-11581762601.

[47] INDIRECT AUTO LENDING, *supra* note 39, at 1–2 (describing the indirect loan process).

charge higher rates in order to receive more compensation from the selected lender who purchases the retail installment contract.[48] As Adam Levitin observes, "higher markups correlate with higher rates of default and repossession."[49] Historically marginalized consumers have been victims of discriminatory interest rate pricing connected to these dealer markups.[50] For instance, a CFPB and Department of Justice investigation found that one lender's dealer markup program enabled discriminatory pricing which injured approximately 235,000 racial minority borrowers.[51] These borrowers were subject to "higher dealer markups for their auto loans than similarly-situated non-Hispanic white borrowers."[52]

The CFPB further attempted to address this topic by issuing a bulletin that contained guidance and recommendations to indirect vehicle lenders on the use of dealer markups.[53] However, in 2018 Congress passed a joint resolution, which was signed by the President, rendering the bulletin of "no force or effect."[54] The CFPB's authority and structure was previously challenged before the Supreme Court.[55] Some state lending frameworks may be useful in filling this regulatory gap. In 2018, New York released guidance for indirect automobile creditors on dealer markups.[56]

ASSET COLLECTION TECHNOLOGY IN THE IOT ERA

Recall that connected automobiles are part of the IoT. Business Insider Intelligence estimates that there will be 293 million IoT vehicles in use by 2025.[57] Car

---

[48]   See *id.*; see also Adam J. Levitin, *The Fast and the Usurious: Putting the Brakes on Auto Lending Abuses*, 108 GEO. L.J. 1257 (2020).

[49]   Levitin, *supra* note 48, at 1277 (citing Delvin Davis & Joshua M. Frank, *Under the Hood: Auto Loan Interest Rate Hikes Inflate Consumer Costs and Loan Losses*, CTR. FOR RESPONSIBLE LENDING, Apr. 19, 2011, at 12–13).

[50]   See *CFPB and DOJ Order Ally to Pay $80 Million to Consumers Harmed by Discriminatory Auto Loan Pricing*, CONSUMER FIN. PROT. BUREAU (Dec. 20, 2013), www.consumerfinance.gov/about-us/news room/cfpb-and-doj-order-ally-to-pay-80-million-to-consumers-harmed-by-discriminatory-auto-loan-pricing/.

[51]   *Id.*

[52]   *Id.*

[53]   See generally INDIRECT AUTO LENDING, *supra* note 39.

[54]   See *id.*; see also S.J. Res. 57, 115th Cong., 132 Stat. 1290 (2018).

[55]   See Seila Law LLC v. Consumer Fin. Prot. Bureau, 140 S. Ct. 427 (2019); Jon Hill, *Justices Take Up CFPB Constitutionality Case*, LAW360 (Oct. 18, 2019, 2:58 PM), www.law360.com/california/articles/1204756/breaking-justices-take-up-cfpb-constitutionality-case?nl_pk=52c85548-3a20-4e78-813b-c72f07378e7d&utm_source=newsletter&utm_medium=email&utm_campaign=california.

[56]   N.Y. EXEC. LAW § 296-a (McKinney 2019); Letter from Maria T. Vullo, Superintendent of Fin. Servs., N.Y. State Dep't of Fin. Servs., to Indirect Automobile Lenders (Aug. 23, 2018), www.dfs.ny.gov/system/files/documents/2020/03/il180823.pdf; *New York Revives Rescinded Fair Lending Policy on Indirect Auto Lending*, MAYER BROWN (Sept. 10, 2018), www.mayerbrown.com/en/perspectives-events/publications/2018/09/new-york-revives-rescinded-fair-lending-policy-on?utm_source=Mondaq&utm_medium=syndication&utm_campaign=LinkedIn-integration.

[57]   Rachel Green, *Honda and AutoNavi Are Partnering on a Connected Car Platform*, BUS. INSIDER (Jan. 4, 2018, 8:04 AM), www.businessinsider.com/honda-autonavi-partnership-connected-car-platform-2018-1.

manufacturers are increasingly building cars that are connected to the Internet with infotainment systems that collect large amounts of consumer-generated data.[58] Indeed, one consulting firm suggests that "today's car has the computing power of 20 personal computers, features about 100 million lines of programming code, and processes up to 25 gigabytes of data an hour."[59]

In the era of the internet-connected vehicle, automobile creditors use various types of asset collection technology when extending credit to borrowers. Creditors frequently require subprime borrowers to consent to the installation of a starter-interrupt device (SID) or other tracking device in their vehicles prior to extending a loan.[60] Starter-interrupt devices and other types of GPS tracking devices can be used in both subprime vehicle lease and sale transactions. A SID could also be installed in a consumer's vehicle after a default.[61] Subprime vehicle lenders can receive direct fees from automobile dealers' use of SIDs. For instance, Credit Acceptance's 2020 annual report filed with the Securities and Exchange Commission notes that through several contractual arrangements it previously received fees from third-party SID providers for each SID dealers purchased and installed on consumer vehicles financed through the company.[62] Those fees totaled $1.9 million in 2019 and $6.4 million in 2018.[63]

PassTime, an asset collection technology provider, advertises its devices to sub-prime creditors as being essential to "mitigate the risk of financing" consumers with subprime credit.[64] In 2016, PassTime's vice president stated that approximately 70 percent of automobiles acquired by subprime borrowers are accompanied by a device that has SID features, among other things.[65] The company touts that its

---

[58] *See* McKinsey & Co., Connected Car, Automotive Value Chain Unbound 13 (2014); Andrew Meola, *Automotive Industry Trends: IoT Connected Smart Cars & Vehicles*, Bus. Insider (Dec. 20, 2016, 12:57 PM), www.businessinsider.com/internet-of-things-connected-smart-cars-2016-10.

[59] *What's Driving the Connected Car*, McKinsey & Co. (Sept. 1, 2014), www.mckinsey.com/industries/automotive-and-assembly/our-insights/whats-driving-the-connected-car.

[60] *See* Atlanticus Holdings Corp., Form 10-K for the Year Ended December 31, 2018 (2019), www.sec.gov/Archives/edgar/data/1464343/000143774919005717/atlc20181231b_10k.htm (noting that the "auto finance segment" of the company's business uses SIDs to decrease deficiencies); Atta-Krah, *supra* note 6, at 1190; Max Raskin, *The Law and Legality of Smart Contracts*, 1 Geo. L. Tech. Rev. 305, 308 (2017); Sweeting, *supra* note 6, at 819–20. *See generally* Edward J. Markey, Tracking & Hacking: Security & Privacy Gaps Put American Drivers at Risk (2015); Elaine S. Povich, *Late Payment? A 'Kill Switch' Can Strand You and Your Car*, Pew Charitable Tr. (Nov. 27, 2018), www.pewtrusts.org/en/research-and-analysis/blogs/stateline/2018/11/27/late-payment-a-kill-switch-can-strand-you-and-your-car.

[61] Eric L. Johnson & Corinne Kirkendall, *Starter Interrupt and GPS Devices: Best Practices*, PassTime (Jan. 14, 2016), https://passtimegps.com/starter-interrupt-and-gps-devices-best-practices/.

[62] Credit Acceptance Corp., Annual Report for the Fiscal Year Ended December 31, 2019 (Form 10-K) 9, 70 (2020), www.sec.gov/ix?doc=/Archives/edgar/data/885550/000088555020000021/cacc-20191231x10k.htm (also noting that the company "allowed [d]ealers to install previously purchased GPS-SID on vehicles financed by us until September 1, 2019").

[63] *See id.* at 70.

[64] *TRAX*, PassTime, https://passtimegps.com/solutions/trax/ (last visited Mar. 18, 2020).

[65] Jaeah Lee, *Wait, Banks Can Shut Off My Car?*, Mother Jones (Mar. 2016), www.motherjones.com/politics/2016/04/subprime-car-loans-starter-interrupt/.

devices are being used worldwide, and it is the winner of several industry awards for its IoT products.[66] The *New York Times* estimates that SIDs were installed in approximately 2 million vehicles in 2014.[67] Starter-interrupt device technology is also in use in Canada's vehicle lending industry.[68]

Once installed in a vehicle, SIDs allow automobile creditors to remotely disable a vehicle. As John Rothchild notes, SID technology may have "its antecedents in remote disablement of computers when the vendor believed that the owner owed money on the hardware or software."[69] Starter-interrupt devices can also be used to send multiple payment reminders to subprime borrowers and track a vehicle's current and past location, among other things.[70] In one reported bankruptcy case involving an older model SID, the consumer could only operate the vehicle if the lender provided him with new codes approximately every month that could be entered on the device after receipt of payments.[71] Previous codes would expire twenty days after they were provided to the consumer.[72] The court described the SID as a "doomsday machine."[73]

---

[66] *See 2015 IoT Evolution Product of the Year Award Winners Announced*, IoT Evolution (May 6, 2015), www.iotevolutionworld.com/newsroom/articles/402891-2015-iot-evolution-product-the-year-award-winners.htm (noting that PassTime is a 2015 award winner); *GPS Solutions to Connect Your Vehicles & Protect Your Assets*, PassTime, https://passtimegps.com/about/ (last visited Mar. 18, 2020); PassTime, https://passtimegps.com/ (last visited Dec. 20, 2019); *The Right Vehicle Intelligence & GPS Tracking Solution for Your Business*, PassTime, https://passtimegps.com/solutions/ (last visited Mar. 18, 2020) [hereinafter *Solutions Overview*].

[67] Michael Corkery & Jessica Silver-Greenberg, *Miss a Payment? Good Luck Moving that Car*, N.Y. Times: DealBook (Sept. 24, 2014, 9:33 PM), https://dealbook.nytimes.com/2014/09/24/miss-a-payment-good-luck-moving-that-car/?ref=dealbook.

[68] *See* Yvonne Colbert, *Privacy Group Wants Better Regulations for GPS Starter Interrupt Devices*, CBC News (Aug. 13, 2018, 5:30 AM), www.cbc.ca/news/canada/nova-scotia/gps-starter-interrupters-privacy-technology-laws-1.4780860.

[69] John A. Rothchild, *Net Gets Physical: What You Need to Know About the Internet of Things*, Am. B. Ass'n (Nov. 17, 2014), www.americanbar.org/groups/business_law/publications/blt/2014/11/03_rothchild/.

[70] *See, e.g.*, Kashmir Hill, *People with Bad Credit Can Buy Cars, but They Are Tracked and Have Remote-Kill Switches*, Forbes (Sept. 25, 2014, 2:25 PM), www.forbes.com/sites/kashmirhill/2014/09/25/starter-interrupt-devices/#69bdd21a7733; *ControlIt*, Ituran, www.ituranusa.com/control-it/ (last visited Dec. 20, 2019); *DefenderGPS*, Skypatrol, www.skypatrol.com/defender/ (last visited Dec. 20, 2019) (discussing the features of the Skypatrol SID); *LMU-600 GPRS Series*, CalAmp, www.calamp.com/wp-content/uploads/resources/LMU-600.pdf (last visited Dec. 20, 2019) (discussing the company's wireless SIDs); PayTeck, www.payteck.cc/ (last visited Dec. 20, 2019) (discussing the company's SID); *Solutions Overview*, *supra* note 66 (discussing the company's SID and Automated Collection Technology products); Spireon, www.spireon.com/goldstar-gps-vehicle-tracking (last visited Dec. 20, 2019) (discussing the company's SID).

[71] Dawson v. J & B Detail, L.L.C. (*In re* Dawson), No. 05-22369, 2006 WL 2372821, at *1 (Bankr. N.D. Ohio Aug. 15, 2006). For another case with similar facts regarding the operations of a SID, *see In re Horace*, No. 14-30103, 2015 WL 5145576, at *1 (Bankr. N.D. Ohio Aug. 28, 2015). *See also* Carter et al., *supra* note 38, at 213, discussing the various types of SIDs.

[72] *In re Dawson*, 2006 WL 2372821, at *1.

[73] *Id.* at *7.

Many SIDs and other GPS tracking devices are installed in used and older model vehicles that lack infotainment systems and a direct internet connection. However, the installation of a SID or other tracking device in older used vehicles establishes a connection to external devices that are connected to the Internet (and other networks), thereby bringing these older vehicles into the IoT. These external devices can be used to remotely control the vehicle's operations through the SID. For instance, lenders can control a SID installed in a consumer's vehicle via a smartphone. Additionally, the "onboard diagnostics" ports that have been included in vehicles manufactured since 1996 can be used to connect and usher older model vehicles into the IoT.[74]

Consider that AirWire Technologies with the help of IBM Garage has enabled vehicles with an "onboard diagnostic port" to access IoT services and transmit data to cloud systems.[75] Once connected, these older model vehicles can have access to "a voice-activated in-vehicle personal assistant."[76] Consumers can also receive data on their driving habits and the vehicle's operations.[77] In the same way that cathode ray tube televisions have become obsolete, eventually almost all vehicles will be directly connected to the Internet, making older non-connected automobiles a thing of the past. Thus, in the near future, all used and older model vehicles that are financed in subprime lending marketplaces will likely have a more direct connection to the Internet.

Starter-interrupt devices and other GPS tracking devices enable the collection and storage of extraordinary amounts of data about vehicle owners. Since subprime borrowers are more likely to be required to accept the installation of asset collection technology in their vehicles, these groups of consumers are more likely to be victims of resulting harms. We will come back to this point in later subsections of this chapter. Our daily driving activities and locations visited can be constantly monitored through these devices. For instance, once installed in a consumer's car, PassTime's "TRAX" device reportedly provides creditors with "pin-point GPS tracking," automatic vehicle location updates "every 73 hours," and speed alerts.[78] The

---

[74] Alan McQuinn & Daniel Castro, A Policymaker's Guide to Connected Cars 3, 12 (2018) (describing vehicles with SIDs as "connected cars" that are part of the IoT); Lothar Determann & Bruce Perens, *Open Cars*, 32 Berkeley Tech. L.J. 915, 955 (2017) (discussing the history of regulations regarding the use of onboard diagnostics ports in cars beginning in 1996); Antuan Goodwin, *A Brief Intro to OBD-II Technology*, CNET (Apr. 14, 2010, 3:13 PM), www.cnet.com/roadshow/news/a-brief-intro-to-obd-ii-technology/; Liz Slocum Jensen, *Onboard Diagnostics Will Connect Cars to the Internet of Things*, VentureBeat (Aug. 7, 2016, 5:13 AM), https://venturebeat.com/2016/08/07/onboard-diagnostics-will-connect-cars-to-the-internet-of-things/.

[75] Debashis Bagchi, *AirWire Technologies Builds Connected Car App with IBM Garage*, IBM (Nov. 1, 2018) https://www.ibm.com/blogs/cloud-computing/2018/11/01/airwire-technologies-ibm-cloud-garage/;*Connecting the World One Car at a Time*, IoTool (Jan. 3, 2018), https://iotool.io/news/industry-4-0/connecting-the-world-one-car-at-a-time; *AirWire Enables Intelligent Vehicles with the IBM Cloud Garage*, https://www.youtube.com/watch?v=Ak4byzRZrVA (last visited Dec. 20, 2019).

[76] *Connecting the World*, *supra* note 75.

[77] *Id.*

[78] See *TRAX*, *supra* note 64.

device also has an optional SID feature. The product of another SID provider includes "odometer readings" and "accelerometer" features.[79] PassTime's "Select GPS" SID also has "tow and tamper detection" features and the ability to send "payment reminder" notifications to drivers.[80] These products also have geofencing and remote disablement capabilities.[81]

A device with a geofencing feature allows a party to establish a geographic boundary for a vehicle and receive notifications once the vehicle exits or enters the predefined geographic area.[82] Such a feature (together with other mechanisms) enables a party to remotely disable a vehicle once a geofencing violation alert is received.[83] Asset collection technology and devices can also react to pre-established thresholds established by a dealer, such as motion and date and "other event combinations."[84]

While vehicle lenders and lessors have historically retained some degree of control over automobiles post transaction, the extent to which these parties can exert their influence over us and our lives has increased steadily in the IoT setting. In fact, one SID provider labeled its device "ControlIt."[85] Spireon, another SID maker, touts that its "goldstar" products allow dealers and lenders to obtain historical and current vehicle data to "predict [the] most probable ... location" of a vehicle at any point in time to facilitate recovery and payments.[86] The company's devices and systems continuously collect vehicle data and can determine how long vehicles have been in motion and parked.[87] The company also offers multiple daily reports and alerts, including "geofence violations" and "excessive mileage" reports, speed alerts, and "battery disconnect" alerts.[88] The "goldstar" product has remote disablement and payment reminder features, and the company allows dealers to receive notifications of individuals' driving behaviors, including mileage history.[89] In addition to collecting and storing driving history, asset collection devices and systems can also automatically collect and analyze

---

[79] *3.5G Locate/Recover-S*, IMETRIK, www.imetrik.com/pdf/Imetrik_3.5g_product_sheet_FINAL.pdf (last visited Dec. 20, 2019); *Vehicle Trackers*, CALAMP, www.calamp.com/products/vehicle-trackers/ (last visited Dec. 20, 2019).

[80] *Select GPS*, PASSTIME, https://passtimegps.com/solutions/selectgps/ (last visited Dec 21, 2019).

[81] *Id.*

[82] *See* Hill, *supra* note 70.

[83] *See id.*

[84] *LMU-600 GPRS Series*, *supra* note 70.

[85] *ControlIt*, *supra* note 70.

[86] *Meet the New Goldstar*, SPIREON (May 25, 2017), www.spireon.com/meet-new-goldstar/.

[87] *Features Making Your Life Easier & More Profitable*, SPIREON, www.spireon.com/goldstar-gps-vehicle-tracking/#1529615953806-b6588b4a-1703 (last visited Dec. 20, 2019); *The Most Trusted GPS Recovery Solution*, SPIREON, www.spireon.com/goldstar-gps-vehicle-tracking/ (last visited Mar. 18, 2020).

[88] *See Features Making Your Life Easier & More Profitable*, *supra* note 87; *The Most Trusted GPS Recovery Solution*, *supra* note 87. Other companies also offer SIDS with similar features. *See, e.g., Features*, RCI, www.rciwirelesscontrol.com/features/ (last visited Dec 21, 2019).

[89] *See Features Making Your Life Easier & More Profitable*, *supra* note 87; *The Most Trusted GPS Recovery Solution*, *supra* note 87.

"home and work address data."[90] Other SID products that companies offer include "parking behavior" reports and other features that allow dealers and creditors to "schedule commands" for future dates.[91] Thus, a creditor could schedule in advance the date on which a vehicle will be remotely disabled.

In addition to SIDs and other tracking devices, companies are also using automated license plate reader (ALPR) technology and resulting data to extend their power post transaction and facilitate repossessions.[92] ALPRs are "high-speed, computer-controlled camera systems that ... automatically capture all license plate numbers that come into view, along with the location, date, and time."[93] Automated license plate reader technology is widely used by both state and non-state actors, but is insufficiently regulated.[94]

Automated license plate reader cameras can capture more than "1,600 license plate images an hour."[95] An ALPR camera can also capture images of drivers and passengers.[96] Increasingly, ALPR technology is becoming more affordable, complex, and invasive.[97] Automated license plate reader software can be purchased for as little as $5 per month, and can be added to existing IoT security cameras.[98] Connecting ALPR systems and cameras directly to the Internet or to IoT devices makes them even more powerful. The American Civil Liberties Union (ACLU) reports that there are various mobile apps that allow individuals to use their smartphones to scan license plate images and submit them to ALPR databases.[99] ALPR-generated data can be stored in various databases and can be sold to third parties without our even knowing that the data were collected. Automated license plate reader data access can be purchased from ALPR vendors whose databases frequently include billions of license plate records.

Combining ALPR and SID data with the deluge of data that will be generated from our use of static objects that are embedded with sensors and connectivity increases lenders' and repossession companies' access to data that can be used as

---

[90] *See Features Making Your Life Easier & More Profitable*, *supra* note 87.

[91] *ControlIt*, *supra* note 70; *GPS/Payment Protection Devices*, FEX DMS, www.fexdms.com/payment-protection-gps.asp (last visited Dec. 20, 2019).

[92] *Automated License Plate Readers (ALPRs)*, Electronic Frontier Foundation, www.eff.org/pages/automated-license-plate-readers-alpr (last visited Dec. 20, 2019).

[93] *Id.*

[94] Axon AI & Policing Tech. Ethics Bd., Automated License Plate Readers 5 (Oct. 2019), https://static1.squarespace.com/static/58a33e881b631bc60d4f8b31/t/5dadec937f5c1a2b9d698ba9/1571679380452/Axon_Ethics_Report_2_v2.pdf.

[95] Lisa Bartley, *Hidden Surveillance Powered by Repo Industry – Eyewitness News Investigation*, ABC (Nov. 4, 2014), https://abc7.com/news/repo-industry-collecting-data-on-you/379656/.

[96] *Id.*

[97] Elizabeth E. Joh, *The New Surveillance Discretion: Automated Suspicion, Big Data, and Policing*, 10 Harv. L. & Pol'y Rev. 15, 22 (2016).

[98] Igor Bonifacic, *Anyone with a Camera and $5 Can Now Have a License Plate Reader*, Engadget (Jan. 30, 2020), www.engadget.com/2020/01/30/watchman-openalpr-homeowners-launch/.

[99] Am. Civil Liberties Union, You Are Being Tracked: How License Plate Readers Are Being Used to Record Americans' Movements 4 (2013) [hereinafter ACLU ALPR Report].

a proxy for our reputation and creditworthiness. This could impact the lender's decision to grant a loan, the terms of any such loan, and the post-default repossession process.

ASSET COLLECTION TECHNOLOGY DISCLOSURE FORMS

Subprime vehicle lenders can require consumers to execute one-sided SID installation disclosure forms as part of the loan process. Lenders provide disclosure forms to consumers in an attempt to ensure compliance with statutes and regulations that apply to consumer lending transactions as well as those that apply specifically to SIDs. The various state statutes specifically addressing SIDs and electronic self-help are discussed in more detail later in this chapter.

The model lending SID and tracking device disclosure forms found on several lenders' websites suggest that in practice the data hoarding features of asset collection technology may not always be adequately communicated to consumers.[100] To the extent used, these SID disclosure forms may notify consumers of the presence of a SID in the vehicle, and briefly describe the collection of location data, but fail to describe in sufficient detail how these data can be analyzed to generate driver reports and mined to predict consumer habits.[101] These documents may not always contain provisions regarding who can obtain access to the SID data, sell the data, or disclose the data, and may place few if any restrictions on companies' ability to use the data. These activities could be viewed as unfair and deceptive trade practices. In a consumer complaint to the CFPB, one consumer expressed concern about several inadequacies in a SID lending disclosure form, which allegedly did not sufficiently inform the consumer about the types of data that would be collected, where the data were held, and whether the SID and its GPS capabilities would track the vehicle continuously.[102] The consumer reported being unaware of whether the vehicle was being tracked while it is was parked.[103]

---

[100]   *See, e.g., Disclosure Statement and Agreement for Installation of a GPS Device*, PEOPLES CREDIT, https://peoplescredit.net/wp-content/uploads/10-4-17-corrected-PCI-GPS-Disclosure-without-starter-interrupt-06-07-17-fillable-pdf.pdf (last visited Feb. 24, 2020); *Disclosure Statement and Agreement for Installation of a Starter Interrupt and GPS Device*, HERITAGE ACCEPTANCE, www.heritageacceptance.net/media/uploads/0/150_GPS-Addendum.pdf (last visited Feb. 24, 2020) [hereinafter *Heritage Form*].

[101]   *See, e.g., Customer Agreement and Disclosure Statement for Installation of Starter Interrupt/GPS Device*, RIGHTSIZE FUNDING, www.creditsmarts.com/creditsmarts/db.images/7629.PDF (last visited Dec. 21, 2019); *LoanPlus GPS and Starter Interrupt System Disclosure and Agreement for Installation*, NATIONWIDE, www.nac-loans.com/sites/default/files/pdf/NATIONWIDE%20CAC/Funding%20Forms/WEB%20CAC%20GPS%20SID%201-16.pdf (last visited Dec. 21, 2019) [hereinafter *Nationwide Form*].

[102]   *See Consumer Complaint No. 2736951*, CONSUMER FIN. PROT. BUREAU (Nov. 24, 2017), www.consumerfinance.gov/data-research/consumer-complaints/search/detail/2736951.

[103]   *Id.*

Even when a model disclosure form provides additional details about data collection the consumer can still be required to waive any objections to data collection and monitoring.[104] For instance, a model disclosure form in the industry currently goes so far as to state that the buyer "waives any claim to confidentiality or a right to privacy" and is "solely responsible for providing notice" to third parties in buyer's vehicle "that their movement and/or location may be tracked while in the [v]ehicle."[105] Loan transactions that require subprime borrowers to accept the installation of asset collection technology in their vehicles also contribute to the unequal access to privacy and security problem. Another model disclosure form notes that buyers "have no right to privacy in the location of the [v]ehicle."[106] The form also contains provisions requiring the buyer to indemnify certain parties as well as clauses waiving the company's responsibility for all losses, harms, damages, delays, or interruptions the consumer incurs due to the SID.[107] Although installation of the device is a condition for the loan, no warranties are given regarding the merchantability or fitness of the device.[108] The model disclosure form states that the location feature of the SID can be used to "periodically test for the location of the [v]ehicle."[109] Yet, a SID can provide continuous twenty-four-hour location status rather than periodic location history and tracking.[110] Another form notes that tampering with the SID device constitutes a breach of contract and the consumer can be liable for costs associated with repairing the device.[111] To the extent not prohibited by law, an additional possible concern is companies' subsequent use of unilateral amendment provisions to revise asset collection technology provisions more strongly in their favor.[112]

With respect to federal data protection regulation that may be applicable to this issue, various financial institutions, including some automobile creditors, must comply with the Gramm Leach Bliley Act (GLBA) and its associated

---

[104] See *Disclosure Statement and Agreement for Installation of a GPS Vehicle Tracking/Starter Interrupt System*, GREATER CHICAGO, www.greater-chicago.com/Document/GPS%20Tracking%20Agreement .pdf (last visited Feb. 24, 2020) (providing detail about data collection and use).

[105] *Id.*

[106] *Nationwide Form, supra* note 101.

[107] *Id.*

[108] *Id.*

[109] *Id.*

[110] TRAX, *supra* note 64; *see also Select GPS, supra* note 80 (describing a "24/7/365" SID location feature).

[111] *Heritage Form, supra* note 100.

[112] Several sources of law discuss unilateral amendment provisions in financial transactions. *See, e.g.,* UNIF. CONSUMER CREDIT CODE § 3.205 (UNIF. LAW COMM'N 1974); Jim Hawkins, *Earned Wages Access and the End of Payday Lending*, B.U. L. REV. (forthcoming 2020), https://papers.ssrn.com/sol3/papers .cfm?abstract_id=3514856 (discussing the use of unilateral amendment provisions in fintech products); David Horton, *The Shadow Terms: Contract Procedure and Unilateral Amendments*, 57 UCLA L. REV. 605, 625 n.129 (2010) (discussing unilateral amendment provisions in financial transactions and noting that "the Truth in Lending Act and its implementing provision, Regulation Z, require creditors to disclose changes to fees and interest rates, but do not mention changes to procedural terms").

regulations.[113] The FTC has provided specific guidance to automobile creditors on the GLBA's Privacy Rule.[114] The Privacy Rule regulates the disclosure of "nonpublic personal information" (NPI), which, according to the FTC, includes "any information you get about an individual from a transaction involving . . . financial product(s) or service(s)," but does not include information that a financial institution has "a reasonable basis to believe is lawfully made 'publicly available.'"[115] Other GLBA rules establish various standards for the security of NPI, such as the development of a "comprehensive information security program."[116] It is unclear whether data gathered from asset collection technology would consistently qualify as NPI for purposes of GLBA rules since one could plausibly argue that consumer vehicles are operated on public roads and highways, and therefore SID data is public. To the extent that the GLBA rules do not apply, then any corresponding limitations may be inapplicable to the disclosure of asset collection technology data.[117]

Even if consumers were provided with more information regarding SID data collection and analytics in lending disclosure forms, many may not understand the implications of the disclosure. We are already inundated with a plethora of mandatory lending disclosure forms, and SID disclosure forms are likely one of many forms that we do not carefully review. A consumer complaint narrative submitted to the CFPB suggests that in some cases vehicle salespeople may not provide consumers with sufficient time to review lending documents, and may not verbally disclose the

---

[113]   *See* Fed. Trade Comm'n, The FTC's Privacy Rule and Auto Dealers: Frequently Asked Questions (2015), www.ftc.gov/system/files/documents/plain-language/bus64-ftcs-privacy-rule-and-auto-dealers-faqs.pdf; *see also* 15 U.S.C. §§ 6801–6827 (2020); FTC Privacy of Consumer Financial Information Rule (Privacy Rule), 16 C.F.R. § 313 (2018); FTC Standards for Safeguarding Customer Information Rule (Safeguard Rule), 16 C.F.R. § 314 (2018). The CFPB has also released principles applicable to covered consumer financial data sharing practices. However, it is unclear whether the principles would be applicable to the asset collection technology context. See Rory Van Loo , *Technology Regulation by Default: Platforms, Privacy, and the CFPB*, 2 Geo L. Tech. Rev. 531, 535 (2018); Rory Van Loo, *Digital Market Perfection*, 117 Mich. L. Rev. 815, 839 (2019) (critiquing the CFPB's data principles); *CFPB Outlines Principles for Consumer-Authorized Financial Data Sharing and Aggregation*, Consumer Fin. Prot. Bureau (Oct. 18, 2017), www.consumerfinance.gov/about-us/newsroom/cfpb-outlines-principles-consumer-authorized-financial-data-sharing-and-aggregation/ (stating that the CFPB's principles are aimed at "protecting consumers when they authorize third party companies to access their financial data to provide certain financial products and service"); Consumer Fin. Prot. Bureau, Consumer Protection Principles: Consumer-Authorized Financial Data Sharing and Aggregation (2017), http://files.consumerfinance.gov/f/documents/cfpb_consumer-protection-principles_data-aggregation.pdf.
[114]   *See* Fed. Trade Comm'n, *supra* note 113.
[115]   Fed. Trade Comm'n, How to Comply with the Privacy of Consumer Financial Information Rule of the Gramm-Leach-Bliley Act 4–5 (2002), www.ftc.gov/system/files/documents/plain-language/bus67-how-comply-privacy-consumer-financial-information-rule-gramm-leach-bliley-act.pdf; *see also* 16 C.F.R. § 313.3(n) (defining NPI).
[116]   16 C.F.R. § 314.3(a); *id.* § 314.2(b) (defining "customer information" as NPI).
[117]   For instance, Daniel Solove and Paul Schwartz contend that under the GLBA, "[f]inancial institutions can share personal information with nonaffiliated companies only if they first provide individuals with the ability to opt out of the disclosure." Daniel J. Solove & Paul M. Schwartz , Consumer Privacy and Data Protection 88–92 (2015); *see also* 15 U.S.C. § 6802(b).

presence of a SID in a vehicle even when the consumer asks directly.[118] Another CFPB complaint narrative indicates that vehicle salespeople may describe devices with GPS features as being beneficial in that they help borrowers keep track of minors who drive the vehicle without informing the borrower that lenders can use the device's capabilities to repossess the vehicle.[119] Similarly, in a 2005 bankruptcy case, a consumer alleged that when she purchased the vehicle, she thought the SID was an anti-theft device installed in the vehicle for her benefit, and only discovered that she would need monthly SID codes from the lender to operate the vehicle after the first payment was due.[120] Other CFPB consumer complaints also suggest that consumers may be unaware of the possible consequences or presence of an SID until after the creditor disables the vehicle.[121] Dealers may also surreptitiously install tracking devices in our vehicles without obtaining prior consent, as evidenced by a lawsuit brought by Florida's department of legal affairs of the office of the attorney general against an automobile lender.[122] The FTC has sent civil investigative demands to at least two auto finance companies regarding their use of SIDS.[123]

PRE-DEFAULT PRIVACY AND DIGITAL DOMINATION HARMS

Asset collection technology may offer some benefits to both consumers and lenders. It may decrease repossession expenses, permit consumers to immediately cure defaults by making payments, allow consumers quick access to their vehicles after a cured default, and increase subprime consumers' "access to credit."[124] It could also reduce collateral depreciation associated with subprime consumers' use of the vehicle.[125] Vehicle location tracking could also aid consumers in proving possible misconduct by dealers and repossession companies.[126] However, there are

[118] *See Consumer Complaint No. 1387772*, CONSUMER FIN. PROT. BUREAU (May 21, 2015), www .consumerfinance.gov/data-research/consumer-complaints/search/detail/1387772.

[119] *See Consumer Complaint No. 2059131*, CONSUMER FIN. PROT. BUREAU (Aug. 11, 2016), www .consumerfinance.gov/data-research/consumer-complaints/search/detail/2059131.

[120] *See* Hampton v. Yam's Choice Plus Autos, Inc. (*In re* Hampton), 319 B.R. 163, 166–67 (Bankr. E.D. Ark. 2005).

[121] *See Consumer Complaint No. 2586071*, CONSUMER FIN. PROT. BUREAU (July 26, 2017), www .consumerfinance.gov/data-research/consumer-complaints/search/detail/2586071;   *Consumer Complaint No. 2391282*, CONSUMER FIN. PROT. BUREAU (Mar. 16, 2017), www .consumerfinance.gov/data-research/consumer-complaints/search/detail/2391282.

[122] State v. Beach Blvd Auto. Fin., Inc., 139 So. 3d 380, 383 (Fla. Dist. Ct. App. 2014). *See generally* Leah Altaras, *Follow That Car! Legal Issues Arising from Installation of Tracking Devices in Leased Consumer Goods and Equipment*, 3 SHIDLER J.L. COM. & TECH. 8 (2007).

[123] CREDIT ACCEPTANCE, 2017 ANNUAL REPORT add. at 12 (2017), www.ir.creditacceptance.com/static-files /def41d4d-3d83-483d-8039-8cd2dc35ddf3; Matt Scully, *FTC Looks for Abuses in Auto Lenders' Use of Kill Switches*, BLOOMBERG, www.bloomberg.com/news/articles/2017-02-17/u-s-regulator-looks-for-abuses-in-auto-lenders-repo-gadgets (last updated Feb. 17, 2017).

[124] Povich, *supra* note 60.

[125] RUSCH & SEPINUCK, *supra* note 14, at 158.

[126] *See* Justin Wilfon, *Woman Says Dealership Was Supposed to Repair Truck, but She Tracked It to Employee's Home*, WSB-TV (Feb. 24, 2020, 11:15 PM), www.wsbtv.com/news/local/woman-says-

significant privacy and digital domination harms that can result from companies' use of asset collection technology. These harms can arise both before and after a consumer's default. This section explores pre-default harms.

Vehicle lenders and dealers have historically had information about us, including our home and workplace addresses. Asset collection technology and IoT devices expand the volume, types, and quality of data these entities can now collect. Today's vehicles have been transformed into "data harvesting" tools. Almost every vehicle component is a possible data generator, including the wheels, seatbelts, windshield wipers, blinkers, brakes, engine, and more.[127] Recall from earlier discussions in this chapter the various types of data and driving reports about users that asset collection technology can collect and produce. For instance, now, data about our daily frequent locations and driving habits (including odometer and accelerator readings and duration of time spent parked and in motion), among other things, are also being collected. Starter-interrupt device sellers, car dealers, lenders, and other companies all potentially have access to this wealth of data. Powerful and potentially accurate inferences about us and our families could be made using these data. These inferences can be used to shape our behaviors and impact how companies treat us and the opportunities we receive.

A survey conducted by the AAA Foundation for Traffic Safety concluded that in 2016, consumers drove approximately 31.5 miles daily.[128] In 2018, the U.S. Department of Transportation Federal Highway Administration reported that on average consumers drive 13,476 miles per year.[129] In light of the remarkable amounts of time we spend in our vehicles each day, the combination of newly connected vehicles, asset collection technology, and vehicle infotainment systems allow companies to amass vast quantities of data about us and our daily behaviors.

By having access to the vehicle location history data asset collection technology collects, a lender or dealer could determine if a debtor is no longer frequently driving to their place of employment during regular business hours.[130] Thus, location history can conceivably disclose our employment status, along with other sensitive information, and therefore our capacity to make loan payments. Location data can also be used to deduce our purchasing and entertainment preferences. Existing location data companies already insert software into mobile apps to continuously track every place

---

dealership-was-supposed-repair-car-she-tracked-it-employees-home/OEID7V575ZBI
DCY4E4YZ2SZ4HM/.

[127] Christina Rogers, *What Your Car Knows About You*, WALL ST. J. (Aug. 18, 2018, 12:01 AM), www .wsj.com/articles/what-your-car-knows-about-you-1534564861?redirect=amp#click=https://t.co/ vI4H9mCrmF.

[128] AAA FOUND. FOR TRAFFIC SAFETY, AMERICAN DRIVING SURVEY, 2015–2016 (2018), https://aaafoundation .org/wp-content/uploads/2018/02/18-0019_AAAFTS-ADS-Research-Brief.pdf.

[129] *See Average Annual Miles Per Driver by Age Group*, U.S. DEP'T TRANSP., FED. HIGHWAY ADMIN., www .fhwa.dot.gov/ohim/onh00/bar8.htm (last modified Mar. 29, 2018).

[130] Corkery & Silver-Greenberg, *supra* note 67.

we visit daily,[131] and ultra-wideband communications technology allows them to do so with unparalleled precision.[132] The possibility of combining vehicle location data with smartphone location data could reveal even more intimate details about us.[133] Despite the frequency with which companies collect our location data, a recent empirical study evaluating consumer perceptions of location data determined that consumers have strong privacy expectations even in public spaces and "[m]isleading labels in device and system interfaces may . . . deceive users about underlying data practices."[134]

Several Supreme Court cases have addressed the sensitive nature of location data in the Fourth Amendment context. In *United States v. Jones*, concurring justices stated that "the use of longer term GPS monitoring . . . impinges on expectations of privacy."[135] In *Carpenter v. United States*, the court acknowledged "that individuals have a reasonable expectation of privacy in the whole of their physical movements."[136] Thus, there is a reasonable expectation of privacy in location data held by third parties in certain contexts. Although *Carpenter* involved the detailed collection of cell phone location data and raised Fourth Amendment concerns, the case's holding may have important implications in the commercial law context as companies are increasingly collecting and processing location data generated from our use of IoT devices and asset collection technology.

Starter-interrupt devices enable lenders, dealers, and other third parties to track our location throughout the life of the vehicle loan and engage in the type of "longer term GPS monitoring" referenced in *United States v. Jones*.[137] One model SID disclosure form requires the consumer to explicitly acknowledge that the SID must remain on the vehicle for the duration of the loan period established by the retail

---

[131]   Stuart A. Thompson & Charlie Warzel, Opinion, *Twelve Million Phones, One Dataset, Zero Privacy*, N.Y. TIMES (Dec. 19, 2019), www.nytimes.com/interactive/2019/12/19/opinion/location-tracking-cell-phone.html.

[132]   Colleen Josephson & Yan Shvartzshnaider, *Every Move You Make, I'll be Watching You: Privacy Implications of the Apple U1 Chip and Ultra-Wideband*, FREEDOM TO TINKER (Dec. 21, 2019), https://freedom-to-tinker.com/2019/12/21/every-move-you-make-ill-be-watching-you-privacy-implications-of-the-apple-u1-chip-and-ultra-wideband/; *see also* Stephen Shankland, *Apple Built UWB into the iPhone 11. Here's What You Need to Know (FAQ)*, CNET (Sept. 14, 2019, 5:00 AM), www.cnet.com/news/apple-built-uwb-into-the-iphone-11-heres-what-you-need-to-know-faq/.

[133]   *But see* Jon Henley, *Denmark Frees 32 Inmates over Flaws in Phone Geolocation Evidence*, GUARDIAN (Sept. 12, 2019, 6:13 AM), www.theguardian.com/world/2019/sep/12/denmark-frees-32-inmates-over-flawed-geolocation-revelations (noting issues "about the reliability of geolocation data obtained from mobile phone operators"); Yuan Yang et al. *China, Coronavirus and Surveillance: The Messy Reality of Personal Data*, FIN. TIMES (Apr. 1, 2020), www.ft.com/content/760142e6-740e-11ea-95fe-fcd274e920ca (noting that *"location data is not always accurate* depending on cell tower coverage").

[134]   *See* Kirsten Martin & Helen Nissenbaum, *What Is It About Location?*, 35 BERKELEY TECH. L.J. 251, 308 (2020).

[135]   United States v. Jones, 565 U.S. 400, 430 (2012) (Alito, J., concurring).

[136]   Carpenter v. United States, 138 S. Ct. 2206, 2217 (2018).

[137]   *Jones,* 565 U.S. at 430 (Alito, J., concurring).

installment contract.[138] The average duration of a vehicle loan is over sixty-nine months.[139] In contrast, the average automobile loan length was forty-six to fifty-two months in the 1980s.[140] Today, location data could be collected daily for five years or more. Since subprime lenders can require the installation of SIDs in a consumer's vehicle as a condition of the loan on a take-it-or-leave-it basis, subprime consumers have no choice but to agree to the installation of the device in order to obtain a vehicle. For many of us, vehicles are a crucial means of transportation to places of employment and, like smartphones, are "indispensable to participation in modern society."[141] Thus, a subprime consumer's "consent" to the installation of a SID and the collection of associated data may not be voluntarily provided. Additionally, companies can also abuse SIDs to disable vehicles for reasons that are unrelated to a default under the lending agreement. For instance, in *Hanes v. Darar*, the dealer refused to accept the consumer's monthly payment and disabled the consumer's vehicle after the consumer had a verbal altercation with the dealer's wife.[142]

Vehicle dealers can use geofencing technology to send real-time targeted advertisements to our smartphones when we are perusing competitor vehicle dealers' lots.[143] In addition to targeted advertisements, geofencing can now be used for more insidious purposes. Geofencing allows companies to wield significant control over our location and the location of our vehicles. Recall that a geofencing feature (coupled with a disablement mechanism) gives lenders the ability to disable a vehicle when it enters or exits an area that it finds unacceptable. Once a lender receives a geofence violation alert, the lender has the capacity to restrict the driver's and the vehicle's mobility. This geofencing power could be exercised both before and after a default. Thus, creditors have a disproportionate amount of influence over the geographic area in which vulnerable groups of debtors may travel, thereby extending their dominance over these consumers and their vehicles post transaction. Consider that a lender reportedly disabled the vehicle of a domestic violence victim

---

[138] *See GPS Locator Device Acknowledgement*, PINNACLE FIN. GROUP, www.pinfingroup.com/pdf/ Payment_Device_Acknowledgment.pdf (last visited Dec. 20, 2019) ("I understand that keeping the Device in my vehicle over the life of my contract is a condition of the extension of credit to me."); *see also Starter Interrupt and Locator Device Acknowledgement*, PINNACLE FIN. GROUP, www .pinfingroup.com/pdf/GPS_Customer_Acknowledgement.pdf (last visited Feb. 24, 2020).

[139] *See* Phil LeBeau, *A $523 Monthly Payment Is the New Standard for Car Buyers*, CNBC, www .cnbc.com/2018/05/31/a-523-monthly-payment-is-the-new-standard-for-car-buyers.html (last updated May 31, 2018); Matt Tatham, *Sticker Shock Is Real: Car Payments Hit a Record High!*, EXPERIAN (June 11, 2018), www.experian.com/blogs/ask-experian/sticker-shock-is-real-car-payments-hit -a-record-high/.

[140] Tatham, *supra* note 139.

[141] *Carpenter*, 138 S. Ct. at 2210.

[142] Hanes v. Darar, No. COA11-627, 2012 N.C. App. LEXIS 345, at *2 (N.C. Ct. App. Mar. 6, 2012).

[143] Justin Croxton, *Case Study: How a Luxury Dealership Won with Geofencing Marketing*, DEALER MARKETING MAG. (Apr. 6, 2018), www.dealermarketing.com/case-study-how-a-luxury-dealership-won -with-geofencing-marketing/; Charles Mazzini, *The Five Ws (and One H) of Geofence Marketing*, FORBES (Dec. 13, 2019, 6:00 AM), www.forbes.com/sites/forbesagencycouncil/2019/12/13/the-five-ws- and-one-h-of-geofence-marketing/#4ee0ed6749aa.

who drove her vehicle outside of the lender's established geofence zone to escape her abusive spouse.[144] Asset collection technology geofencing and disablement capabilities can enable "geoslavery" – a term used by Jerome Dobson and Peter Fisher to describe the dangers of continuous location surveillance, which allows companies to exercise coercive control over our movements and activities.[145]

It is also important to note that the consumer harms described earlier are more problematic than those that might arise in secured transactions solely between corporate entities. Secured lenders have historically used various contractual provisions to preserve their interests in corporate debtors' collateral. Some companies have had their operations remotely disabled or paralyzed during contractual disputes with other entities.[146] If a lender requires a corporate debtor to accept the installation of asset collection technology in its collateral, the constant location tracking of this collateral is likely less pernicious than the personal privacy invasions that vulnerable consumers suffer when they are required to consent to the lender's use of such technology. When compared to vulnerable groups of subprime borrowers, most corporate entities are in a better position as debtors to negotiate with, and protect their interests against, secured lenders. Corporate entities likely have more resources to legally challenge the validity of any such remote disablement.

Although less problematic than the concerns noted earlier, the payment reminder feature of SIDs is also potentially invasive and provides an additional method through which lenders can continue to exert control post transaction before a default. Recall that asset collection technology devices can send payment reminder notifications to debtors. In a CFPB consumer complaint narrative, one consumer who accepted the installation of an asset collection device in their vehicle alleged harassment after being inundated with payment alert reminders, emails, phone calls, and text messages reminding the consumer of payment deadlines.[147] The cost of receiving frequent phone calls and text messages is also likely borne by the consumer. In another complaint to the CFPB, a consumer reported that timely payments confirmed by the consumer's bank were sent to the lender, but the lender still disabled the consumer's vehicle for lack of payment.[148] Consumers may bear the cost of lender inaccuracies and payment disputes. Without the use of asset collection technology, a lender who has misplaced a consumer's monthly payment would not have the ability to quickly disable the vehicle's operations or immediately force the

---

[144] Clifford Atiyeh, *Subprime Blues: How Auto Lenders Can Track and Disable Your Vehicle*, CAR & DRIVER (Sept. 30, 2014), www.caranddriver.com/news/a15361238/subprime-blues-how-auto-lenders-can-track-and-disable-your-vehicle/.

[145] Jerome E. Dobson & Peter F. Fisher, *Geoslavery*, IEEE TECH. & SOC'Y MAG. 47, 47–48 (2003), https://pdfs.semanticscholar.org/c0e1/0fa50dfb89b571e7e9dd1817f165d50f4a0a.pdf.

[146] Esther C. Roditti, *Is Self-Help a Lawful Contract Remedy?*, 21 RUTGERS COMPUTER & TECH. L.J. 431 (1995).

[147] *Consumer Complaint No. 2736951, supra* note 102.

[148] *Consumer Complaint No. 2830855*, CONSUMER FIN. PROT. BUREAU (Mar. 2, 2018), www .consumerfinance.gov/data-research/consumer-complaints/search/detail/2830855.

consumer to make another payment (which may not be due under the loan agreement) to operate the vehicle. Limitation of liability clauses in credit contracts and state law requirements may limit the amount of damages that consumers may receive when a lender breaches the lending agreement.[149]

The installation of a SID with GPS capabilities in a vehicle can negatively impact the functionality of other vehicle components. One CFPB consumer complaint narrative describes how after a contractually required tracking device was installed in the consumer's vehicle, the electrical components of the vehicle malfunctioned, creating safety concerns for several months that could not be resolved by the dealer.[150] The consumer reported incurring multiple rental, towing, taxi, and repair costs, and daily inconveniences, including missing work due to vehicle defects and safety issues caused by installation of the tracking device.[151] The complaint narrative suggests that the consumer was still required to make payments on the vehicle, and the vehicle may have been repossessed by the lender.[152] Starter-interrupt device consumer lending disclosure forms can require subprime consumers to make their vehicles available in the event that the SID needs repairs.[153] Additionally, the firmware of some SIDs can be upgraded "over the air."[154] To the extent that these upgrades occur after the device is installed in a vehicle, the consumer may have purchased the vehicle but lacks the ability to regulate upgrades to a device that can be used to control the vehicle's operations.

Companies frequently monetize consumer-generated data. As we will discuss in Chapter 7, unless specifically prohibited by law, consumer data can be transferred and disclosed to third parties in various corporate transactions. Data transfers in corporate transactions can also occur in the asset collection technology context as well. For instance, cooperative agreements involving dealers, creditors, and SID manufacturers could facilitate the transfer and disclosure of the consumer data asset collection technology and IoT devices collect. These transfers can occur before, and be unrelated to, a consumer's default under a lending agreement. Additionally, these data, along with driving behavior reports, could be sold to mapping companies that offer real-time traffic reports. The manufacturer of one SID advertises that users

---

[149] *See* N.C. Gen. Stat. Ann. § 25A-25(a) (West 2020) (limiting consumer recovery in "consumer credit sale" transactions to "amounts paid by the buyer under the contract"); *see also* Hanes v. Darar, No. COA11-627, 2012 N.C. App. LEXIS 345, at *10–11 (N.C. Ct. App. Mar. 6, 2012). *But see* U.C.C. § 2-719(3) (Am. Law Inst. & Unif. Law Comm'n 2017) ("Limitation of consequential damages for injury to the person in the case of consumer goods is prima facie unconscionable.").

[150] *Consumer Complaint No. 2101580,* Consumer Fin. Prot. Bureau (Sept. 8, 2016), www .consumerfinance.gov/data-research/consumer-complaints/search/detail/2101580.

[151] *Id.*

[152] *See id.*

[153] *Buyer's Agreement for Installation and Disclosure of GPS Device,* People's Credit, www .peoplescredit.com/fileserver1/peoplescredit/eforms/E278A1AD-ECE9-A1E9-0C7B-E302E82D849A.pdf (last visited Dec. 20, 2019); *see also Customer Agreement and Disclosure Statement for Installation of Starter Interrupt/GPS Device, supra* note 101.

[154] *See 3.5G Locate/Recover-S, supra* note 79; *Vehicle Trackers, supra* note 79.

of its product can share vehicle location data with any party of their choosing via email or phone.[155] The constant threat of hacking of the databases and cloud systems in which these data are likely stored is also problematic.

Lastly, automobile recovery companies and their agents have used ALPR to collect data on passing motorists.[156] This includes collecting the license plates, images, location, date, and time of vehicles for motorists that have made timely payment to lenders as well as those that do not have a contractual relationship with an automobile creditor.[157] This type of surreptitious and hidden surveillance diminishes our ability to control what happens to information about us and decreases our already limited capacity to monitor and understand the types of data multiple entities collect about us. Companies' deep understanding of our limited ability to monitor and understand their data practices incentivizes companies to be less accountable with our data.

POST-DEFAULT PRIVACY AND DIGITAL DOMINATION HARMS

The very nature of a consumer lending transaction facilitates an ongoing relationship between debtors and creditors. Asset collection technology and IoT devices allow lenders to expand their reach and exercise their power in new ways after a consumer default. Automobile creditors can frequently control a SID installed in a vehicle through a mobile app. These SID users can locate and identify subprime consumers and disable consumers' vehicles for nonpayment with ease by using their smartphones and other web application services that accompany a SID. The *New York Times* reports that a credit union representative disabled a consumer's car by using SID technology on his mobile phone while shopping in Walmart.[158]

One might posit that a lender's use of asset collection technology is no different from a scenario in which a lender uses a repossession agent to repossess a vehicle in accordance with the terms of a lending agreement, and as a result, there are no harms. One response to this critique is that asset collection technology allows creditors to virtually and permanently place debt collectors and repossession agents in subprime borrowers' vehicles, and continuously collect data about such debtors that a traditional repossession person would have a difficult, if not impossible, time obtaining on a consistent basis.[159] A lender has the capacity to govern and digitally restrain a consumer's daily activities with a simple click of a button. Given the vast amount of time consumers spend in their vehicles per year, users of SIDs can exert a remarkable degree of control over subprime consumers' lives post default. It is the

---

[155] *See Controllt, supra* note 70.

[156] *See* Bartley, *supra* note 95.

[157] *See* Todd C. Frankel, *A Surprise, Data-Driven Return of the Repo Man*, Press Herald (May 15, 2018), www.pressherald.com/2018/05/15/a-surprise-data-driven-return-of-the-repo-man/.

[158] Corkery & Silver-Greenberg, *supra* note 67.

[159] *Id.*

creditor, rather than the consumer, who retains the ultimate control over the vehicle's operations. After a default, creditors operating a SID may allow a non-paying consumer to operate a vehicle for a limited twenty-four-hour period for some emergencies.[160] This is potentially beneficial to consumers. However, unless state law requires otherwise, it is the creditor who determines what constitutes an emergency and whether to grant the request. This is further evidence of vulnerable consumers' decreasing dominion and autonomy with respect to their vehicles and lives.

The "repo mode tool" of one SID company allows creditors to provide repossession agents with device access and generate location alerts that are shared with these agents "every 5 minutes for up to 72 hours."[161] The website of another SID seller suggests that some of its products are also "right to cure compliant."[162] This is likely an attempt to comply with state laws that require companies to allow us to cure defaults within a statutorily defined time period prior to exercising the right of repossession.[163] Lenders may not always provide consumers with a sufficient opportunity to cure payment delinquencies prior to disabling a vehicle. Lenders have disabled consumers' vehicles using SIDs after even just three days of missed payments.[164]

There have been several reports of consumers who have experienced serious daily and lifestyle interruptions when their vehicles have been remotely disabled. Manufacturers of SIDs suggest that their installed devices cannot turn off a car while it is being driven by a consumer.[165] Yet, there have been reports of consumers who have had their cars disabled for nonpayment by auto lenders while the car is in motion or at a stoplight.[166] Other consumers have reported that they were unable to drive minors to educational institutions or attend doctors' appointments after their vehicles were disabled and did not receive pre-disablement notifications.[167]

---

[160]   *See id.*

[161]   *DefenderGPS, supra* note 70.

[162]   *Passtime Elite: GPS + Automated Collection Technology,* PassTime https://passtimegps.com/elite/ (last visited Aug. 17, 2018).

[163]   Unif. Consumer Credit Code § 5.111 (Unif. Law Comm'n)("[A]fter a default consisting only of the consumer's failure to make a required payment, a creditor, because of that default, may neither accelerate maturity of the unpaid balance of the obligation, nor take possession of or otherwise enforce a security interest in goods that are collateral until 20 days after a notice of the consumer's right to cure (Section 5.110) is given."); *see also* Colo. Rev. Stat. Ann. § 5-5-111 (West 2019); Kan. Stat. Ann. § 16a-5-111 (West 2019); S.C. Code Ann. § 37-5-111 (2019).

[164]   Corkery & Silver-Greenberg, *supra* note 67. A CFPB complaint narrative describes an instance in which a consumer allegedly had a vehicle repossessed twice after being only three days late on payments. *Consumer Complaint No. 2676559,* Consumer Fin. Prot. Bureau (Sept. 17, 2017), www .consumerfinance.gov/data-research/consumer-complaints/search/detail/2676559. A device with GPS tracking capabilities was installed on the vehicle as a condition of the loan. *Id.*

[165]   Sean Patrick Farrell, *The Remote Repo Man,* N.Y. Times (Sept. 24, 2014), www.nytimes.com/video/ business/100000003095109/the-remote-repo-man.html.

[166]   *Id.; see also* Corkery & Silver-Greenberg, *supra* note 67.

[167]   Corkery & Silver-Greenberg, *supra* note 67.

Similarly, in *In re Horace*, a bankruptcy case involving a SID, the consumer alleged that the device was used to disable the vehicle on several occasions, including when she was at a medical appointment after surgery.[168]

Automobile repossession companies have amassed hundreds of license plate records using ALPR technology.[169] Recall that access to these data can also be obtained from ALPR vendors. These data can be used after consumers' default to more easily enable vehicle repossessions. News reports suggest that ALPR data and technology have generated a boom in the repossession industry.[170] One ALPR vendor boasts that its ALPR data "has helped lenders recover over $5 billion in assets" and can "reduce days to recovery by 50%."[171] The company's network reportedly "grows by over 160 million [license plate] sightings every month."[172]

As with SID data, lenders and repossession companies with access to ALPR data can discover intimate details about our lives. Data captured by ALPR technology could be used to reveal or infer our political and religious affiliation, social connections, and marital, familial, health, and employment status, among other things.[173] Lenders and repossession companies can use ALPR and SID data to paint a detailed history of us and our vehicles' whereabouts and possibly predict when we may become delinquent on payments, and whether we are likely to make additional payments after an initial default. Automated license plate reader technology can also be used to target low-income and racial minority neighborhoods for data collection, surveillance, and collateral repossession.[174] Research suggests that even mundane data generated from our online digital footprint, such as the websites we access, "equal or exceed the information content of credit bureau (FICO) scores" and could be used to predict default rates.[175] Automated license plate reader technology and data combined with SIDs and IoT devices further skew the default and repossession process in favor of lenders.

---

[168]   *In re* Horace, No. 14-30103, 2015 WL 5145576, at *6–8 (Bankr. N.D. Ohio Aug. 28, 2015).

[169]   Steve Orr, *License Plate Data Is Big Business*, USA TODAY, www.usatoday.com/story/news/nation/2014/11/02/license-plate-data-is-big-business/18370791/ (last updated Nov. 2, 2014, 5:13 PM).

[170]   Frankel, *supra* note 157; Kaveh Waddell, *How License-Plate Readers Have Helped Police and Lenders Target the Poor*, ATLANTIC (Apr. 22, 2016), www.theatlantic.com/technology/archive/2016/04/how-license-plate-readers-have-helped-police-and-lenders-target-the-poor/479436/.

[171]   *Smart Recovery*, DIGITAL RECOGNITION NETWORK, https://drndata.com/products/smart-recovery/ (last visited Dec. 20, 2019).

[172]   *Id.*

[173]   *See* Randy L. Dryer & S. Shane Stroud, *Automatic License Plate Readers: An Effective Law Enforcement Tool or Big Brother's Latest Instrument of Mass Surveillance? Some Suggestions for Legislative Action*, 55 JURIMETRICS J. 225, 227 (2015).

[174]   Waddell, *supra* note 170.

[175]   Tobias Berg et al., *On the Rise of the FinTechs – Credit Scoring Using Digital Footprints* 1 (Fed. Deposit Ins. Corp., Ctr. for Fin. Research, Working Paper No. 4, 2018), www.fdic.gov/bank/analytical/cfr/2018/wp2018/cfr-wp2018-04.pdf.

EXPANDING POST-TRANSACTION CONTROL

As the IoT becomes more ubiquitous and asset collection technology continues to evolve, there may be new technological developments that make it much easier for creditors to monitor, disable, and control vehicles and other IoT devices after an event of default. Imagine a future where, after a consumer defaults on a vehicle loan, the creditor's collection agent or employee can disable the vehicle's ignition, operate the vehicle's smart lock components to prevent the consumer from accessing the vehicle, or instruct the vehicle to drive directly to the dealership or a repossession garage, simply by verbally sending a request to an internet-connected smart speaker, assistant, robot, or watch.

Companies' increasing reach post transaction is not just limited to subprime borrowers. With the IoT's rise, companies' ability to observe and control us and our IoT devices post transaction is expanding. Recall from Chapter 5 that the maker of an IoT "garage door opener" remotely disabled a consumer's device in response to the user's negative review of its product.[176] Similarly, recall that Tesla remotely disabled the autopilot feature in a customer's vehicle after the vehicle was sold.[177] Also consider that insurance companies have offered consumers discounts in exchange for consumers agreeing to download mobile apps that can connect to their IoT vehicles or install telematics devices in their vehicles, which can track their location and collect various forms of data.[178] Insurance companies' collection of data from these devices, related mobile apps, and our vehicles raises several problems, including cybersecurity issues as well as concerns about how collected data will be used against us. These problems are significant, but perhaps distinct from the asset collection technology context in which the lender has the capacity to not only collect data about the borrower, but also to remotely disable the vehicle.

To the extent that surveillance insurance discount programs are offered to low-income borrowers, this could mean that their movements are tracked by both their vehicle lender and their insurance company. More economically advantaged

---

[176] Rob Price, *The Maker of an Internet-Connected Garage Door Disabled a Customer's Device over a Bad Review*, Bus. Insider (Apr. 5, 2017, 3:51 AM), www.businessinsider.com/iot-garage-door-opener-garadget-kills-customers-device-bad-amazon-review-2017-4.

[177] Jason Torchinsky, *Tesla Remotely Removes Autopilot Features from Customer's Used Tesla Without Any Notice*, Jalopnik (Feb. 6, 2020, 4:10 PM), https://jalopnik.com/tesla-remotely-removes-autopilot-features-from-customer-1841472617.

[178] John M. Vincent & Cherise Threewit, *How Do Those Car Insurance Tracking Devices Work?* US News (Feb. 26, 2018), https://cars.usnews.com/cars-trucks/car-insurance/how-do-those-car-insurance-tracking-devices-work; Mike Juang, *A New Kind of Auto Insurance Technology Can Lead to Lower Premiums, but It Tracks Your Every Move*, CNBC (Oct. 6, 2018, 2:00 PM), www.cnbc.com/2018/10/05/new-kind-of-auto-insurance-can-be-cheaper-but-tracks-your-every-move.html; Julie Jargon, *The Terror of Teen Drivers: Parents Track Their Kids Without Being in the Car*, Wall St. J. (Mar. 3, 2020), www.wsj.com/articles/the-terror-of-teen-drivers-parents-track-their-kids-without-being-in-the-car-11583231401; Comments from the Future of Privacy Forum to the Fed. Trade Comm'n & U.S. Dep't of Transp. (May 1, 2017), https://fpf.org/wp-content/uploads/2017/05/Future-of-Privacy-Forum-Comments-FTC-NHTSA-Workshop.pdf.

borrowers may have more bargaining power in transactions with their insurance companies, and could be more willing to forego discounts to avoid insurance companies' surveillance. Also, consider that consumers who live in racial minority neighborhoods are subject to higher vehicle insurance premiums.[179] Historically marginalized consumers could also be enticed to accept vehicle insurance companies' surveillance in an effort to mitigate discrimination.[180] Auto insurance companies' surveillance activities also highlight the unequal access to privacy problem, as low-income and historically marginalized borrowers could be more willing to accept insurance companies' surveillance in exchange for discounts. Recall that a somewhat similar concern related to unequal access to privacy and security also arises when dealers and lenders require subprime borrowers to accept the installation of SIDs in their vehicles as part of a loan transaction.

Additionally, it may ultimately become possible for asset collection technology to be used not only in subprime lending transactions involving vehicles, but also more widely in other transactions in which we purchase, rent, or lease IoT devices and obtain financing. Companies already use radio frequency identification to tag and locate various objects and devices in supply chain, retail, storage, and production processes.[181] Consider that an FTC enforcement action against several companies, including a software developer that provided asset collection technology with remote disablement features to rent-to-own companies, appears to have been primarily concerned with the surreptitious monitoring features of the software installed on consumers' rent-to-own computers rather than its asset collection capabilities.[182] The FTC's complaint alleging substantial injury to consumers based on hidden data collection suggested that the remote disablement features of the software provided effective alternative methods for collection that rendered the surveillance features unnecessary.[183]

Unless clearly prohibited by law, IoT refrigerators, stoves, televisions, thermostats, and other devices purchased or leased on credit could be embedded with various forms of asset collection technology and used by creditors to extend their control

[179] Julia Angwin et. al, *Minority Neighborhoods Pay Higher Car Insurance Premiums than White Areas with the Same Risk*, ProPublica (Apr. 5, 2017), www.propublica.org/article/minority-neighborhoods-higher-car-insurance-premiums-white-areas-same-risk.

[180] Edwin Lombard III, *Telematics: A Tool to Curb Auto Insurance Discrimination*, Capitol Wkly. (Feb. 18, 2020), https://capitolweekly.net/telematics-a-tool-to-curb-auto-insurance-discrimination/.

[181] Christopher G. Bradley, *Disrupting Secured Transactions*, 56 Hous. L. Rev. 965, 971–72, 988–89 (2019).

[182] *See* Complaint, *In re* Designerware, LLC, No. 112-3151 (F.T.C. Apr. 11, 2013), www.ftc.gov/sites/default/files/documents/cases/2013/04/130415designerwarecmpt.pdf [hereinafter Designerware Complaint]; Complaint, *In re* Aaron's Inc., No. 122-3264 (F.T.C. Mar. 10, 2014), www.ftc.gov/system/files/documents/cases/140311aaronscmpt.pdf; Press Release, Fed. Trade Comm'n, FTC Halts Computer Spying (Sept. 25, 2012), www.ftc.gov/news-events/press-releases/2012/09/ftc-halts-computer-spying.

[183] Designerware Complaint, *supra* note 182. *See also*, Decision & Order, *In re* Aaron's Inc., No. 122-3264 (F.T.C. 2014), www.ftc.gov/system/files/documents/cases/140311aaronsdo.pdf.

over us and these devices.[184] For instance, what if a consumer fails to make payment on a financed IoT refrigerator, and the purchase money creditor is allowed to remotely disable the refrigerator until payment is received? In such a setting, ordinary private creditors will have the power to behave in the same manner as utility providers that have historically easily turned utilities on and off based on our payment status. Additionally, the data generated by quickly depreciating and lower-cost IoT devices could become more valuable to PMSI lenders than the devices themselves. If this does happen, it could incentivize a large number of PMSI lenders to insist on the installation of asset collection technology systems in IoT devices, or require device owners to share data collected by IoT devices, or provide discounts to device owners to entice them to willingly share IoT device data.

Lastly, more devices with so-called consumer "kill switch" capabilities (somewhat akin to the remote disablement features of asset collection technology) are coming to the market.[185] These devices include smart displays with speaker capabilities, smartphones, and laptops and are aimed at empowering consumers to secure stolen devices, disable specific device features, and prevent data acquisition.[186] As of the date of writing it is not entirely clear if all of the companies designing devices with kill switch features will have the capacity to remotely operate these features as well. It is also unclear if these devices will be designed to sufficiently guard against unauthorized third-party (for example, hackers) manipulation of the kill switch features.

A REPOSSESSION UNDER THE LAW

As we have discussed, asset collection technology streamlines the repossession process. A lender that uses asset collection technology to locate and physically acquire a vehicle through its repossession agent has exercised its right of repossession. However, an important legal issue in dispute in some jurisdictions is whether a lender's use of asset collection technology to remotely disable (rather than physically repossess) a vehicle qualifies as a repossession without a breach of the peace under state law.

Recall that Article 9 and other state and federal laws govern consumer lending transactions. Under Article 9, a lender may disable "equipment" after default, but

---

[184]   *See* CAL. CIV. CODE § 1799.100 (West 2019). Federal regulation and state law also limit the creation of non-purchase money security interests in household goods, such as appliances. 16 C.F.R. § 444.1 (2018); W. VA. CODE ANN. § 46A-4-109(3) (West 2019).

[185]   Katharine Schwab, *The Hardware Trend Google and Apple Are Throwing Their Weight Behind*, FAST COMPANY (May 15, 2019), www.fastcompany.com/90349731/the-hardware-trend-google-amazon-and-apple-are-throwing-their-weight-behind.

[186]   *See id.; see also Hardware Kill Switches*, PURISM, https://puri.sm/learn/hardware-kill-switches/ (last visited Mar. 2, 2020); Marc Saltzman, *Webcams Are Infiltrating Your Home. Here's How to Secure Those on Your Computers*, USA TODAY,www.usatoday.com/story/tech/columnist/2020/02/15/webcam-security-heres-some-simple-tips-protect-your-privacy/4749529002/ (last updated Feb. 17, 2020).

must do so without breaching the peace.[187] Some commentators have suggested that using a SID to disable a vehicle is akin to the equipment disablement provisions of Article 9, and, as such, SID usage should be permissible under Article 9 by analogy to these provisions.[188] However, the term "equipment" is specifically defined in Article 9, and it is unlikely that consumer vehicles meet this definition.[189] It is more probable that consumer vehicles are "consumer goods" rather than "equipment" under Article 9.[190] Thus, a lender cannot rely on Article 9's equipment disablement provisions to justify its use of a SID to disable a consumer's vehicle, although a lender could obtain consumer consent to the disablement.

Article 9 also permits a lender to take possession of the motor vehicle after the consumer defaults without first going to court. However, the creditor may exercise the remedy of "self-help" only if it does not breach the peace.[191] Some jurisdictions also impose additional requirements for the repossession of motor vehicles.[192] The term "breach of the peace" is not defined in the UCC.[193] If a lender's repossession is improper, the lender may be subject to civil and criminal liability, and the lender's ability to collect a deficiency judgment in a consumer transaction could be restricted.[194] Recall also that asset collection technology, such as SIDs, can be used in vehicles that are subject to lease (rather than sale) agreements. Article 2A of the UCC generally applies to the lease of goods, including possibly consumer motor vehicle leases,[195] and authorizes lessors to exercise the remedy of self-help and "take possession of the goods" (subject to not breaching the peace) in the event the lessee defaults.[196] Lenders may also use the remedy of self-help in motor vehicle lease transactions, subject to applicable consumer protection laws.[197]

The use of SIDs could be viewed as "electronic self-help" on the part of the lender. However, some sources of contract law restrict the use of "electronic-self-help" measures as a remedy for contract disputes. The ALI Software Principles, for example, prohibit automated electronic disablement in consumer

---

[187] U.C.C. § 9-609(b) (AM. LAW INST. & UNIF. LAW COMM'N 2017).

[188] *See* Hudson & Laudicina, *supra* note 6, at 846.

[189] U.C.C. § 9-102(a)(33) (defining equipment as "goods other than inventory, farm products, or consumer goods").

[190] *Id.* § 9-102(a)(23) (defining consumer goods as "goods that are used or bought for use primarily for personal, family, or household purposes").

[191] *See id.* § 9-609(a)–(b).

[192] RUSCH & SEPINUCK, *supra* note 14, at 157–58.

[193] U.C.C. § 9-609(a)–(b) cmt. 3 (stating in the Official Comments that "this section does not define or explain the conduct that will constitute a breach of the peace").

[194] CARTER ET AL., *supra* note 38, at 179; JAMES J. WHITE & ROBERT S. SUMMERS , UNIFORM COMMERCIAL CODE 1335–36 (Hornbook Series 6th ed. 2010) ("[T]he creditor's commission of a breach of the peace may expose it to: (1) tort liability, including punitive damages; (2) criminal penalties; (3) liability under 9-625; and (4) in a consumer case, it also may deprive the creditor of its right to a deficiency judgment.").

[195] U.C.C. § 2A-102; 1 Consumer Credit Law Manual § 3.08 (2020).

[196] *Id.* § 2A-525.

[197] *Id.* § 2A-104.

transactions.[198] Similarly, UCITA restricts the use of electronic self-help.[199] However, recall from Chapters 4 and 5 the limited impact of these sources of law. A few jurisdictions also place limitations on self-help repossessions, subject to certain exceptions, such as the debtor voluntarily surrendering the collateral.[200]

Once a consumer is in default, state law may require a lender to provide the consumer with written notice of a right to cure the default and observe a statutorily defined time period within which the default can be cured (usually by making a payment) before exercising its right to repossess the collateral.[201] Failure to comply with such consumer protection statutes may lead to lender liability.[202] If a repossession is defined as requiring a lender to have "physical possession" of the collateral, disabling a vehicle using a SID would not qualify as a repossession.[203] Additionally, it is unclear whether disabling a vehicle using a SID would constitute a breach of the peace, which, as previously stated, is not defined in the UCC.[204] There is scant case law specifically addressing the UCC and SIDs in consumer transactions.[205] However, though not always clear on these issues, case law generally discussing repossessions and the few state statutes that specifically address SIDs and electronic self-help are indeed instructive.

Several courts have addressed the question of whether a lender must take "physical possession" of collateral in order for a repossession to occur.[206] These courts have generally found that a repossession may be physical or constructive. For instance, in *Van Wormer v. Charter Oak Federal Credit Union*, the court indicated that a repossession should not be narrowly defined to require a physical taking and instead suggested that a repossession can occur when the lender "takes steps consistent with the exercise of dominion or control

[198] Am. Law Inst., Principles of the Law of Software Contracts § 4.03(b), Ill. 4, Westlaw (database updated Oct. 2019) ("automated disablement is not available in a consumer agreement"); Juliet M. Moringiello & William L. Reynold, *What's Software Got to Do with It? The ALI Principles of the Law of Software Contracts*, 84 Tul. L. Rev. 1541, 1551 (2010); Florencia Marotta-Wurgler & Robert Taylor, *Set in Stone? Change and Innovation in Consumer Standard-Form Contracts*, 88 N.Y.U. L. Rev. 240, 255 n.46 (2013); Robert A. Hillman & Maureen O'Rourke, *Defending Disclosure in Software Licensing*, 78 U. Chi. L. Rev. 95, 111 n.84 (2011).

[199] Unif. Comput. Info. Transactions Act § 816, 605(f) (Unif. Law Comm'n 2002) ("This section does not authorize use of an automatic restraint to enforce remedies because of breach of contract or for cancellation for breach.").

[200] *See, e.g.*, La. Stat. Ann. § 10:9-609 (West 2019); Wis. Stat. Ann. § 425.206 (West 2019); *see also* Carter et al., *supra* note 38, at 187.

[201] *See, e.g.*, S.C. Code Ann. § 37-5-111 (2019).

[202] *Id.* (providing for conversion liability).

[203] *See generally* Dawson v. J & B Detail, L.L.C. (*In re* Dawson), No. 05-22369, 2006 WL 2372821 (Bankr. N.D. Ohio Aug. 15, 2006).

[204] *See supra* note 193and accompanying text.

[205] Carter et al., *supra* note 38, at 213.

[206] *See, e.g.*, McMillen v. Pippin, 27 Cal. Rptr. 590 (Cal. Ct. App. 1963); Avery v. Chrysler Credit Corp., 391 S.E.2d 410 (Ga. Ct. App. 1990); Van Wormer v. Charter Oak Fed. Credit Union, No. 114865, 2000 WL 1281530, at *2 (Conn. Super. Ct. Aug. 25, 2000).

o[ver]" the collateral.[207] Some commentators have attempted to distinguish the *Van Wormer* holding and other similar cases by arguing that a consumer retains physical possession of the vehicle when a lender remotely disables the vehicle using a SID, and that remote disablement fosters consumers' "continued possession and ownership by encouraging contact with a creditor and making arrangements to pay past due amounts."[208] However, as discussed earlier in this chapter, lenders using SIDs exercise significant control over consumers and their vehicles in various ways. This control is even more dominant and evident when the lender elects to disable a vehicle. In a typical repossession, for example, once the repossession agent takes physical possession of the vehicle, the consumer can no longer use the vehicle. Similarly, once the vehicle is remotely disabled via a SID, the consumer is unable to operate the vehicle. Thus, a lender that has used a SID to remotely disable the vehicle should be viewed as conducting a constructive repossession.

Lenders can continue to use and operate a SID in a consumer's vehicle even after the consumer files for bankruptcy. The question of whether a lender has committed a repossession is also a disputed issue in bankruptcy proceedings. Once a consumer files a bankruptcy petition, an automatic stay is created which prevents "any act to obtain possession . . . or to exercise control over property of the [bankruptcy] estate," among other things.[209] Parties that violate the automatic stay can be liable for damages.[210] If a lender repossesses a debtor's vehicle before a bankruptcy filing, most, but not all, courts have found that once the automatic stay is issued the lender should return the vehicle to the debtor.[211]

---

[207] *Van Wormer*, 2000 WL 1281530, at *3; *see also* 6Q UCC REPORTER-DIGEST A318 (Mathew Bender & Co. 2018) (discussing the *Van Wormer* case).

[208] *See* NICOLE MUNRO, PARTNER, HUDSON COOK, LLP, AUTO FINANCE INDUSTRY PERSPECTIVES ON STARTER INTERRUPT & GPS TRACKING TECHNOLOGY USED AS PART OF AN AUTOMOTIVE COLLATERAL MANAGEMENT SYSTEM, ADDRESS AT THE AMERICAN BAR ASSOCIATION BUSINESS LAW SECTION SPRING MEETING – LOSING CONTROL: WHO OWNS YOUR DEVICES NOW THAT THEY ARE CONNECTED TO THE INTERNET? (Apr. 17, 2015), www.americanbar.org/content/dam/aba/events/business_law/2015/04/ spring/materials/losing-control-201504.authcheckdam.pdf. *See generally The Road Ahead: Session 2/4 (Detroit)*, FED. TRADE COMM'N (Jan. 29, 2012), www.ftc.gov/news-events/audio-video/video/road-ahead-session-24-detroit (discussing the SID technology).

[209] 11 U.S.C. § 362(a)(3) (2017).

[210] *Id.* § 362(k).

[211] Pamela Foohey et al., *Driven To Bankruptcy*, 55 WAKE FOREST L. REV. 287, 303 (2020)(observing that "[c]ourts have generally, but not universally, held that, in Chapter 13, the automatic stay requires the return of repossessed (but not yet sold) cars to debtors" and noting that "Chapter 7 likewise can assist debtors in getting their repossessed cars back, provided they reaffirm or redeem the accompanying debt"); Eugene R. Wedoff, *Return of Vehicles Seized Before a Chapter 13 Filing: Does the Debtor Have to File a Turnover Motion?*, AM. BANKR. INSTIT. J., Apr. 2019, at 14 (discussing the circuit split on this issue and noting that most courts have determined that lenders are obligated to return repossessed vehicles to debtors under an automatic stay but other courts have found that the "automatic stay does not apply to vehicles seized pre-petition and that a creditor need only return the collateral to a chapter 13 debtor if the bankruptcy court grans a debtor's motion for turnover").

In *In re Dawson*, the bankruptcy court determined that the lender did not commit a repossession for purposes of the Ohio Retail Installment Act by using a SID to remotely disable a vehicle since the statute required the lender to have "physical possession" of the collateral.[212] However, the court also found that the lender's use of a SID system after the consumer filed for bankruptcy violated the automatic stay. The court reasoned that "simply having the system operational without a payment code or emergency codes available to the debtor is an act to exercise control over property."[213]

In *In re Horace*, the bankruptcy court determined that the lender violated the automatic stay when the SID issued payment reminder beeps and when the consumer's vehicle was disabled using the SID.[214] Similarly, in *In re Mabone*, the court found that disabling a consumer's vehicle after a bankruptcy petition was filed violated the automatic stay.[215] In *In re Grisard-Van Roey*, the bankruptcy court held that "the mere post-petition operation of [a SID] system does not constitute a violation of the automatic stay."[216] The court reasoned that since the lender had provided the consumer with an emergency code, the consumer should have properly entered the code in the system to prevent the vehicle from being disabled.[217] Some bankruptcy cases suggest that as long as the lender provides the consumer with codes to operate the vehicle and disables beeping payment reminders, the lender can continue to use other features of the SID, including tracking the consumer's location and receiving detailed driver history reports. Thus, the privacy violations associated with the use of asset collection devices can continue even after a bankruptcy petition has been filed. Additionally, the holding in *In re Dawson* indicates that in some instances the definition of a repossession under other sources of state law may be limited to a physical repossession. As a result, a lender's use of a SID to disable a vehicle under such statutes does not constitute a repossession, and therefore lender compliance with the consumer-friendly portions of these statutes is not required. At least one SID seller advertises that its device offers a "bankruptcy mode" feature, which allows users to halt the use of certain device features to prevent violations of bankruptcy laws and exposure to liability.[218]

---

212 Dawson v. J & B Detail, L.L.C. (*In re* Dawson), No. 05-22369, 2006 WL 2372821, at *13–14 (Bankr. N. D. Ohio Aug. 15, 2006); Dawson v. J & B Detail, L.L.C., No. 1:06CV1949, 2006 WL 3827459, at *2–3 (N.D. Ohio Dec. 27, 2006).

213 *Id.* at *7; *see also* Hampton v. Yam's Choice Plus Autos, Inc. (*In re* Hampton), 319 B.R. 163, 175 (Bankr. E.D. Ark. 2005).

214 *In re* Horace, No. 14-30103, 2015 WL 5145576, at *4 (Bankr. N.D. Ohio Aug. 28, 2015) (requiring removal of SID).

215 *In re* Mabone, 471 B.R. 534, 538 (Bankr. E.D. Mich. 2012).

216 Grisard-Van Roey v. Auto Credit Ctr., Inc. (*In re* Grisard-Van Roey), 373 B.R. 441, 444 (Bankr. D.S.C. 2007).

217 *Id.* at 444–45.

218 *See* Controllt, *supra* note 70 ("Bankruptcy mode: [a]llows you to suspend GPS based on BK status which protects the dealer from wrong doing & compliance support.").

There are a large number of cases evaluating issues related to a lender's breach of the peace in self-help repossessions. To assess whether a lender has breached the peace, most courts evaluate whether the lender entered the debtor's premises and whether the debtor (or their representative) "consented (or objected) to the entry or repossession."[219] Case law suggests that vehicles can be repossessed on public streets and driveways without breaching the peace in certain circumstances.[220] Whether a debtor orally objects to a repossession is also a factor that a court may consider in evaluating whether a breach of the peace has occurred.[221] Third parties' reactions to a repossession may impact whether a court determines that a repossession breached the peace.[222]

The installation of asset collection technology, such as a SID or other tracking device, in a vehicle decreases the lender's chances of breaching the peace in a repossession. The various reports regarding our driving and behavioral habits generated from such devices can be used by lenders to determine not only the exact physical location of our vehicle, but also periods in which our vehicle is unlikely to be in use. This allows lenders to avoid or decrease the chances of confrontations or oral protests from us and third parties, determine the best location, time, and date to repossess the vehicle to avoid disrupting third parties, and easily repossess vehicles on public streets. When a lender disables a vehicle using SID technology, there is no in-person physical interaction with the consumer. To the extent that an electronic device disablement is viewed as a lender taking "possession of the collateral" in accordance with Article 9, and the disablement occurs while a consumer is driving or at a stoplight or while there are minors and other third parties in a vehicle or causes harm to an individual, one could certainly argue that disabling the vehicle constitutes a breach of the peace. However, it is unclear whether disabling a vehicle using SID technology constitutes a repossession that automatically breaches the peace.

The breach of the peace requirement may aid borrowers in protecting their collateral and avoiding lender abuse. To the extent that self-help measures, such as remote disablement via asset collection technology, avoid breach of the peace issues, borrowers will be stripped of any resulting protections. Additionally, as Jim Hawkins notes, a significant "risk with self-help remedies is that they prevent people from raising affirmative defenses that they could raise in court."[223] When used against consumers, self-help measures can restrict consumers' ability to exercise core legal rights and defenses.

---

[219]   White & Summers, *supra* note 194 at 1336.

[220]   *Id.*

[221]   *See* Hollibush v. Ford Motor Credit Co., 508 N.W.2d 449, 453–55 (Wis. Ct. App. 1993).

[222]   *See* Davenport v. Chrysler Credit Corp., 818 S.W.2d 23, 29 (Tenn. Ct. App. 1991).

[223]   Jim Hawkins, *Law's Remarkable Failure to Protect Mistakenly Overpaid Employees*, 99 Minn. L. Rev. 89, 117 (2014).

Another possible complicating factor for lenders is the application of debt collection statutes. Some laws restrict covered entities' ability to issue threats to disable property when there is no intent to conduct a repossession.[224] A creditor or its agent may not intend to take possession of a motor vehicle when it uses asset collection technology to disable the vehicle, but instead may do so only to force the consumer to make a payment. In such an instance, the electronic disablement of consumer vehicles using asset collection technology could violate the provisions of such statutes. However, to the extent that a company seeking to collect a debt does not meet the statutory definition of a "debt collector" or entity subject to the statute's scope then any restrictions established in those statutes would not apply to the company's collection efforts. The lender would then be free to use asset collection technology to disable consumers' vehicles to incentivize payment without fear of any resulting statutory violations.

ASSET COLLECTION TECHNOLOGY STATE STATUTES

Several state statutes specifically address companies' use of SID technology and electronic self-help.[225] Thus, one must turn to the statutes in these states to evaluate the legality of a lender's use of asset collection technology to disable or repossess a vehicle. New Jersey permits the use of SID technology, but requires lenders to provide detailed notice and obtain consumer acknowledgment of receipt of such notice before or at the time of the transaction.[226] Creditors must wait at least five days if the loan requires one weekly payment or ten days for other transactions after a consumer is in default before disabling the vehicle.[227] The statute also requires lenders to provide consumers with a seventy-two-hour warning grace period before remotely disabling the vehicle, and to permit consumers to operate a disabled vehicle for at least forty-eight hours.[228] Lenders are prohibited from disabling a "vehicle while it is being operated."[229]

California's statute requires BHPH dealers to provide notice and obtain consumer consent in writing to the use of SID technology, and contains provisions requiring warning notices after default prior to disabling the vehicle.[230] The statute also requires covered dealers to provide consumers with the ability to restart the vehicle in the event of an emergency for at least twenty-four hours, and each statutory

---

[224]   CARTER ET AL., *supra* note 38, at 214–15; *see also* 15 U.S.C. § 1692f(6) (2020); ME. REV. STAT. ANN. tit. 32, § 11013 (2017).

[225]   *See, e.g.*, CAL. CIV. CODE § 2983.37 (West 2019); COLO. REV. STAT. ANN. § 4-9-609 (West 2018); CONN. GEN. STAT. ANN. §§ 42a-9-609, 42a-2A-702 (West 2019); NEV. REV. STAT. ANN. § 598.9715 (West 2017); N.J. STAT. ANN. § 56:8-206 (West 2019); 11 R.I. GEN. LAWS § 11-69-1 (West 2019).

[226]   N.J. STAT. ANN. § 56:8-206.

[227]   *Id.*

[228]   *Id.*

[229]   *Id.*

[230]   CAL. CIV. CODE § 2983.37.

violation can lead to a fine of $2,000.[231] Oklahoma and Rhode Island seemingly authorize the use of SIDs as long as the vehicle buyer or lessee consents in writing.[232] Nevada's statute also permits SID use, subject to specific notice and consumer acknowledgment requirements, but requires creditors to wait until thirty days after a late payment to disable a vehicle.[233] The statute prohibits creditors from disabling vehicles while they are in operation.[234] In 2018, New York amended the state's version of Article 9 and debt collection laws to address SIDs.[235] The statute implicitly requires lenders to provide SID disclosures to consumers as part of the lending transaction and explicitly obligates lenders to provide prior notice to debtors at least ten days before disabling a vehicle.[236]

Connecticut and Colorado have passed non-uniform amendments to Article 9 to address a secured lender's use of electronic self-help.[237] Colorado prohibits lenders from disabling "any computer program or other similar device embedded in the collateral" if doing so would cause immediate reasonably foreseeable injury.[238] This provision appears only to be applicable to lenders that seek to exercise their right to disable "equipment."[239] Recall that in the consumer context a motor vehicle is likely consumer goods rather than equipment for Article 9 purposes. Connecticut's electronic self-help amendments to Article 9 apply to secured lenders that seek to "take possession of the collateral" as well as those that seek to "render equipment unusable."[240] The Connecticut statute requires a secured lender to obtain the debtor's agreement to the use of electronic self-help, provide notice of its intent to use this method, and wait at least fifteen days after such notice is provided before using such measures.[241] Additionally, the statute also prohibits the use of electronic self-help if the lender "has reason to know" that injury to the "public health" may occur, and permits debtors to recover damages for "wrongful use of electronic self-help."[242] Connecticut's version of Article 2A also contains similar provisions.[243]

---

[231]   *Id.*

[232]   *See* OKLA. STAT. ANN. tit. 21, § 1173 (West 2018); 11 R.I. GEN. LAWS § 11-69-1(b)(4) (West 2018).

[233]   NEV. REV. STAT. ANN. § 598.9715 (West 2017).

[234]   *Id.*

[235]   Daniel B. Pearson, *New York Reins in the Use of Automobile Kill Switches*, MAYER BROWN (Oct. 9, 2018), www.mayerbrown.com/en/perspectives-events/publications/2018/10/new-york-reins-in-the-use-of-automobile-kill-switc.

[236]   *Id.*; N.Y. GEN. BUS. LAW § 601 (LexisNexis 2020); N.Y. U.C.C. LAW § 9-102(60-a) (LexisNexis 2020) (defining a payment assurance device); *see also* Thomas P. Quinn, Jr. & Nicole F. Munro, *Implications of New York Starter Interrupt Device Law Remain Unclear*, HUDSON COOK (Nov. 30, 2018), www.hudsoncook.com/article/implications-of-new-york-starter-interrupt-device-law-remain-unclear/ (discussing the implicit and explicit requirements of the statute).

[237]   *See* COLO. REV. STAT. ANN. § 4-9-609 (West 2018); CONN. GEN. STAT. ANN. § 42a-9-609 (West 2019).

[238]   COLO. REV. STAT. ANN. § 4-9-609(e).

[239]   *Id.*

[240]   CONN. GEN. STAT. ANN. § 42a-9-609; *see also* U.C.C. § 9-609 (AM. LAW INST. & UNIF. LAW COMM'N 2017).

[241]   CONN. GEN. STAT. ANN. § 42a-9-609.

[242]   *Id.*

[243]   *Id.* § 42a-2A-702.

In short, these statutes generally permit the use of SID technology or electronic self-help in lending transactions subject to certain requirements. Many of these statutes overrely on a notice and choice method to protect us in transactions involving SID technology. Recall that legal scholars have frequently highlighted the limitations of notice and choice regimes. As previously argued earlier in this chapter, we must review and execute a large number of documents in connection with lending transactions. Additionally, recall that many of these lending documents are disclosures that are required by both state and federal statutes. It is unlikely that many of us read or understand these disclosures. As such, statutorily requiring an additional disclosure for SID technology or the use of electronic self-help is unlikely to effectively communicate the implications of entering into a transaction that permits the lender to use such measures. Additionally, subprime borrowers have few, if any, alternatives but to agree to a lender's use of SID technology. In some instances, these SID statutes do not definitively address questions related to whether a lender's use of SID technology qualifies as a "repossession." In contrast, Nevada's statute expressly provides that the creditor's use of a SID to disable a vehicle is a "constructive repossession,"[244] and Connecticut's amendment to Article 9 appears to suggest that electronic self-help is a form of repossession.[245] Case law is still instructive on questions of a breach of the peace, particularly in states that have addressed SID use by making non-uniform amendments to Article 9. However, these state statutes do not definitively resolve all issues related to a lender's use of asset collection technology in consumer lending transactions.

The National Conference of State Legislatures reports that sixteen states have passed legislation addressing the use of ALPR technology. Subject to a limited set of exceptions, Arkansas's statute prohibits individuals and private companies from using ALPR technology.[246] There has been at least one previous attempt by automated license plate reader vendors to challenge the validity of the Arkansas statute.[247] Maine also restricts the use of ALPR systems, but authorizes ALPR use for public safety, law enforcement and commercial vehicle screening purposes.[248] Other states permit use of this technology subject to certain requirements, such as the maintenance of reasonable security measures with respect to the data collected.[249] In states that have not addressed the use of ALPRs, the use of this technology is also likely permissible.

---

[244] Nev. Rev. Stat. Ann. § 598.9715(2)(c) (West 2019).

[245] *See* Conn. Gen. Stat. Ann § 42a-9-609(d)(1).

[246] *Automated License Plate Readers: State Statutes*, Nat'l Conf. State Legislatures (2020), www .ncsl.org/research/telecommunications-and-information-technology/state-statutes-regulating-the-use-of-automated-license-plate-readers-alpr-or-alpr-data.aspx (discussing the Arkansas statute and stating "at least 16 states have statutes that *expressly* address the use of ALPRs or the retention of data collected by ALPRs"); Ark. Code Ann. § 12-12-1803 (West 2019); *see also* Margot E. Kaminski, *Privacy and the Right to Record*, 97 B.U. L. Rev. 167, 236–37 (2017).

[247] *See* Dig. Recognition Network, Inc. v. Hutchinson, 803 F.3d 952 (8th Cir. 2015).

[248] Me. Rev. Stat. Ann. tit. 29-A § 2117-A (2019); *see also* ACLU ALPR Report, *supra* note 99, at 4, 31.

[249] Cal. Civ. Code § 1798.90.51 (West 2020).

THE BASICS OF DEFICIENCY LAWSUITS

A consumer that defaults on a vehicle loan will experience not only a significant decrease in their credit score (and likely subsequent financial hardships), but could also be subject to a deficiency action. When a consumer owes an unpaid financial obligation, the creditor has the ability to initiate a debt collection lawsuit. Once a lender physically repossesses a defaulting consumer's vehicle with the aid of asset collection technology, the lender typically sells the asset to cover the amount owed by the consumer. The collateral's sale price may not equal the loan balance. As a result, the consumer may be liable for the deficiency, and the lender may bring a lawsuit against the consumer to recover those amounts. Over a ten-year period, one such subprime vehicle lender filed 25,000 deficiency lawsuits in New York.[250]

Consider that in order to sell more vehicles to consumers, some vehicle dealerships engage in a practice known as "kicking the trade."[251] Without the lender's knowledge, these dealerships encourage consumers to take out new vehicle loans, and default on their old vehicle loans with the false promise that the original lender will simply take the vehicle back.[252] To enable this practice, these vehicle dealerships inaccurately increase borrowers' incomes on their vehicle loan applications, and lenders can fail to adequately review proof of income documents.[253] Consumer victims of this practice are then potentially subject to deficiency lawsuits if they are unable to pay back their original vehicle loans, and the repossessed vehicle is worth less than the loan.

The default and deficiency lawsuits problem in both the subprime and non-subprime auto lending context is complicated by the fact that (1) vehicles are increasingly becoming more expensive, (2) some consumers are having a difficult time affording these vehicles, and (3) successful vehicle dealerships can make significant profits facilitating vehicle loan transactions in addition to selling vehicles.[254] Increasingly, non-subprime borrowers are purchasing used vehicles.[255] Some subprime borrowers are also taking out new vehicle loans and simply rolling the unpaid portion of their original vehicle loan into the new vehicle loan.[256] As

---

[250] Kamat, *supra* note 45. That same lender reportedly brought more than 17,000 lawsuits against defaulting consumers in one state between 2010 and 2017. Jessica Silver-Greenberg & Michael Corkery, *The Car Was Repossessed, but the Debt Remains*, N.Y. TIMES: DEALBOOK (June 18, 2017), www.nytimes.com/2017/06/18/business/dealbook/car-loan-subprime.html.

[251] Andriotis & Eisen, *supra* note 46.

[252] *See id.*

[253] *Id.; see also* Ben Eisen & AnnaMaria Andriotis, *An $809 Car Payment, a $660 Income: How Dealers Make the Math Work*, WALL ST. J. (Dec. 21, 2019, 5:30 AM), www.wsj.com/articles/an-809-car-payment-a-660-income-how-dealers-make-the-math-work-11576924201?mod=article_inline.

[254] Andriotis & Eisen, *supra* note 46.

[255] Melinda Zabritski, *Consumers Continue to Shift Preferences Toward Used Vehicles*, EXPERIAN (Jan. 27, 2020), www.experian.com/blogs/insights/2020/01/consumers-continue-shift-preferences-toward-used-vehicles/.

[256] AnnaMaria Andriotis & Ben Eisen, *A $45,000 Loan for a $27,000 Ride: More Borrowers Are Going Underwater on Car Loans*, WALL ST. J. (Nov. 9, 2019), www.wsj.com/articles/a-45-000-loan-for-a-27-000-ride-more-borrowers-are-going-underwater-on-car-loans-11573295400.

a result, more consumers are buying vehicles that are worth significantly less than the total cost of the associated vehicle loan, and are increasingly vulnerable to defaulting, deficiency lawsuits, and debt criminalization tactics.

Some jurisdictions prohibit or limit deficiency lawsuits in certain consumer transactions, while others do not.[257] Lenders can be obligated to choose either to repossess the collateral or bring a lawsuit against the consumer for the amount of the debt.[258] Thus, consumers can be subject to debt collection lawsuits on outstanding debts if the creditor decides not to repossess the asset. It may still be possible for the lender to use asset collection technology to monitor and collect data on consumers and the collateral, and then subsequently elect to bring suit against the consumer after default instead of conducting a repossession. In such an instance, privacy intrusions and digital control issues would still be applicable even though the collateral is not ultimately repossessed by the creditor. Vehicle finance laws can allow both deficiencies and repossessions.

VEHICLE TITLE LENDING

So far in our lending discussion we have focused on the subprime auto lending industry, and transactions in which the lender obtains a PMSI in a consumer's product. However, with respect to motor vehicles, once the consumer pays off the initial creditor and obtains title to their vehicle, they may also obtain another loan using the vehicle as collateral. This type of transaction is referred to as vehicle or auto title lending and it is also subject to Article 9 as well as other applicable state statutes.[259] The Pew Research Center reports that auto title lending transactions have increased significantly.[260]

These loans are accompanied by exorbitantly high interest rates and are used by a significant segment of low-income consumers.[261] A news report on a consumer who entered into such a transaction indicated that the loan was subject to

---

[257] Mo. Ann. Stat. § 408.557 (West 2019); Nev. Rev. Stat. Ann. § 604A.5078 (West 2017); Carter et al., *supra* note 38, at 376 ("About half the states have enacted statutes that limit deficiencies in at least certain consumer transactions."); Jim Hawkins, *Credit on Wheels: The Law and Business of Auto-Title Lending*, 69 Wash & Lee L. Rev. 535, 586 (2012) (discussing several state statutes that restrict deficiencies in auto title lending transactions).

[258] Carter et al., *supra* note 38, at 376.

[259] Nathalie Martin & Ozymandias Adams, *Grand Theft Auto Loans: Repossession and Demographic Realities in Title Lending*, 77 Mo. L. Rev. 41, 42, 86 (2012); Wis. Stat. Ann. § 138.16 (West 2019).

[260] Nick Bourke et al., *As Payday Loan Market Changes, States Need to Respond*, Pew Charitable Tr. (Aug. 22, 2018), www.pewtrusts.org/en/research-and-analysis/articles/2018/08/22/as-payday-loan-market-changes-states-need-to-respond.

[261] Martin & Adams, *supra* note 259, at 42; *see also* Jessica Silver-Greenberg & Michael Corkery, *Dipping into Auto Equity Devastates Many Borrowers*, CNBC (Dec. 25, 2014, 5:42 AM), www.cnbc.com/2014/12/25/dipping-into-auto-equity-devastates-many-borrowers.html.

a 70 percent interest rate.[262] A study of title lenders in Texas found that "companies price title loans from 119% [annual percentage rate] to 601%."[263] Lenders in these transactions also use asset collection technology to repossess and monitor vehicles and consumers.[264] In its currently delayed auto title lending regulation, the CFPB notes that some vehicle title lenders require consumers to install SIDs and other tracking devices in their vehicles.[265] This suggest that the pre- and post-default consumer harms highlighted in earlier portions of the chapter are also relevant to auto title lending transactions.

Not surprisingly, auto title lenders also bring lawsuits against consumers for deficiencies.[266] An annual report by the California Department of Business Oversight found large numbers of repossessions and deficiency balances in auto title lending transactions.[267] A CFPB report on auto title lending found that "one-in-five loan sequences" ended in repossession of the consumer's automobile.[268] A study involving approximately "450 title lending customers" determined that "many borrowers are overly optimistic and experience self-control problems that affect their ability to make timely loan payments."[269]

PRIVATE DEBT CRIMINALIZATION TACTICS

As mentioned earlier in this chapter, private debt criminalization involves lenders using threats of jail time and pursuing arrest warrants to collect debts, among other

---

[262]   Carolyn Said, *Pink-Slip Car Loans: Quick Cash, High Price Tag*, S.F. CHRON. (June 21, 2018), www .sfchronicle.com/business/article/Pink-slip-car-loans-Quick-cash-high-price-tag-13012118.php.

[263]   Jim Hawkins, *Are Bigger Companies Better for Low-Income Borrowers?: Evidence from Payday and Title Loan Advertisements*, 11 J.L. ECON. & POL'Y 303, 315 (2015).

[264]   Said, *supra* note 262 (noting that auto title lenders use GPS to track consumers' vehicles); *see also Car Title Loans*, FED. TRADE COMM'N (July 2014), www.consumer.ftc.gov/articles/0514-car-title-loans (noting that the car title lenders can also require consumers to accept installation of SIDs in their vehicles).

[265]   Payday, Vehicle Title, and Certain High-Cost Installment Loans, 82 Fed. Reg. 54472 (Nov. 17, 2017) (to be codified at 12 C.F.R. pt. 1041), www.govinfo.gov/content/pkg/FR-2017-11-17/pdf/2017-21808.pdf. The CFPB's auto title lending rules also note that in auto title lending transactions "the lender generally retains the vehicle title or some other form of security interest that provides it with the right to repossess the vehicle, which may then be sold with the proceeds used for repayment." *Id.* In 2019, the CFPB issued proposed rules to rescind and delay these rules. *See Final Rule: Payday, Vehicle Title, and Certain High-Cost Installment Loans*, CONSUMER FIN. PROT. BUREAU, www .consumerfinance.gov/policy-compliance/rulemaking/final-rules/payday-vehicle-title-and-certain-high-cost-installment-loans/ (last visited Mar. 3, 2020); *see also* Jo Bruni, *Car Title Loan Regulation Rollback Leaves Consumers at Risk*, CONSUMER REP. (Aug. 8, 2019), www.consumerreports.org/short-term-lending/car-title-loan-regulation-rollback-leaves-consumers-at-risk/ (discussing the roll back of the auto lending rules).

[266]   Martin & Adams, *supra* note 259, at 78. *But see* Hawkins, *supra* note 257, at 552.

[267]   *See generally* CAL. DEP'T OF BUS. OVERSIGHT, 2017 ANNUAL REPORT: OPERATION OF FINANCE COMPANIES LICENSED UNDER THE CALIFORNIA FINANCING LAW (2018).

[268]   CONSUMER FIN. PROT. BUREAU, SINGLE-PAYMENT VEHICLE TITLE LENDING 23 (2016).

[269]   Kathryn Fritzdixon et al., *Dude, Where's My Car Title?: The Law, Behavior, and Economics of Title Lending Markets*, 2014 U. ILL. L. REV. 1013, 1013 (2014).

things. Asset collection technology and private debt criminalization tactics can be used to pressure defaulting and non-defaulting consumers to make payments under their loan agreements. Several CFPB consumer complaint narratives indicate that auto lenders have allegedly intimidated defaulting consumers with arrest warrants and jail time.[270]

The initial auto creditors in consumer loan transactions frequently transfer their interest in consumers' outstanding debt to collection companies. The transferees then vigorously pursue consumers for payment by filing debt collection lawsuits, among other things. The ACLU reports that "one in three adults" has had a debt "that has been turned over to a private collection agency."[271] Today, debt collection companies are "making a comeback."[272] Debt collectors are increasingly purchasing consumer debt and are more frequently pursing legal action against indebted consumers. As of the date of writing, even individuals' stimulus payments authorized by Congress in response to the COVID-19 pandemic may not be entirely immune from companies' debt collection efforts.[273]

Debt collection companies (as well as the initial lenders on consumer loans) have long used debt criminalization tactics against consumers in various lending transactions. In multiple CFPB complaint narratives, consumers have reported receiving threats of jail time and arrest warrants on old debts from companies that do not appear to be the initial creditors on their loans.[274] Some companies have also used these tactics to force consumers to make payments

---

[270] *See Consumer Complaint No. 1508741*, CONSUMER FIN. PROT. BUREAU (Aug. 7, 2015), www .consumerfinance.gov/data-research/consumer-complaints/search/detail/1508741; *Consumer Complaint No. 1460443*, CONSUMER FIN. PROT. BUREAU (July 9, 2015), www.consumerfinance.gov/data-research /consumer-complaints/search/detail/1460443; *Consumer Complaint No. 1403934*, CONSUMER FIN. PROT. BUREAU (June 3, 2015), www.consumerfinance.gov/data-research/consumer-complaints/search/detail/ 1403934.

[271] AM. CIVIL LIBERTIES UNION, A POUND OF FLESH: THE CRIMINALIZATION OF PRIVATE DEBT 4 (2018) [hereinafter ACLU PRIVATE DEBT REPORT]; *see also* Dalie Jimenez, *Dirty Debts Sold Dirt Cheap*, 52 HARV. J. ON LEGIS. 41 (2015) (discussing debt collectors' purchase of debts).

[272] Yuka Hayashi, *Debt Collectors Wage Comeback*, WALL ST. J. (July 5, 2019, 6:31 AM), www.wsj.com /articles/debt-collectors-wage-comeback-11562319002.

[273] David Dayen, *Your Coronavirus Check is Coming. Your Bank Can Grab It*, AM. PROSPECT (Apr. 14, 2020), https://prospect.org/coronavirus/banks-can-grab-stimulus-check-pay-debts/; Lorie Konish, *Creditors Can Snatch Your Coronavirus Stimulus Check if You Have Outstanding Debts*, CNBC, www.cnbc.com/2020/ 04/14/creditors-can-snatch-your-stimulus-check-if-you-have-outstanding-debts.html (last updated Apr. 14, 2020); Letter from Letitia James, New York Attorney General et al., to Steven Mnuchin, Secretary, U.S. Dept. of Treasury (Apr. 13, 2020), https://ag.ny.gov/sites/default/files/04.13.20_multistate_letter_to_treasur y_re_garnishment_and_cares_act_final.pdf; Katie Lobosco, *Millions of Americans Could Lose Stimulus Payments to Debt Collectors*, CNN (Apr. 16, 2020, 11:58 AM), www.cnn.com/2020/04/15/politics/stimulus-payments-debt-collectors/index.html.

[274] *Consumer Complaint No. 2336599*, CONSUMER FIN. PROT. BUREAU (Feb. 9, 2017), www .consumerfinance.gov/data-research/consumer-complaints/search/detail/2336599; *Consumer Complaint No. 1554113*, CONSUMER FIN. PROT. BUREAU (Sept. 6, 2015), www.consumerfinance.gov/data-research /consumer-complaints/search/detail/1554113; *Consumer Complaint No. 1474258*, CONSUMER FIN. PROT. BUREAU (July 17, 2015), www.consumerfinance.gov/data-research/consumer-complaints/search/detail/ 1474258.

on phantom debts.[275] The CFPB has initiated complaints against some companies that have engaged in this behavior,[276] and the FTC has also pursued some of these organizations for violations of the Fair Debt Collection Practices Act (FDCPA) and the FTCA.[277] Despite CFPB and FTC efforts in this area, the problem persists.

Whether a debt collector is subject to the provisions of the FDCPA is a hotly contested issue. In *Henson v. Santander Consumer USA, Inc.*, the Supreme Court addressed the types of debt collectors that must comply with the FDCPA.[278] In *Henson*, the court held that even companies that bought debts from other entities are not "debt collectors" under the FDCPA to the extent that they collect debts "for their own accounts" rather than third parties.[279] More recently, in *Obduskey v. McCarthy & Holthus LLP*, the court determined that a law firm that sought to enforce a lender's interest through "nonjudicial foreclosure proceedings" was not a "debt collector" under the FDCPA.[280] These cases suggest that there are significant limits to the FDCPA's reach.

Companies' increased access to IoT data, data analytics, and new asset collection technologies will exacerbate consumer concerns in the debt collection process. Creola Johnson's work on debt criminalization tactics documents instances in which companies use consumers' "sensitive personal data," such as birth dates and social security and driver's license numbers, to successfully threaten consumers with criminal prosecution unless payment is received, despite laws prohibiting such activities.[281] Johnson posits that once a consumer is aware that a company has accurate sensitive data about them, they are more likely to take demands for payments and threats of jail time and arrest warrants seriously.[282]

Recall from our prior discussions that in the IoT era, asset collection technology allows companies to collect intimate and long-term data on our activities, including

---

[275]   *See Consumer Complaint No. 2336599, supra* note 274.

[276]   *See generally* CONSUMER FIN. PROT. BUREAU, FAIR DEBT COLLECTION PRACTICES ACT: CFPB ANNUAL REPORT 2016 (2016); CONSUMER FIN. PROT. BUREAU, SEMI-ANNUAL REPORT OF THE BUREAU OF CONSUMER FINANCIAL PROTECTION (2018).

[277]   *See* Press Release, Fed. Trade Comm'n, Phantom Debt Collectors Settle FTC Charges of Deceiving Consumers (June 4, 2018), www.ftc.gov/news-events/press-releases/2018/06/phantom-debt-collectors-settle-ftc-charges-deceiving-consumers; Lesley Fair, *Sounding the Phantom Debt Collection Alarm – Again*, FED. TRADE COMM'N: BUS. BLOG (June 27, 2018, 1:09 PM), www.ftc.gov/news-events/blogs/business-blog/2018/06/sounding-phantom-debt-collection-alarm-again.

[278]   Henson v. Santander Consumer USA Inc., 137 S. Ct. 1718 (2017).

[279]   *See id.* at 1719; *see also* Kirby v. 21st Mortg. Corp. (*In re* Kirby), 589 B.R. 456 (Bankr. D. Me. 2018) (discussing the *Henson* case and stating that the FDCPA applies only to entities that qualify as "debt collectors" under the statute).

[280]   Obduskey v. McCarthy & Holthus LLP, 139 S. Ct. 1029, 1036 (2019) ("A business engaged in no more than nonjudicial foreclosure proceedings is not a 'debt collector' under the FDCPA, except for the limited purpose of §1692f(6)."); Jon Hill, *Supreme Court Says Foreclosure Firms Not Debt Collectors*, LAW360 (Mar. 20, 2019, 10:38 AM), www.law360.com/articles/1140869/supreme-court-says-foreclosure-firms-not-debt-collectors.

[281]   Johnson, *supra* note 2, at 22–29.

[282]   *See id.*

frequently visited locations, and data analytics can be used to generate various reports about us that are likely to be incredibly accurate. Also, recall that internet-connected vehicles and other ordinary objects embedded with sensors can collect large quantities of data about us, and that asset collection technology data could be monetized and disclosed to third parties. Imagine a scenario in which asset collection data reports (even if anonymized), and data from IoT consumer devices are frequently sold or disclosed to debt collection companies along with creditors' interest in consumers' unpaid debts. Data generated from asset collection technology and IoT devices could then be used in the debt collection process to more effectively manipulate and coerce those of us who are indigent into making payments. These data could also be used to manipulate consumers into making payments on time-barred debts and phantom debts.

Once a debt collection lawsuit is filed either by the initial creditor or by a debt collection agency, the threat of private debt criminalization becomes even more real. An ACLU investigation on debt criminalization tactics found approximately 1,000 cases in twenty-six states in which courts issued arrest warrants for consumers in debt collection lawsuits.[283] Similarly, a 2019 ProPublica report found that medical debt collectors use debt criminalization tactics, such as bench warrants.[284] Depending on the jurisdiction, debt collection lawsuits can be presided over by decision makers who lack law degrees, even though they are given the power to issue warrants.[285] Thus, despite our legal system's formal adoption of a debt collection process, in some jurisdictions, we have failed to invest in the resources necessary to ensure that the system functions properly.[286]

---

[283] ACLU PRIVATE DEBT REPORT, *supra* note 271, at 4.

[284] Lizzie Presser, *When Medical Debt Collectors Decide Who Gets Arrested*, PROPUBLICA (Oct. 16, 2019), https://features.propublica.org/medical-debt/when-medical-debt-collectors-decide-who-gets-arrested-coffeyville-kansas/?fbclid=IwAR1Pt153lEHCQgNgjAtf-ZLPUs5oa6NtPem1bzNYv_QaH24lOThCLQU2qhM.

[285] *Id.*; *see also* Joseph Cranney, *These Judges Can Have Less Training Than Barbers but Still Decide Thousands of Cases Each Year*, PROPUBLICA (Nov. 27, 2019, 5:00 AM), www.propublica.org/article/these-judges-can-have-less-training-than-barbers-but-still-decide-thousands-of-cases-each-year (discussing South Carolina's magistrate courts and noting that "three-quarters of the state's magistrates lack a legal degree and couldn't represent someone in a court of law").

[286] *See* HUMAN RIGHTS WATCH, RUBBER STAMP JUSTICE: US COURTS, DEBT BUYING CORPORATIONS, AND THE POOR 39 (2016), www.hrw.org/sites/default/files/report_pdf/us0116_web.pdf (noting that judges are forced to process default judgments quickly "while simultaneously presiding over another proceeding"); Sam Glover, *Has the Flood of Debt Collection Lawsuits Swept Away Minnesotans' Due Process Rights?*, 35 WM. MITCHELL L. REV. 1115, 1132 (2009) (discussing the ease of obtaining default judgments in Minnesota's debt collection lawsuits noting that "the court administrator enters default judgments on claims for a definite amount. No judge sees the case and the debt buyers do not have to provide any proof of their claims."); Lisa Stifler, *Debt in the Courts: The Scourge of Abusive Debt Collection Litigation and Possible Policy Solutions*, 11 HARV. L. & POL'Y REV. 91, 113–15 (2017) (describing the "ill-equipped" nature of state courts and their inability "to adequately handle all of the cases").

Debtors are often unaware that debt collection lawsuits have been brought against them.[287] The Supreme Court's most recent decision on the FDCPA highlights this issue as well as companies' practice of pursuing consumers for possible time-barred debts. In *Rotkiske v. Klemm*, the debt collector received a default judgment against the consumer after service of process was effectuated at the wrong address and accepted by someone other than the consumer.[288] The default judgment was obtained even though the debt may have been time-barred because the state statute of limitations on the debt may have expired, which if true would likely render the debt collector's underlying claim for payment unenforceable.[289] Because of the service of process error, which appears to have been intentional, the consumer in *Rotkiske* was unable to raise the possible statute of limitations defense in the initial debt collection lawsuit and became aware of the debt collection lawsuit only years after the debt collector obtained the default judgment.[290] The FDCPA was intended in part to restrict debt collectors' ability to enforce debts that they do not have the legal "ability to collect."[291] However, the consumer in *Rotkiske* was unable to obtain relief under the FDCPA because he did not discover the default judgment until after the statute of limitations on the FDCPA had expired.[292] The Supreme Court in *Rotkiske* held that the FDCPA's statute of limitations period begins to run once an FDCPA violation occurs rather than when the consumer discovers the violation.[293]

It is estimated that debt collection companies win more than 95 percent of their lawsuits against consumers.[294] After creditors receive judgments in their favor, they may proceed in various ways, including, in some instances, seizing consumers' non-exempt personal property and assets. Asset collection technology and IoT data could be used to facilitate post-judgment seizures of collateral. Creditors can also request that debtors attend mandatory post-judgment hearings. At these hearings, debtors

---

[287] See Presser, *supra* note 284; ACLU Private Debt Report, *supra* note 271, at 5.

[288] Rotkiske v. Klemm, 140 S. Ct. 355, 357 (2019).

[289] See *id.* at 359 ("the sole FDCPA claim in the complaint asserted that Klemm commenced the 2009 debt-collection lawsuit after the state-law limitations period expired and therefore "violated the FDCPA by contacting [Rotkiske] without lawful ability to collect."); First Amended Complaint, Rotkiske v. Klemm NO.: 2:15-cv-03638-GEKP (E.D Pa. Oct. 19, 2015) ("The Virginia law controls the credit agreement between Capitol One and plaintiff the operative statute of limitations for which is three (3) years. Defendants filed the second collection lawsuit in 2009 or in excess of the three (3) years which elapsed after the default date.... Defendants' conduct violated the FDCPA by contacting Plaintiff without lawful ability to collect.")

[290] See *Rotkiske*, 140 S. Ct.. at 359.

[291] *Id.*; 15 U.S.C. § 1692e(5)(2020) (prohibiting a "threat to take any action that cannot legally be taken or that is not intended to be taken"); *Time-Barred Debts*, Fed. Trade Commission, www .consumer.ftc.gov/articles/0117-time-barred-debts (last visited Feb. 2, 2020) ("It's against the law for a collector to sue you or threaten to sue you on a time-barred debt.").

[292] *Rotkiske*, 140 S. Ct. at 362–63 (Ginsburg, J., dissenting).

[293] *Id.* at 357–58 ("absent the application of an equitable doctrine, §1692k(d)s statute of limitations begins to run when the alleged FDCPA violation occurs, not when the violation is discovered"); Bill Wichert, *Justices Say FDCPA Clock Starts When Violation Occurs*, Law360 (Dec. 10, 2019), www .law360.com/articles/1226898/justices-say-fdcpa-clock-starts-when-violation-occurs.

[294] ACLU Private Debt Report, *supra* note 271, at 5; *see also* Presser, *supra* note 284.

provide obligatory answers to questions about their finances and ability to pay, among other things. Civil arrest warrants can be issued for consumers who do not attend post-judgment hearings,[295] which can occur as frequently as every three months.[296] The ACLU has documented multiple cases in which consumers have not appeared at such hearings because of family, work, or health issues and other obligations.[297] Once a warrant is issued, the consumer can be arrested and the creditor may receive any posted bail amounts.[298] Arrest warrants have been issued in cases involving automobile debts, including motor vehicle deficiency lawsuits.[299] The ACLU report describes two consumers whose automobile creditor sued them for a deficiency after repossessing the vehicle.[300] These consumers were subsequently arrested after a warrant was issued for their failure to attend a hearing.[301] As more debt collectors become increasingly emboldened in their use of the court system and asset collection technology, and more consumers fall behind on their debt payments, debt criminalization tactics could become more widespread.

HISTORICALLY MARGINALIZED CONSUMERS

It is well documented that race and income can impact the lending and debt collection process. A Pew Research Center analysis found that the Great Recession worsened the racial wealth gap, with "the median wealth of middle-income blacks [falling] to $33,600 in 2013, down 47% from 2007."[302] The economic impact of the COVID-19 pandemic could also have similar negative results for racial minorities. According to a Federal Reserve Note, although "[v]ehicle loans are fairly evenly distributed across [racial] groups," in general, African-American and Hispanic "families are the most likely to have high debt payment burdens" and "have the highest incidence of credit constraints."[303] The note goes on to state that

---

[295] See Creola Johnson, *Prosecuting Creditors and Protecting Consumers: Cracking Down on Creditors that Extort via Debt Criminalization Practices*, 80 L. & CONTEMP. PROBS. 211, 228–36 (2017); Presser, *supra* note 284. At least one state has attempted to address the private debt criminalization problem. *See* 735 ILL. COMP. STAT. ANN. 5 / 12-107.5 (West 2019) (imposing requirements for the issuance of body attachments); *see also* Kelly M. Greco & Stephanie R. Hammer, *No More "Debtors' Prison": Greater Notice, Protections for Judgment Debtors*, 101 ILL. B.J. 134 (2013)(discussing the Illinois statute).

[296] Presser, *supra* note 284.

[297] ACLU PRIVATE DEBT REPORT, *supra* note 271, at 5.

[298] *Id.* at 6; Presser, *supra* note 284.

[299] ACLU PRIVATE DEBT REPORT, *supra* note 271, at 54.

[300] *Id.*

[301] *Id.* at 54–55.

[302] Rakesh Kochhar & Anthony Cilluffo, *How Wealth Inequality Has Changed in the U.S. Since the Great Recession, by Race, Ethnicity and Income*, PEW RES. CTR. (Nov. 1, 2017), www.pewresearch.org /fact-tank/2017/11/01/how-wealth-inequality-has-changed-in-the-u-s-since-the-great-recession-by-race-ethnicity-and-income/.

[303] Lisa J. Dettling et al., *Recent Trends in Wealth-Holding by Race and Ethnicity: Evidence from the Survey of Consumer Finances*, FED. RES. (Sept. 27, 2017), www.federalreserve.gov/econres/notes/feds-notes

African-American families "are the most likely to be late on payments."[304] Research on subprime lending suggests that subprime borrowers are frequently found in low-income and racial minority neighborhoods.[305]

A study by the National Fair Housing Alliance on indirect automobile lending transactions found that "62.5 percent of the time, Non-White testers who were more qualified than their White counterparts received more costly pricing options [and] [o]n average, Non-White testers who experienced discrimination would have paid an average of $2,662.56 more over the life of the loan than less-qualified White testers."[306] A study conducted by the Center for Responsible Lending on vehicle dealers' practices determined that although African-American and Hispanic consumers tried to negotiate vehicle prices at the same rate as non-minority consumers, these groups of consumers "received worse pricing" and were "nearly twice as likely to be sold multiple add-on products" that significantly increase loan costs.[307] The study goes on to note that dealers may convince consumers that these "add-on products" are a condition of loan approval.[308] Subprime borrowers are particularly vulnerable to these tactics because many of them are limited to indirect lending transactions and do not believe they have access to alternative sources of financing.[309] Various other research on discrimination in automobile lending transactions have reached similar conclusions.[310]

Given the fact that the various pieces of research discussed earlier suggest that historically marginalized consumers are indeed receiving more expensive loans, these consumers could be more likely to default on installment loan agreements. The widening of the wealth gap and less access to financial resources are likely also contributing factors. Payment defaults negatively impact a consumer's credit score. As a result, lending institutions may be more likely to insist that these groups of consumers consent to the use of asset collection technology in their IoT products as a condition of loan approval. Thus, in the IoT setting, historically marginalized consumers are more likely to fall prey to privacy intrusions, invasive data

---

/recent-trends-in-wealth-holding-by-race-and-ethnicity-evidence-from-the-survey-of-consumer-finances-20170927.htm.

[304] *Id.*

[305] U.S. Dep't of the Treasury & U.S. Dep't of Hous. & Urban Dev., Curbing Predatory Home Mortgage Lending: A Joint Report 45–47 (2000); *see also* Consumers Union SWRO, Minorities Pay More for Home Ownership (2002).

[306] Nat'l Fair Hous. All., Discrimination When Buying a Car: How the Color of Your Skin Can Affect Your Car-Shopping Experience 5 (2018).

[307] Delvin Davis , Ctr. for Responsible Lending, Non-Negotiable: Negotiation Doesn't Help African Americans and Latinos on Dealer-Financed Car Loans 2–3 (2014).

[308] *Id.*

[309] *Id.* at 7.

[310] *See generally* Ian Ayres, *Fair Driving: Gender and Race Discrimination in Retail Car Negotiations,* 104 Harv. L. Rev. 817 (1991); Ian Ayres, *Further Evidence of Discrimination in New Car Negotiations and Estimates of Its Cause,* 94 Mich. L. Rev. 109 (1995); Ian Ayres & Peter Siegelman, *Race and Gender Discrimination in Bargaining for a New Car,* 85 Am. Econ. Rev. 304 (1995).

surveillance, and digital restraints associated with asset collection technology than other groups of consumers. This problem is compounded in the automobile context.

Increasingly, consumers are offered longer repayment periods on subprime auto loans, and they are defaulting on these agreements at higher rates.[311] Longer repayment periods generally translate into lower monthly payments for consumers, while allowing interest and fees to accrue in favor of vehicle lenders. Of noteworthy concern is the depreciating nature of vehicle values. As a result, the value of a defaulting subprime auto borrower's[312] automobile is likely to be significantly less than the amount owed to the auto lender, resulting in a deficiency and potential exposure to a deficiency lawsuit. These concerns, as well as discrimination in vehicle lending transactions and higher incidences of repossessions, will be magnified in the IoT age in light of the congressional dismantling of the CFPB's lending guidance on dealer markups.

These racial disparities continue in the bankruptcy context as well.[313] Once a vehicle has been repossessed, the possibility of an individual filing for bankruptcy may increase.[314] Research on automobile loans in bankruptcy proceedings found that African-American consumers filing for bankruptcy tend to have vehicle loans that are higher than the value of their cars.[315] The study also found that African-American consumers are more likely to file for bankruptcy because of automobile loans and are less likely to have other types of assets.[316]

With respect to discrimination in the debt collection process, a ProPublica analysis of debt collection proceedings in various metropolitan locations found that "the rate of [court] judgments was twice as high in mostly black neighborhoods

---

[311]   Cecile Gutscher, *Subprime Auto Debt Is Booming Even as Defaults Soar*, BLOOMBERG, www.bloomberg.com/news/articles/2018-02-02/never-mind-defaults-debt-backed-by-subprime-auto-loans-is-hot (last updated Feb. 2, 2018); Zabritski, *supra* note 42.

[312]   There are varying definitions of a subprime borrower. Jim Akin, *What Are the Different Credit Scoring Ranges?*, EXPERIAN (Jan. 7, 2019), www.experian.com/blogs/ask-experian/infographic-what-are-the-different-scoring-ranges/ (defining subprime borrowers as individuals with credit scores of 580 to 669 and those with a credit score of 579 or lower as "poor credit"); *Segment of Population Using Alternative Loans May Perform Well on Traditional Credit Products*, TRANSUNION (May 24, 2018), https://newsroom.transunion.com/segment-of-population-using-alternative-loans--may-perform-well-on-traditional-credit-products/ (defining subprime borrowers as "consumers with a VantageScore 3.0 credit score of 300 to 600"); *What Is a Good Credit Score*, EQUIFAX, www.equifax.com/personal/education/credit/score/what-is-a-good-credit-score/ (last visited Dec. 21, 2019) (defining subprime borrowers as individuals with credit scores from 580 to 669).

[313]   *See, e.g.*, Paul Kiel & Hannah Fresques, *Data Analysis: Bankruptcy and Race in America*, PROPUBLICA (Sept. 27, 2017), https://projects.propublica.org/graphics/bankruptcy-data-analysis (finding that "[f]or people residing in majority black zip codes who file for bankruptcy, the odds of having their cases dismissed (and failing to attain lasting relief) were more than twice as high as those of debtors living in mostly white zip codes").

[314]   *See* Elizabeth A. Berger et al., *Credit Where Credit Is Due: Drivers of Subprime Credit* (June 25, 2018) (unpublished manuscript), https://ssrn.com/abstract=2989380.

[315]   Foohey et al., *supra* note 211, at 32.

[316]   *Id.* at 33.

as it was in mostly white ones."[317] Similarly, a survey conducted by the think tank Demos and the National Association for the Advancement of Colored People determined that middle-income "African-Americans are more likely to be" contacted by debt collectors than similarly situated White consumers.[318] If, as these pieces of research suggest, these groups of consumers are indeed disproportionately and aggressively pursued by debt collectors, then they are likely more susceptible to experiencing incidences of private debt criminalization tactics than other groups of consumers. Recall that in the IoT context, lenders and debt collection companies have new and more effective methods (such as asset collection technology) to collect and analyze our data and repossess our collateral. In such a setting, minority and low-income consumers are more vulnerable than other groups of consumers than ever before.

Debt collection companies can use information about our financial and employment history to determine whether we are likely to make payments, and their practices could have a discriminatory impact on vulnerable groups of consumers. There is no doubt that developments in data analytics and machine learning in the IoT setting will also be used by the debt collection industry. Various analytics companies already offer similar services to debt collection businesses. One such company touts that through artificial intelligence and voice analytics it "analyzes the emotions and behaviors of debtors to identify [which debtors are] most likely to pay during a follow-up call" and which debtors are least likely to pay.[319] Data obtained from IoT devices and asset collection technology could be analyzed to more accurately identify and target minority and low-income consumers who are more likely to respond to debt criminalization tactics or repeated demands for payment, and determine whether the social and familial networks of these groups of consumers would be able to aid them in making payments. These data could also be used to more effectively identify minority and low-income consumers who are unlikely to attend post-judgment hearings, thereby allowing creditors to avoid several critiques associated with multiple requests for arrest warrants in debt collection lawsuits. Various technological advancements in the IoT era combined with companies' use of our data may worsen predatory behavior and create new proxies for discrimination in the lending and debt collection process.

Private debt collectors sometimes "contract with county district attorney offices" to pursue indigent individuals for payment, particularly for bounced checks.[320]

---

[317] Paul Kiel & Annie Waldman, *The Color of Debt: How Collection Suits Squeeze Black Neighborhoods*, PROPUBLICA (Oct. 8, 2015), www.propublica.org/article/debt-collection-lawsuits-squeeze-black-neighborhoods.

[318] CATHERINE RUETSCHLIN & DEDRICK ASANTE-MUHAMMAD, THE CHALLENGE OF CREDIT CARD DEBT FOR THE AFRICAN AMERICAN MIDDLE CLASS 2 (2013).

[319] *Accelerate Collections*, RANKMINER, www.rankminer.com/product-applications/collections (last visited Mar. 19, 2020).

[320] ACLU PRIVATE DEBT REPORT, *supra* note 271, at 4, 26–31.

These entities threaten individuals with fees, jail and prosecution.[321] What if these "government-contracted" private debt collectors could also access and use IoT and asset collection technology data, and data analytics to more effectively target non-paying racial minorities? It could further contribute to the use of debt criminalization tactics against such consumers, and if warrants are issued it may also contribute to the criminalization of historically marginalized groups. For such consumers, the debt criminalization problem goes beyond the civil debt collection process, and also occurs in criminal cases across the country where defendants are jailed for failing to pay fees and fines associated with court proceedings.[322] Minority and low-income individuals bear the brunt of these fees.[323]

As we have seen in this chapter, the IoT and asset collection technology combined with inadequacies in commercial lending frameworks can enable privacy, digital domination, discriminatory, and debt criminalization harms. However, there are additional deficiencies in commercial lending frameworks. Commercial lending frameworks as well as the Bankruptcy Code and corporate law can also allow companies to disclose, sell, transfer, and profit from our data with impunity. These types of disclosures also raise privacy and security concerns that are magnified by the volume of data the IoT generates, and the ever-expanding pervasive nature of corporate IoT surveillance.

---

[321] *Id.*

[322] Cain v. City of New Orleans, 327 F.R.D. 111 (E.D. La. 2018) (discussing court fees and fines in the Louisiana criminal justice system); Erik De La Garza, *Arkansas Judge Sued for "Debtors" Prison*, Courthouse News Serv. (Aug. 9, 2018), www.courthousenews.com/arkansas-judge-sued-for-debtors-prison/; Debra Cassens Weiss, *2 Federal Judges Find Constitutional Problem with Debtors Prisons and Bail in New Orleans*, Am. B. Ass'n J. (Aug. 7, 2018, 11:54 am), www.abajournal.com/news/article/two_federal_judges_find_constitutional_problem_with_debtors_prisons_and_bai/.

[323] Matthew Menendez et al., Brennan Ctr. for Justice, The Steep Costs of Criminal Justice Fees and Fines: A Fiscal Analysis of Three States and Ten Counties 7 (2019), www.brennancenter.org/sites/default/files/2019-11/2019_10_Fees%26Fines_Final5.pdf.

7

Consumer Data in Corporate Transactions

Data about consumers has long been a prized asset of organizations. As Paul Schwartz has observed, the "monetary value" of consumer data continues to grow significantly and companies eagerly profit from consumer data.[1] The IoT will foster an exponential growth in the volume, quality, and variety of consumer-generated data. As a result, there will be more of our data available for companies to analyze, exploit, and extract value from. As we have seen in previous chapters, several legal scholars have highlighted the limits of companies' privacy policies and conditions of use, and the role of these documents in enabling data disclosures. However, less attention has been given in legal scholarship to consumer data transfers and exposures in business transactions.[2] Consumer data may be transferred or disclosed to unaffiliated entities in mergers and acquisitions, secured financing transactions, and bankruptcy proceedings. Technology giants use certain corporate transactions to expand their market dominance and to acquire data about us.

Whether consumer data can be easily transferred to third parties as part of a corporate transaction depends significantly on the provisions of an organization's privacy policy and conditions of use. A *New York Times* report found that eighty-five of the "top 100 websites in the United States" had privacy policies or conditions of use that authorized consumer data transfers in the event of "a merger, acquisition, bankruptcy, asset sale or other [business] transaction."[3] In this chapter, I argue that in addition to privacy policies, both corporate and commercial legal frameworks play a critical role in facilitating opaque consumer data disclosures in corporate transactions that increase technology giants' dominance in the IoT era. Discussions about the inadequacies of privacy policies and our lack of privacy must effectively

---

[1] Paul M. Schwartz, *Property, Privacy, and Personal Data*, 117 HARV. L. REV. 2055, 2056–57 (2004).

[2] *See* Stacy-Ann Elvy, *Commodifying Consumer Data in the Era of the Internet of Things*, 59 B.C. L. REV. 423, 432 n.36 (2018); Walter W. Miller, Jr. & Maureen A. O'Rourke, *Bankruptcy Law v. Privacy Rights: Which Holds the Trump Card?*, 38 HOUS. L. REV. 777, 807–33 (2001); Xuan-Thao N. Nguyen, *Collateralizing Privacy*, 78 TUL. L. REV. 553, 586–87 (2004).

[3] Natasha Singer & Jeremy B. Merrill, *When a Company Is Put Up for Sale, in Many Cases, Your Personal Data Is, Too*, N.Y. TIMES (June 28, 2015), www.nytimes.com/2015/06/29/technology/when-a-company-goes-up-for-sale-in-many-cases-so-does-your-personal-data.html.

consider the legal frameworks and corporate transactions that further enable data transfers and strip us of our ability to determine what happens to the data we generate while allowing organizations to solidify their control over the IoT market.

THE ROLE OF PRIVACY POLICIES

Not surprisingly, the privacy policies of several IoT companies allow data generated from our use of their IoT devices, services, and mobile applications to be transferred and disclosed to third parties in various business transactions. For instance, Amazon's privacy policy authorizes the transfer of consumer data upon a "business transfer."[4] The privacy policy of Owlet provides: "[w]e reserve the right to transfer your information to service providers, advisors, potential transactional partners, or other third parties in connection with the consideration, negotiation, or completion of a corporate transaction in which we are acquired by or merged with another company or we sell, liquidate, or transfer all or a portion of our assets."[5] Recall from Chapter 2 that Owlet manufactures infant IoT products that collect sensitive health and activity data about infants. In some instances, a company's privacy policy may not explicitly obligate the company to notify consumers when their data will be transferred, allow consumers to opt out of the disclosure of previously collected data, or require the acquiring company to observe the existing privacy policy. Federal Trade Commission guidance on this issue indicates that companies may only decline to continue honoring previously made privacy promises if they obtain affirmative consumer consent to material privacy policy changes.[6] The problem, of course, with only requiring consumer consent is that consumers are forced to accept companies' privacy policies and terms and conditions in order to use offered services and products. This includes amendments and revisions to existing privacy policies.

Ring's privacy policy authorizes consumer data transfers and disclosures in the event of several business transactions, including "a merger, acquisition, joint venture, reorganization, divestiture, dissolution or liquidation."[7] The company's privacy policy indicates that its devices collect geolocation data, facial recognition data, and video and audio recordings and that it obtains the social media data of users that link their social media accounts to its product.[8] Blink, an IoT camera provider, collects

---

4   *Amazon Privacy Notice*, AMAZON, www.amazon.com/gp/help/customer/display.html?nodeId=201909010 (last updated Jan. 1, 2020).

5   *Privacy Policy*, OWLET, https://owletcare.com/pages/privacy (last updated Jan. 2, 2020).

6   *See* Press Release, Fed. Trade Comm'n, FTC Notifies Facebook, WhatsApp of Privacy Obligations in Light of Proposed Acquisition (Apr. 10, 2014), www.ftc.gov/news-events/press-releases/2014/04/ftc-notifies-facebook-whatsapp-privacy-obligations-light-proposed; Letter from Jessica L. Rich, Dir., Bureau of Consumer Prot., Fed. Trade Comm'n, to Erin Egan, Chief Privacy Officer, Facebook, Inc., & Anne Hoge, Gen. Counsel, WhatsApp Inc. (Apr. 10, 2014), www.ftc.gov/system/files/documents/public_statements/297701/140410facebookwhatappltr.pdf.

7   *Privacy Notice*, RING (Nov. 19, 2019), https://shop.ring.com/pages/privacy-notice.

8   *Id.*

several types of data about consumers using its products and services, including images, videos, and audio.[9] Blink also automatically collects location data and "[d] evice metrics such as when a device is in use, application usage, connectivity data, and any errors or event failures."[10] The company's privacy policy notes that it reserves the right to transfer consumer data in a corporate transaction.[11]

MERGERS AND ACQUISITIONS

Various sources of business law provide the mechanisms that govern mergers and acquisitions and asset sales by corporations.[12] Today's dominant technology companies are the product of a large number of mergers and acquisitions.[13] For instance, Google acquired approximately 270 firms over an almost twenty-year period.[14] In the last few years there have been multiple mergers and acquisitions by leading technology companies. Facebook acquired Instagram and WhatsApp in 2012 and 2014, respectively. In 2016, Walmart acquired Jet.com, an e-commerce platform for $3.3 billion.[15] In 2017, Amazon purchased Whole Foods and Verizon acquired Yahoo.[16] In 2020, Apple acquired Dark Sky, a well-liked weather mobile app.[17]

Many of these acquisitions involved the transfer and disclosure of consumer data to the acquiring company.[18] Upon its acquisition of Yahoo, Verizon acquired billions of users and the immense data associated with those user accounts.[19] The

---

[9]   *Privacy Notice*, BLINK, https://blinkforhome.com/pages/privacy-policy#sectionb (last visited Dec. 1, 2019).

[10] *Id.*

[11] *Id.*

[12] *See, e.g.*, 15 U.S.C. § 78m(d) (2019); DEL. CODE ANN. tit. 8, §§ 251, 271 (2019).

[13] Tim Wu & Stuart A. Thompson, Opinion, *The Roots of Big Tech Run Disturbingly Deep*, N.Y. TIMES (Jun. 7, 2019), www.nytimes.com/interactive/2019/06/07/opinion/google-facebook-mergers-acquisitions-antitrust.html.

[14] *Id.*

[15] Press Release, Walmart, Walmart Agrees to Acquire Jet.com, One of the Fastest Growing e-Commerce Companies in the U.S. (Aug. 8. 2016), https://corporate.walmart.com/newsroom/2016/08/08/walmart-agrees-to-acquire-jet-com-one-of-the-fastest-growing-e-commerce-companies-in-the-u-s.

[16] *See* Ingrid Lunden, *Verizon Closes $4.5B Acquisition of Yahoo, Marissa Mayer Resigns*, TECHCRUNCH (June 13, 2017, 7:32 AM), https://techcrunch.com/2017/06/13/verizon-closes-4-5b-acquisition-of-yahoo-marissa-mayer-resigns-memo/; Greg Petro, *Amazon's Acquisition of Whole Foods is About Two Things: Data and Product*, FORBES (Aug. 2, 2017, 12:13 PM), www.forbes.com/sites/gregpetro/2017/08/02/amazons-acquisition-of-whole-foods-is-about-two-things-data-and-product/#2b097afca808.

[17] Brian Barrett, *Apple Buys Dark Sky in an Android Worst-Case Scenario*, WIRED (Apr. 1, 2020, 3:01 PM), www.wired.com/story/apple-buys-dark-sky/amp.

[18] *See* Sarah Berger, *Keeping Track of Your Data Is Getting Harder to Do*, BANKRATE (Aug. 18, 2016), www.bankrate.com/finance/identity-theft/consumer-data-company-acquisition.aspx/amp/; Samuel Gibbs, *Ring: Amazon Aids Smart Home Push By Closing Video-Doorbell Firm Deal*, GUARDIAN (Apr. 12, 2018), www.theguardian.com/technology/2018/apr/12/ring-amazon-smart-home-acquisition-video-doorbell-maker; Petro, *supra* note 16.

[19] David Lazarus, *Your Privacy: Verizon's Takeover of Yahoo Is All About User Data*, L.A. TIMES (Feb 24, 2017, 3:00AM), www.latimes.com/business/lazarus/la-fi-lazarus-verizon-yahoo-privacy-20170224-

revised privacy policy governing Yahoo accounts after the acquisition contains a provision that notes that the company may collect and analyze users' emails, photographs, attachments, and other communications.[20] In contrast to other email providers, such as Google and Microsoft, the company reportedly continues to review users' communications to target them for contracting across the web based on the interest group profiles the company creates.[21] Empowered with Yahoo's volumes of data, and the repeal of the Obama-era net neutrality rules, Verizon (under its Oath unit) now has almost limitless power to profit from our data.

When Nest acquired Dropcam in 2014, the company obtained access to Dropcam's consumer data.[22] Nest, which previously operated independently from Google as a subsidiary of Alphabet, Inc., announced in 2018 that it would join with Google to work with the company's hardware division.[23] This collaboration raises questions about the extent to which Nest's consumer data will be shared with Google. Nest previously promised to refrain from sharing consumers' data with Google. Consumers who use Nest devices in conjunction with the Google Assistant will have their data shared with Google.[24]

Amazon's acquisition of Whole Foods allowed the company to obtain offline information on consumers' food shopping habits, patterns, and preferences.[25] Combining in-store offline data with other sources of data allows Amazon to influence and meet consumer needs with increasing accuracy. The vast quantities of consumer data that Whole Foods holds was likely one of the primary purposes behind Amazon's decision to pay $13.7 billion dollars to acquire the company.[26]

Amazon has also acquired several IoT companies in a bid to expand its influence in the smart home industry. The company acquired Blink in 2017 and Ring in 2018,

---

story.html; Anjali Athavaley & David Shepardson, *Verizon, Yahoo Agree to Lowered $4.48 Billion Deal Following Cyber Attacks*, REUTERS (Feb. 21, 2017, 4:38 AM), www.reuters.com/article/us-yahoo-m-a-ver izon/verizon-yahoo-agree-to-lowered-4-48-billion-deal-following-cyber-attacks-idUSKBN1601EK.

[20] *Welcome to the Oath Privacy Center*, OATH, https://policies.oath.com/in/en/oath/privacy/ (last updated Apr. 2018).

[21] Douglas MacMillan et al., *Yahoo, Bucking Industry, Scans Emails for Data to Sell Advertisers*, WALL ST. J. (Aug. 28, 2018, 10:36 AM), www.wsj.com/articles/yahoo-bucking-industry-scans-emails-for-data-to -sell-advertisers-1535466959.

[22] John Lowensohn, *Nest Buying Video-Monitoring Startup Dropcam for $555 Million*, VERGE (June 20, 2014, 8:21 PM), www.theverge.com/2014/6/20/5829126/nest-and-google-acquire-home-monitoring-company-dropcam.

[23] *See* Wendy Lee, *Nest, Now a Google Subsidiary, Starts Selling Video Doorbell*, S.F. CHRONICLE (Mar. 14, 2018), www.sfchronicle.com/business/amp/Nest-now-a-Google-subsidiary-starts-selling-12754008 .php; Announcement from Rick Osterloh, Senior Vice President, Hardware, & Marwan Fawaz, CEO, Nest, Nest to Join Forces with Google's Hardware Team (Feb. 7, 2018), https://blog.google /inside-google/company-announcements/nest-join-forces-googles-hardware-team/.

[24] Lee, *supra* note 23; Leo Kelion, *Google-Nest Merger Raises Privacy Issue*, BBC (Feb. 8, 2018), https:// www.bbc.com/news/technology-42989073.

[25] *See The Big Prize in Amazon-Whole Foods Deal? Data*, WALL ST. J.: TECH NEWS BRIEFING (June 21, 2017, 12:05 AM), www.wsj.com/podcasts/tech-news-briefing/the-big-prize-in-amazon-whole-foods-deal-data/8ac160cd-6769-477c-9bd0-999fa6b2dd10.

[26] *See id.*

and announced plans to buy Eero, a mesh Wi-Fi networking system provider, in 2019.[27] Amazon's head of devices acknowledged the company's acquisition of Ring users' data as part of the transaction.[28] Amazon's Eero acquisition allows it to potentially gain access to Eero users' data, including IoT device usage patterns and the amount of "time spent online."[29] It also potentially gives Amazon the ability to one day slow down the performance of Eero users' non-Amazon IoT products in favor of their Amazon equivalents.[30] Through its Amazon Alexa Fund, the company has also provided venture capital funding to IoT companies, such as Ring and Ecobee, a smart thermostat manufacturer.[31] Ecobee's IoT thermostat is already Alexa enabled.[32] Amazon's acquisition of multiple IoT firms allows it to obtain more data about the consumers using the products of those acquired companies and further its deep understanding of those consumers' daily lives.

The technology titans of today are increasingly flexing their market dominance by blocking the devices and services of their competitors. For instance, Google previously blocked access to its YouTube app on Amazon's Fire TV and Echo Show.[33] Amazon refused to sell Google's IoT products on its platform, and restricted consumers' ability to use its Prime Video application on Google devices.[34] Consumers were of course caught in the middle until the issue was resolved almost eighteen months later.

Mergers and acquisitions involving large technology firms that hold vast quantities of consumer data, such as Amazon and Google, increases these companies'

---

[27] *See* Darrell Etherington, *Amazon Acquires Connected Camera and Doorbell Startup Blink*, TECHCRUNCH (Dec. 22, 2017, 7:58 AM), https://techcrunch.com/2017/12/22/amazon-acquires-connected-camera-and-doorbell-startup-blink/; Press Release, Amazon, Amazon to Acquire Eero to Help Customers Better Connect Smart Home Devices (Feb. 11, 2019), https://press.aboutamazon.com/news-releases/news-release-details/amazon-acquire-eero-help-customers-better-connect-smart-home.

[28] Gibbs, *supra* note 18.

[29] John Patrick Pullen, *Amazon Buying Eero Could Create Tech's Most Dangerous Data Company*, FORTUNE (Feb. 12, 2019, 4:40 PM), https://fortune.com/2019/02/12/amazon-buys-eero-wifi-acquisition-data-privacy/.

[30] *See id.*

[31] *See* Paul Bernard, *Alexa Fund Invests in Three Early-Stage Voice Startups Showcasing New Alexa Capabilities*, AMAZON ALEXA (Sept. 27, 2018), https://developer.amazon.com/blogs/alexa/post/7a2dd936-a623-4c7e-8591-1f6674eb5d22/alexa-fund-invests-in-three-early-stage-voice-startups-showcasing-new-alexa-capabilities; Lora Kolodny, *Amazon is Backing Ecobee, a Smart Thermostat Company, Just Days After Buying Ring*, CNBC, www.cnbc.com/2018/03/06/amazon-alexa-fund-and-energy-impact-partners-invested-in-ecobee.html (last updated Mar. 7, 2018).

[32] Kolodny, *supra* note 31.

[33] *A Google vs. Amazon Antitrust Lesson*, WALL ST. J. (Dec. 12, 2017, 8:19 PM), www.wsj.com/articles/a-google-vs-amazon-antitrust-lesson-1513125303.

[34] *Id.*; Tony Romm & Abha Bhattarai, *European Regulators Are Looking into Antitrust Concerns at Amazon*, WASH. POST (Sept. 19, 2018, 9:40 AM), www.washingtonpost.com/business/2018/09/19/european-regulators-are-looking-into-anti-trust-concerns-amazon/?noredirect=on&utm_term=.c501b97ae5fd; David Katzmaier & Ty Pendlebury, *YouTube App Now on Fire TV; Amazon Prime Video Arrives on Google Chromecast*, CNET (Jul. 9, 2019, 6:00AM) www.cnet.com/news/youtube-app-coming-to-fire-tv-amazon-prime-video-arrives-on-google-chromecast/.

dominance in the IoT setting.[35] However, as Mark Lemley and Andrew McCreary note, these mergers and acquisitions do not always fit neatly within existing merger review principles and distinctions.[36] These traditional distinctions include horizontal and vertical mergers.[37] Amazon's continued dominance and acquisition of IoT companies may bring about additional antitrust scrutiny.[38] Amazon provides a marketplace for products sold by itself and others, and services that allow competitors to provide and ship their products to consumers, all while collecting significant quantities of data about consumers and competitors' products. These data can be used to entice us to purchase Amazon branded products instead of similar products offered by competitors.[39] For instance, Amazon's Alexa recommends Amazon branded products to users.[40]

Amazon has a unique status in the IoT marketplace. Recall that the company manufactures its own IoT products and sells IoT products manufactured by others on its platform. Recall from Chapter 2 that Amazon also provides cloud services to IoT companies.[41] Amazon now dominates the cloud computing industry and has used its market power to successfully monetize smaller rival companies' software tools while simultaneously ensuring that these companies "have little choice but to work with Amazon."[42] Increasingly, IoT product manufacturers, including small startups, are offering devices that are compatible with Amazon's services and products, including Amazon's DRS and Alexa.[43] In partnership with other entities,

---

[35] *See* Press Release, Fed. Trade Comm'n, Google Agrees to Change Its Business Practices to Resolve FTC Competition Concerns in the Markets for Devices Like Smart Phones, Games and Tablets, and in Online Search (Jan. 3, 2013), www.ftc.gov/news-events/press-releases/2013/01/google-agrees-change-its-business-practices-resolve-ftc; Google Inc., No. 111-0163 (F.T.C. Jan. 3 2013), www.ftc.gov/sites/default/files/documents/public_statements/statement-commission-regarding-googles-search-practices/130103bril lgooglesearchstmt.pdf.

[36] Mark Lemley & Andrew McCreary, *Exit Strategy*, 78–82, https://papers.ssrn.com/sol3/papers.cfm?abstract_id=3506919.

[37] *Id.* at 81. Some technology companies' acquisitions may be viewed as conglomerate mergers. *Id.* at 82; Wu & Thompson, *supra* note 13(noting that Google has had fifty-five conglomerate mergers over a twenty-year period). Conglomerate mergers have been viewed as less deserving of antitrust scrutiny. Abu Bradford et al., *The Chicago School's Limited Influence on International Antitrust*, 87 U. CHI. L. REV. 297, 307 (2020).

[38] *See* John Bowden, *FTC Launches Amazon Antitrust Probe: Report*, HILL (Sept. 11, 2019, 12:21 PM), https://thehill.com/policy/technology/460905-ftc-launches-amazon-antitrust-probe-report (discussing an existing FTC investigation into Amazon practices). *See generally* Lina M. Khan, *Amazon's Antitrust Paradox*, 126 YALE L.J. 710 (2017) (discussing Amazon's market power); Apple Inc. v. Pepper, 139 S. Ct. 1514, 1514 (2019).

[39] Julie Creswell, *How Amazon Steers Shoppers to Its Own Products*, N.Y. TIMES (June 23, 2018), www.nytimes.com/2018/06/23/business/amazon-the-brand-buster.html.

[40] *Id.* (noting that "consumers asking Amazon's Alexa to 'buy batteries' get only one option: AmazonBasics").

[41] *See AWS IoT Core*, AWS, https://aws.amazon.com/iot-core/ (last visited Dec. 1, 2019).

[42] Daisuke Wakabayashi, *Prime Leverage: How Amazon Wields Power in the Technology World*, N.Y. TIMES (Dec. 16, 2019), www.nytimes.com/2019/12/15/technology/amazon-aws-cloud-competition.html.

[43] *See Amazon Dash Replenishment*, AMAZON ALEXA, https://developer.amazon.com/en-US/alexa/dash-services (last visited Dec. 1, 2019); David Nield, *Why (and How) Startups Are Tying Into Amazon's DRS System*, READWRITE (Oct. 7, 2015), https://readwrite.com/2015/10/07/amazon-drs-partners/.

Amazon's DRS has expanded to include IoT packages embedded with sensors that can monitor product use rates, and place subsequent orders for consumers with Amazon.[44] Thus, the company could potentially have the ability to collect data on any product that is accompanied by DRS-enabled IoT packaging. Amazon's Home Key Kit, which is accompanied by a mobile app, allows the company to provide in-home and in-car deliveries of groceries and other goods even when consumers are not home.[45] In effect the company has the keys to access our homes and vehicles, and can collect location data on our vehicles during delivery.[46] It is clear that Amazon wields significant power and control over the emerging IoT market.

Amazon is not alone in using mergers and acquisitions to expand its dominance and control in the market. Recall that Google has acquired more than 200 startup companies, including YouTube and Nest.[47] Google is also increasingly entering the IoT space. Recall from Chapter 5 that through Nest, Google acquired the Revolv IoT home hub in 2014.[48] In 2018, Google announced plans to acquire Xively to boost its IoT cloud offerings.[49] The company also acquired Onward, a firm that provides customer service solutions powered by artificial intelligence.[50] Google's Android Things is a platform for IoT devices and services that the company hopes Android IoT manufacturers will widely use.[51] Google also provides IoT cloud-based services.[52] IoT companies also manufacture products that are compatible with Google Home and Assistant.

[44]   *Jabil Packing Solutions and Amazon Dash Replenishment Services*, JABIL, www.jabil.com/dam/jcr:497af7ff-7133-4855-b263-e98f5edcbc7e/060518-JPS%20Amazon%20DRS%20Fact%20Sheet.pdf (last visited May 19, 2020); Lisa Pierce, *Smart Packaging Helps Boost Amazon's Auto-Replenish Service*, PACKAGING DIG. (June 12, 2018), www.packagingdigest.com/smart-packaging-helps-boost-amazon-s-auto-replenish-service; *Smart Packaging with Dash Replenishment Service*, JABIL, www.jabil.com/industries/packaged-goods/drs.html (last visited May 19, 2020).

[45]   *See Open Freedom*, AMAZON, www.amazon.com/b?node=17735409011&ref_=pe_30107000 (last visited Dec. 1, 2019).

[46]   *See Open Anywhere*, AMAZON, www.amazon.com/b/ref=s9_acss_bw_cg_keyprdpk_12a1_w?&node=17051031011&pf_rd_m=ATVPDKIKX0DER&pf_rd_s=merchandised-search-7&pf_rd_r=3EZ72HAVZMJNYASPSMKJ&pf_rd_t=101&pf_rd_p=527882ff-e265-4a3c-8c6e-e634ba89a2a2&pf_rd_i=17735409011#eligibility (last visited Dec. 1, 2019).

[47]   Steve Kroft, *How Did Google Get So Big?*, 60 MINUTES (May 21, 2018), www.cbsnews.com/news/how-did-google-get-so-big/.

[48]   Aaron Tilley, *Google's Nest Acquires Smart Home Hub Startup Revolv to Control Every Device in Your Home*, FORBES (Oct. 24, 2014, 4:16 PM), www.forbes.com/sites/aarontilley/2014/10/24/googles-nest-acquires-smart-home-hub-maker-revolv/#3b9c6c213761.

[49]   Antony Passemard, *Google Announces Intent to Acquire Xively*, GOOGLE (Feb. 15, 2018), https://blog.google/products/google-cloud/google-cloud-announces-intent-to-acquire-xively/.

[50]   Lucas Matney, *Google Acquires Customer Service Automation Startup Onward*, TECHCRUNCH (Oct. 2, 2018, 10:19 AM), https://techcrunch.com/2018/10/02/google-acquires-customer-service-automation-startup-onward/.

[51]   *See Android Things*, ANDROID DEVELOPERS, https://developer.android.com/things/ (last visited Dec. 1, 2019); Dave Smith, *Android Things Developer Preview 7*, ANDROID DEVELOPERS (Mar. 6, 2018), https://android-developers.googleblog.com/2018/03/android-things-developer-preview-7.html.

[52]   *See Google Cloud*, GOOGLE, https://cloud.google.com/iot-edge/ (last visited Dec. 1, 2019); *Google Cloud IoT Solutions*, GOOGLE, https://cloud.google.com/solutions/iot (last visited Dec. 1, 2019).

In 2019, Google revealed plans to acquire Fitbit, a company that has been a leading provider of IoT wearable devices.[53] Recall from Chapter 5 that Fitbit also acquired Pebble, a former smartwatch competitor.[54] With the Fibit acquisition, Google gains access to current and future Fitbit users' health-related data. Google has promised to "give [current] Fitbit users the choice to review, move, or delete their data."[55] Fitbit has indicated that users' health-related data "will not be used for Google ads."[56] However, it is unlikely that current Fitbit owners who would like to continue to use their Fitbit devices and associated online services will be able to use their devices without sharing some device data with Google going forward. Statements focusing on data usage and advertisements post transaction are also misleading. Data usage is not confined to targeted advertising. Health-related data can reveal deep insights about us and can be used for much more than advertising. Fitbit provides data-driven services to its users, including Fitbit premium (a subscription service) that mines user data to provide fitness coaching.[57] Google is likely to become an integral player in the provision of Fitbit data-driven services.

Similarly, when Nest was brought under Google's umbrella in 2018, Nest owners who needed to renew the IoT camera's online video recording and storage subscription service were strongly encouraged to merge their Nest accounts with their Google accounts.[58] Nest users are also required to merge their accounts with Google in order to access new device-related IoT services.[59] The Nest subscription service is a central feature of the IoT camera. Nest owners who elected to merge their accounts became subject to Google's privacy policy.[60] In light of the integral connection between the functionality of IoT devices and online services, technology companies' promises to allow consumers to delete or move data before an

---

[53] Lauren Goode, *What Google's Fitbit Buy Means for the Future of Wearables*, WIRED (Nov. 2, 2019, 7:00 AM), www.wired.com/story/google-fitbit-future-of-wearables/; Rick Osterloh, *Helping More People with Wearables: Google to Acquire Fitbit*, GOOGLE (Nov. 1, 2019), www.blog.google/products/hardware/agreement-with-fitbit.

[54] Press Release, Fitbit, Inc. Acquires Assets from Pebble, FITBIT (Dec. 7, 2016), https://investor.fitbit.com/press/press-releases/press-release-details/2016/Fitbit-Inc-Acquires-Assets-from-Pebble/default.aspx.

[55] Osterloh, *supra* note 53.

[56] Goode, *supra* note 53.

[57] Press Release, Fitbit to be Acquired by Google, FITBIT (Nov. 1, 2019), https://investor.fitbit.com/press/press-releases/press-release-details/2019/Fitbit-to-Be-Acquired-by-Google/default.aspx.

[58] *See* David Nield, *Why Nest Accounts Are Becoming Google Accounts and What You Can Do About It*, GIZMODO (Aug. 23, 2019, 10:10 AM), https://gizmodo.com/why-nest-accounts-are-becoming-google-accounts-and-what-1837473764; *What's Happening at Nest?*, NEST, https://nest.com/whats-happening/#what-happens-if-i-dont-migrate-to-a-google-account (last updated Nov. 27, 2019).

[59] *See What's Happening at Nest?, supra* note 58.

[60] *Our Commitment to Privacy in the Home*, GOOGLE, https://store.google.com/us/category/google_nest_privacy?hl=en-US&GoogleNest (last visited Dec. 1, 2019); *see also* Victoria Song, *Nest, As You Knew It, Is No More*, GIZMODO (May 10, 2019, 12:10 PM), https://gizmodo.com/nest-as-you-knew-it-is-no-more-1834667689; *What's Happening at Nest?, supra* note 58.

acquisition may be hollow. Google is also expanding its Nest line of products by combining smart speakers with Wi-Fi routers.[61]

As we have seen, mergers and acquisitions can enable data consolidation. When technology giants acquire other firms, they also acquire more information about us to exploit and profit from. Thus, mergers and acquisitions involving dominant technology companies, such as Google and Amazon, may very well restrict competition and enable privacy intrusions. These transactions could decrease consumer autonomy and choice, create barriers for new companies to enter the market, make it difficult for other existing companies to compete in the market, facilitate predatory pricing, and force other IoT manufacturers to build and offer products that are compatible with the products, platforms, and services technology giants offer.[62] Mergers and acquisitions can also decrease the number of competitor products that are on the market, and with fewer robust alternatives more consumers may turn to technology giants' products.[63] By consolidating their control of the market through the acquisition of smaller firms, technology giants can more effectively utilize invasive data collection practices and lax security measures that we are required to accept by virtue of the decrease in acceptable competitors providing similar services and products. We are then all corralled into acquiescing to privacy intrusions and surveillance in order to access the services and products technology giants provide.

One could argue that because data consolidation from mergers and acquisitions allows only a select group of companies to access our data, some privacy concerns may be alleviated. Stated differently, if fewer companies have access to our data then there are fewer opportunities for others to exploit and profit from our data. One response to this point is that technology giants, like other companies, have the ability to disclose and transfer our anonymized and identified data to third parties as well. Thus, data consolidation may not decrease other firms' access and ability to profit

---

[61] Dieter Bohn, *Nest Wifi First Look: Google Finally Combined a Smart Speaker and a Router*, VERGE (Oct. 15, 2019, 11:00 AM), www.theverge.com/2019/10/15/20908082/nest-wifi-smart-speaker-router-assistant-hands-on-photos-video-price.

[62] *See* NAT'L ASS. OF ATTORNEYS GEN., FED. TRADE COMM'N HEARINGS ON COMPETITION AND CONSUMER PROTECTION IN THE 21ST CENTURY, PUBLIC COMMENTS OF 43 STATE ATTORNEYS GENERAL (June 11, 2019) [hereinafter PUBLIC COMMENTS OF 43 STATE ATTORNEYS GENERAL], https://games-cdn.washingtonpost.com/notes/prod/default/documents/280a441c-bc99-4467-99ee-3dae197458c4/note/7fdfc363-2e70-4dd1-9680-1638de00f531.pdf#page=1; Sean Moran, *43 Attorneys General Urge FTC to Take Action on Big Tech Competition, Privacy*, BREITBART (June 11, 2019), www.breitbart.com/politics/2019/06/11/43-attorneys-general-urge-ftc-to-take-action-on-big-tech-competition-privacy/; *see also* U.S. DEP'T OF JUSTICE & FED. TRADE COMM'N, HORIZONTAL MERGER GUIDELINES (2010), www.ftc.gov/sites/default/files/attachments/merger-review/100819hmg.pdf; D. Bruce Hoffman, Acting Director, Bureau of Competition, Vertical Merger Enforcement at the FTC, Remarks at the Credit Suisse 2018 Washington Perspectives Conference (Jan. 10, 2018), www.ftc.gov/system/files/documents/public_statements/1304213/hoffman_vertical_merger_speech_final.pdf.

[63] For a detailed discussion of consumer lock-in concerns *See* Chris Jay Hoofnagle et al., *The Tethered Economy*, 87 GEO. WASH. L. REV. 783, 839–43 (2019).

from our data, and it may not automatically lead to more privacy protections. Instead, data consolidation may allow technology giants to have even more power to determine who gets to benefit from our data, while we are left with no choice but to further trust them with our data.

Technology startup firms are often complicit in technology giants' data consolidation.[64] As Lemley and McCreary note, "the venture capital funding model that dominates the tech industry is focused on the 'exit strategy' – the ways funders and founders can cash out their investment."[65] This exit strategy is often realized through a merger with a dominant firm.[66] Once the exit strategy is realized, the dominant technology firms that acquire startups can further solidify their market power by subsequently shutting down the smaller innovative firm after incorporating the best features of the acquired startup into their big technology products.[67] Examples of this tactic include Microsoft's acquisition of Wunderlist and Sunrise.[68]

When large technology companies acquire smaller firms, they also obtain the technical talent and expertise of startup firms' employees.[69] These employees, like other workers, may be subject to contractual restraints that decrease their job mobility.[70] Thus, talent consolidation can also be a side-effect of mergers and acquisitions. This may decrease the number of talented workers with the expertise to address privacy and security concerns who are available in the technology market, and who do not already work for dominant technology companies.

In 2018, European antitrust regulators launched a preliminary investigation into Amazon's use of merchant data.[71] Google was also fined $5 billion by European regulators in 2018 for several antitrust violations, including obligating companies to preinstall Google apps as a condition of Google app store licensing.[72] In 2019, the

---

[64] Lemley & McCreary, *supra* note 36, at 1–24.

[65] *Id.*; MARGARET O'MARA, THE CODE: SILICON AND THE REMAKING OF AMERICA 391 (2019).

[66] Lemley & McCreary, *supra* note 36, at 1–24 ("Most companies that succeed instead exit the market by merging with an existing firm.").

[67] *Id.*

[68] Richard Waters, *Big Tech's "Buy and Kill" Tactics Come Under Scrutiny*, FIN. TIMES (Feb. 13, 2020), www.ft.com/content/39b5c3a8-4e1a-11ea-95a0-43d18ec715f5.

[69] O'MARA *supra* note 65; Suresh Naidu et al., *Antitrust Remedies for Labor Market Power*, 132 HARV. L. REV. 536, 590–91(2018).

[70] Orly Lobel, *Gentlemen Prefer Bonds: How Employers Fix the Talent Market*, 59 SANTA CLARA L. REV. 663, 678–85 (2020). *See generally*, ORLY LOBEL, TALENT WANTS TO BE FREE: WHY WE SHOULD LEARN TO LOVE LEAKS, RAIDS AND FREE RIDING (2013).

[71] Romm & Bhattarai, *supra* note 34.

[72] Press Release, European Comm'n, Antitrust: Commission Fines Google €4.34 Billion for Illegal Practices Regarding Android Mobile Devices to Strengthen Dominance of Google's Search Engine (July 17, 2018), http://europa.eu/rapid/press-release_IP-18-4581_en.htm; *see also* Lauren Hirsch, *Google Antitrust Probe Expands as Bipartisan State AGs Beef Up Staff and Resources*, CNBC, www.cnbc.com/2020/02/07/google-antitrust-probe-expands-as-states-beef-up-staff.html (last updated Feb. 7, 2020) (noting that Google has appealed the $5 billion EU fine); Valentina Pop & Sam Schechner, *Google Appeals Against EU Antitrust Fines*, WALL ST. J. (Feb. 12, 2020, 11:38 AM), www.wsj.com/articles/google-starts-appeal-against-eu-antitrust-decisions-11581516872 (same); Sam Schechner, *Google Appeals $5 Billion EU*

FTC announced a new task force to monitor technology companies' anticompetition activities, including mergers.[73] Several state attorneys general have also urged the FTC to more actively regulate technology companies' acquisition activities by requiring "prior approval and/or prior notice for future acquisitions as part of more consent decrees in technology platform markets."[74] State attorneys general, the U.S. Department of Justice (DOJ), and the House Judiciary Committee's antitrust subcommittee have also launched investigations into technology companies' expanding market power.[75] The FTC has also previously investigated some technology companies, including Google and Facebook, for privacy violations.[76] Whether technology giants will actually face stringent antitrust repercussions in the United States remains to be seen.

To date, existing antitrust law and the federal authorities charged with its enforcement have been unable to curb technology companies' rapid market power expansion and domination.[77] Tim Wu has observed that "over the span of a generation" antitrust law "has shrunk to a shadow of itself, and somehow ceased to have a decisive opinion on the core concern of monopoly."[78] Wu and others have convincingly argued that antitrust law's narrow conception of, and overreliance on, the consumer welfare standard have proven ineffective at curtailing and grasping technology giants' current market power.[79]

Fine in Android Case, WALL ST. J. (Oct. 9, 2018, 2:58 PM), www.wsj.com/articles/google-appeals-5-billion-eu-fine-in-android-case-1539109713 (discussing Google's appeal of EU antitrust fines).

[73] Matthew Perlman, *FTC's New Tech Task Force Is a Warning to Industry*, LAW360 (Mar. 26, 2019, 8:44 PM), www.law360.com/articles/1143122/ftc-s-new-tech-task-force-is-a-warning-to-industry.

[74] *See* PUBLIC COMMENTS OF 43 STATE ATTORNEYS GENERAL, *supra* note 62, at 2.

[75] *See* Hannah Albarazi, *DOJ Makes Antitrust Probe of Big Tech Companies Official*, LAW360 (July 23, 2019, 10:25 PM), www.law360.com/articles/1181339; *see also* Bryan Koenig, *Google, Amazon, Others Face House Antitrust Scrutiny*, LAW360 (June 3, 2019, 9:49 PM), www.law360.com/articles/1165223; Steve Lohr, *Google Antitrust Investigation Outlined by State Attorneys General*, N.Y. TIMES (Sept. 9, 2019), www.nytimes.com/2019/09/09/technology/google-antitrust-investigation.html?module=inline; Steve Lohr, *House Anitrust Panel Seeks Documents From 4 Big Tech Firms*, N.Y. TIMES (Sept. 13, 2019), www.nytimes.com/2019/09/13/technology/amazon-apple-facebook-google-antitrust.html?module=inline; Diasuke Wakabayashi, *Google Wants Safeguards for Information in Antitrust Fight*, N. Y. TIMES (Oct. 31, 2019), www.nytimes.com/2019/10/31/business/google-antitrust-case.html.

[76] Seth Fiegerman, *Google, Facebook and Apple Could Face US Antitrust Probes as Regulators Divide up Tech Territory*, CNN BUSINESS (June 3, 2019, 4:31 PM), www.cnn.com/2019/06/03/tech/facebook-google-amazon-antitrust-ftc/index.html; Press Release, Fed. Trade Comm'n, Google and YouTube Will Pay Record $170 Million for Alleged Violations of Children's Privacy Law (Sept. 4, 2019), www.ftc.gov/news-events/press-releases/2019/09/google-youtube-will-pay-record-170-million-alleged-violations (discussing FTC investigation and settlement with Google); Press Release, Fed. Trade Comm'n, FTC Imposes $5 Billion Penalty and Sweeping New Privacy Restrictions on Facebook (July 24, 2019), www.ftc.gov/news-events/press-releases/2019/07/ftc-imposes-5-billion-penalty-sweeping-new-privacy-restrictions (discussing FTC investigation into Facebook).

[77] JOHNATHAN B. BAKER, THE ANTITRUST PARADIGM: RESTORING A COMPETITIVE ECONOMY 119 (2019).

[78] TIM WU, THE CURSE OF BIGNESS: ANTITRUST IN THE NEW GILDED AGE 16 (2018). *See also* Carl Shapiro, *Protecting Competition in the American Economy: Merger Control, Tech Titans, Labor Markets*, 33 J. ECON. PERSP. 69, 70 (2019) (noting antitrust failures in the merger context).

[79] *Id.* at 17; Lina M. Kahn, Note, *Amazon's Antitrust Paradox*, 126 YALE L.J. 710, 710 (2017) (contending that "the current framework in *antitrust* – specifically its pegging competition to 'consumer welfare,' defined as short-term price effects – is unequipped to capture the architecture of market power in the

Today, antitrust law's failings are even more glaring. Technology giants will likely continue to solidify their market power through acquisitions, all while obtaining unprecedented access to vast quantities of data that flow from the IoT's proliferation.

FTI Consulting, an advisory firm, reports that through the third quarter of 2016 "more than 150 IoT companies were mergers & acquisitions targets."[80] Price Waterhouse Coopers notes that the pace of IoT mergers and acquisitions has quickly increased over the last few years, and in the IoT context mergers and acquisitions is a core "offensive strategy in protecting" Fortune 500 firms' turf against competitors.[81] As the previous section of this chapter demonstrates, privacy policies routinely contain provisions that authorize data transfers in business transactions. These provisions are standard and common to IoT privacy policies and once present these provisions allow for the seamless transfer of consumer data in mergers and acquisitions. The transfer of these data, and the acquisition of smaller IoT companies, allows technology giants to expand their dominance and influence over our lives and activities.

SECURED FINANCING TRANSACTIONS

Secured financing arrangements also provide multiple avenues for consumer data to be disclosed and transferred to unaffiliated entities. Recall from Chapter 6 that these transactions are normally governed by Article 9 of the UCC. Also remember that in a secured transaction, a debtor allows a lender to impose a lien (a security interest) on its collateral (personal property) to obtain funding. In the IoT setting, companies' customer databases will expand to include biometric, health-related, and other types of highly sensitive data about consumers. Rights in these new types of data, which were not previously widely accessible to multiple companies, can be part of companies' assets.

With respect to biometric data, these data can be stored in various ways and in some instances, rather than storing actual biometric scans, some companies store only the authentication codes or mathematical representations of associated biometric identifiers.[82] Companies that store only audio voice recordings or photographs in their databases can transform these data into biometric identifiers that can be used to

modern economy"); Frank Pasquale, *Paradoxes of Digital Antitrust: Why the FTC Failed to Explain Its Inaction on Search Bias*, HARV. J.L. & TECH. OCCASIONAL PAPER SERIES, July 2013, at 1 (arguing that "[i]f antitrust law continues to decline in power and scope, we should expect a digital replay of the domination of monopolistic trusts in the late nineteenth century").

80   *IoT Driven M&A*, FTI CONSULTING TECH. INSIGHTS, www.fticonsulting.com/~/media/Files/us-files /insights/articles/internet-of-things-m-and-a.pdf.

81   *The Internet of Things: Using M&A to Deliver IoT Strategies*, PwC (2017), www.pwc.com/us/en/ technology/publications/assets/the-internet-of-things-using-ma-to-deliver-iot-strategies.pdf.

82   *About Touch ID Advanced Security Technology*, APPLE SUPPORT (Sept. 11, 2017), https://support .apple.com/en-us/HT204587; Claire Gartland, *Biometrics Are a Grave Threat to Privacy*, N.Y. TIMES (July 5, 2016), www.nytimes.com/roomfordebate/2016/07/05/biometrics-and-banking/biometrics-are -a-grave-threat-to-privacy; Anna Myers, *Can the U.S. Legal System Adapt to Biometric Technology?*,

accurately identify individuals at any time. Recordings of a person's voice and pictures of a person's face can, with the necessary computing power, be quickly converted into biometric identifiers, such as face prints or voice prints.[83] Biometric identifiers can enable facial recognition technology "to identify one face from millions in under one second."[84] Recall that the Amazon Echo records consumers' "voice requests" and these data could be retained on Amazon's servers.[85] These audio recordings could be converted into voice prints to identify individuals.

A company's intellectual property rights associated with its customer database or list can be used as collateral (along with other types of personal property) to facilitate an Article 9 secured transaction. Intellectual property rights are general intangibles (a type of collateral) under Article 9.[86] Customer lists can qualify as trade secrets, which are governed by both state and federal law.[87] It may also be possible to use the servers that store and run the database for financing purposes. It is also important to acknowledge, of course, that some technology companies store consumer data in "data shards" in multiple servers (including cloud networks) across the world rather than as a single complete file in a single location and on a single server.[88] In some instances, all or just a significant portion of a company's rights in personal property could be encumbered by a lender's security interest, and those rights could also include rights associated with a database.

Questions regarding data ownership and rights in data are vexing and complex.[89] For Article 9 purposes, all that is necessary to create an enforceable security interest

INT'L ASS'N PRIVACY PROF'LS (Aug. 12, 2016), https://iapp.org/news/a/can-the-u-s-legal-system-can-adapt-to-biometric-technology/.

[83] *See generally* Sercan Ö. Arik et al., *Neural Voice Cloning with a Few Samples*, 32ND CONF. ON NEURAL INFO. PROCESSING SYS. (2018), https://arxiv.org/pdf/1802.06006.pdf.

[84] *Facial Recognition: Why 2018 Will Be a Landmark Year for Artificial Intelligence*, ECONOMIST: FILMS, http://films.economist.com/the-world-in-2018.

[85] Tim Moynihan, *Alexa and Google Home Record What You Say. But What Happens to That Data?*, WIRED (Dec. 5, 2016, 9:00 AM), www.wired.com/2016/12/alexa-and-google-record-your-voice/; *see* Jing Cao & Dina Bass, *Why Google, Microsoft and Amazon Love the Sound of Your Voice*, BLOOMBERG (Dec. 13, 2016, 3:00 AM), www.bloomberg.com/news/articles/2016-12-13/why-google-microsoft-and-amazon-love-the-sound-of-your-voice; Kim Komando, *How to Listen to Everything Amazon Echo Has Ever Heard*, FOX NEWS (Apr. 15, 2017), www.foxnews.com/tech/2017/04/15/how-to-listen-to-everything-amazon-echo-has-ever-heard.print.html.

[86] U.C.C. § 9-102(a)(42) cmt. 5(d) (AM. LAW INST. & UNIF. LAW COMM'N 2017).

[87] Defend Trade Secrets Act of 2016, 18 U.S.C. § 1836 federal statute applicable to trade secrets); Avery Dennison Corp. v. Kitsonas, 118 F. Supp. 2d 848, 854 (S.D. Ohio 2000) ("[C]ustomer lists, pricing information, [and] sales strategies" are trade secrets under state law.); David S. Levine & Christopher B. Seaman, *The DTSA at One: An Empirical Study of the First Year of Litigation Under the Defend Trade Secrets Act*, 53 WAKE FOREST L. REV. 105, 113 (2018)(noting that prior to the adoption of the Defend Trade Secrets Act, "[h]istorically, trade secrecy has been governed by state law"); Emily Newhouse Dillingham, *How to Protect Your Company's Customer Lists as Trade Secrets*, LAW.COM (Jan. 2, 2018, 12:00 AM), www.law.com/nationallawjournal/sites/nationallawjournal/2018/01/02/misappropriation-of-your-customer-lists-make-a-federal-case-out-of-it/ (discussing trade secret protection of customer lists under the Defend Trade Secrets Act of 2016); Nguyen, *supra* note 2, at 578.

[88] Paul M. Schwartz, *Legal Access to the Global Cloud*, 118 COLUM. L. REV. 1681, 1694–96 (2018).

[89] *See* Pamela Samuelson, *Privacy as Intellectual Property?*, 52 STAN. L. REV. 1125, 1130–31 (2000).

is that the company have "rights in the collateral or the power to transfer rights in the collateral."[90] Thus, data need not be "owned" in order for rights associated with the data to be assigned. One might argue that whether a company can grant a security interest directly in its data (rather than the associated intellectual property rights) is potentially unsettled given Article 9's use of the term "personal property." However, Article 9's structure acknowledges that collateral can be both intangible and tangible. Further, in defining general intangibles the UCC's drafters "sought to make it clear that, even though collateral did not fit into one of the other definitional categories contained in Article 9, and even though it was intangible, it would nevertheless be governed by Article 9, unless the transaction was excluded."[91] Thus, the UCC's drafters intended for general intangibles to serve as a "broad residual category" for multiple types of collateral.[92] This history suggests that the term general intangibles can be interpreted broadly to allow for the creation of security interests in data and customer databases.[93] Moreover, case law suggests that a customer list is a general intangible under Article 9 and can be used for secured financing transactions.[94] One court concluded that a debtor had valuable commercial "property rights" in its book of business, which contained information about the debtor's commercial relationships.[95] The court found that the book of business was "akin to a customer list."[96] A customer database is "the modern version of the customer list."[97] Organizations have previously used their customer lists and intellectual property rights as collateral in secured financing deals.[98] Data have been described as "the world's most valuable resource."[99] Data brokers frequently treat consumer data as an asset by selling and transferring the data. As organizations' customer databases expand to include various types of valuable IoT data, corporate

---

[90] U.C.C. § 9-203(b)(2) (Am. Law Inst. & Unif. Law Comm'n 2017).

[91] Frederick H. Miller & Carl S. Bjerre, 9A Hawkland's Uniform Commercial Code Series § 9-102:9, Westlaw (database updated Dec. 2019).

[92] *Id.*

[93] U.C.C. § 9-102(a)(42) (Am. Law Inst. & Unif. Law Comm'n 2017).

[94] *In re* Emergency Beacon Corp., Nos. 77-B-980, 76-B-356, 1977 WL 25608 (S.D.N.Y Dec. 28, 1977) (determining that customer lists are general intangibles); Levitz v. Arons Arcadia Ins. Agency (*In re* Levitz Ins. Agency), 152 B.R. 693, 697 (Bankr. D. Mass. 1992) (suggesting that customer lists are general intangibles); Charlene Brownlee & Blaze D. Waleski, Privacy Law § 7.02 (Law Journal Press ed. 2019) ("[T]he courts have acknowledged a lender's security interest in a customer list.").

[95] GE Capital Corp. v. Wickard (*In re* Wickard), 455 B.R. 628, 633–34 (Bankr. W.D. Mich. 2011) (finding that debtor had "property rights" in the book of business "[r]egardless of whether the court classifies it as an account or general intangible within the meaning of the Uniform Commercial Code, it nevertheless qualifies as valuable commercial property").

[96] *Id.* at 633.

[97] Jonathan C. Lipson, *Financing Information Technologies: Fairness and Function*, 2001 Wis. L. Rev. 1067, 1081 (2001).

[98] Elvy, *supra* note 2, at 459; Miller & O'Rourke, *supra* note 2, at 788–89; Nguyen, *supra* note 2, at 577.

[99] *Regulating the Internet Giants: The World's Most Valuable Resource Is No Longer Oil, but Data*, Economist (May 6, 2017), www.economist.com/news/leaders/21721656-data-economy-demands-new-approach-antitrust-rules-worlds-most-valuable-resource.

financing transactions involving customer databases and intellectual property rights associated with same will likely become more widespread.

The ALI's *Principles for a Data Economy* project, if adopted and finalized, could provide recommendations on whether Article 9 should be interpreted in a manner that permits security interests to be established in data that are not subject to a property regime, such as intellectual property law.[100] As discussed earlier, there are strong arguments that Article 9 as written does in fact cover such transactions. Further, if a lender and a company possessing consumer data execute a contract containing provisions that clearly indicate that the consumer data secures the loan and the agreement provides for enforcement mechanisms in favor of the lender in the event of the debtor's default, such transactions could be enforceable. Article 9's scope provision clearly states that it applies to "a transaction, regardless of its form, that creates a security interest in personal property."[101]

Under Article 9, lenders can create enforceable liens (security interest) in organizations' general intangibles by having the organization authenticate a security agreement that meets certain requirements.[102] Parties are not required to describe the type of collateral that is subject to the lien in detail in their security agreement. Instead, subject to some exceptions, the parties can generally use the appropriate Article 9 collateral label to describe the collateral. Under Article 9, the term general intangible refers to several different types of collateral and can be used to describe collateral in the security agreement. To obtain priority and provide public notice of its lien, lenders typically file a financing statement in the appropriate filing office. The financing statement can also describe the collateral as a general intangible, but in some instances the collateral could also be described as "all assets or all personal property" of the debtor. As Xuan-Thao Nguyen has persuasively written, because Article 9 does not require the lender to specify that it has a security interest in an organization's customer database or intellectual property rights associated with the same, "the public will not know whether 'general intangible' means trademarks, patents, . . . payment intangibles, . . . or consumer databases."[103] The result is that consumers are unable to determine whether rights associated with their highly sensitive IoT data have been assigned in a secured financing transaction.

Recall from Chapter 6 that once a lender creates an effective lien on an organization's collateral, if the organization defaults on the loan (for instance by failing to make timely payments), the lender has the ability under Article 9 to foreclose on the collateral. If rights associated with a customer database are used as collateral, the lender could sell and dispose of the collateral in the event of a default. Remember

---

[100] *Principles for a Data Economy*, AM. L. INSTIT., www.ali.org/projects/show/data-economy/#_status (last visited Mar. 28, 2020)

[101] U.C.C. § 9-109(a) (AM. LAW INST. & UNIF. LAW COMM'N 2017).

[102] U.C.C. § 9-108, 9-203(b)(3)(A) (AM. LAW INST. & UNIF. LAW COMM'N 2017) (providing the requirements for "reasonably identify[ing]" collateral).

[103] Nguyen, *supra* note 2, at 586.

from Chapter 6 that an event of default is not limited to failure to make payments, but includes any event defined as a default in the security agreement. For example, breaching a representation or warranty in the security agreement, insolvency, loss of a license, and failing to timely provide requested information to the lender could constitute a default under a security agreement. Thus, multiple circumstances could permit highly sensitive consumer data to be disclosed to a secured party and ultimately transferred to an unaffiliated entity. Many security agreements are not publicly distributed, making it difficult to determine all of the circumstances that may trigger a default.

Admittedly, a general intangible may be difficult to repossess in light of its intangible nature.[104] There are other enforcement mechanisms available under Article 9 that may be an imperfect fit for secured transactions involving consumer data.[105] However, upon a default, a lender who becomes a judgment creditor could convince the debtor company to settle by voluntarily assigning its rights in the general intangible to the lender.[106] The lender could also attempt to obtain a court order requiring the debtor company to transfer or assign the collateral for sale.[107] As such, the concerns noted earlier regarding the disclosure of consumer data are still potentially applicable despite the intangible nature of general intangibles.

In addition to data disclosures involving the initial lender, there are other avenues for data disclosures in secured financing transactions. An organization could monetize its customer database containing highly sensitive IoT data by licensing it or by hiring an unaffiliated service provider to process and store the data. Under Article 9, these entities could be viewed as having rights in the customer database or in the data product derived from the data. If a lender subsequently qualifies as an entity to whom such rights can be assigned, these unaffiliated providers could use their rights in the database or derived data product as collateral to obtain financing from another lender. In such an instance, consumer data would then be at risk of transfer and

---

[104] Juliet M. Moringiello, *False Categories in Commercial Law: The (Ir)Relevance of (In)Tangibility*, 35 FLA. ST. U. L. REV. 119, 126–27 (2007) (noting that "nothing in the plain language of Article 9 limits the repossession remedy to goods and other tangible assets … [as] the U.C.C. does not define possession. Commentators, however, including the authors of some of the leading casebooks and treatises in the field, contend that the repossession remedy is limited to tangible property]").

[105] U.C.C § 9-607 (AM. LAW INST. & UNIF. LAW COMM'N 2017); *Remedies Outside the Box: Enforcing Security Interests Under Article 9 of the Uniform Commercial Code*, AM. B. ASS'N (Aug. 31, 2012), www .americanbar.org/groups/business_law/publications/blt/2012/08/03_cabral/ ("UCC § 9-607 provides secured parties with the remedy of collection. This remedy applies to certain types of liquid assets, including accounts receivable, general intangibles, chattel paper, notes, deposit accounts, and other intangible assets that oblige an underlying obligor to make payment or render performance to the debtor.").

[106] Craig Weiner and Michael Kolcun, *Protecting and Enforcing Judgment Creditor Interests in IP*, LAW360 (Jun. 30, 2017, 11:42 AM), www.law360.com/articles/934855/protecting-and-enforcing-judgment-creditor-interests-in-ip.

[107] *Id.*

disclosure to another lender in addition to the original lender. This can occur without consumers' knowledge.

State statutes that provide service providers with a lien on personal property for improving, transforming, and enhancing property are also potentially problematic.[108] If companies employ service providers to analyze and transform consumer-generated data, and these service providers are not compensated in accordance with their contract, a statutory lien could be imposed on the data product. Once a lien is imposed and other statutory requirements are met, the service provider could foreclose on the data product. If that occurs, consumer data could then be transferred and disclosed to third parties.

BANKRUPTCY PROCEEDINGS

Bankruptcy proceedings can involve both secured and unsecured lenders, although the former typically fare better in bankruptcy. Recall from Chapter 6 that once a company or individual files for bankruptcy, attempts by secured lenders to enforce their Article 9 interests are normally enjoined. In bankruptcy, many of a company's assets will normally become part of what is called the "debtor's estate." Not surprisingly, customer databases and intellectual property rights are assets that can be included in the estate. For instance, when Pay by Touch, a biometric company, filed for bankruptcy, its assets included its customer database containing the "biometric templates of over two million" consumers.[109]

Once the customer database containing highly sensitive consumer data is part of the bankruptcy estate, it can be disclosed and sold to unaffiliated entities. First, a bankrupt company in possession of its customer database may be able to continue existing uses of its database in the "ordinary course of business."[110] If data transfers and disclosures and other types of data usage are within "the ordinary course of business" (and potentially authorized by the company's privacy policy) these practices may continue even after the bankruptcy petition is filed. Thus, in theory, a company may continue to transfer and disclose consumer data even after it has filed for bankruptcy. Second, an unaffiliated entity could also purchase and obtain access to consumer data in connection with purchasing the bankrupt company's assets. For example, when FiLIP, an IoT company, filed for bankruptcy, its assets included data about the children and parents who used the company's products. The bankruptcy court approved the sale of the company's assets to an unaffiliated

---

[108]   Elvy, *supra* note 2, at 468–69.

[109]   Report of Consumer Privacy Ombudsman at 5, *In re* Solidus Networks, Inc., No. 2:07-bk-20027-TD (Bankr. C.D. Cal. Mar. 26, 2008) [hereinafter Pay by Touch CPO Report]; Danielle Keats Citron, *Reservoirs of Danger: The Evolution of Public and Private Law at the Dawn of the Information Age*, 80 S. CAL. L. REV. 241, 250 (2007).

[110]   11 U.S.C. § 363(b)–(c); LINDA J. RUSCH & STEPHEN L. SEPINUCK, PROBLEMS AND MATERIALS ON SECURED TRANSACTIONS 133 (3rd ed. 2014).

entity.[111] When RadioShack initiated bankruptcy proceedings, the company's assets, which included some of its database of 117 million customer records, were purchased by Standard General.[112] A bankrupt Sports Authority sold its customer database for $15 million.[113]

Third-party cloud service providers that store IoT data on behalf of companies could also go bankrupt. Assuming that the provider's customers are unable to timely retrieve their data from the provider's servers, this scenario raises the question of whether the bankrupt storage provider has any transferable rights in the data held on its servers and data storage equipment that should be part of the bankruptcy estate and potentially transferred to third parties. When cloud provider Nirvanix filed for bankruptcy, it gave customers approximately one month to transfer all of their data.[114] In light of the extent to which companies' databases will expand to include vast quantities of sensitive IoT consumer data, there are concerns associated with the exposure and transfer of these data to third parties in bankruptcy proceedings. Consumers have little control over how they will subsequently be treated by data purchasers once their data are analyzed and monetized after bankruptcy. If data is indeed the "new oil," then a company's customer database will be one of the most precious and valuable assets in a bankruptcy proceeding.

Recall from Chapter 3 that it is difficult to define privacy and its associated harms and that a narrow version of privacy has dominated privacy law discourse. It is not surprising that many aspects of commercial law have not been revised to sufficiently account for these harms. Even when commercial law has been revised to address privacy concerns, it is the narrow version of notice and choice that has dominated

---

[111] Order (I) Approving Asset Purchase Agreement; (II) Authorizing and Approving Sale of Acquired Assets Free and Clear of Liens, Claims and Encumbrances; (III) Authorizing the Assumption and Assignment of Certain Executory Contracts; and (IV) Granting Related Relief, *In re* FiLIP Technologies, Inc., No. 16-12192 (KG) (Bankr. D. Del. Nov. 9, 2016) [hereinafter FiLIP Sale Order]; Exhibit A to Sale Approval Order at 41, *In re* FiLIP Technologies, Inc., No. 16-12192 (KG) (Bankr. D. Del. Nov. 9, 2016) ("ser data of existing current and past customers"); Jeff Montgomery, *Sale of Bankrupt Kid-Tracking Firm to Smartcom OK'd*, LAW360 (Nov. 8, 2016, 7:08 PM), www .law360.com/articles/860757/sale-of-bankrupt-kid-tracking-firm-to-smartcom-ok-d.

[112] Chris Isidore, *RadioShack Sale Protects Most Customer Data*, CNN: MONEY (June 10, 2015, 4:16 PM), http://money.cnn.com/2015/06/10/news/companies/radioshack-customer-data-sale/index .html; *see also* Michael Hiltzik, *The RadioShack Bankruptcy Shows You Can't Trust a Company's Privacy Pledge*, L.A. TIMES (May 19, 2015, 11:50 AM), www.latimes.com/business/la-fi-mh-radioshack-you-have-no-privacy-left-20150519-column.html.

[113] Kathryn Rattigan, *Sports Authority Sells Its Customer Database to Dick's Sporting Goods for $15 Million*, DATA PRIV. & SECURITY INSIDER (July 7, 2016), www.dataprivacyandsecurityinsider.com/2016/ 07/sports-authority-sells-it-customer-database-to-dicks-sporting-goods-for-15-million/; Alex Schiffer, *In Sports Authority Bankruptcy, Customer E-mail Data Commands Hefty Sum*, L.A. TIMES (June 30, 2016, 3:05 PM), www.latimes.com/business/la-fi-sports-authority-auction-20160629-snap-story.html; *see In re* Sports Auth. Holdings, Inc., No. 16-10527, 2016 Bankr. LEXIS 4565 (Bankr. D. Del. May 24, 2016).

[114] *See* Klint Finley, *IBM Cloud Storage Partner Nirvanix Files for Bankruptcy*, WIRED (Oct. 2, 2013, 1:58 PM), www.wired.com/2013/10/nirvanix-bankrupt/amp; SILVERTON CONSULTING, INC., LESSONS FROM THE RAPID CLOSURE OF NIRVANIX 2 (2014), https://sci-zones-silvertonconsult.netdna-ssl.com/cms1/wp-content/uploads/filebase/archive/article/SCI-Nirvanix_Lessons-v040B.pdf.

such revisions. For example, the Bankruptcy Abuse Prevention and Consumer Protection Act of 2005 (BAPCPA) amended the Bankruptcy Code and was partially intended to address concerns related to the transfer and disclosure of consumer data in bankruptcy proceedings. The BAPCPA is also hampered by a limited view of privacy that overrelies on notice and choice

The BAPCPA suffers from several glaring limitations, which are all the more apparent in the IoT setting. Under the BAPCPA, the sale or lease of "personally identifiable" consumer data is restricted when a transfer of the data violates the debtor's previously provided privacy policy.[115] In many instances, data generated from our use of IoT devices can qualify as personally identifiable information since IoT data can lead to the identification of a specific individual and can be connected to other types of identifiable information, such as names and addresses. However, if the IoT data does not constitute personally identifiable information under the statute, then the intended statutory protections may not be triggered.[116] One might argue that anonymized and aggregated data are not personally identifiable information because they are unlikely to lead to the identification of a specific individual and may not satisfy any of the statutorily enumerated categories. Recall the limitations of anonymization discussed in Chapter 2.

The BAPCPA also relies heavily on the notice and choice principle. Under the BAPCPA, if a company's privacy policy at the commencement of the bankruptcy proceeding prohibits "the transfer of personally identifiable data" to third parties, a transfer is permissible only if it is consistent with the privacy policy or "after the appointment of a consumer privacy ombudsman" (CPO) and court approval of the transfer, along with compliance with relevant statutory requirements.[117] If a company has not provided a privacy policy or if the transfer of the data is in compliance with the privacy policy, it is unlikely that a court will appoint a CPO to provide guidance on whether and under what conditions the sale should be approved. Recall from the earlier sections of this chapter that IoT companies and other types organizations routinely include language in their privacy policies that authorize the transfer and disclosure of consumer information in the event of a bankruptcy. Thus, companies can "contract" around the statutory protections of the BAPCPA. As I have observed elsewhere, "the language in the debtor's privacy policy controls the level of scrutiny that will be given to the sale of consumer data in bankruptcy proceedings."[118] Stated differently, it is the notice that the company provides that determines the applicability of statutory provisions. With respect to choice, consumers can be said to have been given the ability to consent to or reject and select

---

[115]   11 U.S.C. § 363(b)(1)(B)(ii) (2012).

[116]   *In re* Graceway Pharm., LLC, No. 11-13036 (PJW), 2011 WL 6296791, at *4 (Bankr. D. Del. Sept. 30, 2011).

[117]   11 U.S.C. § 363(b); *see also* Luis Salazar, *Privacy and Bankruptcy Law: Part II: Specific Code Provisions*, Am. Bankr. Inst. J., Dec./Jan. 2006, at 58, 59.

[118]   Elvy, *supra* note 2, at 478.

another company's offerings if they object to a privacy policy that contains language authorizing a transfer of data during bankruptcy proceedings. Recall the Pay by Touch bankruptcy mentioned earlier. The court appointed a CPO to address the possible sale of consumers' data because the company's privacy policy provided that personally identifiable data would not be transferred to third parties without the company first obtaining consumer consent.[119] If the company's privacy policy had allowed for the transfer of the biometric data of millions of consumers in a bankruptcy proceeding, it is unlikely that the court would have appointed a CPO given the BAPCPA's provisions. Such a result should concern us all. In contrast, in *In re Boscov's Inc.*, the debtor's privacy policy allowed consumer data to be transferred to third parties as part of a business transition and the bankruptcy court did not appoint a CPO.[120] When FiLIP filed for bankruptcy, the court approved the sale of the company's assets (likely including consumer data) and determined that the transfer was "consistent with the [d]ebtor's privacy policy" in light of the provision permitting data transfers during bankruptcy.[121]

Additionally, because CPO protection and related statutory requirements are only applicable if a company provides a privacy policy that restricts the transfer of personally identifiable information, and that policy is effective when the bankruptcy proceeding commences, a company could amend its privacy policy at any time to authorize a data transfer. A privacy policy could be amended immediately before bankruptcy to skirt the BAPCPA's limited protections. As long as consumers consent and are notified of the amendments (notice and choice), nothing prevents a company from engaging in this behavior, except for possible FTC scrutiny.

Some courts may also be reluctant to appoint a CPO even when the transfer of consumer data conflicts with the terms of a debtor's privacy policy.[122] These courts have reasoned that a CPO is unnecessary if the data purchaser agrees to be the company's successor-in-interest and consents to using the customer data under the existing privacy policy.[123] In the FiLIP bankruptcy, the court noted that the buyer had consented to the adoption of the company's privacy policy.[124] These courts overrely on the language of the company's privacy policy. By focusing on the data

---

[119] Pay by Touch CPO Report, *supra* note 109, at 3–4.

[120] *See generally* Order Granting Motion of Debtors for an Order (A) Approving Bidding Procedures for the Sale of Substantially [*sic*] of Their Assets, (B) Approving the Form and Manner of Notice Thereof, (C) Scheduling an Auction and Sale Hearing and (D) Approving Breakup Fee at 7, *In re Boscov's Inc.*, No. 08-11637 (Bankr. D. Del. Oct. 2, 2008); S. Jason Teele et al., *The Impact of Privacy on FDIC Resolution Plans*, Law360 (Nov. 17, 2011, 1:00 PM), www.law360.com/articles/286179/print?section=banking.

[121] FiLIP Sale Order, *supra* note 111, at 5.

[122] Lucy L. Thomson, *Personal Data for Sale in Bankruptcy: A Retrospective on the Consumer Privacy Ombudsman*, Am. Bankr. Inst. J., June 2015, at 32, 33.

[123] *In re* Reader's Digest Ass'n, No. 09-23529 (RDD), 2010 Bankr. LEXIS 5682, at *17 (Bankr. S.D.N.Y. Jan. 14, 2010); *In re Escada (USA) Inc.*, No. 09-15008 (SMB), 2010 Bankr. LEXIS 4362, at *11 (Bankr. S.D.N.Y. Jan. 7, 2010).

[124] FiLIP Sale Order, *supra* note 111, at 5.

buyer's agreement to comply with the company's existing privacy policy, courts may not adequately evaluate the impact of non-bankruptcy law on the transfer, a topic that CPOs frequently consider in making their recommendations to the court.[125] Declining to appoint a CPO because a data buyer agrees to adopt a previous privacy policy reinforces deference to the notice and choice regime – the notice being the bankrupt company's original privacy policy, and the choice being consumers' previous consent to the bankrupt company's terms and conditions and privacy policy.

Consumer privacy ombudsmen can play an invaluable role in bankruptcy proceedings involving the potential sale of consumer data. They are independent third parties that can help bankruptcy courts in determining whether to approve a sale or lease of consumer data. They have also previously coordinated with state attorneys general, and requested and received official responses from the FTC. They have taken these responses and positions into account in their recommendations to bankruptcy courts.[126] However, a CPO's appointment by a bankruptcy court does not always guarantee sufficient protection of our data. Consumer privacy ombudsmen also recommend that data purchasers comply with the data seller's existing privacy policy as a condition of transfer.[127] This recommendation seemingly originates from the FTC's proposed Toysmart settlement agreement, which could be why some courts have also failed to appoint CPOs when the data buyer agrees to observe the data seller's prior privacy policy.[128] In doing so, CPOs and courts fail to adequately consider the limitations of the existing privacy policy which may authorize other types of data monetizations and disclosures that are harmful to consumers.

Consumer privacy ombudsmen frequently recommend that data purchasers obtain consumer consent in order to change the company's previous privacy policy.[129] This also reflects incorporation of the notice and choice principle. Data buyers could amend the privacy policy and obtain consumer consent for additional data disclosures and monetizations. Relying primarily on consumer consent to privacy policy amendments does not sufficiently protect consumers. Additionally, some CPOs have recommended opt-out rather than opt-in consumer consent for

---

[125]　Thomson, *supra* note 122, at 33.

[126]　Report of the Consumer Privacy Ombudsman at 6, *In re* RadioShack Corp., No. 15-10197 (BLS) (Bankr. D. Del. May 16, 2015) [hereinafter RadioShack CPO Report]. *See generally* Letter from David C. Vladeck, Dir., Bureau of Consumer Prot., Fed. Trade Comm'n, to Michael St. Patrick Baxter & Yaron Dori, Esqs., Covington & Burling LLP (Sept. 14, 2011).

[127]　RadioShack CPO Report, *supra* note 126, at 3–5.

[128]　Press Release, Fed. Trade Comm'n, FTC Announces Settlement with Bankrupt Website, Toysmart.com, Regarding Alleged Privacy Policy Violations (July 21, 2000), www.ftc.gov/news-events/press-releases/2000/07/ftc-announces-settlement-bankrupt-website-toysmartcom-regarding; Letter from Jessica L. Rich, Dir., Bureau of Consumer Prot., Fed. Trade Comm'n, to Elise Frejka, Consumer Privacy Ombudsman for *In re* RadioShack Corporation, No. 15-10197 (BLS) (May 16, 2015), www.ftc.gov/system/files/documents/public_statements/643291/150518radioshackletter.pdf (discussing FTC Toysmart proposed settlement conditions).

[129]　RadioShack CPO Report, *supra* note 126, at 5; Thomson, *supra* note 122, at 33.

some data transfers.[130] This too is evidence of the presence of the notice and choice principle in the bankruptcy context. Consumers may also be given a limited time period within which to opt out of data transfers in bankruptcy proceedings.[131] Also, recall from Chapter 3 that the CCPA gives consumers the right to opt out of data sales.[132] Consumer privacy ombudsmen could also consider the CCPA's provisions in making recommendations about data transfers in bankruptcy proceedings. However, recall from Chapter 3 that the CCPA's corporate transaction provisions are in need of improvement.

As we have seen, the Bankruptcy Code is limited by its overreliance on a notice and choice model and the provisions of companies' privacy policies. The BAPCPA's language empowers companies to easily avoid its limited consumer protections by including provisions in their privacy policies that authorize data transfers and disclosures in any business transaction.

Once consumer data are disclosed or transferred to unaffiliated entities in bankruptcy proceedings and in connection with corporate transactions, such as mergers and acquisitions and secured financing deals, several potential consumer concerns are likely to follow. The databases and servers of data transferees are not immune from hacking. These entities face the same information security concerns discussed in Chapter 2. Transferees can also subsequently disclose IoT data to other third parties, including data brokers, advertisers, and other technology companies. Transferees that obtain data through the frameworks discussed in this chapter can also use data analytics techniques to monetize their newly acquired data assets and use the data in harmful ways, including to determine our opportunities, shape our behaviors, and target us for further contracting. These entities could also begin using online PFP models to further extract value from the data, which may exacerbate concerns about unequal access to privacy and security for vulnerable consumers.

This chapter has demonstrated that more attention is needed to address the disclosure of consumer data in corporate transactions. As the IoT expands, more data will be available for companies to monetize in various corporate transactions and bankruptcy proceedings. There is a pressing need to rethink legal frameworks that presently allow companies to transfer and disclose our data in corporate transactions with ease while expanding their market dominance.

---

[130] RadioShack CPO Report, *supra* note 126, at 6; Joshua A. T. Fairfield, *The End of the (Virtual) World*, 112 W. VA. L. REV. 53, 90–91 (2009).
[131] RadioShack CPO Report, *supra* note 126, at 3–4.
[132] CAL. CIV. CODE § 1798.120 (2019).

PART III

Concrete Legal Solutions for a Commercial Law of Privacy and Security

8

Establishing Baseline Privacy and Security Frameworks

In 2015, the US Senate passed a resolution recommending the adoption of a national strategy for IoT development (IoT Resolution).[1] Currently, the proposed Developing Innovation and Growing the Internet of Things Act (DIGIT) would establish a federal working group and a steering committee within the Department of Commerce.[2] If the act is adopted, the working group, under the guidance of the steering committee, would be charged with evaluating and providing a report containing recommendations to Congress on multiple IoT aspects.[3] These areas include identifying federal statutes and regulations that could inhibit IoT growth and impact consumer privacy and security.[4]

The current proposed DIGIT and prior efforts to adopt similar legislation provide evidence of some federal legislators' interest in IoT-specific issues. The DIGIT and the IoT Resolution also suggest that Congress to some extent supports the further development and expansion of the IoT. Historically, federal support for emerging technologies has sometimes led to inconsistent results. Consider that the CDA was adopted in part to ensure that a clean Internet would blossom, and "to allow a new industry to grow with minimal interference from courts and regulators."[5] However, Congress's adoption of Section 230 of the CDA, and courts' expansive interpretation have immunized platforms from a host of liabilities, including resulting illegal discrimination and certain products liability claims as discussed in Chapter 5.[6]

---

[1]   S. Res. 110, 114th Cong. (1st Sess. 2015), www.congress.gov/bill/114th-congress/senate-resolution/110/text ("develop a strategy to incentivize the development of the Internet of Things").

[2]   S. 1611, 116th Cong. (2d Sess. 2020), www.congress.gov/bill/116th-congress/senate-bill/1611/text. There have been previous attempts to enact a DIGIT-like statute. *See, e.g.*, Developing Innovation and Growing the Internet of Things Act, H.R. 5117, 114th Cong. (2d Sess. 2016).

[3]   S. 1611.

[4]   *Id.* § 4.

[5]   Jeff Kosseff, The Twenty-Six Words That Created the Internet (2019); Danielle Keats Citron, *Section 230's Challenge to Civil Rights and Civil Liberties*, Knight First Amend. Inst. (Apr. 6, 2018), https://knightcolumbia.org/content/section-230s-challenge-civil-rights-and-civil-liberties.

[6]   Olivier Sylvain, *Intermediary Design Duties*, 50 Conn. L. Rev. 203 (2018); Citron, *supra* note 5; Olivier Sylvain, *Discriminatory Designs on User Data*, Knight First Amend. Inst. (Apr. 1, 2018), https://knightcolumbia.org/content/discriminatory-designs-user-data.

As this book has argued, the IoT and companies' data business models and commercial practices raise large-scale privacy, security, and digital domination concerns, and several existing legal frameworks fail to sufficiently address these issues. The IoT allows companies to erode our anonymity in both the public and private spheres while simultaneously colonizing our homes and bodies with insecure devices and connected services and systems. It can also facilitate unequal access to privacy and cybersecurity, further enable corporations to determine the opportunities we receive and shape our behaviors, and allow some companies to exploit vulnerable consumers. Several existing privacy and security frameworks have also failed to adapt to the growing overlap of the privacy and commercial law worlds in a manner that sufficiently protects consumer interests. Given these concerns and the congressional interest in the IoT evidenced by the proposed DIGIT and the IoT Resolution, I argue that the law can do more to directly protect consumer interests against privacy, security, and digital domination harms, and must adequately address the increasing connection between privacy law and commercial law. An extensive approach is necessary to achieve these goals.

An extensive approach that addresses consumer concerns and accounts for the blending of the commercial law and privacy law worlds requires both the adoption of a federal baseline privacy and security statute, and revisions to various sources of law impacting commercial practices that raise privacy, security, and digital domination concerns. This two-pronged approach could limit, and in some cases prevent, consumer harms, while possibly addressing at least one of the problematic results of previous congressional support for emerging technology – the CDA. We will discuss amendments to the CDA in Chapter 9 as well as amendments to various sources of commercial law that raise privacy and security issues. In this chapter, I recommend specific provisions that can be incorporated into a federal baseline statute to aid in correcting the deficiencies of the current approach to privacy and security issues.

In the absence of an adequate baseline federal privacy and security statute, states must continue to play an important role in adopting, and revising existing, privacy and security legislation. Additionally, recall our standing discussion from Chapter 2, and the ways in which standing requirements have been fatal to consumer claims. As I argued in Chapter 2, there is a strong need for courts to expand their perception of consumer harm to account for intangible harms where constitutional requirements permit. Despite *Spokeo*, there is some room for Congress to shed additional light on standing issues in the privacy context as well.

Recall that the FTC, the GAO, some academics, and consumer advocates have all supported calls for various versions of a comprehensive federal privacy and security statute. Such a statute is long overdue. In this chapter, I contend that both domestic and international legal frameworks and proposals could be used as inspirational sources for drafting a baseline privacy and security federal statute. I posit that despite significant differences in legal systems, GDPR principles are not entirely foreign to US privacy law, and certain GDPR provisions could be used to inspire a baseline federal privacy statute.

This chapter joins the earlier recommendations of privacy scholars and advocates in support of relying on some aspects of the European data privacy and security approach to reformulate US data protection frameworks.[7] I also argue that the CCPA and other current and proposed domestic frameworks, such as the Principles of the Law of Data Privacy (ALI's Data Privacy Principles) are all useful sources as well. Federal legislation can shed light on permissible data practices and impose prohibitions on certain data-related activities. The goal of this approach is in part to move us away from excessively relying on notice and choice as well as to significantly impact companies' willingness to adopt certain data business models and commercial practices, and design products that enable wide-scale invasive data collection and unrelenting and unnecessary surveillance. Admittedly, not all technology companies have exploited consumer data in ways that harm consumer interests. Some companies may act in good faith on privacy and cybersecurity issues. However, this does not negate the need for privacy and security legislation to guard against corporate abuse. Additionally, I also note that the "information fiduciary framework" proposed by Jack Balkin and Jonathan Zittrain could also be used to partially address the inadequacies of notice and choice. However, for several reasons discussed in detail later, I ultimately suggest that selective incorporation of some GDPR and other domestic principles is likely a more viable proposal. If GDPR-like principles are imported, the United States can learn from the GDPR's deficiencies and adapt federal legislation and regulation.

Privacy and security harms are also multifaceted and multilayered and there are various harms (both individual and societal) that occur outside of the IoT context, and which are beyond the scope of this book. These include, for example, privacy harms associated with revenge pornography. Despite this, I propose a broad federal baseline statute rather than one that applies only to the IoT for several reasons. It is time to correct our privacy laws' overreliance on the notice and choice model, and the largely sectoral approach to privacy and security, the effects of which are not just limited to the IoT. A statute that regulates only the consumer IoT industry would fully continue the sectoral approach to privacy. Additionally, IoT harms may have some similarities with privacy harms that occur in the non-IoT data trade context. For instance, corporate surveillance enabled by data business models in the traditional online setting, in which companies use various techniques to track our activities while we access the Internet via our computers, also impacts our ability be to be anonymous in online transactions and decreases our ability to determine

---

[7] *See, e.g.,* PRISCILLA M. REGAN, LEGISLATING PRIVACY: TECHNOLOGY, SOCIAL VALUES, AND PUBLIC POLICY 234 (1995); David H. Flaherty, *The Need for an American Privacy Protection Commission,* 1 GOV'T INFO. Q. 235 (1984); James P. Nehf, *Recognizing the Societal Value in Information Privacy,* 78 WASH. L. REV. 1 (2003); Alexander Tsesis, *The Right to Erasure: Privacy, Data Brokers, and the Indefinite Retention of Data,* 49 WAKE FOREST L. REV. 433 (2014).

what happens to information about us. Although the proposals I offer are primarily geared towards addressing privacy and security harms the IoT raises, they could also have broad implications and be used to address other types of similar privacy harms that occur in consumer and corporate data trade transactions in the non-IoT context as well. If Congress intends to address privacy issues, the resulting legislation should address privacy and security harms in both the IoT and non-IoT context. However, here is not the right place for a full discussion of the ways in which legislation can attempt to remedy all privacy and security harms in the non-IoT context. Thus, rather than providing a detailed legislative proposal that covers all privacy and security issues, my goal in this chapter is to provide specific recommendations that any baseline privacy statute could include to address deficiencies in laws that govern privacy and security, and commercial practices in order to address the consumer concerns discussed in earlier sections of this book.

Although this book has in some instances highlighted concerns associated with IoT government surveillance, this book's primary focus has been on the actions of corporate entities in the IoT context, particularly in data trade arrangements impacting consumer data. As such, the proposals offered later do not address in extensive detail privacy harms associated with government surveillance and the IoT. Nonetheless, despite existing constitutional protections and other legal frameworks, which affect state actors' surveillance activities, consideration should be given to the extent to which existing frameworks can be reimagined and privacy legislation can be used to bolster existing protections in this area. Government surveillance is incredibly important but too vast a topic to fully address here. It is also important to note that several sources of legal scholarship have previously tackled the issue of government surveillance in the IoT context.[8]

SEVERAL RECOMMENDED PROVISIONS FOR A BASELINE PRIVACY AND SECURITY STATUTE

In the last few years, multiple federal privacy and data security bills have been proposed but have failed to be finalized, including federal data breach notification bills.[9] There is also consideration at present of various proposed federal privacy laws

---

[8] *See generally, e.g.,* ANDREW GUTHRIE FERGUSON, THE RISE OF BIG DATA POLICING: SURVEILLANCE, RACE, AND THE FUTURE OF LAW ENFORCEMENT (2017); Andrew Guthrie Ferguson, *The Internet of Things and the Fourth Amendment of Effects,* 104 CALIF. L. REV. 805 (2016); Andrew Guthrie Ferguson, *The "Smart" Fourth Amendment,* 102 CORNELL L. REV. 547 (2017); Eldar Haber, *The Wiretapping of Things,* 53 U.C. DAVIS L. REV. 733 (2019); Ira S. Rubinstein, *Privacy Localism,* 93 WASH. L. REV. 1961 (2018); Anne Toomey McKenna et al., *The Role of Satellites and Smart Devices: Data Surprises and Security, Privacy, and Regulatory Challenges,* 123 PA. ST. L. REV. 591 (2019).

[9] *See* Joseph P. Facciponti & Maxwell T. S. Thompson, *Will New Congress Pass a National Data Protection Law?,* LAW360 (Jan. 4, 2019, 2:02 PM), www.law360.com/articles/1115448; *see also, e.g.,* Consumer Data Protection Act, S. 2188, 115th Cong. § 2, at 21 (2d Sess. 2018) (Discussion Draft), www.wyden.senate.gov

and an IoT Cybersecurity Improvement bill for federal devices that could influence the consumer market.[10] Large technology companies are formidable opponents of consumer-friendly privacy and security legislation. In 2019, Facebook and Amazon spent almost $17 million each on federal lobbying.[11] The lack of comprehensive privacy legislation has made the US "an outlier among regulatory approaches around the world."[12] Weak sectoral federal laws that to some extent continue to enable an ineffective self-regulatory approach to data protection coupled with the absence of a federal statute that establishes baseline privacy rights has fostered an environment in which companies are free to disclose, and monetize our data with impunity. Consider, for example, that a 2019 comparative study of IoT devices in the United States and the United Kingdom found that IoT devices in the United States shared more IoT data with third parties than did those devices used in the United Kingdom.[13] The authors of the study suggest that this difference may be due in part to weaker privacy laws in the United States.[14]

/imo/media/doc/Wyden%20Privacy%20Bill%20Discussion%20Draft%20Nov%201.pdf; Consumer Data Protection Act of 2018 (Sen. Wyden, Discussion Draft), www.wyden.senate.gov/imo/media/doc/Wyden%20Privacy%20Bill%20one%20pager%20Nov%201.pdf ("It permits companies to charge consumers who want to use their products and services, but don't want their information monetized."); Jason Auman, *Hacking Our Securities Disclosure System: The Need for Federal Broker-Dealer Disclosure Requirements Vis-à-Vis Cyber Incidents*, 2018 Colum. Bus. L. Rev. 952, 969–70 (2019) ("Since 2005, senators have introduced several pieces of legislation that would impose federal data breach notification requirements on businesses and federal agencies, but each failed.").

10　Consumer Online Privacy Rights Act, S. 2968, 116th Cong. (1st Sess. 2019); *Fact Sheet: Chairman Wicker's Discussion Draft The United States Consumer Data Privacy Act*, U.S. Senate Committee on Com., Sci., & Transp. (Dec. 3, 2019), www.commerce.senate.gov/2019/12/chairman-wicker-s-discussion-draft-the-united-states-consumer-data-privacy-act; Cameron F. Kerry, *Game On: What to Make of Senate Privacy Bills and Hearing*, Brookings (Dec. 3, 2019), www.brookings.edu/blog/techtank/2019/12/03/game-on-what-to-make-of-senate-privacy-bills-and-hearing/; See Press Release, U.S. Congresswoman Zoe Lofgren, Eshoo & Lofgren Introduce the Online Privacy Act (Nov. 5, 2019), https://lofgren.house.gov/media/press-releases/eshoo-lofgren-introduce-online-privacy-act; Press Release, U.S. Senate Comm. on Commerce, Sci., & Transp., Wicker, Thune, Moran, Blackburn Announce Plans to Introduce Date Privacy Bill (Apr. 30, 2020), www.commerce.senate.gov/2020/4/wicker-thune-moran-blackburn-announce-plans-to-introduce-data-privacy-bill; Kim Lyons, *Senators' Plan For Reining in Contact Tracing Apps Doesn't Make a Lot of Sense*, Verge (May 1, 2020, 2:08 PM), www.theverge.com/2020/5/1/21243977/gop-senators-contact-tracing-data-coronavirus-covid-19-privacy.

11　Tony Romm, *Tech Giants Led by Amazon, Facebook and Google Spent Nearly Half a Billion on Lobbying over the Past Decade, New Data Shows*, Wash. Post (Jan. 22, 2020, 6:32 AM), www.washingtonpost.com/technology/2020/01/22/amazon-facebook-google-lobbying-2019/.

12　Daniel J. Solove & Paul M. Schwartz, *ALI Data Privacy: Overview and Black Letter Text*, 68 UCLA L. Rev. (forthcoming 2020) (manuscript at 5), https://papers.ssrn.com/sol3/papers.cfm?abstract_id=3457563.

13　*See generally* Jingjing Ren et al., *Information Exposure from Consumer IoT Devices: A Multidimensional, Network-Informed Measurement Approach*, Internet Measurement Conf. (2019), https://moniotrlab.ccis.neu.edu/wp-content/uploads/2019/09/ren-imc19.pdf (finding that "US devices tend to contact more non-first parties").

14　*Id.* ("[W]e note that US devices tend to contact more non-first parties, possibly due to more relaxed privacy regulations with respect to the EU."). Despite "Brexit," the GDPR will continue to have a significant impact on UK data protection law. *See also* Roger Bickerstaff et al., *How Technology Communications Companies Should Prepare for Brexit*, Law360 (Feb. 4, 2020, 2:22 PM), www

The IoT will leave no industry untouched. The IoT will impact almost every major American industry, including healthcare, manufacturing, financial services, communications, transportation retail, and energy, as well as COVID-19 pandemic response efforts. The global pandemic illustrates the various ways in which IoT devices can be used to generate volumes of sensitive data about us, including our temperatures, heart rates, daily steps, and sleep patterns and much more. Recall that IoT rings, thermometers, and fever detection cameras are already being used in pandemic relief efforts. The pandemic provides further evidence that Congress should enact privacy and security legislation that goes beyond notice and choice. Thus, more than ever before, there is a strong need to adopt federal privacy and security legislation that fills regulatory gaps, cuts across all industries, provides baseline privacy rights to natural persons, defines the contours of acceptable and unacceptable data practices, and imposes on companies granular cybersecurity requirements and privacy obligations.

In subsequent sections, I suggest that provisions from the GDPR can be useful in drafting baseline privacy legislation. Before turning to those provisions, it is important to acknowledge that some GDPR principles are not completely unfamiliar to US privacy law. First, the FIP principles discussed in Chapter 3 contemplated data access rights, among other things.[15] Several GDPR provisions, including the "transparency measures are derived from the FIPs."[16] Second, long before the GDPR (and its immediate predecessor) came into being, in 1974 several Senators proposed a federal privacy bill (1974 Federal Privacy Bill), akin to some aspects of the GDPR, to address "new systems of information gathering" and "sophisticated computer technology."[17] When introducing the bill in 1974, Senator Samuel J. Ervin, Jr. astutely observed that "male or female, whatever one's cultural style or religious or political views, each of us is the subject of cumulative records being stored by a variety of Government agencies and private organizations."[18] This observation remains true today, but the volume of our cumulative records has increased exponentially with the IoT's rise.

.law360.com/articles/1240241/how-tech-communications-cos-should-prepare-for-brexit (noting that the GDPR "will continue to apply in the U.K. through the transition period. Afterward, the derogated regulation will be enacted into U.K. law" and discussing instances in which the GDPR will continue to apply post-transition).

15   U.S. Dep't of Health, Educ., & Welfare, Records, Computers, and the Rights of Citizens: Report of the Secretary's Advisory Committee on Automated Personal Data Systems 41–42 (1973), www.justice.gov/opcl/docs/rec-com-rights.pdf.

16   Woodrow Hartzog, *The Inadequate, Invaluable Fair Information Practices*, 76 Md. L. Rev. 952, 956 (2017) ("Even when entire regimes change, as with the GDPR, the fundamental framework is still built around the FIPs and control, with changes at the margins."); Margot E. Kaminski, *Binary Governance: Lessons From the GDPR's Approach to Algorithmic Accountability*, 92 S. Cal. L. Rev. 1529, 1610 (2019).

17   S. 3418, 93d Cong. (1974); *see also* Flaherty, *supra* note 7; Paul M. Schwartz, *Preemption and Privacy*, 118 Yale L.J. 902 (2009); Gabriela Zanfir-Fortuna, *A U.S. Bill from 1974, Shares So Much DNA with the GDPR, It Could Be Its Ancestor*, Medium (Mar, 3, 2020), https://medium.com/@gzf/a-us-bill-from-1974-shares-so-much-dna-with-the-gdpr-it-could-be-its-ancestor-7952c8e4adea.

18   S. 3418; *Sam Ervin: A Featured Biography*, U.S. Senate, www.senate.gov/senators/FeaturedBios/Featured_Bio_ErvinSam.htm ("In the 1960s and '70s, as he continued to oppose civil rights for

The 1974 Federal Privacy Bill proposed a statute that would have (i) applied to both private and public entities with some exceptions, (2) established a federal privacy board to oversee covered entities' data practices, (3) imposed restrictions on data disclosures and data processing that would prejudice individuals, and (4) included several GDPR-like rights, such as access rights.[19] The bill also included a private right of action.[20] A significantly watered-down version of the bill would eventually be adopted as the Privacy Act of 1974, which applies only to federal agencies.[21] Despite this, the 1974 Federal Privacy Bill remains a useful source for drafting privacy legislation today. The bill also provides evidence of an early federal perspective on data privacy issues in the United States that shares some characteristics with the current European approach.[22]

Preemption and Scope

Turning now to the possible provisions of a federal baseline privacy and security statute, federal legislation could serve as a floor, rather than a ceiling, for privacy and

African Americans, Ervin investigated privacy issues, authored the Privacy Act of 1974, and emerged as a prominent defender of civil liberties.").

[19] S. 3418. The following are several notable excerpts from the 1974 bill: "Any federal agency, State or local government, or any other organization maintaining an information system that includes personal information shall (1) collect, maintain, use and disseminate only personal information necessary to accomplish a proper purpose of the organization.... (4) maintain information ... as necessary to assure fairness in determinations relating to a data subject; ... (12) comply with the written request of any individual ... to remove such name or address, or both from such lists; (13) collect no personal information concerning the political or religious beliefs, affiliations, and activities of data subjects ... unless authorized by law." *Id.* § 201(a). Organizations subject to the proposed statute that "disseminate[] statistical reports or research findings based on personal information ... [would have been obligated to] (A) make available to any data subject or group (without revealing trade secrets) methodology and material necessary to validate statistical analyses." *Id.* § 201(b). Covered entities "upon request and proper identification of any individual who is a data subject, grant such individual the right to inspect, in a form comprehensible to such individual (A) all personal information about that individual ... (C) the recipients of personal information about such individual including the identity of all persons and organizations involved and their relationship to the system when not having regular access authority ... (5) upon receipt of notice from any individual who is a data subject, that such individual wishes to challenge, correct, or explain information about him in such system – (A) investigate and record the current status of such personal information; (B) purge any such information that is found to be incomplete, inaccurate, not pertinent, not timely nor necessary to be retained, or can no longer be verified." *Id.* § 201(d).

[20] S. 3418 §§ 304, 306.

[21] Privacy Act of 1974, Pub. L. No. 93-579, 88 Stat. 1896 (codified as amended at 5 U.S.C. § 552a (2012)); Comm. on Gov't Operations, U.S. Senate & House of Representatives, Legislative History of the Privacy Act of 1974 S. 3418 (Public Law 93-579): Source Book on Privacy (1976), www.loc.gov /rr/frd/Military_Law/pdf/LH_privacy_act-1974.pdf; Erin Murphy, *The Politics of Privacy in the Criminal Justice System: Information Disclosure, the Fourth Amendment, and Statutory Law Enforcement Exemptions*, 111 Mich. L. Rev. 485 (2013) (noting that the Privacy Act of 1974 applies only to federal agencies); Rubinstein, *supra* note 8, at 1981 (noting that the Privacy Act of 1974 applies only to federal agencies and was the first federal statute to incorporate FIPs); Zanfir-Fortuna, *supra* note 17.

[22] Zanfir-Fortuna, *supra* note 17.

information security rights and obligations. Federal legislation need not preempt state legislation that grants individuals more rights or imposes additional legal obligations on companies. Although this approach may not provide complete legal uniformity, it can allow states to continue to innovate and respond to new privacy and data security threats.

With respect to the issue of scope and covered entities, federal privacy legislation could apply to all private entities who "determine[] the purposes and means of the processing" of personal data as well as those that process the data.[23] As is the case with the GDPR, exclusions can be made for natural persons that process data for personal or household purposes, criminal investigations, and public safety.[24]

The definition of personal data is also critical to any privacy statute's application. Federal statutes have historically defined personally identifiable information using several reductionist approaches, including listing specific categories of data that are protected by a statute and defining protected data as non-public data.[25] An overly narrow approach to personally identifiable information can leave certain categories of data unprotected by legislation.[26] European regulation covers data that are associated with an identified or identifiable person.[27] The CCPA lists specific categories of data subject to the statute and, like the GDPR, includes identifiable data within its scope.[28] The ALI's Data Privacy Principles, the most recent effort by the ALI to provide guidance on data privacy issues, also broadly define personal information to include identifiable data, even though they treat identified data differently from identifiable data.[29] The 1974 Federal Privacy Bill defined personal information to include, among other things, any information "that affords a basis for inferring personal characteristics, such as finger and voice prints and photographs."[30]

In light of the rate at which we shed data and the frequency with which companies vacuum our data up, a comprehensive and flexible definition of personal information or data is needed. Personal data covered by baseline federal legislation could be broadly defined. The definition of personal information contained in the GDPR,

---

[23] Regulation 2016/679, of the European Parliament and of the Council of 27 April 2016 on the Protection of Individuals with Regard to the Processing of Personal Data and on the Free Movement of Such Data and Repealing Directive 95/46/EC, 2016 OJ (L 119) 1 at art. 4 [hereinafter GDPR].

[24] *Id.* at art. 2; *see also* Principles of Law, Data Privacy § 1(b)(2) (Am. Law Instit. 2019) (excluding "purely interpersonal or household relationships" and "personal activities").

[25] *See* Paul M. Schwartz & Daniel J. Solove, *The PII Problem: Privacy and a New Concept of Personally Identifiable Information*, 86 N.Y.U. L. Rev. 1814, 1817 (2011).

[26] *See, e.g., id.;* Paul Ohm, *Broken Promises of Privacy: Responding to the Surprising Failure of Anonymization*, 57 UCLA L. Rev. 1701 (2010).

[27] *See* Schwartz & Solove, *supra* note 25, at 1873–74; *see also* GDPR, *supra* note 23, at arts. 4(1), 9 and Recitals 26–30. *See generally* Paul M. Schwartz & Daniel J. Solove, *Reconciling Personal Information in the United States and European Union*, 102 Calif. L. Rev. 877 (2014).

[28] *See* Cal. Civ. Code § 1798.140 (Deering 2019).

[29] Principles of Law, Data Privacy § 2(b); *see also* Solove & Schwartz, *supra* note 12, at 14.

[30] S. 3418, 93d Cong. § 304 (1974).

the CCPA, the ALI's Data Privacy Principles, and the 1974 Federal Privacy Bill could all be used as a starting point for drafting a federal statute. For example, in any baseline federal legislation, personal data could be defined to include identified data, identifiable data (both directly and indirectly), biometric data, health-related data, device data, internet or network data, data about an individual associated with commercial transactions, and inferences drawn from any source of data, among other things.

Despite the possible risk of ossification, the scope of federal privacy legislation should be broad enough to adequately deal with current and future technological developments that allow companies to target us without knowing our identities or track us across multiple devices, and that impact data identifiability. The vast quantities of data that can be collected and processed in the IoT context increase "risks of re-identification."[31] Federal legislation must adequately deal with these risks. It should also be clear that if anonymized data can be used in any way to identify an individual it is subject to the statute. Recall from Chapters 1 and 2, the various reports and studies revealing how anonymized and aggregated data can be easily de-anonymized to reveal people's identities. In such an instance, federal legislation could extend to protect individuals' rights with respect to such data.

Selective Use of GDPR and Domestic Privacy Principles

As I have argued in earlier chapters, several sources of privacy legislation rely heavily on the notice and choice model to the detriment of consumers. This heavy reliance on the control narrative of privacy also fails to fully capture privacy's social importance.[32] Most persons value some level of privacy and likely have some common views of privacy.[33] Privacy is central to the functioning of our democratic system.[34] Baseline federal privacy legislation should attempt to correct the overreliance on notice and choice. Recall from Chapter 3 that my argument is not that we should completely do away with notice and choice in all instances. Instead, notice has value and so does choice, but overrelying on notice and choice as the primary means of protecting privacy and consumers is inadequate.

As Priscilla Regan observes, "if information privacy concerns are of broader societal importance, then additional support exists for an institutional mechanism to protect information privacy as is found in most European countries."[35] Several of the GDPR's core rights and legal principles could be used to address privacy law's

---

[31] *Opinion 8/2014 of the Working Party on the Protection of Individuals with Regard to the Processing of Personal Data on the Recent Developments on the Internet of Things*, at 11, 14/EN WP 223 (Sept. 16, 2014), https://ec.europa.eu/justice/article-29/documentation/opinion-recommendation/files/2014/wp223_en.pdf [hereinafter *Working Party IoT Recommendations*].

[32] REGAN, *supra* note 7, at 213–34.

[33] *Id.*

[34] *Id.*

[35] *Id.* at 234.

current overreliance on the US version of notice and choice. The GDPR does not use the notice and choice model as the exclusive means of protecting consumers.[36] Admittedly, several GDPR rights and principles are in keeping with traditional notice requirements, but the GDPR also imposes restrictions on consent.

Under the GDPR, consent can serve as a legal basis for processing, but consent is not unfettered. The GDPR provides that consent should be affirmative and be "freely given, specific, informed and unambiguous."[37] This language discourages the use of browsewrap agreements and disfavors opt-out consent approaches.[38] In contrast, recall from our Chapter 4 discussion that in the United States browsewrap agreements can be valid even though a consumer has failed to provide affirmative consent. The GDPR guidance issued by the United Kingdom's Information Commissioner's Office provides that companies should not use "opt-out boxes."[39] Further, consent is invalid under the GDPR if individuals would face "negative consequences" if they elected not to consent and consent that is "bundled-up" with

---

[36]   *See* Lisa M. Austin & David Lie, *Safe Sharing Sites*, 94. N.Y.U. L. Rev. 581, 589–90 (2019) (contending that the FTC's notice and choice regime fails to fully incorporate FIPs principles and noting that the GDPR goes beyond the notice and choice regime); Kevin E. Davis, & Florencia Marotta-Wurgler, *Contracting for Personal Data*, 94. N.Y.U. L. Rev. 662, 667 (2019) (contrasting the GDPR framework with the FTC's approach to privacy and security, and describing the GDPR as providing a regulatory framework that imposes "financial consequences for failure to comply" in contrast to the FTC's "Notice and Choice" approach, "which relies mostly on self-regulation"); A. Michael Froomkin, *Big Data: Destroyer of Informed Consent*, 21 Yale J.L. & Tech. 27, 35 (2019) (noting that the GDPR "includes significant limitations on data storage and re-use" in contrast to much of US privacy law which focuses on consent); Paul Ohm, *Forthright Code*, 56 Hous. L. Rev. 471, 480 (2018) (noting that the GDPR provides "much thicker regulation of personal data use than the FTC's authority"); Paul M. Schwartz & Karl-Nikolaus Peifer, *Transatlantic Data Privacy Law*, 106 Geo. L.J. 115, 142–44 (2017); Gabriela Zanfir-Fortuna, *10 Reasons Why the GDPR Is the Opposite of a "Notice and Consent" Type of Law*, Future Privacy F. (Sept. 13, 2019), https://fpf.org/2019/09/13/10-reasons-why-the-gdpr-is-the-opposite-of-a-notice-and-consent-type-of-law/. *But see* Hartzog, *supra* note 16, at 955–56; Charlotte A. Tschider, *Regulating the Internet of Things: Discrimination, Privacy, and Cybersecurity in the Artificial Intelligence Age*, 96 Denv. L. Rev. 87, 132 (2018); Ari Ezra Waldman, *Safe Social Spaces*, 96 Wash. U. L. Rev. 1537, 1569–70 (2019).

[37]   GDPR, *supra* note 23, at art. 4(11); *see also* Article 29 Data Protection Working Party, Guidelines on Consent Under Regulation 2016/679 (Apr. 10, 2018) [hereinafter GDPR Consent Regulation Guidelines], www.google.com/url?sa=t&rct=j&q=&esrc=s&source=web&cd=2&ved=2ahUKEwjjl8iAoovnAhWRMXoKHVooCaoQFjABegQIBRAB&url=https%3A%2F%2Fec.europa.eu%2Fnewsroom%2Farticle29%2Fdocument.cfm%3Faction%3Ddisplay%26doc_id%3D51030&usg=AOvVaw3d37uQbnEgUE7XlX1PiIob. Several of the W29 guidelines, including the GDPR Consent Regulation Guidelines, have been endorsed by the European Data Protection Board. *See, e.g., GDPR: Guidelines, Recommendations, Best Practices*, European Data Protection Board, https://edpb.europa.eu/our-work-tools/general-guidance/gdpr-guidelines-recommendations-best-practices_en (listing previously issued and endorsed guidelines) (last visited Feb. 1, 2020).

[38]   Schwartz & Peifer, *supra* note 36, at 144 (contending that "the GDPR disfavors the use of silence or inaction to constitute consent"); *see also* Solove & Schwartz, *supra* note 12, at 19 (stating that "opt out is not valid consent under the GDPR" in contrast to US law).

[39]   *Consent*, Info. Commissioners Off., https://ico.org.uk/for-organisations/guide-to-data-protection/guide-to-the-general-data-protection-regulation-gdpr/lawful-basis-for-processing/consent/ (last visited Feb. 5, 2020).

form contracts is not presumed to be "freely given."[40] Consumer consent cannot be used to validate "fundamentally unfair" data practices.[41] The GDPR also provides individuals with the ability to withdraw their consent.[42] Under the GDPR, "consent will not be considered to be free if the data subject is unable to refuse or withdraw his or her consent without detriment."[43]

Additionally, the GDPR imposes purpose and necessity limitations.[44] For instance, the GDPR provides that personal data should not be "further processed in a manner that is incompatible with" the original and specific legitimate purpose of data collection.[45] The GDPR contains restrictions on tying consent to data usages beyond what is required or necessary for contract performance with the end user.[46] However, even if the GDPR's consent approach is adopted, Contract Distancing and information asymmetry concerns must be addressed. In Chapter 9, I offer additional recommendations to remedy both concerns.

The GDPR's core data protection rights and the specific default legal obligations it imposes on companies (such as privacy by design and default) regardless of consumer contracting choices enables movement away from an overreliance on notice and choice.[47] These obligations (and in some cases the limitations on consent) could ameliorate the "privacy self-management" problem, in which consumers bear most of the burden of protecting their privacy and ensuring cybersecurity.[48] Recent proposed guidance on the GDPR's contracting provisions supports these points and states that "personal data cannot be considered as a tradeable commodity. Even if the data subject can agree to the processing of personal data, they cannot trade away their fundamental rights through this agreement."[49] Federal legislation could incorporate this principle.

There are several GDPR-like rights and legal obligations that could be incorporated into federal baseline privacy legislation. These include: (1) a right to request that

---

[40]   *GDPR Consent Regulation Guidelines, supra* note 37, at 5 ("As a general rule, the GDPR prescribes that if the data subject has no real choice, feels compelled to consent or will endure negative consequences if they do not consent, then consent will not be valid. If consent is bundled up as a non-negotiable part of terms and conditions, it is presumed not to have been freely given.").

[41]   *Id.* at 3–4.

[42]   GDPR, *supra* note 23, at art. 7.

[43]   GDPR *Consent Regulation Guidelines, supra* note 37, at 5.

[44]   *See, e.g.,* GDPR, *supra* note 23, at arts. 5(1), 6, 7.

[45]   *Id.* at art. 5.

[46]   *See, e.g.,* GDPR, *supra* note 23, at art. 7(4); *see also* THE EU GENERAL DATA PROTECTION REGULATION (GDPR): A COMMENTARY 19 (Christopher Kuner et al. eds., 2020) [hereinafter GDPR COMMENTARY] ("[C]onsent cannot be 'bundled' to cover a service which is not necessary for the performance of a contract."); Schwartz & Peifer, *supra* note 36, at 143 (under the GDPR "[u]se of information beyond that which is necessary for the contract is impermissible").

[47]   *See, e.g.,* GDPR, *supra* note 23, at arts. 5, 25, 32, 35.

[48]   *See generally* Daniel J. Solove, *Privacy Self-Management and the Consent Dilemma,* 126 HARV. L. REV. 1880 (2013).

[49]   EDPB Guideline Article 6(1)(b) (2019); EUROPEAN DATA PROTECTION BOARD, GUIDELINES 4/2019 ON ARTICLE 25: DATA PROTECTION BY DESIGN AND BY DEFAULT (Nov. 13, 2019), https://edpb.europa.eu/sites/edpb/files/consultation/edpb_guidelines_201904_dataprotection_by_design_and_by_default.pdf.

companies delete our data, subject to some exceptions;[50] (2) a right to obtain information about the data that companies collect and process about us;[51] (3) a right to object to and restrict data processing and automated decision making;[52] (4) data portability rights;[53] and (5) a right to correct inaccurate data.[54] The 2019 privacy principles released by Democratic members of Congress also reflect many of these rights.[55] Also, recall from our earlier discussions that the 1974 Federal Privacy Bill included several GDPR-like rights. Federal legislation could also explicitly require data minimization, and privacy and security by design and default.[56] These obligations could extend not only to companies that we deal directly with, but also to companies who obtain our data through various contracts with other companies. Privacy by design in the IoT setting should to some extent mean that strong privacy settings are implemented by default, and devices are designed to function without always having to connect to the Internet and collect and transmit data. Also, privacy and security by design, and privacy and security by default obligations, could also restrict large technology giants' ability to force IoT device makers to design devices to send them continuous streams of data. Requiring privacy and security by design and default, and data minimization principles, could incentivize companies to largely offer devices and services with consumer-friendly privacy and cybersecurity features. This could help to tackle the unequal access to privacy and security problem. Companies could also ensure that data "in the context of the IoT [are] kept for no longer than is necessary for the purpose for which the data were collected or further processed."[57]

Building on the GDPR rights and obligations mentioned earlier, federal legislation could expressly permit organizations to use and collect consumer data to the

---

[50] *See, e.g.*, GDPR, *supra* note 23, at arts. 12, 17; CAL. CIV. CODE §§ 1798.105, 1798.130(a)(1)(A), 1798.145 (g) (West 2020). *See generally* Robert C. Post, *Data Privacy and Dignitary Privacy: Google Spain, the Right to Be Forgotten and the Construction of the Public Sphere*, 67 DUKE L.J. 981 (2018).

[51] *See, e.g.*, CAL. CIV. CODE §§ 1798.100(b), 1798.130(a), 1798.135; GDPR, *supra* note 23, at arts. 5, 12, 13, 14; *see also* Margot E. Kaminski, *The Right to Explanation, Explained*, 34 BERKELEY TECH. L.J. 189, 199 (2019) ("Article 13 [of the GDPR] establishes a series of notification rights/requirements when information is collected directly from individuals. Article 14 [of the GDPR] establishes a similar set of notification rights/requirements when information about individuals is collected from third parties. Article 15 [of the GDPR] creates an individual right of access to information held by a company that can be invoked 'at reasonable intervals.'").

[52] GDPR, *supra* note 23, at arts. 18, 21, 22.

[53] *Id.* at arts. 13, 20.

[54] *Id.* at art. 16.

[55] *See Privacy and Data Protection Framework*, SENATE DEMOCRATS, www.democrats.senate.gov/imo/media/doc/Final_CMTE%20Privacy%20Principles_11.14.19.pdf; *see also* Cameron F. Kerry, *Senate Democratic Privacy Principles: Endgame or Game Over for a Bipartisan Privacy Bill?*, BROOKINGS (Nov. 22, 2019), www.brookings.edu/blog/techtank/2019/11/22/senate-democratic-privacy-principles-endgame-or-game-over-for-a-bipartisan-privacy-bill/.

[56] *See, e.g.*, GDPR, *supra* note 23, at art. 5.

[57] *Working Party IoT Recommendations*, *supra* note 31, at 17. *See also* Michael L. Rustad, *How the EU's General Data Protection Regulation Will Protect Consumers Using Smart Devices*, 52 SUFFOLK U. L. REV. 227, 248 (2019).

extent needed to (1) ensure the operations of consumer-requested or purchased devices and services, and (2) make improvements to product security and safety. Companies should at all times ensure the security of consumer data and protect consumers' privacy even when using consumer data to improve product safety and security. This obligation should extend to contractually related third parties, and companies' partners and affiliates who have access to our data. Other recognized and legitimate data uses, retentions, and practices that are required by law and those that do not harm consumer interests and privacy rights could also be made expressly permissible. The GDPR's approach to the concept of legitimate interest as well as alternative proposals offered during the GDPR's creation on this issue could also be helpful as well.[58]

A possible concern with this approach is that expressly permitting companies to use consumer data to improve product safety or security could enable companies to continue to vacuum up our data in the same manner that they do today. Stated differently, companies could attempt to justify their data collection and processing habits by claiming that such practices are necessary to improve the security and safety of current and future products. This is a valid concern. One response is that regulators charged with enforcing the statute could ensure that companies do not abuse expressly authorized categories by attempting to fit all of their data collection and use practices within said categories. Companies could be required to justify their data collection and use practices as falling within authorized categories. The express authorizations should also be considered in light of the other proposed provisions of a federal statute, including data minimization, necessity and purpose limitations, privacy and security by default and design, and the restrictions on harmful data practices discussed later. Data collection that is unnecessary for device and service functionality and that is not connected to a legitimate interest, such as fraud prevention, could be restricted. For example, many IoT devices need not collect our precise location data or consistently monitor our activities to function. Additionally, a company's data collection and use practices should not be deemed to fit within express authorized categories simply because the collection and processing

---

[58] GDPR, *supra* note 23, at art. 6, Recitals 47–49 ("[T]he legitimate interests of a controller, including those of a controller to which the personal data may be disclosed, or of a third party, may provide a legal basis for processing, provided that the interests or the fundamental rights and freedoms of the data subject are not overriding, taking into consideration the reasonable expectations of data subjects based on their relationship with the controller."); GDPR COMMENTARY, *supra* note 46, at 17–18 (noting that "[w]hilst the Albrecht Report had limited the use of legitimate interest to 'exceptional cases,' the compromise text allowed controllers to rely on their legitimate interest to process data when it met individuals' 'reasonable expectations' (Article 6)"); *What Does "Grounds of Legitimate Interest" Mean*, EUROPEAN COMMISSION, https://ec.europa.eu/info/law/law-topic/data-protection/reform/rules-business-and-organisations/legal-grounds-processing-data/grounds-processing/what-does-grounds-legitimate-interest-mean_en (last visited Mar. 3, 2020) ("[Y]our company/organisation must also check that by pursuing its legitimate interests the rights and freedoms of those individuals are not seriously impacted, otherwise your company/organisation cannot rely on grounds of legitimate interest as a justification for processing the data and another legal ground must be found.").

of consumer data is integral to the company's data business model or programs. The statute could also clearly indicate that these express authorizations should not be interpreted to automatically authorize all forms of targeted advertising and data processing, including to create discriminatory profiles that reveal insights about individuals, or otherwise harmful data practices.

Rather than solely allowing the narrative of privacy as control manifested through notice and choice to continue to dominate privacy law frameworks, baseline privacy legislation could also reflect a view of privacy as the right of our society to obligate corporate entities using our data to respect our interests in the data they collect and process about us.[59] As such, data practices that harm consumer interests both individually and collectively could be expressly restricted using a non-exhaustive list and could apply regardless of whether a company obtained consumer consent. These prohibitions could apply broadly to companies who collect data directly from us as well as entities who obtain access to our data through contracts with other entities. Examples of impermissible and harmful data practices that could be prohibited include those that (1) are associated with a failure to implement data minimization and privacy and security by design and default principles, and companies' ability to use data collected in violation of these principles could be restricted, (2) violate consumers' statutorily granted privacy rights (subject to reasonable exceptions, such as a company's denial of access rights when it is unable to verify a consumer's identity), (3) cause disability, age, price, gender, LGBTQ, religion, national origin, pregnancy, ethnicity, and racial discrimination, and other forms of traditionally recognized illegal discrimination, and (4) are associated with companies' use of dark patterns and other measures to mislead consumers.

The 1974 Federal Privacy Bill's provisions on data processing that could prejudice data subjects could also be instructive in this area.[60] The prohibited harmful data practices discussed earlier could address several of the privacy harms and limitations discussed in earlier chapters. For instance, the prohibitions on discrimination could help to ameliorate the exclusion problems discussed in Chapter 1. The limitation on consent and misleading data practices could aid in correcting the overreliance on notice and choice. The prohibited price and economic discrimination mentioned earlier is primarily aimed at addressing discrimination that exploits consumers' vulnerabilities. For example, recall the Uber dynamic price discrimination issue described in Chapter 1, in which the company reportedly has the ability to charge higher prices to individuals with low smartphone battery power. With respect to other forms of discrimination, companies' ability to use big data and various other

---

[59] Regan, *supra* note 7, at 231–32.

[60] S. 3418, 93d Cong. (1974). Organizations subject to the proposed statute that "disseminate[] statistical reports or research findings based on personal information ... [would have been obligated to] (B) make no materials available for independent analysis without the guarantee that no personal information will be used in a way that might prejudice judgments about any data subject." *Id.* § 201(b).

technological developments to intentionally or unintentionally develop or use proxy traits that enable discrimination and have a disparate impact should also be restricted. For instance, recall our discussion in Chapter 1 of how Facebook enabled exclusion by using users' liked posts and group membership. These restrictions could also be helpful in protecting consumer interests in some of the COVID-19-related data that technology companies are increasingly collecting and processing from IoT devices and other sources as part of pandemic response efforts.

Returning now to the GDPR-like individual privacy rights, with respect to data deletion rights, consumers could be clearly granted the right to request that a company destroy their data. This obligation could extend to contractually related third parties, and companies' partners and affiliates. If a consumer elects to terminate their use of the company's devices or services, companies could then be obligated to refrain from future uses of such data that are not authorized or required by law, that harm consumer interests and privacy rights, or that cannot be justified by a legitimate business interest, such as fraud prevention and cybersecurity protection. Consideration should also be given to whether an exception should also be made for "public interest, scientific or historical research purposes or statistical purposes."[61]

Admittedly, data deletion rights and obligations remain controversial. There are also potential practical difficulties, such as determining how a right to delete should apply to information about an individual shared by others and when multiple individuals share an account or device. Additionally, in some cases even if data are deleted from a company's live system, they could remain in backup systems.[62] Despite these difficulties, data deletion rights and obligations can be particularly useful in the IoT setting. Recall that IoT devices, mobile apps, and related systems, which have colonized our lives, collect and process unprecedented amounts of detailed and real-time data about us and our families. Having the ability to have some of these data deleted within reason from live and backup systems, and obligating companies to do so could limit concerns about IoT data being stored indefinitely, transferred and disclosed to multiple third parties, and used against us in various ways, including to negatively impact the opportunities we receive and to erode our anonymity. Data deletion rights and obligations could to a limited extent also mitigate unequal access to privacy concerns. Such a right and obligation could allow those of us who cannot afford to shield ourselves from data collection and surveillance – by, for instance, purchasing Privacy Wearables and other protective privacy and security products – to have some of the data that companies collect about us deleted. While data deletion rights and obligations would not stop the initial collection of data about the "privacy have nots," it could limit subsequent data

---

[61] PRINCIPLES OF LAW, DATA PRIVACY § 10 (AM. LAW INSTIT. 2019); *see also* Solove & Schwartz, *supra* note 12, at 39.

[62] *Right to Erasure*, INFO. COMMISSIONER'S OFF., https://ico.org.uk/for-organisations/guide-to-data-protection/guide-to-the-general-data-protection-regulation-gdpr/individual-rights/right-to-erasure/ (last visited Apr. 2, 2020).

uses. With respect to the live and backup system issue noted earlier, one approach that could be taken is to require companies to ensure that they do not continue to use the backup data for other purposes and that the data in backup systems are eventually overwritten within a reasonable time period.[63]

A right to obtain information could obligate companies to adopt effective cyber-security and verification practices to ensure that third parties, including hackers, do not abuse data request and access rights to obtain our data.[64] Companies could also be required to disclose to us not only the data we knowingly supply directly to them, but also data obtained from third parties (such as data brokers, and other companies); data about us that we supply indirectly (for example, browsing history); raw and interpreted data from IoT devices;[65] and data analytics reports generated from the use of such data, including insights used for targeting and advertising. Access to these data could help to address information asymmetry concerns discussed in Chapter 4. Access rights and obligations can also include a right to challenge and correct inaccurate data and obtain an explanation about algorithmic decision making that has legal or significant effects.[66] These rights could also be used to some extent to address exclusion concerns. For instance, once we are able to have access to information concerning us that companies use to make decisions that impact us, we can exercise our ability to correct inaccurate data that may negatively impact the opportunities we receive. Consideration could also be given to the extent to which access rights would require companies to make data identifiable.[67]

Even if we are given a right to object to algorithmic decision making, companies could be permitted to use solely algorithmic decision-making systems as long as they are able to ensure that these systems are bias free and our core data rights are protected.[68] Consideration could also be given to the desirability of incorporating

---

[63]   *Id.* Info. Comm'r's Office, Deleting Personal Data (1998), https://ico.org.uk/media/for-organisations/documents/1475/deleting_personal_data.pdf.

[64]   *See* Mariano Di Martino et al., *Personal Information Leakage by Abusing the GDPR "Right of Access,"* Usenix (2019), https://dl.acm.org/doi/10.5555/3361476.3361504 (a study of the GDPR's data access rights and finding that due to the lax verification processes of "15 out of 55" studied organizations, researchers were able "to impersonate a subject and obtained full access" to individuals' personal data); *see also* Kashmir Hill, *Want Your Personal Data? Hand Over More Please,* N.Y. Times, www.nytimes.com/2020/01/15/technology/data-privacy-law-access.html#click=https://t.co/kHVtRvLEPm (last updated May 22, 2020).

[65]   *Working Party IoT Recommendations, supra* note 31, at 19–20.

[66]   *See, e.g.,* GDPR, *supra* note 23, at art. 22(1); Article 29 Data Protection Working Party, Guidelines on Automated Individual Decision-Making and Profiling for the Purposes of Regulation 2016/679 (2018) [hereinafter GDPR Automated Decision-Making Guidelines]; Danielle Keats Citron & Frank Pasquale, *The Scored Society: Due Process for Automated Predictions,* 89 Wash. L. Rev. 1 (2014) (calling for algorithmic decision making due process rights in the United States).

[67]   Solove & Schwartz, *supra* note 12, at 14.

[68]   *See, e.g.,* Algorithmic Accountability Act of 2019, S. 1108, 116th Cong. (1st Sess. 2019), www.congress.gov/bill/116th-congress/senate-bill/1108/text; GDPR, *supra* note 23, at arts. 15(h), 22, Recital 71 (noting that even if an individual has provided explicit consent to data processing, the automated processing of personal data, such as profiling, should still be "subject to suitable safeguards, which

established exceptions to the GDPR's restrictions on solely algorithmic decision making.[69] As mentioned earlier, a practice that causes actual discrimination could be viewed as an impermissible and harmful data practice. Other types of possible algorithmic fairness and ethical concerns could also be considered, including the amplification of pre-existing biases, "quality of service, stereotyping, [and] denigration."[70] These issues may be exacerbated in the IoT setting in light of the increasing amounts of data that companies can collect and process about us.

One possible critique of this proposal is that requiring companies to disclose detailed information about their data analytics reports would negatively impact their intellectual property rights and overburden consumers with additional information.[71] Somewhat similar access right provisions contained in the text of the GDPR appear to be subject to an exception for intellectual property rights.[72] However, in light of the overall aims of the GDPR, the core individual rights contained within the GDPR appear to supersede intellectual property rights.[73] A similar approach could be taken in the United States in light of the individual and societal concerns the IoT presents. Additionally, to address concerns about the usefulness of algorithmic decision-making explanations and consumer burdens with

should include specific information to the data subject and the right to obtain human intervention, to express his or her point of view, to obtain an explanation of the decision reached after such assessment and to challenge the decision"); GDPR AUTOMATED DECISION-MAKING GUIDELINES, *supra* note 66, at 19–23.

[69] *See Rights Related to Automated Decision-Making Including Profiling*, INFO. COMMISSIONER'S OFF., https://ico.org.uk/for-organisations/guide-to-data-protection/guide-to-the-general-data-protection-regulation-gdpr/individual-rights/rights-related-to-automated-decision-making-including-profiling/ (last visited June 8, 2020) (Under the GDPR, "you can only carry out . . . [solely automated] decision-making where the decision is: necessary for the entry into or performance of a contract; or authorized by Union or Member state law applicable to the controller; or based on the individual's explicit consent" and discussing additional obligations applicable to children.); Kaminski, *supra* note 16, at 1591–92 (noting that the GDPR restricts "solely algorithmic decision making").

[70] Michael A. Madaio et al., *Co-Designing Checklists to Understand Organizational Challenges and Opportunities Around Fairness in AI*, 2020 CHI CONF. ON HUM. FACTORS COMPUTING SYSTEMS 318 (2020), www.jennwv.com/papers/checklists.pdf; Nicole Turner Lee et al., *Algorithmic Bias Detection and Mitigation: Best Practices and Policies to Reduce Consumer Harms*, BROOKINGS (May 22, 2019), www.brookings.edu/research/algorithmic-bias-detection-and-mitigation-best-practices-and-policies-to-reduce-consumer-harms/; EUROPEAN COMM., ETHICS GUIDELINES FOR TRUSTWORTHY AI (2019), https://ec.europa.eu/digital-single-market/en/news/ethics-guidelines-trustworthy-ai.

[71] GDPR AUTOMATED DECISION MAKING GUIDELINES, *supra* note 66, at 19 ("Data controllers have an interest in not sharing details of their algorithms to avoid disclosing trade secrets, violating the rights and freedoms of others (e.g. privacy), and allowing data subjects to game or manipulate the decision-making system.").

[72] *See, e.g.*, GDPR, *supra* note 23, at Recital 63, art. 22(2) (listing several exceptions); Lilian Edwards & Michael Veale, *Slave to the Algorithm? Why a "Right to an Explanation" Is Probably Not the Remedy You Are Looking For*, 16 DUKE L. & TECH. REV. 18, 21 (2017); Kaminski, *supra* note 51, at 200.

[73] Kaminski, *supra* note 51, at 189 (discussing the work of several scholars who have contended that GDPR "fundamental rights such as the right to data protection take precedence over trade secrecy"); *see also* GDPR AUTOMATED DECISION MAKING GUIDELINES, *supra* note 66, at 17 (noting that entities "cannot rely on the protection of their trade secrets as an excuse to deny access or refuse to provide information" and shedding light on the limits of the consent exceptions).

additional information, companies could be incentivized to audit and design bias-free automated decision-making systems. Companies could also be obligated to provide explanations in a manner that consumers can understand. Federal and state actors could be explicitly given the power and resources to actively monitor and review companies' algorithmic decision-making systems and hold companies accountable for implementing biased systems.[74] Companies can be further encouraged to test their proposed systems to guard against bias prior to implementing them.

Turning now to data portability, one possible objection to a data portability right is that such a right could negatively impact consumers' privacy. Following this line of reasoning, increasing other companies' access to our data means that more companies have the ability to exploit our data. Additionally, startup companies may not need all of our historical data in order to succeed.[75] There are also possible data security concerns as well.[76] Non-dominant firms could have less robust information security practices. There is also the issue of whether one should be able to transfer data that includes information about other individuals or data generated by others about an individual.

Although a data portability right may have some drawbacks, such a right could be useful in addressing technology giants' ability to confine us to their platforms, products, and services. For instance, recall from Chapter 7 that one of the possible impact of mergers and acquisitions involving dominant technology companies is the corresponding decline in competitor products, and with fewer alternatives, consumers may be more likely to turn to technology giants' products. While data and product lock-in concerns are found in various contexts, such as the social media setting, these concerns are acutely problematic in the IoT setting. Recall from Chapter 5 that because IoT devices depend on an intricate provision of ongoing software and services we must maintain our relationships with the companies that provide these services in order for our devices to function. Additionally, technology giants have recently agreed to take steps to develop open standards for IoT devices.[77] If we have the ability to transfer our data to different platforms and interoperability, and data formatting problems are resolved, dominant firms' ability to lock us into their products

---

[74] *See, e.g.,* Edwards & Veale, *supra* note 72, at 23; GDPR AUTOMATED DECISION MAKING GUIDELINES, *supra* note 66, at ANNEX I.

[75] Matthew Lane, *Recognizing and Dealing with the Tension Between Competition and Privacy Policies,* DISCO (Oct. 22, 2019), www.project-disco.org/privacy/102219-recognizing-and-dealing-with-the-tension-between-competition-and-privacy-policies/.

[76] Peter Swire & Yianni Lagos, *Why the Right to Data Portability Likely Reduces Consumer Welfare: Antitrust and Privacy Critique,* 72 MD. L. REV. 335, 338–40 (2013) ("[C]ompetition law, in both the U.S. and E.U., recognizes important efficiencies that can occur from lock-in for some situations; notably, a certain level of switching costs can encourage investment in new products and services, creating efficiency over time.").

[77] *Amazon, Apple, Google, and the Zigbee Alliance and Its Board Members Form Industry Working Group to Develop a New, Open Standard for Smart Home Device Connectivity,* ZIGBEE ALLIANCE (DEC. 18, 2019), https://zigbeealliance.org/news_and_articles/connectedhomeip/.

could be decreased.[78] Although there may be certain possible market benefits to consumer lock-in, such as increased investment in new goods and services, a data portability right could also enable the creation of more acceptable alternative IoT products and services by non-dominant firms, thereby benefiting both consumers and non-dominant IoT firms.[79] The GDPR guidelines addressing the data portability right could be helpful in this area.[80] Additionally, companies that receive our data could be clearly obligated to ensure the security of the data once it is received. From a policy perspective, and to possibly address data portability privacy concerns, consideration could also be given to whether data portability rights should extend primarily to certain types of data that would be more likely to promote competition.[81] A right to delete could also serve to balance privacy harms related to data portability rights. Lastly, data portability is likely here to stay. The CCPA already contains data portability provisions.[82] Federal legislation should also address data portability rights.

The CCPA's provisions on data sales, augmented by the improvements discussed in subsequent sections of this chapter addressing state legislation, could also be included in federal legislation. Federal legislation could also contain an additional anti-discrimination provision and address companies' use of financial incentives. This anti-discrimination provision (with some improvements) could be borrowed from the repealed FCC Privacy Rules. Recall from Chapter 3 that the repealed FCC Privacy Rules would have prevented broadband internet access service providers from denying us access to services if we refused to waive our privacy rights. Also, remember that the CCPA contains its own anti-discrimination and financial incentives provisions that could also be of use in addressing this issue in federal legislation. The CCPA's provisions on these topics could be more robust, and I will discuss these points in the state privacy legislation section. Federal privacy legislation could prevent companies from denying us access on an equal basis to devices, software, and services if we refuse to consent to a waiver of our privacy rights, the sale, license, or disclosure of our data, or the use of our data for data analytics purposes related to profiling or advertising. A federal privacy statute could also directly opine on privacy issues associated with ISPs, including requiring adherence to net neutrality

---

[78]   Mehmet Bilal Ünver, *Turning the Crossroad for a Connected World: Reshaping the European Prospect for the Internet of Things*, 26 Int. J.L. & Info. Tech. 93 (2018); Maureen K. Ohlhausen, *Privacy and Competition: Friends, Foes, or Frenemies?*, CPI (Feb. 25, 2019), www.competitionpolicyinternational .com/privacy-and-competition-friends-foes-or-frenemies/.

[79]   Swire & Lagos, *supra* note 76, at 340.

[80]   *See* Article 29 Data Protection Working Party, Guidelines on the Right to "Data Portability" (2017), https://ec.europa.eu/newsroom/article29/item-detail.cfm?item_id=611233.

[81]   *See, e.g.*, Lane, *supra* note 75; Eric Null & Ross Schulman, *The Data Portability Act: More User Control, More Competition*, New America (Aug. 19, 2010), www.newamerica.org/oti/blog/data-portability-act-more-user-control-more-competition/.

[82]   Cal. Civ. Code § 1798.100 (West 2020).

principles and extending the core privacy rights and obligations established by the federal statute to cover ISPs' activities.

Selective Use of GDPR and Domestic Security Principles

A baseline federal privacy statute could also address security concerns. As mentioned earlier, the GDPR requires "data protection by design and default."[83] The GDPR also requires that subject companies adopt appropriate data security measures "to ensure a level of security appropriate to the risk."[84] Recall from Chapter 3 the drawbacks of primarily relying on a reasonable data security approach. Even courts have recognized the need for granular cybersecurity guidance. In *LabMD, Inc. v. FTC*, the Eleventh Circuit vacated an FTC cease and desist order requiring a company to adopt reasonable cybersecurity practices.[85] The court reasoned that the order lacked specific guidance and did not instruct the company to "stop committing a specific act or practice."[86]

The National Institute of Standards and Technology's cybersecurity framework and recommendations can serve as a blueprint for guidance that could be specifically incorporated into federal legislation. Recall from Chapter 2 that NIST's cybersecurity frameworks are currently only voluntary. Companies' cybersecurity obligations must extend to both physical IoT devices as well as to connected services and systems, including mobile applications. The United Kingdom's Code of Practice for Consumer IoT Security could also be a helpful source for drafting security guidance.[87] Possibly useful provisions contained in the code of practice include recommendations that companies (i) make associated IoT systems resilient to data networks and power outages; (ii) guarantee the integrity of IoT software; and (iii) decrease exposed security attack surfaces.[88]

Additionally, as cybersecurity threats and algorithmic decision making evolves, so too should regulatory cybersecurity guidance. Federal legislation can be drafted to both simultaneously provide a non-exhaustive list of granular cybersecurity guidance as well as grant powers to regulatory bodies to adopt new rules to address technological changes that pose security risks that are not fully captured by the express language of a statute.

---

[83] GDPR, *supra* note 23, at art. 25.

[84] *Id.* at art. 32.

[85] LabMD, Inc. v. FTC, 894 F.3d 1221 (11th Cir. 2018).

[86] *Id.* at 1236 ("In the case at hand, the cease and desist order contains no prohibitions. It does not instruct LabMD to stop committing a specific act or practice. Rather, it commands LabMD to overhaul and replace its data-security program to meet an indeterminable standard of reasonableness. This command is unenforceable.")

[87] UK Dep't for Dig., Culture, Media & Sport, Code of Practice for Consumer IoT Security (2018), https://assets.publishing.service.gov.uk/government/uploads/system/uploads/attachment_data/file/773867/Code_of_Practice_for_Consumer_IoT_Security_October_2018.pdf.

[88] *Id.*

Baseline federal privacy legislation could also deal with data breaches. The term "breach" could be broadly defined to encompass unauthorized data access, uses, disclosures, and losses. The ALI's Data Privacy Principles and the GDPR are useful sources for such a broad definition.[89]

Companies should also be subject to federal data breach notification obligations. Like the GDPR, existing laws in some states include a risk of harm analysis in their data breach notification requirements.[90] For instance, Alaska's data breach notification statute contains a risk analysis provision and also permits businesses to provide the attorney general with written risk of harm reports.[91] The GDPR requires a notification to enforcement authorities "without undue delay" within a specified time frame, if feasible, and it also imposes an obligation to provide reasons for any delays beyond that time frame unless "the data breach is unlikely to result in a risk to the rights and freedoms of natural persons."[92] Notifications to individuals are required if there will likely be a "high risk to the rights and freedoms of natural persons."[93] The GDPR Article 29 Working Party guidance, which was subsequently endorsed by the European Data Protection Board (EDPB), sheds light on when a company will be deemed to become "aware" of a data breach, provides guidance on assessing risk, and gives a non-exhaustive list of examples of data breaches that may constitute a high risk to individuals.[94]

While the risk assessment approach to data breach notification could be used as a framework for federal legislation, the drawback of this approach is that it allows

---

[89] *See* PRINCIPLES OF LAW, DATA PRIVACY § 11(b)(1) (AM. LAW INSTIT. 2019); GDPR, *supra* note 23, at art. 4(12).

[90] Emily Westridge Black, *What to Know About the 48th State Breach Notification Law*, LAW360 (Apr. 17, 2017, 5:15 PM), www.law360.com/articles/912677/what-to-know-about-the-48th-state-breach-notification-law. *See generally* FOLEY & LARDNER LLP CYBERSECURITY TEAM, STATE DATA BREACH NOTIFICATION LAWS (2019), www.foley.com/en/insights/publications/2019/01/-/media/409938b300d2452a85671df61679acf8.ashx [hereinafter FOLEY DATA BREACH SUMMARY] (summarizing state data breach notification statutes).

[91] *See* ALASKA STAT. § 45.48.010 (2019); *see also* FOLEY DATA BREACH SUMMARY, *supra* note 90.

[92] GDPR, *supra* note 23, at art. 33; GDPR CONSENT REGULATION GUIDELINES, *supra* note 37, at art. 4.

[93] GDPR, *supra* note 23, at art. 34(1) ("When the personal data breach is likely to result in a high risk to the rights and freedoms of natural persons, the controller shall communicate the personal data breach to the data subject without undue delay."); *see also* ARTICLE 29 DATA PROTECTION WORKING PARTY, GUIDELINES ON PERSONAL DATA BREACH NOTIFICATION UNDER REGULATION 2016/679, at 20 (Oct. 3, 2017) [hereinafter GDPR DATA BREACH GUIDELINES] ("The threshold for communicating a breach to individuals is therefore higher than for notifying supervisory authorities and not all breaches will therefore be required to be communicated to individuals, thus protecting them from unnecessary notification fatigue.").

[94] *See* GDPR DATA BREACH GUIDELINES, *supra* note 92, at 27–29; *see also Article 29 Working Party*, EUR. DATA PROTECTION BOARD, https://edpb.europa.eu/our-work-tools/article-29-working-party_en (last visited June 8, 2020) (noting that the Article 29 Working Party "dealt with issues relating to the protection of privacy and personal data until 25 May 2018"); *GDPR: Guidelines, Recommendations, Best Practices*, EUR. DATA PROTECTION BOARD, https://edpb.europa.eu/our-work-tools/general-guidance/gdpr-guidelines-recommendations-best-practices_en (last visited Mar. 4, 2020) ("During its first plenary meeting the European Data Protection Board endorsed the GDPR related WP29 Guidelines . . . on Personal data breach notification under Regulation 2016/679, WP250 rev.01.").

companies to play a central role in determining when to provide notice of a data breach to consumers. This is particularly true if the legislation does not require that a company consult with government authorities in making the determination.[95] A company's definition of high risk, or risk for that matter, may differ from consumers' expectations and beliefs about risks in data breaches. Also, limiting a risk analysis to harms associated with identity theft ignores the intangible harms that are associated with data breaches and surveillance. As such, a blanket rule requiring notification to individuals (regardless of risk impact) when there is a data breach is preferable even if consumers may be overwhelmed with breach "notification fatigue." Once notified of a breach, a consumer could, for instance, choose to stop using an insecure device and the consumer could have the option to bring suit.

Enforcement

Baseline federal privacy legislation could be enforced simultaneously by multiple actors. Consumers could be given a private right of action when companies violate the provisions of, and rights granted by, the baseline privacy and security federal statute. In *Spokeo*, the Supreme Court expressly noted the limits of Congress's impact on standing issues, but the court also acknowledged that "because Congress is well positioned to identify intangible harms that meet minimum Article III requirements, its judgment is also instructive and important."[96] Federal baseline privacy legislation could expressly address concrete privacy interests, and the concrete impact of intangible privacy harms.

Consider the Ninth Circuit's notable application of *Spokeo*. Most recently, in *Patel v. Facebook*, a case involving BIPA, the Ninth Circuit applying *Spokeo* held that "an invasion of an individual's biometric privacy rights 'has a close relationship to a harm that has traditionally been regarded as providing a basis for a lawsuit in English or American courts.'"[97] The court relied on the common law history of privacy and Supreme Court cases on technology and privacy.[98] The Ninth Circuit also held that the plaintiffs "alleged a concrete and particularized harm" because violations of BIPA's requirements "actually harm or pose a material risk of harm to" the plaintiffs' concrete privacy interests.[99] The court's opinion is also notable because it highlights the importance of consent. The court found that collecting biometric data without an individual's consent, as the plaintiffs alleged, in violation of BIPA "invades an individual's private affairs and concrete interests" for standing purposes.[100] Thus, whether an individual consented to data collection can be a central issue. As I will argue in

---

[95] See Black, *supra* note 90.

[96] Spokeo, Inc. v. Robins, 136 S. Ct. 1540, 1549 (2016) (explaining that despite Congressional instruction, "Article III standing requires a concrete injury even in the context of a statutory violation").

[97] Patel v. Facebook, Inc., 932 F.3d 1264, 1273 (9th Cir. 2019).

[98] *Id.*

[99] *Id.* at 1275.

[100] *Id.* at 1273.

Chapter 9, in determining consent to data collection and other contract terms, courts could expressly and effectively consider Contract Distancing even if the GDPR's approach is adopted.

Existing federal enforcers, such as the FTC, the FCC, and the CFPB could all be tasked with ensuring compliance with a baseline federal privacy statute in the industries they regulate. To fill regulatory gaps, entities and data that are arguably not currently and sufficiently subject to existing legislation and the jurisdiction of federal enforcers could be made expressly subject to the FTC's authority and covered by baseline federal privacy legislation. State attorneys general could also be permitted to enforce the statute. A violation of consumers' baseline privacy rights or any provision of the privacy statute, as well as a failure to comply with required cybersecurity obligations, could be viewed as a deceptive and unfair practice. These activities could be actionable by the FTC and other agencies, regardless of the implicit or explicit promises made by a company in its privacy policy and other communications with consumers. In assessing statutory violations, federal agencies could also be tasked with considering long-standing evidence about the ways we make privacy choices and companies' power to influence these choices. Federal agencies must not be cabined by narrow conceptions of privacy harms and could be given the power to consider and address unequal access to privacy and cybersecurity concerns.

The resources (staff and funding) and power of federal agencies enforcing baseline privacy legislation could be significantly expanded. Within each agency there should be a large, well-established privacy and security unit dedicated to enforcing the federal baseline privacy statute. As of 2019, the FTC only had forty full-time employees working on privacy and cybersecurity issues.[101] In contrast, the United Kingdom's Information Commissioner's Office has approximately 500 employees devoted to privacy and security topics even though the United Kingdom is a significantly smaller jurisdiction than the United States.[102] The FTC has asked Congress for more funding to hire additional staff, and Congress must commit to doing this.[103] The federal agencies mentioned earlier can be given the power to adopt rules to achieve the goals of the baseline privacy statute. The FTC's rulemaking authority could be widened. The FTC must be released from the rulemaking yoke of the Magnuson Moss Warranty Act.[104] The FTC and other federal agencies enforcing baseline privacy legislation could also have the ability to issue large fines (civil penalties) even for first-time privacy and cybersecurity violations. These fines

---

[101] Letter from Joseph Simons, Chairman, Fed. Trade Comm'n, to Frank Pallone, Jr., Chairman, House Comm. on Energy & Commerce (Apr. 1, 2019), https://energycommerce .house.gov/sites/democrats.energycommerce.house.gov/files/documents/FTC%20Response%20to% 20Pallone-Schakowsky.pdf.

[102] *See id.*

[103] *See id.*

[104] *See, e.g.,* CHRIS HOOFNAGLE, FEDERAL TRADE COMMISSION: PRIVACY LAW AND POLICY 334 (2016) (discussing the Magnuson Moss Warranty Act & the FTC).

could be made large enough to make a strong dent in violators' annual revenue and bottom line to encourage compliance.

The adoption of a baseline privacy statute that multiple existing federal agencies have the capacity to enforce with respect to industries within their scope has the benefit of partially correcting our sectoral approach to privacy by creating a unified framework for privacy and security enforcement, and establishing privacy and security rights and obligations that are applicable to all industries. Admittedly, there are alternative enforcement approaches that could be adopted. Recall that the 1974 Federal Privacy Bill would have established a federal privacy board.[105] A new data protection agency could be created to enforce the baseline privacy statute. Alternatively, sole enforcement authority could be given to the FTC, and the agency's reach could be expanded to cover entities not currently subject to its jurisdiction. However, since the multi-agency enforcement approach does not require a complete overhaul of the current US enforcement approach to privacy and security, it may be viewed as a less radical approach. The multi-agency enforcement approach allows existing agencies to use their unique industry expertise to ensure proper enforcement and privacy protection while simultaneously filling gaps left open by the sectoral approach. It also avoids dependence on a single agency to address all privacy and security issues. Additionally, there is precedent for extending enforcement power under a federal statute to more than one federal agency. Both the FTC and the CFPB enforce the FDCPA.[106] Although there may be challenges associated with coordinated enforcement efforts, the FTC's and CFPB's joint efforts with respect to the FDCPA suggest that multiple federal agencies can coexist and work together on enforcing a single piece of legislation.[107]

Further Objections to Selective GDPR Importation

So far, I have argued that several GDPR provisions could be incorporated into federal legislation. Our legal system is distinct from the EU legal landscape, which recognizes data protection and privacy as core individual rights, and views privacy as

---

[105] S. 3418, 93d Cong. § 101(a) (1974); *see also* Flaherty, *supra* note 7, at 237.
[106] Press Release, Fed. Trade Comm'n, FTC and CFPB Report on 2018 Activities to Combat Illegal Debt Collection Practices (Mar. 20, 2019), www.ftc.gov/news-events/press-releases/2019/03/ftc-cfpb-report-2018-activities-combat-illegal-debt-collection ("The CFPB and the FTC share enforcement responsibilities under the FDCPA.").
[107] *See id.* (noting that the FTC and CFPB "reauthorized their memorandum of understanding" in 2019); *see also* Bureau of Consumer Fin. Protection, Fair Debt Collection Practices Act: BCFP Annual Report 2019 (2019), https://files.consumerfinance.gov/f/documents/cfpb_fdcpa_annual-report-congress_03-2019.pdf (joint congressional report by CFPB and FTC on the FDCPA); Memorandum of Understanding Between the Consumer Fin. Protection Bureau and the Fed. Trade Comm'n (Feb. 25, 2019), www.ftc.gov/system/files/documents/cooperation_agreements/ftc-cfpb_mou_225_0.pdf.

an important value.[108] Some of the proposed data rights and prohibitions on data uses, such as the right to delete, may compete with rights grounded in other important sources of law, such as the First Amendment.[109] One solution to concerns about the right to delete is to simply make this right (and other possible conflicting federal baseline statutory provisions) subject to the First Amendment.[110] However, it is clear that in today's age we face unprecedented privacy and cybersecurity harms, and there are more data about us available today than ever before. We must grapple with companies' ability to use the First Amendment as a tool to further their colonization of our homes, lives, and bodies.

Additionally, as Neil Richards convincingly argues, "[i]nstances of contractual commercial regulation are well outside the scope of the First Amendment."[111] An extensive approach to correcting our current legal system's privacy and cybersecurity failures also requires us to consider the ways in which contract law both facilitates, and could potentially correct, data exploitation. Legislators could adopt "both default and mandatory" contractual rules applicable to consumer data transactions.[112] These rules could include provisions addressing consent (such as the GDPR rules discussed earlier), Contract Distancing, information asymmetry, and the application of non-waivable implied warranties to the terms of service, and

---

[108] *See* Charter of Fundamental Rights of the European Union, arts. 7 and 8, 2012 OJ (C 326) 2, https:// eur-lex.europa.eu/legal-content/EN/TXT/PDF/?uri=CELEX:12012P/TXT&from=EN; *see also Data Protection*, EUR. DATA PROTECTION SUPERVISOR, https://edps.europa.eu/data-protection/data-protection_en (last visited Feb. 2, 2020).

[109] *See, e.g.*, Sorrell v. IMS Health Inc., 564 U.S. 552, 552–59 (2011) (holding that a Vermont statute that restricted specific companies' ability to transfer or use "prescriber-identifying information" for "marketing or promoting a prescription drug, unless the prescriber consents . . . impose[d] content- and speaker-based burdens on protected expression [and was] subject to heightened judicial scrutiny"); Jane Bambauer, *Is Data Speech?*, 66 STAN. L. REV. 57, 71 (2014) (contending that the *Sorrell* "opinion suggested that the restriction on transfers of data between willing givers and receivers was automatically a restriction of speech"); *Ashutosh Bhagwat, Sorrell v. IMS Health: Details, Detailing, and the Death of Privacy*, 36 VT. L. REV. 855, 856 (2012) (noting that "hints" left by the *Sorrell* court may negatively impact the validity of rules aimed at protecting privacy); Woodrow Hartzog & Neil Richards, *Privacy's Constitutional Moment and the Limits of Data Protection*, 61 B.C. L. REV. 1687 (2020) (contending that there are significant First Amendment concerns associated with privacy regulation and proposing a new privacy framework); CONG. RESEARCH SERV., DATA PROTECTION LAW: AN OVERVIEW 36 (2019), https://fas.org/sgp/crs/misc/R45631.pdf (discussing First Amendment objections to privacy legislation). *But see* Neil Richards, *Why Data Privacy Law Is (Mostly) Constitutional*, 56 WM. & MARY L. REV. 1501, 1506, 1521–24, 1532–33 (2015) (arguing that "the right to be forgotten runs into First Amendment problems when it starts to resemble the old disclosure tort," and contending that the *Sorrell* decision does not upset the well-established understanding that "general commercial regulation of the huge data trade [is] not censorship").

[110] *See* GDPR, *supra* note 23, at arts. 12, 17.

[111] Neil M. Richards, *Reconciling Data Privacy and the First Amendment*, 52 UCLA L. REV. 1149, 1204 (2005).

[112] *Id. But see* Eugene Volokh, *Freedom of Speech and Information Privacy: The Troubling Implications of a Right to Stop People from Speaking About You*, 52 STAN. L. REV. 1049, 1058–62, 1062 n.42 (2000) (citing Cohen v. Cowles Media Co., 501 U.S. 663, 671 (1991).

privacy policies governing consumer data trade arrangements. I will explore some of these issues in more detail in Chapter 9.

Also, consider that Senator Ervin argued in his remarks introducing the 1974 Federal Privacy Bill, which contained data removal provisions, that "[t]he Constitution creates a right to privacy which is designed to assure that the minds and hearts of Americans remain free. The bulwark of this constitutional principle is the [F]irst [A]mendment. The [F]irst [A]mendment was designed to protect the sanctity of the individual's private thoughts and beliefs."[113] This suggests that the First Amendment may not always have been viewed as an insurmountable obstacle to strong privacy and security legislation, but instead could serve as a justification for such legislation.

Admittedly, the GDPR itself is not immune to criticism, including concerns about the costs of GDPR compliance, which can be more easily borne by larger firms, and the possible entrenchment of large companies' market power as a result.[114] There are also enforcement gaps associated with the GDPR.[115] Ari Ezra Waldman convincingly argues that "privacy law [including the GDPR] is experiencing a process of legal endogeneity [in which] mere symbols of compliance" (such as companies' use of data protection officers) "are standing in for real privacy protections" because the law grants too much power to "compliance professionals" to apply and define the law in practice.[116] Several of the GDPR's provisions, including the requirement of privacy by design and consent provisions, may leave room for enforcement gaps.[117] A study (CMP Study) evaluating compliance with the

---

[113] S. 3418, 93d Cong. (1974).

[114] *See, e.g.,* McKay Cunningham, *Exposed,* 2019 MICH. ST. L. REV. 375, 407 (2019) (contending that the GDPR "principally targets the process of data collection rather than its after-captured use"); Tal Z. Zarsky, *Incompatible: The GDPR in the Age of Big Data,* 47 SETON HALL L. REV. 995, 996 (2017) (contending that "the GDPR fails to properly address the surge in big data practices"); Garrett A. Johnson & Scott K. Shriver, *Privacy & Market Concentration: Intended & Unintended Consequences of the GDPR* (Mar. 20, 2020) (unpublished manuscript), https://papers.ssrn.com /sol3/papers.cfm?abstract_id=3477686 (a study of the GDPR's impact finding that the GDPR "reduced data sharing online, but had the unintended consequence of increasing market concentration"); Roslyn Layton, The 10 Problems of the GDPR, Statement Before the Senate Judiciary Committee on the General Data Protection Regulation and California Consumer Privacy Act: Opt-ins, Consumer Control, and the Impact on Competition and Innovation (Mar. 12, 2019), www .judiciary.senate.gov/download/03/12/2019/layton-testimony; ALEX MARTHEWS & CATHERINE TUCKER, BROOKINGS, PRIVACY POLICY AND COMPETITION (2019), www.brookings.edu/wp-content/uploads/2019/ 12/ES-12.04.19-Marthews-Tucker.pdf (contending that "evidence suggests that the cost of GDPR per employee will be proportionally greater for smaller firms" but noting that there "are few tools or accepted methods of measuring the potential benefits of privacy regulation" and as such it is difficult to determine definitively whether privacy regulation will negatively impact competition).

[115] *See, e.g.,* Shmuel I. Becher & Uri Benoliel, *Law in Books and Law in Action: The Readability of Privacy Policies and the GDPR,* CONSUMER L. & ECON (forthcoming 2020), https://papers.ssrn.com /sol3/papers.cfm?abstract_id=3334095 (an empirical study of the GDPR's impact finding that "in spite of the GDPR's requirement[s], European citizens often encounter privacy policies that are largely unreadable").

[116] Ari Ezra Waldman, *Privacy Law's False Promise,* 97 WASH. U. L. REV. 4, 31 (2019).

[117] *See id.* at 22–23. *But see, e.g.,* EUROPEAN DATA PROTECTION BOARD, *supra* note 49.

GDPR's consent obligations through the use of third-party consent management platforms (CMPs) found that "dark patterns and implied consent [designs] are ubiquitous [and] only 11.8% [of studied designs] meet minimal requirements ... based on European law."[118]

The GDPR's deficiencies provide an opportunity for US lawmakers to learn from and address gaps in any imported provisions of the GDPR's text, practical application, and enforcement. Guidance issued by the EDPB can be useful in clarifying ambiguities. Effective and robust antitrust enforcement could mitigate concerns about market power concentration. State actors rather than companies could have the power to define the meaning of federal legislation in practice. Admittedly, state actors may be unable to define every single instance and circumstance covered by federal legislation, and so companies will still have an important role to play. However, state actors rather than companies should play the primary role in this area. In light of the CMP Study mentioned earlier, federal legislation could ensure that companies are responsible for statutory violations even if they outsource their obligations to CMPs.

Another study discussing the GDPR's impact indicates that most consent notices "provide too few or too many options, leaving people with the impression that their choices are not meaningful and fueling the habit to click any interaction element that causes the notice to go away instead of actively engaging with it and making an informed choice."[119] Consent notices can also be used to nudge consumers toward consenting to data collection. The study indicates that there is a strong need for legal frameworks to do more than simply require consumer consent. Legal frameworks must also establish intelligible requirements or guidance for how to achieve consent in a manner that ensures "users can make free and informed choices."[120] This guidance can include recommendations on the position of consent notices, and restrictions on nudging by "highlighting 'Accept' buttons or pre-selecting checkboxes."[121] As mentioned in our earlier discussions of harmful data practices, companies could also simply be prohibited from using "dark patterns" to manipulate and shame consumers into consenting to data collection and data processing practices.

With respect to data breaches, companies may not always comply with the GDPR's 72-hour data breach notification requirement to authorities, and given

---

[118] Midas Nouwens et al., *Dark Patterns After the GDPR: Scraping Consent Pop-ups and Demonstrating Their Influence*, Ass'n for Computing Machinery (2020), https://arxiv.org/pdf/2001.02479.pdf; *see also* Iskander Sanchez-Rola et al., *Can I Opt Out Yet?: GDPR and the Global Illusion of Cookie Control*, Ass'n for Computing Machinery (2019), http://dx.doi.org/10.1145/3321705.3329806 (a study evaluating the GDPR's impact and finding that there are "a large number of websites that present deceiving information, making it very difficult, if at all possible, for users to avoid being tracked").

[119] Christine Utz et al. *(Un)informed Consent: Studying GDPR Consent Notices in the Field*, Ass'n for Computing Machinery (2019), https://arxiv.org/pdf/1909.02638.pdf (also noting that "the widespread practice of nudging has a large effect on the choices users make").

[120] *Id.*

[121] *Id.* at 13.

the shortness of this period companies may be unable to successfully evaluate the scope of data breaches before providing notice.[122] Federal baseline legislation could adopt a longer or more reasonable data breach notification time frame to address this issue. Florida's data breach notification statute provides for a thirty-day period.[123]

Despite the many critiques of the GDPR (some of which are warranted) and its short tenure, some research suggests that the GDPR is improving consumer privacy and tackling companies' vast appetite for surveillance and data. A study evaluating the GDPR's impact on online cookies found that "EU consumers encounter significantly less unconditional usage of persistent cookies when surfing the web than US visitors."[124] Other research evaluating the GDPR's impact found improvements in mobile app privacy, and more adherence to data minimization principles post GDPR implementation, which suggests that the GDPR is having a positive impact on EU consumers' privacy.[125] Another study using the dataset of an intermediary in the "online travel industry" determined that "the GDPR resulted in approximately a 12.5% reduction in total cookies," but that consumers who did not exercise their GDPR rights were more identifiable for an extended period of time.[126]

Information Fiduciary Framework

In addition to selective GDPR and domestic incorporation discussed in detail earlier, a federal statute could also attempt to correct the current deficiencies of notice and choice through incorporation of the privacy as trust and information fiduciary framework proposed by several scholars.[127] This approach is also in keeping

---

[122]   GDPR, *supra* note 23, at art. 33; Kalev Leetaru, *Facebook's Latest Breach Illustrates the Limits of GDPR*, FORBES (Dec. 14, 2018, 3:52 PM), www.forbes.com/sites/kalevleetaru/2018/12/14/facebooks-latest -breach-illustrates-the-limits-of-gdpr/#272a752c74a5.

[123]   FOLEY DATA BREACH SUMMARY, *supra* note 90; FLA. STAT. § 501.171 (2019).

[124]   Adrian Dabrowski et al., *Measuring Cookies and Web Privacy in a Post-GDPR World*, SBA RESEARCH, https://publications.sba-research.org/publications/201903%20-%20ADabrowski%20-%20Measuring% 20Cookies.pdf.

[125]   *See* Nurul Momen et al., *Did App Privacy Improve After the GDPR?*, 17 IEEE SECURITY & PRIVACY 10, 10–20   (2019),   https://ieeexplore.ieee.org/stamp/stamp.jsp?tp=&arnumber=8845749   (finding "changes in app behavior and in user feedback that point toward the positive impact of the GDPR on apps").

[126]   *See generally* Guy Aridor et al., *The Economic Consequences of Data Privacy Regulation: Empirical Evidence from GDPR* (Jan. 24, 2020) (unpublished manuscript), https://papers.ssrn.com/sol3/papers .cfm?abstract_id=3522845.

[127]   *See, e.g.*, S.B. 5642, 2019–2020 Leg., Reg. Sess. (N.Y. 2019), https://legislation.nysenate.gov/pdf/bills/ 2019/S5642; ARI EZRA WALDMAN, PRIVACY AS TRUST: INFORMATION PRIVACY FOR AN INFORMATION AGE (2018); Jack M. Balkin, *Information Fiduciaries and the First Amendment*, 49 U.C. DAVIS L. REV. 1183 (2016) [hereinafter Balkin, *Information Fiduciaries and the First Amendment*]; Neil Richards & Woodrow Hartzog, *Privacy's Trust Gap: A Review*, 126 YALE L.J. 1180 (2017); Jack M. Balkin, *Information Fiduciaries in the Digital Age*, BALKIN.COM (Mar. 5, 2014, 4:50 PM), https://balkin .blogspot.com/2014/03/information-fiduciaries-in-digital-age.html; Allison Grande, *NY Lawmakers Say Time Is Now for Consumer Privacy Law*, LAW360 (Nov. 22, 2019, 10:12 PM), www.law360.com /consumerprotection/articles/1222713/ny-lawmakers-say-time-is-now-for-consumer-privacy-law?

with conceptualizing privacy as the right of our society to require businesses using our data to respect our interests in the information they collect and process about us. Somewhat similarly, the ALI's Data Privacy Principles also contain a duty of confidentiality that is predicated on "relationships of trust," but consent can be used to avoid claims involving breaches of confidentiality.[128] The ALI's Data Privacy Principles' incorporation of a duty of confidentiality also illustrates that a fiduciary framework is not entirely incompatible with an approach that also relies on certain GDPR provisions.

Under a fiduciary approach, companies that offer IoT devices and associated services, systems, and software would be viewed as "information fiduciaries" of our data. These entities would be obligated to act in a trustworthy and loyal manner, and must safeguard our interests in data transactions by, for instance, ensuring that they do not use our data "in unexpected ways to ... disadvantage [us]" or disregard "important social norm[s]."[129]

How could this data fiduciary approach work in the IoT context? Recall our discussion of Samba TV from Chapter 1. Internet of Things television manufacturers that permit built-in apps to engage in hidden and widespread data collection for multiple unexpected purposes under the guise of viewing recommendations could be seen as violating their fiduciary duties.[130] The information fiduciary approach could also be used to address companies' possible use of granular IoT data to engage in predatory advertising, and to manipulate and exploit our emotional weaknesses.[131] Such practices could be viewed as a breach of fiduciary obligations. Internet of Things companies' fiduciary obligations (whether created by state or federal legislation or by courts) could also extend to all third parties who obtain consumer IoT data, including those who do not have direct relationships with consumers. Violations of fiduciary obligations could be enforced by state or

---

nl_pk=o6do6a2b-64f8-4c4c-b81d-6950221f7573&utm_source=newsletter&utm_medium=emai l&utm_campaign=consumerprotection&read_more=1; Tim Wu, *An American Alternative to Europe's Privacy Law*, N.Y. TIMES (May 30, 2018), www.nytimes.com/2018/05/30/opinion/europe-america-privacy-gdpr.html.

[128] PRINCIPLES OF LAW, DATA PRIVACY § 6 (AM. LAW INSTIT. 2019).

[129] Balkin, *Information Fiduciaries and the First Amendment*, *supra* note 127, at 1227.

[130] *See* Jonathan Zittrain, *How to Exercise the Power You Didn't Ask For*, HARV. BUS. REV. (Sept. 19, 2018), https://perma.cc/W233-C7Q6 (noting that the information fiduciary approach "would preclude predatory advertising" and "prevent data from being used for purposes unrelated to the expectations of the people who shared it").

[131] *Id.*; *see also* Ariel Dobkin, *Information Fiduciaries in Practice: Data Privacy and User Expectations*, 33 BERKELEY TECH. L.J. 1, 17 (2018) (elaborating on "the information fiduciary duty by defining four categories of behavior: manipulation, discrimination, third-party sharing, and violating a company's own privacy policy"); Jack M. Balkin, *Fixing Social Media's Grand Bargain*, HOOVER INSTITUTION 14 (2018) (Aegis Series Paper No. 1814), www.hoover.org/sites/default/files/research/docs/balkin_webrea dypdf.pdf (describing manipulation as "techniques of persuasion and influence that (1) prey on another person's emotional vulnerabilities and lack of knowledge (2) to benefit oneself or one's allies and (3) reduce the welfare of the other person").

federal agencies as unfair and deceptive practices, and a private cause of action could also be created.[132]

While the information fiduciary approach has some merit and would likely be an improvement on the privacy approaches codified by existing legislation, this approach is not free from criticism. Under an information fiduciary approach, certain companies collecting our data would have a duty of loyalty and "a duty to not create potential or actual conflicts of interest that might undermine their duties of loyalty."[133] Recall our discussion of agency principles from Chapter 4. Under agency law, agents also have a duty of loyalty, but liability for breaches of that duty can be limited if the principal consents (although the agent must act in good faith and deal fairly with the principal in acquiring that consent).[134] If an information fiduciary approach is adopted and a possible conflict of interest arises despite the information fiduciary's efforts, significant attention and care should be given to determining whether and to what extent an information fiduciary should be able to avoid breach of fiduciary duty claims by contending that consumer consent was provided. As we have seen, consent can be abused and used to justify surveillance and intrusive data collection practices. Like the earlier GDPR proposal, a fiduciary approach still requires that Contract Distancing and information asymmetry problems be addressed.

Another concern with the information fiduciary approach is how best to balance the competing duties that corporations have to their shareholders.[135] It would be necessary to address these possible tensions in order to give effect to the data fiduciary proposal. Although the fiduciary framework is a valuable proposal it would need to be augmented by additional approaches. Even if a fiduciary framework is adopted it would still be necessary to ensure that consumers are provided with core privacy rights similar to those in the GDPR, such as access and deletion. Thus, a fiduciary approach could be combined in a federal statute with the earlier selective GDPR and domestic importation approach discussed previously. However, a solely GDPR importation approach together with reliance on earlier-discussed domestic frameworks may be a more viable alternative for several reasons. The GDPR is already operational and important lessons can be learned from its operational deficiencies, which can be addressed at the federal level. Many companies are also already familiar with the GDPR's requirements, which could to some extent allow for frictionless integration. Lastly, it is also important to acknowledge that the GDPR framework is not completely devoid of trust concepts. Although the GDPR's

---

[132] *See, e.g.,* WALDMAN, *supra* note 127, at 89–92.

[133] Balkin, *Information Fiduciaries and the First Amendment, supra* note 127, at 1208; Jack M. Balkin, *The Three Laws of Robotics in the Age of Big Data*, 78 OHIO ST. L.J. 1217, 1228–29 (2017).

[134] RESTATEMENT (THIRD) OF AGENCY § 8.06 (2006); *id.* § 8.03 cmt. c.

[135] *See generally* Lina M. Khan & David E. Pozen, *A Skeptical View of Information Fiduciaries*, 133 HARV. L. REV. 497 (2019)(critiquing data fiduciary proposals).

recitals may not establish new law, Recital 7 acknowledges "the importance of creating . . . trust" in the digital economy.[136]

ADDITIONAL PROTECTIONS FOR SENSITIVE DATA

A federal baseline privacy statute should provide special protections for biometric data, health-related data, and children's data. The GDPR also contains provisions applicable to certain types of sensitive data.[137] Children are perhaps the most vulnerable members of our society. Corporate entities can begin collecting data on children when they are very young. Children are particularly vulnerable to data exploitation. As of the date of writing, there is currently at least one proposed federal bill that would impose design, content, and marketing restrictions on covered companies' online interactions with children.[138] The bill implicitly recognizes the deficiencies of the existing framework governing children's data. Biometric and health-related data are highly sensitive as well. Biometric data are largely immutable and share certain characteristics with human body parts, such as kidneys, which the law prohibits from being sold. Further, certain types of data may one day become indistinguishable from personhood. BIPA can serve as a starting point for specific biometric data provisions in a federal privacy statute.[139] Data minimization in this area is critical. Companies should collect and store only minimal and necessary amounts of biometric, health-related, and children's data.

Despite data minimization principles, adequate protection of these types of data requires explicit prohibitions on certain uses involving such data. An outright prohibition on the processing of biometric, health-related, and children's data for the purpose of profiling, behavioral targeting, obtaining insights, and identifying preferences could be adopted. Exceptions could be made for medical and scientific research. Companies should not be able to make decisions that impact the types of opportunities we receive based on the inferences they glean from our biometric, health-related, or children's data. With respect to children's data, even the United

---

[136] GDPR, *supra* note 23, at Recital 7; *see also* EUROPEAN DATA PROTECTION BOARD, *supra* note 49 (discussing certification seals and the possibility of enhancing "data subjects' trust in the processing of their personal data"); Kaminski, *supra* note 16, at 1586.

[137] GDPR, *supra* note 23, at arts. 8–9, 12, 22, Recitals 38, 51, 58; *What Are the Rules on Special Category Data*, INFO. COMMISSIONER'S OFF., https://ico.org.uk/for-organisations/guide-to-data-protection /guide-to-the-general-data-protection-regulation-gdpr/special-category-data/what-are-the-rules-on-special-category-data/ (last visited Apr. 15, 2020) (noting that the GDPR allows special category data to be processed with explicit consent).

[138] Kids Internet Design and Safety Act, S. 3411, 116th Cong. (2d Sess. 2020), www.markey.senate.gov /imo/media/doc/KIDS%20Act%202020.pdf; Press Release, U.S. Senator Ed Markey, Senators Markey and Blumenthal Introduce First-of-Its-Kind Legislation to Protect Children Online from Harmful Content, Design Features (Mar. 5, 2020), www.markey.senate.gov/news/press-releases/sen ators-markey-and-blumenthal-introduce-first-of-its-kind-legislation-to-protect-children-online-from-harmful-content-design-features.

[139] *See* 740 ILL. COMP. STAT. ANN. 14/15 (West 2018).

Nations Children's Fund recognizes that in order for children's privacy to be sufficiently protected in the online setting, children must be free from "online profiling."[140]

A federal baseline statute could also prohibit companies from licensing, selling, or assigning rights in biometric, health-related, and children's data or databases, even if such data are anonymized or aggregated and even if consumer consent is received. Disclosures to third-party service providers that companies hire to perform functions directly associated with consumer-requested services could still be permissible. Commercial entities could also be obligated, to the best extent possible, to delete biometric, health-related, and children's data after the consumer-requested services have been provided or after a three-year period, whichever is later. With respect to the live and backup system issue, an approach similar to the one discussed earlier could be used for sensitive data as well. BIPA contains somewhat similar provisions that could also be helpful in crafting statutory language on this issue.[141] Additionally, when possible, devices and services should be able to function without requiring consumers to provide or consent to the collection, disclosure, and transfer of their biometric data.

With respect to statutory definitions, consideration should be given to whether federal privacy legislation should define biometric data to cover not only face prints and voice prints, but also the sources of such data, including photographs and voice recordings. The term "child data" could be broadly defined in a baseline privacy statute to include any data, including IoT data (whether identified or identifiable), about children under the age of eighteen.

Consider that a study of student data brokers found that subject to a few exceptions, school districts generally indicate that they do not sell student data, yet student data brokers were able to obtain access to various types of data about students.[142] The study identified multiple student data brokers that collect and sell student data, and found that "student lists are commercially available for purchase on the basis of ethnicity, affluence, religion, lifestyle, awkwardness, and even a perceived or predicted need for family planning services."[143] Basic student data such as names, zip codes, and addresses can also be sold.[144]

---

[140] UNICEF, Industry Toolkit: Children's Online Privacy and Freedom of Expression 8 (2018), www.unicef.org/csr/files/UNICEF_Childrens_Online_Privacy_and_Freedom_of_Expression (1).pdf.

[141] *See* 740 Ill. Comp. Stat. Ann. 14/15(a) ("A private entity in possession of biometric identifiers or biometric information must develop a written policy, made available to the public, establishing a retention schedule and guidelines for permanently destroying biometric identifiers and biometric information when the initial purpose for collecting or obtaining such identifiers or information has been satisfied or within 3 years of the individual's last.").

[142] N. Cameron Russell et al., *Transparency and the Marketplace for Student Data*, 22 Va. J.L. & Tech. 107, 116, 138–39 (2019).

[143] *Id.* at 107, 125–29.

[144] *Id.* at 141–42.

The restrictions discussed earlier on the use of children's data could also apply to data about children produced in educational settings. A baseline federal privacy statute could clearly indicate that all commercial entities are prohibited from selling, licensing, or assigning rights in children's data gleaned from educational settings, and from using these data for the purpose of profiling and advertising.[145] To be clear, these prohibitions should not restrict educational institutions' ability to use other forms of traditional student data in the same manner in which they have long used such information for educational purposes. Lastly, exceptions can be made for certain activities, such as school yearbook pictures and research.[146]

Facial Recognition and Detection Technologies

In addition to providing rules applicable specifically to all types of biometric data, federal legislation should also directly address facial recognition and detection technologies. While these technologies may have some benefits, they pose a significant threat to our privacy and civil rights. Facial recognition and detection technologies can negatively impact both children and adults.

With respect to children, recall from Chapter 1 that schools have used facial recognition technology to monitor children and to supposedly ensure their safety. The COVID-19 pandemic has led to school closures and a transition to online learning. Once the pandemic is over schools will eventually reopen and the use of facial recognition technology in educational settings is likely to continue. Subjecting underage children at educational institutions to facial recognition technology has vast negative implications which outweigh any potential benefits of this technology. It could further enable educational institutions to disproportionately discipline students from historically marginalized groups. It could facilitate harmful interactions between racial minority students and law enforcement if the school's facial recognition technology automatically contacts law enforcement officials. It conditions children (and therefore future adult members of our society) to accept data collection, privacy intrusions, and surveillance as a normal part of everyday life. It moves us in the direction of social rating systems, by entrenching facial recognition technology into our society. It forces parents to accept surveillance of their

---

[145] *See FERPA General Guidance for Students*, U.S. DEP'T EDUC., www2.ed.gov/policy/gen/guid/fpco/ferpa/students.html (noting that "[p]arochial and private schools at the elementary and secondary levels generally do not receive ... funding [administered by the Department of Education] and are ... not subject to FERPA") (last visited Feb. 2, 2020); U.S. DEP'T OF EDUC. PRIVACY TECH. ASSISTANCE CTR., PROTECTING STUDENT PRIVACY WHILE USING ONLINE EDUCATIONAL SERVICES: REQUIREMENTS AND BEST PRACTICES (2014), https://tech.ed.gov/wp-content/uploads/2014/09/Student-Privacy-and-Online-Educational-Services-February-2014.pdf (discussing targeted advertisements and noting that "if the school or district has shared information under FERPA's school official exception, however, the provider cannot use the FERPA-protected information for any other purpose than the purpose for which it was disclosed"). *See also*, CAL. BUS. & PROF. CODE § 22584(a)–(b) (West 2016).

[146] FUTURE OF PRIVACY FORUM, THE POLICYMAKER'S GUIDE TO STUDENT DATA PRIVACY 8 https://ferpasherpa.org/wp-content/uploads/2019/04/FPF-Policymakers-Guide-to-Student-Privacy-Final.pdf.

children and the collection of their children's biometric data in order to provide their children with an education. Potentially relevant federal guidance indicates that parents should generally not be required to waive their FERPA rights in order to obtain educational services.[147]

The use of facial recognition technology in schools also creates more data about children for corporate and government exploitation. Many institutions can barely keep the data of adults secure. It is certainly not wise to trust all companies with the biometric data of children. A further complicating factor is the large-scale transition to online learning in response to the COVID-19 pandemic and schools' use of various technology platforms. Similar concerns arise in the pandemic online learning environment as well, including requiring parents to consent to their children being recorded during online lessons.

Turning now to adults, recall from Chapter 1 that Clearview AI provides a mobile app that can be used to instantly evaluate an uploaded picture of a person and connect that picture to other images of the individual obtained from various social media websites.[148] Companies, wealthy individuals, and government actors have all used the company's mobile app.[149] Even though we did not consent to this collection and in many instances social media websites' settings require us to make our profile pictures public, the company claims that it has a First Amendment right to scrape and profit from public images of us.[150]

An individual's decision not to post a profile picture on a social media website, such as LinkedIn, could impact the opportunities the person receives. Corporate actors and individuals (including criminal actors) could one day easily identify us (as well as obtain our work and home addresses and other background information) using similar services by simply taking a picture and uploading it to a Clearview AI-like app.[151] There is also the potential for wealthy and elite individuals with early access to similar technology to use the technology and resulting disclosed information against less well-off members of society.[152] As Senator Edward Markey observes, ubiquitous use of this technology "could facilitate dangerous behavior and could

---

[147] *See* Letter from Dale King, Dir., Family Policy Compliance Office, to U.S. Dep't of Educ. 6–7 (Nov. 2, 2017), https://studentprivacy.ed.gov/sites/default/files/resource_document/file/Agora%20Findings%20letter%20FINAL%2011.2.17.pdf.

[148] Kashmir Hill, *The Secretive Company that Might End Privacy as We Know It*, N.Y. Times (Jan. 18, 2020), www.nytimes.com/2020/01/18/technology/clearview-privacy-facial-recognition.html; *see also* Craig McCarthy, *Rogue NYPD Cops Are Using Facial Recognition App Clearview*, N.Y. Post (Jan. 23, 2020, 12:23 PM), https://nypost.com/2020/01/23/rogue-nypd-cops-are-using-sketchy-facial-recognition-app-clearview/.

[149] Kashmir Hill, *Before Clearview Became a Police Tool, It Was a Secret Plaything of the Rich*, N.Y. Times, www.nytimes.com/2020/03/05/technology/clearview-investors.html#click=https://t.co/M2d4aH7f5g (last updated Mar. 6, 2020).

[150] Alfred Ng, *Clearview AI Says the First Amendment Lets It Scrape the Internet. Lawyers Disagree*, CNET (Feb. 6, 2020, 12:13 PM), www.cnet.com/news/clearview-says-first-amendment-lets-it-scrape-the-internet-lawyers-disagree/.

[151] *See* Hill, *supra* note 149.

[152] Hill, *supra* note 150.

effectively destroy individuals' ability to go about their daily lives anonymously."[153] Also, what if a company, such as Clearview AI, is able to access databases or servers storing the biometric data of children at educational institutions and then exploit it for profit?

It is increasingly clear that there are strong reasons for prohibiting or limiting educational institutions' and non-state actors' (individuals and commercial entities) ability to use facial recognition technology.[154] As of the date of writing, the city of Portland is mulling a possible ban on both private and state actors' use of facial recognition technology.[155] Oakland and San Francisco have already restricted the use of facial recognition technology.[156]

Additionally, recall from Chapter 1 that facial detection technology (which lacks additional facial *recognition* capabilities) also presents privacy concerns and allows companies to unmask our emotions and target us in insidious ways for their profit. Companies could be prohibited from using facial detection technology in this manner even if they do not directly identify us.

OBSTACLES TO EFFECTIVE FEDERAL LEGISLATION

There are several possible objections to recommending that Congress adopt a baseline privacy and security statute. There is a significant risk that the federal legislative process will be hijacked by corporate interests, resulting in a statute that preempts stronger state laws, fails to contain a private right of action, and validates the existing status quo in favor of industry. There is also the risk of ossification. Once adopted, a federal statute may be difficult to amend and new technological developments could render the legislation obsolete. These are all valid concerns. However, these concerns do not render invalid the need for federal legislation in this area.

---

[153]   *See* Letter from Edward Markey, U.S. Senator, to Hoan Ton-That, Founder & CEO, Clearview AI, www.markey.senate.gov/imo/media/doc/Clearview%20letter%202020.pdf.

[154]   Other privacy law scholars have also called for a prohibition on facial recognition technology. *See, e.g.*, Evan Selinger & Woodrow Hartzog, *The Inconsentability of Facial Surveillance*, 66 Loy. L. Rev. 101 (2019); Evan Selinger & Woodrow Hartzog, *What Happens When Employers Can Read Your Facial Expressions?*, N.Y. Times (Oct. 17, 2019), www.nytimes.com/2019/10/17/opinion/facial-recognition-ban.html?action=click&module=Opinion&pgtype=Homepage.

[155]   Sean Captain, *Portland Plans to Propose the Strictest Facial Recognition Ban in the Country*, Fast Company (Dec. 2, 2019), www.fastcompany.com/90436355/portlands-proposed-facial-recognition-ban-could-be-the-strictest-yet?partner=feedburner&utm_source=feedburner&utm_medium=feed&utm_campaign=Feed%3A+fastcompany%2Fheadlines+%28Fast+Company%29; *see also Vote to Ban Facial Recognition Technology in Portland Put on Hold*, WGME (Jan. 7, 2020), wgme.com/news/local/vote-to-ban-facial-recognition-technology-in-portland-put-on-hold.

[156]   Kate Conger et al., *San Francisco Bans Facial Recognition Technology*, N.Y. Times (May 14, 2019), www.nytimes.com/2019/05/14/us/facial-recognition-ban-san-francisco.html; Christine Fisher, *Oakland Bans City Use of Facial Recognition Software*, Engadget (July 17, 2019), www.engadget.com/2019/07/17/oakland-california-facial-recognition-ban/; Caroline Haskins, *A Second U.S. City Has Banned Facial Recognition*, Vice (June 27, 2019, 6:15 PM), www.vice.com/en_us/article/paj4ek/somerville-becomes-the-second-us-city-to-ban-facial-recognition.

Recall that various federal agencies and other consumer advocates, including the FTC, have long called for the adoption of federal privacy legislation. The federal agencies tasked with enforcing a federal statute can be given the power to amend their regulations to give full effect to the goals of the statute and account for new technological developments. Congress must have sufficient political will to adopt privacy and security legislation that adequately protects consumers. In light of the current political environment and the COVID-19 pandemic, Congress may not soon adopt baseline privacy and cybersecurity legislation. States will have to continue to play a key role in protecting our privacy.

STATE PRIVACY LEGISLATION

In the absence of adequate federal baseline privacy and security legislation, more states could follow in California's footsteps and adopt statutes that grant us various rights with respect to the data we generate, and impose specific obligations on businesses with respect to how they handle our data. State legislation could ensure that we are given several GDPR- and CCPA-like rights. The potential privacy and security harms that we all face in the IoT age outweigh criticisms regarding the potential costs of statutory compliance and any possible negative impact on the data industry.

Although the CCPA may serve as a model for privacy legislation in other states, the statute is still a work-in-progress and as of the date of writing, the final text of the CCPA Regulations discussed in Chapter 3 have not yet been filed with the Secretary of State.[157] There is a new 2020 ballot initiative attempt to expand the CCPA's provisions through the adoption of the proposed California Privacy Rights Act (CPRA).[158] If adopted, the CPRA would establish a California data protection agency and provide certain protections for sensitive data, among other things.[159]

Additionally, recall from Chapter 3 that there are several CCPA provisions that could be improved upon. For example, ambiguities and gaps in the statute's definition of the term "sale" must be addressed. A sale could be defined to clearly include the data collection and processing activities of technology companies, such as Facebook. The CCPA and other state legislation could also clearly define a sale or

---

[157] *Proposed Regulations Package Submitted to OAL*, available at https://oag.ca.gov/privacy/ccpa (last visited Jun. 10, 2020).

[158] *See* The California Privacy Rights Act of 2020, No. 19-0021 (amended Nov. 2019), https://oag.ca.gov /system/files/initiatives/pdfs/19-0021A1%20%28Consumer%20Privacy%20-%20Version%203%29_1 .pdf; *Californians for Consumer Privacy Submits Signatures to Qualify the California Privacy Rights Act for November 2020 Ballot*, CALIFORNIANS FOR CONSUMER PRIVACY (May 4, 2020), www .caprivacy.org/californians-for-consumer-privacy-submits-signatures-to-qualify-the-california-privacy -rights-act-for-november-2020-ballot/; Jeremy Greenberg, *CCPA 2.0? A New California Ballot Initiative Is Introduced*, FUTURE PRIVACY F. (Sept. 26, 2019), https://fpf.org/2019/09/26/ccpa-2-0-a-new- california-ballot-initiative-is-introduced/.

[159] CALIFORNIANS FOR CONSUMER PRIVACY: WHY CPRA https://s25kktkjvr2g7bnh48bvn812- wpengine.netdna-ssl.com/wp-content/uploads/2020/04/WhyCPRA.pdf.

transfer of data to include all data asset transfers that occur in connection with a corporate transaction. At a minimum, consumers should clearly have the right to be notified of a sale or disclosure, and the right to prevent their data from being disclosed or transferred from one corporate entity to another as part of a corporate transaction, such as a merger. Notice without the ability to prevent a company from transferring your data as part of a corporate transaction is meaningless.

Since the CCPA became effective on January 1, 2020, almost every online website provides California residents with a "Do Not Sell My Information" option. To exercise their statutory rights, California residents must actively select the opt-out option on every single website they visit, and provide additional information to companies as part of the verification processes that are likely needed in order to prevent third-party abuse of data sale rights. This is an onerous burden in light of the frequency with which we access the Internet. There are several ways to relieve this burden. An opt-in approach, in which all consumers are automatically opted out of data sales (including data transfers as part of a corporate transaction), could be adopted. Currently, under the CCPA, the opt-in approach for data sales applies to minors and their parents.[160] Extending the opt-in approach to all consumers would better ensure that consumers do not bear the burden of requesting that companies refrain from transferring or disclosing their data. Such an approach may also more effectively impact companies' data business models. Consider that an empirical estimate of the financial impact of opt-in and opt-out privacy approaches found that "online publisher revenues" and "advertisement surplus" may decrease more under an opt-in approach than under an opt-out approach.[161]

The opt-out versus opt-in debate is old and still relies heavily on consumers having notice and choice.[162] This suggests that alternative or supplemental solutions are necessary. First, courts could more adequately address the Contract Distancing and information asymmetry concerns discussed in Chapter 4. I will come back to this point in Chapter 9. A second alternative is to extend the data sale prohibition discussed earlier for sensitive data to other types of data sales. As I have argued throughout this book, technology companies wield significant influence over our privacy expectations. These companies often skew the narrative in their favor and shift the blame for their privacy-invasive tactics and cybersecurity failures onto us. Technology companies also shape our perceptions about privacy legislation. Consider that YouTube has successfully encouraged its content creators to express their opposition to the FTC's COPPA enforcement activities against it and has attempted to shift the burden of COPPA compliance onto its

---

[160] CAL. CIV. CODE § 1798.120(c) (Deering 2019).

[161] Garrett A. Johnson, *The Impact of Privacy Policy on the Auction Market for Online Display Advertising* (Bradley Policy Research Ctr. Fin. Research & Policy, Working Paper No. FR 13–26, 2013), https://papers.ssrn.com/sol3/papers.cfm?abstract_id=2333193.

[162] *See, e.g.*, Jeff Sovern, *Opting In, Opting Out, or No Options at All: The Fight for Control of Personal Information*, 74 WASH. L. REV. 1033 (1999).

content creators.[163] Legislation intended to protect children is now being opposed by online content creators (some of whom are parents) at the behest of a technology company. All of this indicates that even if we have the ability to opt in or opt out of data sales or data collection, companies could exert their influence to ensure that we choose options that undermine our own interests. When drafting laws in this area, legislators must take this powerful influence into account. There is no level playing field between consumers and technology companies when it comes to data, and it is high time that the law recognized this.

In light of unequal access to privacy concerns, the CCPA's anti-discrimination and financial incentives provisions could be more robust.[164] Companies already extract data from us unwillingly under the artifice of notice and choice. Recall from our Chapter 3 discussions that inadequacies in the CCPA and in the Draft Regulations on this issue leave companies with room to continue to coerce and manipulate consumers into trading away their data rights to obtain better prices while shopping. Covered entities could be prohibited from attempting to charge different prices for goods and services even when those differences are connected to the value of the data. A blanket prohibition on financial incentives that use privacy-invasive discounts and discrimination involving personal data could be adopted. The term "privacy-invasive discount" could be defined as an offering that requires consumers to trade in highly sensitive data, including, but not limited to, biometric, and health-related data, in order to receive a discount. Even if a financial incentive program does not involve a privacy-invasive discount, it should be clear that we cannot trade away our statutory privacy rights through such a program.

State legislation could ensure that our data rights are not contingent on the language contained in companies' privacy policies. State laws could also provide adequate guidance on prohibited data uses and non-consensual data collection and surveillance. As we discussed in earlier sections of this chapter, harmful data practices could be prohibited. State legislation in this area could also clearly require

---

[163] *Why It's Google that Deserves the Anger of YouTubers*, Ctr. for Digital Democracy (Nov. 27, 2019), www.democraticmedia.org/article/why-its-google-deserves-anger-youtubers; *see also* Harsimar Dhanoa & Jonathan Greengarden, *Misinformed YouTubers Are Undermining the Fight for Children's Privacy Online*, Slate (Nov. 27, 2019, 7:25 AM), https://slate.com/technology/2019/11/youtube-coppa-google-ftc-settlement-children-privacy.html.

[164] Cal. Civ. Code § 1798.125 ("(1) A business shall not discriminate against a consumer because the consumer exercised any of the consumer's rights under this title, including, but not limited to, by: (A) Denying goods or services to the consumer. (B) Charging different prices or rates for goods or services, including through the use of discounts or other benefits or imposing penalties. (C) Providing a different level or quality of goods or services to the consumer. (D) Suggesting that the consumer will receive a different price or rate for goods or services or a different level or quality of goods or services. (2) Nothing in this subdivision prohibits a business from charging a consumer a different price or rate, or from providing a different level or quality of goods or services to the consumer, if that difference is reasonably related to the value provided to the business by the consumer's data.").

companies to disclose the identity and contact information of data buyers and transferees, including data brokers. Our data disclosure and sale rights could clearly apply to data broker transactions. We could have a broad private right of action for privacy and security failures and statutory violations as recommended in earlier sections of this chapter. In the absence of adequate federal legislation, states must adopt legislation that sufficiently regulates companies' collection and use of sensitive data, such as biometric, health-related, and children's data. This legislation could incorporate the recommendations for these types of data discussed earlier in this chapter.

In addition to the CCPA, other sources of law, such as the Uniform Law Commission's proposed uniform model data law, once drafted and finalized, could also provide guidance to states on privacy issues.[165] This, of course, presumes that any such model law or other sources of law contain adequate protections for consumers, and does not incorporate the many failures of previous privacy legislation, such as an overreliance on the notice and choice model.

STATE DATA SECURITY LEGISLATION

Recall from Chapters 2 and 3 that states have adopted data breach notification laws and data security laws.[166] As with federal privacy legislation, in addition to data breach notification obligations, state legislation must also require privacy and security by design and default as well as provide specific data security guidance, which imposes legal obligations on businesses to protect consumer data and ensure device and system-related security. This non-exclusive granular guidance could be in addition to requiring companies to adopt reasonable cybersecurity measures. One state framework that adopts a somewhat similar approach is New York's Stop Hacks and Improve Electronic Data Security (SHIELD) Act.[167] The SHIELD Act imposes a reasonable data security requirement and provides specific guidance on what businesses should minimally include in their reasonable security programs, including disposing of covered data, providing workers with necessary security training,

---

[165] *See Collection and Use of Personally Identifiable Data Committee*, ULC (2019), www.uniformlaws.org/committees/community-home?CommunityKey=9aadc6d7-0020-4df2-821d-19aa34084532.

[166] William McGeveran, *The Duty of Data Security*, 103 MINN. L. REV. 1135, 1153 (2019) ("some states have moved beyond notification mandates to impose other particular data security obligations").

[167] N.Y. GEN. BUS. LAW § 899-aa–bb (McKinney 2019); *id.* § 899-bb; *see also* Christopher A. Iacono & Gabrielle I. Weiss, *New SHIELD Act Provisions Take Effect in March, Additional Legislation Pending*, N.Y. L.J. (Feb. 26, 2020, 11:00 AM), www.law.com/newyorklawjournal/2020/02/26/new-shield-act-provisions-take-effect-in-march-additional-legislation-pending/ (discussing the SHIELD Act and other proposed NY privacy legislation); *New York Passes SHIELD Act Amending Data Breach Notification Law*, JONES DAY (Aug. 2019), www.jonesday.com/en/insights/2019/08/new-york-passes-shield-act (noting that the SHIELD Act amended NY's data breach notification law). Oregon's data security statute also provides additional guidance on reasonable data security measures. OR. REV. STAT. ANN. § 646A.622 (West 2020).

adjusting cybersecurity programs given "business changes or new circumstances," and selecting third-party service providers that provide appropriate cybersecurity protections and incorporating those obligations into third-party service contracts.[168] New York's data breach notification framework also extends to instances in which data are viewed or accessed without authorization.[169] Even the FTC has recognized the need to improve specificity and guidance in its data security orders.[170] As is the case with federal legislation, the NIST cybersecurity framework can be used to shed light on reasonable cybersecurity features as well.[171] Similarly, the provisions of the SHIELD Act discussed earlier could also be useful in drafting a baseline federal statute.

State legislation must also go beyond the hard-coded password issue found in California's IoT cybersecurity statute, must consider the interconnected nature of IoT devices, services, and systems, and could obligate companies to maintain and update device software. Cybersecurity legislation aimed at IoT devices could define devices to include not only physical objects, but also associated online services and mobile applications. Companies' cybersecurity obligations could extend not only to the physical device, but also to mobile applications and connected systems, including cloud-based systems and related authentication systems.

In this chapter, I have argued that adopting a federal baseline privacy statute that provides certain rights to individuals and imposes certain obligations on companies is an important step in addressing the privacy, digital domination, and security IoT harms that lie at the unique intersection of commercial law and privacy law. I have also argued that in the absence of adequate federal legislation, states must continue to play an active role in protecting our privacy and security in the IoT age. However, as we have seen, multiple sources of law impact privacy and data security–related issues, including contract law, tort law, and state and federal statutes.[172] A comprehensive solution to addressing privacy, digital domination, and security

---

[168]   N.Y. GEN. BUS. LAW § 899-bb.

[169]   N.Y. GEN. BUS. LAW § 899-aa ("'Breach of the security of the system' shall mean unauthorized access to or acquisition of, or access to or acquisition without valid authorization, of computerized data that compromises the security, confidentiality, or integrity of private information maintained by a business."); *see also* FOLEY DATA BREACH SUMMARY, *supra* note 90(comparing various state data breach notification laws); Allison Grande, *NY Data Security Law to Make State a More Active Enforcer*, LAW360 (Nov. 7, 2019, 10:08 PM), www.law360.com/articles/1217998/ny-data-security-law-to-make-state-a-more-active-enforcer ("Most state laws are either silent on whether unauthorized access to data constitutes a breach or take the approach that only the disclosure of such data triggers reporting obligations."). The SHIELD Act's breach notification requirements extend "not only [to] instances where data has been acquired but also where it has been viewed without authorization." *id.*

[170]   *See* Jack Queen, *FTC Details "New and Improved" Data Security Orders*, LAW360 (Jan. 6, 2020, 5:02 PM), www.law360.com/articles/1231573/ftc-details-new-and-improved-data-security-orders.

[171]   Ohio's data security law references NIST and other federal frameworks. OHIO REV. CODE ANN. 1354.03 (West 2018); McGeveran, *supra* note 166, at 1157.

[172]   DANIEL J. SOLOVE & PAUL SCHWARTZ, INFORMATION PRIVACY LAW 31–40 (6th ed. 2018).

harms in the IoT era must account for the blurring of the lines between the privacy law world and the commercial law world by addressing deficiencies in other areas of the law that impact privacy and security. Chapter 9 offers several solutions to remedy inadequacies in various sources of law governing commercial practices that affect our privacy and security.

9

Towards a Robust Commercial Law of Privacy and Security

As we have seen, the law wields considerable influence over the rights and remedies available to us as consumers. Several areas of commercial law are ill-equipped to sufficiently protect our consumer interests in the IoT age. This is because various legal frameworks governing commercial practices have not been sufficiently reformulated to account for the growing connections between the world of privacy and the world of commercial law. As earlier sections of this book have demonstrated, there are multiple legal frameworks impacting commercial practices at the federal and state level that are ripe for significant legal reform. These sources of law include contract law, the FAA, products liability law, the CDA, debt collection law, the Bankruptcy Code, and secured financing laws. An extensive approach to correcting existing deficiencies in commercial law at the state and federal level is needed to fully account for the commingling of the privacy, security, and commercial law worlds, and to better address consumer harms in the IoT age. In this chapter, I offer solutions that can be implemented in various sources of state and federal law to remedy inadequacies and usher in a more robust commercial law of privacy and security that protects consumers' interests.

ADDRESSING CONTRACT DISTANCING AND INFORMATION ASYMMETRY

Recall from Chapter 4 that contract law has a significant impact on our legal rights as consumers, including, for instance, determining the validity of contractual provisions, such as warranty disclaimers. Also, remember from our Chapter 4 discussions that Contract Distancing and increased levels of information asymmetry are a significant problem in the IoT era. As consumers, we are overburdened with a plethora of online agreements and company policies that we must review and assent to daily. Contract law must adapt to these realities.

Contract law could require courts to assess the level of Contract Distancing and information asymmetry, which favors corporations at the expense of consumers, when evaluating whether a consumer has assented to an IoT contract (and its terms) or whether a consumer has expressed consent to a data practice as required by either a federal or state baseline privacy law. Elsewhere in 2016, I argued that in assessing the level of Contract Distancing and information asymmetry, courts could consider several factors, including the type of IoT device at issue, the extent to which the consumer understands the implications of the contract terms, the amount and type of data the device maker (and related third parties and service providers) obtain from the consumer's IoT devices, and the extent to which consumers have access to the IoT data they generate and the data analytics reports companies use to target consumers for contracting.[1] If US baseline privacy legislation borrows some provisions from the GDPR as discussed in Chapter 8, this approach to addressing Contract Distancing can bridge the existing gap between US contract law's framework for evaluating consent in consumer contracts and the GDPR's external reliance on the European Union Directive on Unfair Terms in Consumer Contracts.[2]

As consumers, we should not be deemed to assent to one-sided contract terms based solely on the fact that we have continued to allow an IoT device to place successive orders on our behalf, clicked an "I agree" button, or have continued to use the IoT device. To the extent that companies use data to target vulnerable consumers for contracting, such consumers should not be bound to one-sided and anti-consumer contract terms if it is clear that they failed to fully understand the agreement's terms and implications. To be clear, under such an approach, IoT contracts can still be enforced even if a specific term in the contract is rendered unenforceable in light of Contract Distancing and information asymmetry concerns.

Nancy Kim has recently proposed a novel consentability theory, which reconceptualizes traditional consent. Some aspects of the consentability theory provide a useful framework that could be used to address Contract Distancing and information asymmetry concerns, and offer a concrete approach to apply and expand on my earlier-mentioned recommendations. Consentability evaluates whether and under what circumstances state actors should prohibit individuals from engaging in certain activities despite apparent consent.[3] Recall from Chapter 4 that in application, contract law is often constrained by restrictive views of a "manifestation of assent." Traditional contract formation principles do "not require a high level of knowledge" or "actual assent."[4] In contrast, Kim adopts a relative and sliding scale consent

---

[1] Stacy-Ann Elvy, *Contracting in the Age of the Internet of Things: Article 2 of the UCC and Beyond*, 44 Hofstra L. Rev. 839, 911 (2016).

[2] Regulation 2016/679, of the European Parliament and of the Council of 27 April 2016 on the Protection of Individuals with Regard to the Processing of Personal Data and on the Free Movement of Such Data and Repealing Directive 95/46/EC, 2016 OJ (L 119) 1, at Recital 42; European Data Protection Board, Guidelines 2/2019 on the Processing of Personal Data under Article 6(1)(b) GDPR in the Context of the Provision of Online Services to Data Subjects 6 (2019), https://edpb.europa.eu/sites/edpb/files/files/file1/edpb_guidelines-art_6-1-b-adopted_after_public_consultation_en.pdf.

[3] *See* Nancy S. Kim, Consentability: Consent and its Limits 53 (2019).

[4] *Id.* at 98.

approach that considers the cognitive biases plaguing modern-day consumer consent, and reformulates the following "three consent conditions: a manifestation of consent, knowledge and voluntariness."[5] In exploring the meaning of these conditions under a consentability framework, Kim contends that these conditions require an evaluation of: (1) the consenting individual's purpose for entering into the transaction, (2) whether the consenting individual grasps the "nature of the act" and the "material facts involved in making his or her decision," (3) whether the act of consent is involuntary, and (4) whether the party seeking to obtain consent has withheld information from the consenting party or acted in bad faith.[6] There is valid consent when each of these consent conditions is "robust" enough that they outweigh the potential harm to the consumer's autonomy interest.[7] Under Kim's framework, autonomy interests include, but are not limited to, body and integrity harms (both mental and physical) and "a waiver of rights."[8]

Additionally, in evaluating the validity of consent, Kim proposes an "[o]pportunism [c]orollary" under which the law can prohibit persons from reaping the benefits of activities that "knowingly harm or exploit others."[9] Such opportunistic conduct decreases the firmness of the consent conditions and impedes a functioning society, while simultaneously restricting "the value of individual autonomy for all members of society."[10] This opportunism corollary shares similarities with the information fiduciary framework discussed in Chapter 8, which also attempts to address data manipulation and exploitation concerns. However, as Kim notes, the opportunism corollary does not mean that individuals and entities must act as fiduciaries for each other, but instead recognizes that corporate actors and individuals should not enrich and attempt "to benefit themselves by persuading others to act in a way that harms their self-interest."[11] Additionally, Kim's opportunism corollary and consent conditions seek to directly tackle opportunistic and exploitative behavior facilitated by contract law principles. As such, Kim's opportunism corollary and consent framework can complement the alternative information fiduciary and GDPR proposals discussed in Chapter 8.

Kim's opportunism corollary and consent conditions perfectly capture several concerns associated with the proliferation of IoT devices and resulting Contract Distancing and information asymmetry. Recall from Chapters 1 and 2 the various

---

5   *Id.* at 71, 81, 117–18 (observing that the consent conditions "consider the impact of the most common cognitive biases and shortcomings on the consenter" and "[a] relative theory of consent is a reconceptualization of consent that shifts the focus away from the *manifestation* of consent to the conditions of consent").

6   *See id.* at 71–73.

7   *Id.* at 81. Kim identifies four core autonomy interests that are served by a consent doctrine: "bodily integrity, freedom of movement, various civil and political rights, and the rights of private property ownership." *Id.* at 53.

8   *Id.* at 75.

9   *Id.* at 69.

10 *Id.* at 69, 81.

11 *Id.* at 70.

ways that the IoT can harm our self-interest by limiting our access to privacy and cybersecurity. For instance, the IoT can, among other things, restrict and reduce our ability to (i) protect ourselves from cybersecurity incidents, (ii) prevent individuals and corporate actors from distorting information and appropriating our likeness, (iii) conceal aspects of our personalities, events, and emotions from corporate actors who seek to monetize every aspect of our lives and bodies, and (iv) determine what happens to information about us. Also, recall from Chapter 6 the digital domination, loss of device control, and debt criminalization harms that may flow from companies' use of IoT and asset collection technology. Additionally, as we discussed in Chapter 5, limitations in products liability law and warranty principles can allow IoT companies to escape liability for defective products that harm us.

As consumers, most of us are unaware of how our data are processed and used. Companies often obscure the details of these practices in their privacy policies and use privacy settings aimed at lulling us into sharing and authorizing as much data collection as possible. As a result, Kim's knowledge condition, mentioned earlier, is deficient. A PwC consumer survey found that 81 percent of US consumers believe that providing their data to corporations "is a necessary evil in today's modern economy."[12] We are often forced to agree to surveillance and data collection and processing in order to obtain fully functional IoT devices. This indicates a weak voluntariness condition.

In addition, IoT technology and advancements in machine learning create multiple opportunities for companies to profit not only from the initial sale of an IoT device, but also from the ongoing services required for the buyer to operate the device and the data that the buyer generates from using the device and associated services. IoT product makers are increasingly participating in pandemic response efforts, often in partnership with government actors and employers. Fears regarding the COVID-19 pandemic may also contribute to an environment in which some of us may be more willing to accept privacy-related tradeoffs, including giving corporate actors access to data from IoT devices, smartphones, and other objects. Internet of Things technology and the pandemic create a setting that is ripe for opportunism. Companies' data business models and commercial practices facilitate this opportunism and exploitation. Firms are manufacturing IoT devices to colonize every portion of our homes, schools, lives, and bodies, as well as those of our children. Companies are advertising IoT devices to us as modern conveniences critical to life in the twenty-first century and essential to pandemic relief efforts. Yet, they are using our data and designing these devices to influence our decisions to consent to their data harvesting practices.

---

12   *Consumers Trust Your Tech Even Less than You Think*, PwC, www.pwc.com/us/en/services/consult ing/library/consumer-intelligence-series/trusted-tech.html?WT.mc_id=CT1-PL52-DM1-TR1-LS4-ND30-TTA4-CN_PwC.CISTrustedTech.xLoS-PTW&eq=CT1-PL52-DM1-CN_PwC. CISTrustedTech.xLoS-PTW [hereinafter *PwC Survey*].

As this book has argued throughout, by transforming what was once offline activity to online activity, IoT device manufacturers and other corporate actors can, among other things, erode our anonymity in both public and private settings, further enable unequal access to privacy and cybersecurity, significantly influence and shape our opportunities and behaviors, and prey on those of us who are weakest. Vulnerable consumers include low-income consumers, historically marginalized groups, children, and those of us with weak data literacy skills. These are significant individual and collective harms that outweigh the economic interests of technology companies.

By requiring an analysis of the extent to which a consent-giver purportedly understands the nature and implications of a company's contract and whether the consent-giver has access to data to better inform this understanding, Kim's relative and sliding scale consent conditions can also be used by courts to consider Contract Distancing and information asymmetry in IoT contracts.[13] These conditions, as well as the opportunism corollary, go beyond the traditional requirement of a manifestation of assent and enable a shift away from blanket assent to all online terms and narrow conceptions of the reasonably prudent smartphone user discussed in Chapter 4, toward a consent analysis that considers "the realities of how humans make decisions in given contexts, instead of presupposing a rational actor making decisions under ideal circumstances."[14] The global pandemic highlights the need to reformulate consent doctrine to consider the realities of individuals' contracting circumstances.

Under this approach, even if the IoT contract is enforceable, there may be no valid consent to specific IoT contract terms and privacy policy provisions that enable abusive data collection, disclosure, processing, and transfer practices. Such an approach is necessary to stem the increasing tide of IoT devices that continue to inundate the consumer market. Technology companies must be disincentivized from imposing on us devices and services that require us to connect to the Internet to function and consent to ongoing invasive data collection, while simultaneously failing to fully guarantee device and service security and functionality. For instance, consider that Amazon's Alexa terms of use provide "[w]e do not guarantee that Alexa or its functionality or content (including traffic, health, or stock information) is accurate, reliable, always available, or complete."[15]

In practice an individual might consent by clicking "accept" to the terms of a company's return policy, order quantity limits, contact information provisions, or service fees and payment provisions, as these terms may not significantly decrease or impact the individual's autonomy.[16] On the other hand, if a company adopts data

---

[13] Kim, *supra* note 3, at 124.

[14] *Id.*

[15] *Alexa Terms of Use*, Amazon, www.amazon.com/gp/help/customer/display.html?nodeId=201809740 (last updated Apr. 28, 2020).

[16] Kim, *supra* note 3, at 119.

collection and processing practices that are not prohibited by statute and which pose a strong threat to our privacy and bodily integrity, a single click of an "accept" option should not automatically suffice to justify the company's conduct. Instead, consent to such terms could be presumed to be "defective."[17] This presumption of defective consent can also coexist with, and enhance the incorporation of, GDPR principles recommended in Chapter 8. Recall that GDPR guidance on consent indicates that consent that is "bundled-up" with adhesive contracts is not presumed to be "freely given."[18] If consent is defective, the manifestation of assent could be more definite and the consumer should have had reasonable alternatives and access to information in a manner and at a time which aids the consumer to fully understand important and relevant information and the implications of consent.[19] In no event should an individual be deemed to waive fundamental privacy rights established by baseline privacy legislation. To the extent that a company's terms of service, privacy policy, or data practices violate the requirements of a baseline privacy framework, consumer consent should not be used to legalize the violation. Deference to corporate practices should not be used to justify overcoming the presumption.

With respect to the issue of reasonable alternatives, the PwC survey mentioned earlier found that 90 percent of US consumers wished that there were more businesses that could be trusted with their data.[20] This suggests that there is some demand for companies to adopt business models centered around protecting our data, rather than profiting from and exploiting our data by, for instance, requiring or enticing us to accept privacy-invasive discounts, transfer rights in our data in exchange for meager payments, or to pay higher prices for privacy-protective products.

Turning now to the possible future agency issues discussed in Chapter 4, courts must be cautious in applying agency principles to IoT consumer transactions. If IoT devices are eventually manufactured with the capacity to think and act independently, and therefore qualify as agents under agency principles, the extent to which we should be bound to transactions involving IoT agents could depend, in part, on whether IoT devices can fulfill the required fiduciary duties and the degree of control we can exert over such devices. Such an analysis could consider the amount and types of data the device collects, whether such data will be disclosed to the manufacturer, retailer, or other third parties while simultaneously contracting on our behalf, and whether we have the ability to prevent the IoT device from disclosing these data.

---

[17] *Id.* at 163–66.

[18] Article 29 Data Protection Working Party, Guidelines on Consent Under Regulation 2016/679, at 5 (Apr. 10, 2018).

[19] *Id.* at 124, 128.

[20] *PwC Survey, supra* note 12.

PROHIBITING MANDATORY ARBITRATION PROVISIONS

In this chapter and in Chapter 8, I propose several solutions to address many of the consumer harms the IoT generates. In order to give full effect to these solutions, federal law must ensure that companies do not use mandatory arbitration and class action waiver provisions to prohibit consumers from obtaining legal recourse in courts. Federal law should prohibit the use of mandatory arbitration provisions and class action waivers in consumer transactions. The FAA could be amended to give effect to a mandatory arbitration prohibition. As of the date of writing, there is at least one proposed federal bill, the Forced Arbitration Injustice Repeal Act, that if passed would restrict the use of mandatory arbitration provisions in consumer agreements.[21]

A FUNCTIONAL APPROACH TO PRODUCTS LIABILITY

Products liability law and warranty principles are central to consumer remedies for the sale of injurious goods. As I argued in Chapter 5, these areas of the law suffer from several glaring limitations that are increasingly problematic for consumers in the new, intangible world of the IoT. Courts and legislators must adopt a functional approach to products liability law and warranty rules that accounts for the vital role that services and software play in IoT device operations. Physical items can no longer be divorced from services, software, and online systems. Products liability law's and the UCC's patchwork and sectoral coverage based on the severability of services and software from physical objects must come to an end. In short, the law in this area must evolve to recognize and incorporate the convergence of physical objects, services, software, and online systems. This will be a challenging task, and it requires revisions to different sources of law.

First, a functional approach requires us to rethink products liability laws' definition of the term products, and Article 2 of the UCC's definition of the term goods. The specific areas of products liability law and Article 2 of the UCC that depend on these definitions to guarantee a consumer's access to a cause of action must encompass services and software that are integral to device functions. Second, traditional theories of product defects and warranty breaches must extend to cover IoT problems rooted in services and software that are needed to maintain device functionality. This expansion could also cover defects related to data breaches and other cybersecurity concerns. The providers of software and services that are necessary for IoT devices to function could be viewed as "product sellers" or "sellers of goods" under products liability law and Article 2 of the UCC. This includes companies that offer online platforms and marketplaces for the sale of defective devices.

---

[21] Forced Arbitration Injustice Repeal Act, H.R. 1423, 116th Cong. (1st Sess. 2019); Patrice Simms, *Bill Limiting Forced Arbitration Is Critical to Real Justice*, Law360 (Sept. 22, 2019, 8:02 PM), www.law360.com/articles/1200791/bill-limiting-forced-arbitration-is-critical-to-real-justice.

Functional Products and Goods

Recall from Chapter 5 that the definition of products under products liability law is generally limited to "tangible personal property" and "objects." Article 2's definition of goods is also limited to "movable" things. Services and software do not always qualify as products or goods. Under a functional approach, products or goods include services and software that are used to operate or access features of IoT devices and ensure device functionality (whether external to or embedded within a device, or subsequently downloaded after the device is acquired) in addition to the physical devices themselves. Functionality could be defined as or assessed by reviewing companies' descriptions of the products, companies' advertising materials and websites, and most importantly, the device's operations. For example, a company can advertise that an IoT device can be remotely operated through a mobile application, that a subscription service allows data associated with the device to be stored in the cloud or on a company's server, or that a device can reorder goods through a reordering service – all of these services and software would be viewed as products or goods. Viewing these items as goods or products allows us to access the various causes of action that depend on the definition of goods and products under products liability law and the UCC.

Implementing a functional approach to defining goods and products requires amendments to state laws as well as an adjustment in the way that courts evaluate and assess related issues. For instance, Article 2's definition of goods can be amended so that the services and software that are used for device functionality (whether external, internal, or subsequently downloaded) would be covered under the definition of goods. A similar approach could be taken in the various torts restatements and state statutes that define products, as discussed in Chapter 5. Another alternative with respect to Article 2 is for courts to abandon their use of the predominant purpose test and instead adopt a functionality test when evaluating Article 2's applicability to transactions involving goods and non-goods.[22] Under this test, courts would apply Article 2 to a hybrid transaction when the services and software that are provided in connection with the provision of an IoT device are connected to device functionality. In applying this test, courts could consider the advertising materials that companies provide, as well as how integral the services and software are to device operations. Regardless of the label that is attached to the parties' agreement (for instance, "terms of service" or "license"), Article 2 would apply to an entire transaction involving the provision of IoT devices, services, and software where the non-goods aspect of the transaction is used in device functions. Another complicating factor is that only a handful of states prohibit warranty disclaimers in consumer transactions. Thus, to ensure the viability of warranty breach claims, it is also necessary to limit parties' ability to disclaim implied warranties in consumer

---

[22] *See* Stacy-Ann Elvy, *Hybrid Transactions and the INTERNET of Things: Goods, Services, or Software?*, 74 WASH. & LEE L. REV. 77, 148 (2017).

agreements under Article 2 to the extent that other sources of state law or federal law do not effectively curtail such disclaimers.

Functional Defects and Warranty Breaches

Once a product is defined to include services and software under tort law, a consumer could potentially have a cause of action for strict liability for harms associated with such offerings. This strict liability claim would be in addition to a possible claim for negligence under existing tort law principles. In furtherance of the functional approach, in addition to manufacturing, design, and warning defects, it may be necessary to establish and recognize a new type of defect in the IoT setting – a "maintenance" or "functional" defect. This would encompass certain defects and problems related to the ongoing services and software that companies must provide for device functionality, and would not rely exclusively on whether the device is rendered "unreasonably dangerous."

For instance, if the network and cloud systems of a company that manufactures an IoT camera are hacked and a consumer's video history is disclosed, or if a party can remotely turn on the consumer's IoT camera and surreptitiously observe the consumer, these occurrences could be viewed as maintenance or functional defects. This defect category could also include software and service terminations. Consumers who suffer from data breaches associated with IoT devices and services could have a cause of action under products liability law and the UCC (and such a cause of action should not depend on whether the data is anonymized, encrypted, or contains information that is traditionally viewed as personally identifying, such as social security numbers), as well as any private causes of action that may be established under applicable statutes.[23]

This solution joins earlier calls to extend the concept of strict liability to data breaches.[24] As Daniel Solove and Danielle Citron have persuasively written, state "[d]ata-breach-notification laws require provision of notice to people about data breaches, but they do little to redress any injuries caused."[25] In light of the documented inadequacies of traditional privacy torts, including constitutional concerns and an excessive focus on the public exposure of private data and significant offenses to a reasonable person, products liability law and warranty principles could

---

[23]   *See, e.g.,* CAL. CIV. CODE §§ 1798.82–84 (West 2019); *id.* § 1798.150. *See generally* DANIEL J. SOLOVE & PAUL M. SCHWARTZ , PRIVACY LAW FUNDAMENTALS 206–09 (2017) (stating that "only a minority of state statutes provide a private right of action" and listing data breach statutes that provide a private cause of action); *2018 Security Breach Legislation,* NAT'L CONF. STATE LEGISLATURES (Feb. 8, 2019), www.ncsl.org /research/telecommunications-and-information-technology/2018-security-breach-legislation.aspx #2018reach%20Matrix%20June%202018.pdf (listing state data breach laws).

[24]   *See, e.g.,* Danielle Keats Citron, *Reservoirs of Danger: The Evolution of Public and Private Law at the Dawn of the Information Age,* 80 S. CAL. L. REV. 241, 243–44, 263–67 (2007).

[25]   Daniel J. Solove & Danielle Keats Citron, *Risk and Anxiety: A Theory of Data-Breach Harms,* 96 TEX. L. REV. 737, 781 (2018).

potentially serve as a source of remedy in data breaches.[26] Nonetheless, in assessing standing requirements, more courts must be willing to acknowledge the various types of harms that consumers incur in data breaches, including "risk and anxiety" and other subjective privacy harms.[27] Although some states have adopted legislation addressing companies' data security practices, we must not succumb entirely to arguments that companies cannot guarantee or secure devices from intrusion, as such arguments simply lower our cybersecurity expectations.[28] If a company offers a product that relies on interconnectivity, services, software, and networks to function, the company could have an ongoing obligation to maintain the security of the product, the data, and the network. If the company is unable to do this successfully, the product should not be offered to the public or the company could be exposed to products liability claims for associated defects.

There are two potential limitations on the foregoing discussion. First, the Supreme Court's holding in *Riegel v. Medtronic, Inc.* may restrict the viability of products liability actions involving medical IoT devices that receive pre-market approval from the FDA.[29] In *Riegel*, the court held that federal law preempted certain state tort law claims (negligence and strict liability) related to an alleged defective product.[30]

Second, recall that the economic loss doctrine restricts certain products liability claims.[31] The application of Article 2 to a consumer transaction becomes even more important when the economic loss doctrine prevents a viable strict liability or

---

[26] *See, e.g.*, Julie E. Cohen, *Privacy, Ideology, and Technology: A Response to Jeffrey Rosen*, 89 GEO. L.J. 2029, 2043 (2001) (discussing the failures of traditional privacy torts); Neil M. Richards, *The Limits of Tort Privacy*, 9 J. TELECOMM. & HIGH TECH. L. 357, 357, 365–74 (2011) (same); Neil M. Richards & Daniel J. Solove, *Prosser's Privacy Law: A Mixed Legacy*, 98 CALIF. L. REV. 1887, 1919 (2010) (same); Alicia Solow-Niederman, *Beyond the Privacy Torts: Reinvigorating a Common Law Approach for Data Breaches*, 127 YALE L.J. F. 614 (2018) (same); Lior Jacob Strahilevitz, *Reunifying Privacy Law*, 98 CALIF. L. REV. 2007, 2033 (2010) (same).

[27] *See* Solove & Citron, *supra* note 25, at 744–45; *see also* M. Ryan Calo, *The Boundaries of Privacy Harm*, 86 IND. L.J. 1131, 1133 (2011) (discussing anxiety as a harm and subjective and objective privacy harms).

[28] *See, e.g.*, ARK. CODE ANN. § 4-110-104 (West 2019); CAL. CIV. CODE § 1798.81.5 (West 2019); Jeff Kosseff, *Defining Cybersecurity Law*, 103 IOWA L. REV. 985, 1012 (2018).

[29] *See* Riegel v. Medtronic, Inc., 552 U.S. 312, 312 (2008).

[30] *Id.* ("Petitioner's common-law claims are pre-empted because they are based upon New York 'requirement[s]' . . . that are 'different from, or in addition to' the federal ones, and that [relate to safety and effectiveness . . . Common-law negligence and strict-liability claims impose 'requirement-[s]' under the ordinary meaning of that term."); *see also* Romer v. Corin Group, PLC, No. 2:18-cv-19-FtM-99MRM, 2018 WL 4281470, at *2 (M.D. Fla. Sept. 7, 2018) (stating that "[a]fter *Riegel* a plaintiff injured due to use of a Class III device approved through a PMA can escape preemption only if he asserts a 'parallel' state law claim."); Charlotte Tschider, *Preempting the Artificially Intelligent Machine*, BYU L. REV. (forthcoming 2020), https://papers.ssrn.com/sol3/papers.cfm?abstract_id=3443987 (discussing the preemption impact of the *Riegel* case).

[31] RESTATEMENT (THIRD) OF TORTS: LIAB. FOR ECON. HARM §§ 2–3 (AM. LAW INST.); Pauline Toboulidis, *Restatement of the Law Third, Torts: Liability for Economic Harm Approved*, ALI ADVISER (May 21, 2018), www.thealiadviser.org/economic-harm-torts/the-american-law-institute-membership-approves-restatement-of-the-law-third-torts-liability-for-economic-harm/; *Restatement of the Law Third, Torts:*

negligence claim. The UCC's provisions can be more robust and consumer friendly. This includes not only defining "goods" to include services and software, as previously described in this chapter, but also prohibiting implied warranty disclaimers in consumer transactions and extending the merchantability warranty to cover pre- and post-transaction harms associated with IoT devices, services, and software.

To limit regulatory arbitrage, other provisions in Article 2 impacting warranty provisions will also need to be evaluated. For instance, Article 2 could be amended to ensure that companies cannot use contractual provisions, including express and limited warranty terms, to displace, void, or limit the effect of the implied warranty of merchantability.[32] A sale could also encompass transactions that involve a license as well as the provision of services (whether free or purchased) that impact device functionality and are necessary for the consumer to enjoy all advertised features of a device. Nor should a lack of privity serve as a bar in cases involving the merchantability warranty. Additionally, the implied warranty of merchantability must not be limited to the condition of IoT devices, services, or software at the time of delivery to the consumer. The warranty could be expanded to clearly recognize the ongoing provision of software and services in the IoT context. Thus, it should be clear that the warranty is not limited to the device's condition at the time of sale but can also extend to cover actions by sellers and service providers post transaction. This would then mean that software and service vulnerabilities or defects that arise after concluding the transaction could still be subject to a breach of implied warranty claim. If a company fails to adopt adequate cybersecurity measures to ensure the security of IoT devices services, networks, and software, then these offered items are not fit for their ordinary purpose and the warranty could be viewed as breached. The warranty's duration need not be tied to the express or limited warranty that companies provide.[33] While the warranty should not last forever, it should extend long enough to allow consumers to obtain the benefit of their bargain by being able to use contracted-for devices, services, and software. The average life expectancy of an equivalent non-IoT household product could be a relevant factor in such a determination. Further, consideration should also be given to whether additional limits should be placed on sellers' cure rights in certain instances, and whether consumers should continue to be required in the IoT setting to provide sellers with notice of warranty breaches in light of the fact that companies can collect data on device functionality.[34]

In addition to providing a breach of implied warranty claim for cybersecurity vulnerabilities, a functional approach could also allow products liability law to serve

---

Liability for Economic Harm – Now Available, ALI ADVISER (Mar. 18, 2020), https://ali.org/news/articles/restatement-law-third-torts-liability-economic-harm-published/.

[32] U.C.C § 2-317(c) (AM. LAW INST. & UNIF. LAW COMM'N 2020).

[33] *See e.g.*, CAL. CIV. CODE § 1791.1(c) (West 2019).

[34] U.C.C §§ 2-508; 2-607; Banh v. Am. Honda Motor Co., No. 2:19-cv-05984oRGK-AS, 2019 U.S. Dist. LEXIS 230700, *4 (C.D. Cal. Dec. 17, 2019) (noting that some courts "have applied this U.C.C. provision [2-607] to require that a plaintiff give the defendant reasonable pre-suit notice before asserting a breach of warranty claim in court").

as a source of remedy for other IoT consumer harms. If a company elects to terminate services and software integral to the device functionality or fails to provide software updates, or if there are glitches in the software updates the company provides that cause harm, consumers could have a cause of action for breach of the implied warranty of merchantability under Article 2. Since a company's express warranty expires after a specified period of time, it is important that a company has an ongoing obligation to ensure the merchantability of integral services and software that are connected to device functionality. Under this approach, consumers of the Revolv, Pebble, and Logitech devices discussed in Chapter 5 would have had a cause of action for breach of the merchantability warranty when their devices were fully or partially bricked. These consumers would no longer be at the mercy of companies who can unilaterally decide how much compensation, if any, to provide to them.

Once a functional approach to Article 2 is adopted, it becomes much easier to answer pressing liability questions in a manner that makes sense. Consider, for instance, the *In re Sony Gaming* decision discussed in Chapter 5. If the court applied a functional approach to the transaction at issue, the online services provided in connection with the consumer's acquisition of the video console would be viewed as a central part of the "goods." As a result, the court could not then easily dismiss the breach of implied warranty claim using the rationale that the implied warranty of merchantability applied only to "goods" and not services. If Article 2's definition of goods is amended and adopted by states as suggested earlier, a court facing a similar issue would have to conclude that the transaction is subject to Article 2. This would then give rise to the implied warranty of merchantability, assuming that the company providing the device and services qualifies as a merchant.

Application of the functional approach to *In re Sony Gaming* and other similar cases allows courts to address specific types of harms that consumers may face in the IoT context. Chief among these harms are cybersecurity harms. In the *In re Sony Gaming* case, the plaintiffs alleged that the defendant's online services and network were not adequately secured, which resulted in the disclosure of their personal information after the company's network was hacked.[35] If IoT transactions involving goods, services, and software are subject to Article 2, then breach of the implied warranty of merchantability becomes a more viable claim when a device or a company's database or network is hacked, or when sensitive data collected by companies and IoT devices are disclosed to third parties. Again, this presumes that state or federal law also effectively prohibits disclaiming implied warranties in the transaction at issue.

Although the FTC has played an important role in addressing cybersecurity problems, if companies do not believe that they will be held accountable through consumer lawsuits for securing data, services, and networks, they may not effectively

---

[35] *In re* Sony Gaming Networks & Customer Data Sec. Breach Litig., 996 F. Supp. 2d 942, 954–56 (S.D. Cal. 2014).

address cybersecurity concerns associated with their offerings. Regulatory agencies cannot pursue every claim involving lax security measures, even if their staff and resources are expanded, as recommended in Chapter 8. As it currently stands, many data breach lawsuits are unsuccessful, and, in some cases, this is because of limits found in various sources of law, such as the economic loss doctrine and Article 2's limited definition of goods. Exposure to liability via direct lawsuits from consumers can serve as a powerful incentive to design devices and maintain services and networks with security in mind and to adopt appropriate data collection practices.[36] To make this happen, we would need to address not only defects in products liability law and the UCC, but also laws, such as the FAA, that limit consumers' access to courts by validating anti-consumer contract terms, such as mandatory arbitration and class action waiver provisions. Further, as recommended in earlier sections of this chapter, courts must also consider Contract Distancing and information asymmetry in determining whether consumers are subject to contract terms applicable to IoT services and software.

Functional Sellers and Merchants

Article 2 defines a seller as "a person who sells or contracts to sell goods" and it also contains a provision defining merchants.[37] Recall from our discussion in Chapter 5 that tort law sources of products liability law also contain definitions of "product sellers." Under a functional approach, the terms "distributor," "product seller," "seller" of goods, or "merchant" would encompass all commercial parties providing services and software that are necessary for IoT devices to function as advertised. Thus, when Amazon provides its dash replenishment service, goods or a mobile app to owners of the GE IoT products discussed in Chapter 5, Amazon would be viewed as a seller or merchant with respect to those services, goods or software. GE would be viewed not only as the manufacturer with respect to the physical dishwasher, but also as a seller with respect to the services and external software that it provides for consumers to use in conjunction with operating their IoT devices.

Similarly, when a company, such as Nest, provides an internet-connected camera along with a subscription service that stores video history in the cloud, and a mobile app to control the device, the company would be viewed as a maker of the device as well as a seller with respect to the associated services and the internal and external software that it provides. If a bug or glitch in a software update damages the device or other property within the home, or causes harm to individuals within the home, products liability law should provide adequate remedies to consumers. A software update glitch impacting an IoT thermostat could lead to frozen or burst pipes and

---

[36] Several scholars have explored the role of products liability in the privacy law context. *See generally, e.g.*, Ari Ezra Waldman, *Privacy's Law of Design*, 9 U.C. IRVINE L. REV. 1239 (2019) (exploring the role of products liability law in addressing privacy by design gaps).

[37] U.C.C. § 2-103(1)(d) (AM. LAW INST. & UNIF. LAW COMM'N 2002); *see id.* § 2-104.

flooding in a consumer's home as well as physical injury to consumers and others in their homes due to drastic temperatures changes.[38] By viewing the providers of software and services as sellers or merchants, it is more likely that consumers who suffer harms that originate from or are connected to those aspects of an IoT consumer transaction will be able to access causes of actions under products liability law and the UCC that depend on a party qualifying as a seller, distributor, or merchant.

E-commerce platforms are the modern-day version of shopping malls. Traditional shopping mall owners are not completely immune from tort liability lawsuits,[39] and neither should e-commerce platforms be. Where appropriate, courts could broadly interpret state statutes defining sellers under products liability law. For example, to the extent that a statute's definition of product seller relies on a company "placing a product in the line of commerce" or being involved in the "distribution chain," such language could be interpreted to cover companies that provide an online marketplace for the sale of defective products, even if the products are offered for sale by third-party sellers. An exception could be made for third-party sales conducted by individual consumers, rather than commercial entities on such platforms. In other words, e-commerce platforms would not be viewed as product sellers when a product is sold by one individual to another on their platform. As such, they would be exposed to liability when they permit commercial entities to offer defective products for sale on their platforms.

Not only could e-commerce companies be viewed as sellers of the products provided by third-party sellers that they permit to conduct business on their platforms, but they could also be viewed as merchants who "deal in goods of th[at] kind" for purposes of the merchantability warranty under Article 2.[40] This is arguably a drastic step that exposes e-commerce companies to multiple sources of liability for products that they do not manufacture, particularly if the consumer can identify the manufacturer and seller of the product. Indeed, one might posit that e-commerce platforms cannot police or ensure the quality of all of the products that third-party sellers offer for sale on their platform and should not be burdened with the exorbitant costs associated with the same. Following that line of argument, requiring platforms to do so would derail innovation and block access to online marketplaces for lesser-known manufacturers and sellers.

A potential compromise solution to address these concerns is to authorize liability for e-commerce platforms as product sellers for products sold on their platforms by third-party sellers only if: (1) the e-commerce platform's actions in connection with handling, storing, packaging, or shipping the product led to the defect, (2) the third-party seller and manufacturer cannot be identified and brought within the court's

---

[38] Nick Bilton, *Nest Thermostat Glitch Leaves Users in the Cold*, N.Y. TIMES (Jan. 13, 2016), www .nytimes.com/2016/01/14/fashion/nest-thermostat-glitch-battery-dies-software-freeze.html.

[39] *See* DAN DOBBS ET AL., HORNBOOK ON TORTS 465–73 (2nd ed. 2015).

[40] U.C.C. § 2-104(1); *see id.* § 2-314.

jurisdiction or, if these parties are known and identified, they are judgment-proof at the time the judgment is enforced, or (3) if the e-commerce platform has not obtained valid documentation from third-party sellers and manufacturers indicating that the product at issue meets all applicable safety and security standards established under relevant domestic and international law.[41]

While this compromise solution would permit e-commerce platform liability under certain circumstances, it is likely best from a consumer protection perspective to impose liability without conditions when a product is sold by a third-party seller and causes harm to consumers. As the IoT expands, third-party sellers will have the capacity to collect sensitive consumer data and control consumers' activities post transaction. This creates a stronger argument for blanket e-commerce platform products liability. This is even more true when Amazon sells and makes Alexa-enabled IoT devices that do not have a screen to display contract terms, and which have the capacity to order additional IoT products from Amazon and third-party sellers on Amazon's website.[42] Amazon's influence and reach in the IoT context is ever-expanding. A 2018 NPR and Edison Research report found that 16 percent of American consumers purchased an IoT smart speaker and 11 percent of those consumers owned Amazon's Alexa devices.[43] A 2019 report on smart speaker ownership found that Amazon's Echo has "a 61% market share among smart speaker owners."[44] Amazon is also attempting to expand its reach to the automotive industry through the "Echo Auto," a small device that can be placed in and used to enable

---

[41] Several state products liability statutes contain a similar liability exclusion for product sellers, but these statutes do not adequately deal with e-commerce platform liability, and a similar approach is also discussed in the comments of the Products Restatement. RESTATEMENT (THIRD) OF TORTS: PRODUCTS LIABILITY § 1 cmt. e (AM. LAW INST.); *see also, e.g.,* KAN. STAT. ANN. § 60-3306 (West 2019) ("A product seller shall not be subject to liability in a product liability claim arising from an alleged defect in a product, if the product seller establishes that: ... (5) any judgment against the manufacturer obtained by the person making the product liability claim would be reasonably certain of being satisfied."); TENN. CODE ANN. § 29-28-106 (West 2019) ("No product liability action ... shall be commenced or maintained against any seller, other than the manufacturer, unless: ... (5) [t]he manufacturer has been judicially declared insolvent."); WASH. REV. CODE ANN. § 7.72.040 (West 2019) ("A product seller, other than a manufacturer, shall have the liability of a manufacturer to the claimant if: (a) [n]o solvent manufacturer who would be liable to the claimant is subject to service of process under the laws of the claimant's domicile or the state of Washington; or (b) [t]he court determines that it is highly probable that the claimant would be unable to enforce a judgment against any manufacturer.").

[42] *See* David Carnoy, *How Is "Amazon's Choice" Chosen? Amazon Won't Say,* CNET (Mar. 21, 2018, 4:00 AM), www.cnet.com/news/do-humans-choose-what-products-get-amazons-choice/; Nicolas Towner, *CNET Asks: Are You a Fan of the New Amazon Smart Home Devices?,* CNET (Sept. 28, 2018, 4:37 PM), www.cnet.com/news/cnet-asks-are-you-a-fan-of-the-new-amazon-smart-home-devices/.

[43] EDISON RESEARCH, CES 2018: THE NPR AND EDISON RESEARCH SMART AUDIO REPORT, FALL/WINTER 2017 (2018), www.edisonresearch.com/ces-2018-npr-edison-research-smart-audio-report-fall-winter -2017/; NPR & EDISON RESEARCH, NAT'L PUB. MEDIA, THE SMART AUDIO REPORT (2020), www .nationalpublicmedia.com/uploads/2020/01/The-Smart-Audio-Report-Winter-2019.pdf (noting that 24 percent of US adults have smart speakers).

[44] Bret Kinsella, *U.S. Smart Speaker Ownership Rises 40% in 2018 to 66.4 Million and Amazon Echo Maintains Market Share Lead Says New Report from Voicebot,* VOICEBOT.AI (Mar. 7, 2019, 8:00 AM),

Alexa in consumers' vehicles.[45] Amazon's "smart plug," another IoT device, allows consumers to control their non-Amazon devices through Alexa and reportedly brings "regular devices like lights, coffee makers or fans . . . into the smart home."[46] In 2018, home building giant Lennar Corporation announced that every home built by the company will be "equipped with Alexa," and it is projected that "about 35,000 houses across 23 states will be sold with built-in Amazon devices."[47]

These developments suggest that more consumers are likely to utilize Amazon's IoT devices, services, and online platform to not only manage and control their homes and devices, but also to purchase products directly from the company's website. Amazon's IoT devices, such as the smart plug, may impact the functionality (and perhaps even the express warranty) of devices manufactured and sold by other companies. Insulating e-commerce platforms, such as Amazon, from products liability for third-party sales fails to consider these companies' unique position, influence, and sweeping dominance in the IoT setting. Imposing liability on e-commerce platforms encourages them to be more selective about the types of products that are offered for sale on their platforms as well as the types of third-party companies that can conduct business on their platforms. The exception for consumer third-party sellers would permit companies such as eBay to continue to provide a marketplace for consumers to sell goods to each other.

Many of the cases discussed in Chapter 5 illustrate the need to hold e-commerce platforms responsible for the products that they permit to be sold on their websites. In the *Fox* case, discussed in Chapter 5, the defective hoverboard caused a fire destroying the plaintiffs' home.[48] Amazon obtained more than $200 million in hoverboard sales sold on its platform between September 2015 and November 2015, yet Amazon was shielded from a products liability claim because it was not viewed as a seller under the Tennessee products liability statute.[49] The court also dismissed the plaintiffs' claim under Tennessee's consumer protection statute.[50] Further, as to the cost concerns discussed earlier, which may potentially be

---

https://voicebot.ai/2019/03/07/u-s-smart-speaker-ownership-rises-40-in-2018-to-66-4-million-and-amazon-echo-maintains-market-share-lead-says-new-report-from-voicebot/.

[45] Kyle Hyatt, *Amazon Echo Auto Puts Alexa on Your Dash*, CNET (Sept. 20, 2018, 11:52 AM), www.cnet.com/roadshow/news/amazon-echo-auto-puts-alexa-on-your-dash/.

[46] Molly Price, *Amazon Smart Plug Showcases Simple Setup*, CNET (Sept. 20, 2018, 1:11 PM), www.cnet.com/reviews/amazon-smart-plug-preview/; *see also* Jacob Kastrenakes, *Amazon Announces $25 Smart Plug that Lets You Control Appliances with Alexa*, VERGE (Sept. 20, 2018, 1:42 PM), www.theverge.com/2018/9/20/17882918/amazon-smart-plug-price-release-date-alexa-voice-control-routines-lights-ac.

[47] Grace Donnelly, *Amazon Alexa Will Come Built-In to All New Homes from Lennar*, FORTUNE (May 9, 2018, 12:44 PM), http://fortune.com/2018/05/09/amazon-alexa-lennar/.

[48] Fox v. Amazon.com, Inc., No. 3:16-cv-03013, 2018 WL 2431628, at *3 (M.D. Tenn. May 30, 2018).

[49] Fox v. Amazon.com, Inc., 930 F.3d 415, 428 (6th Cir. 2019); *Fox*, 2018 WL 2431628, at *2–3, *10; Mike Curley, *Amazon Settles Suit over Hoverboard House Fire*, LAW360 (Apr. 10, 2020, 6:08 PM), www.law360.com/articles/1262643/amazon-settles-suit-over-hoverboard-house-fire (noting that the case was settled).

[50] *Fox*, 930 F.3d at 428–29; *Fox*, 2018 WL 2431628, at *37–39.

associated with requiring e-commerce platforms to ensure the quality of third-party products, in the *Fox* case, Amazon required third-party sellers of hoverboards to provide evidence of legal compliance with applicable international requirements only after becoming aware of electronic and safety problems associated with the product and months after making millions from hoverboard sales.[51] The district court's opinion in *Fox* noted that "Amazon had no safety certifications from any of the sellers placing hoverboards for sale on the Amazon website."[52] At a minimum, e-commerce platforms that allow devices to be sold on their websites could be required to obligate third-party sellers to provide documents indicating that the device complies with applicable international and domestic regulations and guidance. This is particularly important in the IoT setting, as IoT devices are comprised of multiple electrical components. A similar obligation could also be imposed in sales between consumers.

A Critique of the Functional Approach

A possible objection to the functional approach to products liability law and warranty rules proposed earlier is that products liability law has historically primarily addressed issues related to physical harm and should not be extended to cover all IoT harms.[53] Following this line of argument, privacy, digital domination, and cybersecurity concerns are abstract, and are beyond the traditional scope of products liability law. One response to this critique is that although products liability law has gone through phases of expansion and retraction, products liability law has historically evolved from and adapted to new contexts.[54] Even *MacPherson v. Buick Motor Co.*, a 1916 case that "la[id] the foundation for the modern era of products liability law," and revised the legal principles of that era to expose manufacturers to liability, was decided in response to consumer harms caused by the dawn of mass-manufactured automobiles.[55]

---

[51] *See Fox*, 2018 WL 2431628, at *3 ("In December 2015, Amazon's product safety team demanded sellers provide legal compliance documentation for the hoverboards offered for sale. This demand included documentation that the hoverboards complied with Underwriters Laboratory requirements and United Nations transportation regulations.").

[52] *Id.*

[53] DAVID OWEN, OWEN'S PRODUCT LIABILITY LAW 2 (3rd ed. 2015) ("[P]roducts liability law governs liability for the sale or other commercial transfer of a product that causes physical harm because it is defective or its properties are falsely represented.").

[54] *Id.* at 18–30 (discussing the history of products liability law).

[55] MacPherson v. Buick Motor Co., 217 N.Y. 382 (1916); OWEN, *supra* note 53, at 21–22, 247 ("Tort law's major contribution, launched in 1916 by *MacPherson v. Buick Motor* was its rejection of the privity-of-contract requirement in tort law claim."); Sally H. Clarke, *Unmanageable Risks*: MacPherson v. Buick *and the Emergence of a Mass Consumer Market*, 23 LAW & HIST. REV. 1 (2005); Steven P. Croley & Jon D. Hanson, *Rescuing the Revolution: The Revived Case for Enterprise Liability*, 91 MICH. L. REV. 683 (1993); Jonathan Kahn, *Product Liability and the Politics of Corporate Presence: Identity and Accountability in* McPherson v. Buick, 35 LOY. L.A. L. REV. 3, 20–42 (2001).

Business historian Sally H. Clarke observes that at the time of *MacPherson* automobile manufacturers used the privity requirement to insulate themselves from liability and transfer the costs of defective vehicles to consumers.[56] This transfer of risk occurred because of manufacturers' "inability to control the technology" associated with the rise of a "new complex consumer product" – the automobile – and "their ability to innovate in a market context."[57] Internet of Things consumer devices are the "new complex consumer product[s]" of our time. Instead of waiting to perfect automobile technology to limit possible defects, *MacPherson*-era automobile manufacturers were eager to place their vehicles on the market.[58] Similarly, many IoT companies have flooded the consumer market with insecure and privacy-invasive devices that rely on software, services, and external systems to function, while simultaneously using their ability to innovate to retain control over us and our devices post transaction. These companies have rushed to place the Internet into a plethora of modern objects, without taking sufficient precautions to guard against possible resulting harms. Today's companies are exploiting limitations in existing liability rules to shield themselves from liability in a manner that is similar to *MacPherson*-era automakers. Clarke's study of the early automobile market also evaluated the impact of the decision in *MacPherson* and found that the case, in combination with several other factors, contributed to a decline in vehicle defects.[59] In the same way that the law evolved to respond to the consumer harms that flowed from the rise of automobiles, so too can products liability law evolve to fully address IoT harms. A functional approach to products liability law can better ensure that companies do not continue to shift the costs of innovation and harmful IoT products to consumers.

Lastly, even if one were to concede that the tort theories of products liability law should not be expanded to cover the various IoT harms discussed in this chapter, warranty liability is flexible enough to adapt. Moreover, a consumer protection statute could be adopted to fully implement the functional approaches I have recommended.

CLOSING THE CDA'S PRODUCTS LIABILITY GAP

As we discussed in Chapter 5, some courts have interpreted the CDA to provide products liability immunity to online companies for defective products. Scholars disagree on Congress's intent in passing the CDA. Jeff Kosseff suggests that the statute's drafters intended to give "sweeping immunity" to website

---

[56] Clarke, *supra* note 55, at 6, 49; *see also* SALLY H. CLARKE, TRUST AND POWER: CONSUMERS, THE MODERN CORPORATION, AND THE MAKING OF THE UNITED STATES AUTOMOBILE MARKET (2007).

[57] Clarke, *supra* note 55, at 8.

[58] *Id.* at 4.

[59] *Id.* at 5–6, 34–45 ("*MacPherson* intensified [existing] market pressures: Manufacturers reduced their chances of being sued and improved their chances of defending themselves successfully by making good on Cardozo's demand that they undertake careful inspections and tests of their products.").

owners.[60] In contrast, Michael Rustad and Thomas Koenig have persuasively argued that Section 230 of the CDA was intended to give ISPs "protection from online defamation claims."[61] Regardless of Congressional intent, the CDA was adopted decades ago.[62] There have been significant technological developments since the CDA's enactment that require a new approach to technology platforms' liability for defective products. Additionally, even the former chairman of the FCC, who oversaw Section 230's creation, has publicly acknowledged that today the statute should be revised to limit technology companies' immunity.[63] Companies' use of CDA immunity to dodge certain products liability lawsuits must be restricted. The most efficient solution is to amend the CDA to expressly carve out products liability actions.

There have been discussions and hearings in Congress concerning potential amendments to Section 230, but as is the case with baseline federal privacy legislation, it is unclear whether Congress will move in that direction.[64] As such, where appropriate, courts must be willing to reign in their overly broad interpretation of the CDA. In the absence of legislation amending the CDA to carve out products liability actions from its coverage, courts must recognize the limited purpose of the CDA and when possible cease broadly applying the CDA's provisions to e-commerce platforms in products liability suits. Doing so would limit companies' ability to use the CDA as a shield in products liability suits and complement the functionality approach to products liability law discussed earlier.

REGULATING ELECTRONIC SELF-HELP AND DEBT COLLECTION HARMS

State and federal legal frameworks must effectively regulate the use of asset collection technology and debt collection abuses in light of the concerns discussed in Chapter 6. There are several possible ways to achieve this goal. The FTC has repeatedly recommended that Congress amend the FDCPA to more adequately address debt collection abuses.[65] It is time for Congress to answer these calls. Recall

---

[60] JEFF KOSSEFF, THE TWENTY-SIX WORDS THAT CREATED THE INTERNET (2019).

[61] Michael L. Rustad & Thomas H. Koenig, *Rebooting Cybertort Law*, 80 WASH. L. REV. 335, 340 (2005).

[62] Danielle Keats Citron, *Section 230's Challenge to Civil Rights and Civil Liberties*, KNIGHT FIRST AMEND. INST. (Apr. 6, 2018), https://knightcolumbia.org/content/section-230s-challenge-civil-rights-and-civil-liberties (noting that "[t]he CDA, which was part of the Telecommunications Act of 1996, was not a libertarian enactment"); Mary Anne Franks, *"Revenge Porn" Reform: A View from the Front Lines*, 69 FLA. L. REV. 1251 (2017) (discussing the CDA).

[63] *See* Guy Rolnik & Eytan Avriel, *"We Were Naïve," Says FCC Chair Who Oversaw the Creation of Section 230*, PROMARKET (Jan. 23, 2020), https://promarket.org/we-were-naive-says-the-fcc-chair-who-oversaw-the-creation-of-section-230/.

[64] *See, e.g., Hearing on "Fostering a Healthier Internet to Protect Consumers,"* HOUSE COMM. ON ENERGY & COMMERCE, https://energycommerce.house.gov/committee-activity/hearings/hearing-on-fostering-a-healthier-internet-to-protect-consumers (last visited Feb. 2, 2020).

[65] *See, e.g.,* Staff of the Fed. Trade Comm'n's Comment Before the Bureau of Consumer Protection 11 (Sept. 18, 2019), www.ftc.gov/system/files/documents/advocacy_documents/comment-staff-federal-trade-commissions-bureau-consumer-protection-matter-proposed-rule-request/final_-_cfpb_debt_

from Chapter 6 that despite the FDCPA's prohibition on conduct that will "harass, oppress or [cause] abuse," companies continue to engage in debt criminalization tactics.[66] Consideration should be given to whether the definition of debt collector should be revised to specifically address the limitations in the statute's provisions that led to the Supreme Court's decision in the *Henson* case discussed in Chapter 6.[67] The FDCPA could also be amended to address the problem in the *Rotkiske* case discussed in Chapter 6. The FDCPA's statute of limitations period could begin to run upon discovery of a violation, rather than when the violation occurs. The resources and funding of federal agencies charged with enforcing the FDCPA must be expanded to enable active pursuit of entities that engage in debt criminalization tactics. The FTC and CFPB must also continue their enforcement efforts on phantom debts.[68] State and government actors must also proactively pursue debt collectors that engage in debt criminalization tactics.

The FDCPA could be amended to explicitly prohibit covered entities from requesting or using warrants in debt collection lawsuits.[69] State law debt collection frameworks could also impose a similar limitation. One possible critique of this proposal is that it significantly encroaches on courts' ability to ensure timely and orderly compliance. This unique power of courts has been weaponized and abused by creditors to the detriment of consumers. The harms associated with this weaponization outweigh concerns about protecting the traditional power of courts.

The FDCPA could also be revised to more effectively address debt collection efforts associated with time-barred debts.[70] Consider that in *Stimpson v. Midland Credit Management*, the Ninth Circuit rejected a claim by a consumer that

coll_draft_comment_9-13_v2_1pm_ver_to_comm.pdf; Fed. Trade Comm'n, Collecting Consumer Debts: The Challenges of Change (2009), www.ftc.gov/system/files/documents/advocacy_documents/comment-staff-federal-trade-commissions-bureau-consumer-protection-matter-proposed-rule-request/final_-_cfpb_debt_coll_draft_comment_9-13_v2_1pm_ver_to_comm.pdf.

[66] 15 U.S.C. § 1692d (2019).

[67] Henson v. Santander Consumer USA Inc., 137 S. Ct. 1718, 1725 (2017) ("these are matters for Congress, not this Court, to resolve").

[68] *See, e.g.*, Bureau of Consumer Fin. Protection, Fair Debt Collection Practices Act: BCFP Annual Report 2019 (2019), https://files.consumerfinance.gov/f/documents/cfpb_fdcpa_annual-report-congress_03-2019.pdf; Press Release, Fed. Trade Comm'n, Phantom Debt Brokers and Collectors Settle FTC and New York AG Charges (July 1, 2019), www.ftc.gov/news-events/press-releases/2019/07/phantom-debt-brokers-collectors-settle-ftc-new-york-ag-charges?utm_source=govdelivery.

[69] The ACLU has also made a similar recommendation. Am. Civil Liberties Union, A Pound of Flesh: The Criminalization of Private Debt 40 (2018), www.aclu.org/report/pound-flesh-criminalization-private-debt. Currently the FDCPA prohibits companies from representing or implying "that non-payment of any debt will result in the arrest or imprisonment of any person or the seizure, garnishment, attachment, or sale of any property or wages of any person unless such action is lawful and the debt collector or creditor intends to take such action." 15 U.S.C. § 1692e(4) (2019).

[70] *See, e.g.*, 15 U.S.C. § 1692e(5) (prohibiting debt collectors from threatening to "take any action that cannot legally be taken"); Midland Funding, LLC v. Johnson, 137 S. Ct. 1407, 1418 (2017) (Sotomayor, J., dissenting) ("Every court to have considered this practice [of filing suit in ordinary civil courts to collect debts that they know are time barred] holds that it violates the FDCPA."); *Time-Barred Debts*, Fed. Trade Commission, www.consumer.ftc.gov/articles/0117-time-barred-debts (last visited Feb. 2,

a company had violated the FDCPA by sending him a letter attempting to collect on a time-barred debt.[71] The court reasoned that "there is nothing inherently deceptive or misleading in attempting to collect a valid, outstanding debt, even if it is unenforceable in court."[72] If a debt is time barred by the applicable statute of limitations, debt collectors could be prohibited from initiating contact with consumers about the payment of the debt, even if such initial communications indicate that the debt collector will not sue because of the time-barred nature of the debt.[73] Allowing debt collectors to initiate contact with consumers to request payment on time-barred debts, as long as they notify consumers that they will not sue, is an inadequate consumer protection measure.[74] The simple act of requesting payment on a legally unenforceable debt is deceptive and could convince unsuspecting and vulnerable groups of consumers to pay them. In some states, making such payment on a time-barred debt can revive the debt.[75] Debt collectors repeatedly initiate contact with consumers on time-barred debts with the hope that consumers will

2020) [hereinafter *FTC Time-Barred Debts*] ("Collectors are allowed to contact you about time-barred debts.... It's against the law for a collector to sue you or threaten to sue you on a time-barred debt . . . the collector can continue to contact you to try to collect, unless you send a letter to the collector demanding that communication stop.").

[71] *See* Stimpson v. Midland Credit Mgmt., 944 F.3d 1190, 1201 (9th Cir. 2019) ("Congress could prohibit, or otherwise restrict, attempts to collect time-barred debts, but it has not done so . . . Stimpson has not identified anything false, deceptive, or misleading in Midland's letter, so his FDCPA claim fails"). *But see* McMahon v. LVNV Funding, LLC, 744 F.3d 1010, 1019 (7th Cir. 2014) (reasoning that "the proposition that a debt collector violates the FDCPA when it misleads an unsophisticated consumer to believe a time-barred debt is legally enforceable, regardless of whether litigation is threatened, is straightforward under the statute").

[72] *Stimpson*, 944 F.3d at 1200; *see also 9th Circuit Rules Letter's "Benefits" of Paying Time-Barred Debt Not Misleading Under FDCPA, CFPB to Address SOL Disclosures*, CONSUMER FIN. SERVICES BLOG (Dec. 30, 2019), www.lexology.com/library/detail.aspx?g=b4fa07c8-ed1b-4144-a5ed-9335739adc4c (discussing *Stimpson* and CFPB & FTC activities on time-barred debts).

[73] In *Stimpson*, the debt collector's communications with the consumer noted that it would not sue on the debt. *Stimpson*, 944 F.3d at 1194; FED. TRADE COMM'N, REPAIRING A BROKEN SYSTEM, PROTECTING CONSUMERS IN DEBT COLLECTION LITIGATION AND ARBITRATION 26 (2010), www.ftc.gov/sites/default/files/documents/reports/federal-trade-commission-bureau-consumer-protection-staff-report-repairing-broken-system-protecting/debtcollectionreport.pdf (noting that consumer protection advocates contend that the FDCPA should prohibit collection attempts of time-barred debt).

[74] *See, e.g.*, Pantoja v. Portfolio Recovery Assocs., LLC, 852 F.3d 679 (7th Cir. 2017) (finding an FDCPA violation because the debt collector's "letter did not make clear to the consumer that the law prohibited the collector from suing to collect the old debt"); Consent Decree, U.S. v. Asset Acceptance, LLC, No. 8-12-cv-00182-JDW-EAJ (M.D. Fla. Jan. 31, 2012), www.ftc.gov/sites/default/files/documents/cases/2012/01/120131assetconsent.pdf (FTC consent decree mandating that company provide notice of the time-barred nature of the debt).

[75] *See, e.g.*, KAN. STAT. ANN. § 60-520 (2019); *Midland Funding*, 137 S. Ct. at 1419 (Sotomayor, J., dissenting) ("In many States, a consumer who makes an offer [of partial payment on a time-barred debt] like this has – unbeknownst to him – forever given up his ability to claim the debt is unenforceable. That is because in most States a consumer's partial payment on a time-barred debt – or his promise to resume payments on such a debt – will restart the statute of limitations."); Zeehlu Yang v. Midland Credit Mgmt., No. 15-2686-JAR, 2016 U.S. Dist. LEXIS 12177, at *3 (D. Kan. Feb. 2, 2016) ("Kansas has a revival statute, which states that a partial payment on a debt revives the statute of limitations, regardless of how long the debt has been stale.").

be induced into making a partial payment, which then allows the debt collector to sue for the full debt amount even though it was initially time barred.[76] State laws could prohibit debt revival upon partial payment on time-barred debts in consumer transactions. State laws could also provide that before obtaining a default judgment, all debt collectors are required to submit evidence to prove to the court that the creditor is still entitled to enforce the loan and the statute of limitations has not expired.[77]

Opponents of these proposals may contend that they incentivize non-payment of debts and that payment of time-barred debts can improve consumers' credit scores.[78] One response to this critique is that all creditors have the ability to pursue debtors for non-payment before the statute of limitations runs. Additionally, removing debts from consumers' credit reports is an inadequate justification for duping consumers into paying unenforceable debts. If a time-barred debt remains on a consumer's credit report, the consumer has the option of contacting the credit bureau or the creditor to resolve the issue. In such an event, the creditor could then be obligated to inform the consumer that it is legally unable to file suit to collect the debt, and that the consumer could simply wait until expiration of the reporting period for the time-barred debt to be removed from the credit report. A consumer's decision to contact a creditor holding a time-barred debt should not permit the company to subsequently inundate the consumer with requests for payment.

There is currently at least one legislative attempt to revise the Fair Credit Reporting Act (FCRA) to address the reporting period for adverse events, among other things.[79] Proper consideration could also be given to the ways in which the FCRA can be revised to more effectively address companies' ability to use data (including IoT data) to discriminate against vulnerable groups of consumers and engage in predatory lending activities in various types of consumer lending transactions and which ultimately may have an adverse effect on consumers' credit scores.[80] When companies engage in such practices, consumers' credit scores should not suffer as a result, regardless of the transaction type.

---

[76] See *Midland Funding*, 137 S. Ct. at 1419 (Sotomayor, J., dissenting); *see also* Marc C. McAllister, *Ending Litigation and Financial Windfalls on Time-Barred Debts*, 75 WASH & LEE L. REV. 449, 455 (2018) ("[A] debtor who makes a partial payment on the debt, however small, will revive the statute of limitations on the debt and permit judicial recovery of the entire balance for many years to follow.").

[77] The ACLU has also made a similar recommendation to state actors. *See, e.g.,* AM. CIVIL LIBERTIES UNION, *supra* note 69, at 43; *see also* APRIL KUEHNHOFF ET AL., NAT'L CONSUMER LAW CTR., ZOMBIE DEBT: WHAT THE CFPB SHOULD DO ABOUT ATTEMPTS TO COLLECT OLD DEBT (2015), www.nclc.org/images/pdf/debt_collection/report-zombie-debt-2015.pdf (discussing recommendations for time-barred debts).

[78] *FTC Time-Barred Debts, supra* note 70 ("Not paying a debt may make it harder, or more expensive, to get credit, insurance, or other services because not paying may lower your credit rating.").

[79] See generally Comprehensive CREDIT Act of 2020, H.R. 3621, 116th Cong. (2d Sess. 2020), https://rules.house.gov/sites/democrats.rules.house.gov/files/BILLS-116HR3621-RCP116-47.pdf; Andrew Kragie, *House to Vote This Week on Dem Changes to Credit Reports*, LAW360 (Jan. 27, 2020, 9:50 PM), www.law360.com/consumerprotection/articles/1237982/house-to-vote-this-week-on-dem-changes-to-credit-reports?nl_pk=06d06a2b-64f8-4c4c-b81d-6950221f7573&utm_source=newsletter&utm_medium=email&utm_campaign=consumerprotection.

[80] *See, e.g.,* H.R. 3621, *supra* note 79.

Given the privacy and digital domination harms associated with the use of SIDs and GPS tracking devices, and the possible disproportionate impact on low-income and minority consumers, baseline federal privacy legislation could also prohibit companies from impliedly or explicitly conditioning product sales and services and loan approvals on consumer consent to the use of asset collection technologies in products or engaging in manipulative or dark pattern tactics to obtain such consent. The drawback of such an approach is that there may be challenges in factually proving that the lender impliedly conditioned the loan. A neater solution, although perhaps more controversial, could be to simply prohibit the use of asset collection that enables the types of pre- and post-default privacy and digital domination harms discussed in Chapter 6. Financial incentives (such as discounts) in exchange for consumer consent to the installation of asset collection devices could also be prohibited. In the absence of federal legislation incorporating these recommendations, state lending laws could be amended to include them. If companies begin using asset collection technology in financial transactions involving other types of consumer IoT devices, similar prohibitions could also be applicable to such transactions. Additionally, the use of ALPRs and other types of non-consensual tracking technology could be more widely confined to government entities with appropriate restrictions.

One possible critique of these proposals is that companies use asset collection technology in subprime transactions to decrease their repossession costs, and these cost savings are passed on to consumers in the form of lower interest rates and deposits. As such, restricting the use of such technology will increase costs for consumers. However, the extent to which asset collection technology decreases subprime lenders' transactional costs is unclear, and it is also unsettled whether such decreased costs are actually passed on to consumers. The history of discriminatory dealer mark-ups discussed in Chapter 6 calls this hypothesis into question. Additionally, a CFPB empirical study on the pass-through savings argument in the arbitration context found that "there [was] no evidence of arbitration clauses leading to lower prices for consumers."[81] This may also be true in the subprime lending asset collection technology context, but more empirical work in this area is needed. The pernicious consequences that flow from asset collection technology justify restrictions on the use of such technology in consumer transactions and outweigh unproven arguments about increased costs.

To the extent that companies are permitted to use asset collection technology, private entities and debt collectors could also clearly be prohibited from using data and insights generated from debtors' use of IoT devices and services and asset

---

[81] Consumer Fin. Prot. Bureau, Arbitration Study: Report to Congress, Pursuant to Dodd-Frank Wall Street Reform and Consumer Protection Act § 1028(a), § 10.3, at 15 (2015); *CFPB Study Finds that Arbitration Agreements Limit Relief for Consumers*, Consumer Fin. Protection Bureau (Mar. 20, 2015), www.consumerfinance.gov/about-us/newsroom/cfpb-study-finds-that-arbitration-agreements-limit-relief-for-consumers/.

collection technology in the debt collection process to enable debt criminalization and abusive practices. This prohibition could apply to initial creditors and to traditional debt collectors subject to the FDCPA. Baseline privacy legislation applicable to all industries, and which specifically addresses asset collection technology, could further enable federal agencies to actively regulate this issue.[82]

Another possible alternative to remedy the harms associated with the use of asset collection technology can be found in Article 9 of the UCC. States could adopt non-uniform amendments to Article 9 to prohibit electronic self-help measures in the consumer goods context (such as remotely disabling IoT goods). Additionally, Article 9 could be revised to indicate that in a consumer transaction a secured party's use of asset collection technology constitutes a repossession and a breach of the peace.

LIMITING DATA TRANSFERS IN CORPORATE TRANSACTIONS

Recall from Chapter 7 that several corporate and commercial law frameworks allow companies to solidify their market power and enable the disclosure and transfer of our data in business transactions. These transactions include mergers and acquisitions and possibly secured financing arrangements. Bankruptcy proceedings can also permit opaque consumer data transfers between corporate entities.

Mergers and Acquisitions

Robust antitrust merger review and enforcement has the capacity to play a key role in addressing resulting privacy harms and data monopoly concerns in the mergers and acquisitions area. Admittedly, this book is not the right place for a detailed discussion of the ways in which antitrust enforcement can attempt to remedy all resulting privacy harms associated with corporate transactions. Instead, in this section I join earlier calls for continued and detailed evaluations by antitrust scholars, regulators, and lawmakers of existing antitrust doctrine to determine the ways in which antitrust rules can evolve to address modern concerns, such as those noted in this book. There are ongoing discussions and proposals at the federal level to craft antitrust legislation to deal with mergers involving large firms.[83] As one antitrust scholar, Tim Wu, convincingly argues, legislative action by Congress could clarify and expand the reach of existing antitrust statutes and the power of antitrust enforcers.[84] Legislation

---

[82]   *See, e.g.,* Cong. Research Serv., Data Protection Law: An Overview 35 (Mar. 25, 2019), https://fas .org/sgp/crs/misc/R45631.pdf (discussing the Consumer Financial Protection Act and contending that with few exceptions the CFPB has not widely used its "unfair, deceptive, or abusive act or practice" authority in the privacy space and "the CFPB has generally been inactive in the data privacy and security space").

[83]   Thomas Franck, *Elizabeth Warren Is Preparing a Plan to Ban Mega Mergers, Allow Gig Workers to Unionize,* CNBC, www.cnbc.com/2019/12/05/elizabeth-warren-preparing-plan-to-ban-mega-mergers-review-past-deals.html (last updated Dec. 9, 2019).

[84]   *See* Tim Wu, The Curse of Bigness: Antitrust in the New Gilded Age 127–29 (2018).

in this area could expressly and sufficiently account for consumer privacy and cybersecurity harms. Mark Lemley and Andrew McCreary have argued that antitrust enforcers could "presumptively block acquisitions of directly competitive startups by dominant firms."[85] Additionally, perhaps, antitrust enforcers could also be more willing to resort to undoing mergers.[86] Large technology companies' multiple acquisitions of IoT companies are ripe for these types of antitrust enforcement. If baseline federal privacy legislation is adopted, there is room to include provisions to address companies' transfer and disclosure of our data in corporate transactions. For instance, large technology companies' ability to use privacy policies to obtain automatic permission and authorization for data transfers and disclosures in mergers and acquisitions could be restricted.

Recent efforts by data titans to address privacy concerns which may at first glance appear consumer friendly could be likely to further cement large technology companies' marketing power. Consider that Google has announced plans to, over time, eliminate third-party websites' ability to deploy cookies to track our activities.[87] This announcement may have significant competition implications. Google already possesses a treasure trove of consumer data and the announcement to limit tracking does not appear to impact Google's data collection and processing practices. While this new effort may limit other companies' ability to surveil and profit from our online activities, it may further cement Google's seemingly untouchable digital dominance and market power. This illustrates the pressing need for robust antitrust regulation and enforcement as well as effective privacy legislation.

In early 2020, the FTC and DOJ released draft vertical merger guidelines for public comment.[88] The draft guidelines are an attempt both to provide more clarity on enforcers' approach to vertical mergers and to update previously issued outdated guidelines.[89] However, the draft guidelines do not clearly define which vertical mergers are presumptively invalid.[90] Despite the release of the draft vertical merger guidelines, a lack of sufficient harmony and coordination between the FTC and the

---

[85] Mark Lemley & Andrew McCreary, *Exit Strategy* 85 (Stanford Law & Econ. Olin, Working Paper No. 542, 2019), https://papers.ssrn.com/sol3/papers.cfm?abstract_id=3506919.

[86] Wu, *supra* note 84, at 131.

[87] Justin Schuh, *Building a More Private Web: A Path Towards Making Third Party Cookies Obsolete*, CHROMIUM BLOG (Jan. 14, 2020), https://blog.chromium.org/2020/01/building-more-private-web-path-towards.html.

[88] *See generally* U.S. DEP'T OF JUSTICE & FED. TRADE COMM'N, DRAFT VERTICAL MERGER GUIDELINES, REQUEST FOR PUBLIC COMMENT (Jan. 10, 2020), www.ftc.gov/system/files/documents/public_state ments/1561715/p810034verticalmergerguidelinesdraft.pdf.

[89] Christopher Cole, *FTC's Phillips Says Vertical Merger Rules Badly Need Refresh*, LAW360 (Feb. 5, 2020, 6:26 PM), www.law360.com/articles/1241097/ftc-s-phillips-says-vertical-merger-rules-badly-need-refresh.

[90] *Id.* For additional discussions on the draft vertical merger guidelines, *see* Steven Salop, *The 2020 Vertical Merger Guidelines: A Suggested Revision* (Apr. 1, 2020) (unpublished manuscript), https://papers.ssrn.com/sol3/papers.cfm?abstract_id=3550120.

DOJ may hamper antitrust enforcement activities[91] – cohesive antitrust actions by both federal actors are necessary. Additionally, as noted in Chapter 7, technology giants' acquisitions may not always fit neatly within existing antitrust merger distinctions. As of the date of writing, recent antitrust inquiries into technology giants' acquisition activities are unresolved.[92] The IoT's rise, and companies' acquisition efforts, suggest that antitrust enforcers could do more to effectively regulate large technology companies' unchecked market power and the frequency with which these companies transfer and disclose our data in mergers and acquisitions. Tensions between privacy and competition are ripe for resolution. A detailed proposal of the ways in which antitrust law can be revised is left to other experts in this area.

Bankruptcy Code Amendments

Data transfers and disclosures in bankruptcy proceedings must also be limited. The Bankruptcy Code can be amended to more effectively address this issue and remedy existing gaps in the BAPCPA, including correcting the overreliance on notice and choice, and other areas of the code. Several different approaches could be adopted. First, the Bankruptcy Code could be amended to require that courts appoint CPOs whenever consumer data are offered for sale or lease in bankruptcy proceedings.[93] Stated differently, a CPO can be appointed to provide guidance to the court on whether the transfer and disclosure of the data should be approved, even if (1) the company in bankruptcy does not provide a privacy policy, or its existing privacy policy contains language that authorizes the transfer and disclosure of consumer data, or (2) the consumer has consented to the privacy policy or the terms and conditions.[94] This approach could correct the Bankruptcy Code's provisions that heavily rely on notice and choice to protect consumer data in bankruptcy proceedings. When consumer data transfers are involved in a bankruptcy proceeding, bankruptcy courts must be wary of exclusively focusing on attempting to extract as

---

[91] *See, e.g., Factbox: Big Tech Faces Growing Number of U.S. Probes*, THOMPSON REUTERS (Dec. 5, 2019, 10:56 AM), www.reuters.com/article/us-tech-antitrust-probe-factbox/factbox-big-tech-faces-growing-number-of -u-s-probes-idUSKBN1Y92G8; John D. McKinnon & Brent Kendall, *U.S. Antitrust Enforcers Signal Discord over Probes of Big Tech*, WALL ST. J. (Sept. 16, 2019, 10:11 PM), www.wsj.com/articles/u-s-antitrust-enforcers-signal-discord-over-probes-of-big-tech-11568663356; Monica Nickelsburg, *FTC Chair Aims to Resolve Big Tech Antitrust Probes This Year, Ending Investigations or Taking Action*, GEEKWIRE (Jan. 7, 2020, 1:23 PM), www.geekwire.com/2020/ftc-chair-aims-resolve-big-tech-antitrust-probes-year-ending-investigations-taking-action/.

[92] Bryan Koenig, *In FTC Probe of Small (Big) Tech Deals, Knowledge Is Power*, LAW360 (Feb. 19, 2020, 9:15 PM), www.law360.com/cybersecurity-privacy/articles/1245307/in-ftc-probe-of-small-big-tech-deals -knowledge-is-power?nl_pk=8bca81a9-bf53-40e6-b4c6-4d8c2eda4ebe&utm_source=newsletter& utm_medium=email&utm_campaign=cybersecurity-privacy.

[93] Stacy-Ann Elvy, *Commodifying Consumer Data in the Era of the Internet of Things*, 59 B.C. L. REV. 423, 520–22 (2018).

[94] *See id.* at 520.

much value as can be gained from the debtor company's assets for the benefit of creditors to the detriment of consumers' interests. Instead, bankruptcy courts must actively consider the implications of consumer data transfers and disclosures and they must be willing to follow and give significant weight to CPO recommendations that adequately protect consumers' data.

Second, an outright prohibition on transfers involving consumers' information in bankruptcy proceedings could be adopted.[95] However, companies' databases and rights in consumer data are valuable assets and imposing a blanket restriction on the transfer of all types of consumer data (or rights associated with such data) in corporate bankruptcies could solidify the power of existing technology giants. To address this concern and strike a balance between corporate and consumer interests, a bankruptcy data transfer and disclosure prohibition could be limited to highly intimate and sensitive data, such as biometric, health-related, and children's data, and the CPO's review powers could be extended to other types of consumer data. The Bankruptcy Code could be amended to expressly require companies in bankruptcy to destroy highly sensitive consumer data before the sale or transfer of a customer database or consumer data to a third party.

One possible critique of these proposals is that allowing consumer data to be easily sold or transferred to third parties as part of a bankruptcy sale is beneficial to consumers, particularly when data is transferred to a third party that will continue the bankrupt company's operations or is in the same industry as the bankrupt entity. The transfer of the data may allow consumer devices and consumer services to continue to function and prevent service interruptions. While exceptions could be made for such specific transfers, to the extent that this information is transferred to a third party during bankruptcy in the same line of business, the business acquiring the data could be prohibited from further monetizing and transferring the data and could be permitted to use the data only to the extent necessary to meet consumer needs. The potential dangers of repeatedly disclosing and transferring highly sensitive consumer data from party to party and server to server justify the imposition of transfer and disclosure restrictions.

Secured Transactions

Recall from Chapter 7 that Article 9 of the UCC has the capacity to facilitate unchecked consumer data transfers as part of a secured transaction. To the extent that companies elect to assign interests in their databases, which contain consumer data, or the associated rights in those data, such a transaction could be subject to Article 9 of the UCC. Given this, the UCC could be amended to more adequately deal with such transactions. The UCC is primarily a creature of state rather than federal law, and as such this is an area ripe for non-uniform state legislative action,

---

95 *See id.* at 504.

although a uniform approach is preferable. Just as in the bankruptcy context, there are several ways to go about limiting possible data disclosures and transfers in Article 9 transactions.

Section 9-201 of the UCC provides that contracts governed by Article 9 are also subject to laws that provide distinct rules for consumers (such as consumer protection statutes) and any such laws control in the event of a conflict with Article 9.[96] If privacy and cybersecurity legislation is adopted as recommended in Chapter 8, which restricts companies' ability to freely transfer our data in corporate transactions, one could contend that Article 9's provisions must automatically defer to any such legislation in accordance with Section 9-201. However, one might argue that consumers are unlikely to be directly associated with a deal between the debtor company and the creditor even though consumer-generated data may be involved in the transaction.[97] Revisions to Article 9 may still be necessary to promote consistency across all related statutes and, to the extent that Section 9-201 is applicable, avoid disputes about whether the state privacy and security statute conflicts with Article 9.[98]

First, Article 9 could be amended to explicitly provide that if a company's rights in consumer data are subject to a creditor's security interest, judicial intervention is the only method by which the creditor can enforce its rights with respect to the data. If state legislation grants consumers only an opt-out right for data sales (including those in corporate transactions and possible Article 9 arrangements), Article 9 could be revised to provide that creditors and third parties are prohibited from accessing the data of consumers (held by the debtor) who have exercised their opt-out rights. The debtor and creditor must be responsible for ensuring that the data of consumers that opt out of corporate data transactions are not transferred or disclosed as part of the secured transaction. If consumers are provided with more robust data sale rights, Article 9 could be amended to provide that even if consumer consent to a privacy policy authorizing data disclosures and transfers as part of a secured transaction is received, the creditor and other third-party entities will be prohibited from using Article 9's mechanisms to access the consumer data.[99] Where appropriate,

---

[96] *See* U.C.C. § 9-201(b)–(c) (AM. LAW INST. & UNIF. LAW COMM'N 2020). At the federal level, "the UCC does not apply to the extent that it is preempted." *Id.* at § 9-109(c)(1); Elvy, *supra* note 93 at 507; U.S. CONST. art. VI, cl. 2.

[97] *See* Tex. Lottery Comm'n v. First State Bank of Dequeen, 325 S.W.3d 628, 637 (Tex. 2010).

[98] *See id.* at 637–39 (finding that the state lottery statute at issue applied to all individuals and was "not a statute or rule of law that establishe[d] a different rule for consumers within the meaning of 9-201(b)" and that section 9-406's anti-assignment provisions negated the anti-assignment provisions of the lottery statute); *see also* U.C.C. § 9-201(c) ("Failure to comply with a statute or regulation described in subsection (b) has only the effect the statute or regulation specifies."); LINDA J. RUSCH & STEPHEN L. SEPINUCK, PROBLEMS AND MATERIALS ON SECURED TRANSACTIONS 146 (3rd ed. 2014) ("In the rare instance when the rules on enforcement in Article 9 conflict with some other applicable rule of law (such that compliance with both laws is not possible), the creditor might need to file a declaratory action to seek a court determination of which set of requirements is paramount.").

[99] *See* Elvy, *supra* note 93, at 500–22.

consideration could be given to whether limitations could also be imposed on possible judgment creditors' access to consumer data. Alternatively, rather than an outright prohibition on data transfers in secured transactions, such a prohibition could be limited to highly sensitive data, such as biometric and health-related data.[100] Recall that in Chapter 8, I also suggest a similar approach in a baseline privacy statute with respect to the assignment of rights in sensitive data.

If a comprehensive prohibition on data transfers is not adopted, Article 9 could minimally require that a CPO – akin to bankruptcy CPOs – be appointed to provide guidance to the court in deciding whether to issue an order requiring the debtor to disclose, transfer, or assign rights in the consumer data. CPOs could be encouraged to make several recommendations to the court, including recommending that: (1) the data cannot be sold or transferred in a piecemeal manner to third-party data buyers; (2) the creditor be authorized to operate the indebted company's business as a "going concern"; and (3) the creditor or data buyer be required to adopt consumer-friendly privacy policies and data collection and processing practices that limit disclosures and transfers after data acquisition.[101]

CONCLUDING WORDS

While commercial law and privacy law may have historically focused on distinct issues and questions, the world of commercial law and the world of privacy law are now inescapably linked together in a marriage of sorts. This union predates the IoT's rise, but the IoT further solidifies the permanency of this coupling. This book has highlighted the various ways in which the existing commercial law of privacy and security heavily favors corporate interests to the detriment of individuals. As I mentioned, these failures have been with us for some time, and before the coming of the IoT. However, the mountains of data IoT devices collect combined with the ubiquitous and unrelenting nature of IoT surveillance and the resulting digital domination threats exacerbate the consumer concerns that result from the blending of the commercial law and privacy law worlds. Technology companies have the power to use commercial law frameworks to exploit and profit from our COVID-19–related data. The pandemic illustrates the pressing need to revise commercial law and privacy and security law frameworks to protect the privacy and security of individuals. It is the unique combination of the failings of privacy law and commercial law which allow companies to use IoT devices and services and other technological developments to digitally dominate, surveil, and exploit us and our data.

The various legal frameworks of privacy and security law discussed in this book do not effectively and consistently deal with the privacy and security concerns that result from commercial's law encroachment into the privacy space. Technology

---

[100]   *Id.* at 504.
[101]   *Id.* at 518.

companies have played a critical role in facilitating this encroachment. United States privacy law has largely continued to rely excessively on the notice and choice framework reflected in the sectoral approach to privacy. Privacy law's overreliance on the notice and choice regime as the primary mechanism of consumer data protection has enabled corporate actors to force us to consent to their dubious data collection and use practices, while surveilling our every move and collecting increasingly accurate and intimate volumes of data about us that they use to determine how to treat us.

Several areas of law impacting commercial practices fail to sufficiently account for the movement of privacy and security issues into the commercial law arena in a manner that protects individuals from corporate exploitation. Many of the sources of commercial law discussed in this book inadequately deal with the consumer privacy, security, and digital domination harms the IoT and other technological developments raise. To be clear, my argument is not that the drafters of the various sources of commercial law have been oblivious to, or have historically never considered, privacy or security-related issues. Commercial law frameworks have long struggled to adequately address consumer protection issues and there are also flaws in several sources of consumer protection legislation. Attempts to adapt various sources of commercial law to deal with technological developments have in notable cases either been unsuccessful or partially ineffective. The BAPCPA and the failed Article 2B UCC project and resulting UCITA are all examples of this.

Commercial law is a crucial source of corporate actors' power over us in the IoT era. It is commercial law that gives teeth to privacy law's notice and choice framework. It is commercial law's inability to sufficiently grapple with privacy and security issues that has allowed companies to exploit privacy law's heavy dependence on the notice and choice regime to extract almost limitless rights from our data through illusory consent and has blessed corporate data collection and use practices at almost every turn. It is the contract law and lending frameworks of commercial law that allow corporate actors to use IoT devices and various other technological developments to extend their domination over us in various transactions. It is products liability law's and the UCC's inability to account for the interconnected nature of IoT devices, services, and systems as well as other technological advancements, that allows many companies to be free from various forms of liability for privacy, security, device failures, and digital domination harms. Similarly, it is the UCC, the Bankruptcy Code, and other sources of law that enable firms to opaquely and easily transfer and monetize our data in corporate transactions, solidify their market power, and consolidate our data, all to primarily advance their interests. The IoT evidences the pressing need for various sources of commercial law to fully come to terms with the privacy and security problems of today.

By no means do I argue that this book has covered all sources of commercial law, privacy and security law, or consumer protection laws. Indeed, it is unlikely that any single article or book could achieve that goal. There is much left to be explored and resolved. What is clear, though, is that several sources of commercial law have primarily served as a source of power that many companies deploy in their efforts to use technological developments, such as the IoT, to extend their dominion over us. My hope is that this book will serve as a new beginning and will foster renewed discussions of how best to develop a commercial law of privacy and security that also protects our interests as individuals.

This book has largely painted a bleak picture of current and possible future harms in the IoT era, but there is hope. The law can evolve to effectively deal with privacy, security, and digital domination harms in the IoT age and beyond. This book has offered a path forward to begin the process of creating a commercial law of privacy and security that acknowledges and safeguards our interests. Recall that the concerns I describe in this book are enabled by inadequacies in both commercial law and privacy law. As such, I argue that we need a comprehensive approach that offers solutions that are connected to both areas of the law and that recognizes the growing overlap of the privacy and commercial law worlds.

A baseline privacy and security statute is a crucial step in correcting privacy law's overreliance on notice and choice and inability to deal with commercial law's invasion of the privacy space. While I do not purport to offer a complete and comprehensive legislative proposal for a baseline privacy and security statute, I do offer recommendations that can be incorporated into such a statute to aid in correcting the deficiencies of the current approach to privacy and security issues that arise in data trade arrangements between individuals and companies that I discuss in this book. A baseline privacy and security statute can grant certain privacy rights to individuals, define the contours of permissible and impermissible data collection and use practices, and impose specific obligations on corporate actors who seek to use our data. Revisions to various sources of commercial law can reign in corporate actors' use of commercial law frameworks to exploit privacy law's failings and to empower themselves to our detriment. The UCC and other sources of contract law and lending law, products liability law, the Bankruptcy Code, and debt collection law can be adjusted in accordance with this book's many recommendations. There is room for legislative actors, regulatory bodies, and, in some instances, courts to tackle these issues.

Some corporate actors and their advocates may object to a commercial law of privacy and security that also sufficiently protects individuals. Many of them will likely call for more continued deference to commercial practices, whether through maintenance of a self-regulatory and heavily dependent notice and choice regime in privacy and security frameworks, or through maintenance of commercial law's continued respect for private ordering, prior notice of contract terms and commercial practices, and exploitation of the complicated UCC revision process. We must ensure that they do not win. The stakes for us, our families, and our society are too high. The time is ripe for a revolutionary approach to the commercial law of privacy and security.

Index